CLASSICAL LITERATURE AND POSTHUMANISM

Also published by Bloomsbury

POSTHUMANISM IN THE AGE OF HUMANISM: MIND, MATTER, AND THE LIFE SCIENCES AFTER KANT
Edgar Landgraf, Gabriel Trop and Leif Weatherby

THE NEW HUMAN IN LITERATURE: POSTHUMAN VISIONS OF CHANGES IN BODY, MIND AND SOCIETY AFTER 1900
Mads Rosendahl Thomsen

THE MATERIALITIES OF GREEK TRAGEDY: OBJECTS AND AFFECT IN AESCHYLUS, SOPHOCLES, AND EURIPIDES
Mario Telò and Melissa Mueller

CLASSICAL LITERATURE AND POSTHUMANISM

Edited by Giulia Maria Chesi and Francesca Spiegel

BLOOMSBURY ACADEMIC
LONDON • NEW YORK • OXFORD • NEW DELHI • SYDNEY

BLOOMSBURY ACADEMIC
Bloomsbury Publishing Plc
50 Bedford Square, London, WC1B 3DP, UK
1385 Broadway, New York, NY 10018, USA
29 Earlsfort Terrace, Dublin 2, Ireland

BLOOMSBURY, BLOOMSBURY ACADEMIC and the Diana logo are trademarks of
Bloomsbury Publishing Plc

First published in Great Britain 2020
This paperback edition published in 2021

Cover design: Terry Woodley
Cover image © Valeria Shukhova, Konstantin Korchuk

A catalogue record for this book is available from the British Library.

Library of Congress Cataloging-in-Publication Data
Names: Chesi, Giulia Maria, editor. | Spiegel, Francesca, editor.
Title: Classical literature and posthumanism / edited by Giulia Maria Chesi and Francesca Spiegel.
Description: London, UK : Bloomsbury Academic, 2019. | Includes bibliographical references and index.
Identifiers: LCCN 2019014054| ISBN 9781350069503 (hb) | ISBN 9781350069527 (epdf)
Subjects: LCSH: Classical literature—History and criticism. | Animals in literature. | Monsters in literature. | Machinery in literature. | Machine theory in literature. | Cyborgs in literature. | Philosophical anthropology in literature. | Object (Philosophy) in literature.
Classification: LCC PA3009 .C54 2019 | DDC 880.09—dc23 LC record available at https://lccn.loc.gov/2019014054

ISBN: HB: 978-1-3500-6950-3
PB: 978-1-3502-3154-2
ePDF: 978-1-3500-6952-7
eBook: 978-1-3500-6951-0

Typeset by RefineCatch, Limited, Bungay, Suffolk

To find out more about our authors and books visit www.bloomsbury.com and sign up for our newsletters.

to
Pat Easterling
for her fine mind and her gentle heart

and

Michael Silk
for his love of breaking new grounds and the care
for good writing everywhere

CONTENTS

CONTRIBUTORS

Roland Baumgarten is Lecturer in Classics at the Humboldt University of Berlin. His research interests include Greek cultural history (especially religion and education), Ancient Historiography and translation studies. His monography 'Heiliges Wort und Heilige Schrift bei den Griechen. Hieroi logoi und verwandte Erscheinungen' (1998) deals with some of the issues of his paper.

Virginia Burrus is the Bishop W. Earl Ledden Distinguished Professor of Religion at Syracuse University, where she moved in 2013 after teaching for many years at Drew University. She specializes in the literary and cultural history of Christianity in late antiquity, with special focus on gender, sexuality and the body; martyrdom and asceticism; ancient novels and hagiography; ecology and the posthuman. Among her most recent publications is *Ancient Ecopoetics: On Cosmologies, Saints, and Things in Early Christianity* (2019).

Giovanni Ceschi has a PhD in Classical Philology from the University of Trento. He teaches Greek and Latin at 'Giovanni Prati' high school in Trento. His research interests include dramatic poetry of the fifth century BCE and Greek medicine, as well as Sophoclean tragedy, ᾿Αρχαία comedy, Hippocratic therapy and the relationship between poetry and science in classic Greece. As for specialized language related to tragedy, he wrote the monograph *Il vocabolario medico di Sofocle* (2009). He also wrote the entry *Medical Vocabulary* for *Encyclopedia of Ancient Greek Language and Linguistics* (2014).

Giulia Maria Chesi is Lecturer of Greek at the Humboldt-Universitaet zu Berlin. She has written a book on the *Oresteia* and she is currently writing a monograph on technology in the *Odyssey*.

Mireille Courrént is Professor in Latin Literature and Language at the University of Perpignan. Her research focuses on Vitruvius's treatise De Architectura as a literary and philosophical work. She has edited and contributed to *Vitruve* (Cahiers des Etudes Anciennes, 2011) and published *De architecti scientia. Idée de nature et théorie de l'art dans le De Architectura de Vitruve* (2011) and *Vitruuius auctor. L'œuvre littéraire de Vitruve et sa réception dans la littérature antique (Ier- Ve siècles)* (forthcoming, 2019).

Martin Devecka is an assistant professor in the Classics Programme and the Department of Literature at the University of California, Santa Cruz. His research is focused on Graeco-Roman cultural history and especially on the place of non-human forms of life in the ancient imagination. He is currently finishing a book on Roman zoology.

Alex Dressler is Associate Professor of Classics at the University of Wisconsin – Madison, and the author of *Personification and the Feminine in Roman Philosophy* (2016), as well as numerous articles ranging from comedy and exemplarity to psychoanalysis and the hermeneutics of suspicion. Current projects centre around the late fourth century CE Christian poet and ascetic, Paulinus of Nola, and include a verse a translation of Paulinus' correspondence with Ausonius of

Bordeaux and a monograph on 'Paulinan' aesthetics with special attention to the role of money in the development of aesthetic autonomy and concepts of value in classical literature.

Katherine Fleming is Lecturer in Twentieth-Century and Contemporary Literature at Queen Mary, University of London, UK. Her most recent co-edited volumes include *Seneca in the English Tradition*, Special Volume of Canadian Review of Comparative Literature (forthcoming) and *The Reception of Classical Antiquity in German Literature* (forthcoming).

Maria Gerolemou is a Leventis postdoctoral research associate at the Classics and Ancient History Department of the University of Exeter. Her research focuses on Ancient Greek drama, Wunderkultur and, most recently, ancient sciences. She is the author of the book *Bad Women, Mad Women: Gender und Wahnsinn in der Griechischen Tragödie* (2011) and the editor of the collective volumes *Recognizing Miracles in Antiquity and Beyond* (2018) and *Mirrors and Mirroring: From Antiquity to the Early Modern Period* (with L. Diamantopoulou, Bloomsbury, forthcoming). She is now preparing a book on ancient Greek drama and technology (*Automatic Theatre in Ancient Greek Drama: Distinguishing Technology and Humanity*, Bloomsbury) and works on the collective volume, *The Body as Machine in Antiquity: Towards an Early History of Iatromechanics* (with G. Kazantzidis).

Y. N. Gershon received his doctorate from the University of Cambridge for examining the narrative techniques of Dionysius of Halicarnassus. With the support of the DAAD he was Kurt Hahn Scholar at Universität Erfurt, and was later Henry Procter Visiting Fellow in Classics at Princeton University. His research interests include historical narratives of Rome, Greek historiography more generally, and the Second Sophistic. His current project examines narrative vitality, variety and variegation in Greek historical and non-historical texts

Manuela Giordano is Associate Professor in Greek Literature at the University of Siena. She is particularly interested in interdisciplinary approaches and has published on a range of topics relating to Homer and tragedy, as well as on historical-anthropological issues. Her current research interests focus on early fifth century Athens, orality and literacy.

Elena Giusti is Assistant Professor in Latin Literature and Language at the University of Warwick. She is the author of *Carthage in Virgil's Aeneid: Staging the Enemy under Augustus* and is currently writing a book for Bloomsbury on Dido of Carthage and her reception.

Simon Goldhill is Professor of Greek at the University of Cambridge. His book *Victorian Culture and Classical Antiquity* won the Robert Lowry Patten award for the best book on Victorian literature in 2012; his book *Sophocles and the Language of Tragedy* won the Runciman Prize for the best book on a Greek subject, ancient or modern, in 2013. His most recent book is *A Very Queer Family Indeed: Sex, Religion and the Bensons in Victorian Britain*. He is a fellow of the American Academy of Arts and Sciences and Foreign Secretary of the British Academy. He was director of the Cambridge Centre for Research in the Arts, Social Sciences and Humanities (CRASSH) from 2011 to 2018.

Tom Geue lectures in Latin at the University of St Andrews. He has just finished a book on anonymous Roman literature (Author Unknown: The Power of Anonymity in Ancient Rome). His interests float across the Latin literature of the early Roman principate, from Virgil to Juvenal, and creep some way beyond, from Elena Ferrante to Alice Oswald to Marxist criticism.

He is currently in planning mode for a new project on the Italian philologist and Marxist Sebastiano Timpanaro.

Marianne Hopman is Associate Professor of Classics and Comparative Literary Studies at Northwestern University. Her research focuses on Homer, Athenian tragedy, mythology, literary theory, feminism, animal studies and posthumanism. She is the author of *Scylla: Myth, Metaphor, Paradox* (2012) and the co-editor of *Choral Mediations in Greek Tragedy* (2013). Current projects include a study of interactions between human and non-human animals in Homer, as well as a monograph on *Prometheus Bound* and the conceptualization of technai in fifth-century Athens.

Yuk Hui currently teaches at Bauhaus University, Germany. He is the author of *On the Existence of Digital Objects* (2016), *The Question Concerning Technology in China: An Essay in Cosmotechnics* (2017) and *Recursivity and Contingency* (2019).

Aaron Kachuck is Junior Research Fellow at Trinity College, Cambridge. He works on the development of political and religious symbolism and their literary form in the early Principate, as well as on their intertwined reception in later periods, especially Early Modern Europe. His first book is on *The Solitary Sphere in the Age of Virgil*; he is currently writing a book on the Latin dream-form in literary history.

Alexander Kirichenko is a Heisenberg senior research fellow at the Humboldt University in Berlin. He is the author of *A Comedy of Storytelling: Theatricality and Narrative in Apuleius' Golden Ass* (2010) and *Lehrreiche Trugbilder: Senecas Tragödien und die Rhetorik des Sehens* (2013), as well as articles on Pindar, Callimachus, Virgil, Horace, Propertius, Seneca, Petronius, Statius, Apuleius and the cult of Mithras.

Tua Korhonen is a senior research fellow at the Department of Languages (Latin and Greek), University of Helsinki, Finland. Her research interests have ranged over Greek philosophy and rhetoric, classical tradition in early modern Europe, medieval Greek manuscripts, and human-animal studies. Korhonen's more recently published work in the latter field includes the monograph, with Erika Ruonakoski, *Human and Animal in Ancient Greece: Empathy and Encounter in Classical Literature* (2017). Currently she is working with descriptions of addressing and anthropomorphising animals in Greek literature as well as epic animal similes.

Genevieve Liveley is a Turing fellow and reader in Classics at the University of Bristol, where her particular research interests lie in narratives and narrative theories (both ancient and modern). She has published widely in books, articles, and essays on narratology, on chaos theory, cyborgs, AI and how ancient myth might help us to better anticipate the future.

Anne Tuttle Mackay completed her PhD in Spring 2019 at University College London with her thesis 'Animals and Animal-Human Dynamics in Valerius Flaccus' *Argonautica*'. She is currently working on an expansion of the thesis for a monograph. She has previously published on augury in Statius (under Anne Tuttle), and her other research interests include Flavian Epic, non-human subjectivity and empathy, narratology, and Roman religion and historiography.

Agis Marinis is Assistant Professor of Greek Philology and Drama at the University of Patras (Greece). He studied Classics in Athens and Cambridge (BA, MPhil) and received his PhD from the University of Cambridge in 2008. The focus of his doctoral dissertation is the intersection of Pindaric poetry and religion, on which a monograph is forthcoming from Routledge. He is also working on Aeschylus' *Seven against Thebes*, as well as on the presence of Theban myth in Greek and Roman poetry.

James McNamara completed his PhD at the University of Cambridge on oratory and rhetoric in the works of Tacitus. He has held postdoctoral positions at Cambridge and Victoria University of Wellington, a lectureship at Trinity College, Oxford, and lately a Research Fellowship with the DAAD at the universities of Potsdam and Florence. He has taught widely in Latin language and literature, and has research interests in imperial Latin literature, in historiography, oratory, ethnography and the history of classical education.

Kirstin Mertlitsch is Senior Scientist (Postdoc) and director of the University Center for Women and Gender Studies at the University of Klagenfurt. Her research interest range over Feminist Philosophy, Gender Epistemology, Gender and Queer Studies, Intersectionality and Diversity Studies, Critical Posthuman Studies and New Materialism. Her first monography was published in 2016: *Sisters, Cyborgs, Drags. Das Denken in Begriffspersonen der Gender Studies*. Her current research focuses on epistemic diversity.

Anne-Sophie Noel has taken up a position of assistant professor in Greek at the École Normale Supérieure of Lyon in 2018 (research unit HiSoMA). Before that, she has taught Classics and French in France, England, and the USA and was a junior fellow at Harvard's Center for Hellenic Studies. She has published on a range of topics related to Greek tragedy and its modern reception, with a focus on objects in the performance of Greek tragedy, ancient objects and the history of emotions, as well as objects and cognitive theory. Her monograph, which is currently being completed, combines these three perspectives. Her current work also includes the co-edition of a special issue of the French online journal *Agôn* dedicated to matter and materiality in the performing arts (ancient and modern), which engage critically with the concepts of new materialism and posthumanism.

Luciano Nuzzo is Associate Professor in Philosophy of Law and Theory of Law at the Università del Salento. His last book was published in 2018: *Il mostro di Foucault. Limite, legge, eccedenza* (Meltemi, Milano).

Antonietta Provenza is Junior Research Fellow in Ancient Greek Literature at the University of Palermo (Dep. "Culture e Società"). She is the author of *La medicina delle Muse. La musica come cura nella Grecia antica* (2016) and of many articles in journals and volumes mainly concerning ancient Greek music and its contexts, Attic drama, ancient Greek medicine.

Laura Rosella Schluderer obtained her PhD in Ancient Philosophy from the University of Cambridge in 2014. Since then, she has been affiliated to the University of Pisa and then continued pursuing her research interests as an independent scholar. Her work focuses on Plato's late metaphysics and its relationships with the thought of fifth century Pythagoreans such as Philolaus and Archytas, in particular on the notion of musical harmony as an explanatory model in ontology and as a pattern of goodness in ethics. She has also written about the microcosm and macrocosm model, pervasive in ancient thought, in order to disclose its ontological bases and its ethical implications. She has published a number of articles in international journals on various issues in Ancient Philosophy, from Heraclitean ethics to Plato's cosmological model for virtue, from harmony as a model for health in Hippocratic texts to Philolaus' metaphysics of structure.

Giacomo Sclavi majored in English and German Literature at the Università degli Studi di Siena before moving to the Department of Classics of the Humboldt-Universität zu Berlin in 2013. His research covers a wide range of interests from Latin Grammar and Linguistics to Greek myth and its Roman reception.

Francesca Spiegel is writing a book on the reception of Greek and Roman narratives in modern medical writing on sexuality, technology and gender. Together with Giulia Maria Chesi, she helms the Technosomata research network in Berlin. Francesca has worked extensively on the concept of agency, and has a monograph forthcoming on distributed agency in the plays of Sophocles. She also edits the website distributedagency.net.

Jenny Strauss Clay is William R. Kenan, Jr. Professor of Classics emerita at the University of Virginia, is the author of *The Wrath of Athena: Gods and Men in the Odyssey*, *The Politics of Olympus: Form and Meaning in the Major Homeric Hymns*, Hesiod's *Cosmos*, and Homer's *Trojan Theater*. She has also published numerous articles on Greek and Roman poets. She is currently writing a commentary on Hesiod's *Theogony* in collaboration with Athanassios Vergados for the Cambridge Green and Yellow series.

Chiara Thumiger is a classicist and historian of ancient science, currently holding a Wellcome Trust fellowship at Warwick, UK. On the medical side of her research, her interests lie in the area of history of psychiatry and of the representations of mental health. As a classicist, she has worked on Greek tragedy, ancient views about the self, and ancient animals. Recent publications are *A History of the Mind and Mental Health in Classical Greek Medical Thought* (Cambridge, 2017) and *Mental Illness in Ancient Medicine* (co.-ed. W. P. Singer, 2018). Among current projects there is a monograph about the ancient disease phrenitis and its afterlife in the Western medical tradition, and a volume on the topic of 'holism', 'connectionism' and 'localization' in ancient medicine and its reception (Ancient Holisms).

Oxana Timofeeva is a doctor of Science, a professor at the European University at St. Petersburg, a senior research fellow at the Institute of Philosophy of Russian Academy of Science (Moscow), a member of the artistic collective "Chto Delat?" ("What is to be done?"), a deputy editor of the journal "Stasis", and the author of books *History of Animals* (Jan van Eyck, 2012; Moscow, 2017; Bloomsbury Academic, 2018), and *Introduction to the Erotic Philosophy of Georges Bataille* (Moscow, 2009).

Johan Tralau is Professor of Government at Uppsala University, Sweden. He is currently working on a monograph in English on the origins of political philosophy in ancient Greece – specifically, on the evolution of techniques of argumentation from Homer to Sophokles. His most recent book, *Havets väldiga ryggar: Offret och de flytande bildernas gåta* (*The Broad Backs of the Sea: On Sacrifice and the Enigma of Liquid Images*, 2018) deals with cognitively disturbing metaphors in Greek poetry.

Katherine Wasdin is Assistant Professor of Classics at the University of Maryland. Her research interests include reception studies, Greek and Latin poetry, gender in the ancient world, and the Greek novel. She has published a monograph, *Eros at Dusk: Ancient Wedding and Love Poetry* (2018), as well as articles on Claudian, Catullus, and Heliodorus, and is currently writing a book about the reception of Catullus in contemporary female writers and artists.

Nancy Worman is the Ann Whitney Olin Professor of Classics at Barnard College, Director of Graduate Studies at Columbia University, and affiliated with Barnard's Program in Comparative Literature and Department of Women's, Gender, and Sexuality Studies. Her research focuses on style and the body in performance in classical Greek drama and its reception, as well as rhetoric and ancient and modern literary criticism and theory. She has published books and articles on these topics, including most recently *Landscape and the Spaces of Metaphor in Ancient Literary Theory and Criticism* (2015) and *Virginia Woolf's Greek Tragedy* (2019). She is currently working on a book-length project entitled *Embodiment and the Edges of the Human in Greek Tragedy*, which is forthcoming from Bloomsbury

THEORETICAL INTRODUCTION: THE SUBJECT OF THE HUMAN

Giulia Maria Chesi and Francesca Spiegel

> In everything that lives, if one looks searchingly, is limned the shadow line of an idea [. . .] Do not imagine that I speak of human life alone.
>
> Voltairine de Cleyre

'Modernity' starts with planets. What course do they follow? How far do they travel from each other, and from us? What frame of reference – if any – should be privileged, and why? How do we conceptualize the space in between? With the astronomical Copernican revolution in the sixteenth century, a world-view was shaken and a new frame of reference emerged as a paradigm shift.[1]

Astronomical metaphors become ubiquitous and produce dislocations, off-centre motion and disarticulation, unsettling and upsetting the human Self. 'The time is out of joint';[2] in fact, ''tis all in pieces, all cohaerence gone';[3] we feel 'a strange infirmity',[4] as we found ourselves 'aweary of the sun', wishing 'th' estate o' th' world were now undone';[5] the tools are ready for 'An Anatomy of the World', and at the same time the individual himself becomes 'a little world made cunningly / of Elements, and an Angelike spright',[6] and in this rearrangement of senses and perceptions, he wishes to 'sleepe a space'.[7] This *metaphorein* is a process of pouring together and confounding (*confundere*: put together, mix up). The human is an interiority, which pours itself into toys ('there's nothing serious in mortality /All is but toys'[8]) – even 'dreams are toys'[9] – and into machines ('most small fault [. . .] like an engine wrenched my frame of nature / from the fixed place';[10] 'repaire me now'[11]).

In pouring itself together in the dominion of objects, forms of life, abstract patterns, the human behaves like an 'outward Soule' (John Donne, *The Funerall*), like the orbital eccentricity of a satellite around a dark planet – the two celestial bodies' barycentre still undetermined, the geometrical centre, however accurately located, void and lost in deep space.

It is in this confounding, metaphorizing outpouring of the 'outward Soule' that we detect the postmodern territories of the Posthuman, and the signs of an emancipatory subject which is confounded with alterity and is 'be-monster'-ing its features (*King Lear*, IV. ii. 63).

We take emancipation to be the *trait d'union* between Humanism and Post/humanism. For this reason, we start this Introduction by exploring the relation between Humanism and Post/humanism (section 1). Beginning with a history of emancipatory thought, we will introduce the notion of a Post/human subject as a heterogeneous self (section 2) – a hum*an*imal with a culturally and technologically constructed body (section 3), and a huma(n)chine (section 4) – opening up perspectives on how reading classical texts will lead to a critical understanding of Post/human subjectivity. Sections 5 and 6 come back to emancipation, investigating the emancipatory agency of the heterogeneous self envisaged as a huma(n)chine. Section 7 closes our discussion, focusing on the ethical-political challenge that the classical studies presented here pose to readers.

The purpose of this volume, then, is not to find out whether or to what extent Classical texts fit into a Post/human discourse, but to demonstrate how reading Classical literature challenges mainstream views in the Posthuman debates.

Posthumanism is an umbrella term that covers different notions (Cultural Posthumanism, Antihumanism, New Materialisms, Transhumanism and AI Takeover).[12] From the point of view of the history of ideas, Posthumanism can be considered as an intensification of Postmodernism in the sense that it continues the postmodern deconstruction of the notion of the human:[13] according to Grusin (2015), if Postmodernism deconstructed the idea of a human unified self and paved the way for emancipatory discourses on gender, race, ethnicity and class, the Posthuman turn inaugurates a liberatory discourse for groups of non-human entities (such as animals, objects and machines).

This has generated a reluctance to award ontological priority to any shared characteristics of human beings, and has triggered the radical criticism of speciesm and human exceptionalism (Wolfe 2009): the line between humans and animals, humans and objects, is challenged towards the idea of humans and non-humans as entities existing in terms of interacting parts and emergent wholes, which for DeLanda (2002) leads to a flat ontology, i.e., an ontology 'made exclusively of unique singular individuals, differing in spatio-temporal scale but not in ontological status' (47).

There are lively debates among classicists on how Posthuman studies can apply to classical learning. Several conferences have recently been organized (e.g., Edinburgh 2017 on Materiality and Representation; Bristol 2017 Cyborg Classics Symposium; announced UCLA 2019, Metamorphosis and the Environmental Imagination), yet very few materials are published. There are only three books: Bianchi, Brill and Holmes (2019), *Antiquities Beyond Humanism*; Telò and Mueller (2018), *The Materialities of Greek Tragedy*; and Mueller (2016), *Objects as Actors*. There are also only a few papers: Purves (2015), Holmes (2015) and Mueller (2016a) on Homer; and Payne (2016) on Aristophanes' *Wasps*. In these pre-existing works – with the exception of Payne, according to whom the meaning of human and animal hybridity is not about breaking down boundaries but exposing historical practices of domination – the blurring of the boundaries between humans and non-humans seems to translate into a process of saming alterity: animals are perceived as possessing a cognition that should be paradigmatic for humans;[14] feelings pertain to humans and material objects alike;[15] the 'life' of objects is not another in respect to the life of humans;[16] divine natural forces, like Scamander, are 'a particular kind of person';[17] theatrical props are agents like actors.[18] In particular, Holmes et al. consider Posthumanism to be a turn beyond Humanism.

Our volume departs from this existing research and maintains the crucial relevance of difference, which Posthumanism's flat ontologies often level. It is also the first comprehensive Posthuman reference collection in Classical literature, and the first to bring together studies on animals, monsters, machines and objects in Classical literature. While tracing what continuities (and what breaks) exist between these categories and the human, this collection inches towards uncovering the notion of a *heterogeneous self* in Classical literature, of an ontology of the human as inhabited by difference, and a subjectivity that embodies this alterity. It also questions the ideological move of 'saming the difference', by which equality between self and other is achieved by negating differences. Intellectually, this only conceals another strategy of domination over weaker subjects.

The collection invites us to appraise the animal, monstrous and machinic otherness within the human: we need animals, monsters, objects and machines in order to define a space for the human. In this sense, the chapters compel us to ask whether discourses of Posthumanism might exceed the question of what it means to be human – just like they question the view by which the human is the centre of everything. Presupposing an understanding of difference whereby the self exists necessarily and only in function of the Other, this Posthuman reading of Classical literature continues a critical tradition already initiated by Redfield's (1975) *Nature and Culture in the Iliad: The Tragedy of Hector* and Zeitlin's (1996) *Playing the Other*. This volume asks if, and to what extent, a Posthuman decentred view of the human forms part of a Humanistic inquiry.

This book has four Parts. Part I (De/Humanization and Animals) engages with the relation of humans and animals in the context of human and animal identity and subjectivity (Hopman on Odysseus and the boar in *Odyssey* 19; Korhonen on Lucius in Pseudo-Lucian's *Onos*; Mackay on animal voices in Valerius Flaccus), illness and physical suffering (Thumiger on Sophocles' *Philoctetes*), power and social order (Geue on the 'imperial animal' in Virgil's *Georgics*; Giordano on flocks and shepherds in the *Iliad* and Aeschylus' *Persians*; Baumgarten on lions and dogs in Herodotus and Plato). Particular attention is given to the dynamics of de/humanization with reference to discourses of inclusion/exclusion between animal and human. These chapters build on cutting-edge research on human/animal studies in classical antiquity, which challenges human speciesism and exceptionalism by acknowledging that animals also have the capacity for socialization, feeling and empathy, cultural production, knowledge transmission and cognition and, at the same time, by acknowledging the radical alterity of the animal in respect to the human (Alexandridis et al. 2008; Franco 2014; Korhonen and Ruonakoski 2017; Fögen and Thomas 2017).

In Part II (The Monstrous), the chapters by Strauss Clay on Typhoeus in *Theogony*, by Ceschi on demonic disease in Greek Tragedy, by Fleming on the Sphinx, by Kachuck on weeping elephants in Virgil, by McNamara on Cato in Lucan's *Civil War* and by Gerolemou on Aristophanes' *Birds* show that monstrosity is the Other of human and at the same time a constitutive element of human heroism and technology, as well as the crucial attribute of divine and cosmic order. While this Part responds to the increasing popularity of monster studies in classics (Lowe 2015), these chapters are the first to consider the monstrous in its capacity of inhabiting and defining the human in an integrated way.

Chapters 14–20 in Part III (Bodies and Entanglements) cover bodies and entities that are made of human and non-human parts, exposing the emergence and submersion of the human within the non-human. Devecka and Tralau write respectively on constructed bodies in Herodotus and Euripides' *Cretans*, Gershon on body politics in Dionysius of Halicarnassus' *Antiquitates Romanae*, Provenza on the female cyborgic body and identity in the myth of Io, Rosella Schluderer on the notion of cosmos and animal/human becomings in *Philolaus*; Dressler on personification in Seneca's epistles and *Happy Life*; Burrus on Saint Simeon the Stylite and hagiography without humans. While the notion of entanglement is a keyword of the Posthuman research in classics mentioned above, these chapters are the first to ask whether and to what extent human/non-human entanglements are embedded in a discourse of otherness and difference.

Chapters 21–30 in Part IV (Objects, Machines and Robotic Devices) explore the representation of objects, machines and robotic devices, their mutual relation and impact on human and machinic life. Worman and Noel write on props and technical objects in Greek tragedy; Spiegel and Giusti discuss technical objects such as weapons in Antiphon and Virgil's

Aeneid 12; while Wasdin explores speaking objects in Martial's *Xenia* and *Apophoreta*. Courrént discusses automated machines and the creation of a new post-natural world in Vitruvius 9; Chesi and Sclavi write on Pandora in Hesiod as a robotic device; Marinis and Liveley discuss automata in Pindar *Olympian* 7, and Ovid's myth of Pygmalion; Kirichenko writes on the written text of Plato's *Symposium* and *Phaedrus* and Horace's *Ars Poetica* as a technical device for information processing. While there exists extensive literature on machines and technological devices in Greek and Roman culture from the point of view of science fiction and the history of science,[19] these chapters are the first to investigate the literary and cultural reflection on the status of technology vis-à-vis the human and non-human continuity. When it comes to objects such as theatrical props and weapons, the chapters in this Part challenge the current debate on materiality (cf. Telò and Mueller 2018) by asking whether something other than human is equivalent to or rather complements the human.

Our volume is addressed to students and researchers in Classics and correlated disciplines. We chose to proceed by themes rather than by chronology in order to highlight the syncretism of Posthuman themes and engagements with its forms across Greek and Latin literature. Some pairings, such as Homer and Virgil (on animals), continue a long tradition of comparative readings, whereas other combinations are more unprecedented, but equally capable of producing contrasts and opening up new perspectives of reading. Four philosophical papers (Introductions to Post/human theories) deepen the theoretical frame underlying this volume, which we present in this Introduction, by tackling the central notions of our theoretical discussion: difference (Nuzzo), exclusion and inclusion (Timofeeva), cyborg (Mertlitsch), and human feelings of guilt and shame in relation to the human *cupio dissolvi* in technology (Hui).

In what follows, we will elucidate our idea of the Post/human subject as a *heterogeneous self* and its emancipatory agency, and how it emerges from the studies in this volume. We will begin with a historical positioning of the relation between Humanism and Posthumanism, as we understand the heterogeneous self as a Post/human subjectivity, which is a continuation of the *relational* Humanist subject.

Section 1: Humanism and Post/humanism

Posthumanism is often understood as a critique of Humanistic tradition, anchored in the idea that Humanist thought was anthropocentric and phallocentric, meaning that it conceptualized man – more particularly, the European white man[20] – as the norm and measure of all things.[21] Provocatively, Mousley (2007: 14) has called this 'mainstream humanism'. Certainly the Humanist tradition promoted essentialist narratives of human subjectivity that posit the human being as the exception, as the only rational and autonomous being.[22] Thereafter, only *the man* is essentially human – the woman is less fully human, representing the Other to the norm.[23] One thoroughgoing critique was made by Althusser in 'Marxisme et Humanisme': conceptualizing all humans as rational, free and autonomous was deceptive and a tool of domination, which created the illusion of freedom and autonomous subjects where there were none.

And yet, a look at the historical circumstances from which Humanist thinking arose uncovers quite a different positioning of Humanism: there is an other Humanism, one that endlessly promoted critical thinking and preserved the idea of the inviolable dignity of the Other.

To begin with, in the Italian Renaissance, Humanist thought took the form of a protest. Many Humanist thinkers exerted their thinking in opposition to the Church orthodoxy, facing censorship of their work, even capital punishment. To give just a few examples, the Dominican monk Campanella was censured and imprisoned for his 'heresies'; Ficino taught only for a short time at the university in Florence; Pico della Mirandola was refused an institutional venue for the disputation of the 900 theses, the introduction of which is the oration *De hominis dignitate*. Similarly, in the case of Spinoza, the *Tractatus theologicus-politicus* earned him the expulsion from Amsterdam's Jewish community, a family feud, and the condemnation of Luther and representatives of the Catholic Church.

Humanism also created the circumstances for the beginning of Feminism in Europe. In the fifteenth century, Laura Cereta's letter to Bibulus Sempronius is a defence of women's right to public education. In 1509, at the university of Dôle, Agrippa von Nettesheim gave his inaugural lecture '*De nobilitate et praecellentia foeminei sexus declamation*', and it is mirrored by Lucrezia Marinella in *La nobiltà, et l'eccellenza delle donne, co' diffetti, et mancamenti de gli huomini* and by Moderata Fonte in *Il merito delle donne*: *ove chiaramente si scuopre quanto siano elle degne e piu perfette de gli huomini*. Tullia d'Aragona wrote *Dell'inifinità d'amore*, in which she reclaims women's sexual and emotional autonomy. Marie de Gournay and François Poullain de La Barre authored a defence of the equality of women and men, respectively *L'égalité des Hommes et des Femmes* (1622) and *De l'égalité des deux sexes* (1673).

At a second important juncture in the combined history of emancipatory thinking and Humanism – the French Enlightenment – the Encyclopaedists raised their voices against the wrongs of established institutions such as slavery[24] and the death penalty.[25] To identify oneself as an enlightened citizen in these circumstances was not to submit to a tool of domination. It was rather a liberatory gateway to well-reasoned discussion, and it was in these historical circumstances that Olympe de Gouges authored the *Déclaration des droits de la femme et de la citoyenne*.

At this juncture, the production of knowledge through public discussion networks, independent of religion or royal power, enabled the citizen to fashion himself (still only 'himself', despite de Gouges) as a subject able to be free from the authority of the established institutions. In a broader social and political sense, participation in these networks created what Habermas would later call the *Öffentlichkeit* or 'public sphere'.

The prominence of women in the 'public sphere' should not be underestimated. Contemplating the case of France, David Hume wrote: 'In a neighbouring Nation [...] the Ladies are, in a Manner, the Sovereigns of the *learned* world [...]; and no polite Writer pretends to venture upon the Public, without the Approbation of some celebrated Judges of that Sex' ('Of Essay Writing', cited in Keen, 2013: 161). Hume is thinking here, e.g., of the illustrious salons of Mmes de Rambouillet, de Lambert, de Tencin, Mme d'Epinay.

At these turning points in the conjoined histories of emancipatory thought and Humanism, the subject is specifically and even provocatively conceptualized by its relation to others (women, slaves, incarcerated people) rather than being the centre of the universe, the 'homo mensura'. As with early feminist thought entering the sphere of public discourse and the condemnation of slavery and death penalty, openness to foreign cultures further emphasizes the conception of the self as standing in relation to others. For example, Averroism comprises a syncretic view of cultural production,[26] as practised by early comparatist scholars, such as Pico della Mirandola whose *Heptalus* is the first kabbalistic reading of *Genesis.* Humanist scholarship engaged itself not only with Arabic and Hebrew, but also with the cultural heritage of ancient Egypt. Francesco Colonna authored the *Hypnerotomachia Poliphili*, which tells the oneiric travels of Poliphilo and his encounters with Egyptian inscription; Giovan Pietro della Fosse writes *Hieroglyphica*; Giordano Bruno[27] grounds his religious universalism in the Egyptian magical tradition. The polymath and philosopher Leibniz becomes probably the first Western scholar of Confucian and Chinese philosophy and the first comparative mathematician. While it is true that the Humanist scholars of early modern Europe brought renewed enthusiasm to studying ancient Greek texts, Humanistic scholarship is nonetheless comparatist at heart. In this light, a challenge arises to the received view that the Humanist project somehow prioritized the ancient Greeks with the agenda of promoting their 'superiority'.[28]

The Humanist discourse within the Classical tradition

Also the Humanist discourse within the Classical tradition can be read as a vigilant critique of anthropocentrism that posits the human subject as inherently open to the Other. Aristotle's definition of the human being as a rational animal (*Pol.* 1253a9–10) posits the human as the only creature endowed with the faculty of *logos*, from which it follows that humans alone are autonomous and free.[29] A particularly famous example of this is the first stasimon of *Antigone*, which distinguishes between the 'races of wild animals' (*Ant.* 344) and the 'most ingenious man' (*Ant.* 346). Conversely, when a human loses the faculty of *logos*, this is evaluated as a loss of identity. In the myth of Procne and Tereus, the three characters who turn into birds lose their faculty of speech, which gets reduced to bird song. We say 'reduced', because both in the Greek and the later Ovidian version, this exchange of human speech for bird song presents a terrifying aspect of the transformation, symbolizing the ultimate loss of humanity, and implying a view of *logos* as that which differentiates the human from the animal.

Yet, this assessment reflects the way modern scholars have understood Greek authors more than it reveals the 'real intent' of Greek writers or the 'real meaning' of myth. In 'The Intentional Fallacy', 'The Death of the Author' and 'What Is an Author?', Wimsatt and Beardsley, Barthes and Foucault have laid out the fact that authorial intent is not available to the reader: whatever meanings the reader of a text may understand, these meanings say much more about the reader than they say about the writer of the text. As such, in a chauvinistic anthropocentric world-view, a narrative of transformation and losing speech like the myth of Tereus and Procne would signify the loss of humanity. This is not the only interpretation. When it comes to ancient myths of transformation, one can also see that Greek writers are most interested in understanding the whole procedure of metamorphosis rather than making a value judgement about it. Seen this way, human chauvinism is not how ancient Greek cultural and literary production frames its own narratives of animal metamorphosis. Instead, the Classical literary imaginarium approaches animal transformation from an investigative viewpoint that wants to understand what would happen if a human were to be transformed into an animal. This is an instance of perspectival anthropocentrism,[30] according to which humans relate to the world from a human perspective, without for this reason elevating the human to the determining norm.[31]

Framing Graeco-Roman attitudes to animal metamorphosis in this way leads us to uncovering how Greek and Latin authors have often conceptualized the shift from human to animal identity as a result of physical or sexual violence. Greek tragedy furnishes us with examples where characters bemoan their 'bestialization'. In the myth of Tereus and Procne, the rape of Philomela and the cannibalistic supper are at the root of their transfer into the world of an animal existence. The Sophoclean Philoctetes, who will temporarily lose his faculty of articulate speech, considers himself 'wildified', and makes clear that, for him, the whole situation is the result of Odysseus' abuse. Although Philoctetes becomes what a man should *not* be, Sophocles' play presents itself to us as an inquiry into life on the edges of human dignity, rather than a condemnation of human bestiality. Violence and abuse can reduce a human to an animal, but, in tragedy, this reduction to the bestial incites sympathy rather than condemnation. A third example is *Hecuba*, where the spectacle of Hecuba's reduction to the bestial comes across as disturbing, because it jars so much with the noble character as whom Hecuba is first introduced.

These examples show how the Greek tragic subject is a relational one, and as if to prove it, her/his language is such: in the extant plays, the keyword *dike* has different meanings, depending on context and who uses it.[32] Here, the tragic self as speaking and thinking subject is open to the Other[33] and conceptualized as residing in a web of relations, where every interaction with the Other leaves traces on the self, and vice versa.

Our brief excursus into the history of the Humanist subject has allowed us to see that the Humanist model is fundamentally critical of anthropocentrism, like critical Post/humanism itself, which is at heart a critique of anthropocentrism, and not of Humanism. For us, the relationality of the thinking subject is common to both Humanist *and* Post/humanist thought, and is a defining feature of both. As we shall see more in detail in the next section, the Post/human concept of relationality takes from Humanism the idea of the self's absolute respect for the Other, as well as the idea of the inviolable dignity of the human, and all forms of life. From our perspective, Posthumanism should oppose the centrality of man without disregarding his/her humanity in the first place.

Further, with Clarke and Rossini in *The Cambridge Companion to Literature and the Posthuman* (2017: xiv), we contend that 'posthumanist discourses promote neither the transcendence of the human nor the negation of humanism. Rather, critical posthumanisms engage with the humanist legacy to critique anthropocentric values and worldviews'. In this sense, in the history of thought, Post/humanism critically traces the history of the *relational subject* – as inherently decentred and defined by difference – from Humanist thought properly speaking (including its debts to Graeco-Roman antiquity) of the early modern period, to postmodern theory of the relational self, and takes it one step further, by introducing the idea of the subject as *the heterogeneous self*. With Herbrechter (2012: 2), we argue that, '"Posthumanism" is still some form of humanism, after all.'

Section 2: The heterogeneous self

The conceptualization of the Post/human subject as a heterogeneous and relational self calls for further refinement and perspective. How exactly may we envision a heterogeneous self?

Difference and the Post/human subject

The heterogeneous self does not only stand *in relation* to the Other, but it *embodies* it: it *becomes* animal, it *becomes* machine. As it has the Other *within*,[34] it is hum*an*imal, huma(n)chine. The hum*an*imal and the huma(n)chine, or as Haraway puts it, the *cyborg*,[35] acknowledges a displacement of subjectivity in the Other, not the death of the subject.[36] By disentangling the divide between nature and technology (huma(n)chine) and between the human and the animal (hum*an*imal), the cyborg affirms the emergence of a technologized and animalized subject who decentres the human Self by situating the human at the intersection of the organic and the technical, of the human and the animal. Since being human is being animal, and being machine, the essence of the human is co-essential: a sharing, or assemblage.[37] The Post/human subject, then, is not identical to itself; it has no *essential* identity.[38] The technologized and animalized human being becomes an inherently *heterogeneous Self* who embodies the machinic and animal difference within himself. This is why the Post/human subject makes it possible to re-think the epistemological value of contradiction.[39] By overcoming the dialectic of identity, the *heterogeneous Self* instantiates *difference differentially* (cf. Nuzzo on Foucault in this volume). Difference here is not in opposition to but in continuity with identity.[40]

The heterogeneous self does not reassess each entity on the same ontological plane, which some have described as a 'flat ontology'.[41] By embodying difference differentially, the idea of a heterogeneous self keeps intact the epistemological value of difference and identity. This is crucial: difference without identity erases diversity. As Haraway puts it (2016: 27): 'in the consciousness of our failures, we risk lapsing into *boundless difference* and giving up on the confusing task of making *partial, real connection*. Some differences are playful; some are poles of world historical domination. "Epistemology" is about *knowing the difference*' [italics ours]. Here, the consideration of differences between Self and Other does not create dichotomies; on the contrary, it poses the question of how we are supposed to make ourselves what we are to become.

Classical literature invites us precisely to think about 'boundless difference' and 'knowing the difference' when it comes to the Post/human subject as a hybrid construct (hum*an*imal; huma(n)chine). While hybridity is a welcomed quality, during the darker moments of human experience it can become an unexpected threat to dignity: Noel in this volume discusses instances where human corpses become assimilated with things in the natural environment and demoted to infra-human states that open the floodgates to disrespectful behaviour. Taking stock of the negative connotations of hybridity, it is necessary to make finer distinctions between modes of hybridity: not all hybridizations are helpful. This sentiment is explored also by Tralau, who takes Euripides' *Cretans* to study the disruptive and unpleasant nature of metaphors where the components do not fit together but highlights the displeasure in experiencing or viewing a woman's body as a human-animal-machine conglomerate.

Difference, emancipation and flat ontology

The notion of boundless difference amounts to the reduction of the Other to the norms of the self – Levinas (1957) would talk about *égologie*. If we are to accept that only difference is ontologically cogent, we have to agree also that 'we are all, and *must* be, monsters' (MacCormack 2012: 294): in doing so, aren't we paradoxically *erasing* alterity, and thus repeating intellectually and ethically the very imperialism that Posthumanism sought to confront – the colonization of the Other as the self?

In promoting a critical thinking which scrutinizes the regime of sameness inherent to a flat ontology – a philosophical gesture deeply rooted in the Classical tradition – the Post/human subject takes up the critical stance so distinctive of the Humanist tradition. Indeed, an ontology, which posits humans, animals and objects on the same plane of immanence appears to be associated with a blind belief in the tenets of contemporary capitalism. Erasure of difference looms large over the economy of digital identities, if we conceptualize the formation of a 'nomadic subject'[42] susceptible of entering an abstract and mobile trade in the commodified features of gender, culture, nationality, religious beliefs, social belonging and personal habits, mimicking the unrestricted circulation not just of commodities and services, but also of identities.[43]

In the Classical texts under scrutiny a very sophisticated discourse on ontological entanglements emerges, one that pushes us to ponder critically if and to what extent the categories of difference and ontological intersection can co-exist. In her discussion of Philolaus' cosmology, Rosella Schluderer (Chapter 18) argues that all living beings within the *cosmos* share the same ontological structure, and yet there is between them an equally undeniable distinction. At each level of the *scala naturae* new aspects emerge, 'which, far from disappearing as the complexity of the system increases, are subsumed and combined to endow each new emergent becoming with different powers and capacities'. Dressler (Chapter 19) discusses a Senecan idea of the human as characterized by unity with entities other than human: consistent with the Stoic idea of panpsychism, there is an inalienable continuity between the human and the non-human. Like the humans, so too stone and beast are free of fear and anger. Yet, only humans can be happy because thanks to their self-reflexivity they have an understanding of their own prosperity. Moreover, human foresight is provocatively thought 'as doing the action that the person presumably does with it'. Yet, foresight is distinct from the human as it is a human possession and therefore a commodity owned by the self-reflexive human agent. Chapter 20 by Burrus on Simeon the Stylite and Chapter 17 by Provenza on Io show how an ontologically founded continuity between human and non-human entities relates to the divine, and the female. In particular, the figure of Io as a female cyborg becomes an elucidation of ontological entrapment (like the hybridity of the cyborg Helen in the epic tradition,[44] Io's new hum*an*imal ontology fails to be emancipatory).

There is another reason why the Post/human subject takes up the critical stance of the Humanist subject. In resisting an ontology of boundless difference, the Post/human subject asks if such an ontology does not run the risk of annulling both the alterity of the human in respect to the object and the alterity of the object in respect to the human. If objects and humans exist on the same ontological plane, the object exists independently from human perception and cognition – it is 'already there'. Yet, if the object is already there and exists on the same ontological plane as the human being, it follows that the human being too has to be 'already there'. Yet, the human being is not 'already there': it is the product of cultural discourse, which perpetually makes and re-remakes the human. Equally so, the object is not 'already there': objects are made by humans, come into existence and endure time.[45] Humans and objects, then, have their specific mode of existence.[46]

Classical literature shows a way of conceptualizing object–human interconnectedness that preserves alterity. Wasdin (Chapter 25) takes a close look at what assumptions are behind human–object interactions in the case of presents: the gift that is inscribed with the name of its intended owner, or with instructions as to its proper use, gives the appearance of being able to speak. One gets the impression of an object telling the person what to do; this anthropomorphizing of an object-turned-thinking-subject drives home the inseparability of things from humans. Yet, even if inscribed objects can have verbal agency, the act of verbalization necessarily still has human authorship. Wasdin's discussion pushes us to ponder about the radical alterity of the object: if human–object interconnectedness relies upon anthropomorphization, the object *in itself* remains unknown to humans. Worman (Chapter 21) focuses on the extension that material textures, especially clothes, can give to human bodies and how the synergy of textile and human lays bare a Greek tragic sensibility to the mechanics and thing-ness of human bodies, melted together in a Posthuman condition. However, the fusion of human and textile materials is a semiotic locus 'for pondering identity, entrapment, proximity, family history'.

Equally importantly, Classical literature makes us think about the complexity of human–object entanglements by addressing the theme of unwanted interconnectedness. In Chapter 23, Spiegel focuses on malfunctions of man–weapon entanglements, where weapons fail to be a seamless extension of masculine human agency, and instead cause damage. Here, malfunctioning entanglements are considered in the light of ideologies underwriting Greek embodiment of masculinity. Giusti (Chapter 24) deals with the symbiotic relationship of arms and men in the *Aeneid*, comparing how this combination materializes in Aeneas and Turnus, taking the networkedness of things and humans to interpret the ambiguities of Augustan ideology in Virgil's epic.

To recap

To think of the Post/human subject as hum*an*imal and huma(n)chine is to decentre the human by conceptualizing it as interconnected in inextricable entanglements.[47] Hence, we have never been *essentially human* because we have never been *human enough*. By its interconnection with the animal and the machinic, a heterogeneous self is responsible for these Others. This is not meant in the essentialist sense that only the human subject as self is capable of taking responsibility and thus once again inhabits a dichotomous power relation where the self cares for the Other, which then becomes an object. Quite the converse: this is to state the moral priority of the Other over the self in an asymmetrical ethical relation which language cannot contain.[48]

In showcasing the relationality of *human* with *other* as a state of hybridity, the Post/human heterogeneous self is embodied and *unified*: it incorporates its own de-centralization (= liability to marginalization) into a unified configuration of subjectivity that is certainly heterogeneous and hybridized, but *integrated* and not at all dismantled or displaced. The Post/human heterogeneous self does not dispute human identity in its essence as a dubious substance falling apart. By *re-figuring* the boundaries of human/animal/machine, the Post/human subject challenges the human acting as a complex, convoluted extension of itself, pushing the boundaries of its own imagination to the point of a radical alterity. We might picture prehistoric people in a cave, in front of the fire casting an ambiguous light on the wall and ceiling; a shadow-play which they assumed as the intervention of imaginary creatures, like spirits of the forest. In their dream-like, symbolic mind, alterity was conserved, even fostered. In an activity similar to this, the Post/human subject does not 'break up boundaries' in order to reassess each entity on the same plane of immanence as itself, but establishes itself within a context of radical alterities. Becoming animal and becoming machine does not mediate the distance between technology and nature, but shows that there never was a binary dichotomy. In this sense, the hum*an*imal and the huma(n)chine, or the cyborg, is not a 'borderline figure', as much as it is the reclaiming of the human's extension in mythical form. Cyborgs are *dramatic devices, theatrical arrangements* that tell of the human's nostalgia for devices and forms of existence from which humans are different.

In a history of emancipatory thinking, Post/humanism is a further step into Humanist thinking, because it affirms the emergence of the human subject as the emergence of the Other. In doing so, Post/humanism is also a Feminism: 'the emergence or the occurrence of the other', as Irigaray puts it in *Éthique de la différence sexuelle*, equals 'the mourning of the self as an independent entity'.[49] The Post/human heterogeneous subject, as the Humanist subject that preceded it, is a critical subject intent on emancipation from ideological discourses of identity and of alterity: it recognizes that there can be no 'Self' without an 'Other' (and that the self is not autonomous), but simultaneously, that it is not logical to say that the self *is* the Other.

We now will unpack the heterogeneous self as Becoming-animal (section 3); Becoming-machine (section 4).

Section 3: Becoming-animal

For humans, becoming-animal is becoming animal in a human body. From a phenomenological perspective, humans experience themselves primarily as having a sentient body, which acts as the norm of embodiment, along with a norm of the first-person sensuous and mental awareness: because human thinking takes place within a body, mind is the consciousness of a body, and thinking is embodied.[50] By having a body, humans also become sympathetic with other humans – and non-human animals – to the extent that the human body feels the body of the Other. In other words, embodiment is what enables humans to recognize the subjectivity of another, and therefore to perceive them as a subject of life. Humans, then, have the animal difference within them:[51] like animals, humans can feel through their body, and this is how humans can understand that, even if it does not suffer exactly in the same way, an animal *can* suffer. Thus, human embodiment leads to an ethics that is not about justice in the sense of following laws, but about responsibility and care, so not about calculation, prohibition or compulsion, but about emotion, desire and feelings.[52] And yet, although animals are subjects of life as much as humans, humans can relate to them only according to human norms, only according to human ethics. The inter-subjectivity of the human being conceptualized as a hum*an*imal is still based on the rationality of ethics: to paraphrase Agnes Heller (1994) in 'A Reply to My Critics', humans have to think together how to think, how to act, how to live. In this sense, human language, for the hum*an*imal, is not the basis of an exceptionalism, but the *conditio sine qua non* for embodying the Other.

We do not mean that animals do not have their own ethics. We mean that the human being who embodies animal difference, but ceases to define itself as in part *human*, abandons an ethical perspective that for her/him can only be human. Animals do not speak in human language;[53] therefore, for the human being who, in her/his capacity as a hum*an*imal, talks human language, they remain fundamentally an enigma: animals will never answer the hum*an*imal[54] – even if we suppose that they understand him. Paradoxically, the existential condition of the interconnected hum*an*imal is that of an abyssal solitude.

In safeguarding the radical alterity of the animal, the hum*an*imal resists human discourses of animal domestication. Those are, as Timofeeva puts it in this volume, discourses of inclusion and exclusion:

> The discourse of exclusion starts with the ethical and ontological predominance of the human, whereas the discourse of inclusion insists on the affinity of all levels of being. But these two discourses are related and their function is the same: to establish or to conserve a certain order of things. As Bataille pointed out, the basis of this rational order is the transcendence of the human that requires the sacrifice of irreducible animal nature.

Human embodiment as the way to becoming-animal also points to the limits of the hum*an*imal subjectivity – *Schmerz* is a private business; my body is only my body: not the body of an animal and not the body of another human being.

In Part I, 'De/Humanization and Animals', the chapters invite us to ponder the problems inherent in conceiving of the human/animal relation as a continuity or as a dichotomy. The human is constructed through animality and the animal through humanity (Hopman, Chapter 1), also in a cultural gesture of shared domestication (Baumgarten, Chapter 7); humans and animals are both centres of subjectivity (Korhohen, Chapter 2, and Mackay, Chapter 3) and shared embodiment is the condition for the empathic encounter between humans and animals (Korhohen), human suffering even intersects with animal suffering (Thumiger, Chapter 4), yet human empathy with animal suffering can also be a function of domination by the ruling class (Geue, Chapter 5); a rhetoric of complementarity between humans and animals enables a strategy of dehumanization of the Other when it comes to conflicts between humans, and a legitimization of the idea that some people are 'naturally born' to lead (Giordano, Chapter 6).

Hum*an*imal bodies

For the hum*an*imal, the human body is not just the centre of human consciousness and therefore the centre of the empathic encounter with the animal other. The human body is a product of cultural and social practices, and it is hybridized, because culture is hybrid. The hum*an*imal subject prevents us therefore from all too easily adopting a materialist-biologist view of the human. History has shown that the socio-political consequences of a materialist-biologist view of the human are disastrous.

In the context of the industry 4.0, characterized by accelerated technological innovation and potentiated pharmacological feasibility – in terms of human lifespan, human sexuality, human mental stimulation and performance – Nikolas Rose in 2007 had coined the notion of 'neurochemical selves' in the context of psychopharmacology and how the molecules of psychotropic drugs encroached on human subjectivity in a way that invisibly merged the human with an added molecule. For the psychologist Oyama (2000), all developments and behaviours of both humans and animals are biologically and physically constructed, and not at all related to cultural transmission.

We take issue with such a material-biological idea of the human body, for the reason that it does not acknowledge the disciplinarian aspect of pharmacology, the historic synergies of pharmacology and ideology. The xenofeminist collective Laboria Cuboniks writes of 'pharmacological tools', and one itches to complete the phrase with the words 'of domination', as the Xenofeminist manifesto, much like Haraway's Cyborg manifesto, is concerned with the politics and the economy of accelerated technological – particularly pharmacological – feasibility. In studying the history of medical testosterone and contraception in modern culture, Preciado (2008) shows its origin in eugenics programmes of the 1930s; the adaptation to the mass-market in the 1960s and 1970s was an afterthought; and right into the present time, the approval of uses of testosterone in legislation is a highly politicized and polarizing subject.

As early as 1966, Canguilhem had argued that medicine's abilities to correct or improve the human body make medicine a normative, regulatory and constructivist science. In *Surveiller et punir*, Foucault put forward the concept of a 'docile body', i.e., a body that can be submitted, utilized and enhanced for efficacy or productivity. Preciado, in 2008, spoke of 'micro-prosthetics'; but it is the ethics of prosthetics, the ideology of domination that could, and often does, inhabit the conception and application of *pharmaka* (psychiatry being the most discussed example: Foucault; Szasz; Whitaker), where it is not enough to settle for a materialist-biologist view of the human. It still is, as Rabelais had his novelistic character Gargantua write to his son, 'La sagesse ne peut pas entrer dans un esprit méchant, et science sans conscience n'est que ruine de l'âme'.

Classical literature plays with the awareness that human bodies are culturally produced. Greek literature presents an image of medicine as the technological knowledge for constructing bodies according to a cultural norm of health (Devecka, Ceschi). Bodies are also constructed by language (Tralau) and body technologies, like rejuvenation, serve as a *topos* in political discourse (Gershon).

Section 4: Becoming-machine

What does it mean, for humans, to become a machine, a huma(n)chine? The huma(n)chine is 'a cybernetic organism, a hybrid of machine and organism',[55] 'a fusion of the organic and the technical forged in particular, historical, cultural practices'.[56] As argued by Chesi and Sclavi (Chapter 27), the figure of Pandora is readable as a huma(n)chine – she is described as a product of technology, and yet human at the same time – and disentangles a technocratic logic of domination perpetrated in the idea of a tyranny of machines over humans. It is this Pandora which in this section is our source of inspiration for our view of the huma(n)chine as a Post/human emancipatory subject.

The human and the machinic difference

Indeed, humans embody the machinic difference. The fabrication and elaboration of mechanism as functional working units is a specific organic trait. *Techne* is an expression of *bios* – it is not out there towering upon the individual.[57] The machinic is by its nature 'human', abstracted from deambulation, heartbeat, breathing pattern, language. As McGurl in 'The Posthuman Comedy' puts it (2012: 550), 'The second act of the posthuman comedy is in this sense a turn (and continual return) to naturalism, one in which nature, far from being dominated by technology, *reclaims* technology as a human *secretion*, something human beings under the right conditions naturally produce and use.' In fact, the mechanization of humans, who are the *artifex* of their own world, 'has long preceded the mechanization of their working instruments, in the far more ancient order of ritual' (Mumford 1967: 190), and of politics: the resolution of the nature/culture divide is already implicit in Aristotle's claim that human beings are *by nature* urban (viz. technological) animals (*Politics* 1253a2–3: *anthropos phusei politikon zoon*).

Humans embody the machinic also because they share a profound intimacy with the technical object. As Heidegger has shown in *Die Frage nach der Technik*, both are 'Bestand' (standing-reserve): as the airplane is ordered ('bestellt') to fly, so the human being is ordered to challange ('herausfoerdern') nature by exploiting its resources. Yet, humans and technical objects are profoundly different. What distinguishes humans is their specific epistemic operation of inventorying and ordering the world into a 'Bestand'. Humans think and speak, and, in doing so, they reveal the 'Gestell' (the enframing) to be the mode of technological uncovering of the world as 'Bestand' (i.e., of bringing something from being not at all into being that which it is). The enframing exposes humans to a double danger: by using technology to exploit nature (to discover what lies hidden in nature), humans posit themselves as masters ('Herr') over nature, and, thus end up knowing only themselves (the technological world they build).

The shared intimacy between humans and technical objects is also measured in human creativity. Technical objects are not just an extension of the human body, they are an extension of human creativity, as Simondon (2012: 334–340) has spelled out. Thus, even if we assume, with Hutchins (1995) in *Cognition in the Wild*, that a technical activity like, say, navigation is a distributed cognitive network made of pilots, navigating tools and other individuals, the navigating tools still function according to the cognitions of the humans who built them.

In Chapter 26, Courrént makes us aware, once more, that the resolution of the nature/culture divide and the view of the human being as inherently technological has a long and in fact ancient history: in her discussion, she exposes the Vitruvian man as one who lives in an artificial world that he construes and constructs by technology, while distancing and alienating himself from the world of nature.

The machinic difference and the limits of the human

The human subject, conceptualized as a huma(n)chine, is not a machine. The notion of a radical difference between humans and machines points to the ontological and epistemological limits of the human and prevents us from lapsing into discourses which anthropomorphize the machine and assimilate the Other to the self.

Human ontological limits. The huma(n)machine is still a mortal and ephemeral being. Ethics of prosthethics should insist on the human inviolable right to death (the 'droit à la mort', as Blanchot phrased it), for death is the condition of alterity.

Human epistemological limits. Machines are not intelligent as we are. Bostrom (2006, 2014) argues that the achievement of a human-level AI translates straightforwardly into replicating human intelligence in a digital environment (the so-called bottom-up approach). Yet, our knowledge of the human brain is extremely poor. We are far from a sophisticated understanding of the human unified field of consciousness (how our cognitive and motor activities happen at once). The lack of knowledge in the field of neuroscience alone makes the creation of a digital replica of the human mind dubious at best. Even assuming that neuroscience is about to reach an exhaustive knowledge of the brain, we still would not be any closer to replicating human intelligence in a digital environment. The entire sum of all scientific data regarding brain functions does not amount in any significant sense to an explanation of how consciousness actually occurs. Elucidating a phenomenon, scientifically, involves always something more than just annotating numbers, or even acknowledging objective 'facts'. Mathematicians recognize a restricting boundary of this sort as they explain the impossibility of devising a coherent, and at the same time complete system of representation, even in the relatively simple realm of first-order arithmetic (Gödel 1931). In other words, 'intelligence' alone – whatever we might mean by that notion – cannot explain itself on its own terms.

In this light, our inability to give an exhaustive explanation of the brain's activity seems to hinge less on the amount of data and the efficiency of simulation than on the epistemological difficulties of defining what human consciousness is. And if this is the case, certainly any of our artifacts, however technologically advanced, will rather display a necessarily non-human intelligence. This implies that robotic machines as embodied agents,[58] with sensorimotor skills, will display a necessarily non-human embodied cognition.[59]

Contrary to a widespread Posthuman view of artificial intelligence as dis-embodied information processing – a view which perpetrates a devaluation of the body and 'disincarnates' the mind as an abstract pattern (in the Cartesian tradition of the Cogito) – Classical literature invites us to appraise robotic information processing as corporeal and incarnate features of machinic cognitive processes. In Chapter 29, Kirichenko argues that the written texts of Plato and Horace are information-processing devices transforming the embodied consciousness of the speaker into an 'information pattern' which enters a symbiotic relationship with the reader's embodied subjectivity by way of a metaphorical process of biological imageries.

The imitation game

The radical difference of machinic intelligence from human intellingence points out that the human being envisaged as huma(n)chine must have the absolute moral priority of the Other's dignity: we do not want 'intelligent' machines to be our slaves. Again, the Posthuman subject embodies the cultural heritage of Humanism: s/he prioritizes otherness and its dignity, while scrutinizing the limits of the human subject.

Like the Flatlanders of Abbot's novella who, inhabiting a two-dimensional plane, cannot distinguish between between squares and circles by sight only, so we seem unable to overcome our own cognition, and are compelled to understand any machinic apparatus that we build in terms of human categories. Thanks to a projection of this sort, a machine might become 'human-like' only in successfully replicating activities that *we* tend to assess as constitutive parts of ourselves: talking, moving and even feeling, dreaming, loving. So 'human-like' becomes a crucial term which requires a critical assessment. The 'human-likeness' which is at stake here implies similarity, as in some manifest resemblance, but not an identity of inner states of cognition; a conformity of external behaviour to the human model, and nothing more, however perfect the replica might appear. The likeness might even border on indiscernibility; but, as Leibniz says, identity of indiscernibles only occurs when each and every property is in common, and this is not the case. In other words, a failure to distinguish does not prove an equivalence of inner states. What actually occurs, on the other hand, is a success in what Turing (1950) emphatically and unequivocally named the 'imitation game' in 'Computing Machinery and Intelligence'. Thus, the debate on human-like machines is really about understanding the status quaestionis of the human: the machine and human connection in terms of simulation. It is precisely simulation as a philosophical notion that should be under scrutiny in the scholarship, if we want to comprehend the game at the core of today's technology.

Classical authors like Homer and Pindar invite us to think about the interralation between humans und human-like robotic devices precisely in the term of a simulation game. In Chapter 28, on the moving statues built by the Heliadae in *Olympian* 7, Marinis argues that these statues, like the Homeric golden maidens, only fake a similarity with human beings. Moreover, in Pindar as in Homer, technology determines the place of humans in the world as it is at the core of the divide humans/gods. Only gods can create life technologically: the maidens built by Hephaestus are endowed with sensory perception (*phrenes*) and intelligence (*noos*) and, like the singing statues built by Hephaestus and Athena for Apollo's temple in Delphi (*Paean* 8. 65–71), they possess language (*aude*); the statues of the Heliadae, instead, only possess movement, which alone is not a prerequisite of life in Greek thought.

In what follows (sections 5 and 6), we will focus on the emancipatory power of the heterogeneous self envisaged as a huma(n)chine.

Section 5: Disentangling technophobia

If machines replicate human intelligence, they are not a stronger system that threatens us. If they threaten us, we would have the means to defend ourselves; they would not be more dangerous than a lion to whose attack we *can* but need not succumb. For humans as huma(n) chines who embody the machinic difference, technophobia is unfounded: machines do not threaten human survival.

Contrary to technophobic attitudes widely spread in contemporary debates on technological innovation, Classical authors invite us to foster technophilia. As Marinis argues in Chapter 28, in Pindar, the moving statues built by the Heliadae are the product of a technological knowledge which is a *sophia adolos*, that is, within the Pindaric world, a knowledge that does not push humans towards *hybris* and social injustice. Similarly, as argued by Chesi and Sclavi (Chapter 27), the narrative about Pandora in Hesiod invites us to criticize the credo that machines will outlive humans in a near future: as a hybrid of machine and organism, the figure of Pandora points to the continuity between these two different species rather than to their violent oppositions.

As an emancipatory subject that does not fear technology but understands what machines are, the Post/human heterogeneous self also embraces feminist thinking. The idea of super-intelligent machines replacing humanity stems from a patriarchal and masculinist understanding of evolution simply as the assault of the strong on the weak. Evolutionary psychology scholar Blaffer Hrdy (2009), in *Mothers and Others*, posits that the human world did not come about by belligerence and competition, but out of empathy, and is a product of the exclusively female capacity of 'cooperative breeding', which enabled shared intentionality and pro-social behaviour among humans. We think that especially women, who have a special connection with the issues of computing technology[60] and 'reproduction', are in a place to challenge the ideological bias inherent in the existential-risk scenarios of super-intelligent machines attacking humans or disposing of them – like all ideologies, which thrive on conflict.

Patriarchal and masculinist assumptions are shown also in the industrial production of sex robots, as Liveley discusses in Chapter 30. Classical literature is a privileged place to tackle human–sex robot interactions. The myth of Pygmalion – as Liveley illustrates – frames these interrelations not as *how* one might relate to a sex robot, but *what* one might relate to it (what suppositions about women, prostitutes, sex and the right to a sexuality).

Section 6: Informatics of domination

Against the background that the machinic has little to do with materialism and determinism, but has instead much to do with consciousness and finalism – with a purposeful organization of a predetermined and human-determined end – we argue that the huma(n)chine is not the robotic human who has finally overcome the physical and cognitive limitations of his biological humanity.[61] The huma(n)chine does consider the nature of the action and does not look solely to its consequences; s/he does not replace common sense with something better, the right algorithm ethically superior to the human being and her/his fallibility.[62] The huma(n)chine is a subjectivity that resists the reduction of humans to a machine and subverts all rules of informatics domination (the translation of human labour into robotics and word processing; sex into genetic engineering; human mind into artificial intelligence and decision processing),[63] since s/he understands that the machinic is not about command and control but presupposes the notion of design, purpose and *telos.*

Classical literature offers post-apocalyptic visions of a world in which the informatics of domination has prevailed. In Lucan's *Civil War*, as McNamara argues in Chapter 12, the military desert-crossing dramatizes the dystopic condition of humans following a script that leads them to their death in an environment unfit for human life, envisioning a dystopia of consequences of superimposing technological advancement on existing structures of domination.

And now, how does the huma(n)chine disentangle the logics of command and control? By posing dilemmas: for instance, do humans 'humanize' automata, or do automata 'robotize' humans? To these questions, Bataille maybe would say that 'it is the subject at his boiling point'; Virillio would perhaps talk of the accident inherent in the technological development of AI (by inventing ships, we also invented shipwrecks; by enhancing the intelligence of machines, we might lessen our own). There is always an excess of energy, an 'accursed share', to be spent in some way, to pursue, to get rid of, to atone for. We name robots as 'children' and 'mothers' of each other, not *at the cost of* dehumanizing ourselves, but *for* this precise reason. In other words, this nomenclature fills a psychological need to share out and disperse a portion of our own humanity, which so often appears as the source of error, makes us guilty and, as Hui explains in his introductory chapter in this volume, lets us feel full of shame. The more technology develops, the more it seems to unfold a 'cupio dissolvi' among humans, a desire to join some universal, abstract scheme larger and mightier than ourselves, even at the cost of dissolving ourselves into it.

All this brings us back to the question of whether a Post/human enquiry of the relation between humans and machines is really a theorethical move beyond Humanism or rather represents a further step into the inquiry of what it means to be human, and, therefore, returns us to a critical appraisal of the Humanist heritage of concepts such as human dignity, the respect of alterity and free thinking. As we have seen, the human being conceived of as huma(n) chine is not an 'idolâtre de la machine': s/he does not advocate the equation 'man=machine' and, in doing so, s/he makes us aware that the machinic is radical difference, while showing that technophobia is not fear of the new techologies but rather the refusal of the radical alterity of the machine, through a strange anthropomorphic gesture that bends the otherness of machines to the human norm of the self.[64]

Section 7: Post/humanism and anarchy

The Post/human subject conceptualized as a hum*an*imal and huma(n)chine is an anarchic subject where 'anarchic' points towards her/his ethical responsibility for the Other within her/him: the Other – following Levinas – is an 'anarchic intrusion into the world' that shatters all normative frames because the essence of her/his alterity cannot be grasped.[65]

As ethically anarchic, the Post/human subject is not cannibalistic, in the 'symbolic' sense of this term. Universalizing a singular being under the name 'human' contains a portion of symbolic sacrifice, for there is necessarily a loss of identity and a symbolic sacrifice whenever those singular beings that we call 'human' are named and configured *as* human.[66] Rather, by remapping the boundaries of the human, the animal and the machinic, the Post/human subject affirms complexity and hybridity as the main characteristic of the symbiotic dimension of life apt for overcoming the violence and authoritative calls to order of domination and capital today. *Remapping the boundaries* does not mean, then, to question the norm but to recognize that life does not teach us order.[67] Life is mutation; as Deleuze and Guattari put it, the symbiotic relationships between forms of life are not a form of evolution but rather monstrous becomings.[68]

On an epistemological and political level, the monstrous produces normal subjects by acting as a contrasting foil to what is supposed to be the norm; even more importantly, monstrosity brings human knowledge to its limits and in this way it deactivates its normative discourses making possible a resistance to norms (cf. Nuzzo's introductory chapter in this volume). In Part II of this text, The Monstrous, the chapters explore classical representations of monstrosity in its ambivalent role. In a discourse of inclusion, monsters are used to show up the normative limits of the human and the non-human. In a discourse of inclusion, they dissolve the boundaries between normal and abnormal. Acting as the defining category of the human and the non-human in a conceptual framework where one cannot exist without the Other, the monstrous works on multiple levels. It relates to the divine and is always on the verge of emerging, and as such is a constitutive element of cosmogonies (Strauss-Clay, Chapter 8); it is an agent of civil war and cosmic disruption (McNamara, Chapter 12) or the demonic force of disease (Ceschi, Chapter 9) whose agency scatters human intentionality. The monstrous is also an integral part of technological prosthetics (Gerolemou, Chapter 13) and an emblem of political power and empathy between species (Kachuck, Chapter 11).

As an ethically anarchic subject who defends the radical alterity of the Other, the Post/human subject refuses a political code that legitimizes the view of all human beings – and living creatures and non-human entities – as being essentially the same[69] and therefore worthy of the same rights. An emancipatory policy, abandoning the discriminating factors between humans, animals and robotic devices, criticizes the risk of continuing a tradition of thinking in which some people are routinely denied their human status and rights, and are ignored or marginalized. People who have never been considered as humans with full rights will only be further ignored, mistreated and marginalized in an uncritical Posthuman context: migrants and asylum seekers are frequently seen to be demanding to be treated as humans rather than as animals.[70] As the postcolonial theorists Mills (1997) and Wynter (2003) for instance show, Posthumanist ideas can be interpreted as anti-human, and used as an excuse to dismiss the existence of human victims today.[71] Also, twentieth-century history should be a cautionary tale about denying the radical difference between humans, animals and objects: persecuted Jews, political opponents of the Nazi regime, gays and Roma people were deported to the camps on trains meant for animals and commodities. Critical Post/human theory should not dismiss the differences that the Other poses to the Self as a challenge, but accept them in all their confrontational divergence from one's own criteria – still devoted to the Humanist idea that it is humans' responsibility to make the world a decent place to live. Thus, relying on Heidegger in the *Brief über den Humanismus*, if Posthumanism should criticize Humanism, it is because Humanism has not yet evaluated highly enough the humanness of humans ('Gegen den Humanismus wird gedacht, weil er die Humanitas des Menschen nicht hoch genug ansetzt').

As Hui argues in this volume, Post/humanism has to talk about politics. Confronted with the challenges of globalization – the precariousness of workers' rights in Europe, the decline of the middle class, modern slavery (like work conditions in factories all around the world, human trafficking) – the Post/human subject *perhaps* invites us to go back to the founding basis of humanity: sharing and *mutual help as a factor of evolution* in the form of small communities whose social spontaneity – as Buber calls it – translates in self-organized social welfare and labour. Is this a possible way to emancipation? As an inherently decentred subject, can we envisage the Post/human subject as a subject promoting political decentralization? We have no intent to evaluate the worth and merits of specific political discourses: we pose these questions as an exercise in critical theory, not an assessment of fixed beliefs.

What has Classical literature got to do with all this? The chapters in this volume show how a Post/human interpretation of classical texts calls into question ideological discourses on animals, objects and robots, re-casting boundaries and differences. Of course, this remapping is not just a literary or aesthetic phenomenon. By posing an anthropological conceptualization comprising the irreversible continuity between the human and the non-human, and therefore by unravelling a narrative of liberation and emancipation, the Classical texts under scrutiny pass on to the reader an ethical-political question: how shall I live with the Other in me? – *la déconstruction de la langue est coupée par le dire politique* (Barthes 1973, *Le plaisir du texte*).

INTRODUCTIONS TO POST/HUMAN THEORIES

THE QUESTION OF THE ANIMAL AND THE ARISTOTELIAN HUMAN HORSE

Oxana Timofeeva

The question of the animal is one of the central issues in current debates within contemporary philosophy, comparative literature, cultural studies, media studies, critical animal studies and, in general, the entire field of the so called human sciences, which, by confronting a challenging figure of the non-human as its other (animal being a paradigmatic example of such a figure of alterity), revises and reestablishes its borders, and paves the ways of crossing or transgressing them.[1] It is precisely these crossings and transgressions that are the main focus of this chapter.

The problem of the border between the human and the non-human animal has its practical and theoretical sides. On the practical side there are various strategies of inclusion of non-human animals in the domain of the law, rights, subjectivity, politics, language, art, communication, collaboration, recognition and culture – in a word, in the domain of the human. Such intention comes from the animal rights movement, from ethical concern and political activism. On the theoretical side there is a whole new tradition of critique of the old metaphysical philosophy with its notorious human/animal distinction and exclusion of animals from the domain of reason, logos, language, truth, etc. This new tradition appears in the second half of the twentieth century, and is inspired mainly by poststructuralism, Deleuzian ideas of becoming-animal,[2] or Derrida's deconstruction of the very notion of the animal as opposed to the human.[3] It further develops through Agamben's reflections on bare life and his critique of the anthropological machine,[4] in the work of Donna Haraway,[5] Cary Wolfe,[6] Elisabeth de Fontenay,[7] Akira Mizuta Lippit[8] and many other contemporary thinkers who elaborate new interdisciplinary approaches to a radical reconsidering of the problem of species.

An extensive critique of anthropocentrism and anthropocene in posthumanist thought,[9] new materialisms, etc. takes as its target the classical metaphysical model of the predominance of humanity over non-thinking, non-speaking and non-working animals. From Aristotle and Plato, through Kant and Hegel, to Heidegger and Levinas, a ubiquitous tendency of philosophical 'maltreatment' of animality in the hierarchy of beings (and of reproducing such hierarchy in general) is now laid bare, and this has already become a commonplace of theorizing humans, animals and their relations, where questions of power, law, violence, subjectivity, body, unconscious, etc. are at stake.

The explosion of alterity, of which contemporary zoophilosophy is the case, derives, first of all, from breaking the old ties between Western philosophy and theology, which happens in the nineteenth and twentieth centuries. In this period, the motif of the Other emerges to replace the God of traditional metaphysics deeply rooted in Christian monotheism. The vertical relation between the human and God as a guarantor of the truth of being is replaced by a horizontal relation to the Other – the other human being, the other non-human being, etc.

If the twentieth century was characterized by the so-called anthropological turn, today, another turn is on the way – a turn to the non-human Other (that at some point merges with a new materialist turn), that requires not just a new ethics and politics, but also a new ontology. It is within this tectonic shift from the transcendent God to the immanent Other that the theme of the animal takes a special place in contemporary philosophy. In this movement towards the Other, the human has to meet itself – but will it recognize itself?

Animal being has been a subject of reflection since antiquity. However, separating the philosophy of animals from the philosophy of nature in its classical sense (where animal organisms are considered a natural phenomenon), but also from metaphysics and philosophical anthropology (where animal life and animal being is compared with the human), is a relatively recent move. Long after the Cartesian equation of thought with existence (*cogito ergo sum*), philosophy poses the question of thinking animal existence, which supposedly does not think itself. In this regard, the philosophy of nature, metaphysics and philosophical anthropology became a domain the analysis of which outlines new approaches to animality.

For such analysis, one has to differentiate between animal as a concept, an image, an object, and a subject. Animal as a concept is born from the system of philosophical definitions and is linked to other concepts, such as human being (to whom animal is often opposed as the Other), life, body, soul, intelligence, mimesis, etc. Animal as an image belongs to the order of symbolic mediations and appears as an element of metaphoric language on which humans talk to themselves either about themselves (thus, in humanist tradition the figure of the animal can refer to some human passions) or about the Other (in this case the animal is to be found on the one side with the excluded, vulnerable, etc., with migrants, or minorities, or the poor). When the image and the concept are bonded, i.e. when there is a concept or a system of concepts behind the image, the animal appears as a conceptual metaphor.

The animal as an object, or real animal, is at stake mostly in natural sciences, such as ecology, zoology or zoo-psychology, and those departments of philosophy that are the closest to these sciences. A special role in this regard is played by ethology that borders on anthropology, social philosophy and psychology: it emerges at the end of the nineteenth and beginning of the twentieth centuries and studies the behaviour of animals in their natural environments.

Animals as subjects are the focus of the animal rights movement and practical philosophy that rethinks human attitudes towards other biological species.[10] If for the natural sciences the animal is an object, then for contemporary practical thought and struggles animals are treated mainly as subjects – in particular, subjects of law. The question of the animal rises at the borders of such domains as ethics and politics, on the one hand, and ecology and economics, on the Other.

At a crossroads between ecology and economics, the problem starts with human activity on earth and its huge influence on the environment that is generally characterized as damaging, producing climate change, the large-scale extinction of various animal species, and other alarming aspects of the Anthropocene.[11]

At the crossroads of ethics and politics, one encounters the problem of humans' cruel and exploitative attitudes towards other species, based on the idea of the human's superiority and in the absolute value of human life, which has to maintain itself through industrial-scale consumption and extermination of animals. The struggle for animal liberation, for the equal and respectful attitude towards them, presents an important agenda for public discussion. One of its leading motifs is the violence of humans against other animals as the model for violence of humans against other humans.

In this practical sense, the animal is one of the names of the Other, together with some people whose political, legal, or citizen status is in doubt. The struggle for animal rights, the necessity of which is reinforced by the arguments borrowed from the data of natural sciences about the presence in animals of some forms of communication, intellect, sensitivity, etc. is another step in a wider humanist movement of expansion of the domains of rights and freedoms, that follows such important shifts as decolonization, the abolition of slavery, the struggle for women's rights, etc.

My work is dedicated to the theoretical and cultural representations of animals, and it focuses mostly on analysis of the animal as an image, a notion and a conceptual metaphor. The bestiary of philosophy presents a set of such metaphors or masks of the Other – of God, of the other human being, of the other animal and, finally, of oneself as the Other. Thus, I concentrate on the theme of difference, of the boundary between human and animal, which will eventually show its own instability, fluidity and elasticity. Dialectical interplay happens at this border, between the same and the other, where a non-human other can present itself as a shifted centre of the human 'I', close to the Freudian unconscious.

Theoretical philosophy interrogates the conditions of possibility of those phenomena that are related to animality and criticized by practical philosophy. Whereas ethics poses the questions about the measure of our responsibility towards the Other, and politics that of the limits of violence against it, philosophical ontology looks to the very being of the Other, to deconstruction of the mechanisms of differentiation between self and other, phenomenology to the living worlds and the forms of perception, psychoanalysis to the drives and instincts of the human animal, anthropology to the cultural invariants of human self-determination.

'Nothing in nature is as distinct in itself as is the animal, but as its nature is the speculative Notion, nothing is so difficult to grasp,' Hegel writes in his *Philosophy of Nature*.[12] However, even before being a notion, the animal in philosophy is first a construction or a metaphor. But a metaphor of what? Of the other life that is not human, but is a basis of humans' self-determination and self-relation, or designates its limit – an inner limit when it concerns our corporeal existence, instinctual life, etc., or an outer limit when it concerns the other animals.

We do not have an immediate access to the Other that is supposed to stay beyond this limit: it is possible scientifically to investigate the animal organism or how the animal body functions, but we cannot penetrate 'the soul' of the non-human animal, of the bird, of the fish, of the insect, to have the same verbal conversation as we do with other human animals with whom we try to establish mutual understanding and recognition (among the attempts to break or overcome this barrier one could list our communication with domesticated animals whose world might stay inconceivable for us but at the same time influence us and is translatable). In *Humankind: Solidarity with Nonhuman People*, Timothy Morton marks this 'basic social, psychic and philosophical foreclosure of the human-nonhuman symbiotic real' with the 'dramatic' word 'Severing':

> What the Severing names is a trauma that some humans persist in reenacting on and among ourselves (and obviously on and among other lifeforms). The Severing is a foundational, traumatic fissure between, to put in it stark Lacanian terms, reality (the human-correlated world) and the real (ecological symbiosis of human and nonhuman parts of the biosphere). Since nonhumans compose our very bodies, it's likely that Severing has produced physical as well as psychic effects, scars of the rip between reality and the real.[13]

Within a culturalist framework we deal with the human construction of animality. Moreover, the human world is constructed in such a way that it won't be too much to say that real animals gradually become replaced by their own representations or representatives. The difference between the two is that representation gives us an external idea of what an animal is as an object (in arts, science or mass culture), whereas representatives speak in the name of the animal treated as a subject with its interests and a kind of will (in the animal rights movement, as well as in animal studies critically relating themselves to human sciences).

But in what now seems a bygone cultural tradition, animals played a much more distinctive role, acting themselves as representatives of something human or divine. It would be hard not to mention in this regard the favourite horse of Caligula, Incitatus, who was named not only a citizen of Rome, but a member of the Roman senate.[14] This gives us a perfect idea of the very essence of the embodiment of the representative power. In classical narratives animals traditionally represent human merits or defeats: fables are the best example. In psychoanalysis animals might represent human figures associated with the idea of family, order and law. Thus, in Freud's famous Wolf-man case wolves in the dream represent the father of the patient.[15]

However, the very inevitability of the representational frame provides viability to the utopia of a real animal, which rather than being represented or re-presenting something in the symbolic field reveals the immediate innermost truth of the real of human being itself, or can be described in terms of will, power or desire. The ambiguity of the animal, which is representation par excellence, yet at the same time also unrepresentable, provokes a particular tension between ontology, politics and psychoanalysis, and it is interesting to track how in this unstable field animality is being produced and reproduced. A critical genealogy of the discourse of animality in its philosophical, aesthetic and political aspects looks back at the metaphysical tradition, which is based on the humanist and anthropocentric model of subjectivity. The hidden figure of the animal occupies a strange place in the shadow of this tradition from antiquity to modernity.

Many years ago I came to this subject in a roundabout way. I was working on my first book, dedicated to the theme of eroticism in Georges Bataille. Trying to answer the question, 'what does the word eroticism mean for Bataille?' I paid attention to the fact that he constantly repeats one formula: eroticism is something that distinguishes humans from animals. Bataille is original at this point: as a criterion for such a distinction philosophers usually considered rational thought, language or, for example, consciousness of death, and some are still doing that. As for me, I would not engage myself in a search for the true criterion of distinction between humans and animals. Instead, I started to analyse how such a borderline is produced in one or another philosophical system or ideological narrative.

One can indicate two types of classical philosophical discourses that focus on the animal. The discourse of exclusion starts with the ethical and ontological predominance of the human, whereas the discourse of inclusion insists on the affinity of all levels of being. But these two discourses are related and their function is the same: to establish or to conserve a certain order of things. As Bataille pointed out, the basis of this rational order is the transcendence of the human that requires the sacrifice of irreducible animal nature.

For Foucault, animality is the internal truth of madness that shows the limits of the human.[16] Animality is like an unthinking, unthinkable mirror-twin of subjectivity. According to Lacan, looking into the mirror, the human being appropriates its own image from without, from the other.[17] But what if it is the animal that exists outside of the mirror, where the human being has to recognize itself and at the same time cannot do so? Criticizing Lacan, Derrida specifies that the enigma is to be found not in the human being looking at himself, but rather in the animal that stares back at it.[18]

The play of inside and outside, of inclusion and exclusion, is a sort of device, which Agamben calls an 'anthropological machine': it establishes a borderline between the self and the animal other.[19] This is not only a metaphysical but also a political operation: sometimes, certain humans marked as animals find themselves abandoned beyond the border. According to Agamben, the question of the animal is not the question of its essence and nature, but the question of the human/non-human distinction and its practical, juridical and political implications. The examination of this borderline passes through concepts such as power, sovereignty, order and law and demands a historical analysis.

It is important to note, in this regard, that animals are not represented in official history, because animality has traditionally been consigned to non-historical nature. Nevertheless, it has its own historical materiality, at least as a labour force. From my point of view, there is a kind of injustice in this neglect of the animal in history: that's why quite a while ago I initially decided to dedicate my book[20] to the history of animals, and borrowed the title from Aristotle, a reference to whom is the focus of this chapter.

In his *History of Animals* Aristotle describes the habits of animals. His animal world is clearly humanlike: human beings are not only part of this world, but also its universal model. Other creatures approach this model to a greater or lesser extent, and are endowed with certain human merits – friendliness or aggression, slyness or simple-mindedness, nobleness or baseness, audacity or timidity.

Aristotelian animals are not only humanlike, but they imitate humans. Thus, a swallow building itself a nest imitates a human building a house: 'in the mixing of straw into mud she keeps the same order' (Aristotle 1991: 612b23–24; trans. D. B. Balme). I have to say that the word 'order' is really important here. Keeping order, Aristotle's swallow imitates human intelligence, or prudence, because human beings, too, keep a certain order in their life. It is as if a bird and a human kept some general order, as if they shared some reasonably ordered world.

In this world, there is a sort of continuity of all living things. Plants imitate animals, animals imitate humans and humans imitate gods. Mimesis makes it possible to organize an interchange between different levels of being. Animals, humans, plants – everyone is involved in a cause, which could be described as maintenance of a cosmos. Everyone has their own way to maintain a kind of general world order. This order was not established by humans, but it is measured by humans. And we might note that all individuals in their own way already conform to certain general laws and prohibitions, which in addition seem all-too-human.

One of the stories, told by Aristotle in *Historia animalium* (631a2–8), deserves special attention:

> It is said too that the king of the Scythians had a high-quality mare all of whose colts were good; the king, wishing to breed from the best out of the mother, brought it to her to mate; but it refused; but after she had been concealed under a wrap it mounted her in ignorance; and when the mare's face was uncovered after the mating, at sight of her the horse ran away and threw itself down the cliffs.
>
> *Aristotle 1991; trans. D. B. Balme*

Of course, this strange story refers us to a well-known myth. I could say that the gesture of a groom covering up the mare is a kind of parody of the blind fate that brings Oedipus into his mother Jocasta's embraces. The scene of animal suicide is really impressive: one can imagine this lonely, absurd figure of a fast horse flitting to the brink of an abyss. What is the impulse of the animal soul that pushes it forward?

Apparently, the theme of the prohibition of incest is so widespread in ancient Greek culture that it is easily projected onto animals. But I have to specify that what is frightening is not incest as such, but the fact that it provokes a break in a certain world order (in the case of Oedipus the King, his incest has such catastrophic consequences as the pestilence of the city of Thebes). We should not forget that Oedipus the Horse was born in a reasonably ordered world: the stability of the harmonious structure of this world is guaranteed by the participation, even if passive, of all its functional elements; a local failure imperils the system as a whole.

A harmonious cosmic structure is so fragile that it can lose its balance at any time, whenever a local breach in this order happens. Such breach in the order has to be considered not as a crime, but rather as a kind of error, a failure of a certain creature to maintain the order or to observe the law. It can be rather done by ignorance, or blindly. Nobody will do ill of his own volition, because the prudence of Aristotelian humans and humanlike animals consists in pursuing good. Those who do ill simply do not understand what is good, or they are not reasonable enough, or they are blinded by passion, or they are not acquainted with the law.

As concerns the highest good and highest laws, one might suspect that they are known only by the select few, and these few are at the head of the state. The hierarchical state system, according to Aristotle, corresponds with human nature itself, in which the soul rules the body and the mind rules the feelings. Animals, as considered less prudent, must be subordinate to humans, because it is through humans that they approach the highest good. Further, an obscure god's will has the power even over those who are at the top of the social pyramid. It may seem absurd or unjust, but it has the force of law. Observing the laws which are beyond their understanding, both Oedipus the King and Oedipus the King's Horse participate in the maintenance of the cosmos, which is – for the Greeks – more or less common, and which is still not finally appropriated by men.

Aristotle's human recognizes himself in the animal and sees in animals' behaviour a kind of parody of his own gestures. He feels a deep affinity with the animal. This feeling obviously relates both to totemism and to the ancient Greek belief in metempsychosis, the fantastical circulation of anima, living soul, between vegetable, animal and human bodies. One can imagine the unanimous ensemble of creatures being involved in a kind of common production of the strong effect of unity of the ancient cosmos. And the horse occupies a really important and honourable place in this ensemble. It is even represented on the obverse side of Greek gold coins.[21] In his early chapter 'The Academic Horse', Bataille reflects upon this representation and emphasizes the mathematical precision and nobility of the equine expression of harmony.[22]

Bataille compares the academic horse as the embodiment of *eidos* with improbable, demented horses represented on Gallic coins. Approximately from the fourth century BCE the Gauls began to mint their own coins imitating Greek originals. But the image of the horse has been seriously deformed, and its deformations, according to Bataille, are not random. 'Barbarian' horses are the illustration of a disordered life, which is alien to the high ideals of harmony and perfection. As Bataille describes it, for this life, full of excess and danger, such ideals appear as something like 'police regulations are to the pleasures of the criminal classes'.[23]

Bataille describes the transformation of the horse image as the form of a transgression and a rebellion against the 'platitude and arrogance of idealists'.[24] Demented horses on the Gauls' coins can be interpreted as the signs of the process known as falling into barbarism or as a return to the animal condition: in the so-called civilized world the least allusion to the possibility of such a process legitimates even the strongest forms of maintaining the order and the social hierarchy. Indeed, those who are at the top represent chaos as the single bad alternative to the status quo. Were it not for wise police regulations, the world would cease to be intelligible and anthropomorphic, and sweet humanlike Aristotelian animals would be displaced by insane barbaric monsters.

There is an impression, related to the fear of entropy, that the reproduction of the conditions of human life requires permanent efforts, and harmonious ancient forms illustrate the fact that such efforts were not in vain. But it seems at once that the forces of chaos, such as floods, invasions, war, revolution, epidemics or volcanic explosions, have taken over. Thus, the same harmonious forms illustrate the fragility of the cosmos and the difficulty of maintaining its order.

The academic horse, represented on the golden coin, is allied to the Oedipalized horse from Aristotle's book. However, the initially 'good' Aristotelian horse transgresses the order, turns mad and becomes the absurd suicidal animal. One could say, of course, that such a depiction of an animal is too anthropocentric. It humanizes the horse in its very dehumanization or digression towards insanity. But what if avoiding anthropocentrism is, after all, a false target?

Among many questions about what animals can or cannot do there is one that is still without an answer: do animals commit suicide? Positivist scientists tend to reply that they don't, and all animal gestures that can remind us of a suicide can be explained by their instinctive behaviours that eventually cause their death. Thus, for instance, the mystery of the Overtoun Bridge in Scotland, from which a great number of dogs have leapt, was unravelled: there were a lot of mice and mink burrows under the bridge, and the dogs were leaping there attracted by the smell of the rodent's urine.[25]

It is said that animals behave naturally. Suicide is unnatural, therefore they do not commit suicide, with some exceptions: when death occurs as a result of mental disorders or major stress, mainly caused by proximity to humans, or captivity, etc. According to this scientific point of view, interpreting certain gestures of animals as suicidal means romanticizing and humanizing them, projecting on them our own fantasies. But what is more anthropocentric, in this regard – Aristotelian humanizing projection or the scholarly verdict that animals, in contrast to humans, do not die of their own accord; that is, to translate it into the language of philosophy, they are not able to negate themselves as living beings?

In my own *History of Animals*, I am trying to say that this negative gesture is intrinsically animal. It is the animal in us that breaks the order of things or the circle of natural and immediate existence. The animal way of being is negative; we share it with other species. By this, I do not intend to argue against natural sciences and to claim that non-human animals do commit suicide the same way as humans do for whatever romantic reasons. What I want to say is that the borderline between the human and the animal, the one and the other, passes through this very creature, be it Oedipus the King or Oedipus the Horse. The negation starts from the animal that, in an Oedipal situation, or some other exceptional situation, takes the side of the human and attacks the animal that it is. Even if, according to the laws of nature, horses do not kill themselves, there will be at least one that does.

FOUCAULT, THE MONSTROUS AND MONSTROSITY

Luciano Nuzzo (translated by Giulia Maria Chesi)

1.

In this chapter, I would like to provide a reading of Foucault's thought from the perspective of monstrosity. The thesis I would like to argue for is that the monster and the monstrous play a strategic role in Foucault's thought. Such an assertion might seem risky considering how rarely he addresses the topic. A detailed analysis of the monster is present, in fact, only in the chapter 'Monstres et fossiles' in *Les mots et les choses*, and in the course at the Collège de France, *Les anormaux*. Although Foucault mainly analyses the monster in the context of these two texts, all his philosophical production seems crossed by the 'monster's line'. We can trace it in many of his texts,[1] including *Folie et déraison* (1961), the inaugural lecture at the Collège de France, *L'ordre du discours* (1986), the Courses '*Pouvoir psychiathrique*' (1973–1974) and '*Il faut defendre la societé*' (1975–1976). It also reveals a plurality of philosophical, juridical and political issues in his analyses: the relationship between transgression and limit, between reason and madness, between processes of veridiction and forms of power, as well as the problem of norm and of the technologies of production of normality, the question of resistance and counter-conduct. All major Foucauldian themes seem to gain further significance through the question of the monster and the monstrous. The monster functions as a 'heuristic device' by showing, better than any other concept, the processes of constitution of the material and symbolic world.[2] It is the place for the emergence and convergence of a series of epistemic questions and reflections concerning the disciplinary construction of the human sciences, the relationship between the categories of normality and anomaly, and the symbolic representation of these categories.[3] Thus, this chapter is not just about tracing back what Foucault says about the monster and the monstrous; it is about letting the theme of monstrosity emerge as the defining prospect of his enquiry.

The discourse on monstrosity has a sustained and tortuous history, which poses a variety of questions to the conceptual vocabulary of Western thought. The issue of monstrous difference seems to indicate the very form of a discourse that escapes classifications and disciplines, which 'rejects its identity, without previously stating: I am neither this, nor that'[4] and, just like a monster, makes fun of that 'civil status morality' that cares about identity. Foucault's monster is intertwined with the monstrosity of a philosophical practice, which is played out on the limits of devices of knowledge and power. Archaeology and genealogy, and then the ontology of the present, not only show the contingent and aleatory character that lies behind the consolidated forms of knowledge and institutions of power, but also reactivate those who have been possibly excluded from the selections of those forms and institutions.[5] Foucault's method, therefore, seems diagonally crossed by the monster's line. The monster, before being the product of a device of knowledge/power, is the materialization of a space of experience where thought experiments with its own limits, reckoning with its own un-thought. When the human being appears on the scene of Western culture, the un-thought constitutes the other of man, his counter-figure. As Foucault himself says,

> Man has not been able to describe himself as a configuration in the *episteme* without thought at the same time discovering, both in itself and outside itself, at its borders yet also in its very warp and woof, an element of darkness, an apparently inert density in which it is embedded, an unthought which it contains entirely, yet in which it is also caught.[6]

If modern thinking directs itself towards transforming 'man's Other' into 'the Same as himself',[7] apparently Foucault and his monstrous thought move in the opposite direction, towards thinking 'difference differentially', disentangling consolidated unity and identity. The task of thinking does not consist, then, in recovering the human, taking it from the dark background from which it emerges, in order to return it to its profound truth, and finally reconcile it with its own essence. Rather, with a tangential movement, which decentres and displaces, thinking brings out the multiple singularities irreducible to the law – that of the Model, that of Identity, that of the Same – and ultimately returning the human, out of every anthropocentrism, to that 'boundless diversity which eludes specification'.[8] If, then, the monster *of* Foucault presents itself in the ambivalence of the genitive, subjective and objective, what seems to emerge is monstrosity as an unstable and ever-changing form of difference – a difference that cannot be thought of as a lack, as an absence of form, and therefore a difference that escapes all those strategies of knowledge and power to assume it as negativity and, consequently, to overcome it dialectically.

2.

In the *résumé* of *Les anormaux*, the monster is described as the opaque background against which 'the large, ill-defined, and confused family of abnormal individuals' will slowly take shape.[9] This statement – although in a different frame of reference – alludes to the closing sentence of the paragraph dedicated to the monster in *Les mots et les choses*: 'the monster provides an account, as though in caricature, of the genesis of differences'.[10]

With monstrosity, we understand the constitutive processes of the discursive orders and of the power devices. It is the result of discourses and practices that concern both the epistemic forms and the historical-political conditions, which allow us to construct difference, give it a name, classify, normalize, manage and make it productive. Monstrosity can therefore be understood as the discursive space in which the question of difference, and the question of the techniques through which difference is constructed, subdued, neutralized and used, emerges with greater force. Difference, in the Foucauldian analysis, has a structural and constitutive function. In fact, it occupies a strategic position because it allows us, as Rosi Braidotti puts it, to 'illuminate the complex and dissymmetrical power-relations at work within the dominant subject-position'.[11] Like a distorting mirror, the monster reflects the discursive processes and practices whereby a specific historical epoch establishes the play of truth and falsehood, constituting the human being as the subject of knowledge. From the opaque background of monstrosity and its incessant threat, the subject and its rationality emerge as transcendental conditions of any knowledge that claims to be true. And it is always in an oppositional relationship to monstrosity that the subject of reason is constituted as a social and a juridical subject. The monstrous and the monster indicate everything that the subject does not have to be in order to be first and foremost a subject, and therefore rational, social, legal.

If the concept of monstrosity escapes any definition, the only way to define it, as Filippo del Lucchese observes (2011: 111), is to let it emerge from the conflicting movement that tends to eliminate it, to neutralize or include it in the order of speech and in power devices. The word monster, or better the classification of an entity as monstrous, has no reference, does not indicate something, has no real signifier, rather it establishes a difference.[12] The monster is a species we can't name yet; however, at the same time, as Derrida remarks, 'as soon as one perceives a monster in a monster, one begins to domesticate it; one begins, because of the "as such" – it is a monster as monster – to compare it to the norms, to analyze it, consequently to master whatever could be terrifying in this figure of the monster'.[13] The monstrous difference, then, inaugurates a double movement. The monster signals a difference and, at the same time, this difference is captured, neutralized, objectivized within the discursive and power devices. When the monstrous difference is named, it is captured in language, in its rules and its divisions. In other words, it is subjected to a standardization process.

The strategic character of the monster I mentioned at the beginning of this chapter manifests itself, therefore, in the liminal position that it entertains with the device of knowledge-power that produces it from time to time. The monster as a limit belongs and does not belong to the discursive regime and to the practices of power that have drawn the *figure* of a monster. It belongs to it because the definition of monster depends on a discursive regime that allows us to identify what the monster's monstrosity consists of, and therefore who can be considered a monster. It belongs to the discursive regime because the discursive regime, which defines the conditions of the possibility of monstrosity, is the result of power games and determines, in turn, effects of power, that is, practices of exclusion, internment, normalization. The monster is that on whose exclusion a certain order is organized and, for this reason, belongs to the order albeit as its limit. At the same time, however, the monster does not belong to the discursive regime because the difference that the monster signals (and which it also preserves in its linguistic embedding – the monster is a sign without meaning and for this reason it inspires terror and wonder at the same time) can never be completely neutralized by the device that builds the monster, which describes its monstrosity and defines its linguistic or institutional space of existence. The monster retains, in spite of everything, a subversive character.

3.

The monster is a *Grenzbegriff*; it constitutes the limit of a given order of discourse and power because it signals the point of crisis of the power devices by including, managing, controlling the difference. But, even more radically, the monster is a *Grenzbegriff* because difference is monstrous to the extent that it brings thinking and language to its limits. The very possibility for thinking to be critical is here at stake. This is a pivotal point in Foucault's enquiry: on the one hand, it refers to the relationship between thinking and its outside and, on the other hand, to the relationship between transgression and limit. As far as the relation between thinking and its outside is concerned, the central question involves the very possibility of thinking the outside of thinking. Is the difference that monstrosity signals always captured within the conditions of meaning traced by the order of reason or is it possible to think 'difference differentially', escaping the insidious mesh of a metaphysical device that has always thought difference starting from identity?[14] With regard to the relationship between transgression and limit, the question is whether the transgression of the rule that the monstrous difference signals is able to escape the dialectic of transgression and limit, or rather whether it is condemned to confirm and reinforce the norm.

This is not a matter of simple resolution. The difficulty of responding unequivocally to this problem does not depend, in fact, only on the interpreter's 'bad will' or on the author's lack of 'clarity'. Rather, it seems that this difficulty has a structuring dimension, internal to the movement of Foucault's texts, which are more concerned with presenting the problem than with identifying solutions. Foucault, therefore, does not seem to decide on one or the other solution of the problem, perhaps also because thinking problematically means maintaining ambivalence and constantly renewing its problematicity. It is as if in the texts of Foucault we witnessed a continuous oscillation between opposing hypotheses without the author opting for one or the other. Rather, one has the feeling that Foucault, either in the same text or in texts published a short time apart from each other, supports opposing hypotheses, producing, as Esposito has observed (2004: 27), a characteristic doubling effect 'that gives to his text a slight vertigo from which the reader is simultaneously seduced and disoriented'. For this reason, the solution provided by Unterthurner, which radicalizes the thesis of a discontinuity in Foucault's thinking, simplifies the theoretical problem underlying Foucault's notion of monstrous difference. According to Unterthurner (2012: 199–218), in Foucault there would be two distinct orientations in the way of thinking about difference and monstrosity. A first orientation would emerge in the texts in which Foucault deals with literature, and in *Histoire de la folie*. Here, the monstrous difference would indicate a radical experience of the outside that comes before any mode and technique of capture and objectification of the monstrous in the network of knowledge and powers. A second orientation, instead, would emerge with *L'ordre du discours* and in the course of *Les anormaux*. Here, on the contrary, difference and monstrosity would always be captured and functioning within the knowledge and power devices.

It is not just a dispute about continuity and rupture in Foucault's thinking. Rather, the question concerns the character of Foucault's inquiry. As highlighted by Revel (2008: 136), how does one make sure that a subjective expression is not immediately identified, objectified and subjected to the system of powers of knowledge in which it is inscribed? If the human being is the result of a twofold objectification, of knowledge and of practices that define him within a certain horizon, how is it possible to refuse to participate in the social and cultural configuration to which, after all, he has always belonged?

These questions, which Foucault formulates between the end of the 1950s and the end of the 1960s in *Histoire de la folie* and in the writings and interventions that go by the name of literary writings, are never completely abandoned; indeed, they constitute a counter-discourse that is present throughout Foucault's entire philosophical production. The question of resistance, of the counter-conduct, of transgression, in fact, returns between the end of the 1970s and the early 1980s in his research on ethics and the processes of subjectivation. To signal the presence of such questions does not mean, as Revel warns us (1996: 12), to make 'the apology of a newfound clarity, or of an ultimately revealed secret'; on the contrary, it means understanding Foucault 'as a problematic manifestation of an intellectual history'. The two distinct orientations following one another in a precise chronology suggested by Unterthurner are, on the contrary, constantly intertwined in Foucault's work. This overlap does not depend on a contradiction, but rather on the fact that these orientations are the expression of a problematic knot around which Foucault's inquiry is structured. If it is true that in the texts on disciplinary power and devices of normalization Foucault reconstructs the totalizing space of a normative order, it is also true that he does not cease to point out, in certain forms of speech or in certain counter-conduct practices, forms of resistance and alterity which indicate that the regulatory system is never completely clear from glimmers and counter-tendencies (Ravel 1996: 11).

Returning, then, to the question that interests us here – the monstrous – it seems important, once again, to underline how the monster and its monstrosity thematize the problem of the limit and the outside. The question of the limit and the outside, moreover, is not restricted to a period in Foucault's production but is present, as a problematic node, in all of his work. Finally, the very possibility of criticism and resistance depends on the problem of the limit.

4.

Foucault argues for the ambivalence of the limit, its being both delimitation and openness to the outside. By the same token, the limit defines the movement of thought itself. The limit, like the outside, does not indicate something fixed but constitutes a moving matter animated by peristaltic movements, folds and corrugations. The analysis of the limits of thinking, of reason, of disciplines and powers becomes thought from outside – a thought that produces continuous repositioning, making the limits of reason, disciplines, and powers fragile and porous.[15]

A critical discussion must take the question of the limit seriously. In Foucault, the question of the limit, like that of monstrosity, is posed in an ambivalent way. The radical question of 'how' to think and 'how' to practise the lines of escape from the mechanisms of control is intertwined with an analytic of modes of knowledge and powers, i.e. of the epistemic forms and the historical practices through which the limits are constituted. This 'double movement' is constitutive of the Foucauldian enquiry. In the Preface to the first edition of *Histoire de la folie*, Foucault writes:

> We could write a history of limits – of those obscure gestures, necessarily forgotten as soon as they are accomplished, through which a culture rejects something which for it will be the Exterior; and throughout its history, this hollowed-out void, this white space by means of which it isolates itself, identifies it as clearly as its values. [. . .] To interrogate a culture about its limit-experiences is to question it at the confines of history about a tear that is something like the very birth of its history.[16]

The construction of identity passes through the identification of the limits of what must be excluded to produce identity. What emerges with modern rationalism, using Foucault's temporalization from the *âge classique*, is a way to produce and deal with difference: difference is identified as difference, as waste or deviation, and thus included, through its exclusion, in the order of discourse or in the order of the institutional political system within which the discourse is produced and functions. In this way, what threatens the order is made productive and assimilated within the order.

At the same time, however, the analysis of the mechanisms by which reason captures madness and forces it to silence is not limited to reaffirming the insuperability of the limit, of reason and language, but rather pushes thought 'to its extreme, putting it to the test of its exterior'.[17] Reconstructing the limits implies a reconstruction of the unconscious of knowledge that opens thinking to an extremely radical option, that of making madness speak as such, before and after its capture, making it emerge from the silence to which reason has condemned it. Returning the word to the mad human being means trying to think difference differentially by escaping the dialectic of identity.

If *Histoire de la folie* is the history of the Other, of the way in which a culture determines the difference that limits it, in *Les mots et les choses*, and in *Archéologie du savoir*, the analysis is addressed to those 'identity spaces' that are the result of the *partage* through which a culture defines the face of its own positivity (*le visage de sa positivité*). As Foucault (2002: XXVI) puts it, this means to do 'the history of the Same – of that which, for a given culture, is both dispersed and related, therefore to be distinguished by kinds and to be collected together into identities'. Through an archaeological analysis, Foucault tries to reconstruct how reason constituted figures of knowledge and determined the conditions of truth of certain statements by rejecting others, and how and under what conditions certain objects of knowledge were constituted. It is a question of entering the space between the already codified gaze and the reflective knowledge, in which the order appears in its being itself: the concatenation of words, their power of representation, the laws of exchanges, and the regularities in the life of living beings are made possible and manifest themselves within a certain mode of order. For Foucault (2002: XXIII) this means to rediscover 'on what basis knowledge and theory became possible; within what space of order knowledge was constituted; on the basis of what historical a priori, and in the element of what positivity, ideas could appear, sciences be established, experience be reflected in philosophies, rationalities be formed, only, perhaps, to dissolve and vanish soon afterwards'.

What is at stake are the historical and structural conditions that define a given enunciative field and, therefore, how a given epistemic configuration identifies, controls, excludes chance, the random, the dispersed. Now, this enquiry into the naked experience of the order is analogous, in many respects, to the bare experience of difference, which the history of madness tries to attain. Here, too, it is a matter of defining the space for the possibility of critical thinking, where once again criticism means to push thinking to play with its own exterior. As Esposito (2016: 138) observes, *Les mots et les choses* and *L'archéologie du savoir* confront us with a process of radical externalization that invests the object as well as Foucault's own philosophical perspective. This externalization process, according to Esposito, takes the shape of a radical distance from the Humanistic tradition. In the final pages of *Les mots et les choses*, Foucault, on the one hand, undermines the centrality of the human being by reconstituting the recent conditions of its appearance: the human being is only that transcendental allotrope which is the product of modern *episteme*; on the other hand, he identifies in those 'counter-humanistic sciences', such as psychoanalysis and above all ethnology, the lines of escape that decentralize not only the sovereignty of the subject but the sovereignty of Western thought. On the methodological level, we find this same decentralization of the subject in *L'archéologie du savoir* (Foucault 2002: 103). There, an enunciation is analysed as a set of linguistic signs that defines the subjective dimension, instead of being the intentional result of a speaking subject.

This relationship between thinking and the outside is particularly significant in the transition from archaeology to genealogy, from the linguistic setting of utterances to their material and political conditions of existence. Foucault abandons the reference to the Husserlian notion of historical a priori, understood as historical-transcendental condition of utterances. Certainly, his reading of Nietzsche[18] and the new interpretations of Nietzsche's work allow Foucault to discard the transcendental paradigm. In fact, the a priori archive continued to function as transcendental, although without possessing the characteristics of timelessness and rigidity, as it was assumed as a condition capable of providing meaning to experience.

In the inaugural lecture held at the Collège de France entitled *L'ordre du discours* (1986: 149), Foucault underlines how in every society 'the production of the discourse is at once controlled, selected, organized and redistributed according to a certain number of procedures, whose role is to avert its powers and its dangers, to cope with chance events, to evade its ponderous, awesome materiality'. Among different discursive procedures that serve to control the event, Foucault identifies the disciplines. The discipline is defined by a field of objects, by a set of methods, by a corpus of propositions considered as true, therefore by a corpus of doctrines and teachings. At the same time, however, discipline is a principle of regulation of behaviour. It indicates the conditions of production of new statements as well as the rules that must be followed in order to produce new propositions. If the rules that govern the formation of discourses have the objective of averting the event and its contingency, then the task of an enquiry that wants to be critical is to posit itself at the limit and, following a double movement, to reconstruct the limits, *ces gestes obscurs*, that define the identity of a given order by excluding that which threatens the order – and to introduce 'into the very roots of thought a notion of *chance*, *discontinuity* and *materiality*'.[19]

As is well known, in 'Nietzsche, la généalogie, l'histoire' Foucault tells us with extreme clarity about the meaning of a thought capable of decentralizing the perspective on things, of producing a continuous displacement – a thought, to put it as Nietzsche once did, able to overthrow the enchanted castle of Olympus and to watch its underground. Genealogy is opposed to the search for an origin; it opposes, in other terms, any form of metaphysics that intends to follow the development of an essence or of a principle over time, allowing us to discover 'that truth or being does not lie at the root of what we know and what we are, but the exteriority of accidents'.[20]

5.

It is within this critical history of the limit that Foucault's analysis of the monster must be placed. An apparently marginal reference may probably clarify the issue at stake. In *L'ordre du discours* Foucault writes: 'Within its own limits, every discipline recognizes true and false propositions, but it repulses a whole teratology of learning'; beyond the limits that the discipline fixes so that the propositions can be recognized as being part of their discursive sphere 'there are monsters on the prowl, however, whose forms alter with the history of knowledge'.[21]

The monstrous indicates a heterogeneity, an aleatory event that breaks into the discourse and that the discourse, through the techniques that Foucault accurately describes, including the disciplines, must keep under control. This happens by including in the discourse the aleatory event as waste, deviation, difference. The monster is a sign of a difference and, at the same time, this difference does not seem to be a radical difference because it is taken, captured, objectified within the order of discourse or within the order of power in which it is inscribed.

In this perspective, *L'ordre du discours* is particularly significant. It represents the point of arrival of an archaeological research on the forms of production, limitation and appropriation of the discourse, initiated with *Les mots et les choses* and continued with *L'archéologie du savoir*. At the same time, it indicates the starting point of a genealogical research that deals with the conditions of appearance, growth and variation of discursive techniques, by considering the discourse no longer as something external to power relations, but rather as embedded within the political-institutional context in which it produces its effects. The reference to the monster and the monstrous in *L'ordre du discourse* allows us, therefore, to understand not only how the question of which the monster is a sign – the experience of the limit – permeates Foucault's philosophical work, but how this question remains an open and problematic knot: difference is the space of a clash, of a struggle within discursive orders and power devices.

In *Les mots et les choses* and *Les anormaux*, Foucault shows how from the end of the eighteenth century the classical notion of the monster begins to change, in the sense that the subversive and disturbing power of the monstrous becomes an anomaly whose causes can be explained and reproduced in laboratory experiments. The same happens with the new forms of knowledge and powers, between the end of the eighteenth and the beginning of the nineteenth century, which seek to explain, control and treat abnormality. Yet, the process of capturing and objectifying monstrous difference is not accomplished once and for all. It is, indeed, the result of a struggle, that which is at stake in a conflict between opposing forces. As we have seen, Foucault himself is ambivalent in dealing with the difference to which the monster refers.

Beside the interpretation that underlines the pervasive nature of devices and the impossibility of dismantling them, and that which sees in the monster a difference always caught in the order of discourse and managed through normalization techniques, it is possible to identify another path of thinking that goes through those texts – a path that puts the accent on the escape routes from the devices and sees in the monster an excess. Through this latter interpretation, the outside and the experience of the limit reappear. Here, the question is how to force the limits, how to bring knowledge and power to their limits, that is, to the point where devices that capture our lives can be deactivated.

This deactivation, however, does not take place once and for all. It is not eschatological; on the contrary, it is achieved in the contingency of the event in which the possibility of criticism and resistance is produced. We are distant from a political theological perspective; the direction is, rather, that of a radical immanentism. On the one hand, Foucault seems to say that it is impossible to think and practise the outside. In the system of language, but also in social devices such as the hospital, the madhouse, the prison, no real transgression is possible that is not already captured by the discourse that fixes the division between an inside and an outside. On the other hand, however, Foucault underlines different figures of a possible 'passage to the limit'. Figures of this 'passage to the limit' are those literary languages that bring language to its limit, transgressing the laws that regulate it, but also, moving from the practice of language to the order of power, all those counter-conducts that constitute acts of resistance, pushing the limit further and further, and emerging on the outer edge of the system of knowledge/power that they contest.

Following the 'monster line' means to observe both the discursive techniques and the practices of power which construct and capture difference, which constitute it in order to capture it, metaphysically and politically, as 'difference of or difference in'; it also means to listen to the roar of the struggles fought at the margins and in the folds of devices, to recognize the glow of the clash between the multiple singularities of bodies and power. On the one hand, the difference that the monster signals is assimilated within an utterance and a discourse that intends to neutralize it, reaffirming the truth and authority of the model and of the norm; on the other hand, however, the attempt to capture and neutralize never completely succeeds, because difference is metamorphic, not only in the sense that it is capable of being different from what it is but above all in the sense that difference is given only in the continuous deferment of itself. For this reason, difference implies a politics of excess, capable of disturbing and making unstable the discourse that establishes the boundary between identity and difference, as well as the practices of power that assume the task of governing it.

Foucault does not merely propose an analytic of the power/knowledge devices that govern our lives. Instead, there is a radical question throughout its production which does not ask 'what is' and 'why it is' but rather 'how': 'how to think', 'how to practise' the lines of escape from the mechanisms of (state) control. Along these lines, I would like to highlight two issues we have been discussing. First, monstrosity signals an open question in all Foucault's reflection: the problem of difference and limit. The monstrous difference makes it possible to address the question of the limit – the limit of the forms of knowledge that regulate the production of the utterances in a given epoch; the limit of the practices of power that constitute subjected subjects. Thinking about the monster means thinking about an experience of the limit and beginning to think starting from such an experience. This experience of the limit can be considered not only what the monster triggers, but the very basic matrix of Foucault's philosophical investigation. Second, the monster is heterogeneous materiality. It is, using a language different from that of Foucault, becoming without denial, a life that does not want to live but simply lives.[22] The power devices analysed by Foucault are constantly crossed by lines of escape. This means, in my opinion, that what is at stake in the analysis of knowledge and power proposed by Foucault is the identification of the points of rupture in the pervasive meshes of the devices that govern our lives. The intellectual is a topographer and a geologist. His role is to provide tools for analysis, which allow us to identify where the scape lines and the strengths of power are. In other words, the intellectual is supposed to make a topographical and geological survey of the battle.[23] For this reason too, reading Foucault through the monster is productive. The monster is political in the sense that it is that difference that escapes control and its devices by differentiating itself in its continuous metamorphosis. It is the emerging space of the ungovernable – the space in which the laws of the possible and the impossible are altered, where the logic that governs these partitions is deactivated and new combinations become possible.

HOW TO BECOME A CYBORG[1]

Kirstin Mertlitsch (translated by Francesca Spiegel)

'A cyborg is a cybernetic organism, a hybrid of machine and organism, a creature of social reality as well as a creature of fiction.'[2] Donna Haraway spoke of her own invention of conceptual characters that embodied notions, theories, or sociological phenomena, as a 'menagerie of figurations'. In addition to her most famous *Cyborg* figure, first introduced in 'A Cyborg Manifesto', Haraway created a cast of characters, such as the FemaleMan, the Modest Witness, OncoMouse and Dogs. Haraway anticipated post-anthropocentrism long before posthumanism became *en vogue*, representing it through her cast of conceptual characters. She writes on the cyborg: 'By the late 20th century, our time, a mythic time, we are all chimeras, theorized and fabricated hybrids of machine and organism; in short, we are cyborgs.'[3]

For Haraway, the work of natural scientists, in particular when they are developing scientific theories, comes down to telling stories (cf. Haraway 1994), to designing myths ('ironic political myth').[4] Haraway's philosophical figures come into existence as intersections, as nodes or knots in a network of different theoretical approaches from cultural studies to science studies, via projects of feminist and anti-racist science. This theoretical orientation could be understood as a form of critical posthumanism (Braidotti 2013), which takes as its point of departure the end of man as the measure of all things, valorizing instead, and laying emphasis on, the connectedness of human and non-human subjects.

This chapter will provide an introduction to network theory, which lays the foundation for engendering cyborgs in a twofold manner. First, the cyborgs embody and mediate the very notion of networking. They do so by standing in relation with objects, machines, things, people, and the environment more globally. Second, Haraway calls her methodical approach of theory development a form of narrative (cat's cradle), which brings together different threads and case scenarios from which creatures like the cyborg ultimately emerge. The methodological approach of storytelling as a form of discursive practice, and the networked process through which the cyborg materializes, both contribute to the cyborg eventually manifesting herself as a material-semiotic agent.

Cyborg: A short biography

> So my cyborg myth is about transgressed boundaries, potent fusions, and dangerous possibilities which progressive people might explore as one part of needed political work.[5]

The philosophical figure of the cyborg is at the centre of 'A Cyborg Manifesto: Science, Technology, and Socialist-Feminism in the Late Twentieth Century', first published by biologist and scientist Donna Haraway in 1985 and then revised several times.[6] As a hybrid of human, machine and animal, the cyborg breaks with Western dichotomies and stands as an emblem of different ways of thinking, of living, of working. This in turn opens up pathways for feminist critical engagement with technology and technoscience.

The cyborg finds its literary ancestry in fictions of the eighteenth and nineteenth centuries, with references to figures such as the automata Olympia in E.T.A Hoffmann's *Der Sandmann*, which refer to Pygmalion's Galatea and other figures like dolls, homunculi or the Golem.[7] Cybernetic organism, or *Cyborg*, refers to an entanglement of organic and technological materials. In the context of 1960s space travel, scientists Manfred E. Clynes and Nathan S. Kline published a paper titled 'Cyborgs and Space'. The paper looks at precisely this entanglement of organic and technological materials in the case of the astronaut, whose body connects to mechanical devices in order to produce oxygen, body warmth and gravity.[8]

Haraway critically analyses the blurring of boundaries between human and machine within the concept of an animal-human-machine, which is precisely what the cyborg stands to personify. The first part of the manifesto (which has a total of six parts) puts the cyborg body centre-stage, highlighting the entanglements of organic and mechanical parts in an analysis serving to help grasp the concept of nature–culture hybridity (natureculture).

Being creatures 'in a post-gender world' the cyborgs do not stem from unity and fullness, but rather 'the dichotomies between mind and body, animal and human, organism and machine, public and private, nature and culture, men and women, primitive and civilized are all in question ideologically'.[9] For Haraway, a cyborg identity is a fragile one, a partial and strategic one, an identity arising from and taking shape in the absence of an essential unity of gender, race or class. Here, Haraway simultaneously challenges assumptions of natural femininity uniting all women. Instead, Haraway advocates for coalition, elective and political affinity among women. Haraway ascribes 'women of color' (borrowing Chela Sandoval's term) an oppositional consciousness, an awareness that is critical of power structures, rejecting essentialist concepts of selfhood.[10]

In the next two sections, titled 'The Informatics of Domination' and 'The "Homework Economy" Outside "the Home"', Haraway turns to socio-political, technological and economic change in the 1980s and its deep implications for the working conditions, and consequences for the physical bodies of workers. Haraway calls this phase the transition from the industrial economy society to an information economy society. She uses the term *informatics of domination* to speak of new emerging networks in which it is possible that different components, so long as they are appropriately codified, can be networked together. Haraway envisages the possibility of networking the entire world through communication technologies of which the codes are appropriately translated: 'The organism has been translated into problems of genetic coding and read-out.'[11] Micro-electronics are at the foundation of all communication technologies and, thus, micro-electronics influence all areas of society, the State, multi-national corporations, but also, for instance, the medical construction of our bodies.

Through the interplay of communication technologies and biology, the body becomes a construction of machine and living organism. To highlight this, Haraway uses the image of women in what she calls 'the integrated circuit'. Haraway describes the precarity of work for women – especially women of color – in the technocratic world as 'homework economy'. This refers to the growing precariate always under the threat of unemployment and poverty, whose work time is always available (reserve corps) and is not adequately paid. Looking at the bigger picture of a society governed by science and technology, Haraway conceptualizes it as a network: 'I prefer a network ideological image, suggesting the profusion of spaces and identities and the permeability of boundaries in the personal body and in the body politic. "Networking" is both a feminist practice and a multinational corporate strategy – weaving is for oppositional cyborgs.'[12]

Finally Haraway positions the cyborg in a highly technologized world as workers in south-East Asian, Japanese or American electronics companies. She calls 'Sister Outsiders' (after Audre Lorde) or 'Bastard-Race of Cyborgs' (after Cherrie Moraga) those who work under exploitative conditions. And yet, she writes, the relation between human and machine is a blurry one, and it is unclear who or which is the producing entity, and who or which is the entity that is being produced, in such a scenario.

Haraway outlines the particular position of the cyborg through the example of female workers in the electronics industry. They are determined by their physicality in a specific historical environment, they are 'situated' in it. Herein in fact lies a critical point in Haraway's cognitive-theoretical approach to the situation, or location, of knowledge. Her final call to action, 'I would rather be a cyborg than a goddess', is an expression of her feminist critical engagement with technology and technoscience, expressed through a criticism of technophobic eco-feminist veterans, and through the sceptical affirmation of techno-science.

Haraway's piece was first published in the United States in the 1980s. It was written in the context of the cold war (*Star Wars*), in a time marked by technological breakthroughs and transition periods towards a global information age. The same time period saw the publication of Haraway's most important contribution to feminist epistemology, 'Situated Knowledges: The Science Questions in Feminism as a Site of Discourses on the Privilege of Partial Perspective' (1988), establishing cognitive-theoretical positions already also visible in the *Manifesto*. The writing style is inspired by avant-garde manifestoes (perhaps also the communist manifesto), which establish time frames and temporalities of their own, and follow their own, conceptualized timeline. As Harasser has written, Haraway's text suggests futurity, and suggests a desired and utopian and/or an *un*desired, dystopian, future to be manifest, present and real. Haraway's short text describes both imaginative and real political situations. Manifestoes, Harasser writes, are performative: they produce politically relevant, historically powerful subjects.[13] With 'A Cyborg Manifesto', Haraway triggered a hype in the 1980s both within and outside of feminist academic circles, drawing in its trail a vast number of new contributions and handbooks, all the way up to playing a key role in the emergence of Cyborgs-Studies and Cyberfeminism.

Polymorphic information systems

'A Cyborg Manifesto' traces the line between an organic age of industrial production and the age of polymorphic information systems.[14] In the chapter 'Informatics of Domination', Haraway lays out how exactly this change occurs, and becomes manifested and personified by the conceptual figure of cyborgs. As a historian of science, Haraway assesses the state of affairs in her own contemporary present. First, she calls into question the commonly held distinctions between nature and culture; then, she conceptualizes the globalized and neo-liberal world as a large-scale networked information system (today we would say world wide web, or internet), in which the layout of a digital age is already embedded.

Haraway profoundly shifts the understanding of nature vs. culture and its differences, by arguing along the lines of class, race and gender. She writes that 'ideologies of sexual reproduction can no longer reasonably call on notions of sex and sex role as organic aspects in natural objects like organisms and families'.[15] The dimension of race, Haraway continues, must similarly be re-appraised: 'likewise for race, ideologies about human diversity have to be formulated in terms of frequencies of parameters, like blood groups or intelligence scores. It is "irrational" to invoke concepts like primitive and civilized'.[16] The paradigm shift is very markedly evident in Haraway's chart of material and ideological dichotomies in transition to new networks, or informatics of domination. Examples are transitions from representation to simulation; from organism to biotic components; from physiology to communications engineering; microbiology, tuberculosis to Immunology, Aids; from scientific management in the home and at the factory to a global factory or electronic cottage; from family/market/factory to women in the integrated circuit; from public/private to cyborg citizenship; from paid labour work to robotics, etc.[17] Haraway draws attention to how electronics is the foundation of all communication technologies: 'Modern states, multinational corporations, military power, welfare state apparatuses, satellite systems, political processes, fabrication of our imaginations, labour-control systems, medical constructions of our bodies, commercial pornography, the international division of labour, and religious evangelism depend intimately upon electronics.'[18]

The most important tools of power in the informatics of domination are communication and bio-technologies, as they inaugurate new kinds of social relations, especially for women. Here, the entire globalized world is understood as an integrated circuit information system that merely needs to be coded correctly. Here, Haraway anticipates, very early on, the concept and idea of a world wide web that currently forms the basis of communication. Telecommunications networks, computers, the production of weapons, and database management all follow the same principles of communication technology, which Haraway terms a Cyborg-semiology. She writes: 'The key operation is determining the rates, directions, and probabilities of flow of a quantity called information. Information is just that kind of quantifiable element (unit, basis of unity) which allows universal translation, and so unhindered instrumental power (called effective communication).'[19]

The figure of the cyborg, then, is embedded in a post-modern and posthuman age, which is determined by the neo-liberal values of growth rate, costs and degrees of freedom. Haraway's analysis lavishes capitalism with a profound critique, yet, at the same time, argues that the capitalist market alone is capable of creating such a basis of connectivity and networkedness, integration in a circuit.

Thus, for Haraway, cyborgs are not so much subjects to a Foucauldian bio-politics, but, rather, to a *simulation* of politics, and can be almost infinitely integrated and networked. In other words, the cyborg for Haraway impersonates the being networked and integrated into a circuit. With this, she breaks down hegemonic boundary lines: between animal and human, between humanimal (organism) and machine, and in suspending the boundaries between the physical and the non-physical.

Networks and nodes

> Along with other science studies scholars, I use the terms actors, agencies and actants for both human and nonhuman entities. Remember, however, that what counts as human and as nonhuman is not given by definition, but only by relation, by engagement in situated, worldly encounters, where boundaries take shape and categories sediment.[20]

> Cat's cradle is about patterns and knots; the game takes great skill and can result in some serious surprises. One person can build up a large repertoire of string figures on a single pair of hands; but the cat's cradle figures can be passed back and forth on the hands of several players, who add new moves in the building of complex patterns.[21]

The philosophical figure of the cyborg comes to be through Haraway's connectivity, through being networked with her outer environment. This interwebbing with the environment ultimately collapses some classic Western dichotomies: binary pairs of opposites like nature vs. culture, subject vs. object, material vs. immaterial, self vs. other, human vs. machine, male vs. female, all dissolve and fold into one, united in a creature that embodies the hybridization of human organisms with machines. In her role as a post-gender creature, this figure is fractational, full of contradictions, and promises a 'post-modern' collapsing of all those dichotomies that have shaped modern/modernist thought. Yet, finding ways to collapse those dichotomies does not equate to their total deconstruction. Precisely because Haraway grounds her concepts in materiality and materialism (machines and actants), the cyborg philosophical figure cannot be understood just as a product of discourse. Re-uniting opposites (and dichotomies) is to give rise to a plethora of new creatures, artifacts, materialities, networks and discourses, not entailing a complete obliteration of classic dichotomies. Everything is not conceptualized as material; nor is everything understood as pure discourse. Both ontological states are imbricated within each other, predicated upon each other. This conceptualization tilts sideways a traditional understanding of nature vs. culture. Haraway favours the image of a network for its ability to convey the mixture of identities and spaces of existence. She terms this process of hybridization differently across several passages, using different verbs: knotting together, tangling, interknitting, stringing, unbinding. The entanglement of nature and culture (natureculture) is central to the essay 'The Promises of Monsters' (1992), in which Haraway speaks of 'artificial' and 'social' natures. The essay highlights the relationality of human, organic, inorganic and other actors. In 'A Cyborg Manifesto', Haraway had specified: 'It is not clear what is mind and what body in machines that resolve into coding practices. In so far as we know ourselves in both formal discourse (for example, biology) and in daily practice (for example, the homework economy in the integrated circuit), we find ourselves to be cyborgs, hybrids, mosaics, chimeras.'[22]

The connections between humans, artifacts, things, objects and devices cluster into a node, which is characteristic of network theory, and which forms the philosophical figure of the *Cyborg*. From the 1980s onwards, Haraway's approach is influenced especially by the theoretical work of historians of technology and sociologists Bruno Latour and Michel Callon. The *Cyborg* connects with mechanical, human and animal components, and what is more, she *is* the connection between human and non-human agencies. Factory workers in the global South become *Cyborgs* for instance because in the electronics factories they are docked into various machines. This practice of situating human agents in such a relation is discussed in Haraway's essay 'A Game of Cat's Cradle: Science Studies, Feminist Theory, Cultural Studies' (1994). She reads this as a game of threads, and compares it with the network-agent theory: I prefer cat's cradle as an actor-network theory. The issues here are not 'mere' metaphors and stories; the issues are about the semiosis of embodiment, or, in Judith Butler's nicely punning phrase, about 'bodies that matter'.[23]

In 'A Game of Cat's Cradle', published after 'A Cyborg Manifesto', Haraway presents her own approach to the production of theories. Taking the cat's cradle as a feminist approach to actor-network theory (ANT), one can retrospectively interpret the earlier work of Haraway. ANT formed the conceptual backdrop of Haraway's research already in the 1980s, as Haraway scholars have written.[24] However, in *Modest Witness* (1997a), Haraway criticizes network theorist Bruno Latour for, as the title suggests, being too 'modest' or purportedly unprejudiced and neutral as an observer. The modest witness represents the idea of an 'objective', unsituated, seemingly genderless scientist or researcher. Haraway calls this position self-invisibility intended to dissociate scientists from their situatedness as specifically modern, European and masculine:

> many science studies scholars, like Latour, in their energizing refusal to appeal to society to explain nature, or vice versa, have mistaken other narratives of action about scientific knowledge production as functionalist accounts appealing in the tired old way to preformed categories of the social, such as gender, race, and class. Either critical scholars in antiracist, feminist cultural studies of science and technology have not been clear enough about racial formation, gender-in-the-making, the forging of class, and the discursive production of sexuality through the constitutive practices of technoscience production themselves, or the science studies scholars aren't reading or listening – or both.[25]

Haraway's interest is not only in adopting a 'situated' perspective on research, and one in which the researcher him or herself becomes part of a specific context. It is also to force androcentric positions to come face to face with feminine humanity, and the representation of her philosophical figures also shows this.

In her research, Haraway ties together different threads of analysis from Cultural Studies, Science Studies, feminist, multicultural and anti-racist theory and projects. Additionally, she relates these with different dimensions, where the mythic, textual, technical, political, organic and economic dimensions implode.[26] On this method, she writes: 'That is, they collapse into each other in a knot of extraordinary density that constitutes the objects themselves. In my sense, story telling is in no way an "art practice" – it is, rather, a fraught practice for narrating complexity in such a field of knots or black holes.'[27]

She describes the cat's cradle as a setting in relation to networks, wherein promising knots and figures are invented. Central to Haraway's approach to actor-network theory is the understanding that objects, things, technology and knowledge are all acting subjects/agents or, rather, that they acquire their agency by entering an interaction: 'Actors and agents act; they author action; all real agency is theirs.'[28]

The network theorist Birgit Peuker points out that agents only become agents through the process of establishing connections. The point is not the equivalence of nodes, but the unity of actor and network, as the term itself suggests. In other words, the actor only becomes an actor through the process of being networked.[29] We begin to see how in this concept the 'modern separations' (or Western dichotomies) between nature and culture – or rather, nature and society – are elided, just as they are in the philosophical figure of the *Cyborg*. The Science and Technology Studies researchers and professors Bammé, Berger and Kotzmann write that in actor-network theory the 'grand dichotomies' that have characterized Western philosophy and history of science are deactivated, such as 'nature and society, micro and macro, technical and social, internalism and externalism, human and non-human actors'.[30]

Such crossings also inhabit the *Cyborg*, who comes into existence through a networking process that connects human and non-human components, as well as Haraway's ideas.

Haraway terms this concept of entangled natural and cultural elements natureculture, or uses the expression 'material-semiotic entities'. The philosophical figure of the *Cyborg*[31] is constituted through the interconnection of communication technologies and bio-technologies, through machines and through devices, as Haraway reiterates throughout the *Manifesto*: 'Communications technologies and biotechnologies are the crucial tools recrafting our bodies. These tools embody and enforce new social relations for women world-wide.'[32]

Embodied knowledge: Material-semiotic actors

> Feminist embodiment, feminist hopes for partiality, objectivity and situated knowledges, turn on conversations and codes at this potent node in fields of possible bodies and meanings. Here is where science, science fanatasy, and science fiction converge in the objectivity question in feminism.[33]

Haraway's *Modest Witness* (1997a), published after 'A Cyborg Manifesto', is a kind of post-script to her methodological approach, and to how this approach relates to her conceptual figures. In this book, creatures are designed and introduced into a (scientific) narration, in which they are networked and situated. Haraway writes: 'Modest_ Witness@Second_Millennium. FemaleMan©_Meets_OncoMouse™ is an e-mail address. Let us see how its nodes and operators map out the tropes and topics of this book. My title contains three syntactical marks: @, ©, ™. Each little modifter signs us into history in particular ways.'[34]

Haraway's aim, as she explains in an interview, is to establish for herself what she understands as figurations and narrations. It is also to explore how discursive constructs and materiality can be thought together without producing oppositions. In the interview, Haraway discusses how different kinds of tropes work and who are the actors on the stages of the construction of knowledge. Haraway's objective is to develop a clearer understanding of the overlap and permeability of boundaries between different agencies: the human and the non-human, the machinic and the non-machinic, etc.[35]

Thus the philosophical figure of the *Cyborg* is not only made on a content-material plane through the act of networking, but also on a methodical-semiotic (and cognitive-theoretical) plane. Haraway speaks, for instance, of practising 'materialized refiguration' (Haraway 1994, 63). According to her, storytelling (i.e. conducting research, or producing knowledge) does not stand in contrast or opposition to materiality, because storytelling ties together different dimensions. Figures like the *Cyborg*, which acts in Haraway's narrative, are material-semiotic actors – and doubly so. They are engendered by the networking of human, animal and mechanical parts as hybrids, and as such are foils for a nature-vs-culture concept. At the same time, this philosophical figure emerges out of a cognitive-theoretical perspective by its materiality and through assignations of meaning that one might also describe as a process of interconnection. The resulting *Cyborg* is not just a term, but also a thinking figure. As Gender Studies researcher Cecilia Åsberg has written: 'These figure have by Haraway been described as a co-constructed, entangled or "imploded knots" of *naturecultures*, of both fleshy materiality and discursive constructions of the humanist imagination.'[36]

With Haraway, the so-called objects of knowledge become material-semiotic actors capable of acting. With this, Haraway lifts the 'traditional' cognitive-theoretical difference between researcher and object of research, for both the subject and the object are active and capable of taking action. In other words, so-called 'objects of knowledge' for Haraway are material-semiotic knots materializing in social interaction.[37] Haraway gives an example from literature that shows how so-called objects of science actively acquire an agency of their own. She discusses Gender and Technology researcher Katie King, for whom poems become objects of literary production. For King, Haraway writes, language becomes an independent actor: 'Like King's objects called "poems", which are sites of literary productions where language also is an actor independent of intentions and authors, bodies as objects of knowledge are material-semiotic generative nodes. Their *boundaries* materialize in social actions.'[38]

In different places, Haraway interprets the process of conducting research as a specific type of scientific narration, i.e. as a cultural practice of creating meaning. But the objects of science too can produce meanings and convey those meanings performatively. Hammer and Stieß explain how for Haraway, not all activities in the process of this construction are purely based in language or discourse. Rather, the relation between discourse, language, referentiality and the body must be re-thought to highlight how knowledge is conceptualized as a node of bodies and significance. The point is, Hammer argues, that constructed knowledge is the result of interactions between scientists and their activities, as well as the objects of their knowledge.[39]

According to Hammer and Stieß, for Haraway, the power of an agency cannot be limited to just the inquiring and cognizant subject, nor are bodies thought of as passively presenting nature. Situated knowledge much rather is built by the interactive process of material-semiotic actors, where bodies are capable of producing meaning, and can bring forth new bodies. In other words, bodies cannot be set out and determined once and for all, for Hammer and Stieß, bodies have a surplus of meaning.[40]

Questioning the difference between the subject and the object of scientific research, i.e. the difference between materiality and discursivity (material-semiotic) and between culture and nature, once we relate this to the philosophical figure of the *Cyborg*, means that there is no univocal difference between recognition and recognizer, between concept and conceptualizer. Haraway creates that which she recognizes. In her scientific storytelling she creates the *Cyborg*, which she and 'we' simultaneously *are*. In other words: there is no clear opposition between the subject of cognition (Haraway) and the object of cognition (Cyborg), because the *Cyborg* is part of the scientific narration, which she herself performs and brings into view through her performance. Carmen Gransee argues that for Haraway the strict distinction between a creative, narrating subject of learning and the constructed, passive object of learning is not tenable, since 'we inhabit narratives, and narratives inhabit us'. According to Gransee, Haraway assumes an immanent discursivity in all cognition, since no object of any cognition whatsoever can exist outside of narrative and discourse.[41]

Gransee highlights that as an object of knowledge 'Nature' is not external to the modes of narration and construction of scientific knowledge. Simultaneously, the object of knowledge itself must be understood as a material-semiotic actor inside of a narrative pattern. Therefore, for Gransee, the narrative field of knowledge production is marked by interaction between the different material-semiotic actors: (Lab-)Animal, Human, Machine, Lab-technology, Institutions, etc.[42] Or, to conclude with the words of Donna Haraway: 'we are all chimeras, theorized and fabricated hybrids of machine and organism [. . .] in short, we are cyborgs. The cyborg is our ontology.'[43]

ANDERS, SIMONDON AND THE BECOMING OF THE POSTHUMAN

Yuk Hui

It is said that we have entered the posthuman epoch. Humans are awoken from their own illusion of being at the centre of the world surrounded by beings such as animals, plants, objects and even phantoms. However, isn't this something that *already happened* at the very beginning of humanization since man is an existence without essence, without quality (Stiegler 1998)? And did the concept of the posthuman only become transparent with the emergence of a technological consciousness after modernity (Hui 2017)? We must start by contesting that the arrival of the 'posthuman' epoch is not simply out of an awakening by a brand-new ontology, but because humans are rendered obsolete by the technological artifacts produced by humans themselves. It is a dialectical movement partly compelled by the industrial revolutions, in which an internal negation is produced. Humans cease to be the centre of the world, and become just parts of gigantic technical systems, in which they are functions or mere operators. Given this *fact*, the question that follows is: what is meant by such a renunciation of the human? Like Nietzsche's announcement of the death of God, the question is less about the fact of the death of a transcendent being, but more about what it really means to live without God. It means the re-cognition of the fate of human beings, and the re-structuralization of all domains in order to create and maintain a new coherence. One can celebrate this outdatedness of the human under different names, posthuman or transhuman, European Prometheanism (Brassier 2014: 467–488) as well as accelerationism.

Posthuman as pharmakon

This chapter aims to elucidate the relation between the concept of the posthuman and technicity, and proposes that like technology, which is a pharmakon, the concept of the posthuman is intrinsically pharmacological; *pharmakon*, in the sense that it is at the same time, and irreducibly, poison and remedy (Derrida 1972b; Stiegler 2011).[1] It is under this pharmacological condition that I propose that after having realized the decentring of the human, it is necessary to re-consider the becoming of the posthuman in the 'fourth industrial revolution' characterized by smart environment, robotics, artificial intelligence, genetic technologies, etc. The concept of pharmacology has been recently invoked by Stiegler to elaborate on the double nature of technology, in order to open the question of the 'evil' and reconstitute the question of the 'good'. On the one hand, the posthuman gives us an impression of liberation, freeing ourselves from the older category of human; on the other hand, 'being liberated' is nothing other than the fact that humans became obsolete in relation to their own products. I am very sympathetic with the posthuman discourse, and that the humanities must fight against any human centrism for what Braidotti (2013) calls *posthumanities*. However, certain posthuman discourses in some ways also show a naïve attitude towards technology and see it simply as secondary to a 'true' and 'good' posthuman ontology, as if all oppositions can be neatly resolved by a theoretical canon – whether this be a process philosophy or a relational ontology, while completely ignoring the question of industrialization which is the other of the self of the modern human or posthuman.

The transhumanists take an opposite position and exploit technology to an extreme. They embrace functionalism (seeing the human as a composition of functions that can be improved individually) and an interdisciplinary programme for human enhancement, including information technology, computer science and engineering, cognitive science and the neurosciences, neural-computer interface research, materials science, artificial intelligence, regenerative medicine and life extension, genetic engineering and nanotechnology (More 2013: 4–5). They emphasize the importance of technology as a means of *extropia* (as opposed to the 'static utopia'), an open-ended perfection of the human species (More 2013: 5–6). There is an ambiguity between the term transhuman and posthuman, for example transhumanists like Nick Bostrom see the transhuman as a form of the posthuman, which possesses some posthuman abilities to transcend the limits of the human, for example, life span, cognition and emotion (Bostrom 2013: 29). We may recognize that the transhuman sounds like a typical 'scientific humanism' (Dupuy 2013: 82).[2] However, both the posthuman and the transhuman epoch cannot be judged according to a simple divide between a clean posthumanities and the outdated humanism (Braidotti 2006a), or between an enthusiastic open transhumanism and a closed dualist humanism. It seems that both jump too quickly to a 'futurist' vision without a historical analysis of the relation between humans and technology since the industrial revolutions and its dynamics.

Against these two extreme takes on the role of technological progress in the construction and deconstruction of the human species, this chapter would like to first address the reflections on the relation between humans and technology against the backdrop of industrialization from two philosophers of technology: Anders and Simondon. Industrialization is a metaphysics, which constantly reduces beings into calculable elements, be it resources, desires or tastes. We propose to consider the posthuman as a *pharmakon*, since it at the same time distances itself from the dualist humanism and reveals two psychopathologies. Second, we will attempt to reflect on these reflections, in order to raise the question of the posthuman's becoming in view of a new industrial revolution often 'modestly' referred to as Industry 4.0. Largely due to the delay of translations, both Anders' and Simondon's thoughts haven't gained the amount of attention that they deserve.[3] The assessment of Anders and Simondon directly confronts the current discourses of the posthuman as well as the transhuman. The works from these two thinkers are responses to the intensive industrialization and are also prophecies of the posthuman. In a rigorous and somewhat satirical way (especially the former), they not only reveal a certain symptomatology of the posthuman, but also demand new conceptualization of relations between technology and the posthuman.

For Anders, the obsolescence of human beings is expressed as a deeply psychological defeat before the technical apparatus, for the reason that these objects have reversed the master–slave relations between human and machine. This outdatedness is not only psychological, but also fundamentally existential. It is a technical reality that covers all domains of knowledge and historical concepts, such as materialism, ideology, freedom, history, etc. In other words, Anders described an industrial technological condition of existence, which transformed both ways of being and the knowledge of such being. Anders' analysis of modern technology is fundamentally

Heideggerian, in the sense that the human being, in the framing of technology, becomes raw material or mere resource (Anders 1980: 32);[4] while he also dramatizes the Heideggerian critique by turning man's inquietude about machines into an existential shame in front of the technical being made by man himself. Simondon shares a similar view concerning the decentring of the human being in the context of productivity. For him, the industrial technical objects are in the process of forming their own autonomy, and consequently they are closing themselves and leave human beings as outsiders, if not yet redundant. The failure to understand the technological progress and its renewed relation with human beings is the source of alienation; this alienation is not shame but a psychosomatic and existential malaise. Simondon for his part goes further and proposes to reintegrate technology into culture, and therefore to construct a programme for the development and pedagogy of technical knowledge. We will try to outline the critique of Anders and Simondon on technical objects, in order to clarify the relation of humans and industrialization, before arriving at resituating their critiques according to the evolution of technical objects driven by the new wave of industrialization dominated by technical/digital objects (Hui 2016).

Promethean shame and the obsolescence of man

In the section titled 'The Obsolescence of the Human World' of the second volume of *Obsolescence of the Human*, Anders described the Japanese playing Pachinko in Tokyo. The humans are synchronized with the machine in front of them, craving the falling of the coins, while the machine will never stop. These coin hunters cannot go home since the game will never end. Winning is always possible, though one doesn't know when exactly. Anders described that from Shimbashi to Ginza, these machines are everywhere, even inside the glass buildings (Anders 1980: 59–60). These machines, once called fixed capital by Marx, have moved outside of factories and pervade urban spaces; they are no longer autonomous machines that are passively commanded by workers, but they are 'players', 'opponents' who enter into games with human beings. Here we can locate Anders' main thesis concerning the obsolescence of human beings: the evolution of technical apparatus following the industrial revolutions displaces the human being from the centre of the world that it used to be, in other words, it becomes obsolete.

Before we enter into a closer look at Anders' arguments, we need to say a few words concerning the periodization of the industrial revolution. The following would be the typical periodization of the three industrial revolutions according to the commentator of Anders, Édouard Jolly: the first industrial revolution is marked by the invention of machines powered by steam engines, which are able to produce on their own; the second industrial revolution is known as re-structualization of the technological condition of production, in which human beings are reintegrated to aid the functioning of the machines, e.g. monitoring or repetitive working on the assembly line; the third industrial revolution is the informational and computational revolution, which took place around the mid-twentieth century (Jolly 2010: 15–16). However, the classification is not so clear-cut when it is presented in Anders' writings. We can also derive the following reading: the first industrial revolution is the use of massive employments of machines in production; the second industrial revolution is to use machines to produce machines; the third industrial revolution is the production of needs (*Mangel*), which includes material and psychological need (Anders 1980: 19). However, consumerism was already implemented by the time of the second industrial revolution. The production of needs leads to needs without 'real need', as Anders writes, 'the symbol of the third industrial revolution is nuclear energy'. In this sense, the third industrial revolution is nothing but the prophecy of an immanent apocalypse in view of the historical events such as the bombings of Hiroshima and Nagasaki, the Chernobyl disaster and more recently Fukushima.

Culture has never anticipated the impacts of the industrial revolution – not to mention that German Romanticism was concurrent in time with the industrial revolution towards the end of the eighteenth century – it underestimated the psychosocial perspective of technical objects (Anders 1980: 58).[5] Following the second and third industrializations, the incompatibility or tension between culture and technology has only been amplified. The advancement of automation machines resulted in the rapid obsolescence of human beings as if the latter are more and more vulnerable to be replaced by the former. In Anders' cultural pessimism, the obsolescence is not simply a condemnation of the domination of the human subject, but also the symptom resulting from the inability to resolve this incompatibility. Now we are entering the fourth industrial revolution marked by the digital and smart objects, and in order to deal with the posthuman condition, we cannot avoid facing its further obsolescence.

Confronting the rapid technological development: a symptom developed since the first industrial revolution continues to intensify and amplify. Anders called it the Promethean shame, meaning that human beings are ashamed in front of the machines created by themselves. Prometheus, the Titan, is closer than god to human beings, either in ancient Greek narratives or in Goethe's poem. Goethe's *Prometheus* mocks Zeus and claims himself to be the creator of the human being, as one reads, 'Here I sit, forming people in my image; A race, to be like me, To suffer, to weep, To enjoy and delight themselves, And to mock you – As I do!' (Goethe 1789, cited in Wellbery 1996: 288–290). Konrad Paul Liessmann, the biographer of Anders, has remarked that 'gestures of the modern man, who has abandoned god, and demonstratively took his destiny in the hand, were Prometheus' (Liessmann 2002: 55), while the revolutionary and emancipatory identification of Prometheus was radically broken. The pride of Prometheus as the creator of man and of technics began to be replaced by a feeling of inferiority (*Minderwertigkeit*) and despicableness (*Jämmerlichkeit*) (Anders 1980: 25). This shame is not only a psychosocial one, but also an existential one: namely the organic becomes inferior in front of the inorganic. In Anders' own words, this shame is 'not because he didn't tolerate anything from himself being made, he wants to make himself; but because he doesn't want to be unmade; not because it will be indignant to be made by others (god, gods, nature); rather because he is not made, and as the non-made he is inferior to all its fabrications' (Anders 1980: 26).

In Anders' diagnosis, the relation between human and things, namely the role of the human as the subject of thinking and acting, and things as objects to be contemplated and made is reversed at the industrial age. It dramatizes the concept of reification at play in the thought of Marx and Lukács concerning commodity. If reification is a form of alienation for Marx and Lukács, which leads to what Lukács calls the 'most extreme dehumanisation' (1971: 149), it is undesirable and has to be combated; now this reification becomes appealing through the social psychology of things that are modern machines. This is a critical moment of the becoming of the posthuman and its complicated psychological identification with its gadgets. The readers may question, even may laugh, that Anders' critique is not significant today since not many users of the iPhone may want to become an iPhone or the rather cute and intelligent Asimo.

The point that Anders raises is that there is an identification between human and machine, and indeed, such identification has only been intensified today, when we think of the discussion on the *replacement* of labours by automats; the concept of replacement is thinkable only because of such an identification.

The 'subject' remains a fundamental reference to the origin of this shame (Jolly 2010: 26). For the idealists, starting with Fichte, the subject is auto-positing in the sense that it can posit itself (*selbst setzen*) without depending on another condition, that is to say it is unconditional. The word for the unconditional in German is *Unbedingt*; it also means not to be reduced to be a thing (Frank 1995: 50). Hence the *Ich* can be unconditional since it cannot be identified with a thing but rather a self-positing act: A=A. The identity of the subjective with the objective becomes clearer and broader in Schelling's identity philosophy. A=A is not only applied to the *Ich* but also to nature (Tilliette 1992: 326–333). The identity is presented as indifference, which marks its absoluteness. Questioning Schelling's identity of the I, Anders reproaches him with his dialectical rhetoric, and makes a scandal of the identification:

> Schelling had said – the dictum was used previously before: 'Man's sense of superiority (or self-conceit, or conceitedness) resists the origin from the cause (or ground)', so one may now formulate as counterpart: 'The origin resists the leap into freedom and into the exposure of the being-I.' And this resisting, also, is 'shame' – and probably not just 'also': since much indicates that the shame of being 'I', is the more general and more original one than the shame of not being-I.
>
> *Anders 1980: 74–75*

In twentieth-century philosophy, the question of the subject takes another form, however the effect is the same. In Heidegger, the subject that he calls *Dasein* is thrown to the world. In an environment of distraction, *Dasein* seeks to retrieve its authenticity (*Eigentlichkeit*) against the distraction of the public (*das man*) (Heidegger 1996: 114). *Dasein* must recognize that it is not the *Ich*, but rather the being-in-the-world as facticity. In Anders' critique, this being-born (*natum esse*) becomes problematic; it becomes a source of shame. Since the world of apparatus presents another structure in which *Dasein* can no longer retrieve its identity, he both is *and* is not himself. He is the being in his own skin that he doesn't want to be. The problem is, as Babette Babich summarized, 'we are born, not made', one 'begins and ends with our awful shame at having been born' (Babich 2013: 76).

Anders continues, 'the shame of not being a thing, is a new, a second stage that man has reached in the history of the reification [*Verdinglichung*]: because of which man acknowledges the superiority of things, put himself in comparison with it, affirms his own reification, respectively rejects his non-reification as a shortcoming' (Anders 1980: 31). The human as maker, in the sense of causal-effect, is transformed into a passive subject, in Anders' words, the difference between 'to make' and 'to do' is sublated (*aufgehoben*). The sublation, and Anders clearly refers to Hegel here, is the synthesis enforced by the industrial technical objects that in turn create a totalitarianism of technical beings. After the second industrial revolution, the reversed human–tool relation is expressed through working conditions. Anders writes: 'today this "sublation" became fully clear, because in our "push-button" epoch, the last effect will be produced by simply pressing a button' (Anders 1980: 70). The question here is the distinction between to do and to make.

'To make' has a *telos*; while 'to do' doesn't have an end, it is *teloslos (telos-less)*. When work is no longer 'to make' but 'to do', it becomes effortless (*anstrengungslos*). As Anders says, reading or playing the piano is an activity of the *entelecheiai* in the Aristotelian sense that it leads to something by actualizing its potentiality (e.g fulfillment); working with a machine implies *an-ergeia* (ἀν-έργεια), Anders turns the *en-ergeia* (ἐν-έργεια, magical operation) into a negativity, excluded from the *ergon* (ἔργον). The difference between the machine and an instrument, for example a musical instrument, lies in the fact that, after repetitive exercises, the musical instrument becomes an extension of the body of the musician; while with an industrial machine, the workers also have to do repetitive work in order to increase efficiency, but they only become part of the extension of the machine (Jolly 2010: 56). This type of work is effortless, in the sense that it is devoid of any pleasure. A worker is no longer 'making' but rather 'monitoring'. What the worker is doing is only part of a larger mechanical process, in the sense that the worker is integrated as a function of it. In the end, the system becomes the true master in the Hegelian sense, while the human complies with the machine and becomes its servant (Anders 1980: 72–74). The work of Anders emphasizes the symptom of the human and the importance of studying the psychosocial aspects of apparatus. Anders was right to point out that 'the triumph of the apparatus world lies in the fact that it has made the difference between the technical and social structure very weak, and the difference between the two insubstantial' (Anders 1980: 110). Hence the industrial technologies became the condition of the social and the technical development. It also determines both social and technical normativity – inaugurating the reign of industrial metaphysics.

Double alienation and the becoming of the technical individual

Although one finds in Simondon a much less pessimistic attitude towards industrial technological development, Simondon also demonstrated the problematic relation between humans and machines. In his *On the Mode of Existence of Technical Objects*, Simondon outlined a programme to study the lineage of technical objects from elements to individuals and then to ensembles. The aim of the book was largely to overcome this monstrous image of machines and to resituate technology in its genesis beyond physical concretization (e.g. technical reality inside a larger cosmic reality). A fundamental difference between Simondon and Anders may be the following: for Simondon, it is not that the machines are rendering human beings obsolete, therefore negative emotions such as fear and hostility emerged; but rather it is the ignorance and misunderstanding of technology that leads to an opposition between culture and technology (Simondon 2012: 10). The eighteenth century corresponds with the epoch of technical elements, in which technological development is associated with the optimism of progress. After the industrial revolution, technical individuals or automatic machines have dismantled this image: 'they are more vast than human beings and determine them, exercising on them an action comparable to ancient supernatural realities like wind and thunder' (Simondon 2013: 107).

In preindustrial times, human beings were the centres of their tools, and hence they could create an *associated milieu* for technical objects, in the sense that they themselves were *technical individuals*. By technical individuals, Simondon means those technical objects that are able to create a recurrent causality with their exterior environment, which allows them to acquire the ability of auto-regulation and auto-stabilization, e.g. creating an associated milieu. Industrial technical individuals possess an associated milieu as their geo-technological milieu (through reticulations, like the Guimbal turbine that uses the river as a cooling agent as well as a driving force), and hence humans who used to be the organizer of the associated milieu become less important in the whole technical composition. The consequence is that machines became strangers and a kind of xenophobia has grown among those who no longer have any knowledge of them and feel helpless in front of them (Simondon 2012: 10).

The population of technical individuals in automatized environments pushed humans away from the centre of production. Simondon shares some of the sentiments that Anders expressed. The shame at the end doesn't come out of the fact that these machines are cleverer than their users, but rather that the users don't understand how they work, and in this way the machines become mere *magical objects* or *black boxes*, another name for a commodity fetish. Simondon wants to overcome the antagonism by going back to technical objects themselves in order to find a resolution to the antagonism between culture and technics, instead of simply ignoring and negating technics. Simondon doesn't only see the alienation of human beings, but also the alienation of technical objects, therefore a *double alienation*. In the working conditions described by Marx, the artisans are forced to leave their workshops and work at factories. These workers, whom Simondon calls labourers of elements in the sense that they are still users of tools, don't understand technical individuals, and are used to their artisanal way of doing things, taming with their tools. They cannot change their mentality to work with technical individuals because they will have to change the gestures that they have developed in their previous experience or in the skill that they have acquired before, and when they work with machines they are merely users, they repeat their gestures according to pre-defined operational procedures and rhythms of machines like the assembly line. The alienation of technical objects is intensified by consumerism after the second industrial revolution. The consumers have the power to determine the destiny of objects, like in Roman times, the dominated people can agree or refuse the life of the defeated gladiator in the arena. In this sense the human imposed a new temporality upon technical objects, detached from the objects' value and function (Simondon 2013: 56–57). For example in the automobile industry, a car can become outmoded, not because it doesn't work anymore, but rather because its symbolic value is depreciated according to the social psychology of the technical object. Hence Simondon claims that Marx's analysis of alienation through surplus value is still valid, however, a new analysis should be put forward in accordance with the second industrial revolution: 'man, as potential buyer, perceives himself as producer of technical objects. In the same person, the function of the buyer alienates the function of the producer; the function of the buyer, and more generally the function of the user, distances man from the product and even the function of production, through a play of recurrent causality' (Simondon 2013: 57).[6] It is on the basis of the attempt to liberate technical objects from alienation that we can understand Simondon's claim on the first page of his treaty on technical objects that a *robot does not exist*: 'We precisely would like to show that a robot does not exist, and that it is not a machine, as much as a statue is not a living being, but only a product of imagination, of active fabrication, and of the art of illusion' (Simondon 2012: 18).

What is fundamental to the diagnosis of Anders and Simondon and their proposal is not a return to humanism, but rather a recognition that the phenomenon of the 'posthuman' is not only an ethical and ontological turn or a mere theoretical conceptuality, but rather a material condition which demands further analysis. When such a rupture happens, it is not enough just to affirm it and celebrate the obsolescence of 'man', but it is also necessary to advance to a renewed relation of humans and machines beyond mere usage and functionality and, at the same time, to develop a critique of industrialization ignoring such questions. For Simondon, the task is to integrate technology into culture, so that the technological development will be compatible with the cultural development, namely that one should go beyond the alienation of and by machines. In order to arrive at this point, or at least to carry out some of these attempts, one should take technological thought and its material realization seriously.

Along the same lines of the analysis of Simondon and Anders, we can observe further intensification of Promethean shame as well as an amplification of the alienating effect of modern technologies. This goes further than the production of technical objects, via the modulation of the milieu through smart objects and architecture. In so doing, one can imagine a totalization of the technological system, as it is described by Jacques Ellul, where the users are no longer able to contemplate the dynamic of the system (Ellul 1980). However, the combat against industrial alienation of human beings cannot simply be interpreted and criticized as a return to banal humanism; since in order to *de-alienate*, it is also necessary to take care of the technical objects, to combat against thoughts and practices that alienate them, which includes seeing them as mere servants or slaves of human beings.

Against naïve posthuman ontologies

We can certainly question if this new transformation of the technical milieu populated with smart objects, sensors and soon robots in our time implies an amplification or intensification of the Promethean shame described by Anders. And if there is such an amplification of shamefulness, how shall the posthuman discourse respond to it? One may reject this question as conservative since it aims to bring back the concept of the human. For example when Anders criticizes industrialization as a metaphysical force rendering human beings superfluous through the implementation of complete automation in offices and factories (Anders 1980: 26), one can easily depreciate his works as a 'humanist' lamentation of the obsoleteness of man (Anders 1980: 26). However, at this point a naïve posthumanism becomes unproductive, in the sense that the real problem concerning industrialization remains hidden, while whoever wants to address the 'human' becomes completely banal and backward.

A similar criticism can be launched against Simondon. What Simondon proposed – as Xavier Guchet has systematically formulated – is to develop a technological humanism. For Simondon, each epoch demands a new humanism pertinent to its technological condition, because 'it aims at the most serious aspect of alienation that a civilisation behaves or produces', so 'each epoch should discover its humanism, orienting it towards the principal danger of alienation' (Guchet 2011: 110; Simondon 2012: 101–102). It would be very easy to jump to the same conclusion that Simondon is fundamentally a humanist, since he proposed a humanism. However, it is a humanism that aims for *a mode of existence*, in which alienation of humans by their own activities can be overcome by acquiring knowledge of the world of technical objects, and by taking care of the non-humans. It comes out of a consciousness of the relation between human beings and the artefacts that they have created.

> All encyclopaedism is humanism, if one understands by the term humanism the will to bring back the status of freedom that human being has been alienated, so that no man-

> made being is stranger to man; but this rediscovery of the human reality is achieved in different ways, and every epoch recreates a humanism which to some extent is appropriate to its actual circumstances because it aims at the most serious aspect of alienation that a civilisation contains or produces.
>
> *Simondon 2012: 144–145*

It doesn't seem to be a problem if one wants to call Simondon's approach a 'technological posthumanism' as long as one agrees that the term 'posthuman' necessarily signifies a critique of anthropocentrism. Technology becomes a source of alienation produced by the exclusion of man in the course of the formation of technical systems. As Simondon, and later more directly Ellul, point out, technical systems have been in the process of formation between human beings and technical objects, which become more and more concrete. Gradually, with mechanization and automation, the concretization of technical objects starts forming a system in which human beings are excluded or self-excluded (Guchet 2011: 109). This is a new condition, which necessarily correlates with a technical reality. And this self-exclusion is a problem, an incompatibility between human and technical objects that leads to shame and malaise.

Technology has surpassed the social, psychological and soon, if not already, the biological, in the sense that it is a means through which these domains could be transformed on a large scale. Human beings will only be made more and more obsolescent in comparison with the evolution of technical objects (in the combination of nanotechnologies, artificial intelligence, biotechnologies and robotics). This shame is further elaborated by some theorists in the guise of an ethics, under the name of the thing-in-itself (*Ding an sich*) – the ungraspable being of objects or simply a black box. Granting them a mysterious status of the thing in itself doesn't necessarily help to give them respect, and hence reconstitutes a new way of living together. However, those objects that are elaborated upon by these philosophers are nothing more sophisticated than a table, a billiard ball, while ignoring most of the objects in the world. For sure, these different attitudes and approaches are based on the understanding of the task of philosophy. But one thing at least is agreeable, which is that philosophy attempts to comprehend the incomprehensible without reducing it or reifying it, without mystifying it or endowing it with a mysterious aura. The black box constituted by algorithms that are not simply a billiard ball or a table (as examples given by David Hume and Plato), can also produce fear, panic, and hence hostility. Within the proposition that we know there is something that we cannot know, and the affirmation that things definitely withdraw and escape from us conceals two social psychologies of technicity. The extreme cases of it would be the development into two psychopathologies, one towards perpetual discomfort, and the other towards unresolvable hostility.

The posthuman is none other than one of the phases of the co-evolution between life and technics, in which technics is 'the pursuit of life by means other than life' as it is put by Stiegler (1998: 17). The philosophical task for Simondon is to identify and launch a fight against alienation by reconstituting the relation between human and technical objects, human and animals, and in order for this to be possible, it is not a regress to return to any sort of human centrism, but rather to search for new relations between human and technical objects. The utopian image that Simondon gave us is that human agents will be the conductor of the orchestra and the machines are the musicians. In this example, Simondon gave human characters to technical objects; and by so doing, it also disturbs the definition of human as what is opposite to the non-humans. How Simondon's programme can be and should be realized is another question that I have addressed elsewhere (Hui 2016, 2017) and continue to address.

To bring together Anders' and Simondon's critique of industrialization as a response to the posthuman and transhuman discourses is an attempt to show that, in between certain neat and clean posthuman ontologies and the enthusiastic and fanatic transhumanist visions, there is a political struggle yet to be further elaborated. The merit of Anders and Simondon is that they attempt to understand the transformation of industrialization beyond mere economic analysis by considering a social psychology of things and humans; and it is for this reason that we understand the posthuman as a pharmacological condition. Anders' thesis that humans will become superfluous in the fourth industrial revolution may appear justified in posthuman discourses, however, one shouldn't overlook that it is also a lament originating from a psychological and existential crisis. Simondon recognizes that the servitude which human beings have attributed to technical objects and the worker's lack of technical knowledge are sources of alienation. Beyond Anders, Simondon wants to suggest a programme, one that concerns neither automation (for the philosopher denounces automation as the lowest level of perfection) nor human enhancement or perfection, but rather a technological culture in which humans and machines don't (and will not attempt to) dominate each another and technology becomes the support of culture.

How far can posthumanism respond to Anders' and Simondon's critiques? And how far can the posthuman as *pharmakon* open up to us new imaginations concerning the development and use of technology? A prompt rejection of Anders' and Simondon's thought as humanist doesn't help avoid and resolve the issues they raised about industrialization. Planetary computation (Bratton 2016) seems to have overcome the antagonism between culture and technics, but in fact what is evident is that in this conceptualization culture is only one of the products or even by-products of technological acceleration; following Simondon, one should situate it within a genesis of technicity, e.g. a broader background in which such a technological condition has emerged. The existence of technical objects (and now systems) remains in the shadows for humans, posthumans, transhumans, etc., and there are modes of existence that have particularly haunting effects, since they cast shadows on what is considered good and bright. It is not at all, as Bostrom imagines, that one can choose to perfect a good posthuman capacity and ignore the bad posthuman capacities (Bostrom 2013: 29–31), since as a *pharmakon* it is always already both good and bad. The task is not to bring the human back to the centre, but rather to take the posthuman as an invitation to resituate the posthuman in this phase of industrialization and to reflect upon the becoming of the posthuman, which I prefer to call inhuman, by following Lyotard.[7]

PART I
DE/HUMANIZATION AND ANIMALS

CHAPTER 1
ODYSSEUS, THE BOAR AND THE ANTHROPOGENIC MACHINE[1]

Marianne Hopman

In his 2015 book, *Learning to Die in the Anthropocene*, American writer Roy Scranton stresses the urgency to rethink what it means to be human in the Anthropocene:[2]

> In order for us to adapt to this strange new world, we're going to need more than scientific reports and military policy. We're going to need new ideas. We're going to need new myths and new stories, a new conceptual understanding of reality, and a new relationship to the deep polyglot traditions of human culture . . . We need a new vision of who 'we' are.[3]

Scranton is quick to question, however, whether the humanities can rise to the task: 'Admittedly, ocean acidification, social upheaval, and species extinction are problems that humanities scholars, with their taste for fine-grained philological analysis, esoteric debates, and archival marginalia, might seem remarkably ill-suited to address.'[4] Thus the rise of the Anthropocene, for all its deeply alarming implications, raises a tremendously exciting challenge – and opportunity – for those of us who identify as 'humanities scholars'. Can we contribute new ideas, myths, and stories that will help redefine what it is to be human? Can we draw on the tools of our trade – the details of philological analysis and the minutiae of close reading – to illuminate, rather than escape from, the project of defining a new humanism?

And what part, if any, may classicists play in those conversations? Shouldn't the ambition to create 'new' ideas, myths and stories for the contemporary world prompt us to focus on the present – and the future – rather than dig into the distant past? Furthermore, haven't Plato, Aristotle and 'the Greeks' provided the 'humanist' tradition with concepts that are among the targets of posthumanist critique, such as human exceptionalism and the great chain of beings? In his book *The Open*, Giorgio Agamben traces to Aristotle one version of the 'anthropogenic machine', by which he means the cultural production of the concept of man through the oppositions man/animal, human/inhuman.[5] And yet that enmeshment of classical texts into the dominant anthropocentric tradition may be precisely what makes classicists relevant and important to the posthumanism debate. There are, as Jacques Derrida has argued, several ways of questioning humanism, one of which involves 'attempting the exit and the deconstruction without changing terrain, by repeating what is implicit in the founding concepts and the original problematic, by using against the edifice the instruments or stones available in the house, that is, equally, in language'.[6] The texts that we have inherited from ancient Greece are complex, dialogical assemblages welding together a variety of linguistic, stylistic, aesthetic and ideological layers. Might our core disciplinary practices – philology and close reading – be harnessed to read those texts against the grain, highlight contrapuntal worldviews that were obscured through their later reception, and thus offer a useful contribution to contemporary conversations?[7]

With this agenda in mind, I turn to my case study – the story of Odysseus and the boar as told in *Odyssey* 19.[8] The context is well known. Penelope has asked the faithful nurse Eurykleia to give a bath to Odysseus disguised as a beggar. As the old servant washes the feet of her master, she recognizes the scar that he received from the white tusk of a boar while hunting on Mount Parnassos with his maternal uncles. Eurykleia's anagnorisis, or recognition process, triggers a flash-back about the origin of the scar that falls into two parts: first an account of how Odysseus' grandfather, Autolykos, came to visit his daughter and son-in-law at the time of Odysseus' birth, gave him a name, and invited him to visit upon the turn of manhood (399–412); and second a narrative of youthful Odysseus' subsequent visit to his grandfather, which includes an elaborate hospitality scene followed by the boar hunt itself (413–466).[9]

As commentators have stressed, the boar hunt represents a crucial step in the psycho-social fabrication of Odysseus as a descendant of Autolykos and as a unique individual.[10] The encounter with the boar takes place when Odysseus is in the vigour of early manhood (ἡβάω, 19.410). Its juxtaposition to the story of Odysseus' birth and naming suggests a thematic relevance to questions of identity and fabrication of the self, as does the fact that Odysseus' name is emphatically combined with two adjectives of praise, 'blameless' and 'god-like', immediately after the killing and wounding (Ὀδυσῆος ἀμύμονος ἀντιθέοιο, 19.456).[11] Specifics of the boar hunt including the role of maternal uncles and the tripartite sequence of separation, transition and reintegration match the anthropological concept of rite of passage studied by Arnold van Gennep and others.[12] Even more broadly, cultural parallels show that – as an extremely dangerous sport where men's lives were at stake – boar hunting could be used as a test of manhood and an indication of readiness for warfare in ancient Greece.[13]

There is ample evidence, therefore, that Odysseus fully becomes Odysseus during and through the encounter with the boar. In other words, the narrative may be approached as a specific instance of Agamben's anthropogenic machine – an Odysseugenesis, so to speak. My goal here is to dissect the specifics of this particular example of the fabrication of the human in relation to the non-human. I propose that the text intricately combines at least three different views of the relation between Odysseus and the boar. Specifically, I argue that the fabrication of Odysseus coincides with the imposition of a violent hierarchy that, in contrast with the analogical perception of boars as paradigms for human warriors in Iliadic similes (I), introduces a concept of Odysseus' technology-based difference from and superiority over the boar (II) while still recognizing his vulnerability and permeability to the non-human (III).[14]

I. Audience expectations and the analogical worldview

The expedition that takes Odysseus and his maternal uncles hunting on Parnassos stands out in the extant Homeric corpus as the most detailed account of a heroic hunt. Warriors do not hunt on the plain of Troy. Odysseus or his crew sometimes hunt for food, but those expeditions target animals – goats, a stag, oxen – that *per se* do not put the men's lives directly at risk. As far as plot is concerned, our passage resembles the Calydonian boar hunt narrated by Phoenix in *Iliad* 9, which similarly involves a boar, a youth and his maternal uncles. Indeed the two stories have been fruitfully analysed together through the anthropological concept of rite of passage.[15] Yet from an aesthetic point of view, the highly compressed account of the Calydonian boar hunt strikingly differs from the leisurely paced narrative of *Odyssey* 19. Poetically, the closest

Homeric parallel for Odysseus' struggle with the boar comes from Iliadic similes that describe the encounters of villagers, their dogs and large and dangerous mammals.[16]

On the morning of the second day of Odysseus' visit, he and his uncles leave the house of Autolykos to go hunting. The narrative opens with a beautifully detailed description of their itinerary as the men and their dogs walk through hills, mountains and dense woods bathed in the horizontal rays of the rising sun (*Od.* 19.428–438). These settings, characters and actions call to mind the diction surrounding encounters between humans and lions or boars in the similes.[17] At *Iliad* 18.318–322, Achilles grieving for Patroklos is compared to an angry lion in search of the hunter who has deprived him of his cubs. The close woods where the action happens (ὕλης ἐκ πυκινῆς, *Il.* 18.320) and the tracking (ἴχνι' ἐρευνῶν, *Il.* 18.321) performed by the lion parallel the density of the boar's lair (πυκνή, *Od.* 19.442) and the action of the dogs (ἴχνι' ἐρευνῶντες, *Od.* 19.436) in the Parnassian boar hunt. Similarly, the mountainside (ὄρος, *Od.* 19.431) and glens (βῆσσαν, *Od.* 19.435) where the young Odysseus ventures with his uncles resemble the setting of a simile that compares Ajax protecting the corpse of Patroklos to a wild boar scattering his youthful pursuers in *Iliad* 17 (ἐν ὄρεσσι, *Il.* 17.282; διὰ βήσσας, *Il.* 17.283).

While the boar of *Iliad* 17 scatters his opponents, the boar of *Odyssey* 19 leaves his well-protected lair to confront the hunting party (*Od.* 19.444–447). Such a counter-attack strategy is typical of the boars of Iliadic similes, who often illustrate the defensive courage or aggressive resistance of leading heroes.[18] The bristled mane and shining eyes (φρίξας εὖ λοφιήν, πῦρ δ' ὀφθαλμοῖσι δεδορκώς, *Od.* 19. 446) of the Parnassian boar are reminiscent of those of a boar in a simile highlighting the courage of the Cretan Idomeneus (*Iliad* 13.471–476): he stands his ground, bristles his back up (φρίσσει δέ τε νῶτον ὕπερθεν), and with eyes shining with fire (ὀφθαλμὼ δ' ἄρα οἱ πυρὶ λάμπετον) eagerly fights off human hunters intruding upon his territory. As Odysseus and his uncles tread the slopes of Mount Parnassus, they intertextually enter the world of hunting similes. The responses of ancient audiences listening to the episode would in part have been shaped by their experience of interspecies relationships in the similes, to which I now turn.[19]

In the vignettes of daily life offered in the similes, human and non-human animals find themselves engaged in power struggles whose never-final outcome is always under negotiation. Unlike the larger-than-life individuals of the heroic narrative, the humans of the similes are anonymous commoners – shepherds, craftsmen, farmers – who usually appear in groups.[20] They compete for food with carnivorous mammals, such as lions and wolves, who attack human-raised cattle and may snatch small game pursued by human hunters. The competition often favours the non-humans. Lions may take advantage of a shepherd's absence to prey on sheep or goats (*Il.* 10.485–486; *Il.* 15.323–325).[21] Terrified shepherds may not dare to confront them (*Il.* 17.61–67). When confrontation does occur, a lion may be overthrown, but only because of the numerical superiority of the adversary (*Il.* 11.548–555). Boars offer an equally dangerous although different kind of challenge. As herbivores they do not prey on cattle or game, but they powerfully resist the hunters and hounds who track them in the depth of wildness. The issue of the encounter is always uncertain. The boar may die, as at *Il.* 12.146–150, but it may also put his pursuers to flight (*Il.* 17.281–283). Two boars wreak havoc upon the hounds that pursue them at *Il.* 11.324–325. Other similes leave the outcome unspecified (*Il.* 13.470–476; *Il.* 11.414–418), thus emphasizing the instability of the power relation across species. When life is at stake, the lions and boars of the similes are on the same footing as their human competitors.[22]

That sense of unsettled competition between human commoners and large mammals correlates with a process of analogy – reflected in and secured through linguistic unity – that connects the similes as rhetorical devices to the heroic narrative. Lions and boars resemble warriors in both their behaviour and the emotions driving them.[23] A warrior at the peak of his *aristeia* – most notably Diomedes, Agamemnon or Hektor – is driven by the same *menos* as a marauding lion attacking cattle or sheep. Like his animal counterpart, he wreaks havoc upon his victims. Major heroes under attack display the same resistance as boars against human assailants. Idomeneus holds his ground against Aineias (μένεν, *Il.* 13.476) just as a mountain wild boar stands up to a great rabble of men advancing upon him (μένει, *Il.* 13.472). Ajax son of Telamon scatters Trojan battalions (Τρώων ἐκέδασσε φάλαγγας, *Il.* 17.285) as a boar easily scatters dogs and youth among the mountains (ῥηΐδίως ἐκέδασσεν, *Il.* 17.283).

Accordingly, Iliadic boars exhibit the same psychological and mental states as human warriors. They are singled out for their courage (ἀγηνορίη, *Il.* 12.46), physical strength (ἀλκή, *Il.* 4.253, *Il.* 13.471, *Il.* 17.728; σθένος *Il.* 5.783= *Il.* 7.257, *Il.* 12.42), and pride (μέγα φρονέοντε, *Il.* 11.325). Like other non-human animals in the similes, they are understood to own a psychological apparatus very similar to that of human beings, although they do not have intelligence, *noos*.[24] As Menelaos grudgingly compares the pride of the sons of Panthoos to the 'fury' (μένος) of the leopard, lion and boar, he singles out the boar for the intensity of his θυμός (*Il.* 17.18–23). Likewise, a simile describing Hektor as he rallies the Trojans through the battlefield highlights the 'proud heart' with which a wild boar or lion unflinchingly faces a pack of hounds and huntsmen (κυδάλιμον κῆρ, *Il.* 12.45). In the rhetoric of the similes, heroes, lions and boars partake into the same vital forces that set them apart from human commoners.[25] In line with the primarily aristocratic ethos of the Homeric poems, the similes suggest an ontological taxonomy that cuts across species to distinguish between heroes and their animal peers on the one hand, and commoners on the other.[26] On that worldview, the boar whom the young Odysseus faces on the slopes of Mount Parnassos is animated with the same vitality, energy and drive as that to which the hero Odysseus aspires.

The relevance of the analogical worldview of the similes to audience expectations at the onset of the Parnassian boar hunt is further confirmed by a specific detail. The boar initially lies hidden in a lair made of bushes so dense that elements cannot go through it (*Od.* 19.439–443):

> ἔνθα δ' ἄρ' ἐν λόχμῃ πυκινῇ κατέκειτο μέγας σῦς·
> <u>τὴν μὲν ἄρ' οὔτ' ἀνέμων διάη μένος ὑγρὸν ἀέντων,</u>
> <u>οὔτε μιν ἠέλιος φαέθων ἀκτῖσιν ἔβαλλεν,</u>
> <u>οὔτ' ὄμβρος περάασκε διαμπερές·</u> ὣς ἄρα πυκνὴ
> ἦεν, ἀτὰρ <u>φύλλων ἐνέην χύσις</u> ἤλιθα πολλή.
>
> Now there, inside that thick of the bush, was the lair of a great boar.
> <u>Neither could the force of wet-blown winds penetrate here,</u>
> <u>nor could the shining sun ever strike through with his rays, nor yet</u>
> <u>could the rain pass all the way through it</u>, so close together
> it grew, with a <u>fall of leaves</u> drifted in dense profusion.

As scholars have often noted, that space resembles the place where Odysseus finds shelter upon reaching the island of the Phaeacians (*Od.* 5.476–485):[27]

. . . δοιοὺς δ᾽ ἄρ᾽ ὑπήλυθε θάμνους
ἐξ ὁμόθεν πεφυῶτας· ὁ μὲν φυλίης, ὁ δ᾽ ἐλαίης.
τοὺς μὲν ἄρ᾽ οὔτ᾽ ἀνέμων διάη μένος ὑγρὸν ἀέντων,
οὔτε ποτ᾽ ἠέλιος φαέθων ἀκτῖσιν ἔβαλλεν,
οὔτ᾽ ὄμβρος περάασκε διαμπερές· ὣς ἄρα πυκνοὶ
ἀλλήλοισιν ἔφυν ἐπαμοιβαδίς· οὓς ὑπ᾽ Ὀδυσσεὺς
δύσετ᾽. ἄφαρ δ᾽ εὐνὴν ἐπαμήσατο χερσὶ φίλῃσιν
εὐρεῖαν· φύλλων γὰρ ἔην χύσις ἤλιθα πολλή,
ὅσσον τ᾽ ἠὲ δύω ἠὲ τρεῖς ἄνδρας ἔρυσθαι
ὥρῃ χειμερίῃ, εἰ καὶ μάλα περ χαλεπαίνοι.

. . . and stopped underneath two bushes
that grew from the same place, one of shrub, and one of wild olive,
and neither the force of wet-blowing winds could penetrate these
nor could the shining sun ever strike through with his rays, nor yet
could the rain pass all the way through them, so close together
were they grown, interlacing each other; and under these now Odysseus
entered, and with his own hands heaped him a bed to sleep on,
making it wide, since there was great store of fallen leaves there,
enough for two men to take cover in or even three men
in the winter season, even in the very worst kind of weather.

In *Odyssey* 5 Odysseus takes refuge in this natural shelter after he almost drowns at sea in the storm sent by Poseidon (*Od.* 5.282–450) and then finds himself at the mercy of the elements and of savage animals upon landing on the coast of the Phaeacians (*Od.* 5.465–473). In contrast with that hostile environment, the intertwined olive tree and bush offer a much-needed space where he can regain some strength, but they also stress Odysseus' distance from civilization.[28] The makeshift 'bed' (εὐνή) of leaves contrasts with the elaborate beddings listed in hospitality scenes (*Od.* 4.296–305; *Od.* 19.317–318) and, even more pointedly, with the bed that Odysseus carved for himself and Penelope from a live olive tree (*Od.* 23.183–204). Naked and remote from the refinements of human culture, Odysseus lies on the shore of Scheria on a par with the wild creatures (θῆρα, *Od.* 5.473) for whom he fears to become prey. As they rest among protective bushes, Odysseus and the boar find themselves in spaces that pre-exist the cultural divide between human and non-human animals – places where 'species meet' on an equal footing.

II. The anthropogenic machine at work

So far I have argued that the setting of the boar hunt narrative (*Od.* 19.428–443) puts it in conversation with a rich network of tropes and passages attentive to analogies between human and non-human animals. I now wish to assess the relation between the expectations raised by this network and the encounter itself (*Od.* 19.444–454). My argument is that the actual fighting between Odysseus and the boar acknowledges the ontological analogy suggested in the similes but overlays it with a hierarchical relation that asserts the superiority of the human over the non-human being.

Alerted by the noise made by the hunting party, the boar leaves his lair and prepares to counter-attack. The action rapidly unfolds into three moments: Odysseus rushes ahead; the boar pre-empts him and is the first to inflict a wound, albeit a non-lethal one; Odysseus transpierces him with his spear (*Od.* 19.447–453). Just as Iliadic similes highlight resemblances between boars and human heroes, so is the encounter between Odysseus and the boar superficially modelled on individual contests in the *Iliad*.[29] Although Odysseus appears to wear no defensive piece of armour, he is equipped with the same 'far-shadowing spear' (δολιχόσκιον ἔγχος, *Od.* 19.438) that Iliadic warriors customarily use on the battlefield (21x *Il.*; 4x *Od.*), and he shakes it in the same gesture as Ajax preparing for his duel with Hektor in *Iliad* 7 (κραδάων δολιχόσκιον ἔγχος, *Od.* 19.438b = *Il.* 7.213b). A few lines later, he engages with the boar with the exact same tactics and driven by the same urge as in a duel on the battlefield. Odysseus is 'eager to stab' the boar as Achilles is 'eager to stab' Lycaon with his spear (οὐτάμεναι μεμαώς, *Od.* 19.449a = *Il.* 21.68a). He hits the boar 'in the right shoulder' as Pandaros hits Diomedes (τυχὼν κατὰ δεξιὸν ὦμον, *Od.* 19.452b= *Il.* 5.98b). His spear cuts through the boar's body (ἀντικρὺ δὲ διῆλθε φαεινοῦ δουρὸς ἀκωκή, *Od.* 19.453) in a line quasi identical to the description of Koon's spear cutting through Agamemnon's middle arm (ἀντικρὺ δὲ διέσχε φαεινοῦ δουρὸς ἀκωκή, *Il.* 11.253). The fact that Odysseus confronts the boar on the model of a war duel thus aligns with the boar's analogy to Homeric warriors described above.

Upon further analysis, however, the encounter subtly departs from the Iliadic model of the war duel to gradually become a narrative of human superiority over a non-human being. As the narrative freezes on the image of the lonely beast standing against the throng of men and dogs, he is described in diction that both subtly alludes to and departs from formulas pertaining to human warriors (19.444–447):

> τὸν δ' ἀνδρῶν τε κυνῶν τε περὶ κτύπος ἦλθε ποδοῖїν,
> ὡς ἐπάγοντες ἐπῆσαν· ὁ δ' ἀντίος ἐκ ξυλόχοιο,
> <u>φρίξας εὖ λοφιήν, πῦρ δ' ὀφθαλμοῖσι δεδορκώς,</u>
> στῆ ῥ' αὐτῶν σχεδόθεν . . .
>
> The thudding made by the feet of men and dogs came to him
> as they closed on him in the hunt, and against them he from his woodlair
> <u>bristled strongly his nape, and with fire from his eyes glaring</u>
> stood up to face them close . . .

The two hemistichs at line 446 are especially significant. The boar 'bristles' as Iliadic phalanxes do, but he does so with his 'hair' while they 'bristle with shields and spears' (σάκεσίν τε καὶ ἔγχεσι πεφρικυῖαι, *Il.* 4.282). Control over weapons, or lack thereof, thus separates the boar from human warriors, a theme to which I will return shortly. In addition, the boar's blazing eyes (πῦρ δ' ὀφθαλμοῖσι δεδορκώς) are characteristic of Iliadic heroes going berserk and raging against the enemies in a pique of fury, anger or pain (*Il.*1.104 [Agamemnon]); *Il.* 12.466 and 15.607 [Hektor]); *Il.* 19.16–17 and 365–366 [Achilles]). Significantly, however, the blazing eyes of the boar are referred to as ὀφθαλμοί (as in the description of the boar of *Il.* 13.474), while formulas about blazing human eyes use the term ὄσσε.[30] Those differences complicate the analogy between boars and heroes established in the similes. The boar resembles, but is not identical with, heroes at the onset of their *aristeia*.

Additional details in the action further demarcate the hunt from individual encounters on the battlefield. The threefold sequence described above – whereby Odysseus rushes on but fails to strike first; the boar wounds but does not kill him; and Odysseus kills the boar – has no equivalent in the *Iliad*, where only a small fraction of individual contests (one out of seven) involves more than one blow.[31] One result is to build up suspense and highlight the valour of the boar. Odysseus' failure to strike first briefly opens up the possibility that he could be killed, in accordance with the pattern of single blow encounters prevalent in the *Iliad*. In addition, the fact that the boar delivers the first blow suggests his superiority in terms of the paradigmatic Iliadic qualities of courage and *menos*. The boar is a worthy match for the youth, making the encounter with him an effective test of the skills closely associated with Homeric *aretē*.[32]

Yet just as the narrative recognizes the boar's rapidity and courage, the specifics of the blow exchange at 450–453 depart from the model of Iliadic warfare to highlight the technical superiority of Odysseus over the boar's anatomy. Both the boar and Odysseus attempt to transfix the body of their adversary with something sharp, but the boar fails where Odysseus succeeds.[33] Moreover, the boar's failure is not due to the resistance of his adversary's defensive equipment, as in Iliadic warfare, but to limitations in his own anatomy. Because of his lower height, he does not hit Odysseus in the favourite targets that are the head and entrails. The shape of his tusks forces him to 'tear sidewise', a phrase otherwise used to describe the defensive move of Polydamas leaping to the side when confronting Ajax (λικριφὶς ἀΐξας, *Od.*19.451a = *Il.*14.463a). And because the tusk is too short to reach the bone (οὐδ' ὀστέον ἵκετο φωτός, *Od.* 19.451b), Odysseus is able to strike back despite his wound, a rare event that occurs only twice in the *Iliad*.[34] In contrast to the shorter tusk, the spear is long enough (cf. δολιχόσκιον ἔγχος, 19.438) for its point to pass right through his adversary (19.452–453).[35] Taken together, the contrasting blows construct both an analogy – whereby the tusk is to the boar what the spear is to Odysseus, – and a hierarchy that highlights technology as the dividing factor between the human and the non-human. The boar fights just as major heroes do, but in comparison with his human opponent his lack of equipment limits the outcome of his actions. The narrative does not challenge the idea that the boar may be similar – if not superior – to Odysseus in the areas of courage, physical strength, energy and drive highlighted in the boar similes, but it introduces technology as both a divider and a marker of hierarchy between them. Furthermore, the functional parallelism between tusk and spear highlights the entanglement of the man and his weapon. Odysseus' victory constructs him as an assemblage of human and artefact.[36]

That identification of technological expertise as a distinctive characteristic of Odysseus' mode of being in the world carries wide resonances throughout the poem.[37] Odysseus' carpentry skills allow him to build the raft on which he departs from Calypso's island (*Od.* 5.234–261). The Cyclops episode further contrasts the technological primitiveness of Polyphemus, who eats his victim raw, and Odysseus' skill in sharpening the olive-wood club into a stake (9.319–328). Odysseus' control over technology is also crucial in the battle against the suitors. With Telemachus' help, Odysseus removes all helmets, shields and spears from the great hall (19.31–33, as announced at 16.281–298) so that when the feast turns into slaughter, the suitors can initially only use their swords. By contrast, Odysseus and his supporters (Telemachus, the oxherd, and the swineherd) each rely on full arming gear, including a shield, a helmet and two spears. In all three episodes, superior technology is crucial in Odysseus' victory and affects the ontological status of his opponents by depriving them of human or human-like features. The boar's resemblance to Iliadic heroes is progressively downplayed. The blind Cyclops turns to his ram as his closest companion. The dead suitors lie in the blood and dust 'like fish whom the fishermen have taken in their net . . . and all of them lie piled on the sand' (*Od.* 22.384–389). The identification of technology as a distinctive feature of Odysseus' coming of age thus proleptically paves the way for his improbable victory over 108 suitors three books later.

Understood in these terms, the Parnassian boar hunt reads as an early precursor for the anthropocentric conceit, well-attested in fifth-century Athens, whereby humans are conceived as distinct from and superior to all other animals because of their intelligence and technological savviness.[38] Just as the spear secures Odysseus' victory over the boar, the first antistrophe of the first stasimon – the so-called 'Ode to Man' – in Sophocles' *Antigone* sets man (περιφραδὴς ἀνήρ) apart from all other animals, which he captures or rules over thanks to 'nets' (σπείραισι δικτυοκλώστοις), 'devices' (μηχαμαῖς), and 'yokes' (332–352). Even more specifically, Odysseus' reliance on his spear to secure victory in spite of the boar's physiological superiority parallels the famous anthropogony in Plato's *Protagoras* 320d–322d, where Prometheus endows humans with fire and technical intelligence (τὴν ἔντεχνον σοφίαν σὺν πυρί) to remedy Epimetheus' failure to give them one or more of the powers (δυνάμεις) that secure a careful balance among, and thus ensure the survival of, non-rational creatures (τὰ ἄλογα).[39]

III. Cross-species entanglements

So far I have argued that the boar hunt of *Odyssey* 19 describes Odysseus' coming of age as an affirmation of difference from and superiority over the boar that is all the more significant because it operates against audience expectations of similarities across human and non-human animals. Yet that reading does not exhaust the complexity of the encounter. The Parnassian boar hunt is inserted in the master narrative as an etiology for Odysseus' scar, meaning that the story of Odysseus killing the boar cannot be separated from that of the boar wounding Odysseus. That reciprocity belongs with a larger pattern whereby Odysseus simultaneously receives and brings trouble to people with whom he interacts throughout the poem.[40] In the context of the boar hunt, however, that reciprocity works across species, therefore extending the scope of Odysseus' enmeshments with other beings.

Let's return, then, to the moment when the boar wounds Odysseus (19.449–451):

> . . . ὁ δέ μιν φθάμενος <u>ἔλασεν σῦς</u>
> γουνὸς ὕπερ, πολλὸν δὲ διήφυσε σαρκὸς <u>ὀδόντι</u>
> λικριφὶς ἀΐξας . . .
>
> . . . but too quick for him the boar drove
> over the knee, and with his tusk gashed much of the flesh,
> tearing sidewise . . .

In terms of narrative economy, that account is the culmination, or *telos*, of the aetiological digression triggered by Eurykleia's discovery of the scar. Its diction echoes the two highly compressed accounts for the origin of the scar that bracket the boar hunt narrative in a ring composition pattern (οὐλήν, τήν ποτέ μιν σῦς ἤλασε λευκῷ ὀδόντι, 19.393; cf. οὐλὴν . . . ὥς μιν θηρεύοντ' ἔλασεν σῦς λευκῷ ὀδόντι, 19.464–465).[41] Yet while the macro- and the micro-narratives intersect at the scar, they offer very different perspectives on it.

In the former, the scar belongs with other signs used as proofs of Odysseus' identity in recognition scenes and has been discussed as such at least since Aristotle (*Poetics* 1454b20).[42] The question of signs has been raised earlier in book 19 when Penelope tested the veracity of the beggar's account by asking for details about Odysseus' apparel when he left for Troy (19.215–217; cf. σήματ' 19.250). In that context, Eurykleia's unplanned and immediate recognition of Odysseus marks the scar as a sign of choice, both directly intelligible and not easily manipulated. The semiotic legibility of the scar is highlighted again later as the poem calls it 'a sign easy to be distinguished' (σῆμα ἀριφραδές, 21.217; 23.73) and uses it in three other recognition scenes (21.217–220 [Eumaeus and Philoitios]); 23.73–76 [Eurykleia's report to Penelope]; 24.331–335 [Laertes]). Here, tellingly, Eurykleia's perception is closely followed by her utterance of the name 'Odysseus' (19.474). The scar points to the name that itself points to the individual. Like the personal name, the scar as a sign relies on the premise that individuals retain a stable identity throughout their lives, no matter how much hardship they endure (16.204–206).

By contrast, the boar hunt micro-narrative casts the scar as the outcome of a process that forever changed Odysseus' body. The highly anticipated line 450 when Odysseus is scarified by the boar stylizes the wound as a near-death experience that for a brief moment turns him into embodied flesh fit for consumption. The compound verb διαφύσσω whereby the boar 'scoops out a large amount of flesh' from Odysseus' thigh can refer to the action of drawing wine from a vessel to drink it (*Od.* 16.110). The simple verb ἀφύσσω occurs three times in the *Iliad* to describe how a bronze spearhead made entrails gush out, resulting in the death of the victim (διὰ δ' ἔντερα χαλκὸς/ ἤφυσ', *Il.* 13.507–508 = *Il.* 17.314–315; cf. *Il.* 14.517–518). That sense of Odysseus' vulnerability is further suggested by the word σάρξ 'flesh' that is the object of the verb διαφύσσω. Elsewhere in Homer, the term occurs in conjunction with other body parts like fat, entrails, bones and sinews in contexts where humans are imagined to be eaten by dogs and birds on the battlefield (*Il.* 8.379–380; *Il.* 13.832) or when the Cyclops eats Odysseus' companions (*Od.* 9.293). Odysseus' dead mother Antikleia also refers to flesh (σάρκας), bones and sinews as those parts of the dead that are burnt on pyres (*Od.* 11.219). In those various contexts, then, σάρξ and σάρκες are associated with the vulnerability of human bodies in their subjection to death, decay and their position as animals that may become part of the food chain.[43] The use of the word σάρξ with reference to Odysseus' body highlights his porousness to other bodies and shatters the notion of a stable self safely cordoned off from the outside. Within the micro-narrative, the scar represents Odysseus as a changing body susceptible to transformation and decay through contact with objects and elements, as well as other animals.[44]

Odysseus' permeability to the boar's agency is confirmed in the compressed versions that bracket off the boar hunt from the macro-narrative. Here is Odysseus' narrative reenactment of the encounter to his parents (19.462–466):

> . . . τῷ μέν ῥα πατὴρ καὶ πότνια μήτηρ
> χαῖρον νοστήσαντι καὶ ἐξερέεινον ἕκαστα,
> οὐλὴν ὅττι <u>πάθοι</u>· ὁ δ' ἄρα σφίσιν εὖ κατέλεξεν,
> ὥς μιν θηρεύοντ' ἔλασεν σῦς λευκῷ ὀδόντι
> Παρνησόνδ' ἐλθόντα σὺν υἱάσιν Αὐτολύκοιο.

> . . . and there his father and queenly mother
> were glad in his homecoming, and asked about all that had happened,
> and how he came by his wound, and he told well his story,
> how in the hunt the boar with his white tusk had wounded him
> as he went up to Parnassos with the sons of Autolykos.

Both Laertes and Antikleia's questions as well as Odysseus' answers highlight the agency of the boar, whose death is conspicuously absent from the account. The boar is the subject of the active verb ἐλαύνω 'strike, wound', while Odysseus becomes the victim (πάθοι). In a striking twist on the predominantly heroic tone of the embedded narrative, the encounter on Parnassos is reinterpreted as culminating not so much with the boar's death, but rather with Odysseus' wound. While the scar points to Odysseus' name in the macro-narrative, here it triggers a mention of the boar as active subject. The boar has become narratively inscribed onto Odysseus' body.

In that context of heightened attention to the contact between the boar tusk and Odysseus, might ancient audiences have heard the Greek syntagm for 'boar tusk' (ὀδοὺς συός) within the name of Odysseus (Ὀδυσσεύς)?[45] The text offers no collocation of the words ὀδούς and συός as a single syntagm. Rather, in all six instances where they occur together, the word for 'boar' in the nominative (σῦς) is the subject of a verb meaning 'hit' for which the word for 'tusk', usually modified by the epithet 'white', serves as a dative of means (ὀδόντι).[46] Yet even though it does not lie at the immediate surface of the text, a re-motivation of Odysseus' name in the light of the wound inflicted by the boar tusk is supported by other interpreting practices in the poem. The *Odyssey* offers many examples of 'significant' names – that is, proper names that bards and audiences are likely to have connected to lexical items through etymology or paronomasia – and Odysseus' names are favourite loci for such puns.[47] Odysseus' victory over Polyphemus famously relies on the paranomasia between his pseudonym Outis (Οὖτις) and the syntagm 'nobody' (οὔ τις, 9.408). His Ithakan pseudonyms, Aithôn and Eperitos, have also been interpreted as significant names.[48] And immediately before the boar hunt narrative, the story of Odysseus' naming by his grandfather Autolykos explicitly etymologizes his name from the verb ὀδύσσομαι (19.407–409), thus confirming implicit puns between the verb and the name throughout the poem (*Od.* 5.340; 5.423; 19.275).

Although not all audience members would have heard the ὀδοὺς συός/Ὀδυσσεύς pun, those who did would have been rewarded with additional layers of hermeneutic pleasure. In a striking response to the etymology offered by Autolykos, the boar hunt narrative would place the boar – rather than 'Self-Wolf' (Auto-lykos) – at the origin of Odysseus' name. In addition, the pun would enrich the semiotic relation discussed above between the scar and the name Odysseus with an iconic quality. The trace of the boar tusk (ὀδοὺς συός) imprints Odysseus' name upon his body. Odysseus becomes 'Odysseus' by becoming an assemblage of human and boar.

The complex negotiations of the boar's ontological status vis-à-vis Odysseus described above are encapsulated in the description of his death (*Od.* 19.454):[49]

> κὰδ δ' ἔπεσ' ἐν κονίῃσι μακών, ἀπὸ δ' ἔπτατο θυμός.
>
> He screamed and dropped in the dust, and the life spirit flitted from him.

This extraordinary line otherwise occurs in Homer to describe the death of two very special animals: Pedasos, Achilles' mortal trace horse, borrowed by Patroklos and killed by Sarpedon with a spear that transpierces his right shoulder (*Il.* 16.468); and the stag killed by Odysseus on Circe's island (*Od.*10.163).[50] Metrically and semantically, it is divided after the first syllable of the fourth foot (hephthemimeral caesura) into two hemistichs, the one focusing on the downward movement of the boar's fall, the other on the upward direction of his θυμός flying away.

The first hemistich re-iterates the boar's subjection to Odysseus by downgrading him from heroic paradigm to abject victim. Picking up on the earlier stylization of the encounter as a war duel, κὰδ δ' ἔπεσ' ἐν κονίῃσι aligns the dying boar with a human being. 'Falling into the dust' is a standard way of describing human deaths in the *Iliad*, and the verb καταπίπτω is commonly used of slain or wounded men (e.g., *Il.* 4.523=13.549; 5.560, 12.23, 16.290, 16.311, 16.414=580, 16.662). Yet in the second colon after the feminine caesura the verb μηκάομαι denotes a sound that – but for the exception of the grotesque beggar Iros knocked down by Odysseus at *Od.* 18.98 – only non-human animals produce in Homer. Specifically, μηκάομαι refers to a cry of pain or fear emitted by weak or powerless animals, like the bleating of ewes waiting to be milked (*Il.* 4.435; *Od.* 9.439), or the cry of a deer or hare running in front of rip-fanged hounds (*Il.*10.362). μηκάομαι further contrasts with the loud bellowing of dying bulls to which dying warriors are sometimes compared (*Il.* 16.487–489 [Sarpedon]; *Il.* 20.403–406 [Hippodamas]). Altogether, by the time we reach the hephthemimeral caesura the boar's heroism has been undermined by the weakness of his last cry.

By contrast, the upward movement of the boar's θυμός in the second hemistich suggests that he is survived by an active principle of vitality. The hemistich may be analysed as a combination of two death-related formulas whose juxtaposition generates an eschatological paradox.[51] While departure of the θυμός is the commonest way of describing death in the *Iliad*, the colocation of θυμός and a verb meaning 'fly' is unique to our line.[52] With one exception, the *Iliad* offers no other mention of a θυμός continuing an autonomous existence once separated from the body.[53] In turn, the verb πέτομαι does occur in death formulas, but in collocation with the noun ψυχή. The deaths of Patroklos and Hektor include identical lines describing the fluttering ψυχή going to Hades and mourning its fate (ψυχή … πταμένη, *Il.* 16.856=22.362). According to the *précis* of eschatology offered to Odysseus by his dead mother Antikleia in the *nekyia*, when the θυμός departs from the bones, the flesh, bones and sinews are burnt but the ψυχή flitters 'like a dream' and flies away. (*Od.* 11.219–222).[54] In addition, with one exception, all instances of the word ψυχή refer to human beings.[55]

Given that formulaic background, the unusual combination of θυμός and ἀποπέτομαι may be interpreted in several ways. One may hear an erasure of ψυχή from the formula attested for the heroic deaths of Hektor and Patroklos, perhaps out of an anthropocentric resistance to the idea that animals may have a ψυχή.[56] On that reading, the second hemistich confirms the de-heroicization of the boar in the first hemistich. But the unusual phrase may also suggest that the boar is uniquely survived by a principle of vitality more active than the pale ψυχαί of the underworld. ψυχή is etymologically connected to ψῦχος and ψυχρός, 'cold', suggesting an original reference to the cold breath of death, and in Homer the word appears in the context of life lost or threatened rather than life held and enjoyed.[57] By contrast, the word θυμός refers to an active psychic organ; as we saw earlier, the boar is singled out among other wild animals for the intensity of his θυμός in the simile of *Iliad* 17.18–23. Other occurrences of the verbs πέτομαι and ἀποπέτομαι suggest that the boar's flitting θυμός may be imagined as a vaporous, perhaps winged entity, in line with its etymological connection with Latin *fumus* and its semantic connection with winds.[58] On that interpretation, the unusual postmortem survival of the boar's θυμός may offer an eschatological counterpart for his ongoing narrative presence and agency, through the scar, in Odysseus' life.

While the encounter with the boar is crucial to the social fabrication of Odysseus among his family and larger community, the entanglement of killing and wounding in the episode relies on ontological relations vastly more complex than a stable hierarchy between man and animal. Unlike Iliadic duels, Odysseus' victory over the boar does not rely on *aretē*, but rather on the fact that his spear is more effective than the boar's tusk. Yet even as technology differentiates them, Odysseus' wound insists on a porosity across his and the boar's bodies. The narrative thus oscillates between the urge to create a stable identity based on the opposition between human and animal, and the recognition of the resistance that embodiment offers to that anthropocentric project. This tension is powerfully captured in the paradox of the scar that is simultaneously a sign of Odysseus' identity, and an index of his permeability to other beings.

As Eurykleia recognizes the mark on Odysseus' thigh, she raises a cry, prompting Odysseus to violently silence her for fear that an early revelation of his identity may cause his doom (*Od.* 19.482–490). This narrowly avoided scenario combines narrative motifs of disguise, ambush and recognition that are central to the plot of the *Odyssey*, but in the immediate context of *Odyssey* 19 it also reconfigures the Parnassian hunt with an intriguing twist: just as the boar was provoked to come out of his lair, confront a youth, and thereby meet his death, so might Eurykleia's cry force the ambushed Odysseus to leave his cover and meet and be killed by the suitors. And there is more: in that scenario, the wound inflicted by the boar on the young Odysseus would ultimately result in his death many years later, thus aligning their experiences, closing the ontological gap created by Odysseus' technology-based victory, and bringing to the surface suggestions of resemblance and reciprocity that run through the scar digression. Recovering this alternative story from a foundational text of Western culture may be one small way to answer Scranton's call for a new understanding of what it means to be human in the Anthropocene.

CHAPTER 2
WHAT IS IT LIKE TO BE A DONKEY (WITH A HUMAN MIND)? PSEUDO-LUCIAN'S *ONOS*

Tua Korhonen

> I cannot say what it was like for the other animals, but as far as I was concerned, being unshod, rather skinny, and quite unused to it, I found it absolute agony trotting over the sharp stones with a weight like that on top of me.
>
> Ps.-Lucian *Onos* (16.16–18)[1]

A young man interested in metamorphoses asks a witch's female slave to change him into a bird. The wrong ointment is used and the man, Lucius, becomes a donkey. The female slave promises that he will become human again if he can manage to eat roses. Before that he is forced to experience being passed from one owner to another, abusive treatment and many dangerous situations. In the most famous and elaborate version of this story, Apuleius' *Metamorphoses* (known as the *Golden Ass*) from the third century CE, Lucius' metamorphosis back to a human corresponds to his initiation to the Isiac mysteries. Apuleius' version may be interpreted as an allegory: one must experience a metaphoric death before a new life as a neophyte of the Mysteries can begin. This implies that the Mysteries are not only a guarantee for immortal life but also salvation from a 'mere' animal life. In this way, the story underlines the human–animal and mind–body divides. However, Apuleius' *Metamorphoses* has recently been read as an autobiography of a donkey by Thorsten Fögen among his other cases of individual animals in the Graeco-Roman literature. Fögen states that *Metamorphoses* is 'a unique literary experiment which forces the narrator to adopt the donkey's perspective and describe the events that he experiences as seen through the animal's eyes'.[2]

Apuleius' novel has a shorter Greek equivalent Λούκιος ἢ ὄνος ('Lucius or the Donkey'), known as *Onos*, in the Lucianic corpus and it is also told from a first-person perspective, like the *Golden Ass*. Both works probably had a common Greek source, which used the tradition of Milesian tales with erotic emphases.[3] The most drastic element in this story model (the sexual encounter between a woman and a donkey) also occurs in papyri and it is depicted in ancient iconography.[4] However, the core of the story used by the writer of *Onos* and Apuleius is a human transformed into the most common pack animal in antiquity, the donkey. *Onos*, the pseudo-Lucian Greek story, is seen as a kind of epitome of the original Greek story. Compared with Apuleius' novel, the elaborate digressive stories (like the story of Eros and Psyche, cf. Apuleius *Met.* 4.28–6.24) and many smaller – and from the animal point of view interesting – episodes are missing (one of the robbers' tales, for example, includes a kind of 'metamorphosis' into a bear: a robber dresses up in a bear's skin as a way to smuggle himself inside a rich man's house, cf. *Met.* 4.14–20). The writer of the *Onos* has surely made choices about what are the relevant incidents and emphases in the story.

This chapter focuses on Lucius the donkey's interaction with and attitudes to humans and other non-humans, like working animals and wild animals, in the pseudo-Lucian's *Onos* – a text much less studied than Apuleius' *Metamorphoses*. It poses questions about how Lucius narrates his experience of getting accustomed to his donkey body, or, of *being* a donkey body – whether Lucius' human subjectivity is blended with his subjectivity as a donkey – and how the life of a non-human animal is portrayed. According to the French phenomenologist Maurice Merleau-Ponty, we are our bodies, which means that consciousness is a bodily consciousness in the way that we are always already located in the world and in interaction with others through our body. This notion precedes the posthuman emphasis on materiality, being in the world and embodiment as presented, for instance, by Rosi Braidotti, Cary Wolfe and Donna Haraway.[5] Although Lucius' responses to his situations as a donkey (or, the narrator's descriptions of them) may seem generic or even stereotyped behaviour of donkeys, it will be argued that the narrative produces the presence of a donkey and, therefore, the possibility – for us as readers – to orientate to animal embodiment and how the body structures experience.

Becoming a donkey

The story begins with Lucius travelling in Thessaly on his father's business and arriving at Hypata, where he has the house of an associate to stay in. The female slave of the house, Palaestra, informs Lucius that the lady of the house happens to be a witch (μάγος), who punishes unlikeable persons by metamorphosing them into living beings (εἰς ζῷα, 4.32). The lady can change her own shape too: when she wants to hasten to her lover, she becomes a bird. Palaestra and Lucius become lovers and she arranges for him an opportunity to see a metamorphosis, by peeping into the master bedroom like a voyeur when the lady of the house undresses herself. While putting some frankincense in the fire, she utters a litany of words and rubs her body with an ointment; feathers begin to sprout, her nose becomes horn-like and finally she has 'all a bird's features and characteristics' (12.23–24). When she is thoroughly feathered, she crows horribly (δεινόν) and flies away through the window (12.25–27). This encourages Lucius himself to try out the ointment; he wants to be able to fly and to know whether his soul would transform into that of a bird (13.7–9). (One may wonder how he would recognize this if he in fact had gained a bird's soul.) Lucius smears the ointment and begins to change, not into a bird, but into a donkey. He notices that his mind (φρήν) and intellect (νοῦς) remain human after metamorphosis (15.1–2), that is, his soul has not transformed into a donkey's soul. Therefore, Lucius is a kind of a hybrid: he keeps his human (or, more accurately, a man's) mind including memory but his body is metamorphosed into a male donkey's body. Thus, although the *Onos* is a becoming-animal tale, the narrative seems to emphasize the mind–body divide as strongly as the Graeco-Roman narratives of reincarnation when the soul, after bodily death, moves into another body.

However, Lucius experiences metamorphosis as something 'vanishing' (like his fingers and toes), and something else growing (13.12–18). Naturally, bodily metamorphosis affects his abilities. When Lucius tries to scold Palaestra for the wrong ointment, he notices that he cannot speak anymore.[6] Instead, he drops his lip and looks angrily at her 'as a donkey does' (ὡς ὄνος, 13.21). Later, when he is kidnapped by robbers, the lack of speech equates with the inability to articulate protest (16.21–24 and 38.7–10).[7] However, it is not depicted as fatally as in Ovid's *Metamorphoses*, where the lack of speech is often seen as a tragic deprivation.[8] At least Lucius has a communicative donkey body to express his protests.

Palaestra promises to bring Lucius the cure for the metamorphosis (roses) the next morning so that Lucius will 'undress the animal from himself' (ἀποδύσῃ μὲν αὐτίκα τὸ κτῆνος, 14.7–8).[9] Semantically it is interesting that when referring to the ability of the lady of the house to metamorphose herself into various animals, the narrator, Lucius, uses the word *zôa*, a neutral word referring to all sensuous living beings. But here, in the account of Lucius' own metamorphosis, the word used for animal is κτῆνος, which has connotations of a working animal owned by humans (< the verb κτάομαι 'to own'). However, although Lucius calls himself miserable (ὁ δυστυχής) because he did not metamorphose into a bird (13.12), he depicts his becoming a donkey quite neutrally and does not underline overtly the acknowledged 'ugliness' of donkeys or the humility of becoming an animal, which was generally despised in antiquity.[10]

Palaestra likes her lover even after he has obtained a donkey's body: she strokes his ears and skin (14.11–12). Palaestra is the first of three women who feel affection for Lucius in his donkey form (the other two are the kidnapped girl and the rich woman of foreign origin). However, Palaestra cannot help him because a gang of robbers attack the house in the night and take Lucius with them. In all, Lucius serves six masters: (A) the robbers (chapters 16–26), (B) the servants of the kidnapped girl's family (27–34), (C) the priests of the Syrian goddess (35–41), (D) the rich baker (42), (E) the poor vegetable grower (43–45) and (F) Menecles, the wealthy arranger of gladiatorial shows (46–54). Lucius' relationships with humans and especially his owners alternate, as do his attitudes to non-humans.

Lucius' relationship with human and non-human animals

At Palaestra's house

Lucius arrives at the house in Hypata riding on a horse. He asks Palaestra to ensure that his horse receives grain in the stable (3.5–7). Besides being a practical concern (Lucius sees to it that his possession gets the proper care), Lucius' genuine caring for his horse's well-being looks forward to the scene where Lucius, after his metamorphosis, goes to the stable and notices his horse and the donkey of the house drop their ears as they seem to prepare to defend their food with their hooves against him (15.6–10).[11] Once in the stable, the metamorphosed Lucius begins to *laugh* probably because he is surprised that his horse does not show any reciprocal generosity to him (cf. *Met.* 3.26). Like the horse and the other donkey, Lucius is a domestic animal now: he needs to socialize with his new group and their ways to share or not share food. Likewise, laughing (and humour) was considered a fundamentally human feature in antiquity.[12] Lucius notices that his laugh is, however, braying (15.11–12), so that his inability to laugh betokens his hybridization: he reacts with humour, with surprised laughter, but is not able to produce vocally correct human laughter due to his new physiology. Thus, at this stage, Lucius has not fully realized his transformation into a (domesticated) donkey.

Moreover, Lucius worries that a wolf or other predators might enter the stable (15.13–15). Although some herbivorous animals like donkeys are able to defend themselves by kicking or at least by running away, Lucius, trapped in the stable and still unaccustomed to his donkey's body, feels himself helpless prey for predators. Lucius' fear tells that human-made shelter does not feel like adequate protection against predators in his new 'status' or role as a prey animal. Consequently, his relationship with domestic animals as well as predators has to change: as a domesticated animal, Lucius may need protection from predators but also new ways to protect himself; so he needs to build a new relationship with other domestic animals as well as with his new body.

The robbers (A)

After his kidnapping, Lucius' life as a beast of burden begins. Soon he speaks of himself and the two animals kidnapped with him (his horse and the donkey of the house) as 'we': 'they saddled *us* and fastened on *our* backs everything they had brought out and *we* carried these heavy loads and they beat *us* with sticks' (16.11–14).[13] Lucius even uses the first person plural in the sense 'we animals' twice later.[14] He also refers to the other two pack animals as 'the other (domestic) animals' (τὰ ἄλλα κτήνη) as he is beginning to identify with his new role as κτῆνος: he cannot say how the other two animals manage but he himself gets very tired, being unshod and unaccustomed to such a way of travelling (16. 16–18). Lucius decides to collapse so that the robbers will leave him there to be eaten by wolves (that is, providing him an opportunity to escape) but suddenly 'the other donkey' (ὁ ἄλλος/ἕτερος ὄνος, 16.11–12, 19.13) drops down. Lucius supposes that the donkey has the same kinds of plans as he does – Lucius is thus humanizing the other donkey – but the donkey gets a horrible beating and dies (19.14–27). Lucius' fellow-feeling is obvious although he realizes that his companion's death was his own salvation: the same would have happened to him if he had dropped first and pretended to be unconscious (20.1–2). Lucius calls the donkey 'wretched' (ἄθλιος, 19.15), 'the wretched companion (κοινωνός) of my captivity and my pack-duty' (19.23–24) and his 'travelling companion' (συνοδοιπορος, 20.1). Thus, Lucius sympathizes and begins to feel a fellow-feeling for his co-sufferer, who is a representative of his new species, the donkey. To use Donna Haraway's concept, Lucius is 'becoming *with*' the nonhuman animal with whom he shares a common destiny.[15]

Lucius also feels sympathy for a beautiful kidnapped girl who is locked inside beside him in the robbers' cave. When the girl weeps, Lucius 'weeps' too (22.12). In the night Lucius tries to escape with the girl riding on his back. The girl for her part calls Lucius 'beauty' (or the good one, ὦ καλὲ σύ, 23.32) and promises him freedom from work and plenty of barley. But the robbers catch them and a torturous death is planned for the girl: after killing Lucius, they will empty his belly of entrails, put the girl inside leaving only her head outside; then they will throw them into the wilds where the rotting body of Lucius would attract vultures, which will eat her still alive (25.19–35). Lucius feels sorry for the 'poor' and 'innocent' maiden but laments his own fate too, for a quite humanly reason: because his 'carcass will not be left unmolested' (μηδὲ νεκρὸς εὐτυχὴς κεισόμενος, 26.3–4). However, the girl is rescued (and Lucius with her) by a group of soldiers, among whom is the girl's fiancé.

The servants and the kidnapped girl's family (B)

Lucius then becomes the property of the girl's family. During the girl's sumptuous wedding, Lucius regrets that he has not been metamorphosed into a dog, seeing the tidbits the housedogs are eating. Lucius thus envies the lot of other domestic animals, which is a common topic in the Aesopic fables.[16] Lucius is, however, rewarded for his attempt to rescue the girl. Her father promises that Lucius will graze free in the meadows with horses and he is allowed to mount the mares in order to produce mules (27.14–17). But the groom, who is now ordered to take care of Lucius, has a wife, Megapole, who ties Lucius to their own home mill and takes for herself the barley that is meant for Lucius. She also lends Lucius to work in their neighbours' mills. Furthermore, Lucius cannot roam free in the meadows because his 'companions who feed together' (σύννομοι, 28.21), the stallions, kick, bite and drive him away not wanting him mounting their mares (which Lucius, however, does not intend to do). Lucius has little to eat and becomes thin. In addition, he is not only working at the small home grinding mills, but is also carrying wood from the mountains, which is a tough ordeal due to the groom's wicked slave-boy who beats and tortures him and falsely accuses him of trying to make love with girls and boys (32.10–21). Lucius escapes punishment (killing or being castrated) for the false accusation because his owners (the kidnapped girl and her husband) are accidentally killed and the servants decide to ransack the house (chapter 34). These runaway servants then sell the animals at a marketplace.

The priests of the Syrian goddess (C), the rich baker (D) and the poor farmer (E)

Lucius is bought by (C) Philebus, a priest of the Syrian goddess Atargatis, whose wooden statue Lucius is supposed to carry, decorated, from village to village.[17] The work is not very hard in itself but Lucius is afraid and indignant for the lascivious sexual habits of Philebus' fellow priests and finally his bray reveals their orgy to the villagers. Therefore, the priests tie him to a tree and flog him (38.23–29). After the priests are thrown into prison for the theft of a golden bowl from a temple, Lucius is sold to (D) a rich baker to work in his big mill house with a great number of 'fellow slave animals' (ὁμόδουλα κτηνά, 42.7–8). Hard work makes him very thin and weak again (42.2–43.2). Lucius is then useless to the baker who sells him to (E) a poor gardener, a farmer of vegetables (43.3–46.2). Although the work consists only in carrying the crop to the market, it is now winter and the owner is so destitute that he cannot build any kind of shelter for Lucius. The poor gardener is not described as cruel to Lucius as such. In contrast, Lucius causes trouble for him. As with the priests of the Syrian goddess, Lucius functions as a 'revealer', this time accidentally: a Roman soldier is offended because the gardener does not answer him and eventually the poor farmer has to escape riding on Lucius. The gardener hides in his friend's house but Lucius reveals their hiding place by peeping out (45.20–34).

Menecles (F)

Lucius is sold again; this time to the cook of a rich arranger of Gladiator shows named Menecles. In this house, Lucius is able to steal left-overs – meat, fish and cakes. When Lucius' strange eating habits has been reported to Menecles, he orders, for the sake of comicality, that a table with wine has to be brought to Lucius. Moreover, Menecles commands his freed slave to instruct Lucius in different tricks. In order to prepare a gladiatorial show, Menecles returns to his native town Thessalonica where Lucius' amazing comic acts (τὰ παράδοξα παίγνια, 49.15) are shown for a fee. A rich foreign lady sees Lucius in the show, 'falls in love', and wants to make love with him (50.10–14). Lucius expresses his anguish as to how to make love in a donkey form: he has had no intercourse even with female donkeys and although he is excited he is afraid that he will kill the woman due to the size of his donkey phallus (51.22–24). When Menecles learns of the successful intercourse, he orders Lucius to do the same in the amphitheatre with a woman who has been condemned to be killed by predators (52.11–19).[18] In the arena Lucius is not only ashamed, but also afraid that a bear or a lion intended for other shows might kill him (53.17–18). Then a man passes carrying flowers and Lucius manages to catch some roses and become a man again. The astonished spectators pose a threat to Lucius, so that he asks for help from the governor. Luckily, the governor knows Lucius' family and because Lucius is still owned by Menecles, the governor declares him free (ἀπολύειν, 55.18). Lucius, now in human form, meets the foreign lady again who asserts that she did not love him but the donkey in him (οὐχὶ σοῦ, ἀλλὰ τοῦ ὄνου τοῦ σοῦ, 56.20–21) – literally: she loved Lucius' donkey, donkeyness – by which, as it becomes clear, she mainly means Lucius' donkey phallus (τὸ μέγα τοῦ ὄνου σύμβολον, 56.20–21).[19] Finally, Lucius embarks on the ship where his brother, who has come to fetch him, is waiting, and they sail to their native city, Patras in Achaia.

Suffering animals

Torture

Like donkeys in the Aesopic animal fables, Lucius suffers constant beating in his life as a donkey.[20] In the first part of the story, when Lucius and the other two animals are being stolen (A), Lucius is unaccustomed to the work of pack animals and stumbles and falls down. He is beaten to continue. He tries to speak but can only bray and is beaten for his braying so that he learns to keep silent (16.24–27). Lucius, and the two pack animals kidnapped with him, are muzzled so that they cannot eat grass and slow down the journey to the robbers' cave. When they have a rest at a familiar farm, some barley is thrown to them. Because Lucius has never eaten raw barley before, he wanders to a garden to find roses and eat vegetables. A gardener punishes Lucius, beating him not only on his ribs and thighs but on his face. Lucius kicks back and runs away. When he has been caught, chased by huge dogs, he is beaten so heavily that he vomits all the vegetables he has managed to eat (18.19–20) and is then loaded with the heaviest items so that he is nearly fainting.[21] This is Lucius' initiation into a donkey's life.

When they continue their journey to the robbers' cave, Lucius' fellow donkey, 'the other donkey', drops down tired of the arduous journey and is then beaten with a stick nearly to its death. When the donkey does not pay any heed to the blows but lays unconscious, the robbers hack off its legs and push it 'still gasping' over a crag (19.25–26). Later on, while Lucius is participating in a robbery on the road, he hurts his foot against a sharp stone and becomes lame due to his painful wound (22.28–29). He has to ignore this and pretend to be healthy because the robbers plan to throw him over the cliff as useless (as had been done to 'the other donkey') and as a bringer of bad luck. Lucius comments (addressing himself as 'you') that 'vultures and their young will have you for dinner' (23.11). The interesting detail here is 'the young': that vultures are not only a threat but feeding parents implies that Lucius the donkey can thus to a certain extent identify with the vultures' situation, even *empathize with* it.[22]

In the second part (B), the slave-boy beats Lucius heavily with a stick sharpened with stubs, hitting always on the same part of the thigh. Lucius is thus not only lame but he has an open sore. The boy piles on too heavy and unbalanced loads of wood, even wickedly putting in stones as an additional load. When he cannot make Lucius move with his beating, he ties thorns on his tail (30.8–18). When Lucius kicks him, the boy ties a load of flax on Lucius' back and sets it on fire (31.8–13). Moreover, because Lucius reveals the lascivious habits of the priests of the

Syrian goddess (C) by his braying, they tie him, for revenge, to a tree and flog him with a whip till 'they have almost killed' him (38.27–28).

For a modern reader the beating and torturing scenes may raise the question of how the ancient audience related to them. Was there any sympathy for a suffering animal? In antiquity, donkeys were stereotyped and ridiculed as lazy and stubborn – and *therefore* as sufferers of abusive treatment – on the one hand, and recognized as enduring violence and hard work on the other. In Semonides' misogynistic poem, the donkey is an image of a lazy and greedy woman: she is an object of repeated 'rubs' (παλιντρίβης, that is: beatings) *because* she needs to be forced to work.[23] However, in the *Onos*, torture of animals is rather equated with low status and low morals: the life of the robbers (A) is violent and they are in turn violent or indifferent to their servants and working animals. Megapole, the groom's wife (B), is using Lucius against the orders of their master for her own benefit, and the slave-boy, as the lowest one in the hierarchy in the kidnapped girl's family, is even sadistic. Priests of the Syrian goddess (C) typify the questionable habits of foreign cults. One Aesopic fable belonging to the Augustana collection, whose written form may be nearly contemporary with *Onos*, describes a situation where a raven picks an open sore on a donkey's back, who is standing on his hind feet because of the pain. The donkey's driver laughs when seeing this. The fable depicts thus a scene of indifference, even laughter for a suffering animal (although the focus of the fable is on the comment of a passing wolf). But the driver here, as a manual worker, may exemplify the behaviour, which was not acceptable for members of higher classes.[24]

Nevertheless, are some violent episodes in the *Onos* meant to be comical, so that the hardships of Lucius the donkey are like those of Chaplin's Little Tramp who constantly experiences humiliation and violence but in a such manner that they induce laughs and sympathy in the audience (cf. the scene of Lucius running with thorns tied to his tail, 30.8–18)? Robert Bresson, the creator of the great modern donkey story in his film *Au Hasard Balthazar* ('Balthazar, for example', 1966), noted the resemblance between the fate of the Little Tramp and his Balthazar the donkey.[25] Lucius is, after all, an active agent (like the Little Tramp, as a matter of fact) with an opportunity to escape from his object-like existence. Although *Au Hasard Balthazar* bears a remarkable resemblance to the story of Lucius' hardships as a donkey shifting from one owner to another,[26] Balthazar's Christ-like passivity makes his abusive treatment especially painful to watch whereas the passing mentions and more elaborate descriptions of beatings of Lucius do not necessarily have the same effect. The beating and killing of 'the other donkey' (19.14–27) is, because of his utmost passivity, more haunting. This scene is narrated by Lucius the donkey who is afraid of the same kind of treatment. Lucius' narration focalizes and guides our sympathies by giving the donkey's viewpoint at the hands of violent humans.

Animals as a source of food

When the slave-boy falsely accuses Lucius of chasing young humans (B), his immediate superior, the groom, orders Lucius to be killed, his meat served to the servants and the entrails to the dogs (33.4).[27] Donkey meat along with dog meat was thought to be of poor quality in antiquity.[28] As a pack animal for the priests of the Syrian goddess (C), Lucius meets the same kind of dangers and threats to his bodily integrity. At first, the other priests ridicule the notion that Philebus has bought Lucius for his own zoophilic pleasure as a 'bridegroom' (36.10). Lucius himself fears that the priests will treat him as a sexual object just because of his changed form (μεταβολή, 38.5–8; namely, into a donkey) in their cinaedic orgies[29] or that he will be mutilated by them because of their custom of cutting their own forearms and tongues in the frenzy of their rites (36.8–13). On the estate of a rich worshipper of Atargatis, where the priests of the Syrian goddess have been welcomed, the house dogs have eaten a ham of wild donkey, a gift to the master of the house (39.6–8). Wild donkey's meat (as game) is thus thought to be a suitable meal for a rich man. The cook's wife suggests that Lucius should be killed and served instead (39.15–22). Lucius is terrified but puns with the situation: the cook will be '*my* cook' (οὑμὸς μάγειρος, 39.27). All in all, at first Lucius is threatened 'only' with being killed (A), then being killed and eaten (B, C) as edible animal meat.

Animal labour

Working conditions may cause suffering for working animals. In Lucius' tale, two episodes, especially, provide suitable examples, namely the mill house of the rich baker (D) and the working with the poor vegetable farmer (E). The duration of the monotonous, mindless labour, as a 'slave' for the mill house is surely longer than the short narrative suggests. First, Lucius has to travel to the mill house with a heavy load, and then, blindfolded and harnessed to the beam of one of the mills, he is struck by a group of millers in order to make him go round and round (42.2–43.2).[30] Thus, Lucius, in the course of his adjustment to a donkey's body and life, becomes a member of a serviceable 'zoo-proletariat', to use Braidotti's expression.[31]

Yet, due to the poverty and because of winter time, the work for the poor farmer (E) is arduous, too: 'I had to tread unshod on damp clay or hard, sharp ice, while all that either of us had to eat was bitter, rough lettuce' (43.13–15).[32] The 'us' (or literally 'both', ἀμφότεροι) here is the poor farmer and Lucius: both have insufficient food to eat. Moreover, the farmer is later treated as a despised animal or a slave by the angry Roman soldier who strikes him with his whip (44.7–8). The poor farmer is, like the kidnapped girl, Lucius' fellow sufferer in the hands of despotic power.

Freak animals

In the care of wealthy Menecles (F), Lucius gains a higher status as a freak animal, from κτῆνος, an owned, domestic animal, to κτῆμα παράδοξον, a 'marvellous asset' (48.1). But Lucius is still owned: the root of both words, κτῆνη and κτῆμα is the verb κτάομαι, 'to own'. Lucius is exceptional because he can do 'undonkeyish' feats with a donkey's body: drink wine and wrestle and dance. Animal performers, often dressed up as humans, were frequent entertainment in antiquity.[33] Lucius' report from the animal performer's point of view does not suggest that these kinds of humanizing performances may be demeaning for the dignity of animals. For Lucius, to become a show animal means simply salvation from the life of a beast of burden, which can be mortal due to the beatings and hard labour.

This part of the tale reminds the modern reader of Kafka's short story 'Ein Bericht für eine Akademie' (1917, 'A Report to an Academy'), where a captive ape named Red Peter decides to learn to behave like a human – for instance, drink whisky – in order to survive. Like Lucius, Red Peter manages to get a comfortable life as a freak animal. However, Red Peter's 'negation of his animal side', as Anna Barcz puts it,[34] tells a tragic story, whereas Lucius the donkey's performance as a donkey acting human is like a return to human life again. Both perform human acts but are still controlled – and in Lucius' case: also owned – by humans. In the end, Lucius' sense of comfort ends when he is forced to act a performance he dreads (the intercourse in the arena).

A donkey's life with a human mind

In his *Against the Stoics on Common Conceptions*, Plutarch refers briefly to a Stoic thought experiment, attributing it to Chrysippus, where Circe had two magic potions, one that makes humans foolish (ἄφρων), but maintains their bodily form, whereas the other potion will not remove the human mind but will change human bodies to those of non-human animals, like donkeys. According to Plutarch, the Stoics would prefer the first potion, the first case – human body at the expense of rationality – which in Plutarch's view is contradictory of general Stoic doctrines stressing rationality.[35] In the Circe episode in the *Odyssey*, it is emphasized that only the bodies of Odysseus' crew became that of pigs, not their minds (*Od.* 10.239–40). Odysseus' men transformed into pigs and Lucius into a donkey are then examples of the second case – Circe's second potion in Chrysippus' thought experiment: a human mind in a non-human body. This kind of hybridity may give many opportunities for fun in a satirical story. However, *Onos* does not play excessively with disparities between Lucius' human wishes and his donkey life. True, Lucius keeps his human appetite and food preferences, which causes some twists in the plot (chapters 17 and 46).[36] When the robbers plan their horrible death for the kidnapped girl, Lucius is concerned about the dignity of his dead body (26.3–4) and Lucius strongly dislikes the placing of the Syrian goddess inside a *Greek* temple (41.3–6). Furthermore, when the groom's neighbour suggests that Lucius is to be castrated, not killed and eaten (due to the false accusation of the slave-boy), Lucius is terrified to the point of being suicidal by the threat to become 'a eunuch', to lose the manhood, literally 'man' *in* his donkey's body, τὸν ἐν τῷ ὄνῳ ἄνδρα (33.23), that is, the (donkey or human) phallus, which is obviously important to Lucius' selfhood and manhood. Lucius' heterosexual drive focuses on women: even as a donkey, he regards the rich foreign lady as desirable (51.18) and he does not want – in fact, he fears – to be the passive, forced partner in the cinaedic orgies of the priests of the Syrian goddess.[37] But the lascivious sexual habits of the cinaedic priests are not just a physical threat to him but an object of contempt. However, his human mind sometimes makes fatally incorrect estimations. Lucius plans to escapes the fate of being butchered and eaten (in place of the lost wild donkey meat) by making havoc in order that he would be thought to be 'insolent' (40.9) and be locked up. This is his 'clever plan (κομψόν τι) to safety' (40.7, 40.11). But if a man would have been imprisoned for insolent (ἀγέρωχος) behaviour, Lucius the donkey is thought to have rabies (λυττᾶ, 40.11) and is expected to be killed on the spot.

In all, Lucius the narrator does not elaborate upon the difficulties of adjusting to a four-footed body or, for instance, eating without hands.[38] Lucius learns quite soon how to defend himself by kicking and biting, although these actions often lead to more severe punishments (18.19–20). Besides the difficulties in intercourse with the foreign lady (51.19–34), the greatest deficiency in his new form is the lack of articulate speech. In antiquity, the basic difference between humans and other animals was considered to be the animals' lack of *logos* (both speech and rationality) since Aristotle.[39] But Lucius is a hybrid: he has rationality but no articulate speech – like a non-Greek speaker or a slave without permission to speak before his masters. Adjusting to the life of a beast of burden is not easy for Lucius simply because he was a free citizen; he is not accustomed to hard manual labour and the low status related to it. In his first attempt to run away, huge dogs are urged to run after him as a runaway slave (18.11–13). Lucius' metamorphosis can thus be read, among other things, as a metaphor for the falling into slavery, which replaces one's former status and freedom.[40] But it is not only a metaphor. Already Aristotle equates domestic animals and slaves (*Pol.* 1.5.1254b23).

Besides becoming more familiar with his non-human body, Lucius identifies with other beasts of burden, expressing sympathy for his fellow-sufferers and fellow-slaves, applying the pronoun 'we' and 'we animals'. Still, when he first meets the donkey in the stable in Hypata, that is, 'the other donkey', which is killed on the journey to the robbers' cave, he uses the expression 'another, real donkey' (ἄλλος ἀληθινὸς ὄνος, 15.6). Lucius thus acknowledges at first that he himself *is* a donkey but not a 'real' (ἀληθινός) one. This discrepancy seems to vanish as the story goes on: Lucius has to experience the common lot of donkeys of constant beating, sexual threats and object-like treatment. All in all, Lucius adjusts and dwells quite naturally in a donkey's body and life so that he achieves a kind of donkey's identity.[41] Only at the end, Lucius' hybridity comes into greater focus again. As a show animal, he is taught to lie on a couch 'on his elbow', wrestle with his instructor and dance standing upright on his two legs; he has to nod yes or no when spoken to (although Lucius cannot speak, he can show that he understands human speech). Lucius congratulates himself that these tasks are easy for him because the audience does not know that there is a human being '*inside* a donkey', ἄνθρωπον ἐν τῷ ὄνῳ κείμενον (48.19–20).[42] Yet Lucius describes the moment of his transformation back to a human form as having a kind of double identity:

> [...] ἀποπίπτει ἐξ ἐμοῦ ἐκείνη ἡ τοῦ κτήνους ὄψις καὶ ἀπόλλυται, καὶ ἀφανὴς ἐκεῖνος ὁ πάλαι ὄνος, ὁ δὲ Λούκιος αὐτὸς ἔνδον μοι γυμνὸς εἱστήκει.
>
> *54.8–11*
>
> [...] bestial appearance left me and vanished, the donkey of old disappeared, and Lucius himself was standing naked on the spot I occupied.

The metamorphosis is described as to be something in-between, a becoming. Lucius sees himself as 'Lucius' who is standing literally 'inside *me*' (ἔνδον μοι), that is, on the spot, in that space, where 'that old (= former) donkey' (ἐκεῖνος ὁ πάλαι ὄνος) had stood.[43] Lucius did not only have a donkey's body – he *was* a donkey body.

The human Lucius was, however, 'inside' himself the donkey. The logic of metamorphosis is that one becomes something which one already is – what is inside becomes outside. The foreign lady who desired Lucius the donkey speaks about the lost donkey inside human Lucius, his lost donkeyness (56.20).[44] The donkey is lost when Lucius has gained his human form. We may then ask what happened to the donkey whose adventures we have been accustomed to follow in Lucius' story. Does he, perhaps, still continue to be part of Lucius, 'inside' him as Lucius the man was 'inside' the donkey's body?[45]

Animal embodiment – being a donkey's body – has if not strictly shaped Lucius' mind but at least taught him to see the world partly from the donkey's point of view. Through Lucius' animal embodiment reported by his human words we readers of the story can orientate to the (imagined) world of a donkey notwithstanding our human embodiment, our 'primordial' human body.[46]

Concluding words

Originally, Lucius wanted to change into a bird, a free, wild animal, which is able to move quickly from place to place, but instead he became a κτῆνος, a domestic animal owned by humans, which has limited freedom, and lacks a human way to communicate, an articulate voice. As a donkey, Lucius experiences being stolen and sold plus various other kinds of abusive treatment as well as the threat of being castrated and of being eaten. His attitude to other domestic animals, those who share the abusive treatment and heavy workload, is that of sympathy and compassion – they are his companions, his fellow-sufferers and fellow-slaves. He also experiences rivalry with his companions, who suspect that he would steal their food and their sexual partners. His experience of humans is mainly that they use him for their own purposes with no regard of the harm resulting to him. Without human protection he perceives himself to be under threat of predators whether they are out in the wild or in the arena. Yet, it is just humans who have forced him to the arena and even urged huge dogs to go after him as he manages to run away. However, a fellow-feeling is evoked in him with those humans who share his suffering.

Lucius the human as a free, moderately wealthy citizen is not accustomed to physical labour. A donkey's life is for him mainly tiring, damaging and dangerous – it is to be a suffering body at the mercy of human owners. However, Lucius has only minor difficulties in 'performing' being a donkey and later on actually performing human-like tricks – being a human donkey – like lying on the couch. Throughout his odyssey as a donkey, Lucius keeps his goal of transforming back into human form again; nevertheless, he becomes used to the new situation and adapts himself more and more easily to the life of a donkey. Despite his human mind, he becomes a donkey's body and therefore adopts a donkey identity. In the end, between his transformation from donkey to man, the unitary identity of 'donkey man' or 'man donkey' is lost. Lucius the man seems curiously less than Lucius the donkey.

All in all, in the *Onos* Lucius blurs the boundaries between human and non-human, experiencing a donkey's life with a human mind. Although Lucius plays the stereotyped 'lazy' donkey seeming to scheme escape and freedom from the workload, we can follow the reasons for his behaviour from the donkey's point of view. From the driver's point of view a stopped donkey represents stubbornness; Lucius knows that it may represent fatigue or fear.

CHAPTER 3

QUAM SOLI VIDISTIS EQUI: FOCALIZATION AND ANIMAL SUBJECTIVITY IN VALERIUS FLACCUS

Anne Tuttle Mackay

Introduction

In his late first-century epic the *Argonautica* (hereafter *Arg.*), Valerius Flaccus (VF) features animals in both simile and narrative which deviate in many ways from their epic tradition counterparts. One example is the prominent role played by his often unprecedented presentation of the non-human in his poetics. More broadly, the author interacts with and participates in the evolution of the treatment of animals in classical epic, including generically typed species of epic animals which were not necessarily standard literary fare, but were nevertheless prominent in the Roman experience and imagination. The development of the portrayal of certain animals in particularly Latin epic is characterized by an increasing sensitivity over time and texts to the physical, emotional and relational experience of the animal.[1] Admittedly, the authors' portrayals are freighted with anthropomorphisms and mediated for the reader via the lens of human categories of experience. Nevertheless, as will be seen, VF invites the reader to explore the possibilities of animal subjectivity for itself and as a vehicle for epic messaging.

VF has scattered instances of animal subjectivity throughout his text, some of which feature the narrator's adoption of the animal gaze for use as a narratorial tool, namely, focalization.[2] The first passage discussed here is a well-known story from myth, the torture of Prometheus by Zeus/Jupiter through a bird, and its subsequent death at the hands of Hercules. The other is a cavalry disaster original to VF's treatment: it has no parallel in other versions of the story. These are not the only cases in VF featuring animal focalization, which in turn suggests subjectivity.[3] But these two cases differ from others in that they exemplify the author's assertion and exploration of an animal subjective experience and affinity with humans within the context of divine activity, wherein the animal is weaponized against the human(oid). The anthropocentric orientation of the epic arguably obviates articulation of the difference between human and animal perceptual worlds, yet I will argue that VF does attempt to represent animal perception beyond just the visual, though he does not elaborate on the animal thought process.[4] Nevertheless, the representations of animal emotions and behaviour in the passages suggest a point of intersection of narratological and post-anthropocentric inquiry. For example, the post-anthropocentric dynamic of pan-human vulnerability as described by Braidotti (2013: 61–63, 66–67) can be figured here as a trans- or pan-species vulnerability,[5] occasioned by divine intervention and human martial enterprise but framed by the perspective of animal participants.

VF's *Arg.* relates the journey of Jason and his Minyae, the Argonauts, from Iolchus to Colchis on a quest for the Golden Fleece. VF loosely follows Apollonius Rhodius' (AR) Hellenistic version in terms of plot, but in many aspects his programme is innovative and 'Romanizing'. Important for the two episodes discussed here is the frequent intervention of the divine on the human plane. In this regard, VF's journey of the *Argo*, breaking natural boundaries and heralding a shift in political power from East to West, represents, and is accompanied by other examples of, change and transition. In addition, on the cosmic level, the disposition and decree of Jupiter (1.531–67),[6] couching the story within a mytho-historical trajectory hurtling toward VF's Rome, reveal the nature and presence of divine justice and benevolence – or cruelty – as a whole.

Animal, human, and the lesser divine are placed in similar positions relative to more powerful gods, and this is clearly seen in the vulture episode. The interaction between animal and anthropoid Prometheus involves an encounter that highlights the shifting between, or constant occupation of both, of the roles of subject and object by vulture and victim alike, and offers a pause in the cycle of violence for them to regard and respond to each other.[7] Of course, the relating of 'companion' species and their humans as discussed by Haraway (2007: 76) is not perfectly reflected in the dynamic between Prometheus and the vulture; if anything, the bird is more properly Jupiter's companion.[8] Nevertheless, the two actors in the passage are familiar with each other, and come face to face before exchanging roles. In the second case, this dynamic of relating can be traced in the transforming influence of trans-species interaction and proximity on domesticated animal species.[9] In the chariot disaster the focalization shows not just the impact of violence on animals drafted into battlefield roles by humans, but also the imagined impact of human myth or literary culture on the animal psyche. Finally, the ethical imperative of the presentation of animals as embodied sufferers, which elicits empathy from the reader as one of its primary effects, is enhanced by their function as focalizers in both passages.[10]

I suggest that animal subjectivity plays a role in the exploring of VF's themes and poetics throughout the epic, including the nature of the divine, the impact of warfare and so on. Here, however, the case studies will focus tightly on the use and consequences of focalization through the animal. I will show that the two passages complement one another in the light they shed on the nature and significance of animal subjectivity in *Arg.*, first as capable of objectifying the non-animal and altering the depiction and perception of the non-animal experience and its connection to that of the animal; and second, the place of animal subjectivity in one aspect of the Valerian programme, the psychologizing of the myth, with important implications for the relationship between animal and human in psychology and agency, and even in interspecies contact in the experience of the 'culture' of myth.

The Promethean vulture

En route to Colchis, Hercules leaves the expedition after the loss of his companion Hylas in book 3. Still, there is a later point at which Hercules' journey almost 'breaks in' on the journey of the *Argo*, with the effects of his action within their view, his nearness felt but not recognized by the crew. VF elaborates on a moment in AR wherein the Minyae pass near the peak where Prometheus is bound and daily tormented by the liver-eating eagle, but they do not understand the cries they hear, nor recognize the shadow of the great bird in the sky (Apollon. 2.1246-59). VF has placed Hercules upon that peak to rescue Prometheus at the moment the Minyae sail past. They are however unaware of Hercules and his triumph over, here, a vulture, seeing only the dying bird overhead after Hercules has struck the fatal blow. Their failure to recognize the bird precludes a meeting of the human and divine spheres. Yet VF does find a way to explore the divide and contact between the celestial and the terrestrial, and with a greater coincidence than in AR, for he has introduced a divine cause for Prometheus' rescue, discussed below. Hercules' parallel journey has thematic significance on several levels, but most important for this brief study, the narration of the rescue comprises a near-seamless virtual transit of the reader's gaze, and engagement of the non-visual senses, between not two but all three spheres – celestial, terrestrial, and infernal – and it is achieved through the animal actor.[11]

The very choice of the species, a vulture rather than an eagle, is marked. Attribution of Prometheus' suffering to a vulture is rare, and VF is the first epicist to attribute Prometheus' suffering to a *lone* vulture.[12] Jupiter's agent is also more transliminal than Zeus' eagle; elsewhere in myth the vulture torments Tityus in the Underworld, while in VF's Roman context, the vulture may be an augural messenger, significant from Rome's Founding.[13] The vulture thus crosses from the celestial to the infernal, and across contexts (cultural and mytho-literary) simultaneously: it signifies communication, connection and causes/effects and consequences across spheres, in small an emblem of the interaction between Roman culture and Greek myth throughout *Arg*. This vulture is part of the liminal exploration of the witnessing of Prometheus' release, and its departure viewed from a distance by the Minyae signals the task's completion. VF harnesses the transliminal aspect of the vulture, mediating and characterizing the contact between the terrestrial and the divine, especially through animal subjectivity demonstrated in focalization. This compels examination of the episode for its implications about the epic's divine machinery, especially the impact of the divine on Prometheus, the vulture and Hercules, and the relationship of all to the divine and to each other.

A multi-sensory traversal of the spheres begins from the moment the episode is triggered by Apollo's appeal to Jupiter early in book 4. At the point of Hercules' decision to go to Troy after Hylas' disappearance, Apollo pleads Prometheus' case to Jupiter (4.62–67) on behalf of humanity (4.64b–66a). Unlike in AR's version, VF's reader is given expository information through Apollo's speech and Jupiter's acquiescence. As will be seen, the shifting back and forth of the reader's gaze from Olympus down to the sea on the human plane – directed by the narrator and filtered through at least one unexpected focalizer – is mirrored in the shift of described perception from that of the gods 'down' to the animal, with corresponding implications for and consequences of the vulture's subjectivity.

Apollo challenges Jupiter's justice generally, but explicitly questions his justice in Prometheus' case, already an occasion for considering the nature of Zeus'/Jupiter's rule in Aeschylus. As if aware of Apollo's argument, Prometheus echoes it with loud cries, and the focus turns earthward:

> dixit ubi, e scopulis media inter pabula diri
> vulturis ipse etiam gemitu maestaque fatigat
> voce Iovem saevis relevans ambusta pruinis
> lumina, congeminant amnes rupesque fragorem
> Caucaseae, stupet ipse dei clamoribus ales.

> When he spoke, from the cliffs in the middle of the meal
> of the dreadful vulture [Prometheus] himself wearies Jupiter
> even with a groan and sorrowful voice, raising eyes burned by the savage

frosts; the rivers and rocks of Caucasus redouble
the crash; the bird itself is stunned by the cries of the god.

4.68–72[14]

Briefly, the framing of the scene involves rapid shifts in perspective, both its origin and its object, from terrestrial/celestial (68–69), to celestial/terrestrial (70–72a), and terrestrial/terrestrial (72b). This is paralleled by shifts in the putative viewer/viewed, often the narrator but from viewing planes occupied by different actors, so, narrator-Prometheus/Jupiter in 68–69, narrator-Jupiter/Prometheus, landscape in 70–72a, and finally narrator-vulture/Prometheus. Additionally, this shift in perception encompasses both vision and hearing (*gemitu, voce, fragorem, clamoribus*), with sound's pathetic effect (*fatigat, stupet*), and touch (*saevis pruinis*), for a pain that is both emotional (*maesta*) and physical. The view implicates and aligns different, spatially separated spectators, especially Jupiter and the vulture, as subjects reacting to Prometheus. Yet the clear example of focalization in the episode is a subtle naming of Prometheus as *pabula* in 68, practically embedded. In the midst of shift of the reader's gaze toward heaven, Prometheus is identified as the object of the animal's interest, its dinner.

Prometheus as object is paired with his function as irritant to Jupiter, but though Jupiter and the vulture are subjects related by a common activity, tormenting Prometheus, all three are related in the reciprocity of affective reaction.[15] The reader is particularly drawn into the vulture's reaction and experience of the event by the bookend to the focalization in line 68, its surprise in line 72. Presumably, this event has happened daily for some time. Yet the vulture is amazed by Prometheus' expression of torment, a response the reader perhaps shares, assimilating the bird's surprise to his or her own. The bird's reaction is incongruous given the familiarity of the activity, and is doubly arresting because its focalized view of Prometheus had previously been so objectifying. It is reasonable, however, given that Prometheus for the animal still functions as food, which *qua* dinner is not expected to express emotion. Furthermore, VF indicates that its perception and reaction is not purely that of instinct to sensory input, but the presentation of the vulture as a companion viewer to both Jupiter – who is bothered (*fatigat)* – and the audience suggests a subjective dynamic. At the same time, the vulture is the agent causing Prometheus' suffering. The sophisticated layers of vision and viewing, crossing of boundaries with the narrator's gaze, reception, reaction and the dynamic between subjectivity and objectification are exemplified in the singling out of the animal agent as the only non-narrator focalizer in the passage. The vulture as agent reflects the earlier disposition of Jupiter toward Prometheus. Still this agent of retribution *sees* Prometheus as a meal, and is capable of being surprised by his emotional expression despite familiarity.

Beyond enhancing Prometheus' suffering and the effect of its relief by Hercules, the narratological device applied through an animal adds dimension to the vulture. The bird is not merely a device or instrument of wrath: like Prometheus, it too is aware, perceives, and like the reader can be moved. It has a life and perception on its own terms.[16] But since Jupiter has changed his mind, the vulture's role changes in the execution of Jupiter's next decree, Prometheus' rescue. Ironically, the vulture has previously served to show Jupiter's displeasure and to punish, but now its death seals the shift in the god's disposition. On the one hand, the freeing of Prometheus means the death of an animal which was doing its divine duty. From its own perspective, however, it was simply eating as animals do. On the other, it exhibits subjective response in its reaction – not necessarily empathetic – to Prometheus' pain. At any rate, the heroic and detached dispatch of an animal menace by Hercules is not an adequate interpretation here, for VF mirrors and reverses Prometheus' experience in that of the vulture. Jupiter has not been overcome with compassion – in fact, the episode as a whole indicates that while he has relented, he has not changed. Only the victim, the object of retribution, has. What had earlier been granted the capacity to objectify Prometheus for the reader as food, has now become the object of Hercules' avenging gaze.

This moment is not narrated. Instead, when the vulture departs from Prometheus, mortally wounded, the Minyae wonder at a vast shadow in the sky, from which blood drips like light rain: *tantum mirantur ... ingentem moribundae desuper umbram/alitis atque atria rorantes imbribus auras* (5.173, 175–176). The bleeding shadow in the sky is a sort of bird-sign, though the Minyae cannot read it.[17] This invocation of the link between vultures and augural practice – with no clear information imparted to the viewers – suggests the decree of Jupiter is rather arbitrary. It also underlines the universal impact of the divine prerogative, on the lesser divine, human and animal life. The vulture had been a special instrument to Jupiter, but now, though unlike Prometheus it has done nothing against him, Jupiter has sanctioned its killing. Jupiter's changeable disposition is felt even by an animal acting as he ordained, its death a reality to be recognized and responded to.

The quick shift of Prometheus from object to subject, proving his subjectivity, eliciting a response from his animal tormentor, prefigures the subtle transition of the vulture from instrument to focalizing agent and watcher. When the animal is dying, it is its previous role as focalizer, capable of reacting to Prometheus, that forces an analogized reading of the bird, its subjective presence twice used to characterize Prometheus. Indeed, its counterpart is its own victim. The animal has become the suffering object of a gaze, now shared by the reader and the Minyae, the animal perspective supplanted by the human. What might have been simply the destruction of a bestial threat is confused and complicated by VF's overt subjectivization of the vulture. The animal focalizer is an audience member as Jupiter and the reader are, and later is a fellow-sufferer of Jupiter's decree as Prometheus, an act which in turn creates a shared subjectivity between tormentor and victim. The sliding scale of agency and victimization is reflected in the transliminal framing of the passage itself: vulture as victim takes the place of the freed Prometheus, while Hercules takes its place as an avenger.[18] The animal is not an obstacle to cosmic progress and civilization, but rather a target for divinely sanctioned suffering, experienced equally and even interchangeably by animals, humans and other gods.

The cavalry of Ariasmenus

The second passage under consideration is from a sequence not found in AR, the Colchian civil war. Thematic implications and reasons for its inclusion, and the theme of civil war in VF generally, have been discussed at length by others;[19] the focus for this chapter is VF's incorporation of animal focalization into a battlefield event. Book 6 sees the Argonauts join Aeetes, the king of Colchis, Medea's father and the keeper of the Golden Fleece, in a war against Aeetes' brother, Perses. Each side is supported by numerous exotic tribes from the East and North. One of these tribes allied to Perses comes to battle under their cavalry leader Ariasmenus. The goddess Pallas, supportive of the Minyae, is present on the field and when Ariasmenus signals his chariots to charge, she steps in, brandishing the aegis, capable of disrupting an entire force upon their sight of Medusa, whose dead gaze drives the viewers mad.

A brief tracing of textual precedents for this intervention of Pallas is in order. In the Iliadic template for divine intervention with the aegis, Apollo targets the Greeks, and the terrified men flee like stampeding livestock – but *not* like horses: δ' ὥς τ' ἠὲ βοῶν ἀγέλην ἢ πῶϋ μέγ' οἰῶν – before a wild beast.[20] A more direct model, in visual terms, is found in the Aeneas–Niphaeus encounter in *Aeneid* 10. Aeneas lays low enemies all around him, and is compared in lines 565–568 to the hundred-handed Aegaeon, many-headed, many-torsoed and monstrous like Medusa. Immediately following the simile, Aeneas faces the four-horse chariot of Niphaeus, and with only his raging movement and visage (*dira frementem*) throws the chariot-team into panic.[21] Niphaeus is thrown down and killed.

VF reverts to the aegis as the inciter of madness, but as in *Aen.* 10, it is the horses – drawing chariots with scythes attached at the axles – rather than the men who are horror-struck:[22]

aegida tum primum virgo spiramque Medusae
ter centum saevis squalentem sustulit hydris,
quam soli vidistis, equi. pavor occupat ingens
excussis in terga viris diramque retorquent
in socios non sponte luem. tunc ensibus uncis
implicat et trepidos lacerat discordia currus.

Then for the first time the maiden raised up the aegis
and the coil[s] of Medusa, scaly with three hundred fierce serpents,
which you alone, horses, saw. Great fear seizes them, their men
knocked backward, and unwillingly they turn back dire ruin
against their allies. Then, with the curved blades
chaos entangles and tears apart the alarmed chariots.

6.396–401[23]

Focalization in this passage functions differently from that in the vulture episode. Here, the reader sees the aegis through the horses' eyes only after the fact, and through not a narration of the horses' experience, but a direct address to the horses *about* it, reinforcing their 'presence'.[24] They are thus focalizers of Pallas' action, and are invited as if narratorial interlocutors to comment on their experience of that action. But they cannot, because provoked by Pallas they immediately react. It has already been shown that animals can cause, witness and experience suffering with an individual subjectivity as humans and gods do. The forcible involvement of horses in visual exchange suggests a further role for animals as participants in reception of myth traditions, here specifically in the use of a mythic object.

The narrator's address to the animals highlights Pallas' choice of target. Her visual assault on the horses with an object laden with meaning and past credits the horses with recognition of the object, inanimate and not immediately obvious as a perceptible threat to animals, which nevertheless triggers a psychological response. Pallas chooses not to command or awe them by revealing her presence, or, like Aeneas, menacing them with gestures. She instead directs toward them a psychological weapon elsewhere used on humans. Her act and its effectiveness underscores an implied shared mental and emotional state of both horses and warriors on the field, and the different ways in which civil war, a prominent theme for VF, might be illustrated are exemplified in the consequences in 6.407–416:[25]

Palladii rapuere metus, sic in sua versi
funera concurrunt . . .
hinc biiuges, illinc artus tenduntur eriles
. . . atroque in pulvere regum
viscera nunc aliis, aliis nunc curribus haerent

dread [wrought by] Pallas seized them, and thus turned toward
their own deaths they rush together . . .
Here are scattered the chariot horses, there the limbs of the masters, 413
. . . and in the black dust
the entrails of kings cling now to some, now to other, chariots.

6.408–409a, 413, 415b–416

The repetition and word order emphasize the confusion and the span of time during which the mayhem continues, as well as embody the noise and extent of the panic.

The chariots drag and are dragged, horses kill and are killed, and their blood darkens the field along with their masters'. *Regum*, 'kings', is an ironic choice, a turn on the previous *dominis* and *eriles*. The humans, before described as *socii*, 'allies' or 'companions' of the horses, are also leaders: the social relationship, especially its hierarchical aspect, between the humans and horses is undermined by the horses' actions against the former, while the status of the humans as masters – from the horses' perspective – is undone by the horses' terror. Instead, the lucid humans' efforts to regain control are ineffectual against the divine appropriation of their animals as weapons against them. Some horses are elsewhere portrayed in VF as the partners and even friends of humans and unique animal partakers in human society, literal *socii*, the term freighted with its generic, personal and political significance.[26] This dynamic is undermined by Pallas' intervention, effaced by trans-species violence in miniature of the larger internecine conflict in which the catastrophe takes place. In addition, the humans watch not simply their deaths but their funerals racing to meet them: *funera* is a perverse echo of communal ritual in which humans and horses have elsewhere in epic participated together, including in VF, which none of the cavalry, totally destroyed, will share.[27] It takes the maddening of only one segment of a force to trigger a civil war, overturning the traditional trans-species relationship, and the awareness of the humans is useless in trying to stop their own destruction. The horses' response to the gaze of Medusa ensures that they share with their human companions not funeral ritual but a violent death.

A closer look at Pallas' deployment of the aegis reveals how this relationship between horse and human has shaped the animal, and as focalizers they are more than substitutes for humans in thematic symbolism. The domestication of a species like the horse, and its incorporation into human culture, causes changes in the culture and shapes the development of the animal, even its very nature. In the case of warhorses, their participation in human society involves an overriding of their most basic instincts, and through interspecies relationships turns them into 'cultural artifact[s] of human society'.[28] Pallas disrupts the efficacy of these animals' training by humans through generating a further shared experience between horse and human, the application of a facet of human culture to alter animal behaviour. Horses as animal brothers turned against human brothers in a model of civil war is supplemented by their participation in their reception of, and response to, mythically significant objects. They do not merely share psychological susceptibility with humans in their reaction to terror. Indeed, their reaction to Medusa, the same as that of humans who throughout myth history have 'seen' Medusa, suggests a recognition on the part of the horses of an object and its significant mythic past. The horses here share in myth culture; or, their participation is shown in a *rupture* of shared culture, in the reaction to Medusa which makes the horses, previously *socii*, enemies of the humans. Like several other ways in which animals participate in human activity, especially when partnered with humans, their vulnerability to Pallas' brandishing of the aegis is to their detriment, and in turn makes their companions vulnerable. In this way, though the horses are subjugated to human enterprise in martial conflict, the horses are harnessed by the goddess to destroy their partners. The partnership between human and animal is confused in the focalization of the aegis by the horses rather than the humans, the sad privilege of the horses noted by the narrator's apostrophe to the panicked animals. After this initial swapping of roles in object reception, the horses take on the role of their masters' enemies, embarking on a wild rampage that destroys them all.

Conclusion

Other Roman writers had expressed a sympathy with animals, and some – like Lucretius, Virgil, and Ovid – seemed to suggest a subjectivity in the experience of the non-human. What these *Arg.* passages together indicate is an even clearer, uniquely Valerian, assimilation of animal and human subjectivity, especially in suffering, and indeed suffering together. The animal and the non-animal may unexpectedly change places, as agents, witnesses and victims in an exchange of visual and audial expression and reaction, and of inflicting pain and punishment. This shift in roles can happen without warning and even without obvious cause, and of course at the behest of a distant divine. In the chariot passage, VF goes even further in interspecies relations: the horses act as recipients of the showing of a mythically significant object, and respond as their human counterparts do. Their proximity to humans is not only in their martial roles; the horses are animals shaped by their human counterparts inhabiting the world of myth. They, like the humans, are subjects interacting with mythic, even literary, tradition. This interaction, however, being a participation in human culture, so often destructive to animal life in VF, is potentially dangerous, and here, it is deadly.

Perhaps the most significant result of these readings – especially the dynamic of shared vulnerability – for a posthuman appraisal of the *Arg.* is a trans-species moral culpability and obligation. The deaths of animals as fellow sufferers with humans at the hands of the gods align them with humans as potential victims of divine activity. Such a shared position relative to the divine can create a sympathetic and empathetic bond between species, a challenge to uncritical human dominion which, for example, puts the horses in danger both on the field and by exposure to human traditions. At the same time, animals are not merely objects, or rather, subjects defined by their victimization: exemplified in focalization, they can objectify and identify the human (or even divine) relative to their own experience and interests. Perhaps surprisingly, animals even enact what would be a morally culpable role for humans fulfilling orders or in an imaging of civil war, though the nature of culpability of humans acting in madness is controversial, and thus that of animals requires further study. These dynamics of subjectivity would pose a provocative counterpoint to the cultural norms of animal–human interactions in VF's context, and suggest a relevant question for posthuman consideration, whether this sophisticated presentation of perception contains a moral imperative: namely, that humans reconsider, and perhaps redefine, their relationship to animals in an anthropocentric world, mythical or real.

CHAPTER 4
ANIMALITY, ILLNESS AND DEHUMANIZATION: THE PHENOMENOLOGY OF ILLNESS IN SOPHOCLES' *PHILOCTETES*[1]

Chiara Thumiger

> Suffering is by no means a privilege, a sign of nobility, a reminder of god. Suffering is a fierce, bestial thing, commonplace, uncalled for, natural as air. It is intangible; no one can grasp it or fight against it; it dwells in time – it is the same thing as time; if it comes in fits and starts, that is only so as to leave the sufferer more defenseless during the moments that follow, those long moments when one relives the last bout of torture and waits for the next. These starts and tremors are not pain, accurately speaking; they are moments of nervous vitality that make us feel the duration of real pain, the tedious, exasperating infinity of the time pain lasts. The sufferer is always in a state of waiting for the next attack, and the next. The moment comes when the screaming crisis seems preferable to that waiting. The moment comes when he screams needlessly, just to break the flow of time, to feel that something is happening, that the endless spell of bestial suffering is for an instant broken, even though that makes it worse.
>
> Cesare Pavese, *This business of living*, 30 October 1940

Much has been said on the Sophoclean Philoctetes[2] as a subject of suffering[3] and despair, on the one hand; and as an object of rejection, victimization and injustice on the other.[4] His positioning within society and vis-à-vis civilization itself has also been scrutinized.[5] In this chapter, I want to look at the play *Philoctetes*, and at its main character specifically as a human being participating in an experience of illness, as a *patient*. The angle I wish to adopt in this exploration, however, is not the most immediate one, the investigation of the hero's *subjectivity* – Philoctetes' pain, his emotions, his reasoning; nor that of the *objectivity* of his situation – the geographies and timescale of his specific destiny, his dramatic and mythological background, his abuse by others, his lack of means. Rather, I shall interpret Philoctetes' illness in this play as a world-changing event in which partake different actors and factors, in a phenomenological perspective; which means, embracing the continuum between the felt experience of the ill subject, the objectivity of the biological changes he is undergoing and the intersubjective feedback he is receiving from the outside. Philoctetes' world is transformed into a radically new shape as a consequence, and it is precisely this all-comprising modification that I would like to address.

In one of the most recent contributions to philosophical studies of pathological experiences, Havi Carel has proposed the phenomenological approach as a perspective to assess illness as a 'disruption of first person experience',[6] as a radically altered form of *being-in-the-world*.[7] This disruption is located in the continuum between the individual as bodily and psychological entity and the living, social and even spatial environment around him or her. I find this an inspiring and valuable perspective on human experiences of annihilation in general, not only pathological, and for a reading of ill-being in Sophocles' *Philoctetes.*

On these premises, I propose to interpret *Philoctetes* as a successful and suggestive representation of a world cataclysm, the catastrophe that the experience of disease ultimately constitutes, beyond the rhetoric and the (necessarily fictitious) literary subjectivity of his central character, the hero Philoctetes, who is famously staged and described through fine details of physical debasement, intense suffering and overall helplessness. This representation is achieved in the drama through a number of devices which progressively decentre the human – intended both as humanistic ideal, the construct of pride and control – the first meaning of the Sophoclean *deinos* – but also in the minor sense of the individual human being Philoctetes. Powerful de-individualizing and de-humanizing expedients (animalization, monstrification, annihilation and dejection) can be found in the play's language, imagery and dramatic developments,[8] and result in an existentially pervasive picture of what it means to exist as an ill human being. This includes, as we shall see, a hyper-awareness of the corporeal reality of the suffering individual – what Carel labels 'loss of transparency'[9] of one's body; and the loss of various existential experiences of identity,[10] with the transition from human into animal being the most scandalous of a series of identity dissolutions – man into woman, Greek into barbarian, warrior into helpless child – to the final extreme of monstrousness, turning into a passive object of revulsion and disgust as apex of the illness experience.

Some of the insights of recent posthumanistic cultural analysis offer us the adequate language and angle to describe these processes and appreciate the meaning of Philoctetes' hyperbolic abjection. What interests me here is precisely that 'ontological decentering of the human'[11] within the world as revision or even subversion of the illusory narratives of anthropocentric control and power through which much of classical antiquity has been traditionally appreciated. Posthuman criticism shifts attention away from a focus on 'subjectivity'[12] as a straightforward aim of inquiry to replace it with the acknowledgement of a diffuse agency as a truer account of human experiences – itself a phenomenological standpoint.[13] From this perspective, the simplistic celebration of the individual self as a stronghold of human identity and freedom is exposed as a sham, and human agency is deeply embedded within a complex net of relationships and external circumstances, often inseparable from paradigms such as the time, or place, of an experience as involuntary players in the game.[14] In such an arena illness, of all conditions – the finiteness and vulnerability of our corporeal existence – is the all-present, if constantly rebuffed reminder of our ultimate marginality and powerlessness as humans.

Illness as hyper-awareness of one's corporeal reality

The process of corporeal debasement and vilification undergone by Philoctetes has been approached by readers, especially in recent times, in ethical and aesthetical terms (as reflection on political belonging, on the values of loyalty and friendship, or as explorations of a grotesque taste).[15] From a phenomenological perspective, such vicissitudes of the hero's wounded body are not just metaphorical devices, instrumental to a more abstract reflection; nor dramatic expedients for an expressionistic effect. Rather, they have a fundamental meaning in themselves. Disease and being diseased in the play, let us not forget, are not a momentary accident waiting to be solved: with a mythological origin *before* the drama (the infraction Philoctetes has committed by trespassing on the sacred ground of Chryse, punished by the bite of a snake with a purulent wound) and a metaphysical, hastened solution only in its aftermath, Philoctetes' disease is posed as a permanent condition, as a mode of existence whose intensity and inescapability reduces to silence any other interpretation, as Budelmann proposes in his analysis of dramatic pain.[16]

This elision of any instrumentality or meaningfulness of pain (no πάθει μάθος here) is evident in how Philoctetes' illness is insistently presented as chronic, a life-condition with rhythms and a periodicity of its own, rather than a stage to be overcome. This clinical narrative differs from what we find in the other known examples of bodily pain in tragedy: the Euripidean *Orestes*, or Sophocles' *Trachiniae*, where physical pain is episodic and acute; even *Prometheus Bound* is a different case, in which, despite the intensity and duration of the pain inflicted on the titan a sense of distance remains, afforded by the cosmological setting of the drama and the divine nature of the character. Interestingly, the absence of illness as 'state of things' extends to the medical writings of the period too: also in the Hippocratic patient reports of the *Epidemics* none of the numerous individual clinical cases preserved deals with life-long illnesses as such, and the interest is firmly on the acute manifestation.

Philoctetes' suffering, thus, is special insofar as it is a long-lasting business: he is 'miserable, *always* alone'; (δύστανος, μόνος αἰεί, 172); he has a 'sickness which returns fiercely and swiftly departs', a rhythm to which he has grown used (ὡς ἥδε μοι / ὀξεῖα φοιτᾷ καὶ ταχεῖ' ἀπέρχεται, 807–808); his illness has become a personified and familiar presence, which wanders away to then make a come-back: 'it has come *in person*, the disease, after a time, perhaps because it is weary of wandering' (ἥκει γὰρ αὕτη διὰ χρόνου, πλάνοις ἴσως / ὡς ἐξεπλήσθη, 758–760). His daily and everyday state of pain has even '*permeated his home*' – an expression heavy with existential weight – ὦ πληρέστατον / αὔλιον λύπας τᾶς ἀπ' ἐμοῦ τάλαν, 1087–1088[17]), effectively modifying the world he inhabits. His own words, as he narrates his own experience, give to his ordeal a sense of temporal depth that is atypical in tragic forms: 'so one period of time went by for me' (285). This sense of duration is acknowledged by others too – most of all, by Heracles and Neoptolemus, at the end of the play, as they envisage the rest of Philoctetes' life, forever haunted by pain: 'you won't have respite from your sickness, *as long as the sun still rises in the east and sets in the west*, until of your own free will you come to the plains of Troy', says Heracles (1329–1331) and Neoptolemus later concludes: 'you will have to go on living as you are living, without deliverance' (1395–1396).

The tragic presentation of illness is thus highly original insofar as it portrays a medical experience even the Hippocratics largely avoided addressing. Also the other two *Philoctetes* plays we know of (Aeschylus' and Euripides'), parenthetically, did not (apparently) address the theme of illness with the same existential force, or give so large a space to staging its psychology.[18] If one looks at this text from the perspective of an historian and anthropologist of medicine, then, this play opens to us a largely uncharted territory.

There is a second important sense in which this territory is uncharted, and this is the central place occupied by the world of a specific diseased individual in the story – the *autopathography* of Philoctetes. We notably lack any such account from antiquity before the first centuries of our era (with Marcus Aurelius and Aelius Aristides as weighty first examples). Philoctetes is thus, we may say, the first speaking patient from ancient literature whose living and first-hand elaborate experience we are invited to observe; and one whose illness is a status quo, a mode of existence. In his case, moreover, no metaphysical anchorage to his experience of pain is to be found – when mentioned, the hero's guilt and the snake's bite in Chryse are presented as mere details, even a pretext devoid of any prominence. The corporeal feelings and sufferings of Philoctetes are the beginning and the end of his world – coterminous with it – and shape his entire existence through a series of radical modifications of his human identity, as we will now explore more closely.

Identity loss: Becoming animal

Chronic illness emerges through a 'dehumanization' of Philoctetes: he is stripped of all that traditionally makes one, in Greek terms, fully 'human' – a free, adult male. Even if these denied identities are finally restored by a solution on a political-ethical level (*ex machina*, at the end of the play), the core of the drama remains untouched by this reinstatement, and Philoctetes is remembered for his refashioning of what it is to be a man defined by his own corporeal illness. The process of dehumanization operates on multiple levels, the expected strong ones in Greek culture: first of all, impacting on human definition against animals. Philoctetes is insistently animalized, both metaphorically (by analogy) and metonymically (by association): he is like an animal, is surrounded by animals, depends on them for survival and addresses them in several apostrophic passages.[19] Animals, in fact, are his companions, a source of food but also ecological equal interlocutors and this proximity constitutes his abjection and misfortune.[20] 'Confined far from all others, with beasts dappled or hairy, and pitiable' in his pain and hunger (κεῖται μοῦνος ἀπ' ἄλλων / στικτῶν ἢ λασίων μετὰ / θηρῶν, 183–185) he addresses his surroundings:

> 'O you inlets and headlands, society
> of mountains beasts, oh jagged rocks,
> I know no other to speak to'
>
> Ὦ λιμένες, ὦ προβλῆτες, ὦ ξυνουσίαι
> θηρῶν ὀρείων, ὦ καταρρῶγες πέτραι,
> ὑμῖν τάδ', οὐ γὰρ ἄλλον οἶδ' ὅτῳ λέγω
>
> *936–937*[21]

and again at the end, voicing his resignation, as he is now sure to be destined to die of hunger, and be devoured by beasts (956–958; 1145–1153).[22] Philoctetes belongs now to the food chain, in a very literal sense. Philoctetes' corporeal presence is evoked in crude terms (his own blood, his 'quivering' or 'discolored' flesh now turned fodder for the beasts) are one thing with his helplessness and exclusion from action: he proclaims his own reduction to matter, and at the same time his own dissolution into the environment he has inhabited until then, the rocks, woods and hills he now chooses to address.

Communication and specifically human language become painfully self-conscious, and play a fundamental role here. This aspect has been thoroughly analysed in different perspectives.[23] On the one hand, Philoctetes screams and grunts like a beast – his cries of pain are a famous feature of the play. At 730–798 an attack of his devouring disease is described and punctuated by inarticulate screams of pain: {ΦΙ.} Ἆ, ἆ, ἆ, ἆ. (732, 739); (743–744); παπαῖ, / ἀπαππαπαππαῖ, παππαπαππαπαππαπαῖ (745–746), and so on. On the other hand, Philoctetes remains attached to, and very conscious of, the Hellenic language he is missing: 'oh dearest of sounds', Ὦ φίλτατον φώνημα (234) – he exclaims upon meeting the Greeks. In fact, he speaks about speaking language a lot, from the first meeting with his Greek visitors; conversely, his overwhelming crying and screaming is remarked on many times by other characters. The disjuncture, his being cut out from a shared language, is rather evident: in his loneliness, it is said, Echo (another character whose presence and, literally, whose body is scattered through the wilderness, according to her *sparagmos* myth) has been his only interlocutor: 'she whose mouth has no bar, Echo, appearing far off responds to his bitter cries of lamentation' (188–190). This is not only a dramatic and geographic isolation, but that ultimate unwiring that accompanies the extremes of agony: as Kristeva formulates it in her claims about a narrative of 'suffering and horror', 'the unbearable subjectivity of the narrator and of the surroundings that are supposed to sustain him can no longer be *narrated* but *cries out* or is *descried* with maximal stylistic intensity (language of violence, of obscenity [. . .])'.[24]

Beast-like overtones are also conveyed in ways other than language: Philoctetes, in his intractable aggressiveness, appears to the other Greeks to pose a 'blind threat' – his anger is cast as involuntary and irresistible, beast-like, just as his agony is: 'no-one dares to approach him' (106), and so on. This element of savagery emerges in the others' inability to decipher him as much as in his own perceived isolation.

Philoctetes not only resembles animals in the way he is perceived by others, or presented through the language of the play: he expresses an intense longing for animals which has however nothing romantic in it, it is no yearning for 'Nature' with a capital N, unlike what one might be tempted to initially think reading the addressing scenes directed to animals and landscapes quoted above: 'O you inlets and headlands, society of mountains beasts' (936–937); or, 'Ah, my winged prey, and you tribes of bright-eyed creatures held by this place in its upland pastures' (1146–1162), and so on. A closer inspection, however, reveals these as rather literal indication of Philoctetes' own being dissolved into the environment around him: he identifies with, and *annihilates himself into landscape*, as far as the literal threat of bodily destruction. The island of Lemnos, we should stress again, is meaningfully depicted as deserted. No contact with fellow-humans is possible, and this is made clear already at the very opening: ('this is the shore of the seagirt land of Lemnos, *untrodden* by mortals, *not inhabited* (βροτοῖς ἄστιπτος οὐδ' οἰκουμένη)' (1–2).[25]

Identity loss: From civilized man to 'primitive'

In his avulsion from a validating context, the dehumanization of Philoctetes also comes through as a regression to a kind of helpless proto-humanity: his state evokes at times a miniature Promethean history of mankind, discovering fire, and fighting for basic survival – and a crooked one at that. As he describes his ordeal:

> So time passed for me . . . and alone in this narrow house, I had to attend to all my wants by my own resources. For my stomach's needs this bow provided . . . And whatever my string-sped arrow might strike, [290] in pain I would crawl to it myself, dragging my wretched foot behind me. Or, again, if water had to be fetched, or, if when the frost had spread, as often happens in winter, a bit of firewood had to be broken, I would creep out in pain and manage it. Then fire would be lacking; but by rubbing stone hard on stone I would at last reveal the hidden spark which preserves me from day to day. Indeed, a roof over my head and a fire inside provides all that I want – except release from my disease.
>
> *285–299*

All these evoke of course the traditional textual parallels (the Aeschylean Prometheus, the Hesiodic narrative, the ode to man in *Antigone*), and at the same time bring these famous progressive tales of human achievement to implosion – all is achievable, expect for the cure for one's disease; and, as humans, we remain only a few steps away from having to start it all over again. In a significant scene, the struggling return home of Philoctetes, a shrieking wretch, at the end of day is contrasted with the civilized icon of the pipe-playing shepherd retiring to his abode after a day of work: 'he is not playing the music of the pipe, like a shepherd living in the wild, but because he stumbles … he utters a far sounding cry' (211–212). We are only one illness away from returning to a precultural, cave-man state.

Identity loss: The house-keeper, the baby and the slave

A third element of debasement has not so much, or not only to do with wilderness, namely Philoctetes' pathetic and grotesque presentation as a house-keeping loner. First, there is an element of gender subtly used as dehumanizing device. We have seen how the dwelling of the hero is first described *in absentia*, as the audience is made to picture the bits and pieces familiar in any household – but a pathetic, miserable one where a bad piece of woodwork stands out, and especially the ill man's dirty rags, the stuff women (especially, low-class women) usually deal with. His wooden cup and his firestones are called by Odysseus and Neoptolemus, with a touch of irony, 'his treasures' or 'store', τὸ θησαύρισμα (35–37); his rugs encrusted with blood and putrefied matter are described with some insistence (38–39). This realism, the intrusion of the everyday is rare and *per se* strongly pathetic in tragedy (a parallel could be the nurse mentioning Orestes' nappies in *Choephoroi*, 755–759) – not by chance a woman, a servant, speaking about a baby. Later, at 534 this same dwelling is called an ἄοικον ἐξοίκησιν, a home-which-is-not-a-home, underlining the estranging, scandalous nature and the discomfort of this ménage.[26]

Not only is for Philoctetes the caricature of a female house-keeper evoked. Next, there is the allusion to infant-like helplessness: through his disease the hero is reduced to less than a man, he crawls and drags himself in search of his medicinal plant just like an infant, or an old man: 'I dragged myself' (290–291); 'he stumbles' (215), he is 'crawling like a child without a loving nurse' (701–703). Finally, his freedom is, literally, taken away from him and he feels reduced to the state of a slave: 'clearly my father gave me life as a slave, not as a free man!' (995–996).

In short, the referents invoked by illness are animal, pre-civilization human, woman or struggling house-keeper, baby or child, and slave: a human being is defiled by illness and dragged by it into each of these pitfalls, alone on an island of despair and exclusion.

Ultimate identity loss: Bodily annihilation

These attacks against the hero's integrity manage to be so radical because they are not only conveyed through the routes of social categories of depreciation – those we have just explored – but because it is precisely the body – not only the status, or the conscience, or the emotions that are manifestly hit. The whole play has a quite unique texture of materiality – and disgusting materiality – that makes this dehumanization unescapable and irredeemable, beyond the reach of ethical discourses. We are made to observe a clinical course that is systematically enhanced by grotesque and emotional effects: a monstrification, as it has been described by Worman,[27] a kind of 'sublimity', with Männlein-Robert[28] not primarily delivered by the mockery received by others but deeply grounded in Philoctetes' own experience of the world. In fact, he anticipates the mockery and almost invites it, he acknowledges it painfully as something to be anticipated. No-one really mocks him on stage; still, he complains that 'those who threw me out quietly mock me' (γελῶσι σῖγ' ἔχοντες, 257–258), with a touch of paranoia; later, at 1023–1024, he again complains 'I am mocked by you and by the two generals' (γελώμενος). This kind of internalised mockery aligns with the insistent references to the stench of his wound, the dripping blood, the dark colour of his affected foot, the pus: 'his foot was dripping from a malady that was eating it away' (νόσῳ καταστάζοντα διαβόρῳ πόδα, 7); 'oozing dark blood dripping from the depths' (783–784, στάζει γὰρ αὖ μοι φοίνιον τόδ' ἐκ βυθοῦ / κηκῖον αἷμα); 'sweat' and 'a vein of dark blood', which 'has burst out from his eel' are mentioned (823–825, ἱδρώς γέ τοί νιν πᾶν καταστάζει δέμας / μέλαινά τ' ἄκρου τις παρέρρωγεν ποδὸς /αἱμορραγὴς φλέψ); the encrusted rags (39):[29] all the remote senses – those available to a theatrical audience: sight, smell and hearing – are summoned to lead us through the disclosure of what Philoctetes is experiencing.

The most natural event of all, illness (and especially the illness of rotting wounds, in a Homeric world) is thus fashioned as a monstrous occurrence, where disgust and abjection loom large. In this respect, the divergence from medical sources of the time could not be starker: as has been analysed, there is a clear elision of disgust in fifth century medicine that provides an interesting contrast with the tones in which Philoctetes' illness is described.[30] In classical medicine, diseases are 'natural' occurrences, not in the philosophical sense of 'nature' but in so far as that they are kept ethically and eudaimonistically neutral by a distant narrative, which is self-styled as objective: this is the image that the clinical cases of the *Epidemics*, for instance, hand over to us. To the experience of an ill person a severe disease, instead, is always – nowadays as much as in ancient times – monstrously exceptional and disruptive, a scandal to the self, *per se* an exception ('why me . . .?'). It is then only appropriate that the first agent of the dehumanization, and alienation in his extraordinary portrayal should be Philoctetes himself, in the words of his auto-pathographical eloquence:[31] he sees his disease as an individual, a *thera* ('I am devoured', βρύκομαι (745); he implores Neoptolemus to 'strike' at his diseased feet, as if to tame the beast (747–749) that is attacking him (787–788, προσέρπει / προσέρχεται τόδ' ἐγγύς) and that he sees as dwelling inside his body (his wounded art is for him an ἐνθήρου ποδὸς, 'a foot inhabited by a beast', 698); the illness διέρχεται, 'goes through him', in his own words (743–744); he 'is being eroded' (266); he ultimately wants to cut himself into pieces, 'to cut off my head and every limb! To kill, to kill is now my wish! (1207–1208, φονᾷ, φονᾷ νόος ἤδη), in a kind of self-inflicted *sparagmos* whereby his body is finally destroyed and dispersed – the fate of Echo had been already mentioned as a suggestive parallel (188–190).

Conclusion

One can look at Sophocles' play as an account of pathological suffering, an account immediately available and relatable for a reader or onlooker, according to which the experience of illness can drag humans into the realm of the animal and the monstrous and is experienced as a 'scandal' that *should have never happened* to us. Diseases constitute an attack against one's perceived humanity at its very core – a humanity predicated upon a form of integrity, however fictional and precarious. This might seem paradoxical, as mortality and illness are, in an important sense, the most 'human' of occurrences; but such is not their psychological reality, not how they *feel*. Sophocles' *Philoctetes* stages this 'unacceptability' of disease, and probes precisely the question of bodily ability and integrity as conditions for humanity, forcing us to face the ever present risk to trespass – into beast? Into a clumsy parody of a house-keeping woman? Into a helpless baby? An abused slave? An uncivilized caveman? A human-disease assemblage? Or objectified, like an inert source of sounds, smells and sights? Many of these insights are well understood by anyone who has experience with severe illness or disability and, as I have tried to illustrate at the beginning of this chapter, resonate in an important way with current phenomenological reflections on 'illness':[32] bodily, or mental suffering is not simply a matter of being a patient afflicted by a named disease, and/or cured by a certain therapy, to finally recover (or not), but the intrusion of a new world, the beginning of an entirely different mode of life that commands the renegotiation of one's existence on all levels.

A broader understanding of 'human', then, must be offered as an alternative to the one based on force, power and presumed bodily integrity that is traditional in the mythological world Philoctetes and his companions belong to – and in which much of Western humanism we are used to is likewise rooted – from the Homeric ideals of *kalokagathia* to the canons of heroic strength that survive as dominant through European literature. Monstrification and de-humanization are nightmares to which, once again, Philoctetes is an accomplice, not a mere victim; his is not the typical – and rather more banal – story of marginalization and stigmatization, but the account of a broader existential change. As such, these nightmares appear to be necessary steps for a man suffering under a severe illness to speak out, live out his invisible pain and put forth a different, more inclusive model for others, but first of all for himself of what it is to be human. MacCormack explores[33] how the 'monster', the *teras* is defined precisely by its 'wonder' – its ambiguous, hybrid, elusive nature; and it is when 'one perceives a monster in a monster, [that one] begins to domesticate it'.[34] And so, in this (slightly Kafkaesque) light, the manifold vilification of Philoctetes is a positive move, which allows the unspeakable internal experience (in Philoctetes' words, δεινὸν γὰρ οὐδὲ ῥητόν, 756) to be accepted by the sufferer in the first place, made congruous with the surrounding world, and ultimately shared with others.

CHAPTER 5
THE IMPERIAL ANIMAL: VIRGIL'S *GEORGICS* AND THE ANTHROPO-/THERIOMORPHIC ENTERPRISE[1]
Tom Geue

Virgil usually comes across as our most 'sympathetic' of ancient poets. I use the term warily, and in both ways: sympathetic insofar as we feel a fellow feeling towards him or his subject;[2] sympathetic in the sense that his chief virtue has often seemed to be his *feeling* for the many victims sprawled across his poems.[3] From Orpheus to Dido, Meliboeus to Turnus, this capacious feeling is said to embrace its victims even as it twists the knife.[4] Animals, too, fall well within the divine bard's 'universal' remit of concern.[5] They are sometimes the vehicles of human-focussed pathos (e.g., Dido's doe, *Aen.* 4.69–73); sometimes they are treated to a long sympathetic gaze, themselves (e.g., the bees of *Georgics* 4).[6] In most cases, the trick pulled is a joint strategy of anthropomorphosis/theriomorphosis,[7] to make animals look like humans, and vice versa. The point of this short piece is to argue that blurring this boundary (at least in antiquity) is not necessarily in the interests of either the human or the animal in question. Rather, it can be a crucial ideological bedrock of violence and domination. In other words: the 'sympathy' is part of the problem.

The structuralist categories[8] still haunting classical studies – human/animal, culture/nature etc. – often mist up the more granular reality: that in the ancient world, from the wannabe Olympian perspectives of the elite, *certain* humans were considered particularly proximate to *some* animals.[9] Around the time of my sympathetic subject, Virgil's *Georgics*, landowner discourse pictured slaves and domestic animals as largely interchangeable;[10] and ethnographic/imperialist discourse did the same with fringe humanity ('The Other') and wild animals.[11] In this chapter, I want to look at how the third book of Virgil's *Georgics* sets its teeth to these dual related tasks of domination. I shall argue that its project of 'domestication' applies both to certain animals, and certain humans; and that the erasure of the human–animal boundary is no proto-ecological love-in, but rather a savvy means of sub*jugation*: that is, a way of bringing specific species *under the yoke*. In Derridean apothegm: 'Politics supposes livestock.'[12]

The deconstructive move of boundary collapse is a key standard of the posthuman political project; in Haraway's signature piece, for example, the erasure of the boundary between humans and animals (among other things) is almost the point of departure enabling the fling-forward into cyborgian humanimal subjectivity.[13] While posthumanism might push the construction of the 'humanimal' – a shared latitude of the biosphere in which the historical categories of 'us' and 'them' are rendered meaningless – as a progressive platform, I want to press here that it need not be, and at certain historical points, it *has* not been. Just as Derrida spotlights the brutal categorization circumscribing the mythical definite-articled group 'The Animal', which pens all non-human beasts into a zoo-like 'space of domestication',[14] so I would like to see Virgil labouring to 'pen' – both write, and enclose – a space for 'The Humanimal'. But this overlapping field between certain animals and certain humans is still a space quarantined from 'true' humanity (read: elite Roman male), a space close enough to communicate expropriated labour, but distant enough not to communicate disease. In other words, boundaries are not necessarily made to be broken; they can also be broken to be made.

Domestication station

Georgics 3 is nominally about animal 'husbandry': in the first half, how to breed and train the horses and cattle; in the second, how to treat the humbler critters, goats and sheep. As always, Virgil spices up the dry didaxis with juicy digressions, this time serving as windows onto the distant world of Libya, Scythia, and finally, onto a vista of a plague that happened in the region of Noricum long ago. These are all ethnographic excurses. Bardolatrous scholars quick to promote Virgil to universal *feeler* often forget that the plague is set in a specific yet distant region, and a remote time[15] – it is emphatically *not* the story of the Roman elite self, but importantly quarantined from it (more on this below).

My starting point here is that writing about animals and writing about far-off humans is *somehow* related in this book. And the key rubric is that of domestication. The clue is there in the opening proem, where Virgil cringeworthily pledges his future poem-temple to a Caesar riding high on recent conquest. Virgil – twice claiming the name *victor* for himself (3.9, 17),[16] jumped up on triumphalist cocaine – ushers all these conquered beings into a choreographed performance:

iam nunc sollemnis ducere pompas
ad delubra iuuat caesosque uidere iuuencos,
uel scaena ut uersis discedat frontibus utque
purpurea intexti tollant aulaea Britanni.

3.22–25

Right now I would relish the chance to lead the official procession to the shrine, and see the cattle slaughtered – or see how the scene flips with the set change, and how the Britons raise the coloured curtain, themselves part of the tapestry.[17]

This stirring pageant leads the cattle to the slaughter spectacle (*uidere*) right alongside the poor captive Britons, who must dance in the Broadway musical of their own oppression.[18] Both these categories of living creature are made to know their place. And that place is not some vague service of or to 'the human'. As usual, 'the human' is a universalist archetype glossing over, and formed in the image of, a very specific *kind* of human – in this case, the Roman ruling class on their merry imperial mission.[19] It is this universalizing notion of the human that Derrida critiques as a cultural gesture of the cannibalistic subject: a subject who performs a kind of symbolic sacrifice by subsuming all individual beings into the category of human.[20]

The symmetry of subjugation only becomes stronger over the course of the book. Virgil promises he will work into the temple design the 'subdued cities of Asia' (*urbes Asiae domitas* 3.30). *Domare* – to tame, domesticate – becomes one of the watchwords of *Georgics* 3. Note how the term comes back to 'training' calves for pliant service. Here the abracadabra of anthropomorphosis is very cynical indeed:

tu quos ad studium atque usum formabis agrestem
iam uitulos hortare uiamque insiste **domandi**,
dum faciles animi iuuenum, dum mobilis aetas.
ac primum laxos tenui de uimine circlos
ceruici subnecte; dehinc, ubi **libera colla**
seruitio adsuerint, ipsis e torquibus aptos

iunge pares, et coge gradum conferre iuuencos;
atque illis iam saepe rotae ducantur inanes
per terram, et summo uestigia puluere signent;
post ualido nitens sub pondere faginus axis
instrepat, et iunctos temo trahat aereus orbis.

3.163–173

But you should school these calves, which you'll hone for the pursuit and profit of the farm, and set them on the fast track to being broken in, while their minds are young and pliant, and their age nice and supple. First lasso their necks with light osier; then, when their 'free' necks are acclimatised to slavery, yoke them in pairs fitted from the collars themselves, and force them to march in lockstep; and now let them make a habit of dragging empty carts over the land, and let them mark the tracks on the dust surface; after, have the beech axle strain and groan under its solid load, and have the brass pole drag the linked wheels.

Scholars better disposed to delightful Virgilian sympathy will note he borrows terms from the language of youth education (*formabis, hortare*)[21] to paint this calf-school in human hues.[22] But this is really about breaking in (*domandi*; cf. *indomitis*) the spritely young things for *slavery* (*seruitio*).[23] The *colla* may be *libera*, but not for long. This is the only place, in a poem famous for wilfully occluding slave labour,[24] where Virgil *doesn't* beat about the bush: domestication of cattle is a form of slavery; and grounding it so helps naturalize both spheres of subjugation.[25] Nor is this unique to the cow.[26] The chariot horse in training gets treatment in kind (*domitis*; *domandum* 206; a 'pliable (i.e. willing) neck' *molli . . . collo* 204). Virgil advocates that this noble creature get treated 'like a labourer' (*sitque laboranti similis* 193). Here simile itself becomes a form of domestication designed not so much for sympathy, as to bring the animals into acceptable human realms of oppression (the enforced labour of slave, or perhaps 'free' tenant worker).[27] The simile strains to break them all in for domination. To work, the lot of you!

What starts as a not-so-innocent spot of anthropomorphosis goes viral. The curse of love is soon said to affect *every* land-stalking beast, humans included:

Omne adeo genus in terris hominumque ferarumque
et genus aequoreum, pecudes pictaeque uolucres,
in furias ignemque ruunt: amor omnibus idem.

243–245

To that extent every race on earth, human or beast, sea types, cattle and bright birds, they rush into burning madness: the same love for everybody.

On the topic of 'same love', Virgil mines material from all over the biosphere: his examples are drawn from the animal kingdom (lioness, bear, boar, horse et al.) and human alike (Hero and Leander 258–263; the former called *iuuenis* 258 after the *iuuenis*-horse of 118, for maximum hum*an*imality).[28] Even Virgil/we are made to come down with the bug, becoming carried away by the *amor* digression itself (*singula dum capti circumuectamur amore.* 285 'while we, charmed with love of our theme, linger around each detail').[29] The heavy anthropomorphizing of early book 3 blossoms into this grand statement of human–animal common ground: love gets *us* all. But this universal flourish fluffs up the transition to the next half of the book, where the strategy of similarity will be slightly different: instead of certain animals becoming certain humans through a domesticating anthropomorphosis, certain humans will cross over into the state of the animal,[30] to get prepped to be broken by their overlords.

Domestication nation

The book's second proem injects Virgil with a dose of *amor* to steel himself for handling the humbler beasts this side of the book.[31] But he reminds us thereby that conquest is still the order of the day:

hic labor, hinc laudem fortes sperate coloni.
nec sum animi dubius, uerbis ea **uincere** magnum
quam sit et angustis hunc addere rebus **honorem**;
sed me Parnasi deserta per ardua dulcis
raptat amor; iuuat ire **iugis**, qua nulla priorum
Castaliam molli deuertitur orbita cliuo.

288–293

This is the real work, from this you should hope for praise, brave farm folk. I have no doubts how big an exercise it is to conquer this with words, and load this honour on to low-brow content: but sweet love bustles me through the steep wastelands of Parnassus; I like roaming the ridges, where no wheel-rut of past travellers twists in a gradual slope down to Castalia.

Officially, we limber up to get our hands dirty. But the plunge into real work keeps *uincere* and *honor* as the main watchwords; the language still traps us in the dominant (dominating) social goals of the Roman ruling class.[32] This is both a lurch up and down,[33] and nothing *captures* the dynamics like the pun in *iugis*: Virgil is moving up onto the ridges (*iugis*), right at the moment he is, effectively, casting off the yokes (*iugis*) of the *armenta*. 'Good to trample the heights; or to leave those yokes behind.' Onwards, and upwards, and downwards!

That high–low double motion is a perfect way to sum the even more ambitious imperial notes of this section, which ends up being as much about humans as it is about sheep and goats. The first fold-out excursus takes us to the Libyan shepherds, where we see more domestication in action. The African sheep graze freely, unyoked, under the watchful eye of familiar looking herdsmen in a far-flung place:

saepe diem noctemque et totum ex ordine mensem
pascitur itque pecus longa in deserta sine ullis
hospitiis: tantum campi iacet. omnia secum
armentarius Afer agit, tectumque laremque
armaque Amyclaeumque canem Cressamque pharetram;
non secus ac patriis acer Romanus in armis
iniusto sub fasce uiam cum carpit, et hosti
ante exspectatum positis stat in agmine castris.

341–348

> Usually – day, night, the whole month long – the flocks graze and amble into the desert spaces, without any hospitality; so vast stretches the plain. The African herdsman drives everything along with him, house, hearth, weapons, Spartan dog, Cretan quiver; in fact just like a fierce Roman kitted out in his fatherland's arms, plucking out a path under an outrageous burden, halting the column and pitching the camp before the enemy has a chance to expect him.

This distant herdsman is swept into a Roman ambit fully and properly. Even before the big simile we see the cultural assimilation coagulating – would a nomadic Libyan shepherd really have *lares*, a dog from Sparta, Cretan trappings?[34] But the point here is not that the Other is rendered legible under the terms of 'the' Roman self (though it is that; and ethnography is a form of epistemological domestication). It is more that this is a specific *kind* of Roman, a rank and file soldier, probably of the lower classes, tramping along with an insupportable burden (in the context of an imperial confrontation against the enemy – *hosti* 347 – perhaps in far-off lands). The point of contact between Roman *miles* and Libyan shepherd is that they are both sufficiently distant from the elite Roman self; and both, in a way, *subject* to that group's burgeoning imperial rule. The big giveaway is the term *acer* applied to the Roman soldier. This dehumanizing adjective ('keen, spirited') only orbits animals or other Others in the *Georgics*.[35] In the plague section, for example, it goes to a Nor-easter, the Gelonian. In fact this passage reverses the domesticating strategies of the *acer Romanus* simile, by making a distant other now the paradigm for what the 'Roman' shepherd (addressee of the section)[36] should do when faced with an infected animal:

> profuit incensos aestus auertere et inter
> ima ferire pedis salientem sanguine uenam,
> Bisaltae quo more solent **acerque** Gelonus,
> cum fugit in Rhodopen atque in deserta Getarum,
> et lac concretum cum sanguine potat equino.
>
> *459–463*

> It helps to turn the flaming heat aside, and to pierce the vein in the inner part of the hoof which is pumping with blood, in the way the Bisaltae and fierce Gelonian tend to do, when the latter escapes into Rhodope and the wastelands of the Getae, and drinks a milk thickened with the blood of a horse.

That Gelonian gets a little too close to the animals in sipping on his bloody White Russian; but he also reprises the same activator epithet, *acer*, reserved for a thrashing beast in close proximity:

> Nec tibi cura canum fuerit postrema, sed una
> uelocis Spartae catulos **acremque** Molossum
> pasce sero pingui. numquam custodibus illis
> nocturnum stabulis furem incursusque luporum
> aut **impacatos** a tergo horrebis Hiberos.
>
> *404–408*

And don't let dog care be lowest priority, but feed quick Spartan puppies with fierce Molossians together, both on fattening whey. With them manning the fort, you'll never be anxious for your stalls – be your worries a thief in the night, a wolf attack, or the untamed Spaniards coming up the back.

So *acer* lashes together a rank-and-file Roman soldier, a frozen Gelonian, but also a keen Molossian hound. These creatures are all, from an elite perspective, potentially recalcitrant beasts which need to be brought under control, bent to the use of (ruling class) Man. From the standpoint of the landowner: thieves, wolves and Spaniards are akin.

What I suspect is happening, here, is that Virgil is shearing the buffer between human and animal only to put certain varieties of animal in close contact with certain kinds of human. The second major ethnographizing passage – on perhaps the next imperial target in Caesar's sights, the Scythians[37] – makes an explicit point of their proximity to animals:[38]

talis Hyperboreo septem subiecta trioni
gens effrena uirum Riphaeo tunditur Euro
et pecudum fuluis uelatur corpora saetis.

381–383

That's what the savage race of men subject to the seven stars of the Hyperboreans is like: pounded by the Riphaean wind, bodies wrapped in the brown furs of beasts.

Again, the similarity isn't just superficial. These Scythians (wishfully described as *subiecta*, mind) are reduced to *corpora*, bodies – and that word thus far has only had the privilege of marking out *animal* bodies.[39] It's only when we come down with the black death at the end of book 3, that we realize what this investment in the creation of a humanimal is really all about.

Conquest and quarantine

The last and loudest way in which Virgil pares back this metaphysical boundary[40] (in practice, I have argued, a way of inscribing a *political* boundary) is the devastating account of plague capping the book.[41] It is brought *on stage* (remember that Briton: the suffering of Others was sport to Virgil, Caesar and their ilk) as another way of thinking the deep 'communicability' between (some) humans and animals. First anthropomorphosis; then *amor*; then theriomorphosis; now this. Epidemic is the flip side of the close encounter.[42] Virgil introduces it as something that breaks rank beyond individual bodies, and steals into whole kinds; but scholars often brush over the fact that it is set a long time ago, in a galaxy far, far away:[43]

nec singula morbi
corpora corripiunt, sed tota aestiua repente,
spemque gregemque simul cunctamque ab origine gentem.
tum sciat, aërias Alpis et Norica si quis
castella in tumulis et Iapydis arua Timaui
nunc quoque post tanto uideat, desertaque regna
pastorum et longe saltus lateque uacantis.

471–477

> Plagues don't pick off individual bodies, but all of a sudden, the whole summer stock, the flock's hope, and the flock itself, the entire family right from the source, everything at once. At that point one should know, if anyone sees (even now, after such a long time) the high Alps and the Noric forts on the hills and the fields of the Iapydes' Timavus, the shepherds' wasted region, their woods uninhabited far as the eye can see.

So this biohazard can wipe out whole populations at a stroke. Almost as a disinfecting reflex, Virgil palms off the story of the worst plague in human history to an area technically beyond the boundaries of the Roman empire: Noricum and surrounds. But the geography is kept fuzzy, for a reason. This was also an area in which Octavian had been stamping out resistance (victory over the Iapydes in 34; part of the triple triumph in 29 BCE).[44] In other words, this region was still a smidgeon *impacatus* (cf. those pesky Spaniards above), but starting to come under the active boot of Roman military dominance. It is no coincidence that Virgil has picked on it as the specific site of the plague.

In one sense, you could say that plague throws up the *limits* of domestication. This is what happens when humans get too close; when the outbreak comes, the shutters have to go down to stop the spread. But in another sense, if we take into account who is actually doing the dying, and where, domestication continues on apace. For what this plague does is carry out the violence of imperialism by other means. The mighty horse, *uictor* (499) once upon a time, crumples beneath the plague's iron grip; but as Virgil describes the illness hitting climax in a horrific self-mauling, he makes sure to tell us this is an apotropaic vignette tailored for the *enemy*: *di meliora piis erroremque hostibus illum!* (513 – 'Heaven grant a happier lot to the good, and such madness to our foes!'). And by killing livestock and freeing up space under the yoke, the plague follows through on the prayer. It brings savage humans and wild animals to heel:

> tempore non alio dicunt **regionibus illis**
> quaesitas ad sacra boues Iunonis et uris
> imparibus ductos alta ad donaria currus.
> ergo aegre rastris terram rimantur, et ipsis
> unguibus infodiunt fruges, montisque per altos
> **contenta ceruice** trahunt stridentia plaustra.
> non lupus insidias explorat ouilia circum
> nec gregibus nocturnus obambulat; **acrior** illum
> cura domat;
>
> *531–539*

> That was the only time, they say, when cattle in those parts had to be sought out to perform Juno's rites, and chariots were led by ungainly buffaloes towards her high treasure chamber. So men laboriously tear up the ground with hoes, and dig the seed in with their own nails, and drag the creaky wagons over the high hills by putting their neck into it. The wolf doesn't search out sorties around the sheepfold, nor stalks the flocks in the night; a fiercer care domesticates him.

The *uri*, wild cattle of an enemy zone (**regionibus illis**) who wouldn't ordinarily be caught dead dragging chariots,[45] are squeezed into gainful employment; the rugged mountain folk themselves are demoted to bearing the yoke with strained necks – exactly how Octavian might have described the upshot of his recent campaigns, except he would have understood *contenta* to mean 'happy'.[46] Even the wolf suffers that key humiliation of above, *domare* – at the hands of something *acrior*, much stronger, wilder than himself (or dog, or Roman soldier, or Gelonian). It seems that if Roman military campaigns miss a spot, imperial plague will mop up the rest; or perhaps it even ravaged the region in preparation, so that Octavian could swoop in and fasten the yoke all the easier. As Virgil says, no one could beat the plague with anything, not even fire: *nec uiscera quisquam / aut undis abolere potest aut* **uincere** *flamma* (559–560 'nor can anyone cleanse the innards with water, or conquer them with fire'). In other words, plague is the ultimate imperial weapon: biological warfare.

This is why, I think, we shouldn't read too much Virgilian sympathy or recoil into the final scene of the book, where the plague does finally come *home* ('human'):

ne tondere quidem morbo inluuieque peresa
uellera nec telas possunt attingere putris:
uerum etiam inuisos si quis temptarat amictus,
ardentes papulae atque immundus olentia sudor
membra sequebatur, nec longo deinde moranti
tempore contactos artus sacer ignis edebat.

559–566

They can't even shear the fleeces – eaten as they are by plague and grime – nor touch the rotting web. If any of them tried on the hated garment, burning pimples and filthy sweat would chase his oily limbs, and in barely a moment the cursed fire would munch his own infected joints.

Critics have talked as if this is some kind of terrifying yet *general* malaise, a cosmic meditation on the human condition.[47] Yet it is very much localized in place and time: it is for a far-off third person plural to deal with (*possunt*), a generic Noric pastor (*si quis*), i.e., a 'someone' who is nowhere near the cosy quarters of the Roman elite self. For a poet of the upper classes,[48] domestication is not about sympathy, or assimilation of self to other; it is about penning together certain forms of human and animal, flinging them beneath you, so they can be rounded up, yoked, and put to work on the estate you will never see.

In a critical discussion of humanimal power relations, it is all well and good to talk of holes in the fence between human and animal; the destructive exceptionalism of humans needs exposing. But we should also stay aware of the historical functions and ideological plots to which boundary-puncturing has sometimes been assigned. When it comes to Virgil's *Georgics*, rampant bardolatry has blinkered us to the mutually back-slapping chumminess between domestication of animals in 'need' of husbandry, the pacification of animals in the 'wild', and the domination of *certain* humans. Those humans – foreign, marginalized populations, who, through conquest, often end up under the yoke, domesticated into Roman homes and yards in the most literal and brutal sense – did not qualify as full card-carrying members of their species, because that membership was jealously protected by a precious few. *Georgics* 3 shows us that thinking animals into humans and humans into animals can be two subsidiaries of the same dark corporation in classical literary fiction: an enterprise seeking to fold them into forced labour and bleed them for all they are worth. Virgil brings that *home* to us – and I'm not sure we should sympathize.

CHAPTER 6
ANIMALS, GOVERNANCE AND WARFARE IN THE *ILIAD* AND AESCHYLUS' *PERSIANS*

Manuela Giordano

Animals have been the subject of numerous questions in recent years, particularly in the new province of human–animal studies, which bears a prominent connection with posthuman approaches.[1] One of the main suggestions these new trends propose is to move away from a separative, post-Cartesian model of inquiry towards a more inclusive one.[2] 'It is the peculiar trait of Westerners that they have imposed,' says Bruno Latour, an inspirational thinker for posthuman studies, 'the total separation of humans and nonhumans – the Internal Great Divide – and have thereby artificially created the scandal of the others.'[3] As far as ancient Greece is concerned, however, the dichotomy implied in such a 'total separation' would be too broad a generalization to be accepted out of hand.

Homeric texts in particular appear to be embedded in an inclusive model of animal-human identity, for reasons which seem to pertain more to cosmology than ethics, and which would seem more in line with the approach advocated by posthuman models than with the 'humanist' one, in the sense that Homeric society tended to see itself as one of those 'inter-specific communities that include human beings and members of other species.'[4] As Clarke has argued, when approaching Homeric representations of animals 'we must do away with any assumption that men and beasts belong in different departments of creation. … Homer's beasts have the same emotional and cognitive apparatus as men'; the links forged by the similes have the effect 'not only to amplify the narrative but even to assimilate aspects of the appearance and personality of the warrior to those of the animal.'[5] Very simply, this entanglement points to a 'fundamental and sometimes intimate relationship between man and animal,' which is testified by the fact that more than half of the Iliadic similes have animal subjects.[6] Not all scholars share this understanding: Heath for one states that: 'They (sc. the Greeks) did not tend to confuse either the human or divine with animals […] when such conflations do occur they signal something dangerous and destructive that threatens to overwhelm *us* all.'[7] The wording of this statement is rather revealing: who is meant by 'us'? It seems that if a dangerous conflation is in order, it would be between the Greeks and 'us Westerners.' The conflation seems moreover to be a historical one: the cultural assumptions of Homeric culture do not overlap with those, say, of classical Athens, where Heath's understanding may well apply. Achilles' mares are endowed with speech, and the gods themselves appear as animals, birds in particular, as in *Il.* 7.58–60, where Athena and Apollo take the form of vultures and perch on a branch of a lofty oak to watch the battle. To say that 'these transformations are manifestations of the gods' power and involvement in the human world, no more surprising than their frequent appearance in the form of particular humans,' falls short of making sense of their transformation into animals, and in fact implicitly admits a continuum between animals and humans.[8] Similarly downplaying the gods' appearance as birds by saying that 'it is usually impossible to tell if this simile refers to a temporary metamorphosis or simply to the speed and ease of flight,' is a less than persuasive explanation that ignores passages where gods do transform themselves into animals.[9]

This is not to idealize Homer as a non-Western voice: the Homeric continuum between animals, humans and gods may well be interpreted as a process of 'saming', that is, another strategy of domination towards weaker subjects.[10] Alternatively, we may envision such a model as a way of conceptualizing animals and humans in a continuous and interconnected, rather than separative, map of animate beings.[11]

As it is true for any subject of study, so for animal studies too, we – 'located scholars' – are bound to deal solely with maps and not with the territory, as the metaphor goes. In a both 'human' and 'posthuman' interpretive scenario, we can only study the map of the territory, the *representation* of the animal. In this respect, a most inspiring theoretical framework comes from Gregory Bateson, a most versatile scholar who developed themes and issues taken up later by posthuman studies, which, to the best of my knowledge, neglect Bateson's contribution. In the 1970s, Bateson broke new ground on the subjects of cybernetics, system theory and animal studies, and challenged from the epistemological point of view the dualism mind–body, self and non-self, in a complex, sophisticated and non-evaluative way.[12] Bateson reminds us that there is no 'ultimate map' of the territory, and no matter how much subjectivity we attribute to that territory (our subject of study), we should keep the awareness that the territory, the animal itself in our case, never gets in at all; as the scholar asserts: 'always the process of representation will filter it out so that the mental world is only maps of maps of maps, ad infinitum'.[13] As such, the study of any representation reverberates and illuminates in the first place the dynamics of anthropopoiesis and of socio-political construction, as we will see in our case-study of the representations of herding animals and their change over time.[14]

In what follows, I will endeavour to sort out the discourses of power and governance mobilized in the representations of collective herding animals, such as sheep and cattle in Homer, and, especially, which elements make a difference in tracing different maps of 'human' and 'animal'.[15] In so doing, rather than looking at the constituent features of each herding animal in isolation, and drawing a Homeric portrait of, say, sheep, I will look at the *relationships* that the use of herding representations constructs and the power relations it creates, with particular attention to battle narratives, which represent the overwhelming majority of animal similes on the whole.[16] In particular, I will focus on the semantics of the larger unit which encompasses both the relationship between the herd and its (human or animal) leader on the one hand, and that between predator and prey on the other, around which meanings tend to cluster. Finally, I will explore a few instances of herding images in Aeschylean tragedy, as a litmus test for changing representations of governmentality.

A sheepish subject

A fair number of works have been devoted to the economic and social history of pastoralism, but close to nothing on sheep, cattle and the like as 'cultural animals', a sheepish subject by all means.[17] In *Lions, héros, masques. Les représentations de l'animal chez Homère* for example, possibly the best available study on Homeric animals, Schnapp-Gourbeillon dedicates just a few pages to the ovine–bovine comparisons, and never as a subject on its own right; much the same holds true for Lonsdale's monograph on Iliadic animals.[18] This fact deserves some attention, especially as the lion similes, to which most works on Homeric animals are dedicated, happen to feature herding animals alongside lions (and sometimes wolves) in most of their occurrences. Why, then, do sheep not deserve the same scholarly attention as lions? The answer seems to lie in a hidden assumption about worthiness and hierarchy: 'the books filled with names of kings', says Brecht in 'A Worker Reads History'; the same goes for lions, we may add, while sheep, as simple soldiers, hardly merit our attention. In contemporary urban societies, sheep come across as not particularly attractive or worthy animals as they display nothing of the heroic demeanour of lions or wolves, no great man can possibly be represented by them, cast as they are in a lowly position in the animal hierarchy – and in whatever this is meant to represent in our human associations. In the contemporary map of sheep, as an entry of an English dictionary reveals, the main highlights are passivity and helplessness, where to be (like) sheep is proverbially 'used with reference to people who are too easily influenced or led' (OED 2019). Closer to objects rather than subjects, more 'them' than 'us', 'sheep are regarded as being as close to an automaton and mindless animal species as can be imagined, and any serious consideration of their cognitive, social and general mental faculties deemed futile'.[19] They are disregarded as subjects because of their 'overt behaviour patterns of a species that is highly fearful of predation, since it has few defences, and which seem content to be led rather than to lead and to adopt a safe group rather than an individual mentality'.[20] These considerations implicitly highlight our cultural taxonomy and criteria for superiority: primacy, excellence, aggression and predator-like behaviour. In contemporary discourse, by consequence, the flock and herd images have either a strong negative connotation of passivity, or a peculiarly positive overtone, as in Christian religious discourse on pastoralism, where the lamb moreover is a Christological and soteriological metaphor.[21]

It may thus come as a surprise that in Homer flocks and herds are meaningful images for warfare and martial qualities: flocks and herds usually represent the army (or should we say the army represents the flock?) where they represent positive and desirable qualities. Far from being disregarded, they certainly were an animal very 'good to think with', as the passage 15.323–325 in the *Iliad* shows most pointedly, where wild beasts stand for Trojans and the herd/flock represents the Achaeans.

The Shepherd of the people: The leader and his flock

The field of pastoralism gives rise to images that designate the relationship of a sovereign or chief over his group as a 'shepherd of the people', a wide and ancient Indo-European metaphor, with a range of diffusion from Vedic *gopá jánasya* to Old English *folces hyrde*, that is, long before it became a key expression for Christian pastorate.[22] The epithet, and the pastoral metaphor, is widespread not only in the Indo-European domain, but also in the whole of the Near East at least from the third millennium, where the image of the good shepherd as a royal epithet is attributed among others, to Hammurabi, Tukulta Ninurti.[23] The use of this epithet/metaphor is foremost and particularly noteworthy, of course, in the Hebrew Bible where God is the *ro'eh*, 'shepherd'. In ancient Greece the metaphor is foremost in Homer, where *poimena/ poimeni laon*, 'shepherd of the people' is an epithet that recurs forty-four times in the *Iliad* as an honorific title of major and minor leaders, both Achaeans and Trojans, and particularly associated with Agamemnon.[24] Sheep (or cattle) as metaphor for people or an army, and shepherds as a metaphor for kings and leaders seem to be used in a vast array of meaningful and interesting parallels throughout varied ancient contexts and surroundings. This suggests that with herding we encounter a case of 'convergence', that is the recurrence of a cultural phenomenon in geopolitical contexts far from each other. As with the general question of 'why certain animal or certain plants and the like are especially suited to serving as meaningful symbolic expressions',[25] as Bettini has suggested, we may look at the *affordances* they provide, that is 'the perceived possibilities or opportunities that an object (such as an animal) offers in relation to a human project of a symbolic and abstract nature'.[26] Throughout the Iron age, herding animals represented the *sine qua non* of human existence, as shown by a wealth of Indo-European expressions such as Avestan *pasu vira*, Umbrian *ueiro pequo* or Latin *pecudesque virosque*, all meaning 'livestock and men', where the association of cattle and men figures more as a symbiotic unit; 'men and livestock' in fact has been considered a merism, a two-part figure referring to the totality of moveable wealth.[27] For a very long period, in both Indo-European and Near Eastern cultures, the survival of small communities depended on livestock, and ancient Greece seems to have been no exception.[28] In the Homeric poems the households 'carried on a necessary minimum of ploughing and planting ... but it was their animals on which they depended for clothing, draft, transport, and much of their food'.[29] This socio-economic situation explains why a typical Homeric war, or a common reason to wage war, was to raid for flocks and herds; in his quarrel with Agamemnon, Achilles reproaches the king that he is fighting the Trojans on Agamemnon's behalf, as 'they have done no wrong to me. Never have they driven off my cattle or my horses' (*Il.* 1.153–154).[30]

Such therefore was the common milieu that gave life to herding metaphors.[31] Far from bucolic or exotic, as they may appear to us, the images evoked by the similes were part of the everyday experience of pastoral communities whose subsistence and wealth largely depended on livestock and whose practices were thereby integrally shaped by considering groups of humans alongside and inseparable from groups of herding animals.[32] The dynamics related to tending a flock, the role of the shepherd, and the structure and hierarchy of the herd thus afforded a powerful model not only for everyday managing of the household and the village, but also for warfare, a matter which becomes paramount to understanding their use in Homeric poems.[33] In the epic narrative flocks are representations of collectives and anonymity, 'animaux aux pluriel', such as swarms of insects and herds.[34] They are organized groups of animals, usually quite large, and like an army they move together in relatively tight ranks.

Martial herding

First, to translate the Homeric *poimena laon* as 'shepherd of the people' is to blur the specific notion that the term *laos* portrays. Whereas *demos* indicates an inhabited district, and hence the 'people' living therein, and *ethnos* refers to a multitude of individuals, which can be either humans or animals, in the *Iliad* the term *laos* has the specific military denotation of 'men, i.e. soldiers, both of the whole army and smaller divisions' (*LSJ*). As Benveniste has remarked, *laos* specifically designates 'le nom du people en tant qu'il porte les armes', whose defining characteristic is its being the retinue of the leader/shepherd.[35] The scholar sees the origin of this relationship in a social structure based on husbandry, where warfare was in the hands of '"bandes" soumises à un chef'. As with a herd or a flock, whose existence by definition depends on a shepherd, a *laos* exists in so far as there is a chief to follow. The *poimena laon* as a shepherd of a people in an army is a two-sided unity, composed of the retinue and its chief: without a *laos* there is no chief, just as there can be no shepherd without a flock. Such a hierarchical martial model is comparable to the historical Spartan *enomotiai*, the 'sworn bands', where the soldiers pledge absolute loyalty to their chief, and can be well adapted to the contingents described in the Catalogue of the second book of the *Iliad*, where the leaders (*hegemones*) and chiefs (*koiranoi*) of the many (naval) contingents are named (*Il.* 2.493 and f., on which see below). Rather than viewing each member of the metaphor on its own, therefore, it may be more instructive to envisage the shepherd-flock image as two parts of a completely interdependent relationship, that is, of a single *complementary* pattern of relationship. In this frame of reference, we can see that the flock simile and the metaphor *poimena laon* exhibit a bipolar complementary pattern of behaviour (or qualities), where, in the words of Bateson, 'the behaviour patterns at one end of the relationship are different from, but fit in with, the behaviour patterns at the other end'.[36] The patterns implied in the *poimena laon* type of relationship can be singled out as submission–dominance, obedience–command, dependence–succouring, where the army-flock exhibits obedience, submission, dependence and faithfulness, and the shepherd-leader command, dominance, leadership and deliverance.

The following passage clarifies this complementary reciprocity particularly well (*Il.* 13.492–495):

λαοὶ ἕπονθ᾽, ὡς εἴ τε μετὰ κτίλον ἕσπετο μῆλα
πιόμεν᾽ ἐκ βοτάνης: γάνυται δ᾽ ἄρα τε φρένα ποιμήν:
ὣς Αἰνείᾳ θυμὸς ἐνὶ στήθεσσι γεγήθει
ὡς ἴδε λαῶν ἔθνος ἐπισπόμενον ἑοῖ αὐτῷ.

And after them followed the host, as sheep follow after the ram
to water from the place of feeding, and the shepherd rejoices in his heart;
even so the heart of Aeneas was glad in his breast,
when he saw the throng of the host that followed after him.[37]

These lines amplify the reciprocity of a well-played pre-constructed dialogue, where the flock follows the trail of the ram, a sort of lieutenant figure of the shepherd, whose expectation is fulfilled. The leading–following dynamic is represented here in the positive emotional response of the shepherd, who rejoices in his heart, *ganytai phrena* (493), and in that of the shepherd-Aeneas who likewise feels joy in his breast in seeing his army following him.

We can apply to this passage the idea of a 'negative reciprocity' proposed by Haubold (2000: 37f.). This is inherent in the complementary nature of the relationship where only the leader is given the subjectivity of feeling, while the perspective of the sheep, emotional or otherwise, is never expressed, just as we do not know what the soldiers feel because their subjectivity is lost in the mass of troops, *ethnos laon* (495). Like the sheep, soldiers are represented 'as automaton and mindless', no mental or emotional faculty is attributed to them but fear. The underlying discourse of power behind this representation instrumentally objectifies the sheep/soldiers as passive, submissive and deprived of any agency. At this point, we face a hermeneutic pitfall: that of inadvertently constructing this slanted dialogue in the evaluative terms of 'victim-executioner' (goodies and baddies), thereby retrojecting into the Homeric world contemporary preoccupations and – more or less hidden – agendas. To this end, it is important not to lose sight of the fact that the discourse of power inherent in the complementary pattern constrains and burdens the leader/shepherd as well: the sheep's obedience and loyalty is countered by the commitment and loyalty of the shepherd, who may risk his life to rescue the flock and ward off the attack of lions and wolves. Some scholars have seen the shepherd-flock image as a lopsided relationship where the flock-army/people serves their master, the recipient of a one-way direction of benefits. This is hardly tenable: not only is it nowhere said that 'Homeric shepherds act in their own interest', but the *Iliad* gives a number of cases in which a shepherd does a risky job, and properly so.[38] In *Il.* 5.136–138, Diomedes is compared to a lion wounded by a shepherd, 'even as upon a lion that a shepherd in the field, guarding his fleecy sheep, has wounded as he leapt over the wall of the sheep-fold, but has not vanquished'. Another instance is *Il.* 17.61–69, where a long simile describes hounds and herd-men clamouring around a raging lion, and yet unable to confront him 'for pale fear takes hold on them'.

The various chiefs of the *Iliad*, with the noteworthy exception of Agamemnon, are also the most exposed on the battlefield; they are the *promachoi*, those fighting on the front line. So does emphasize Sarpedon, the demigod, son of Zeus, the doomed chief of the Licians, when he urges his cousin Glaucus to enter the foray (*Il.*12.310–321). In this passage the role of both parties within the pattern comes to the fore: unlike modern warlords, the Iliadic chief pays his privilege with a pledge to be the first in risking his life. True, such a narrative serves the ends of a hierarchic structure where the leadership of the shepherd-chief corresponds to the weakness of the flock-army, and the exclusive power of the shepherd in delivering the flock by facing predators is mirrored by that of the king/leader of the army, thus legitimizing in pastoral terms the 'rule by the one'.[39] Such rule, however, falls short of being ideal. More often than not, Iliadic shepherds and herdsmen are unable to prevail over predators (as in *Il.* 15.630–634). On this account, Haubold claims 'the shepherd of epic ... is prone to fail. The same holds true for the single agent who leads *laoi*'.[40] Such an assertion seems however far too blunt, as there are cases where shepherds clearly do not fail in guarding and saving their herds successfully: in *Il.* 5. 136–138, quoted above, a shepherd tending his sheep succeeds in wounding a lion, or in the long simile of *Il.* 12.299–309 (see below), the case of a lion who gets hit by the javelin of a herdsman upon attacking a flock is illustrated as a general possibility.

The instances where a shepherd falls short of saving the sheep, moreover, may point to an altogether different conclusion. The discourse of the *Iliad* claims that if they are left on their own, flocks and herds are helplessly doomed to massacre, a narration that stands as a blueprint for the hopeless soldiers badly tended by a witless leader. The absence or inability of a herdsman, therefore, enhances on the one hand the importance of being a good shepherd, but on the other the necessity for an army to have a shepherd at all. The crucial role of the shepherd as instrumental in guarding the sheep-soldiers from the foray of the predator-hero not only legitimizes but also 'proves' the 'natural' necessity for an army to be led by a leader. Homeric kingship is a complex and historically stratified case, but the message conveyed by herding similes is quite coherent and should be kept apart from the question of kingship and political leadership, on which the epic presents us with different models.[41] To gather, to lead, to care for and look after, to deliver, to guard and protect the flock from the attack of wolves or lions: these are the main ideas evoked in the image of the shepherd and his flock.

Prey-predators

The next association created by the representation of the army as cattle and flocks is with prey animals. The image of the prey can only be understood in tandem with their complementary partners and the third component of the similes, the predator, bane of the shepherds. Even beyond guidance and direction, the main role of the shepherd is to deliver the herd from predators.

The marauding lion threatening the enclosure of the cattle is the typical image of the hero described in his might and prowess, 'the beast of war', as a number of studies have well analysed.[42] In many of the similes we have seen, a lion attacks a flock or a herd, for example in *Il.* 12.299–309, where the most valiant Sarpedon enters the foray as a ravenous lion whose fierce moves and unchecked spirit are the object of an extended simile.[43] A comparable unhampered feat is performed by Diomedes 'the lion' in *Il.* 5.136–143, who rages in the sheep-fold, oblivious of the danger, after he receives an infusion of *menos*, 'valour', straight from Athena's hands.[44] The lion stands for a particularly brave or excellent hero (Sarpedon in the first case, Diomedes in the second), whose 'natural' prey is sheep or cattle, the simple soldiers (respectively Achaeans and Thracians). As much as the lion is heedless of danger, the prey are helpless and fearful.[45]

Yet, just as with the relationship between shepherd and flock, here too the complementary relationship holds true. The might and the *aristeia* of the hero as a wild beast are only possible when enacted in the onslaughts on the flock or the herd and are inseparable from them. The complementary pattern one–many governs both the animal image, where the one predator needs many individual prey to sate its hunger, and the martial one, where one great warrior satiates his thirst for blood by massacring countless individuals of the *laos*. The helplessness of the herd in relation to the predators recalls the necessity of a shepherd or the herdsman, who by his strategic and tactical abilities has the 'natural', legitimate and complementary function of safeguarding his army-flock in order to save as many as possible of its components.[46]

The relationship entails additional complementary qualities: courage–fear, attack–flight, single–multitude, superior–inferiors, strong–weak, mighty–helpless, agent–object. But the combined picture of the *aristoi* – lions or wolves who by their individual valour and courage slaughter hundreds of simple soldiers, whose raison d'être seems exactly to become 'cannon fodder' – is not only the basis for an army's organization into *aristoi* (lions and wolves) and sheep/soldiers, but is also instrumental in legitimizing that organization precisely by means of the animal counterparts, thus 'naturalizing' the socio-political power structure of the poems. In the words of Finley, a 'deep horizontal cleavage' characterizes Homeric society: 'above the line were the *aristoi*, literally the best people, the hereditary nobles who held most of the wealth and all the power, in peace as in war. Below were all the other[s]. . . . The gap between the two was rarely crossed except by the inevitable accidents of wars and raids.'[47] This is clearly expressed at the beginning of the Catalogue of the Ships, where the poet says, *Il.* 2.484–487:

> Tell me now, Muses that have dwellings on Olympus – [485] for you are goddesses and are at hand and know all things, whereas we hear but a rumor and know not anything – who were the captains of the Danaans and their lords. But the common folk I could not tell nor name, not though ten tongues were mine and ten mouths [490] and a voice which never breaks [. . .] Now will I tell the captains of the ships and the ships in their order.

The honour of being named and remembered is bestowed solely on captains and lords, the great men, the *aristoi*, 'below were all the other[s]', the nameless mass, to which the poet looks with an 'impersonal regard [. . .] as anonymous members of a larger group', just as with herding animals.[48]

Gender: The bull and the cattle

The appearance of a third type of subject, that is, the leading male individuals of the herd (rams and bulls) serves to illustrate a further classification among peers, the *aristeis*. In *Iliad* 2.480–483, Agamemnon gathers the entire army for review and is represented in his quality of leader of leaders as a bull standing above the cattle. The same vertical hierarchy, which simultaneously pairs and opposes the leader and the mass, the shepherd and his flock, is in this context used to articulate further the military hierarchy, where a 'best over the best' is singled out. Such a scheme duplicates the singular–collective complementary pattern analysed above, and amplifies a clear gender characterization.[49] The single, male and powerful leader, 'chiefest over all', displays his excellence through his bull-like attitude and look, which express a 'natural' superiority over the female cattle. The less powerful leaders are feminized by a dialectic of domination and subjugation.[50]

The gender discourse of male dominance is echoed again, although to a different end, in the *teichoskopia*. The old king Priam asks Helen about the warriors who stand out among the mass of soldiers, and among them he spots Odysseus, whose outward appearance reveals his command in *Il*. 3.195–198, where he is compared to a ram with thick fleece, that goes through a great flock of white ewes. Once again, sheep and cattle suffer the same fate as the human counterparts they are called to designate, women: silenced and objectified.[51]

The extensive use of pastoral imagery might lead us to think that social and economic conditions, that is, the presence of a pastoral economy, would somehow compel such a use. But if everyday experience certainly made a livestock metaphor a major possibility, indeed an affordance, we would be quite wrong in assuming a deterministic relation, as a short but significant look at tragedy will reveal.

Aeschylus' *Persians*: The shattered flock

Let us now turn our attention to tragedy, where my assertions and conclusions must necessarily lose the kind of generalization that epic allows. Not only is every playwright a world of their own, but even more so each single tragedy forms a 'semiotic cluster', and we should be careful in what we deduce. I will subsequently take my examples from one of Aeschylus' tragedies – the *Persians* – which deals with warfare and is thus comparable with the Iliadic examples.

The image of the army as a flock comes in the *parodos* (*Pers*. 73–75), where the chorus of elder Counsellors at the Persian court describe the Persian army 'as a warrior flock' (74: *poimanorion*) and its leader, Xerse, as a 'fiery lord' (73: *thourios archon*).

The *hapax legomenon* '*poimanorion*' is a most interesting word formation composed by the word *poimen*, which relates to herding, and *aner*, 'man'; the term artfully combines the animal and human element into a single identity and a single word, and parallels the Homeric *poimena laon*. The flock is 'divine' (*theion*), as its commander is an '*isotheos phos*' (74).[52] The whole passage is clearly Homeric, as is the entire representation of the Persian army.[53]

The same word formation recurs at line 241 in a context which, it seems to me, disambiguates the word's meaning. Shortly before the messenger enters the scene to report the disaster of Salamis, a rapid exchange takes place between Atossa and the Chorus, where the queen's questions allow a short yet significant description of the Athenians (241–244):

Ἄτοσσα
τίς δὲ ποιμάνωρ ἔπεστι κἀπιδεσπόζει στρατῷ;

Χορός
οὔτινος δοῦλοι κέκληνται φωτὸς οὐδ᾽ ὑπήκοοι.

Ἄτοσσα
πῶς ἂν οὖν μένοιεν ἄνδρας πολεμίους ἐπήλυδας;

Χορός
ὥστε Δαρείου πολύν τε καὶ καλὸν φθεῖραι στρατόν.

Atossa
And who is set over them as shepherd and is master of their host?

Chorus
Of no man are they called the slaves or vassals.

Atossa
How then can they withstand the attack of an invading foe?

Chorus
So well as to have destroyed Darius' great and courageous host.

Returning to Bateson, the Athenian model of relationship that emerges from the exchange between Atossa and the Chorus is of a different category altogether: 'There exists, however, a whole category of human interpersonal behaviour which does not conform to this description [complementary patterns]. We have to recognize the existence of a series of *symmetrical* patterns in which people respond to what others are doing by themselves doing something similar.'[54] The reaction created by applying the Persian–Homeric pattern of governance to the Athenian reality points to a fundamental incompatibility between the two models: the flock is shattered and every soldier is his own shepherd.

In his lecture of 8 February 1978 at the Collège de France, Foucault sets out his inquiry for what he defines 'governmentalism' by dwelling on the subject of pastoral power as a metaphor of governmentalism. He sets one image, that of governing a ship, against another, that of a shepherd of people, heralding 'pastoral power'. If the Persians are ruled by pastoral power in Foucault's terms, that is a shepherd-king, this is clearly much in keeping with Homeric style, where Agamemnon and the king in general is a *poimena laon*, that is, the symbol of the 'rule by the one', whereas the Athenians herald a new, different conception of *kratos* and thus of governmentalism, the 'rule by all', embodied in an army of peer-ranked citizens empowered by their individual responsibility and agency, a far cry from the flock-like army of Homer.

Together with flocks and shepherds, Aeschylus rejects all animal imagery as applied to the Greek side. Whereas the Persians are often described in animal terms (snake, sheep, swarm of bees, fish), the Greeks are never likened to an animal. The fact that only one of the two sides is portrayed by means of animal imagery bears on the other side vividly, by constructing an implicit opposition between animal and human.

If the tragic use of animal imagery can be considered, as differently analysed by Thumiger and Heath, as a distancing procedure for human emotions to be objectified and/or intensified, I would suggest that the animal imagery, applied by Aeschylus as it is exclusively to the enemy's side, is used to objectify the enemy, to distance them and alienate them from what is constructed as a normative map of the 'human' way of being a warrior, and thus, ultimately, a man.[55]

Conclusion

To sum up, my analysis of the herding animals from Homer to Aeschylus has allowed a number of points to emerge both in terms of animal–human relations and posthuman themes. In Homer, herding animals as well as predators are subject to a process of saming, whereby the simile of the army as an orderly herd led by their leader – and/or threatened by a predator-enemy – is the vehicle of a repeated narration about social, military and political hierarchy. In this complementary power structure, some single outstanding individuals are narrated as *naturally* born to be leading, prevailing and ruling components over a passive, submissive and dominated mass and the homology of animals and men 'is invoked to claim the perfect naturalness – and thus necessity – of a human behaviour'.[56] Seen as a larger unit with its diverse articulation analysed above, the relationship of herding animals–human resulting from Homeric examples may be seen as a fundamental device for a discourse about power and domination to be mobilized in different provinces: gender, warfare, politics. The benevolent rule of the pastoral power, furthermore, has proven a solid and long-lasting metaphor of governmentalism up to our day.

The litmus test of the *Persians* has shown us, however, that a dramatic change occurred from Homer to classical Athens in the conceptualization and representation of apparently the same subject, herding animals. Whereas Homer uses the imagery of flocks and herds to map a socio-political and military fixed hierarchy – the rule by the one – and conceptualized that hierarchy in a complementary relationship shepherd-flock/leader-army, Athenian tragedy sharply rejects pastoral imagery and submits it to a process of othering, attributing images of flocks and shepherd to the Persian enemy. The governance of a leader-shepherd is scornfully dismissed as an adequate map for Athenian territory, as well as the discourse of governmentality it implies.

In light of the above, the posthuman framework that Latour calls the 'Internal Great Divide' positing the 'separation of humans and nonhumans' and upon which Western culture is said to rest seems of no, or little consequence to understand Homer, where primary dualisms do not concern human–animal – in the Homeric worldview, a lion may be more akin to a warrior like Achilles than a simple soldier – but rather internal hierarchies – such as predators–prey – and they act within a system where they have a complementary rather than an oppositional relationship. The type of inclusive, immanent cosmology some posthuman theorists put forward where human and non-human animals are seen as deeply interconnected, bears some fundamental similarities with some Greek, 'Western' conceptions, a similarity which blunts considerably the opposition human vs. posthuman, emphasized by some posthuman grandstanding formulations, even if it does not make Homer *ipso facto* politically or ethically correct in posthuman terms, a different province altogether.[57] This may act as an important warning against generalizations or too broad an opposition.

We would be well advised not to lose sight of cultural and historical diversity and specificity, so as not to create, inadvertently, a new 'scandal of the others', colonizing ancient cultures with (ethical and etic) assumptions which, be they humanist or posthumanist, are ultimately and inevitably 'located'.

CHAPTER 7
THE SOVEREIGN AND THE BEAST: IMAGES OF ANCIENT TYRANNY

Roland Baumgarten

The title of this chapter alludes to Derrida's series of seminars from 2001 to 2003, 'The Beast and the Sovereign'.[1] The posthumous edition of these sessions can be regarded as the final outcome of Derrida's years committed to the human–animal issue and might be read as his posthuman manifesto, as it decentres the human by questioning the threshold between animal and human that has been fixed since antiquity.[2]

Although my contribution does not seek to offer an examination of Derrida's theses, it will take its starting point in one of the aspects he discussed. Derrida is not only concerned with the problematization of the human–animal border, but also with the ambivalence of animal metaphor, especially in the socio-political sphere. Equating the sovereign with the beast does not only stand for the purportedly infrahuman aspects of criminal rulership, but also for the superhuman dimension of the ruler's omnipotence:[3]

> The beast and [*et*] the sovereign, the beast is [*est*] the sovereign, that's how our couple seems first to show up, a couple [. . .] but also an alliance, almost a hymen [. . .]. Tête-à-tête or face-to-face [. . .] between, *on the one hand*, the simple conjunction (and [*et*]), which seems to pose, oppose, or juxtapose them as two species of living beings radically heterogeneous to each other, the one infrahuman, the other human or even superhuman, and, *on the other hand*, the copula (is [*est*]), which seems to couple them in a sort of ontologico-sexual attraction, a mutual fascination, a communitarian attachment, or even a narcissistic resemblance, the one recognizing in the other a sort of double, the one becoming the other, being the other (the 'is' then having the value of a process, a becoming, an identificatory metamorphosis), the beast being the sovereign, the sovereign being the beast, the one and the other being each engaged, in truth changed or even exchanged, in a becoming-beast of the sovereign or in a becoming-sovereign of the beast, the passage from the one to the other, the analogy, the resemblance, the alliance, the hymen depending on the fact that they both share that very singular position of being outlaws, above or at a distance from the law, the beast ignorant of right and the sovereign having the right to suspend right, to place himself above the law that he is, that he makes, that he institutes, as to which he decides sovereignly.[4]

Derrida's primary sources for his detailed but often meandering discussion are at first early modern thinkers like Bodin, Hobbes and Rousseau. It is only through their mediation that ancient authors or political figures come into view, such as Caligula through Rousseau,[5] although this Roman emperor who ran his own deification was already branded by ancient authors as *belua* and *monstrum*[6] and was considered a prototype of a tyrant. It is all the more surprising that Derrida only casually talks about the figure of the tyrant. He is more interested in the concept of a 'rogue', as he is obviously strongly under the impression of the first Iraq war and the fresh experience of 9/11. In these circumstances, the term 'rogue state' had been applied by the US administration to the former ally Iraq, and its autocratic ruler Saddam Hussein had been called the 'beast of Baghdad'.[7] In my contribution, however, an attempt should be made to examine Derrida's beast/sovereign couple by exploring the ancient stock character of the tyrant and its associated imagery,[8] focusing on Herodotus' *Histories* and Plato's *Republic*, but also including a short survey of the later Roman developments. The Latin term *monstrum* can serve here as a keyword. Its genuine context is divination. A *monstrum* is a phenomenon deviating from normality, a disconcerting irregularity such as a two-headed calf.[9] In Rome, such prodigies had to be reported to the senate which had to decide whether the *monstrum* had to be interpreted as an evil omen (*prodigium*) against which ritual measures like an expiation (*expiatio*) had to be taken.[10] So, the term *monstrum* refers to the problem of interpretation and thus to the problematization of taxonomies (animal/human, good/evil, etc.).

I start my short study with Herodotus who is renowned both for his fondness of oracles[11] and his catalogue of Greek and non-Greek rulers and leaders, and that is: of their faults and vices, which in extreme cases could be judged as monstrosity.[12] So, closely related to an unveiling of the oracle is the issue of an emergence of the monstrous. The ambiguity of the oracle questions taxonomies of good and evil and the way we deconstruct boundaries between animal and human: the lion-tyrant, or the hum*an*imal ruler, is, as we will see, either good or bad depending on how one reads the oracle. Therefore, reading Herodotus' the sovereign and the beast is not just about disentangling boundaries between human and beast but also about how they are re-erected and re-written.

After acquainting his audience/readers with some of the most famous rulers (Croesus, Cyrus, Cambyses, Periander and Polycrates), Herodotus stages a systematic discussion of political systems in the form of the much discussed constitutional debate.[13] In his plea for democracy and against tyranny, the Persian Otanes presents us with a short but characteristic list of stereotypical tyrannical crimes: disregard of traditional norms, rape of women, killing without trial (3, 80, 5). Both the internal and the external recipient can easily supplement this list with those transgressions which could be found in the previous narration. So, one already knows that the killing of relatives, the breaking of sexual and religious taboos, and the elimination of potential competitors (including family members) belong to the repertoire of the tyrant's misdeeds.[14] These stereotypes were an integral part of public debate, and it is such a heated debate in which Herodotus provides us with an intriguing example of the beast imagery.[15]

Athens, after the expulsion of the tyrants, has become democratic, but Sparta was anxious to support Hippias, the son of Pisistratus, in regaining the rule in Athens. But the Spartan allies, especially the Corinthians, react against this undertaking, since they condemn tyranny as the most repugnant of all forms of rule. Contrary to Otanes, Herodotus grants the Corinthian speaker Socles sufficient time to tell at length the misdeeds of Cypselus the tyrant of Corinth and his bloodthirsty son Periander who is even said to have had sexual intercourse with his dead wife Melissa.[16] Socles has to resort to such loud colours, as his addressees, the Spartans, are regarding Hippias as a potential partner who is, if not honourable, at least reliable and therefore harmless to them. Thus, Socles must make every rhetorical effort to ensure that a situation will never arise again in which the misinterpretation of warnings paves the way for a dangerous tyranny. Therefore, he is going to give us a lesson[17] on the right handling of figurative speech by quoting two oracles, which prophesied the birth of Cypselus. The second one is as follows:

Αἰετὸς ἐν πέτρῃσι κύει, τέξει δὲ λέοντα
Καρτερὸν ὠμηστήν · πολλῶν δ ὑπὸ γούνατα λύσει.

An eagle conceives in a rocky place and will give birth to a lion –
A strong, savage [literally: raw flesh eating] lion which will loosen the knees of many.[18]

In a bold image, two animals are combined, which, from the cultures of the Ancient Near East up to now, are symbols of superiority and power: the eagle and the lion. So, at first glance, the birth of a mighty ruler seems to be announced here.[19] But it is not easy to interpret oracles correctly, as every reader of Herodotus knows.[20] So, Socles points out that this oracle was first considered obscure (ἄσημον) – and that seems to be the case even for modern interpreters. It has, of course, always been stressed that the lion simile is an epic legacy. After all, there are fifty lion similes in the *Iliad* and the *Odyssey*,[21] most of which share a common model: the marauding lion as a threat to human communities and its confrontation with men and dogs.[22] This simile obviously represents the fierce attack of a warrior hero into a hostile phalanx. Thus, the simile is used to illustrate the overwhelming – one could say: superhuman – physical and mental power of heroes like Achilles, Diomedes or Hector. However, it can be considered an expression of archaic warrior ideology.

With the advent of autocratic regimes at the end of the seventh century BC and the connected civil war like conditions, this imagery is given new features. When Theognis speaks of the δημοφάγος τύραννος (1181), he combines the unhomeric word τύραννος (tyrant)[23] with a newly coined epithet: δημοφάγος (people-eater) is supposed to allude to the ὠμοφάγος λέων (raw-flesh eating lion) at Homer (*Il.* 7, 256) and thereby to evoke the image of a man-eating predator, which devours not the enemy, but his own people (δῆμος).[24] The adjective ὠμηστής (raw-flesh eating), used in the Cypselus oracle, might point in this direction too: In Homer, it is the epithet of Priam's dogs, which in his vision of the end of Troy lacerate their own lord.[25]

As interesting as such associations may be, they do not seem to me to observe accurately the exact wording of the oracle. The closest verbal parallel is not found in Homer, but in Hesiod's *Theogony* (310f.) in the list of the children of Echidna and Typhoeus:

Δεύτερον αὖτις ἔτικτεν ἀμήχανον, οὔ τι φατειόν,
Κέρβερον ὠμηστήν, Ἀίδεω κύνα χαλκεόφωνον

second, she [i.e., Echidna] then gave birth to something intractable, unspeakable,
Cerberus who eats raw flesh, the bronze-voiced dog of Hades.[26]

As in the Kypselos oracle, the verb in the first line is τίκτειν, and the beginning of the second line sounds almost identical: Καρτερὸν ὠμηστήν – Κέρβερον ὠμηστήν (the strong raw-flesh eater – the raw-flesh eating Cerberus). In this oracle phrase, therefore, a puzzle may be hidden which any connoisseur of Hesiod can solve. If, in the second verse of the Cypselus oracle, καρτερόν is replaced by Κέρβερον, the lion changes, from the end of the first line to the beginning of the second line, to the well-known underworld monster. The lion of the Cypselus oracle is therefore only a pseudo-lion – which may not be surprising, given his birth from an eagle. It is a hybrid being like the kinship of Cerberus described by Hesiod.[27] There, the mother of these monsters, Echidna, is characterized as an ambivalent being in the proper sense: half a beautiful young woman, half a monster (295: πέλωρον)[28] and equally ὠμηστής (300) as his breed. And she is not only the mother of Cerberus, but also the grandmother of the κρατερή Chimaera (320) who in turn gave birth to the Nemean lion, a 'bane for human beings' (πῆμ' ἀνθρώποισι, 329). That this monster catalogue lends itself to exploitation for political purposes is demonstrated by the epithet of the male producer of monsters: Typhoeus is not only terrible (δεινός), but also outrageous (ὑβριστής)[29] and lawless or 'outlaw' (ἄνομος) (307). The oracle cited by Socles as an effective prelude to his speech can thus be understood as a condensed form of the tyrannical stereotype clothed in riddle language, but it might also point to a particularly insidious aspect of the mode tyrants prefer to appear in. Like Echidna, the tyrant cannot always be seen in his abhorrent appearance, often he is himself a ἄσημος, that is, when he turns his sweet side to the viewer. Herodotus does not hide positive aspects of the Greek tyrannical regimes.[30] Also in the case of Hippias, one does not easily perceive his eventual monstrousness. Thus, the ἄσημον χρηστήριον can be regarded as programmatic for Herodotus' portrayal of Greek and non-Greek autocrats. It does not follow a monotonous stereotype but a discourse that strives to make the vexing multifariousness of the protean form of the ruler discernible.[31] The multifariousness of the autocrat engenders the condition of the ruler as a being which occupies a place between the human and the monstrous: the figure of the tyrant plays out the becoming beast of the sovereign and the becoming sovereign of the beast. The monstrousness of the tyrant figure as something hidden and multiform makes it difficult to capture.

That Herodotus is interested in the tension between the seemingly positive and the hidden dark side of the autocrat can be seen in the way he organized Socles' argumentation, for the already quoted oracle is preceded by yet another one.[32] Here, the oracle tells of a 'boulder' (ὀλοοίτροχος),[33] who will roll in a group of 'sole rulers' (ἀνδράσι μουνάρχοισι), and will set Corinth 'into law' (δικαιώσει). With all the figurative language of the second verse, the third is clearly marked by political vocabulary. This oracle sounds rather as if the birth of a future political reformer, an αἰσυμνήτης, is announced, who will abolish a tyrannical oligarchy – ἀνδράσι μουνάρχοισι may refer to the Bacchiad rule in Corinth – and help justice to break through.[34]

Taking these two oracles together, the Bacchiads seem to think that they have now the right key for the interpretation of the prophecies. Yet, they do not recognize in the lion the monster breed, but an 'heroic' avenger who will call them to account. So, they take the oracles as an appeal to action, but when they seek to eliminate this threat, they do not find a lion cub, but a baby who is looking at them with a friendly smile, which moves them to pity.[35] Their mistake is to cling to the surface of oracular language and not to hear the Hesiodean undertones. If the Bacchiads had understood that an ὠμηστής can have the ambivalent, and seemingly charming form of an Echidna, they might have acted without hesitation.

This interpretation of the Cypselus oracles has some consequences for the assessment of the reliability of Herodotus as a historical source and it draws attention to the role of the oracular tradition in understanding historical events. Barely one commentator assumes that the Socles speech is authentic, but there is an intensive discussion on how the cited oracles[36] may have come into being. However, what makes us certain that the wording of an oracle should be more authentic than that of a political speech or an account of a king's dream? The two Cypselus oracles seem to me so well fitted into the context that at least a revision by Herodotus cannot be ruled out. Such a procedure would not have been indecent. The wording of oracles was by no means sacrosanct. What mattered was the message as such.[37] So, Herodotus would have applied here only the method, which Thucydides asserts for his speeches, that is sticking to the basic statement, the ξυμπάση γνώμη (1, 22, 1). It is precisely this basic form Herodotus uses to provide the prophecy of the birth of another mighty man: Agariste, the daughter of Cleisthenes tyrant of Sicyon and future mother of Pericles, is said to have dreamed of giving birth to a lion (6, 131). How such a terse utterance itself can become a χρηστήριον ἄσημον, everyone can marvel at when looking at the history of the reception of this account: The interpretations range from Herodotus as a Pericles supporter to a harsh Pericles critic.[38] However, the recipient who has learned his lesson in book 5 should not have forgotten it in book 6. My interpretation of Socles' speech can help to support those of Strasburger[39] and his followers who wanted to see here less of an obvious warning against a return of the Pisistratids than a covert warning against the tyrannical rule of the Athenian empire and its leader Pericles. The difficulty of correctly assessing the Athens of the fifth century is due not least to the fact that it could be stylized as a powerful lion in the struggle against the Persian archenemy, but at the same time could appear as an ambivalent monster, both the Athens of the Thucydidean Epitaphios and of his Melos dialogue.[40] But there is also a sort of tragic irony in the Herodotean Socles. In succeeding in preventing the return of the tyrant to Athens he paves the way for a quite dangerous smiling baby: the newborn Athenian democracy.[41]

Also Plato's discussion of tyranny is centred on an ambivalence that ties together the beast and the sovereign in an intimate bond: in the *Republic*, 'the becoming sovereign of the beast and the becoming beast of the sovereign' shapes a discourse on what it means to be human and animal. The background for all this, the question of good and bad rule, has preoccupied Plato during all his life and work.[42] Here I pick out only those elements that can prove Plato's creative dealings with the imagery I discussed. When, in the second book, Socrates describes the character qualities of the newly introduced warrior class, the so-called 'guardians' (φύλακες) from which the philosophical rulers are later to emerge, he does not use the image of the lion but that of a γενναῖος σκύλαξ, a (young) noble dog (375a). This imagery is supposed to stand for the 'spirited' (θυμοειδής) nature of the young guards. Socrates does not neglect to discuss both the advantages and disadvantages of such a nature, which evidently points to the ambiguity of this simile. On the one hand, a θυμοειδής embodies the qualities of the classical hero, he has the necessary fighting spirit (θυμός) so that he will be insuperable in battle (ἄμαχος τε καὶ ἀνίκητος). Yet, there is always the danger that he, being wild and fierce (ἄγριος), will turn against his fellow citizens (375 b), thus contributing to the self-destruction of his own community. To exclude this from the outset, the dog must have a 'philosophical nature' (φιλόσοφος τὴν φύσιν, 375 e), that is in some sense he must be a rational animal. The guard dog is a predator like the lion and it needs the fierceness of the lion to fulfil its task, but it is a domesticated one, able to discern between enemy and friend (376 ab).[43] As this image of the philosophical dog tells us, a good dog is a domesticated dog. When it comes to the animal part of the ruler, the animal part itself is never denied; what we see here is that it makes a difference what kind of animal part it is. To be a good ruler, one has to be a good guardian, a good dog; the good ruler shares not only the ability to be watchful, but also the domestication of the 'philosophical' dog. So, the good ruler is not only a domesticated ruler, but also a domesticated philosopher.[44] Already here we can see that the hum*an*imal analogy is at the core of the argument structure of the *Republic*.[45] If the political imagery of the 'good guardian dog' is an expression of the *condicio humana*, thinking about how a well-ordered society must be shaped relates the question of what makes a human being human at all to the question of the animal.

Analogy plays a major role also in books 8 and 9, where Socrates explicitly parallels the structure of the *polis* with that of the soul. For him, the tyrant is the embodiment of the worst state form and the symbol for the worst condition of the human soul. So, the man who wishes to exercise absolute dominion over others is surrendered to the rule of his desires. This happens because someone who does not consider himself as standing in relation with others, but views others as his property and thus an extension of himself, is not in a position to establish a relationship with others, but remains stuck in an autocratic solipsism of personal passions and desires.

To illustrate that, Plato is using extensively the imagery of beasts in book 9, which is devoted to the description of the tyrannical man. Right at the beginning of this description, Socrates tells us that a person who has problems with restraining his desires will first, in dream form, let free 'the beastly and savage part' of his soul (τὸ θηριῶδές τε καὶ ἄγριον, 571c) and thereby will dream of sexual aberrations like sex with his mother or animals; he is even haunted by cannibalistic fantasies that recall the Theognidean δημοφάγος τύραννος. The somewhat cryptic formulation 'no meat it will not eat' (βρώματος ἀπέχεσθαι μηδενός, 571d) refers to 565d–566a, where the transformation of the 'champion of the people' (δήμου προστάτης) into a τύραννος is paralleled with the transformation of a man into a werewolf, a transformation triggered by tasting human innards from a sacrificial altar.[46]

The account culminates in an image of the soul, which processes all the so far mentioned elements of the beast and monster imagery (588b–589b). The tripartite division of the soul into ἐπιθυμητικόν (desiring), θυμοειδές (spirited) and λόγιστικον (rational) is connected to the images of the hybrid hell monsters Chimaera, Scylla and Cerberus[47] for the ἐπιθυμητικόν (588c), of the lion for the θυμοειδές and of 'man' for the λόγιστικόν (588d). So, man is in its interior a composite being in which the specifically human, rational element is accompanied by a non-human one. Because the latter is subordinated to the human, it is in the proper sense of the word infrahuman. But Plato does not leave it at this quite common two-part division – he subdivides the 'infrahuman' part. The not only wild and ruthless, but rather monstrous desires are opposed to an area that is to be regarded as ambivalent, and precisely in order to emphasize this ambivalence Plato does not use the image of the domesticated dog, which he has created for the young guardians in book 2, but that of the well-known lion. This new combination of the monster and beast image delivers a new image for the self-destructive aspects of the tyrant's life: If the lion is left to itself, the monster and the lion intertwine and entangle themselves. This struggling points to a psychological conflict which is far more dangerous in its effects than the ordinary form of being driven by lower appetites as described for the democratic man (560b–561e). For the tyrant possesses a strong leonine character, which gives him the necessary aggressiveness in the pursuit of his goals, but, on the other hand, pushes him towards a self-destructive competition in his pursuit of his desires and power.

What are the consequences of these insights? If one follows Socles' advice, tyrants are to be eliminated, that is to be kept outside the boundaries of the community by exile or killing. But this would be difficult to apply to the human soul. The living human being, as a composite being, has no choice but to cope both with the lion and the monster. To this end, human reason has to domesticate the lion in such a way that he can use it as a companion in order to curb the wild elements (τὰ ἄγρια, 589b) of the hybrid monster. This model of the human soul does not deny that animal and bestial, even monstrous aspects, are part of the human. Here again we see how animality is a defining part of the human but also we see again the importance of domestication: only the human who embodies the domesticated lion is good. By deconstructing the dichotomy of human and animal, sovereign and beast, the Platonic discourse remaps the hum*an*imal boundary.

To take the Platonic lion-monster as an allusion to Alcibiades is far more appropriate than to refer it to the common tyrant stereotype.[48] Alcibiades is not only an individual torn between striving for honour and pleasure, as Plato presented him in the *Symposium* (216ab), but also a representative of a form of government which is much closer to Plato's contemporaries than the tyrants of the Archaic period or the far away Syracuse: a democracy which over time can become a tyranny. No doubt, the Platonic lion corresponds to the traditional warrior and ruler symbol. To become a danger to its own community, it is in need of interaction with the multifarious and multi-headed beast (θηρίον ποικίλον καὶ πολυκέφαλον, 588c). It is evident that the hybrid monster is not only part of every human soul, but also corresponds to the *demos*, which is likewise composed of wild, but also tame elements.[49] If this *demos* comes into contact with political leaders such as Alcibiades, we'll get, to use a modern metaphor, an explosive mixture. So, Plato's tyrant discourse in the *Republic* aims not so much at describing the disastrous moral condition of actual tyrants, but rather the problematic ambivalence of such lion-like men as Alcibiades. For it is the lion-man as a vital element in the political sphere who is the preferred recipient of the Platonic education programme. It is difficult to tame him, that is to turn him from a potentially raging beast to a vigorous and spirited domestic dog which is prone to right reasoning, but, if successful, the entire *polis* can benefit from such a transformation because it is the only way to keep the ἀμήχανος monster of the *demos* under control. Therefore, not elimination, but cooperation and integration are announced, based on the right use of strength (κράτος). In this light, the tyrant and the beast make us ponder the opposition between being and becoming: domestication is about becoming something else, from the wild to the civilized subject of the *polis*, which does not eliminate monstrosity but tames it. If anthropocentrism is a necessary implication of domestication, in the passage from savage to civilized, at the same time Plato is offering a deconstruction of the idea because monstrosity cannot be eliminated but only tamed.

It is the other renowned pupil of Socrates, Xenophon, who provides us with the best example of such a successful integration. Taking on from the sophist Prodicus the myth of Hercules at the crossroads, he established a new icon, Hercules, as the representative of a more rational, not only warlike virtue.[50] In the aftermath, Hercules' fight against the monsters of the Hesiodic catalogue becomes both psychologized and politicized, so that on the one hand his more or less human opponents were historically reinterpreted as tyrants, which in turn makes possible the equation: monster or beast = tyrant. But on the other hand, the fight could also be interpreted allegorically or psychologically, as a simile for self-control (ἐγκράτεια) and thus as a struggle of the heroic *logos* against the tyrannical *epithymiai*.[51] The conceptualization of monstrosity is always on the verge of emerging in the human and, therefore, the representation of the human as someone who has to struggle for self-control of its own monstrosity draws attention to the limitations of humans' own intentionality. The anthropocentrism inherent to the idea of the self-controlled human being does not give us back the image of the human as essentially human but rather the idea of the self-controlled human who is inevitably co-inhabited by the monstrous.[52]

I will close with a short look at Rome, where we can see that Cicero is equally fond of the tyrant stereotype, which has become a standard motif of the exercises in rhetorical schools.[53] In this way he used these stereotypes in the *Verrine Orations*.[54] But when describing the pernicious influence of Catiline on the Roman youth in *Pro Caelio* (12–14), he combines the 'divinatory' *monstrum* with elements of Plato's image of the tyrannical soul, especially its multiformity (*varia et multiplex natura*). So, the would-be tyrant Catiline is able to present himself as a virtuous man, especially a good warrior (so to say, as a lion), but in reality, he is torn inside by his overwhelming desires.

Cicero had prevented Catiline from destroying the Roman *res publica*, but he failed to stop Caesar. When asking which tyrant image Caesar will decide on, Pisistratus or Phalaris,[55] he seems to see for Rome only the alternative between a somehow civilized or a bestial tyrant, and after Caesar's assassination he uses the image of the latter to denigrate his regime.[56] But at the time of writing the letter to Atticus he may have been less concerned with a frightening tyranny of a Phalaris-*belua* than with the question as to whether Caesar would seek to establish an open tyranny as *rex* or a more covert one in the manner of the Herodotean Pericles lion:[57] Pisistratus was well known for not abolishing the existing constitution,[58] a strategy that was meant to be reissued in the *res publica restituta* of the *princeps* Augustus.[59] So, Cicero tries to cope with the ἄσημος Caesar by using – or better: re-writing – traditional taxonomies, a problem which the Roman historians of the imperial age are still confronted with when they seek to classify their – in the Derridaean sense – sovereign emperors who are placed outside or above the never formally abolished republican constitution. But ultimately these figures elude simple access. Tacitus' Tiberius remains an oracle hard to interpret for the senatorial environment, a sovereign who, in his last years of life, secluded on Capri, in a true den of iniquity, transformed into a monstrous beast haunted by all the vices of the Platonic tyrant. But what is real here, what literary design? And what do we do with Suetonius' self-staging expert Nero who is said to have performed in the amphitheatre once as a lion killer in the outfit of Heracles, that is in the pose of a superhuman *euergetes*, and at another time to have attacked the genitals of prisoners while wearing the skin of a wild animal?[60] The emphatic demarcation against the animal is protective of the *humanum* and thus becomes the core prerequisite for a humane rule. The most unsettling representations of the bestial tyrants Caligula, Nero and Domitian were created at a time when the empire was ruled by 'good' emperors. But even this classification is of course a question of perspective. Trajan, honoured by the Roman senate as *optimus princeps*, fought bitter wars against the Dacians and Parthians, and his successor, Hadrian, the aesthete on the emperor's throne, launched a massacre in Judea to suppress the Bar Kochba revolt to which over 500,000 Jews fell victim. The borderlines are fluid, the ambiguities remain.

* * *

In Herodotus and Plato the image of the tyrant is ambivalent and embedded in a discourse of humanimality: the animal within the ruler (lion in Herodotus; dog and lion in Plato) is always on the verge of emerging, thus opening a space for the becoming sovereign of the beast and the becoming beast of the sovereign. Whereas in Herodotus, the political imagery of the lion-autocrat is framed as oracular – and thus points to humanimality as something difficult to comprehend – in Plato, it defines a discourse of shared human and animal domestication necessary for good political order. Finally, for Cicero, a field of aporetic tensions arises from the task of re-writing traditional taxonomies of the Roman Republican constitution within the context of Roman imperial rule. As my examples have shown, Cicero's prose unfolds the semantic panoply of the word *monstrum* for political castings of the sovereign as beast, hinging on sovereignty's oracular qualities, which leaves open the ambiguities of narrating imperial rule, and which emerge as such in particular in the light of Derrida's late writings.

PART II
THE MONSTROUS

CHAPTER 8
TYPHOEUS OR COSMIC REGRESSION (*THEOGONY* 821–880)
Jenny Strauss Clay

Our theme here is the monstrous, the anomalous, the disruptive. I will leave to others the more theoretical aspects of the emerging field of monster studies, which are, after all, attempts to define and situate the human – even in the context of the so-called posthuman.[1] The early Greeks were especially interested in defining the human in relation to the super- and sub-human, in both their art and in their myths. Hesiod's *Theogony*, which recounts the genesis of the cosmos and genealogies of the gods from their first beginnings until the establishment of Zeus's order, contains perhaps the first sustained reflections on the monstrous. At several stages of the evolution of the cosmos, distinct groups of monsters emerge: the earliest are two pairs of triplets, the Cyclopes and the Hundred-handers. Unlike their siblings, the Titans, who are also the offspring of Gaia and Ouranos, they are not anthropomorphic, or more correctly, they are theomorphic.[2] In describing the Cyclopes, Hesiod is quite explicit (142–145):

οἱ δ' ἤτοι τὰ μὲν ἄλλα θεοῖς ἐναλίγκιοι ἦσαν,
μοῦνος δ' ὀφθαλμὸς μέσσῳ ἐνέκειτο μετώπῳ·
Κύκλωπες δ' ὄνομ' ἦσαν ἐπώνυμον, οὕνεκ' ἄρά σφεων
κυκλοτερὴς ὀφθαλμὸς ἔεις ἐνέκειτο μετώπῳ.

Indeed, in other respects they resembled the gods,
But a solitary eye lies upon the middle of their face;
And their names fittingly were Cyclopes, because
Their single circular eye lies on their face.

Defining the monstrous turns out to be divergence from the theomorphic (which turns out also to be the anthropomorphic); if the Cyclopes are under-endowed with eyes, their brothers, the Hundred-handers, not only have an excessive number of hands, but also fifty heads. Both groups are also characterized by their horrendous strength, which in the final dispensation will be integrated and guarantees the stability of Zeus's regime; the Hundred-handers will play a crucial role in the defeat of the Titans, while the Cyclopes will supply Zeus with the thunderbolts which make him invincible. Another group of monsters emerges somewhat later in the development of the cosmos, but for the most part they intermarry and keep their monstrousness to themselves.[3] Many of them are killed by the heroes while others abide, but at the remote corners of the earth so they no longer trouble neither gods nor men; the monstrous does not completely disappear, but must somehow be accommodated. Perhaps order cannot exist without these emblems of disorder. Thus the monstrous, anomalous and disruptive are either coopted or rendered harmless under Zeus's tutelage.

With the figure of Typhoeus the monstrous suddenly irrupts again at a much later stage and disrupts the orderly pacification of Zeus's cosmos. Indeed that pacification appeared to be complete with the defeat of the Titans and the appointment of the Hundred-handers as their prison wardens. But the unexpected recrudescence of the monstrous in a world which appeared to have received its final order is a reminder that its dissolution remains a possibility and that the monstrous always abides in some form.

With his multiple body parts, hybridity, bizarre sound effects and fifty fire-breathing heads, Typhoeus seems perfectly to embody the chaotic and the anarchic, uncontrolled and uncontrollable. Although he occurs elsewhere as an emblem of disorder in Pindar, Aeschylus and the *Homeric Hymn to Apollo*, here I will be engaging solely with his manifestation in Hesiod's *Theogony*.[4] His very presence there has been deemed anomalous – not to say monstrous – by generations of scholars and critics who see the whole passage as inorganic and as an intrusion into the Hesiodic text.[5] One might, in fact, give some thought to what constitutes a textual anomaly: 'inorganic' suggests a notion of a text that violates textual norms by doubling or multiplying features or importing bits and pieces that do not fit some real or imagined canonical model. In the case of the Typhoeus episode, the main reasons for such a judgement are that it is an unnecessary and redundant doublet of the Titanomachy that precedes it.[6] And indeed many of the terms that describe the two conflicts are similar: the involvement of all areas of the cosmos in the confrontation (693–710 ~ 839–52), the two distinct phases of the battle (665–686, 687–719 ~ 821–852, 853–868) and the decisive victory due to Zeus's thunderbolts (687–693 ~ 853–858). Perhaps the point here is that the forces of disorder all resemble one another. Second, the defeat of Typhoeus is not mentioned in the immediate sequel which seems to pick up from the end of the Titanomachy (881–885):

αὐτὰρ ἐπεί ῥα πόνον μάκαρες θεοὶ ἐξετέλεσσαν,
Τιτήνεσσι δὲ τιμάων κρίναντο βίηφι,
δή ῥα τότ' ὤτρυνον βασιλευέμεν ἠδὲ ἀνάσσειν
Γαίης φραδμοσύνῃσιν Ὀλύμπιον εὐρύοπα Ζῆν
ἀθανάτων· ὁ δὲ τοῖσιν ἐὺ διεδάσσατο τιμάς.

But when the blessed gods had completed their toils,
And stripped the Titans of their honors by force,
Then they urged Olympian wide-seeing Zeus to be king
And to rule in accordance with the advice of Gaia.

Third, Gaia's role in giving birth to the monster appears to contradict her benign role both before the Titanomachy, where she supports Zeus by advising him that his victory depends on his releasing the Hundred-handers (624–628), and afterwards, when she advises the gods to elect Zeus as their king (883–885). To justify the passage on the grounds that Hesiod is incorporating Near Eastern traditions, or more generally dragon-slaying myths, as some do, is no defence at all; nor is it sufficient to claim that, since Zeus's triumph over the Titans required the help of the Hundred-handers, Zeus's defeat of an opponent one-on-one was required to ensure his supremacy.[7]

I suggest we look afresh at the passage through the wider lens of the cosmogonic programme of the *Theogony* and try to grasp its function within the overall economy of the poem and, rather than smoothing over its anomalies, embrace them as necessary components that contribute to its meaning. So: Zeus has defeated the Titans who have been consigned to Tartarus from which they cannot escape. The lengthy description of Tartarus that immediately precedes the Typhoeus episode reveals the architecture and function of the nether world, not only as a prison for the defeated Titans, but also to provide a useful occupation for the potentially dangerous Hundred-handers as their guardians; it also supplies a domicile for Night and several members of her destructive brood and even gives the monstrous Cerberus a useful job as gatekeeper of Hades (717–819); Styx too is accommodated in the lower depth and, through her oath, performs a crucial role in the smooth functioning of Olympus by providing a mechanism for dealing with strife and quarrels among the gods (767–806). Primal Chaos too, the empty space that rendered cosmogony possible, is confined, diminished and transformed into the *chasma mega* (740), the region between earth and the floor of Tartarus in Zeus's final dispensation.

The overthrow of the Titans thus leads into the organization of the underworld; the last part of the cosmos is now subsumed and stabilized under the rule of Zeus. At this point, something quite surprising happens that has precipitated the scholarly controversy outlined above: Gaia mates with Tartarus to produce the monster Typhoeus who intends to 'rule over gods and men' (837) and hence to topple Zeus from power. Gaia's role here is not contradictory as has been claimed, but rather totally in keeping with her character.[8] She has always promoted progress and change and consistently taken the side of the younger: she spurred on Kronos to castrate his father; in turn she prevented Zeus from being swallowed up by his father. In bringing forth her youngest and presumably last son, she behaves in a fully consistent manner. In an act of rebellion and desperation – since who is left for her to mate with? – she mates with Tartarus. It is unpersuasive to see this action as somehow benign. Blaise argues that 'Gaia opposes Zeus, as she did Ouranos and Cronos, when the order she has helped to establish is on the point of becoming immobile and sterile and thus attacks her very nature'.[9] It is difficult to see immobile sterility setting in under Ouranos and Cronos. She further argues that Gaia's union with Tartarus serves to bring the nether regions under Zeus's control.[10] But this has surely already happened as a consequence of the Titanomachy, where Zeus's will is operative (cf. 730), and he appoints the Hundred-handers to be the guardians of the imprisoned Titans.

The bizarre mating of Gaia and Tartarus takes us back to the very origins of cosmogony where along with Chaos, Gaia and Eros, 'murky Tartara in the recess of Earth of the broad ways' (Τάρταρά τ' ἠερόεντα μυχῷ χθονὸς εὐρυοδείης, 119) came into being.[11] In the course of the developing cosmos, Tartarus has been transformed from a primordial neuter plural, a component or feature of Gaia, into a masculine singular (682, 725, 736 = 807, 822, 868, but cf. τάρταρα γαίης, 841) and therefore capable of becoming her mate. While reminiscent of the parthenogenesis of Ouranos and Pontos with whom Gaia subsequently also mates incestuously, nevertheless this union is different: at once, more primordial since Tartarus is part of Gaia, and more advanced since the union involves sexual intercourse and the forward-looking phrase, first used here: ἐν φιλότητι διὰ χρυσῆν Ἀφροδίτην (821). We find ourselves, then, at a strange temporal crossroads, where a recrudescence of the primeval irrupts into the evolved universe.

Typhoeus, the product of this union, closely resembles his nephews and nieces, the offspring of Keto and Phorkys who represent, as I have argued elsewhere, a kind of anti-cosmos that comes on to the cosmic stage at a relatively early phase of the universe's evolution (270–335).[12] For the most part, the monster catalogue is characterized by endogamous unions with the monsters mating with each other, but Typhoeus' mating with Echidna is an exception, and that union produces further monsters (306–333). He shares with them his hybridity, multiplication of body parts, as well as his snake-like and fiery features and thus is a throwback to an earlier more chaotic period of cosmogony (823–835); he likewise resembles the powerful primordial offspring of Gaia and Ouranos, the Cyclopes and the Hundred-handers, but these have, as mentioned above, already been coopted into Zeus's regime.[13] At this later date, Typhoeus becomes a kind of anti-Zeus threatening to undermine the emerging order of Zeus in the evolving cosmos.[14] But Typhoeus' peculiar feature, which receives extended elaboration, is his multiple voices, some comprehensible, others alternatingly frightening (roaring bull and lion) and ridiculous (puppies), thus uniting the sub-human and the super-human. The disordered racket that emanates from Typhoeus' multiple heads and dark tongues offers a raucous anarchic counterpoint to the songs of the Muses, songs that celebrate the coming to be of the cosmos, the ordered universe, and the triumph of Zeus that 'delight the great mind of their father on Olympus' (37).[15] The Muses' harmonious song stands in opposition to the cacophony of the monster's voices, which produce a bizarre chorus of divine and bestial sounds. We may note the similarity to the garland wrought by Hephaestus to crown the Plastic Woman, which contains 'the many monsters that land and sea nurture . . . wondrous, resembling living voices' (κνώδαλ' ὅσ' ἤπειρος δεινὰ τρέφει ἠδὲ θάλασσα . . . θαυμάσια, ζωοῖσιν ἐοικότα φωνήεσσιν, 582–584). The Woman brings along into the human sphere an emblem of the disordered anti-cosmos of which Typhoeus is the divine avatar. On the other hand, at a certain point in human history, the hybrid heroes destroyed the hybrid monsters and thus showed themselves to be a civilizing force.[16] As monster-slayers, Herakles and others had managed to rid the world of their noxious powers and acquired glory for themselves. As will emerge, however, in the case of Typhoeus, no new hero will arise to defeat him. Facets of the monster's chaotic nature will abide and continue to be inflicted on mankind.

But to return to the question of the Typhoeus episode as a whole, besides the auditory dimension of the monster, is there really much to distinguish it from the preceding Titanomachy or must we concede that it is little more than a doublet of the latter as critics have maintained? The claim that Zeus requires the help of the Hundred-handers in the Titanomachy but faces Typhoeus one on one is not quite accurate. In fact it is only when Zeus intervenes and unleashes his thunderbolts that the tide of the battle with the older gods is decisively turned (687, 711). At the very climax of his intervention, we are offered a vision of the undoing of all that has been constructed in the course of cosmogony (700–705):

εἴσατο δ' ἄντα
ὀφθαλμοῖσιν ἰδεῖν ἠδ' οὔασιν ὄσσαν ἀκοῦσαι
αὔτως, ὡς ὅτε γαῖα καὶ οὐρανὸς εὐρὺς ὕπερθε
πίλνατο· τοῖος γάρ κε μέγας ὑπὸ δοῦπος ὀρώρει,
τῆς μὲν ἐρειπομένης, τοῦ δ' ὑψόθεν ἐξεριπόντος·
τόσσος δοῦπος ἔγεντο θεῶν ἔριδι ξυνιόντων.

It seemed to one
Who had eyes to see or ears to hear
Just as when Earth and broad Sky above
Piled up on each other; for such was the great din that arose

Of her collapsing, and of him collapsing from on high:
Such was the din of the gods coming together in strife.

The initial separation of Heaven and Earth is in danger of being undone through a retrogression to that primeval critical moment that permitted the unfolding of the cosmos.

So how, besides being a duel, does the battle with Typhoeus differ? It differs first because the line of Typhoeus has played no direct role in the Succession Myth but poses a threat from a distinct and altogether unique line of Gaia and Tartarus, a line of which he is the sole representative. But perhaps of greater importance is the nature of the conflict. Zeus, as previously in the Titanomachy, fights with his thunderbolts; however, unlike the Titans who like their opponents, the Hundred-handers, share a primitive weaponry in throwing rocks at each other much like Homer's Cyclops, Typhoeus also fights with fire. In the description of the monster, fire is twice mentioned as emanating from his eyes and his heads (825–828).[17] As previously in the Titanomachy, all parts of the cosmos are blanketed in a universal conflagration (839–849):

ἀμφὶ δὲ **γαῖα**
σμερδαλέον κονάβησε καὶ **οὐρανὸς** εὐρὺς ὕπερθε
πόντός τ' **Ὠκεανοῦ** τε ῥοαὶ καὶ **τάρταρα γαίης**.
ποσσὶ δ' ὕπ' ἀθανάτοισι μέγας πελεμίζετ' **Ὄλυμπος**
ὀρνυμένοιο ἄνακτος· ἐπεστονάχιζε δὲ **γαῖα**.
καῦμα δ' ὑπ' ἀμφοτέρων κάτεχεν ἰοειδέα **πόντον**
...
ἔζεε δὲ **χθὼν** πᾶσα καὶ **οὐρανὸς** ἠδὲ **θάλασσα**·

Round about
Earth made a dreadful racket and broad **Sky** above
And the **Sea** and the streams of **Ocean** and the **Tartarean** regions of Earth.
And great **Olympus** shook under the immortal feet
Of its lord as he arose; and **Earth** groaned.
...
Burning from both of them possessed the dark **sea**;
The whole **earth** boiled and the **sky** and the **sea**.

But what sets this encounter apart from the earlier Titanomachy is a crucial difference: here fire battles fire, Zeus's celestial fire confronts Typhoeus' subterranean fire as the chiasmus of lines 845–846 vividly brings out:

βροντῆς τε στεροπῆς τε *πυρός τ' ἀπὸ τοῖο πελώρου*
πρηστήρων ἀνέμων **τε κεραυνοῦ τε φλεγέθοντος**·

The thunder and lightning [of Zeus] and *the fire from the monster*
and tempestuous winds [*Typhoeus*] and **the fiery bolts**.

The celestial fire that belongs to Zeus is the product of the Cyclopes who are usually assigned a place under the earth and associated with volcanic phenomena (cf. *Il.* 2. 782–783).

Hesiod tells us that they had earlier been released from their subterranean bonds by Zeus (503–506):

> οἵ οἱ ἀπεμνήσαντο χάριν εὐεργεσιάων,
> δῶκαν δὲ βροντὴν ἠδ' αἰθαλόεντα κεραυνὸν
> καὶ στεροπήν· τὸ πρὶν δὲ πελώρη Γαῖα κεκεύθει·
> τοῖς πίσυνος θνητοῖσι καὶ ἀθανάτοισιν ἀνάσσει.
>
> And they were mindful of the thanks owed for his benefactions,
> And they gave him thunder and fiery bolts
> And lightening, which huge Gaia had previously hidden.
> And, trusting in these, he rules over gods and men.

Subterranean fire, then, seems to be a primordial possession of Gaia, lodging in her innermost recesses. Zeus receives a share of it as a gift for liberating the Cyclopes, but apparently some remained still available within Gaia and characterizes the fiery nature of her final offspring who is in a sense the product of her union with her own lower depths. This explains a puzzling phenomenon that goes back to the very beginnings of the *Theogony*: the instrument that allows the unfolding of the cosmos. The sickle that liberates Gaia from the suffocating embrace of Ouranos appears rather suddenly and is the first object to be made rather than born in the poem (161–162):

> αἶψα δὲ ποιήσασα γένος πολιοῦ ἀδάμαντος
> τεῦξε μέγα δρέπανον καὶ ἐπέφραδε παισὶ φίλοισι.
>
> Quickly having made the element (*genos*) of grey adamant,
> She wrought a great sickle and showed it to her children.

Hesiod does not explain whence Gaia produced this adamant, presumably a very hard metal, which shares the epithet 'grey' with iron; nor how she was able to form it into a sickle. But it is difficult to conceive of its fabrication without fire, the hidden fire that resides within her, with which the Greeks were well acquainted through their familiarity with volcanic activity.[18]

To return to our passage and the Typhonomachy: its finale first describes the incineration of Typhoeus (857–861), but then focuses on the melting of Earth (861–868):

> πολλὴ δὲ πελώρη καίετο γαῖα
> αὐτμῇ θεσπεσίῃ, καὶ ἐτήκετο κασσίτερος ὣς
> τέχνῃ ὑπ' αἰζηῶν ἐν ἐυτρήτοις χοάνοισι
> θαλφθείς, ἠὲ σίδηρος, ὅ περ κρατερώτατός ἐστιν,
> οὔρεος ἐν βήσσῃσι δαμαζόμενος πυρὶ κηλέῳ
> τήκεται ἐν χθονὶ δίῃ ὑφ' Ἡφαίστου παλάμῃσιν·
> ὣς ἄρα τήκετο γαῖα σέλαι πυρὸς αἰθομένοιο.
>
> Huge Earth burned fiercely
> With the awesome blast, and she melted like tin
> In pierced crucibles, heated by the craft of men,

Or like iron, which is the strongest of all,
In the mountain glens, overcome by blazing fire
Melts in the holy ground at the hands of Hephaestus:
So it was that Gaia melted in the flash of burning fire.

The defeat of Typhoeus is simultaneously the defeat of Earth. The metallurgy simile, unique in the *Theogony*, escalates from the human world of the smelting of tin (449.5°F = 231.9°C) to the elemental world of melting iron (2,800°F = 1,538°C).[19] But in addition to emphasizing the disparity between divine and human craft, the image of Earth's dissolution returns us to the moment prior to the Big Bang, when Earth came into being. And as Hesiod tells it, the essential feature of Earth is her solidity: Γαῖ' εὐρύστερνος, πάντων ἕδος ἀσφαλὲς αἰεί ('broad-breasted Earth, the seat of all, always secure', 117). The very first phase of cosmogony involves Gaia's self-definition as a solid and firm entity with outlines, contours and boundaries: she produces the Mountains and glens that define her surface; she creates Ouranos to enclose her, and Pontos to form boundaries between sea and land (126–132). The melting of Earth, which is the culmination of the Typhonomachy, points to the undoing of all that proceeds from her: retrogression to point zero of the cosmos. Henceforth not only will she put up no further resistance to Zeus's rule, she will in fact ensure it, first, by calling for his election to the kingship, but also by warning him of the potential dangers from his marriage to Metis.

Zeus thrusts Typhoeus back where he came from, back to Tartarus, where Chaos, the dark and formless void in which the cosmos emerged, now diminished and transformed and like its many offspring (e.g., Night, Death and Sleep) is assigned a place in Zeus's domain (740–743).

χάσμα μέγ', οὐδέ κε πάντα τελεσφόρον εἰς ἐνιαυτὸν
οὖδας ἵκοιτ', εἰ πρῶτα πυλέων ἔντοσθε γένοιτο,
ἀλλά κεν ἔνθα καὶ ἔνθα φέροι πρὸ θύελλα θυέλλης
ἀργαλέη· δεινὸν δὲ καὶ ἀθανάτοισι θεοῖσι.

Great is the chasm, nor in a whole year brought to completion
Could one reach the bottom, if first one entered the gates,
But blasts upon horrendous blasts would bear you hither and yon,
Harsh, dreadful even to the immortal gods.

The violent and destructive blasts that Typhoeus unleashes after his incineration by Zeus resemble the hellish gusts that beset the subterranean *chasma* (868; 872–880):

ἐκ δὲ Τυφωέος ἔστ' ἀνέμων μένος ὑγρὸν ἀέντων,
. . .
πῆμα μέγα θνητοῖσι, κακῇ θυίουσιν ἀέλλῃ·
ἄλλοτε δ' ἄλλαι ἄεισι διασκιδνᾶσί τε νῆας
ναύτας τε φθείρουσι· κακοῦ δ' οὐ γίνεται ἀλκὴ
ἀνδράσιν, οἳ κείνῃσι συνάντωνται κατὰ πόντον.
αἱ δ' αὖ καὶ κατὰ γαῖαν ἀπείριτον ἀνθεμόεσσαν

ἔργ' ἐρατὰ φθείρουσι,
πιμπλεῖσαι κόνιός τε καὶ ἀργαλέου κολοσυρτοῦ.

From Typhoeus comes the moist might of winds that blow
. . .
A great bane to mortals, they blow with evil gusts:
Sometimes they blow, shatter ships,
And destroy sailors; and there is no help for men
Who encounter them on the sea.
Others, in turn, throughout the boundless and flowering land also destroy
The lovely works of earth-born men,
Filling them with dust and confusion.

Typhoeus' *acosmia* does not completely disappear with his downfall; a residue remains in the evil winds that emanate from him, winds that destroy crops and cause shipwrecks of men, unlike the more benign and predictable winds (378–380).[20] We are of late all too aware of the cataclysmic destruction precipitated by storms, typhoons, cyclones and hurricanes. By way of contrast, one may recall a passage from the *Odyssey* (6. 41–46):

ἀπέβη γλαυκῶπις Ἀθήνη
Οὔλυμπόνδ', ὅθι φασὶ θεῶν ἕδος ἀσφαλὲς αἰεὶ
ἔμμεναι· οὔτ' ἀνέμοισι τινάσσεται οὔτε ποτ' ὄμβρῳ
δεύεται οὔτε χιὼν ἐπιπίλναται, ἀλλὰ μάλ' αἴθρη
πέπταται ἀννέφελος, λευκὴ δ' ἐπιδέδρομεν αἴγλη·
τῷ ἔνι τέρπονται μάκαρες θεοὶ ἤματα πάντα.

Grey-eyed Athena went off
To Olympus, where they say is the sure seat of the gods forever
Neither is it shaken by winds, nor does rain ever
Dampen it, nor does snow pile upon it, but the sparkling firmament
Cloudlessly spreads out, and a bright beam flits about;
That is where the blessed gods take their pleasure always.

While mankind, χαμαιγενέων ἀνθρώπων, doomed to toil the earth and to sail the seas through Zeus' dispensation (as we know from the Prometheus myth), suffers the consequences of Typhoeus' defeat, the Olympians, who 'live easy', now free of their last rival, remain eternally immune to such perturbations.

To conclude: if at issue in the Titanomachy was the kingship in Heaven, at stake in the Typhonomachy is the very existence of the cosmos itself.

CHAPTER 9
DEMONIC DISEASE IN GREEK TRAGEDY: ILLNESS, ANIMALITY AND DEHUMANIZATION

Giovanni Ceschi

In the fifth century BCE, Hippocratic medicine spreads throughout the Greek world, and widely influences the Greeks' collective imagination, as far as we are allowed to ascertain from literature. Historiography, philosophy, tragedy and comedy all begin to display forms of language deeply influenced by the new Hippocratic theories. This implies a radical transformation in the literary representation of a patient's experience of disease. Archaic Greek thought is characterized by a fatalistic view of evil, seen as a result of divine punitive actions, as an ἄτη impending on the individual, inducing pain to him if he had induced suffering to others. Here, evil affects one's offspring, or falls as a μίασμα upon an entire community, following a ritual impurity caused by the action (even if unintentionally[1]) of an individual. Such a 'chain of guilt' implies a concept of ἦθος where the tragic hero's suffering is an extraneous result of the pain inflicted by an ancestor, and, at the same time, the unavoidable outcome of an inclination he inherited, against which he desperately fights and which nevertheless is part of him, condemning and determining him.[2] From this perspective, tragic νόσος is conceptualized as an entity depriving a human being of self-control and separating him from intentionality. In the case of tragic disease, νόσος is the non-human entity and the progression of disease is not a human agency: humans do not have control over it. So disease is conceptualized as a being with agency: disease-as-being is capable of interfering with human agency.[3]

In contrast, the new Hippocratic perspective analyses νόσος in its phenomenological aspect. It also states a competitive principle: the physician fights against the disease alongside the patient. In the Greek imagination, νόσος is gradually deprived of both its religious and demonic connotations.[4] From an epistemological point of view, this is an historic change, since it implies the idea of a new form of control over disease. Disease can now be objectified, described with the tools of rational thought, and it can be separated from the patient's subjective experience, who – due to his inevitable emotional involvement – does not allow an effective therapeutic intervention.[5] In other words, the 'Hippocratic human being' begins to perceive himself from the outside, and with the new medicine he seeks for models of reproducibility of the nosological event to provide a description as aseptical as possible (see narrative scheme of the clinical pictures in *Epidemics*).

However, the vision of pain and suffering as endowed with the typical features of an ancestral pattern still survives just because it is deeply connected to the most human, visceral fear: the perception of being victims of uncontrollable external forces, despite the increasing emergence of technological and sophisticated defence strategies.[6] This might be the reason why we witness the coexistence of two perspectives on pain in the extant tragic plays: on the one hand, the objective representation of disease, influenced by Hippocratic language[7] and new therapeutic aids; on the other hand, the representation of pain as a subjective experience, which is still perceived in its demonic violence, explosive force and provided almost with a malevolent agency.

In this chapter, a list of examples from extant plays by Aeschylus, Sophocles and Euripides will be provided, even though it cannot claim to be complete. The analysis of tragic passages where physical suffering is a main topic highlights how the new Hippocratic science has influenced the description of νόσος in tragedy, allowing the playwright to achieve growing descriptive precision, yet not incompatible with the unavoidable degree of subjectivity inherent to the characters' representation of the dramatic events in which they are involved. The characters' rhetoric of pain and disease leads the reader to think about the νόσος as an entity with an agency of his own which crossfires with the will of the patient who fights against the disease.

Aeschylus, *Prometheus Bound*

In Aeschylus, 'disease is rooted in the nature of things and is resolved only through the emergence of a just order':[8] disease is a tragic metaphor for an altered order, perceived by the patient as a monstrous and bestial external entity, torturing body and mind. Therefore, an antithesis is established between Health, as the clear and serene universe of order, and Disease, seen as the dark and savage realm of disorder. *Prometheus Bound* is the tragedy in which physical and moral suffering most explicitely emerges, and where pain is inflicted on man according to an unfathomable demonic will. In this chapter, the focus will be not so much on the pain – even if it is physical and tangible – suffered by the hero,[9] but rather on the delusions suffered by the miserable Io, who bursts into the scene dealing with a kind of genetic mutation, that turns her into a heifer. Inachus' daughter 'fires the heart of Zeus with passion, and now, through Hera's hate' (590–592: Διὸς θάλπει κέαρ ἔρωτι, καὶ νῦν … Ἥρᾳ στυγητὸς), she is forced to wander hunted by a gadfly, a torment following her everywhere.

Aeschylus creates a causal relationship between the alleged violation performed by Io and the suffering inflicted on her; however, the play's focus is not so much on the pain etiology, but rather on its bestial and demonic phenomenology. 'A gadfly … is stinging' (566: χρίει … οἶστρος) and it is compared to 'the phantom of earth-born Argus' (567: εἴδωλον Ἄργου γηγενοῦς); the girl is fearful (567: φοβοῦμαι) because she is seeing 'the myriad-eyed herdsman' (568: τὸν μυριωπὸν εἰσορῶσα βούταν); the monster 'travels onward with his deceptive gaze … not even in death does the earth conceal him' (569–570: ὁ δὲ πορεύεται δόλιον ὄμμ' ἔχων, / ὃν οὐδὲ κατθανόντα γαῖα κεύθει). The two verbs attributed to the robber fly, κυναγεῖ and πλανᾷ[10] (572), are related to the semantic sphere of hunting, identifying the patient as a prey.

The torment suffered by Io undoubtedly includes effects both on her body and on her mind: in this passage (from the second stasimon, 566–573) it is difficult to separate the physical perception of pain from its translation into psychological terms;[11] and it is easy to guess that the girl's torture, which is interacting with the protagonist in a dramaturgical function,[12] was a primarily mental θεόσσυτος νόσος, a madness provoked by the divinity which twisted her perception of reality.[13] In lines 673–677, in which Io describes the furious attack of evil and alludes to its metamorphosis into a heifer, we see a clear reference to a painful madness or, more precisely, to a pain making her a fool: 'Immediately my form and mind were distorted (μορφὴ καὶ φρένες διάστροφοι), and with horns, as you see, upon my forehead, stung by a sharp-fanged gadfly I rushed with frantic bounds (ἐμμανεῖ σκιρτήματι).'

The 'epidermal' symptom of mental illness that affects Io consists of her own metamorphosis: μανία in this sense is θηριώδης, and transforms the patient's appearance from human into bestial. Tragic madness is here a metamorphic entanglement of human and not-human, which questions what it means to be human. Somehow, the human appears here to be animalized and in the process of becoming animal. Indeed, the demonic disease that Io suffers from is characterized first of all by ἀμορφία, which is the distortion and destruction of her previous aspect (διαφθορὰ μορφῆς). The distinguishing mark of the demonic nature of this kind of disease is precisely the cancellation of the boundaries that separate human and animal beings.[14]

Io's disease is certainly theurgic from an etiological point of view, but *Prometheus Bound* also contains interesting references to the progress of rational medicine. These references are related to the mythological figure of the Titan, benefactor of humanity with regard to ἰατρικὴ τέχνη (478–483). The greatest gift given by Prometheus to mankind is medicine, the use of φάρμακα, which, for the first time, makes it possible to fight the effects of the disease. By contrast, in describing the suffering that Zeus and Hera inflict on Prometheus and Io, the playwright resorts to a vocabulary of disease with demonic connotations, suggesting an invincible and uncontrollable entity at work. Very effective, from a dramatic point of view, is the antithesis between the inescapable demonic illness that strikes Io on stage and the rational view of νόσος, which in this drama is separate from the divine will for the first time: Prometheus intends to cure human maladies by introducing men to the use of φάρμακα, an action that he will eventually expiate with the terrible punishment imposed by Zeus.

We see how in Greek tragedy, through the progressive influence of Hippocratic medicine, the human body is already conceptualized as an organism which can be modified and manipulated through pharmacological interventions. So already in this ancient text the human body is not seen as a 'natural' given, but is technologically produced. The healthy body is the result of a pharmacological manipulation on the diseased body which is motivated by a cultural idea of health. This theorization of health and medicine finds its full modern expression in the work of physician and philosopher Canguilhem (1966), who, in his discussion of distinction of the normal and the pathological and the role of medicine in correcting or constructing normality/health, argued that a healthy body is the result of a corrective technological measure on the diseased body, which is motivated by an ideology or cultural interpretation of sickness and what it means to be healthy.[15]

Sophocles, *Trachiniae* and *Philoctetes*

In *Trachiniae* and *Philoctetes*, the physical suffering endured by the protagonists is ruthlessy at the centre of the dramatic action, and not – as in most tragedies – filtered by the ῥῆσις delivered by a messenger or by an external character (*Trach.* 1046–1263; *Phil.* 730–885). In situations where the character's body is at the very core of the dramatic events, the text confronts us with the patient's subjective experience of disease. The two 'clinical cases' of Heracles and Philoctetes perform disease as a living, wandering and malevolent entity, assaulting them in gusts, feeding on their blood and consuming them little by little, eventually leaving them exhausted. This dramatic representation of illness is deeply related to the archaic mentality,[16] as it was noted in the subjective description of Io's gadfly. Yet, this does not prevent Sophoclean plays from providing an objective description of the disease, in line with Hippocratic nosology.[17]

The archaic vision of νόσος is clearly functional to scenic effectiveness, but it is not incompatible with the 'diagnostic' precision demonstrated by Sophocles in the staging of Heracles' and Philoctetes' diseases. It has even been conjectured that the dramatic description of spectacular pathologies like these, implemented by exploiting the evocative potential of poetic lexicon, has had an influence on the lexicon of medicine: an excellent example is the word φαγέδαινα, gangrenous ulcers, where the concept of voracity typical of any chronic disease is implicit. Φαγέδαινα occurs four times in *Corpus Hippocraticum* and – not surprisingly, it seems – both in Aeschylus' and in Euripides' *Philoctetes* (*fr.* 253 R.; *fr.* 792 N.). Although this word does not occur in Sophocles' *Philoctetes*, the play offers a wide range of 'variations' on the topic: ἀδηφάγος, βαρυβρώς, διαβόρορς, always referring to disease.[18]

In *Trachiniae*, Heracles is taken asleep on stage, while going through his terrible agony (971f.): his strong and proverbially invulnerable body is devastated by the effects provoked by a tunic imbued with the centaur Nessus' blood. From the beginning, pain is portrayed as a dozing, wild animal – ἀγρίαν ὀδύνην[19] – which should not be woken up. Shortly after, Heracles wakes up, and the pain immediately strikes him with unprecedented violence: during the fluctuations of the crisis, the hero speaks of his illness as a living entity which: 'gnaws, cursed' (987: μιαρὰ βρύκει), 'slithers' (1010: ἕρπει), as 'a cruel pest jumps' to the victim (1027: θρῴσκει δειλαία); 'has eaten away inmost flesh' (1053–1054: ἐκ μὲν ἐσχάτας / βέβρωκε σάρκας); 'sucks the channels of the lungs, making the body its home' (1054–1055: πλεύμονός τ' ἀρτηρίας/ ῥοφεῖ ξυνοικοῦν); 'has drunk away my fresh lifeblood' (1055–1056: ἐκ δὲ χλωρὸν αἷμά μου / πέπωκεν ἤδη); 'consumes' the patient (1088: δαίνυται); and 'has leapt to fury' (1089: ἐξώρμηκεν). In conclusion, it is a διαβόρος νόσος (1084), a 'devouring disease', which gives no respite to the patient who feels 'conquered', at the mercy of the plague (1057: χειρωθείς). Also, terms related to the Dionysian ritual, such as καταρρακεῖν (1103), 'to tear to shreds', and σπαραγμός, 'convulsion, spasm' (1254) occur, referring to the insane violence of the crisis, which 'shreds' the hero.

In these occurrences, disease is described as an autonomous entity, which takes possession of the human being and leads him back to a 'primitive' state, under the control of nature (cf. section 'Identity Loss: From Civilised Man to "Primitive"' in Thumiger's Chapter 4 in this volume). In the case of Heracles (and Philoctetes), under the compulsion of demonic forces, illness means dehumanization and also questions the progressive control of man over his own world: the social and the natural worlds are fused into one through a 'regression to nature'. The posthuman implications of this view are notably sustained by Latour's argument (1993) according to which modernist distinctions between nature and culture are false as this distinction never really existed.

Yet, an attempt was made to show how the cluster of symptoms experienced by Heracles in *Trachiniae* is due to a lung disease, as confirmed by specific clinical courses in the *Hippocratic Corpus*.[20] A series of lexical comparisons allows the identification of correspondences in *Morb.* I 22, which describes the progress of pulmonary disease caused by a traumatic event: several symptoms recorded through the patient's point of view also appear in *Trachiniae* (see the passages just quoted above). Thus, a sort of 'requital' is made with the Hippocratic tradition. In fact, having put on the garment soaked with the blood of Nessus, Heracles succumbs to a disease similar to the one that he had inflicted on the centaur: in order to avenge the harassment of his wife Deianira, the hero had killed him with an arrow that had pierced his lungs. Heracles' 'clinical case' thus testifies Sophocles' versatility in using medical terminology for dramatic ends: the poet does not confine himself to tapping into a series of scattered technical terms from the Hippocratic stock, but shows he can manage a cluster of symptoms with the skill of a professional physician.

The symptoms of Heracles are described with 'scientific' realism, which in this specific situation justifies the juxtaposition of apparently very distant texts such as the tragic (poetic and connotative), and the medical one (technical and denotative). Nonetheless, also the perception of pain by the tragic character and the Hippocratic patient is the same: this simple observation allows us to explain the similar perspective shared by Hippocratic medicine and Greek tragedy. They are unified by the same 'focus' on human suffering,[21] although the two *genera* display a very different view of pain and its etiology: a logical and rational one in medicine as opposed to a supernatural one within tragedy. The identity of focus is the basis of a symptomatological description that draws on a common repertoire of 'amazing' images. Heracles clearly feels the sensation of a διαφθορὰ μορφῆς similar to that of Io in the *Prometheus Bound*. The hero defines himself as ἄναρθρος καὶ κατερρακωμένος (1103), that is he sees himself with disjointed limbs and torn to shreds. Thus, he perceives that he has lost his physical integrity, and possibly his own human nature. As we know, the notion of διαφθορά and the state of being κατερρακωμένος are important Hippocratic issues.[22]

Philoctetes' disease is also a demonic one, with the only difference that the hero speaks of it as a longtime partner, whose rhythms and 'habits' he knows well: an image consistent with the chronic disease – the festering foot wound – which has been haunting the Thessalian hero for a decade.[23] And so, at the first signs of yet another crisis, the hero can reassure Neoptolemus, explaining that the disease 'comes only now and then, perhaps when it has been sated with her roamings elsewhere' (758–759: ἥκει γὰρ αὕτη διὰ χρόνου, πλάνοις ἴσως / ὡς ἐξεπλήσθη); it 'comes sharply, but goes quickly' (808: ὀξεῖα φοιτᾷ καὶ ταχεῖ' ἀπέρχεται). Furthermore, even in this drama the image of the voracious disease is well attested, as it is proved by adjectives such as διαβόρος (gnawing, 7), ἀδηφάγος (voracius, 313), βαρυβρώς (that eats crudely, 694), δακέθυμος (biting at the heart, 706); and the verbs βόσκειν (to nourish, 313), βρύκεσθαι (to be devoured, 745), τρέφειν (to feed, 795), which are consistent with the image of a disease claiming to be 'satiated' by the patient. Finally, Philoctetes' sick foot is further defined by the Chorus through the adjective ἔνθηρος (698), suggestively evoking the presence of a 'ferocious beast' and streghtening the demonic, evil image running throughout the drama.[24] Yet, again, the use of this adjective is emblematic of the possible coexistence in the same term of a technical nuance, attested in the *Corpus*, and of a more popular and evocative meaning. These two semantic aspects are not in antithesis: Philoctetes' wound is 'savage' because it is infected, a semantic value attested e.g., in the treatise *De locis in homine*, and at the same time it is *ferocious*, like a beast that is not satisfied with slaughtering the patient's body.[25]

Occasionally, such semantic overlapping also emerges in other Sophoclean dramas: the adverb φρενοβόρως in *Ajax* (626),[26] to depict a disease – the madness, in fact – *devouring the mind*; the adjective φθινάς, in *Antigone* (819) connected with νόσος to emphasize corrosive and exhausting power of evil; the verb φθίνω, at the beginning of *Oedipus the King* (25, 26), in the description of the devastating effects caused by Theban plague.[27] The feature shared by all these occurrences is the visual evidence, equally suitable for a dramatic *rhesis* and for a medical record. In these or similar terms, the uncommon lexical choice makes the medical connotation clear.[28]

Euripides, *Hippolytus* and *Orestes*

In Euripides, a substantial evolution in the description of νόσος in tragedy is attested: the lexicon draws frequently from Hippocratic terminology because physical suffering appears for the first time on stage devoid of any mythological feature. Evil no longer has an external origin that endows it with a mysterious and autonomous superiority: on the contrary, now evil comes from the body and from the psyche of man himself (Ferrini 1978: 62).[29] Nevertheless, the perception of the patient and the framework of the nosology episodes in the surviving tragedies still maintain a supernatural etiology. Agave, Alcestis, Heracles, Phaedra, Medea, Orestes: mental or physical disease keeps on being inflicted by the gods, or at least by uncontrollable forces transcending the individual. In this section, Phaedra and Orestes will be in the spotlight.

In *Hippolytus* Phaedra's 'lovesickness' is characterized explicitly as a νόσος and it is traced back by the chorus of Troezen young women to a daemonic possession:

> ἦ γὰρ ἔνθεος, ὦ κούρα,
> εἴτ' ἐκ Πανὸς εἴθ' Ἑκάτας
> ἢ σεμνῶν Κορυβάντων
> φοιτᾷς ἢ ματρὸς ὀρείας;
> †σὺ δ'† ἀμφὶ τὰν πολύθη-
> ρον Δίκτυνναν ἀμπλακίαις
> ἀνίερος ἀθύτων πελανῶν τρύχῃ;
>
> 'Has some god possessed you, dear girl? Are you wandering under the spell of Pan or Hecate, the august Corybantes or the Mountain Mother? † . . . † Could it be that you're being tormented by guilt for sinning against Dictynna, the goddess of the wild beasts? Maybe you have forgotten to offer her the sacrificial bread'.
>
> *141–147*

Shortly after, Fedra herself seems to attribute her misfortune to the will of a δαίμων:

> Ἐμάνην, ἔπεσον δαίμονος ἄτῃ
>
> 'I was mad, I fell by the stroke of some divinity'.
>
> *241*

In these passages, the undifferentiated use of θεός and δαίμων appears;[30] also the 'possession' of Phaedra is relevant: in the first section of the tragedy, precisely the indistinct and mysterious nature of the disease is intended to represent lovesickness. As Lanata argued, a careful analysis of the tragic text can offer valuable information about the magical and demonic world of the fifth century. Δαίμων was the religious translation of certain phenomena of human life: δαίμων was the disease, δαίμων was the dream, even without any reference to a particular image or cult. The absence of individuality was characteristic of δαίμονες, as opposed to deities, since the Homeric poems.[31] Therefore, Euripides, in exploiting Hippocratic medicine to describe the symptoms suffered by his 'patients', traces back the etiology of diseases to a completely traditional conception.[32] It can plausibly be argued that dramatic conventions prevented him from innovating in this regard: in Euripides, νόσος still remains θεία and δαιμονία.

Moreover, the perception of disease by the character/patient is traditional as well: despite a symptomatology described almost with the precision of a clinical picture,[33] patients' suffering is outlined with a lexicon which emphasizes the violent, demonic and savage nature of νόσος. In the prologue of the *Orestes,* Electra tells his brother, who lies on his bed worn out by a ferocious disease (34: ἀγρίᾳ ... νόσῳ), that Clytemnestra's blood drives him round and round in frenzied fits (37: μανίαισιν). No longer eating nor washing for many days, when he finds relief from the disease (43: ὅταν μὲν σῶμα κουφισθῇ νόσου) in moments of lucidity, the matricidal son cries wrapped in his cloak; at other times he bounds headlong (45: πηδᾷ δρομαῖος) from his couch, as a colt when it is loosed from the yoke (45: πῶλος ὣς ὑπὸ ζυγοῦ). The occurrence of the adjective ἄγριος (34) is especially significant, because of the demonic implications highlighted by Boulter 1962, describing the symptomatology of a νόσος for which there are precise parallels in *De morbo sacro*.[34] Again, the 'ferine' metamorphosis of the protagonist is significant, and the similarity with the colt clearly emphasizes this image. Thus, in Euripides' plays the diseased body is thought of in terms of transformative change: being human means undergoing a process of making and re-making the body, on the edges of animal and human. For tragic heroes such as Orestes, and Heracles and Philoctetes (as we have seen before), being human includes becoming animal.

In the dialogue with Electra (first episode), Orestes himself, in the midst of a crisis, provides many details concerning his shocking disease. He asks his sister to wipe the drool foaming from the mouth and eyes (219–220: ἐκ δ' ὄμορξον ἀθλίου / στόματος ἀφρώδη πελανὸν ὀμμάτων τ' ἐμῶν), smearing beard and hair (223: αὐχμώδη κόμην; 225: βοστρύχων πινῶδες ἀθλίων κάρα) and giving him a beastly appearance (ὡς ἠγρίωσαι: 'how savage you look' – exclaims Elektra, shocked, at line 226). Going further, madness persists, proving to be unpredictably unavoidable as an epileptic fit. Orestes' sister perceives the first symptom of the crisis, the διαστροφὴ ὀμμάτων:

> οἴμοι, κασίγνητ', ὄμμα σὸν ταράσσεται,
> ταχὺς δὲ μετέθου λύσσαν, ἄρτι σωφρονῶν
>
> 'ah! brother, your eye is growing wild, and in a moment you are turning mad again, when you were just now sane'.
>
> *253–254*

The delirium is described not differently from Io's madness in *Prometheus*:

> ὦ μῆτερ, ἱκετεύω σε, μὴ 'πίσειέ μοι
> τὰς αἱματωποὺς καὶ δρακοντώδεις κόρας·
> αὗται γὰρ αὗται πλησίον θρῴσκουσ' ἐμοῦ
>
> 'Mother, I implore you! Do not shake at me those maidens with their bloodshot eyes and snaky hair. Here they are, close by, to leap on me!'
>
> *255–257*[35]

As for Io, the effect of this demonic νόσος is a distortion of the character/patient's appearance: Io reports διαφθορὰν μορφῆς (*Pr.* 642–643), μορφὴ καὶ φρένες διάστροφοι (*Pr.* 673); Menelaos sees in Orestes a terrible, unexpected ἀμορφία (*Or.* 391). Devoid of a μορφὴ ἀνθρωπίνη, the protagonist seems to lose even his own human identity, so he becomes an easy prey to supernatural forces that threaten to slaughter him, in body and psyche. The idea of νόσος as a demonic power challenges the human being as the self-centred rational being in control of 'nature', his own agency and autonomous decision. In such situations, demonic agency of νόσος is completely separate from human intentionality.

Conclusions: The νόσος as ἀμορφία

Starting from the image of ἀμορφία, some closing remarks will be made. Demonic disease in tragedy is always διαφθορὰ μορφῆς: a ruinous and voracious distortion of human appearance, a kind of bestial metamorphosis. Returning to the cases analysed above, Io is transformed into a heifer; Heracles is reduced to a whimpering prey suffering painful spasms; Philoctetes is forced to catch food in a state of bestial primitiveness (from which he frees himself merely thanks to the precious bow, a gift of Heracles); Phaedra is possessed by an animal impulse towards her stepson; Orestes takes on a beastly appearance.[36] All these characters experience νόσος as καταστροφή, destruction and malign transformation: the supernatural nature of disease admits even physical symptoms, represented through the use of a rational and realistic lexicon, but it will eventually reveal its demonic face in connection with semantic field of θηριῶδες. In this regard, man hit by demonic disease is both ἔνθεος and ἔνθηρος: he has, at the same time, the divinity and the beast within himself.[37]

Being θηριώδης, the demonic νόσος is διαβόρος, insatiable, provided with mobility and autonomous personality. The disease consumes the patient's body and psyche, leaving him ἄναρθρος καὶ κατερρακωμένος.[38] It is a short circuit of human, divine and bestial which destroys human balance, de-forming human appearance, intentionality and rational control. Hippocratic medicine appeared in the spotlight of the fifth century BCE precisely to heal this ἀμορφία.

CHAPTER 10
THE SPHINX AND ANOTHER THINKING OF LIFE
Katherine Fleming

> [The Sphinx] is, as it were, the symbol of the symbolic itself. [. . .] Out of the dull strength and power of the animal the human spirit tries to push itself forward, without coming to a perfect portrayal of its own freedom and animated shape, because it must still remain confused and associated with what is other than itself. [. . .]
>
> [. . .] The Sphinx propounded the well-known conundrum: What is it that in the morning goes on four legs, at mid-day on two, and in the evening on three? Oedipus found the simple answer: a man, and he tumbled the Sphinx from the rock. The explanation of the symbol lies in the absolute meaning, in the spirit, just as the famous Greek inscription calls to man: Know thyself. The light of consciousness is the clarity which makes its concrete content shine clearly through the shape belonging and appropriate to itself, and in its [objective] existence reveals itself alone.[1]

It is tempting to decontextualize Hegel's famous formulation of the Sphinx as 'the symbol of the symbolic itself,' and to infer from it an image of the Sphinx as a coded and coding riddle, a cypher whose profundity and fascination lies self-evidently, precisely, in its opacity, its inscrutability. Regier, in his comprehensive and jaunty Grand Tour of the Sphinx sets off in just this vein: '[The Sphinx] is a symbol of secrets and secret keeping, the symbol that carries messages from the distant past to those precious few (you and I) who can comprehend them. It makes fools of everyone else. It is the symbol of the tease: wherever a Sphinx is, a secret is. It is a nimble symbol, subtle and obsessive.'[2] Such an account must, however, necessarily overlook the significance of Hegel's Sphinx to a philosophical history of subjectivity, to enlightenment. Couched here in his lectures on art, Hegel's interpretation of the Sphinx suggests much about the systematicity of self-conscious reason, of human being. Symbolic (Egyptian) art, here embodied in the form of the Sphinx, can only conceive of its content abstractly, rather than manifest itself sensuously and visibly in the full realization of self-conscious Spirit, as its successor, Greek art, would. The Sphinx's hybrid body, half-animal, half-human, is here the eternally petrified image of imperfect freedom and a futile struggle to accede to self-consciousness. But there is more. Moving from Egypt to Greece, the seminal encounter between Oedipus and the Sphinx becomes the paternity ward of self-conscious reason, while the Sphinx, 'the explanation of the symbol', is schematized as a riddling birth canal from which Oedipus, man, springs to self-knowledge and belonging. By this account, then, the Sphinx is both crucial to, and yet necessarily de-centred from, Hegel's enlightenment narrative of self-consciousness and subjectivity, functioning, on her rock, as the monstrous other of human (masculine) rationality. Hegel's foundational account demonstrates precisely the parameters of the human as located in masculine self-consciousness.

This crucial moment of enlightened reason is revisited in inverse but no less triumphal fashion by Freud, several decades later. Freud's notorious appropriation of the Oedipus story to narrate *unconscious* psychosexual development as universal destiny is much discussed. Less remarked upon is his curious treatment of the Sphinx. In the essay 'Dostoevsky and Parricide', Freud writes of Oedipus that, '[t]he hero commits the deed unintentionally and apparently uninfluenced by the woman; this latter element is however taken into account in the circumstance that the hero can only obtain possession of the queen mother after he has repeated his deed upon the monster who represents the father'.[3]

Here Freud awkwardly reduces the Sphinx to a father substitute (although, since Oedipus has already unwittingly killed his real father, the significance of this second 'parricide' is unclear). Whatever the meaning of this strange sex-change, the obscuring of the Sphinx herself in her specificity is marked. Likewise, his turn to her riddle becomes less an exercise in interpretation and more a superscription: '[T]he first problem with which [the activity of research in children] deals is not the question of the distinction between the sexes but the riddle of where babies come from. (This, in a distorted form which can easily be rectified, is the same riddle that was propounded by the Theban Sphinx)'.[4] Here the riddle is a palimpsest, hidden by Freud's alternative explanation, and the Sphinx is enfolded into the wider psychosexual drama of childhood. Like Hegel before him, Freud privileges Oedipus over the Sphinx.

Recall too Freud's stunned self-recognition when presented with a medallion commissioned by his disciples for his fiftieth birthday in 1906: on one side, a relief portrait of Freud in side-profile; on the other, an image of Oedipus and the Sphinx (in the erotic symbolist style of the era), with an inscription from Sophocles's *Oedipus Tyrannus* (1525): 'ὃς τὰ κλείν' αἰνίγματ' ᾔδει καὶ κράτιστος ἦν ἀνήρ'[5] – 'who knew the renowned riddle, and was a most mighty man'.[6]

The Sphinx, there at the Hegelian and Freudian thresholds of subjectivity, in her feminine, animal hybridity, is the very condition of possibility for masculine universality, for the emergence of self-consciousness.[7] Appositely, Ingres's iconic image – *Oedipus and the Sphinx* – of which Freud was so fond,[8] is also a perfect rendition of the Hegelian Oedipus, with which it is roughly co-eval. Centre-stage, and fully lit, the heroic Oedipus answers the riddle of the Sphinx. She is half in shadow, her animal parts and head cast into darkness, while her human breasts thrust forward into the light, their shape almost recalling a fleshy question-mark.

Yet Ingres's painting, with its depiction of the Sphinx with her paw raised as if in question, rather than simply sexualized aggression, reminds us that she too – and not only Oedipus – is a speaking subject. In this respect, at the very least, even in her most canonical instantiations – the Sophoclean, the Hegelian, the Freudian – the Sphinx calls into question the certainty of the humanist subject position – 'the answer is man' – which she is used to facilitate. Yet the subjectivity of the Sphinx, in some ways essential, has yet to be thought.

In an article urging a reconsideration of the Sphinx precisely as woman, Connell observes this irony, and writes,

> While a Greek Sphinx most commonly has a woman's face, lion's body, and the wings of a bird (Apollodorus *The Library of Greek Mythology* 3.5.8), sometimes a woman's breasts or occasionally other animal features such as a serpent's tail, the Theban Sphinx is heavily marked with a further trait – beyond the body but partly of it she speaks with a human voice. She has language, logic and intellect, the latter of a superior kind (Euripides *The Phoenician Women* 48). In her human aspect she is precisely an adult woman with whom one can talk.[9]

Connell's critique here, and the Hegelian, Freudian or other invocations of the Sphinx all seem to dwell on the Sphinx's almost-humanity, her monstrous half-human form, upon and through which allegories of consciousness and gender are to be played out. What if, instead, we return to the Sphinx as an almost-animal? To do so would be to think the Sphinx in relation to debates around the animal, and cognate with these, debates regarding the machinic, the cyborgic, about what constitutes life.

Taking my cue from Derrida, I will now suggest ways in which we might read the Sphinx as a rich figure for contemporary issues which adhere around the posthuman and ask whether we might deploy her inherent liminality to re-stage critical ethical questions about the relationship between the human and the animal, and about subjectivity. Embodying both human and animal, can the Sphinx be recalled, cyborg-like (we might imagine her as a riddling machine, programmed to repeat her puzzle until short-circuited by Oedipus), to mediate those intellectual networks, perhaps always already existent, between animality and humanity, between the human and what is called the non/in-human?

In *The Animal That Therefore I Am*,[10] Derrida exposes philosophy's reliance upon a foundational, yet unexamined, distinction between the human and the animal, as the first step in discussing, grounding, the human, and asks what structural, systematic difference philosophy always already assumes in order to determine the differences it then seeks to assert as definitional and *as* differences. How far has this (conceptual) violence – paradoxically – in fact legislated for the founding of human reason and ethics, grounded as they are in the domain of what is 'proper' to the human? Within this discussion, Derrida asks if 'another thinking of life' might not be possible. If we recall the Sphinx as an almost-animal, might her hybrid form admit reflection upon the ethical questions which philosophy's definitions of the human and the animal have both raised and concealed?

Concerned before everything about the presuppositions and unacknowledged resolutions by which philosophy – as system and text – comes into being and remains, Derrida's *corpus* addresses philosophy's moments of avowal, how it self-identifies, self-legitimates, self-justifies; those moments which are necessary to philosophy even as they are necessarily disavowed.[11] What, in a philosophical paradigm, is that which functions as the organizational centre for the operability of the whole? It is this analysis of the 'transcendental' which suggests that, philosophy's moment of neutrality is always determined by that which it supposedly determines, explains or legitimates. This, of course, is a long-standing project for Derrida, visible in his earlier critique of structuralism: 'By orienting and organizing the coherence of the system, the center of a structure permits the play of its elements inside the total form. And even today the notion of a structure lacking any center represents the unthinkable itself.'[12]

It is this unthinkable, or that which philosophy has sought to forget which Derrida traces in his work on the animal. In fact, it may be that the history of thought's handling of the animal proves to be a seminal feature of its entire economy:

> it seems to me that the way in which philosophy, on the whole but particularly since Descartes, has treated the question of THE (so-called) animal is a major sign of its logocentrism and of a deconstructible limitation. We are dealing here with a tradition that was not homogeneous, to be sure, but hegemonic, and that in fact proffered the discourse *of* hegemony, of mastery itself.[13]

By this reading, then, Oedipus's, Hegel's, Freud's overthrowing of the Sphinx re-enacts, even as it realizes, this primal, hierarchical gesture of philosophy.

Derrida playfully begins his discussion in *The Animal That Therefore I Am* with a description of his reaction to the presence of his cat while he is naked: 'I often ask myself, just to see, who I am – and who I am (following) at the moment when, caught naked, in silence, by the gaze of an animal, for example, the eyes of a cat, I have trouble, yes, a bad time overcoming my embarrassment.'[14]

Here, Derrida wittily signals – while performing the longstanding humanist trope of the 'nude' – not only his Adamic shame at being seen to be naked (a rich term indeed for theology, epistemology, and so on), but also philosophy's shame *vis-à-vis* the animal. This encounter prompts a reflection on nudity, an 'incomparable experience', which is said to be 'proper to man'.[15] But what *is* proper to man? This question multiplies when we set ourselves the task of distinguishing the human from the animal(s). Despite a very few exceptions, notably Montaigne[16] and Bentham, whose reflections on the potential suffering of animals seem to haunt Derrida, the Cartesian position, upon which Derrida meditates extensively, casts the animal – without feeling, rationality, or a soul – as an automaton. It remained the philosophical paradigm throughout the succeeding centuries.[17] At stake in Derrida's re-reading of Descartes here is also the extent to which Descartes is both founder of and metonym for that persistent philosophical tradition, encapsulated in the entwinement of reason and subjectivity of the *cogito*, which thinks of the human as the complete subject of knowledge, master of nature, and lawgiver (a hegemonic position which, Derrida avers, is predicated on its *a priori* differentiation from 'the animal').

In his *Discourse*, Descartes proposes a thought-experiment, imagining machines resembling humans and animals, and debating how we might determine that they were, in fact, machines. While it would be impossible to distinguish the animal-machines from 'real' animals, Descartes argues, we would soon spot the androids, since they would be incapable of convincing human speech; moreover 'although such machines might execute many things with equal or perhaps greater perfection than any of us, they would, without doubt, fail in certain others from which it could be discovered that they did not act from knowledge, but solely from the disposition of their organs.[18]

Their automaticity, Descartes argues, devoid of reason, would be precisely what would betray them (even if in every other way they perfectly imitated human behaviour), since it could not be programmed with the infinite capacity of reason.

The thought experiment also provides the means of distinguishing humans from animals, since the animals (and also the indistinguishable animal-machines, we must suppose), cannot (truly) speak:

> [T]here are no men so dull and stupid, not even idiots, as to be incapable of joining together different words, and thereby constructing a declaration by which to make their thoughts understood; and that on the other hand, there is no other animal, [. . .] which can do the like. [. . .] And this proves not only that the brutes have less reason than man, but that they have none at all.'[19]

Descartes's brutal remarks here (which – rather extraordinarily – admit even as they disavow the potential for the machinicity of the human) imply a fraught and freighted, intimate and utilitarian conceptual relationship between the animal and the machine, and between speech and reason. Derrida reflects on Descartes' troubled and troubling account:

> Taking this grand mechanicist – and what is also called materialist – tradition back to the drawing board should not involve a reinterpretation of the living creature called 'animal' only, but also another concept of the machine, of the semiotic machine, if it can be called that, of artificial intelligence, of cybernetics and zoo- and bio-engineering, of the genic in general, etc.[20]

In revisiting and revising this weird 'mechanicist' tradition, in Descartes's fantastically wrought animal-automata, then, Derrida finds not simply a delimitation of the animal, but a challenge to thought of the new (re)productive sciences whose offspring disturb the boundary between the living and the non-living.[21] As such, Derrida's 'reinterpretation' hails a 'posthuman' account which calls into question the givenness of the differential categories of the human and the nonhuman.[22]

It is at this intersection, between the human and the nonhuman, the living and the non-living, that we may also once again call the Sphinx into question. The Sphinx's association with death is long-standing, foundational even. In ancient Greece and Etruria, Sphinxes, as funerary monuments, marked and guarded the boundary between life and death. One notable Attic example of this type is the beautiful sixth-century marble grave marker of a youth and a little girl on display in the Metropolitan Museum of Art in New York. Here the Sphinx – lion-haunched, with sharply curved wings folded behind her, and a pacific Archaic smile – sits atop a capital crowning a stele of a young male athlete with a little girl, both in side-relief.

Intriguingly, this relationship transforms from guardianship to predation, as the Sphinx starts to be represented in the pictorial record as an erotic predator – and, pointedly, teacher – of young men (see, for instance, a late fifth-century lekythos by Polion in the National Archaeological Museum of Greece in Athens, on which the leonine, winged Sphinx is depicted flying towards her pedestal perch with a young man clutched between her legs).[23]

This nexus of eros, thanatos, and (secret) knowledge comprises the reception history of the Sphinx. In the (more) modern world, in art and literature, the Sphinx has long denoted fatal eroticism and exoticism, a deadly enigma, a border-crosser and transgressor. Hypertrophically worked up out of the classical Greek image, from the nineteenth century onwards, the Sphinx is a sexualized and dangerous figure, whose barely contained eroticism is marked by her hybrid form with its human breasts and bestial body. The secret which she promises to reveal to Oedipus is that of alluring sexual fatality. Countless artists, from Ingres to Moreau to von Stuck render the Sphinx as an animal–feminine hybrid, erotic provocation and deadly trap.

If the Sphinx is deadly for her eroticism, it might also be said that this lure, this trap (both in its trappings and its association with death, not-life), is also suggestive of her machinic qualities. It could be argued that, futuristically, in addition to her strange assemblage of parts, she shares a sibling resemblance to the machinic cyborg by way of her deadly automaticity, her repeated riddling, her morbid computations. Like the death-driven cyborg of *Terminator 2* ('Have you seen this boy?'), the reiterated questions of this machine ('What goes on four legs in the morning, two legs in the afternoon, and three legs in the evening?') repeatedly foreshadow the unhappy end of those who face her. Adorno and Horkheimer in *Dialectic of Enlightenment* already noted the feminine, repetitive quality of myth and mythical figures and their association with the death of the individuated masculine subject.[24] This repetition, with its undertones of automaticity, of a lack of agency, of 'genuine' freedom, is one of the conundrums of contemporary debates around cybernetics, robotics and artificial intelligence. Curiously, the Sphinx was envisaged as a kind of prosthetic or (might we say?) 'artificial' intelligence, even in antiquity: a common motif of the Sphinx in Greek art, particularly Attic pottery, was to depict her – teacher, predator – on a pedestal, presumably recalling or alluding to her habitual function as a funerary monument. On a famous representation of the iconic confrontation of Oedipus with the Sphinx, the fifth-century Attic kylix of the painter of Oedipus, held in the Vatican Museums, Oedipus, dressed as a traveller, sits cross-legged, listening to the crowned Sphinx as she asks her riddle (teasingly part-inscribed on the kylix itself, as if it, a mere object, could also speak: 'kai tri[poun]'), she who, with her huge wings and lion's body, sits menacingly high above him on a column. The Sphinx, then, is always already envisaged meta-narratively as a sculpture, whose plastic form denotes her artifice.

Not by coincidence, I think, (and here I acknowledge I leap centuries in Sphinxy representation), does Joseph Beuys echo this artificial, machinic Sphinx with his strange drawing, *Electric Sphinx* (in the Tate Scotland collection). Depicted from the waist up, this cat-woman figure, her womanliness clearly marked by her triple pairs of breasts, Diana of Ephesus-like, appears surrounded by radiating spheres of energy, punctuated by shafts flowing from her armpits. A triple – phallic – shape encloses her weird head, pierced with a wire or tube. Pointed ears and a hint of sharp teeth in her open mouth suggest her animal nature, her face, obscured by violent, dark scribblings across the eyes. Above her, on the left, floats a magnet, pointed towards a cross, symbolizing a positive charge. The drawing's full title, scribbled on the reverse – 'Joseph Beuys (electric Sphinx) Motor-Bitch' – signals clearly the malevolent conflation of woman, animal and machine. Condensed in this misogynistic image, then, are most, if not all, of the themes and enigmas which surround this figure. A terrifying composite, a hybrid human, animal, machine, she fascinates and repels. Sexually charged (sex here as a kind of magnetic mechanics), she threatens and entices in equal – fatal – measure.

Returning now to the threshold, the limit of the human, as described by Hegel or Freud, to the riddle that offers the ground for masculine subjectivity and the possibility of ethical life (through universal self-consciousness and the cultural imperatives of the Oedipus Complex), what other thinking of life might be possible if we instead foreground the Sphinx as animal-machine?

Even in the present day, after more than a century of Darwinism, the flourishing of the science of animal cognition, and various international acts and laws (Endangered Species Acts, for instance), which might seem to confer upon animals some of the rights of existence, protection and conservation, which had previously been only human provinces, Descartes' philosophical economy persists. Indeed, the very terms on which these laws are drawn up, proceeding from the opposition between the human and the animal, reveal the Cartesian distinction subtending the entire structure, a structure which endures to possibilize the definition of the human. Yet Derrida's critique of this presumed structure is not to deny that differences exist, but rather to point to the presumption underlying it which violently conceals an ethical demand: 'If I am unsatisfied with the notion of a border between two homogeneous species, man on one side and the animal on the other, it is not in order to claim, stupidly, that there is no limit between "animals" and "man"; it is because I maintain that there is more than one limit, that there are many limits.'[25]

This 'limitrophy' – Derrida's self-declared term designating not only the limit, but that which generates, complicates and multiplies it – and its association with the 'other other', the thinking of which so troubles the anthropocentric ethics whose terms are grounded on exclusion and (we might say animal) sacrifice returns us to Derrida's earlier thinking in *The Gift of Death*:

> I cannot respond to the call, the request, the obligation, or even the love of another without sacrificing the other other, the other others. [. . .] As a result, the concepts of responsibility, of decision, or of duty, are condemned a priori to paradox, scandal, and aporia. Paradox, scandal, and aporia are themselves nothing other than sacrifice, the revelation of conceptual thinking at its limit, at its death and finitude.[26]

The plurality of the interstices between every other, between living and non-living beings is abyssal, because each multiplication is itself, in turn, multiple, fractal. To say as much is not just to acknowledge the differences between the human and each species, nor even between each species and every other species, but to acknowledge that these differences themselves are differential and remain anthropocentrically unthinkable and unthought. Merely to recognize that other species are different from each other still determines those differences as differences.

In a discussion of her theory of agential realism, Barad articulates her understanding of intra-activity, and the temporalities of the production of phenomena which possibilize specific materializations:

> Bodies are not objects with inherent boundaries and properties; they are material-discursive phenomena. 'Human' bodies are not inherently different from 'nonhuman' ones. What constitutes the 'human' (and the 'nonhuman') is not a fixed or pregiven notion, but nor is it a free-floating ideality. What is at issue is not some ill-defined process by which human-based linguistic practices [. . .] manage to produce substantive bodies/bodily substances but rather a material dynamics of intra-activity: material apparatuses produce material phenomena through specific causal intra-actions, where 'material' is always already material-discursive – that is what it means to matter. Theories that focus exclusively on the materialization of 'human' bodies miss the crucial point that the very practices by which the differential boundaries of the 'human' and the 'nonhuman' are drawn are always already implicated in particular materializations.[27]

That materializations might be 'particular' is, I think, precisely Barad's point, and how she hinges her 'posthuman' theory to an ethical (and in her case feminist) perspective (how for her epistemo-ontology might converge with the ethical). Not only are bodies the product of intra-action, not essentially defined, but they are also the products of certain temporally located epistemological parameters. This perspective offers, I think, a way of recouping the posthuman which admits its ethical lessons – its de-centring of the human – while acknowledging both the fact that for the moment at least it is the human who observes and defines the varying materializations which constitute its 'world' (perhaps we need to wait for AI to do philosophy), and also the fact that certain knowledge practices fix the material-discursive in a temporal – historical – 'cut' which both excludes and includes, visibilizes and invisibilizes: our lived experiences therefore come to matter in both senses of that word. In these respects then, the hybrid body of the Sphinx might both enfold its history as a figure which encodes a certain historical interpretation of the female, the animal, and also transcends that history as a symbol for the 'beyond' of that epistemology.

To return to Derrida's *Animal:* in a chapter querying Lacan's certainty regarding the distinction between the human and the animal, he writes:

> It would therefore be a matter of reinscribing this *différance* between reaction and response, and hence this historicity of ethical, juridical, or political responsibility, within another thinking of life, of the living, within another relation of the living to their ipseity, to their *autos*, to their own autokinesis and reactional automaticity, to death, to technics, or to the mechanical [*machinique*].[28]

All we 'know' of the Sphinx's speech is that she asked those who confronted her a riddle. How to define this speech? Is it reaction or response? And, to cut to the point, surely it is – confoundedly – that most 'human' (in Lacanian terms) of responses? A response which seeks a response? A deadly demand? The Sphinx's speech, her ambiguous status as a speaking animal whose question possibilizes masculine self-consciousness, the actualization of Spirit, is here fittingly the ambivalent communication of the autokinetic animal.

What emerges from Derrida's *Animal* is an unsettling reminder of the absolute other. What is more, in his radical restaging of Hegel's seminal master-bondsman scenario and its foundational dialectic of self-consciousness recognized and recognizing, Derrida's new scene, philosopher before cat, becomes also an uncanny re-enactment of Oedipus's encounter with the Sphinx:

> The animal is there before me [. . .] [F]rom the vantage of this being-there-before-me it can allow itself to be looked at, no doubt, but also – something that philosophy perhaps forgets, perhaps being this calculated forgetting itself – it can look at me. It has its point of view regarding me. The point of view of the absolute other, and nothing will have ever given me more food for thinking through this absolute alterity of the neighbor or of the next(-door) than these moments when I see myself seen naked under the gaze of a cat.[29]

This then is the radical ethical challenge of the absolute other, be it the animal, the cyborg, the Sphinx: it can look back. What other thinking of unlimited life does this necessitate?

CHAPTER 11
WHEN ROME'S ELEPHANTS WEEP: HUMANE MONSTERS FROM POMPEY'S THEATRE TO VIRGIL'S TROJAN HORSE

Aaron Kachuck

The Indian elephant is said sometimes to weep.[1]

In late September 55 BCE, celebrations designed to gild Pompey the Great's 'finest hour'[2] turned disastrous, and, in the eyes of learned legend, precipitated the general's death. According to accounts provided at centurial intervals by Cicero (55 BCE), Pliny the Elder (60s to 70s CE), and Cassius Dio (late-second/early-third centuries CE), at these festivities Pompey the Great foundered on something bigger than himself: he had an elephant problem. Inaugurating a new temple complex of 'Venus the Victorious' (*Venus Victrix*) that would feature Rome's first permanent stone theatre[3] and constitute a form of 'continuous triumph',[4] Pompey had endowed an ostentatious 'exhibition hunt' (*uenatio*) to entertain the Roman people; he failed, though, to predict that his elephants would inspire 'the first and the last public protest of which we have knowledge' against cruelty to animals.[5] At this elephant-hunt, Cicero writes, the Roman people saw in these 'beasts' – fearsome monsters, machines of war, symbols of regnal potency – a 'community with the human race' (*illi beluae cum genere humano societatem*, Cic. *Fam.* 7.1).[6] For Pliny, Cassius Dio, and the symbolic tradition upon which they draw, the implications were momentous: this abuse of elephants precipitates Pompey's defeat and the victory of Caesar.

This chapter explores what can be gained by uncovering the shadows of a posthumanist ethics – 'the question of the ethical status of animals in relation to the human'[7] – behind the complex textual record of Pompey's 'elephant fight, a most terrifying spectacle' (ἐλεφαντομαχίαν, ἐκπληκτικώτατον θέαμα, Plut. *Pomp.* 52.4). What are the political, religious, cultural and literary implications of the ways in which this story, and the various ways in which it is told, relies upon a muddling of the traditional separations of human from animal from god? To explore these questions, this chapter first reviews the monstrosity of elephants in the classical imagination, before turning to a close reading of our three principal sources for what transpired on that September day of 55 BCE. Descriptions of this event relate to, and may help to construct, views of the elephant as an animal uniquely similar to humans: if Pompey's Romans can be said to be posthuman, their compassion extends rather narrowly into the animal world.[8] At the same time, the nexus of stories that develop around Pompey's exhibition are informed by the symbolic role of elephants in the cultural and social vocabulary of the ancient Mediterranean and Near East, and, more specifically, of the political machinations and programmes in Rome's Republic and Empire. The intertwining of these two strands – natural philosophy's humane 'beasts' and historical typography's symbols of kingship and apotheosis – finds a literary reflex in Augustan poetry, most especially in Virgil's Trojan Horse. Pompey's elephants thus contribute to the symbolic bestiaries that helped structure literary and political expression in Rome's Republic and Principate.[9]

Given elephants' bellicose utility, the Roman people's humanizing of Pompey's beasts is surprising. Elephants were the prototypical *beluae*, ferocious beasts or monsters: Terence's *Eunuchus* assumes one might think oneself 'fierce' (*ferox*) merely for commanding them (*Eun.* 412–415). *Bellantia monstra*, 'war-waging monsters', Silius Italicus called them (*Pun.* 9.599), differing from horses in also being machines, in the sense of war-like engines, 'a beast bearing turreted munitions and bulwarks on its black back' (*turritas moles ac propugnacula dorso belua nigranti gestans*, 9.240). The elephant, 'towering over all the other beasts' (*super ceteras belua eminens*, Curt. Ruf. 8.13), is, Alain of Lille would later write, 'monstrous by dint of its body's size' (*monstruosa corporis quantitate, De Planct. Nat.* 2.239).

From Romans' first encounter with 'elephants endorst with towers / of archers'[10] in combat – Pyrrhus' invasion of Lucania (281 BCE) – these monstrous war-machines defied classification: 'Fear gripped the Romans,' wrote Pausanias, 'who did not, at any rate, believe them to be animals' (δεῖμα ἔλαβε Ῥωμαίους ἄλλο τι καὶ οὐ ζῷα εἶναι νομίσαντας, 1.12.3–4). Pyrrhus' war-animals – surmounted by tower (*turris*, πύργος, θωράκιον), mahout (*rector*) and other warriors – inspired third-century BCE art;[11] they also informed Lucretius' description of how 'the supreme force of a violent wind across the sea sweeps over the main the generalissimo of the fleet, together with his mighty legions and elephants' (*summa etiam induperatorem classis super aequora uerrit / cum ualidis pariter legionibus atque elephantis*, 5.1226–1228), to whom is forbidden 'the peace of the gods' (*diuom pacem*, 1229). The scene recalls Pyrrhus' invasion, with the Ennian tones of *induperatorem* pointing to the sixth book of that earlier poet's *Annals*.[12] Lucretius' account of armaments' progress includes elephants as climactic nadir (Costa): 'the Lucanian oxen [=elephants] with turreted body, horrible creatures, snake-handed' (*boues lucas turrito corpore, taetras, / anguimanus*, 1302–1303). The monstrously organic ('snake-handed') and technological ('turreted body') convey pure fright (*taetra*) – reflecting Ennius' *Annals* (612 Sk. *tetros elephantos*) – as the most horrifying of those innovations that 'gloomy Discord gave birth to one after another' (*alid ex alio peperit discordia tristis*, 1305). The monstrosity of Discord's youngest is answered linguistically by an apparent neologism – *anguimanus*, 'snake-handed' – whose exceptional morphology – 'a unique fourth-declension adjectival ending' (Costa *ad loc.*) – fits its singular depravity.[13]

Elephants' human community

And yet, while these 'living towers and hills of flesh'[14] could seem the most inhuman, most monstrous, machine of war, Greeks and Romans could also represent elephants, paradoxically, as the most human of animals, as the events at Pompey's theatre demonstrate. Our earliest account of Pompey's elephant spectacle comes from a letter from Cicero to his friend Marius in October of 55 BCE (*Fam.* 7.1 SB 24), a month *ex post facto*. Cicero had advertised Pompey's fanfare earlier that year, in a courtroom attack on Piso, whose Epicurean predilections, Cicero insinuated, would keep him from the games (*Pis.* 65). Cicero's letter to Marius details various 'lavish special effects',[15] including dramatic performances of *Clytaemnestra* and *Equos Troianus* that included 3,000 wine-craters and entire battalions of infantry and cavalry. Cicero's letter inscribes the productions in the cultural conflict between Greek and Roman: it is just as well Marius missed these 'Greek plays' (*Graecos . . . ludos*), seeing how he refuses 'even to take the Greek road to his villa'. He then comes to Pompey's elephants:

> sed quae potest homini esse polito delectatio, cum aut homo imbecillus a ualentissima bestia laniatur aut praeclara bestia uenabulo transuerberatur? quae tamen, si uidenda sunt, saepe uidisti, neque nos, qui haec spectauimus quidquam noui uidimus. extremus elephantorum dies fuit. in quo admiratio magna uulgi atque turbae, delectatio nulla exstitit; quin etiam misericordia quaedam consecuta est atque opinio eius modi, esse quandam illi beluae cum genere humano societatem.
>
> But what pleasure can there be for a cultured man when either an immartial man is torn apart by the strongest of beasts, or when the most splendid beast is transfixed by a hunter's spear? These were the kinds of things that, even if worth seeing, you've already seen, nor did I, who saw them myself, find in them anything novel. The last day was that of the elephants, on the which day there was much wonder on the part of the vulgar crowd, but no enjoyment; indeed, a certain degree of compassion attended the event, and a belief of a kind that there was a sense of community between this beast and the human race.

Cicero poses the paradox boldly: Romans thought beasts (*beluae*) belonged to human community (*societatem*). It is no accident that *societas*, translating the Greek Stoic term οἰκείωσις,[16] was a key component of Cicero's political philosophy: so Scipio, in the third book of Cicero's *Republic*, defines 'people' (*populus*) as necessarily involving 'the consensus and community of those brought together' (*consensus ac societas coetus*, 43). Cicero's people seem to use a philosophical language here that takes up and refuses the conclusions of the Stoics, for whom, in the opinion Cicero's *De Finibus* ascribes to Chrysippus, 'All other things were born for the sake of humans and gods, but that these exist for their own mutual fellowship and community, so that humans may make use of beasts for their own utility, and without injustice' (*cetera nata esse hominum causa et deorum, eos autem communitatis et societatis suae, ut bestiis homines uti ad utilitatem suam possint sine iniuria*, 3.67). Still, Cicero hedges carefully: the people experience 'a certain degree' of compassion, while their judgement amounts to 'belief of a kind'. That the elephants' plight inspires 'compassion' (*misericordia*) makes them effective Ciceronian orators: 'compassion (*misericordia*) is pain from the misery of another person suffering from an injury', Cicero says in his *Tusculan Disputations* (4.8.18), and his *De Oratore* has Antonius claim that 'I did not attempt to move others to compassion (*misericordiam*), before I myself was caught by it' (2.195). Since compassion implies fellow-feeling, elephants inciting compassion in others might feel compassion themselves – a feature modern zoologists have remarked upon in elephants.[17] Bridging the divide between humans and animals allows elephants *a fortiori* to bridge the narrower aesthetic gap between class divisions: neither the 'man of culture' nor 'the vulgar crowd' can find 'pleasure' in this event.

It is precisely elephants' paradoxical *humanitas* that opens Pliny's elephantography: 'The elephant is the largest animal, and also closest to human sensibilities' (*Maximum est elephans proximumque humanis sensibus*, 8.1). The structure of Pliny's work renders this literally true: the seventh book treats humans, the eighth, turning 'to the rest of the animals' (*ad reliqua . . . animalia*, 1), begins with elephants. Pliny's account of the hunt at Pompey's theatre details precisely how the compassion of the people was aroused. Pliny's narrative in the eighth book of his *Natural History* unfolds in three stages. First, one elephant marvellously threw his gladiatorial opponents into the air so that they described a perfect circle, 'as if by art, and not by the fury of a beast, they were thrown' (*uelut arte, non furore beluae, iacerentur*, 8.20). Like Cicero, Pliny hedges, but the impression is of an animal more geometrician than brute. Next, an elephant is killed by a single spear-shot under the animal's eye, straight into its brains (8.21). Finally, the scene is set for conversion to compassion:

> uniuersi eruptionem temptauere, non sine uexatione populi, circumdatis claustris ferreis . . . sed Pompeiani amissa fugae spe misericordiam uulgi inenarrabili habitu quaerentes supplicauere quadam sese lamentatione conplorantes, tanto populi dolore, ut oblitus imperatoris ac munificentiae honori suo exquisitae flens uniuersus consurgeret dirasque Pompeio, quas ille mox luit, inprecaretur.
>
> All of them together attempted to escape, which worried the people, despite the iron bars that closed the animals in. But those Pompeians [i.e., 'elephants'], having lost all hope of escape, supplicated the compassion of the people, groaning in a way that cannot be put into words, together bewailing themselves with a kind of lamentation, with such pain caused to the people that, forgetful of the general and of the public spectacles provided for his own honour, with tears, and all of them together, the people arose and shouted curses at Pompey – the penalty for which he will soon pay.

Pliny, like Cicero, focuses on human 'compassion' for elephants, but thickens the symbolic equivalences undergirding this scene's unexpected climax: the Roman people collectively rise up and cry (*flens uniuersus*), responding to elephants who rose up collectively (*uniuersi*) to bewail themselves (*sese . . . conplorantes*). The Romans are not moved by 'disgust' (*fastidium*)[18] at grotesquerie, as they might have been by the brain-shot beast: it is not merely the prospect of 'beasts in pain'[19] that moves the people, unless by pain we mean not only physical suffering, but, as well, the pains of dejection, sadness and fear.[20] The elephants' complaint, inexpressible in words (*inenarrabili habitu*) resembles Virgil's Aeneas' own 'unspeakable sadness' (*infandum . . . dolorem*, 2.3); the result of 'loss of hope of flight' (*amissa fugae spe*), it recalls one of Virgil's poignant collocations: 'Nor any hope of flight' (*Aen*. 9.131=10.121 *nec spes ulla fugae*).[21] There is 'pain' (*dolor*) for the humans because the voices of the elephants somehow give expression to their own desperation, their loss of hope. These elephants have not yet been tortured, at least not physically: instead, it is imagined sufferings – thwarted effort, dashed expectations, painful prospects – that torture them, and cause their self-pity in such a way as incites human fellow-feeling.

Although Cicero's account unites cultured and uncultured, Pliny's account was more zoophilic than the philosophers'.[22] Cicero's emphasis on 'community' (*societas*) was, we have seen, cast in a Stoic light, but Seneca reflects a more orthodox position by restricting concern to the elephants' human hunters (*Brev*. 13.6). By contrast, when Cicero and Pliny's Roman populaces respectively ascribe and imply 'community' between elephants and humans, they naively adapt an unpopular approach that goes back to Theophratus: his *On Piety* argued against Aristotle that not only Greeks and barbarians, but all animals, shared race (συγγενεῖς) and 'community of sensibilities' (παθῶν οἰκειότης, Porph. *Abst*. 3.25). Had they been touched by Pythagorean or Empedoclean influences, Cicero's and Pliny's crowds might have suspected humans' transmigration into animals: of this there is no hint. Nonetheless, Pompey's elephants are pitied not as disguised humans, but as animals somehow humane. These crowds' compassion thus approach Bion's witticism (Plut. *Soll.* 965B): 'Boys throw stones at frogs for fun (παίζοντα), but the frogs don't die for fun, but for real (ἀληθῶς).'

The Roman crowd is not, however, moved by animals in general, but by elephants: what Achilles Tatius calls the elephants' exceptional 'philanthropy' (4.4.7 φιλανθρωπιάς) provokes an equally exceptional elephantophilia. It was an exception hallowed by natural philosophical tradition. There are, for example, several activities often deemed proper to man in which elephants share: so Plato restricts rhythm to humans (*Leg.* 653E–654A), but Aelian allows it to elephants (*NA* 2.2); so Epictetus thinks only humans feel shame (3.7.27), while Pliny claims that elephants' modesty is wondrous (*HN* 8.12). Although other animals can learn aspects of human oral communication, only the elephant can write: for Latinate Pliny, elephants write Greek (*HN* 8.6), for Aelian the Hellene, in Latin (*NA* 2.11).[23] Elephants' penmanship may lie behind the story about boys poking an elephant's trunk with their styluses (τοῖς γραφείοις, *Soll.* 968D) – the pedagogical elephant then gives the boys a frightening, if ultimately gentle, lesson in respect. Elephants' famed literacy may also inform the story of an elephant as erotic rival of Aristophanes of Byzantium, the famous scholar, for the affections of an Alexandrian flower-seller (Plin. *HN* 8.13; Ael. *NA* 1.38; Plut. *Soll.* 972D).

Elephants' communicative capacities relate to their formation of affective communities among themselves and with humans. They are the only animal Plutarch designates as capable of healing not only through medicaments, but also through surgery (χειρουργίᾳ, *Soll.* 974D), an art which it practised on itself, on other elephants, and on humans (970C–D). According to Aristotle, only the elephant exceeds the human lifespan (*Gen. an.* 777b5), and their mouths produce a sound that is like 'that of a human being expiring or sighing' (ὅταν ἄνθρωπος ἐκπνέῃ καὶ αἰάζῃ, *Hist. an.* 536b22) – one can see how this Aristotelian lens might slip inadvertently into Rome's crowds hearing something human in their laments. For Aristotle, the human is 'the kind of animals that lives in cities'; Cicero would have agreed, while emphasizing in his *Republic* that humans gather together to form communities 'not so much from weakness as from something like a certain natural inclination towards collectivity by humans: for their race is neither individualist nor the kind that wanders in solitude' (*non tam inbecillitas quam naturalis quaedam hominum quasi congregatio; non est enim singulare nec soliuagum genus hoc*, 1.39). Pliny's *Natural History* ascribes the same habits to elephants, who 'always travel around in crowds, of all animals being the least likely to wander in solitude' (*idque cum gregatim semper ambulent, minime ex omnibus soliuagi*, 8.29).[24]

To their natural sociability, elephants add scrupulous religiosity and piety superior to human practice, which informs the 'curses' (*diras*) levelled by the Romans at Pompey,[25] as Cassius Dio's account highlights (39.38):

> ἐπειδὴ τραυματισθέντες τῆς μάχης ἐπαύσαντο, καὶ περιιόντες τάς τε προβοσκίδας ἐς τὸν οὐρανὸν ἀνέτεινον καὶ ὠλοφύροντο οὕτως ὥστε καὶ λόγον παρασχεῖν ὅτι οὐκ ἄλλως ἐκ συντυχίας αὐτὸ ἐποίησαν, ἀλλὰ τούς τε ὅρκους ὅτι οὐκ ἄλλως ἐκ συντυχίας αὐτὸ ἐποίησαν, ἀλλὰ τούς τε ὅρκους οἷς πιστεύσαντες ἐκ τῆς Λιβύης ἐπεπεραίωντο ἐπιβοώμενοι καὶ τὸ δαιμόνιον πρὸς τιμωρίαν σφῶν ἐπικαλούμενοι.
>
> After being wounded, they ceased fighting, and walked about with their trunks raised to heaven, lamenting[26] so bitterly as to give rise to the notion that they did so not by any

kind of chance, that they were bewailing the oaths they had trusted when they crossed over from Libya, and were calling upon their protective spirit to avenge them.

Cassius Dio goes on to laud the elephants' expert knowledge of the heavens, and worship of the sun and moon. Religious themselves, 'they are believed', Pliny notes, 'to possess an understanding of the religion of other people' (*alienae quoque religionis intellectu creduntur*, 8.1); how could Pompey betray creatures so endowed? Pompey should have learned from Ptolemy Philopator, punished with threatening dreams for sacrificing elephants to the Sun after victory at Raphia (217 BCE): as Plutarch notes (perhaps citing King Juba), elephants were 'the animal most loved by the gods' (θεοφιλέστατόν ἐστι τὸ θηρίον, Plut. *Soll.* 972C). In Cassius Dio's account, the elephants have no need for the intermediation of the people's curses: the darlings and connoisseurs of the celestial realm, they can bring down curses upon Pompey's head through their own prayers.

Elephants as the symbol of imperial power

Insofar as the accounts of Cicero, Pliny and Cassius Dio show the Roman people ready to admit elephants into the community of mankind, they might be taken to suggest the possibility, if only for a brief moment, of something resembling a posthuman turn in Roman thought, of a willingness to lower the barriers separating the human from the animal. Still, in the wake of Pompey's spectacle, pachyderm rights broadly construed remained much the same: yes, organizers of public spectacles may have been more chary about presenting elephants in 'exhibition hunts', but the Roman market for ivory continued briskly enough to cause Pliny's contemporaries to substitute elephant bones for scarce ivory (*HN* 8.7–8, 31). In fact, the isolated nature of Pompey's event suggests that to philosophical reasoning we must join explanations of a more immediate, socio-political and symbolic nature.[27] These were, after all, not only elephants, but, as Cicero put it, 'Pompeians' (*Pompeiani*) – a telling identification.

Judged historically, this elephant event fits Pompey's legend – his rise and his fall – suspiciously well. If, as Pliny's 'evidently embroidered'[28] account suggests, the Romans in the arena had 'crying risen together' to curse Pompey, would Cicero have failed to mention so dramatic a display? We cannot know, but it is noteworthy that, a month and a half following Pompey's celebrations, between 13 and 16 November, 55 BCE, as Crassus left Rome to campaign against the Parthians, the tribune C. Ateius Capito pronounced an 'adverse omen' (*obnuntiatio*) and 'curses' (*dirae*) against Crassus' ill-fated expedition.[29] Pliny's account thus effectively conjoins the deaths of Pompey and Crassus, and implicitly links Caesar's sole supremacy to his fellow triumvirs' lack of respect for religious custom. Looking back, 55 BCE's elephantine embarrassment repeats Pompey's thwarted attempt, twenty-six years earlier, triumphantly to enter the city in a four-elephant-drawn chariot – the gate's insufficiencies forced Pompey to dismount.[30] This failed expectation, in turn, would have fulfilled the Homeric etymological *figura* that sent dreams that 'deceive' (ἐλεφαίρονται, *Od.* 19.565) from 'hewn elephantine [=ivory] gates' (πριστοῦ ἐλέφαντος, 564).[31]

Pompey the Great's design stemmed from emulation of Dionysus' return from India and, more immediately, from imitation of his nicknamesake Alexander the Great (cf. Plut. *Pomp.* 2.1) and his cult: in 275/4 BCE,[32] according to the Calixinus of Rhodes (*ap.*

Ath. 5.196a-203b=*FGrH* 627 F 2), Ptolemy II Philadelphus' 'grand procession'[33] included Dionysus' statue drawn by elephants, as well as a golden Alexander flanked by Victory and Athena mounted on chariots drawn by live elephants.[34] Ptolemy Philopator, we've seen, repented his elephant sacrifice; Pompey repeats Philadelphus' parade and Philopator's affront, but, neglecting appeasement, dies on Alexandrian shores. This resting place plays into one of chronology's charming coincidences: 275 BCE saw both Philadelphus' elephant-parade, and elephants' first appearance in Rome, as Manius Curius Dentatus celebrated his triumph over Pyrrhus. To complete this interlocked tale, this latter-day Pyrrhus' failure to get elephants smoothly through a city-gate led to his own death and beheading.[35] In this light, Pliny's Romans' curse is richly overdetermined.

Elephants provoking Pompey's doom are Caesar's gain, and it may not be irrelevant that the obverse of a silver denarius issued by Caesar – perhaps his first coinage during the civil war – displays an elephant trampling a snake, with *CAESAR* inscribed in the exergue.[36] As Nousek (2008) has shown, Caesar's appropriation of elephantine symbols arrogated power and propaganda of 'not one but three of his fiercest opponents: L. Domitius Ahenobarbus, Caecilius Metellus Pius Scipio Nasica, and, most obviously, Cn. Pompeius Magnus'. Julius Caesar's heirs inherited the precedent: under Augustus and Tiberius, following Seleucid example,[37] the elephant turned a significant symbol of the *princeps*' divinity and ascent, as an immortal, to heaven:[38] emblematically, Philip of Thessalonica (*Anth. Pal.* 9.285) celebrates the elephant's transformation from monstrous war-animal to carriage of the dead (and immortal) Augustus. In life, Augustus had already compared himself to an elephant (Suet. *Iul.* 53.2, Ael. *NA* 2.2), and, imitating Philopator, dedicated four obsidian elephants in the temple of Concord *pro miraculo* (Plin. *HN* 36.196), which could mean 'as a curiosity' (Rackham), 'for the portent' (Toynbee 1973, 54) or for 'the marvel'; might Augustus' appropriation of elephants have anything to do with Julius Caesar's defeat of Pompey, and with stories of Pompey's affronts against elephants? If it did, then it would connect to the fantastical notice, shared by the life of Aelius in the *Historia Augusta* (2.3) and Servius' commentary on Virgil's *Aeneid*, that derives the name 'Caesar' etymologically from a respectively Moorish and Punic word, *caesa*, purportedly meaning elephant. In this (likely retrospective) light, Pompey's abuse of the elephant is avenged by the man-god named for that same beast; no doubt Caesar's elephant denarii would have aided such associations.

Elephants, the Trojan Horse, and the origins of Latin literature

Elephants' symbolic capital to the Julian house may explain their apparent role in Augustan poetry. Elephants had been with Roman literature from its beginnings: one of the omens (*monstra*) that had led the Romans to establish literature as an institution was a child born with an elephant's head (Livy 27.11; cf. Val. Max. 1.6). Elephants, symbols for Rome's political houses, were especially important to one of Augustus' sponsored poets, Horace, whose cognomen, Flaccus, drew attention to his ears (Plin. *HN* 11.136), perhaps to their wobbling size (Lyd. *Mag.* 1.23 Φλάκκον τὸν ὦτα μείζονα ἔχοντα).[39] His Lucanian origins (*Sat.* 2.1.34) possibly inspired his interest in the 'Lucanian cow' (*luca bos*), as the elephant was known at Rome (Var. *Ling.* 7.39–40) for the place where Pyrrhus had first introduced them to Italy. His *Epodes* compares the poet unfavourably as a sexual partner to 'black elephants' (*nigris . . . barris*, 12.1), the first (and, for several centuries, only) attestation of another word for elephant, *barrus*,[40] that closely resembles Ennius' term (*Burrus*) for Pyrrhus (*Ann.* fr. 166 Sk.). A topological *puer senex*,[41] the elephant well fits Horace's vision of Rome's literary genius, which, as he notes in his *Epistle to Augustus*, 'turned his wit late to Greek writings' (*serus enim Graecis admouit acumina chartis*, 161).[42] That same poem notes that Democritus would laugh at the crowd that delights in watching a hybrid camel-panther or a white elephant (*elephans albus*, 196), but turns a donkey's tin ear to a poet's words: with elephants' cries in mind, the poet concludes, 'What voices could defeat the sound with which our theatres now resound?' (*quae peruincere uoces / eualuere sonum, referunt quem nostra theatra*, 200–201). Yet more decisively, and autobiographically, Horace's nine-years waiting-period for publishing (*Ars P.* 388–90)[43] resembles the elephants' ten-year gestation (*HN* 8.28) that Pliny himself would use to describe the long gestation of his own *Natural History* (*HN praef.* 28); the fact that Horace there is recommending submitting one's work to the judgment of Spurius Maecius Tarpa (*Ars P.* 387), whom Cicero's letter to Marius (7.1.1 SB 24) notes had been (unfortunately) appointed to choose the theatrical productions for the inauguration of his Theatre, points up this connection:[44] if you are a poet from the land of elephants, then you produce poems at an elephantine pace, and naturally are inclined to submit your works to an experienced elephant hand.[45]

Virgil's *Aeneid* turns Horace's self-oriented elephantine interests imperial. When Virgil narrates his poem's earliest plot-point, he hides Pompey's elephants in plain view, in the form of the Trojan Horse.[46] This contrivance, an erie concatenation of the mechanical and the organic, has a great deal of the elephant about it: it is a mountain-sized horse (*instar montis equum*, 2.15) that is both 'monster' (*monstrum*) and machine of war (*machina belli*, 151; cf. 42, 237) that contains a wooden enclosure (Hexter 1990) that holds a cohort of soldiers among which sits Pyrrhus (263), whose third-century BCE descendent would bring elephants to Italy.[47] If Virgil's Trojan Horse borrows from the *Equos Troianus* of Livius Andronicus or Naevius, Virgil might have recalled the dramatic performance of that play that Cicero notes was part of the inauguration of Pompey's theatre; its famous concluding line, *sero sapiunt* [*sc. Phryges*], 'The Trojans come to wisdom too late' (Cic. *Fam.* 7.16.1 SB 140),[48] applies to Priam and Pompey with equal force, as it would, transversally, to Pyrrhus the Epirot. As Philip Hardie (2013) has noted, Virgil seems to connect, or reflect a connection between, Pompey, Pyrrhus the Epirot and Pyrrhus (=Neoptolemos) the son of Achilles. Virgil's reference to Pyrrhus by patronym (*Aeacides, Aen.* 3.294–297), Hardie suggests (118), recalls the ambiguous oracle that Ennius' *Annals* claims gave the Romans victory over Pyrrhus: 'I say that you the son of Aeacus the Romans will be able to defeat' (*aio te Aeacida Romanos uincere posse*, fr. 167 Sk.). Virgil's headless Pyrrhus-slain Priam 'touches' the parallel fate of Pompey the Great (Serv. *ad Aen.* 2.557), but it also touches Pyrrhus' Epirot descendent.[49] Ascribing Pompey's fall to crimes against elephants may also inform Virgil's account of Laocoon's death: the Trojans claim that 'he had paid rightly for his crime, in that he had harmed the oak with his spear-tip and hurled his criminal spear into its [*sc.* the Horse's] back' (*et scelus expendisse merentem / Laocoonta ferunt, sacrum qui cuspide robur / laeserit et tergo sceleratam intorserit hastam*, 229–231). Laocoon's infliction of suffering upon the animalized Horse is especially evocative: 'its belly struck, its caves sounded, its caverns gave a groan' (*uteroque recuso / insonuere cauae gemitumque dedere cauernae*, 52–53). The lamenting voices of Pompey's elephants were, for Pliny, responsible for the remarkable association of elephants with human society described in Cicero's letters; here, in Virgil's poem, one finds the groans of the elephantine horse behind the people's turn against Laocoon and his cause, thus turning the tide of history.

In Virgil's historical scheme, the Horse dooms Troy, but fulfils Sinon's dubious prophecy (192–194) that is as double-edged as that bestowed on Ennius' Pyrrhus: Greece's Greek-filled horse allows the Greeks to conquer Troy but Rome to conquer Greece. Steven Smith (2014) has shown how Aelian used Italian-born elephants' ability to learn Greek as a model for Roman Hellenization (80–86); similarly, Virgil's elephantine, Pompeian, Trojan Horse points to Rome's path to world empire through the proper integration of Hellenistic symbols of power. Precisely such an integration is operative in Virgil's comparison of the Trojans preparing for departure from Carthage to ants: 'The black line goes over the fields,' (*it nigrum campis agmen*, 4.404). Servius ascribes this hemistich to Ennius' description of elephants (and Accius' of Indians), a humorous juxtaposition Plutarch would also exploit (*Soll.* 968B). Thus, already in Carthage Aeneas represents the Roman turned Hellenistic 'elephant-commander' (ἐλεφαντάρχης, Plut. *Demetr.* 25.5–9); Aeneas' Trojans represent a society as sociable, pious and god-beloved as any elephant herd.[50] Precisely this historical nexus is adumbrated by Jupiter's prophecy in the *Aeneid*'s first book: shortly after the reference to Julius or Augustus Caesar that motivated Servius' note that 'Caesar' derives from the Punic word for 'elephant', we find Jupiter saying to Venus, 'You, care-free, will at last into heaven receive him weighted down with eastern spoils – he too shall be called upon by vows' (*hunc tu olim caelo, spoliis Orientis onustum, / accipies secura; uocabitur hic quoque uotis*, 289–290). Viewed in elephantine light, what heavier Eastern spoils could Romans imagine than elephants, who, per numismatic evidence, would also prove the ideal apotheotic conveyance to heaven, and, quite possibly, the source of Caesar's own name (*uocabitur*)? Whatever the ultimate etymological origin of 'Caesar', these stories turn zoological associations generative:[51] Pompey, abuser of elephants, is laid low by 'Elephant', darling of the gods, symbol of immortal rule. Given this interwoven complex of allusions, it may be significant that Jupiter's own prediction of the conquered Trojans' eventual conquest of Greece (1.284–285) immediately precedes this allusion to Caesar's weighty Eastern spoils.

We cannot get behind Cicero's account of Pompey's exhibition, nor determine the sources of Pliny's and Cassius Dio's elaborations. It is clear, however, that the evolving commentaries upon this unusual event built both on natural philosophical theories of animals and elephants, as well as on the political symbolism of the elephant in Rome's Hellenistic, Mediterranean and Near Eastern worlds, in ways that found expression in Virgil's *Aeneid*. The Roman people are never again said to have objected in such a way to acts of cruelty against animals, but this story suggests that such an articulation, and its shadow of a posthumanist ethics, might have been at least thinkable. If the history of ideas includes paths imagined, but not taken, then stories like that of Pompey's elephants should invite us to welcome these beasts into Rome's cultural bestiary, in which animals served as symbolic currency that bolstered and muddled political programmes and literary forms. Maurizio Bettini has noted that 'monsters are good to think with';[52] true, and even better are animals in equal parts monstrous and compassionate, beasts and gods, and a part, quite possibly, of our human community.

CHAPTER 12
THE MONSTROSITY OF CATO IN LUCAN'S *CIVIL WAR* 9

James McNamara

Introduction

This chapter discusses the monstrosity of Cato in Lucan's *Civil War*, and posthuman facets of his attempt to resurrect *virtus* after the collapse of established *mores*. The rhetoric of the epic lends itself to reflection on the monstrous, and throws into doubt the integrity of the subject in a universe paradoxically unified by its drive to dissolution.[1] In the desert-crossing episode of *Civil War* 9, the war against Caesar, already lost, is occluded by a struggle between the *virtus* of Cato and the hostile environment of Libya (in particular, 9. 368–889).[2] The imagery of civil war as cosmic dissolution has already come to a head in the battle of Pharsalus in book 7 and the ensuing books have a post-cataclysmic character. As Cato marches his army across the Libyan desert, Lucan's celebration of his 'triumph' (9. 593–604) stands in challenging juxtaposition to the disastrous destruction of his soldiers. The concept of *virtus* that Lucan exalts is an attempt to transcend the potentially tragic downfall of *viri*. I argue that the dissolution of the human *vir* as subject is accompanied by the ascent of a monstrous posthuman subject represented by Cato and Medusa. These figures allow reflection on the transcendence of identity and death, major questions in posthumanism. Cato's *virtus*, ostensibly praised by the authorial voice, cannot be regarded as a satisfactory ideal for the humans of the *Civil War*.[3]

The snake attacks on Cato's soldiers, a 'catalogue of carnivalesque bodily distortions without parallel in surviving Roman epic or history'[4] are augmented by Lucan's uncharacteristic excursion into avowedly mythical material. The myth of Medusa has been productively examined as an analogy for the events of the surrounding narrative.[5] As Bexley remarks, a comparison that might be expected of the Medusan excursus – between the heroic *viri* Perseus and Cato – is disrupted by Medusa's dominant role in the digression and by an extended alignment of Medusa and Cato as figures who exert power through their gaze.[6] I suggest that Cato is the dominant monster of book 9. Not only is he physically extraordinary, surpassing all his men in hardihood, but he appears, by means of his philosophy, to exist on a different plane altogether, unthreatened by the snakes, and his ever-present gaze engages in the admonition (cf. *moneo*) and guiding role (cf. *monstro*) associated with a *monstrum*.[7] It is in collusion with the Libyan snakes that Cato's *virtus* becomes the central concern, or problem, of book 9, as *monstra* simultaneously define and destroy the guiding ethics of those who remain after the Pharsalian catastrophe.[8]

Fracturing of the subject

Bartsch offers productive readings of Lucan's *Civil War* as a representation of the fracturing of the subject or the self amidst political, moral and cosmic self-destruction.[9] On every level, Lucan's world is fragmenting through *bella plus quam civilia* (1.1); it is at once the self-destruction of the Roman people and *res publica* and a disaster that calls forth the imagery of cosmic dissolution: the self-destruction of the whole 'mechanism' of the universe (1.80).[10] The integrity of the human being is under threat throughout, as physical destruction and moral corruption destroy both bodily and moral fibre. Lapidge analyses Lucan's use of the imagery of cosmic dissolution in the *Civil War*, strongly grounding it in the language of Stoic cosmology, with its culmination in the battle of Pharsalus (especially 7.812–815). The last three books of the epic, he argues, do not employ the imagery of cosmic dissolution.[11] One of the unexplained consequences of Lapidge's cogent reading of cosmic dissolution is that the epic continues after the cataclysm. In book 9, Cato's decision to cross the desert is an attempt to resurrect an ideal of *virtus* that effectively depends on the destruction of *viri*, undoing the human, as a peculiar version of Stoic ethics takes centre stage. Although Lucan consistently offers overt encomium of Cato, readers have sensed that this position is undermined in various ways.[12] Building on such interpretations, I wish to suggest that Cato's *virtus* has cyborgic qualities that serve the monstrous philosopher but spell disaster for the human beings who follow him.

The last victim of the lurid sequence of snake attacks (9.737–833) is also the only one to survive. Bexley remarks, 'The paradox that the subject must become at least partially objectified in order to retain its subjectivity is played out in Murrus' harsh action against himself.' Only by discarding a part of himself – a monstrous castoff, perfused with venom – can Murrus survive the episode.[13]

quam protinus ille retecto
ense ferit totoque semel demittit ab armo,
exemplarque sui spectans miserabile leti
stat tutus pereunte manu.

9.830–833

Straight away he draws his sword, strikes it [his hand] and separates it from his arm; beholding the wretched exemplar of his own death, he stands safe while his hand perishes.

Scholars have discussed Lucan's obsessive recourse to imagery of decapitation, which in book 9 leaves Pompey a headless *truncus*, whose dismemberment metonymically represents the violent overthrow of political order. That metaphor, going back in Roman culture to the speech of Menenius Agrippa upon the secession of the plebs, is inherently classist.[14] Murrus, whose role was never to be the head but rather the hand, survives bereft of that which defines his place in the destructive Roman enterprise. Paradoxically, in doing so he preserves his life and subjectivity. A cast-off part of himself becomes an edifying *exemplar* to prepare him for his own eventual complete demise. As I shall presently discuss, the episode is dominated by the dynamics of Cato's frighteningly active spectatorship of his soldiers' deaths; not suffering himself in the way his troops do (certainly not being destroyed like Murrus' hand), it is arguably Cato the martyr, back from the future, who serves as such a mighty *exemplar*. After the deaths preceding him, Murrus is described in a strangely serene manner (*stat tutus*) despite his mutilation. Watching what has just been a part of him – now consigned to the status of the abject – he learns from the strange affinity that emerges from the self-destruction of his physical identity.[15]

Affinities and alienation

Cyborgic identity does not observe the boundaries that separate one human subject from another; it is more fluid, existing somewhere between the bounded physical existence of the human and the totally networked existence of a line of code. Haraway remarks in her 'Cyborg Manifesto' on the value of affinities where identities break down: 'The recent history for much of the U.S. left and U.S. feminism has been a response to this kind of crisis by endless splitting and searches for a new essential unity. But there has also been a growing recognition of another response through coalition – affinity, not identity.'[16]

Lucan's *Civil War*, with an eye to identity and its role in political life, shows endless fracturing: any sense of integral wholeness is shattered or turns to self-destruction, from the individual to the cosmic level. At the heart of this self-destructive cosmos is the fatal division between Romans. While traditional social identities are under threat, however, the poet develops strange affinities, most notably with his monsters. Readers have often noted that the poet seems carried away by the horrific glamour of his creations.[17] Posthumanism is open to animal, earth and monstrous subjectivity.[18] The perverse collusion between the poet and his monsters allows Lucan to strike at the heart of Civil War ethics: the problem of *virtus*. This problem, which animates the civil war right up to Pharsalus, continues even after the cataclysm, and it is Cato's struggle with *virtus* in the desert crossing episode of book 9, in which animals, earth and monsters threaten to overshadow the heroic *vir*, that I wish to discuss as an exploration of human problems in a posthuman environment.

After the death of Pompey, the war is effectively already lost, and Lucan now disavows any interest in success. The crossing of the desert is represented, perversely, as a superior kind of triumph that demonstrates what no previous generations of Romans had shown: valour stripped of all exterior considerations, *nuda virtus* with no regard for success (9. 593–596). Now that the outcome of the war is in no doubt, Lucan refocuses his epic away from the fate of the state and onto the personal *virtus* of Cato. The motivation for the desert crossing is difficult to establish in any pragmatic sense, but morally it is justified as necessary for the full expression of Cato's *virtus*:

> *'sola potest Libye turba praestare malorum*
> *ut deceat fugisse uiros.' sic ille paventes*
> *incendit virtute animos et amore laborum.*
>
> *9. 405–407*

> 'Only Libya, through its host of plagues, can provide this: that it will be honorable for men to flee.' Thus he fired their fearful hearts with valour and desire for hardship.

Cato's speech finishes on the emphatic call to honour as men, practically as heroes (*viri*). Cato and Libya are in collusion insofar as each needs the other for the full realization of their nature, *virtus* and *mors* respectively.[19] As I shall show, Cato's manner of replicating his ideas has little to do with the ordinary limits of human *vires*. After extolling Cato as one who may one day be regarded as divine (9.601–604), Lucan casts a shocking light on the nature of that predicted divinity, by aligning Cato with the inanimate and the monstrous, with Libya and its snakes, and with the source of these, the monster Medusa.

Bexley has shown the similarities between Cato's role as spectator of the snake-inflicted deaths and the edifying role of an imagined *sapiens* in Seneca's practical ethics.[20] Cato, sailing unharmed through the perils of the desert, appears as an admonishing *monstrum*. As Seneca put it, 'Do everything as if Epicurus were watching' (Sen. *Ep.* 25.5). Seneca repeatedly invokes the ideal spectatorship of Cato: *Ep.* 11.10; 25. 6; 104.21–22. It is noteworthy that the Cato of Lucan's desert crossing can be closely paralleled by the Cato of Seneca's visualizations. In a sense, Lucan's Cato is behaving not as the flesh-and-blood opponent of Caesar, but already as Cato the martyr, a figure whose significance transcends mortal limitations. Lucan's physically vulnerable soldiers are being exhorted to pluck up their courage by the unremitting gaze of one who is back from the future: Cato as an idea, not Cato as a man. The confrontation serves to throw into stark relief the plight of humans amidst a posthuman paradigm that disastrously combines humanity after the cataclysm with the insufficient redemption of Cato.

Perhaps there is something even more sinister at work. Not only is Cato responsible for taking his army across the desert, but, as Lucan says, in rounding off the series of snake-inflicted deaths, it appears that he *forces* his soldiers to endure:

> *cogit tantos tolerare labores*
> *summa ducis uirtus, qui nuda fusus harena*
> *excubat atque omni fortunam prouocat hora.*
> *omnibus unus adest fatis.*
>
> *9.881–886*

> The supreme valour of the leader forces them to endure such great hardship, as he lies down to sleep on the bare sand and issues his challenges to fortune at every hour. He alone is present at every death.

Sklenář (2003) absolves Cato by shifting responsibility to his *virtus*.[21] This seems, rather, to be precisely the problem: establishing the nature of this *virtus*, and whether it truly serves ordinary *viri* as it serves Cato. The contradictions in his role are exemplified by the way he appears upon the sand (evocative of a battlefield or an arena) as both a duelling champion (*fortunam provocat*) and a spectator (*omnibus ... adest fatis*).[22] The problem is further exemplified in the role of *patientia*, a traditionally laudable quality insofar as it represents endurance, but less obviously so when it signifies passivity. Cato's '*aristeia*' is largely passive, either when he displays his own endurance or when he imparts *patientia* to his men as he witnesses their deaths. Furthermore, the escapade in the desert is itself a consequence of Cato's *impatiens virtus* (9.371), a quality Lucan contrasts with Pompey's restraint in keeping his forces in safer climes. Cato is in tune with the Libyan environment: *impatientia* is a characteristic of the Libyan soil, which does not bear crops; rather than being barren, however, it is productive of all manner of deadly creatures.[23] While Cato is unconcerned, his men react very differently. They complain, but not against nature, since they are out of place, trespassers in a land not intended for humans:

> *inpatiensque solum Cereris cultore negato*
> *damnasti atque homines uoluisti desse uenenis.*
> *in loca serpentum nos uenimus.*
>
> *9.857–859*

> And you [sc. nature] condemned the fruitless soil, forbidding anyone to cultivate it, and it was your will that there should be no human beings where there is venom. We have come into places that belong to the serpents.

The collective complaints of the solders at 848–880 suggest that they do not understand the desert crossing in Cato's terms. When they ask that they be sent to die in battle against Caesar rather than in the desert, they are expressing views quite out of step with Lucan's extolling of *nuda virtus*, with no thought for success. For the soldiers, a struggle against Caesar, however fruitless, is preferable to completely abstracted *labores*.

Virtus *after the* vir

At the oracle of Ammon, Cato proposes the Stoic notion that no force (*vis*) can harm a man possessed of *virtus*. This notion is undermined in a variety of ways by the series of deaths at 9.737–838. The first of the six vignettes of snake-inflicted deaths teaches completely the wrong moral argument. When the *signifer* Aulus is driven by the thirst-inducing *tacitum virus* (9.741) of the *dipsas* to drink his own blood, and there is no way for the incident to be redeemed, Cato is forced to have Aulus' *signa* snatched away to hide the lesson *hoc posse sitim*: that thirst can have this effect. Leigh's argument that the unquenchable thirst that steals upon Aulus is expressed in the language of desire, and demonstrates the failure of a common Stoic precept, suggests the extension of the perverse forms of desire that replicate the power of Lucan's cyborgic monsters.[24] The *tacitum virus* completely obliterates Aulus' ability to display *virtus*.[25] The next victim, Sabellus, is infected with the *virus* of the tiny *seps*, which consumes him so that even his corpse is completely stolen away. As Bartsch has noted, this description throws into doubt the complex existence of a human self or subject: the whole of Sabellus' body is opened up to the world, showing 'what a human being is': *quidquid homo est, aperit pestis natura profana*, 9.777. The heroic status of *vir* is reduced to the more prosaic *homo*, and completely stripped of the physical integrity that allows the human being to exist as a subject. Sabellus, reduced to his disintegrating physical form, is very far from being, like Cato at the oracle of Ammon, *deo plenus tacita quem mente gerebat*, 'full of the god whom he carried in his silent mind' (9.564). The blood of the next victim Tullus is completely transfused for *virus*: *sic omnia membra/ emisere simul rutilum pro sanguine uirus*, 'thus all his limbs at once poured forth red venom instead of blood' (9.809–810). In a world dominated by civil war, the embodied condition of the human is its weakness. At the first hurdle, Cato's lesson – that *virtus* is paramount – falters, as Aulus' suffering drives him to abhorrent extremes. Medusan death has a viral character, replicating in human bodies. While Cato is accorded quasi-divine status, a problem remains: he is an extraordinary exception, who is not susceptible to the weaknesses of embodiment that are so evident in his soldiers. He is *virtus*, rather than *vir.* Cato fails as a talisman for his soldiers because he has less affinity with them than with the monstrous power of Medusan death.

The difficulty of defining Cato's *virtus* is signalled by a striking *recusatio*, when Cato is given the opportunity to consult the oracle of Ammon, and it is suggested he might ask for guidance upon the nature of *virtus*. Cato responds with a series of rhetorical questions to which he knows the answers – but does not state them. Amongst his responses are the following:

an noceat uis nulla bono fortunaque perdat
opposita uirtute minas, laudandaque uelle
sit satis et numquam successu crescat honestum?

9.569–571

Is the good man impervious to all force? Are fortune's threats in vain against valour? Is it enough to want what is praiseworthy? Does right bear no relation to the scale of success?

Although it becomes clear what Cato's answers to most of these questions must be: that no force can do harm to a good man, that fortune's threats are in vain against *virtus*, and that right is concerned with purpose and not with success, nevertheless, the absence of an outright answer allows doubts to remain. The suggestion that wanting *laudanda* is enough may appear as a vainglorious addiction to the external criterion of praise. On the other hand, the disregard for success as an indifferent external criterion is taken to troubling extremes.

Lucan calls the desert crossing a triumph, preferable to the deeds of Rome's renowned heroes, but Cato's *nuda virtus* – stripped, that is, of success – is a difficult ideal to agree with, not only because the costs are so high, but because it is not clear that Cato succeeds in establishing a new approach to *virtus* that is of any service to others beyond himself. The behaviour of Lucan's Cato verges on a perverse idealization of suffering and death as desirable targets rather than indifferent circumstances. When Cato offers his men *ingens meritum maiusque salute*, 'a great benefit, mightier than rescue' (9.885), it is *in letum vires*; the preposition ambiguously, or simultaneously, represents strength *against* death and a powerful drive *towards* death. Seneca warned against *ambitio*, the *perversa via* that led philosophers to advertise their exceptional status through ostentatious asceticism (Sen. *Ep.* 5.2).[26] Tacitus would later reject the attitudes of those who had sought *ambitiosa mors* over a life of service (Tac. *Ag.* 42.5). The contradictions inherent in *patientia* both as hardihood and as 'opting out' of social duties by hurtling towards a fruitless death are constantly apparent in the desert episode. The monstrosity of Lucan's Cato is evident in the paradox of his *patientia*: the tribulations of the *perversa via* through the Libyan desert may raise him to a higher plane, but it is one occupied by disembodied ideas, and in the process he becomes alienated from the embodied suffering humans under his leadership.

There is a disquieting sense that Cato's perverse drive is a cause of suffering. Cato's monstrous beholding, his monstrous *theory* of *virtus*, cannot easily be regarded in isolation from the petrifying gaze of the supermonster Medusa. Her gaze affects all matter, animate and inanimate alike, whether she be alive or dead.[27] For Medusa, death is irrelevant: her severed head in the grip of Perseus or on the aegis of Pallas has as much power to petrify as it did when she lived. To this extent, Lucan is in agreement with earlier versions of the myth, such as Ovid's in the *Metamorphoses*, but the power of his monster seems capable of infinite extension,[28]

hoc potuit caelo pelagoque minari
torporem insolitum mundoque obducere terram.

9.647–648

This [monster] had the power to threaten the sky and the sea with unaccustomed paralysis and cover the world with clay.

This ability to turn the whole world into a barren mineral transcends Medusa's own death and the boundaries between the previously animate and inanimate. Yet the 'unaccustomed paralysis' that Medusa threatens is something more lifeless even than ordinary earth or sea. The image of 'self-replicating death' resembles the fear of various kinds of non-human technological death debated by contemporary technological posthumanists. Increasing automation in technologies of death reaches a new level of terror when the potential of self-replicating robotics is taken into account. Non-living intelligence and strength can replicate itself in the pursuit of the negation of life.[29] In Medusa, nature has incubated its perils and poisons, but a sense of her subjectivity is relatively unimportant – Medusan power is a cyborgic capability, not bound to her as an individual. Her dismembered gaze turns Libya to stone and her blood gives rise to the snakes – not in a metaphor of motherhood, but in a process of replication.[30] When her blood gives rise to snakes, and not to new gorgons, her character as an assemblage of nature's *pestes*, divided against herself, is expressed.[31] Lucan's dystopian vision reveals facets of posthumanism left underappreciated by posthumanist sociologists such as Braidotti: the danger posed to human existence by those technologies that replace reproduction with replication, and human goals of perfection with the cyborgic counterpart of optimization, a danger suggested by Haraway's juxtaposition of the 'organics of domination' and the 'informatics of domination'. Haraway strikingly lays out a vision of the dangers inherent in technological advancement superimposed on existing structures of domination.[32]

Conclusions

While *virtus* gives meaning to the horrific and otherwise senseless deaths of the soldiers, the troubling question remains, whether *virtus* itself disintegrates with Cato's *viri*. In part, the problem is Cato's fixation on an ideal that brings with it the destructiveness of Roman *mores* leading up to the cataclysm of Pharsalus. Lapidge remarks on the difficulty readers of Lucan have faced in trying to gain a correct understanding of his use of Stoic ideas, for want of a deep familiarity with Stoic philosophy. Cato's soldiers might be regarded as suffering under a similar predicament, raised to the level of existential terror. In posthuman terms, the desert-crossing episode dramatizes the disastrous effects on humans in the posthuman world dominated by Medusa and Cato, each of them monstrous, each of them cyborgic in their nature as beings in a state somewhere between a bounded body and a rapidly spreading code.

The episode is marked by strange affinities and fatal rupture. As Johnson has said of Cato, 'This Cato is, in short, something of a pain in the neck, something of a bore. Or rather he would be were he not also fascinating and vital and funny ... If I dislike him ... I find myself nevertheless enjoying him.'[33] In *Civil War* 9, enjoyment – if there is any – derives from Cato's unexpected affinity with Medusa. It is dismaying that Cato's theory remains incomprehensible to his soldiers, and it is his privileged removal from their plight that makes his redemptive role such a failure. The posthuman character of the episode is evident in the obstacles that stand in the way of a tragic reading from the perspective of the soldiers, the bizarre character of the snake attacks distracting from the suffering of the victims. As Mitchell has put it in the chapter 'Cyborg Agonistes': 'The characteristic modern fear is not of barbarians beyond the gates ... but of foreign bodies networked into our midst.' This trouble is especially acute when the foreign body is cast as a *dux*.

CHAPTER 13
WHY CAN'T I HAVE WINGS? ARISTOPHANES' *BIRDS*

Maria Gerolemou

Introduction

The human desire to restore physical characteristics through various kinds of prosthetics is a common and up to a point socially accepted desire. Prosthesis in this chapter, however, deals merely with cases of artificial extension and enhancement of a perfectly proportioned body that seeks through prosthetics to overcome any weakness that the physical body might have.[1] The idea that a healthy organic part could be replaced, increased or improved by a human-like, artificial or non-human limb, which one could use to overcome bodily limitations to one's own advantage and at the expense of others, raises certain questions with regard, generally, to the extent that the prosthetic is allowed to mingle with the natural body and, particularly, to the way this is used.[2]

In Aristophanic comedy, the 'naturalness' of the body is a predominant idea:[3] this idea arises from the fact that here, where the country lifestyle prevails, being 'away from the ills of the city'[4] means to demonize all that is technological or artificial, i.e., everything that does not 'spontaneously' grow on earth (*Ach.* 976, αὐτόματα πάντ' ἀγαθὰ τῷδέ γε πορίζεται). The working class-world of Aristophanic comedy seems to refuse to accept people with intelligence or bodily abilities much beyond the usual human average range: that could lead to rapid social and economic changes that are often scorned in Aristophanic comedy; consider, for instance, the case of a poor citizen suddenly entering the upper classes (see *Peace* 538–550, 1158–1264).[5] This becomes even more outrageous when the poor citizen succeeds in so doing by enhancing his body through unnatural means, which help him to be successful without effort and individual labour and thus gain more profits.[6] This is true not only for Aristophanes' world of labourers; although Athenian society aims to improve intelligence or strength through better education, nutrition, or training, at the same time this cannot reach the point of jeopardizing elementary democratic axioms such as equal access to power and wealth: when only some bodies are enhanced by prosthetics, giving them greater access to resources, opportunities and welfare, this could lead to social inequality through the creation of two groups of citizen, the enhanced and the non-enhanced.

In Aristophanes' *Birds*, what is defined as the desired prosthetic is the wings. Visitors travel to the land of the birds in order to acquire wings which will make their life more comfortable. The fact that in this case prosthetic means do not derive from inorganic matter, i.e., they are not made out of metals, stone, wood, etc.,[7] but from animals, spawns further fears on the risks of prosthetics. Having animal features supplement the human body could create a hybrid body;[8] animal parts could enhance, improve or fix the human body, but, at the same time, they may point towards its vulnerability and inferiority (as it is compared with other life forms).[9] A first step towards identifying animal parts as prosthetic means in ancient literary texts was taken most recently by Samuel Durham Cooper in his doctoral thesis on posthumanism in Aristophanes (2017); in his discussion of *Birds*, he uses the notion of *prosthesis* to briefly describe the function of wings, which, in the play, are prepared to be consumed by desperate humans who want to upgrade their everyday life.[10] However, Cooper, by limiting his discussion to generally defining wings as prosthetic means, discusses neither the incentives behind the demand for wings nor the possible effects of their use. As I argue, in replacing energy derived from human limbs with alternative power sources, the play highlights the threats that may stem from expanding human potential via non-human, animal parts.[11] However, the critical issue with enhancing the human body with animal parts is portrayed in the play not as bodily degeneration but as moral collapse, which relates to effortless wealth and power and the depreciation of physical labour.[12] This approach seems to contradict the view of Arrowsmith, who, in his famous article on Aristophanes' *Birds*, argues that wings in the play are a symbol of Athenian *polypragmosynê*, *pleonexia*, the erotic longing for a good life or, in his own words, the *libido dominandi* that defines the Athenians.[13] Indeed, although the picture of winged men is being mocked in the play – for instance, Tereus in his first appearance on stage thinks that Peisetaerus and Euelpides are laughing at his wings (96–98), and at 801–806 the two protagonists enter the stage laughing at each other's wings (μὰ Δί' ἐγὼ μὲν πρᾶγμά πω γελοιότερον οὐκ εἶδον οὐδεπώποτε),[14] the positive assessment of wings in the play is not threatened. That means, what is being disapproved of here is not the technology of wings as such, but the intention behind it and the way it is used, which are ethically questionable.

Avian technology

Tales of antiquity often refer to wings as attached to human bodies.[15] Wing manufacture goes back to Daedalus and his escape flight. The best-known ancient version of the flight is found in Ovid's *Metamorphoses* 8. 183–235. Daedalus refuses to escape by land or sea, instead choosing to escape through the skies, the only place outside Minos' rule. Ovid meticulously describes the manufacturing process of the wings: Daedalus picks feathers of different sizes, fastens them together with thread and wax and flexes each one into a gentle curve, so that they resemble and function similarly to a real bird's wings. By creating wings Daedalus disrupts, according to Ovid, the natural order of things (188f., *ignotas animum dimittit in artes/ naturamque novat*). The unnatural change of the human body and condition, which allows him to fly to the gods, is marked as an act of hybris. However, while the unfortunate story of Icarus, who soared too close to the sun and melted his wings, functions as a warning on the use of technology, especially when one ignores certain requirements which may render it a threat to nature and/or human nature, it simultaneously presents the beneficial aspects of technology, when used appropriately; in this case it offers freedom to Daedalus and Icarus.[16]

The same can be argued for Aristophanes' *Birds*. The issue here is not whether technological prosthesis is harmful, but how humans use it, or if technology is able to reflect human and civil goals. The beneficial impact of wings on humans is revealed both in the life of the human-bird Tereus (156–160) and in the two protagonists, Peisetaerus and Euelpides (572–576, wings are divine). The former brags about not having to pay for his food as a bird, while the latter says that birds are given him the opportunity to found a city and take on leadership roles. Generally, in the play, wings are promoted as the means to an easy life: according to the Coryphaeus, 'there is nothing more useful nor more enjoyable than to have wings' (785).[17] One can see more new and marvellous things while flying, in faraway countries, and earn more knowledge, for instance about the weather or where treasures are hidden (46–48, 116–119, 599–611, 1470–1472);[18] furthermore, wings keep one warm in winter (1088–1090) and provide access to various kinds of sources – food and wealth (586–603). But more importantly, wings can advance motion and expand its range, thus improving living conditions.[19] The improvement of transport conditions, as travelling was difficult, expensive (bad roads, violence, winds, tides, etc.)[20] and very time-consuming, forms a central topic of discussion in antiquity. Increasing speed techniques in communication seems, for instance, to fascinate Herodotus, particularly where he discusses the Persian couriers (8.98). According to him, 'there is nothing human that accomplishes a journey more swiftly than do these messengers', though he does not mention how they managed to be so fast.

Such improvements primarily aim to reduce the time an activity requires. Wings that speed up action seem, at first glance, to function perfectly in the environment of the *polis*, where time is deadline-directed, i.e., formed according to the timetables of democratic activities (elections, courts, festivals, etc.), where failure to meet various deadlines could be interpreted as a sign of political ineffectiveness.[21] The Clouds in the eponymous play accurately describe such a case, though in a different context. They rebuke the Athenians for meddling with the calendar and describe how people were misled about dinner time and went home having missed a festival or a scheduled sacrifice (615–626).[22] At the same time, however, over-speeding could eventually result in activities that harm the *polis*' institutions. According to the chorus of the *Birds*, if you have wings you don't have to watch a whole tragic performance; you can fly to your house, have lunch, relieve yourself, and then fly back to the theatre to resume (786–789). And if you have an affair with a married woman and notice her husband sitting in the theatre, if you have wings, you can fly to your mistress's house, sleep with her and quickly fly back (793–796). But an empty or partly empty theatre fails to fulfil its role in expressing democratic political ethos or national pride; generally, increased mobility could become an enemy of the *polis*' procedures, as the citizen body presupposes a certain stability; this is a prerequisite for participating in various political procedures and fests,[23] and is made clear by Peisetaerus when he states that if the birds want to be political and found a city, they must stop constantly flying here and there (165, μὴ περιπέτεσθε πανταχῆι, 169f.). There is an agreed perception of what it means to be an Athenian citizen, from which the winged, movable person can be distinguished. The idea of constant movement would appear even more awful in the eyes of peasants whose work on the land demands their constant presence.[24]

Wings as demerit goods

The high demand for wings raises additional issues in the play (1284–1307).[25] Wings give the impression that they are produced in quantity, and that they are the products of a mass production (1305–1311, 1325f.); though, in reality, they originate from moulting the poor birds. They even come in different types:[26] there are musical wings, prophetic or sea-wings (1330–1334). How one can obtain wings? You can either ask for them (1305–1307) or chew a little root and wings grow on your shoulders (654f.). The fact that they are easy to get as well as their oversupply could, furthermore, lower their value. Low-value wings could result in their careless consumption. In the play, such careless consumption is considered degrading and socially undesirable; as argued above, wings seem to obstruct citizen participation in democratic procedures; they, moreover, promote passivity and cause social inequality.

Peisetaerus' plan is to reach a place where things don't happen, τόπον ἀπράγμονα (44), specifically a place where the 'greatest things' (τὰ μέγιστα πράγματα, 128) would be to be invited to a wedding feast with no reciprocal obligations or where fathers criticize those who do not take sexual advantage of their attractive sons (137–142).[27] However, the city that is eventually invented by Peisetaerus does not praise inactivity. The play as a whole, while it allows, in a way, 'machinery' to facilitate labour and activity when this is conducted in a sensible way or, to put it better, in the interests of the *polis*, it rejects the abuse of life-simplified technology.

But let me clarify what I mean by 'machinery'. Peisetaerus' plan to find a city where ease guides people's lives is fulfilled through founding a city where tasks are easily accomplished due to a strictly organized division of physical labour: in the case of the birds, according to each bird's special body type and characteristics, such as long feet or a large beak (1136f., 1164–1167).[28] This is best exemplified in verses 1122–1169: the song depicts the construction of the city wall, and the specific tasks assigned to the birds, in a machine-driven way, according to which the workers' limbs and their tasks imitate the actions of tools (see e.g., 1145f. the geese use their feet like shovels). At the beginning of the song, what is praised is the fact that the birds execute their task with their own hands,[29] αὐτόχειρες; as a result, Peisetaerus cries: 'Is there, then, anything that feet can't do?' In the course of the song, however, what is being underscored is that the mechanized production, in which birds participate, rejects the idea of individual labour; i.e. the song rather portrays an automated society based on the division of labour among team-members.[30] The result is beautiful and magnificent (1125, κάλλιστον ἔργον καὶ μεγαλοπρεπέστατον); for instance, the size of the wall and the fact that it was built so fast impresses Peisetaerus (1131–1132, 1164–1165).[31]

In this automated society, where productivity is increased, its quality is improved and individual labour is, in a way, reduced through the division of tasks, wages are also de-linked from work (1152, τί δῆτα μισθωτοὺς ἄν ἔτι μισθοῖτό τις), although the birds never sold their labour power in exchange for wages, i.e., their labour was never economized (birds don't have wallets, 157).[32] In short, birds were always labouring for free; hence there is no slave class in their land. The slave of the Tereus-bird in the play constitutes an exception. Because Tereus used to be a man, he sometimes has special food requests that require a slave to fulfil them (70–79). Athenaeus in his *Deipnosophistae* states that the old comedy poets depict how people, at first, didn't need anything and thus, didn't have slaves (6.267e). He then cites a number of comic authors and plays where it is noted that goods during these years were automatically provided, hence, there was no need for slaves or other intermediaries between production and human consumption. Crates, for example, in his play *Theria*, describes how a day will come when slaves will not be needed at all as every utensil will be made self-moving, appearing or happening when it is called (Athenaeus 267e).[33] The notion of free wage as an integral part of automatized societies is summarized by Aristotle at the beginning of his *Politics* (1253b33–4a1), where he states that there is only one alternative to slaves and assistants and that is automation; in this context, he parallels Daedalus' animated statues to Hephaestus' moving tripods which are described in the *Iliad* (18.376).[34] However, for Aristophanes' working class, where individual human labour as a means of production is pivotal, an automated production process threatens to transform its participants into mere passive beings; at the end, the 'automatic' birds are deprived of individual responsibility or initiative and end up blindly following the commands of Peisaeterus.[35]

Ornithomania

Let us now consider the reasons behind the human desire for wings. According to the messenger, the desire to imitate everything that has to do with birds (appearance, way of life, names, songs, 1277–1312; 1340) depicts a trend that is translated into a kind of social madness (called *ornithomania*, 1290, though see 1279). That is, the key terms for describing this human need for wings are madness and mimesis. The mimetic faculty, a term coined by Walter Benjamin in his essay 'On the Mimetic Faculty', is defined as the compulsion to copy something or someone else. In *Thesmophoriazusae* Agathon suggests that what we do not own from our natural body can be acquired by mimesis (155f., ἃ δ' οὐ κεκτήμεθα/μίμησις ἤδη ταῦτα συνθηρεύεται). Mimesis is thus defined as a procedure that supplements the physical body; no purpose seems to be served by imitating something of your own nature, since such imitation is unnecessary and ineffective.[36] In a similar vein, Democritus (fr. 154)[37] also argues that humans can develop various abilities by watching the beasts; from the spider they can learn how to weave and mend, from the swallow how to build a house, from swans and nightingales how to sing (cf. also fr. 33).[38] Yet mimesis for the visitors to the land of the birds, who long for wings and wish to imitate everything that birds do, proves to be harmful and a potential threat to the city/citizens, because it is triggered by mania, which results in a careless use of wings (1284f.); this mania proves to be a destructive variation of the force that drove the two protagonists, Peisetaerus and Euelpides, to the land of the birds, that is the positive, inspired kind of erotic madness (324, 412, 1316).[39]

Peisetaerus, who proves to be a 'decent' citizen,[40] suggests that uncontrollable desires for individual profit cannot be trusted to define humanity. Although he seems to acknowledge that wings act as an effective tool that could give citizens an advantage in improving their quality of life,[41] he underlines his concerns that human hands, which differentiate humans from animals,[42] can lose their value when compared with wings (1308–1469). In other words, though hands and wings cannot be juxtaposed, as they each have different functions, there is always the danger that hands could be replaced by the more fortunate wings. Moreover, there are several characteristics that are common to both birds and humans, which could make the switch look natural. According to Aristotle, birds have humanlike capacities for vocal communication (e.g., *PA* 660a 35–661b2, *HA* 504b 1–3) and care for their young ones just as humans do.[43] Nevertheless, in contrast to animals, humans have hands that serve them well in their lives and place them in no worse fate than animals that *prima facie* seem to be more powerful (*PA* 687a 23–26); in addition, human hands work in cooperation with intelligence, while animal limbs merely fulfil mechanically predetermined plans (*PA* 687a2–687b2).[44] What Aristotle could have implied here is the following: the idea of replacing or enhancing human body parts with human-like and manipulable 'tools' appears to reflect the elimination of a creative expression or agency, a component of life that is fundamental to the human essence.

In light of this analysis, we should return to *Birds*, precisely at the moment when visitors start appearing in Nephelokokkygia, requesting wings. There are actually three groups of visitors. The first wishes to sell to the birds what the city has to offer (poetry, prophesies, town plans, quick profit, statutes); the second, which appears after the completion of the wall, frantically asks for wings; the third comes as a delegation sent by Zeus, asking only for a peace treaty with the birds. The willingness of the second group of visitors to give up their hands and physical labour proclaims the collapse of the Athenian social contract, which, as I argued at the outset, largely depends on both the presence of its citizens and their physical labour. By agreeing to transfer physical labour from human to non-human limbs, Athenian maxims like caring for your parents (physical effort), slavery (physical effort), being pure-bred Athenians (natural body), defending your land (physical strength), whose principles lie in the physical body and labour, are at risk. In other words, is it legitimate for an Athenian with wings who is bored in the courtroom to fly away for a while or for a defender of the national borders to desert his post and swiftly fly back home to take a nap? Moreover, what do you imagine would happen if an Athenian were to exchange his hands for Theban wings, or even worse for the wings of a slave bird? The need for a physical body, labour and presence for the proper functioning of the *polis* cannot be ignored.

The first visitor to Nephelokokkygia, a rebellious son, wishes to acquire feathers and live with the birds, because among birds one is allowed to 'throttle and peck his father' (1348). Peisetaerus acknowledges that family bonds don't matter in the land of the birds, but he 'remembers' an ancient law written in the tablets of the storks, which is described as follows: 'When the stork father has raised his young and has taught them to fly, the young must in their turn take care of the father' (1355–1357). What does the ancient law refer to here? This is probably a sophistry that Peisetaerus uses in order to drive away the young man who wishes to advance his body with wings.[45] Later, Peisetaerus gives the rebellious son wings with which he becomes like a fowl, and also offers him a 'patriotic alternative': he advises him to use his hands instead and fight on the Thracian coast as a hoplite (1364–1369).

The dithyrambic poet Cinesias, the second applicant, seeks wings from the birds in search of poetic inspiration (1383–1385). Cinesias comes to the land of the birds searching for 'new paths of songs'; he will need a whole load of wings, which will enable him to perform many flights and see and learn many things. Peisetaerus reacts brutally to the poet, whom he threatens to choke with feathers unless he ends his utterances (1397); finally, he advises him to stop dreaming of flying away with rented wings but to stay with the birds and use his legs to teach them how to dance.[46] The third applicant is an informer to the islanders, a sycophant and a lawsuit-hunter (1410). He is in need of wings to sweep around the world and serve orders. By getting wings, he will be able to rapidly fly to and from court business (1453–1460). He will also have the advantage of eluding pirates and coming back to Athens in springtime with the cranes, laden like them 'with a ballast of lawsuits' (1427–1429). Transportation by wings is more effective than transport by sea and land (233).[47] However, it jeopardizes the potentialities of human energy. Peisetaerus explicitly asks the third applicant: 'Tell me – a strong young man like you – you denounce foreigners for a living?' (1430–1431). The answer is: 'I never learnt how to dig,' meaning, 'I have never used my hands to make an honest living.' Peisetaerus decides to give him wings; but, this is done in the form of advice, and forces him to engage in a lawful occupation (1448–1450). The young man refuses to accept this and Peisetaerus chases him away with whips from Korkyra (1464–1469). The scene ends with the removal of the wing-basket from the stage (1469).[48]

To sum up, the play, though acknowledging the advantages of an enhanced body, cannot but mock the uncritical desire for wings by, generally, underlining the dubious relationship between non-human parts and the physical body. Wings on men seem to provide an unfair advantage over merely using the natural body. After all, isn't it 'cheating' to use wings to accomplish a task easier and faster than the rest of the citizens, instead of training to build up the endurance to perform the same task using human limbs?

PART III
BODIES AND ENTANGLEMENTS

CHAPTER 14
THE SEER'S TWO BODIES: SOME EARLY GREEK HISTORIES OF TECHNOLOGY

Martin Devecka

One of the lasting contributions of posthumanist theory will be to make us stop taking bodies for granted. In place of the body given by nature and modified, technologically, by culture, posthumanism gives us the body as inherently *produced*, not distinguishable from the technologies that act upon it by any nature/culture divide. A society has to *make* the bodies of its members. It does not receive them as raw material.[1]

If this is true for every society, it is true for each of them in different ways – Western practices of childhood vaccination, for instance, having little to do with the intricate facial tattoos of the Amazonian Caduveo, even though both these techniques serve by way of 'remaking' the body according to the idealized image of a *socius*. That is, the technological production of bodies is something that needs to be demonstrated anew for every culture at every time and place. For ancient Greece, this is a task that has yet to be completed.[2]

In what follows, I'll outline an approach to the problem by discussing two ways in which Greek bodies turn out to be shaped – even made – by technology. I'll show that, although there is a distinction in Greek reflection on the body between 'organic' and 'artificial', both these categories correspond to *technai* that effectively form the body in a human image. Moreover, what first appears as an opposition will turn out to be a structural complementarity: for the Greeks, the 'organic' can no more do without the 'artificial' than vice versa.

'Organic' bodily technics proceed by a process of selection and adaptation in response to an *umwelt*. Its activity is organized around a norm of health, which it strives to maintain by the invention and application of technologies according to a *techne* that we could loosely – although, as we'll see, not exclusively – identify as *iatrike*, a 'healing art'.

The crafting of 'artificial' bodies works rather differently and could in fact be understood as a complete structural inversion of the organic. In the Greek imagination, artifice produces android bodies that are mimetic of organic ones even to the extent of being able to move. These bodies are strictly closed off from their *umwelt*, however, and do not work to maintain any norm, because the rule that governs their activity refers, not to a changing environment, but to the moment of their creation as a *mimesis*. The crafting of these artificial bodies, which was thereafter to become the province of the *mechanopoios*, takes its origin from the art of sculpture.[3]

I'm going to flesh out these claims through a close reading of two texts, the Hippocratic *On Ancient Medicine* and the *Peri Apiston* of Palaephatus, which treat organic and artificial techniques respectively. From these texts I intend to demonstrate that artificial and organic bodies stand, for the Greeks, in a properly structural relationship to one another. Then, by looking closely at a pair of passages from Herodotus' *Histories* that dramatize the technological production of bodies, I'll show that the imaginarium of the artificial body not only structurally complements, but also vitally supplements the *iatrike techne* through which the organic body seeks its norm of health. When the organic body breaks down beyond repair, it can only recover its lost wholeness by becoming artificial: at such limit points, the organic production of bodies becomes impossible.

On Ancient Medicine begins by giving a *logos*, a rational account, of the medical *techne*. For the author of this text, medicine has its origins neither in divine revelation nor in speculative reason but in the self-regulation of man's relationship to his *umwelt*. Since *On Ancient Medicine* is a handbook of dietetics, its author specifies this claim by giving a history of eating. In the beginning, people ate like animals, but the diet didn't agree with them. They suffered many terrible things (πολλά τε καὶ δεινὰ) on account of their harsh animal diet ἰσχυρῆς τε καὶ θηριώδεος διαίτης, and the better part of them, weak by nature, probably died from it. Those who survived long enough to think better of eating raw meat and leaves sought out nourishment that was suitable to their nature τροφὴν ἁρμόζουσαν τῇ φύσει. What they ended up with was the food we use now: bread, cooked meat, et cetera.[4]

This 'modern' dietetics is a technological apparatus, and it develops as an adaptive response to an environment in which all the available food makes us ill. Note that our inability to handle the food that nature provides is what sets us apart from the animals, who, because they can eat just whatever grows from the ground, never need to worry about baking bread or roasting meat. They already stand in a state of equilibrium with their environment. We humans, on the other hand, are defined by our selectivity, which requires us to make an adaptive adjustment. This adaptive adjustment takes the form of a technology that helps to produce us as distinctively human.[5]

The same alimentary pressures that drove us to invent cooking act even more forcefully on the sick, who can't even digest food that's been prepared for the consumption of healthy people. Some invalids can tolerate a normal diet, but most of them are harmed by it. They need ἀσθενεστέρου δὲ δή τινος, something that corresponds to their own acquired weakness. Seeking this out, they discover porridge (τὰ ῥυφήματα) by mixing a few solid ingredients with a lot of water (μίξαντες ὀλίγα τῶν ἰσχυρῶν πολλῷ τῷ ὕδατι); those who can't even handle porridge, finally, are reduced to a liquid diet. First alone, and then with the aid of people who possess the medical *techne*, the sick have to make a second or even third adjustment – an adjustment that can properly be called 'cybernetic' – to an alimentary environment that's already been shaped by technology. In this respect, weirdly, sick people appear even further removed from animals than the healthy ones do.[6]

In the idiom of systems theory, cybernetic self-regulation entails the presence of a systemic norm and the capacity of a system to maintain that norm in the face of external pressures by means of negative feedback. In *On Ancient Medicine*, this is exactly what the body does: the norm is health, bad food forces a deviation from the norm, and dietetics provide a negative feedback mechanism that undoes that deviation. It would probably be possible to extend this analysis more broadly across the Hippocratic corpus, which generally and sometimes forcefully rejects surgical or pharmaceutical intervention in favour of techniques that mediate the body's own recuperative mechanisms. *On Ancient Medicine* goes further only by expanding such a theory of treatment into a speculative history of the medical art.[7]

First as cuisine, and then as medicine, *techne* emerges like an excrescence from this process. Both these *technai* persist as necessary prostheses for the maintenance of human life – or at least *healthy* human life, since the author of this text acknowledges that some humans can survive on uncooked food, just as the sick can often survive on food intended for the well.

What the cybernetic response of the organism to its environment in this case actually guarantees is the achievement of a *norm*, since the medical *techne* has been discovered ἐπὶ τῇ τοῦ ἀνθρώπου ὑγιείῃ. This norm is what the dietary devices described in *On Ancient Medicine* aim to support. They work not only to sustain bodies, but to *produce* bodies in a state of health.[8]

For the Greeks, the artificial body stands in a relationship to 'the normal', which is utterly opposed to the one that holds between norms and the organism. Such a body might almost be defined as what exceeds or avoids the norm. Androids, rather than seeking the centre, follow centrifugal lines of flight.

Chapter 22 of Palaephatus' *Peri Apiston* is one of the most succinct of the many Greek texts that could be adduced in support of this claim. The work as a whole is at once a historiography and a critique of what we have come to call Greek myths. I call it historiographic because of Palaephatus' remarks, at the end of his preface, that he has 'seen each of these places, such as it was', and written his accounts 'not from hearsay, but going myself and inquiring'. These remarks, which, like much else in the preface of *Peri Apiston*, signal a generic debt to Herodotus and Thucydides, are nonetheless not only literary decoration. They encapsulate Palaephatus' whole project in this text – which proceeds by reinterpreting according to rationalist and peripatetic canons a set of myths whose historicity it does not call into question. In the passage just quoted, Palaephatus' *historia* or inquiry corresponds to his application of those canons; while in what other way could Palaephatus have assigned a *chorion* – a place, or better yet a location – to each of the myths he treats than by accepting them as grounded in a kernel of historical fact?[9]

The twenty-second item in Palaephatus' catalogue of remade myths is the 'story' – although this is much less a narrative account than the other myths in *Peri Apiston* – of Daedalus' statues. 'It is said regarding Daedalus,' Palaephatus reports, 'that he built statues that moved by themselves.'[10] That claim, however, runs counter to the guiding principle of Palaephatus' investigation, a principle that he attributes in his preface to the presocratics Melissus and Lamiscus: ἐν ἀρχῇ ἔστιν ἅ ἐγένετο, καὶ νῦν ἔσται (whatever existed before will also exist at present); the making of moving statuary is impossible because nobody does that now. This story about Daedalus' statues will have to be otherwise explained.

What, then, is the truth at the heart of this unbelievable tale? Before Daedalus' time, says Palaephatus, statues were sculpted with their hands and feet all perfectly aligned. Daedalus was the first sculptor to introduce a form of *contraposto* and to represent figures *as though in motion*. This is why 'men said "Daedalus made this idol walking, and not standing still," just as now we say "these men are drawn fighting" and "the horses running" and "the ship tossed in a storm." In the same sense, they said that this man made walking statues' (Palaeph. 22.6–7). The story of Daedalus' walking statues thus has its origin in an ecphrastic metaphor. The statues only *look* like they're walking; they no more *actually* walk than a storm-tossed ship in a painting is *actually* about to sink. Palaephatus rewrites what could have been an episode in the development of technology as instead belonging to art history.[11]

For Palaephatus, Daedalus' artificial humans blend across a border of ecphrasis into ordinary statues. The common term between imaginary androids and real statuary is a form of mimesis, the sculptural art, which captures movement either by representing or by reproducing it. The contrast with more recent Western imaginings of 'artificial bodies', distinguished by their filiation with the machine, is worth emphasizing. For fifth- and fourth-century Greeks – a people that we might well call 'pre-mechanical', as Sylvia Berryman and other scholars have done – the field of human endeavour that seems most likely to give rise to an artificial man is not mechanics, but sculpting.[12]

To get at the 'why' of this strange conjunction, we have to appreciate the twofold character of Daedalus' mythic career as a sculptor. Other sources discuss this in greater detail than Palaephatus does. τὸ Δαιδάλου μίμημα φωνῆς δεῖ μόνον (fr. 276), as Aeschylus tells us: Daedalus' sculptures only lack speech. Daedalus is known both for crafting animate statues and for crafting statues of remarkably high mimetic fidelity. Thus Pausanias attributes several statues to Daedalus on aesthetic criteria. All the statues so attributed are *xoana*, a class of 'sacred image' already recognized as archaic by Plato's time. The oldest *xoana* were typically aniconic, not constituting a visual representation of the deities to which they were attached by means other than iconography. Some classical writers seem to have thought that Daedalus had innovated by sculpting these statues mimetically.[13]

Even aniconic *xoana*, though, were sometimes treated by their worshippers as though they could move. The Samians bound their *xoanon* of Hera, for instance, with golden chains, on the assumption that it would flee at the first opportunity, and Pausanias reports a similar practice in Phigalia. Daedalus' androids therefore seem to lie at the confluence of two traditions, one religious and one art-historical, both making *xoana* out to be, or seem, alive. This is how the *xoanon* and the sculptural art that produced it came to play the same role for the Greeks in imagining artificial bodies as machines and mechanism do for us.[14]

What marks these bodies out as 'artificial' – aside from their origin in a human *techne* – is their evident deficiency by comparison with organic bodies of the sort envisioned by the Hippocratic corpus. Whereas organic bodies stand in an adaptive and responsive relationship to their environment, doing whatever it takes to maintain a normative health, Daedalus' artificial bodies only know how to do one thing, which is to move or flee. In any case, toward what norm could they possibly adjust themselves? Their essence is given, in an act of mimetic making, as a likeness – but indeed a likeness to a God or hero, to someone *not present*, so that even further self-adjustment in imitation of a mimetic model is impossible. The organic body has a history of ever-more-effective self-adjustments in pursuit of health; the artificial body has *no* history beyond the moment of its creation, though the achievement of such a creation marks a milestone in the history of the sculptural craft.[15]

The Greeks, then, have two techniques for producing bodies. These techniques, as I've suggested, stand in a structural opposition to each other. The organic body is self-producing and self-regulating in pursuit of the norm of health; the medical art relates to this pursuit orthotically. The artificial body is produced by someone else, a craftsman possessing specialized knowledge, and relates to the norm centrifugally – since it is unable to escape the determinations given to it by the sculptural art that has created it. Each of these bodies is, in a structural sense, the negation of the other.

Like all structural pairings, this one is more than a coincidence. The organic production of bodies, as we'll see, *needs* something like an artificial body as the condition of its possibility. Static opposition becomes narrative correlation. I'd like to illustrate this by looking at two episodes from Herodotus.

The first episode that I'm going to discuss takes place near the end of book three, and begins a rather long narrative sequence in which the Greek doctor Demokedes, first as a prisoner of the Persians and then as a fugitive from them, plays a central role. What brings him to the Persian court in the first place is a foot injury suffered by Darius during a hunting expedition.

The King of Kings has fallen from his horse and twisted his ankle 'quite badly' (κως ἰσχυροτέρως), 'for the ball of the ankle has popped out of its joint' (ὁ γάρ οἱ ἀστράγαλος ἐξεχώρησε ἐκ τῶν ἄρθρων).[16]

Darius immediately takes refuge with *techne* in an attempt to rectify this maladjustment. However, the Egyptians, to whom he appeals first, only make things worse by applying too much force in their efforts to resettle the joint, such that Darius now not only suffers from a twisted foot but is in so much pain that he cannot sleep. Demokedes, fetched and subject to a certain amount of coercion, applies more gentle Greek medical techniques and not only repairs the damage the Egyptians had done to Darius but 'produces him healthy'. We are obviously meant to understand this *hugieia* as equivalent to Darius' being *artipous* again – his recovery of a 'normal' orthopedic function.[17]

Schematically, this is a story about Darius' dislocation from health and his attempts to recover that norm. Undergirding the narrative is an account of organismic technology not unlike the one outlined by the author of *On Ancient Medicine* in a passage I have already discussed. Darius' foot injury triggers an adaptive response, which is to seek out someone who can fix it. He summons the Egyptians first because they are on hand, but also because they are τοὺς δοκέοντας εἶναι πρώτους τὴν ἰητρικήν (scil. *technen*), 'those reputed to be first in the medical art'. This phrase may be taken as indicating the excellence of their craft but also – and especially in an Egyptian context – its antiquity.[18]

The Egyptians apply a forceful cure, one that increases rather than lessens the patient's suffering. Responding to this failure in a 'cybernetic' fashion, Darius looks for another option and eventually battens on a Greek doctor that his courtiers have found for him. Demokedes then treats Darius using Greek cures, ἤπια or mild, which succeed where the ἰσχυρὰ or rough treatments applied by the Egyptians had failed. The terminological opposition puts us in mind of the transition chronicled in *On Ancient Medicine* from ἰσχυρός foods to softer forms of nutriment, and some reference to Hippocratic language is probably intended. Following this second course of treatment, and contrary to his expectations, Darius is restored to health, his foot now straight instead of crooked.

This, then, is the story of an organic body that, with the aid of the medical *techne*, adjusts itself back to a healthy norm. Medicine's promise is that any organic body can, by careful self-correction, recover this norm. There are, however, cases where such a recovery would seem to us to be impossible.

Hegesistratus of Elis is one of the many minor figures that Herodotus introduces into his circumstantial account of the Battle of Plataea. Hegesistratus, a Greek seer serving with the Persians, gives advice that helps persuade Mardonius not to go on the offensive against the badly outnumbered defenders of Hellas. By the time that Mardonius changes his mind, some ten days later, the Greek forces have grown substantially, so that Hegesistratus' prophecy more or less fulfils itself.

Herodotus supplements this account with a biographical note that explains how Hegesistratus has come to prophecy for the Persians even though his home city, Elis, has long been a bulwark of Panhellenism. Hegesistratus had at some point been held prisoner by the Spartans, who were going to execute him. He escaped his fetters by cutting off most of his foot, then fled to Tegeia, where he made himself a new foot out of wood. This experience is the source of the all-consuming hatred of Sparta that has led Hegesistratus to ally himself with the Persians and that, some years after Plataea, will result in his death at Spartan hands.[19]

Herodotus describes Hegesistratus' self-mutilation in the Spartan prison as ἀνδρηιότατον ἔργον, 'the most courageous deed', of any that he knows. This is no idle praise. In the *Histories*, *andreios* turns out to be a surprisingly rare word, and this passage is the only place where it appears in the superlative. What about the *ergon* of Hegesistratus does the historian find so remarkable? Certainly not the bare fact of self-mutilation, since Zopyrus the Persian does something similar, and under less compulsion, in book 3, chapters 155 and following. The really impressive thing about Hegesistratus' *ergon* is not that he cuts his own foot off but what he manages to do without it: flee the Spartans and make the many-miles-long trek to Tegiea.[20]

What makes his deed *andreiotaton*, then, is perhaps this: that Hegesistratus acts with complete indifference to the norms of human function. In a situation where no adaptive response will save his life, Hegesistratus rejects the whole mechanism of adaptive response and actively destroys his own health, trading his own foot for freedom. He then 'runs away' (translating Herodotus' ἀπέδρη) even though he has no feet to run with. In every respect, Hegesistratus rejects the norm of health in favour of a self-consciously 'anti-normal' pattern of behaviour that will keep him alive.

At Tegeia, nonetheless, Hegesistratus becomes *hugies* again. How is this healthy body produced? The *ietrike techne*, as we saw in the case of Darius, can work miracles. It can do so, however, only on the condition that it have at hand a body which is deranged but otherwise 'intact'. Organic techniques can set right a twisted foot, but they cannot – and this is exactly what Hegesistratus needs – conjure a foot out of thin air.

In extremis, organic technology falls short of its own promise, and an artificial crafting of bodies fills its place. Hegesistratus makes a wooden foot and attaches it to himself, filling the gap left by his *andreiotaton ergon*. This is what I meant when I said that organic production of bodies was, in a sense, impossible: it has nothing to offer a body that's been torn apart. Its structural double, sculpture, stands in wait to make up this default and secure the dream of a complete technology for producing health.

On the terrain of myth, this is a suture that can succeed: Hephaestus makes Pelops an ivory shoulder to replace the one that Demeter accidentally ate, and the new one, as far as we know, works as well as the old. History, however, is not just like myth, and Hegesistratus' wooden foot is not the miraculous work of Hephaestus.

In Herodotus, the addition of a mechanical part has important consequences for the body as a whole. Hegesistratus loses the ability to respond adaptively to his *umwelt*: the only thing that he can do is hate Sparta. This hatred can hardly be understood as adaptive, since it leads Hegesistratus to his death, and Herodotus seems to connect its onset closely with Hegesistratus' new wooden foot, syntactically and otherwise. The phrase that describes Hegesistratus' declaration of hostilities is κατεστήκεε . . . πολέμιος. This language is unusual and unnecessarily periphrastic, but it does make Hegesistratus do something – κατεστήκεε, in this context 'set oneself up as' but etymologically 'stand against' – that can't be done without two feet.[21]

If Hegesistratus becomes a composite of artificial and organic, then, he also ends up acting much more like a moving statue than a human being. He no longer works to maintain his own normative health, but only to pursue a goal originating from, and corresponding with the crafting of, his body's artificial part. Through this act of self-making, he has turned himself into the object not of a medical but of a sculptural art. Another way, then, of interpreting Hegesistratus' *andreiotaton ergon*: out of a mad desire to live, he trades the reality of health for its hollow image.

Should these two Greek technologies for making bodies, then, really count only as one? Perhaps so – but in any case, as I hope I've now shown, they need to be understood as a system. The artificial body is a shadow or image of the organic one; the organic body, in turn, needs this image in order to see itself as complete and to extend its promise of health across all possible instances. Artificial bodies are the imaginary miracle lying behind a real Greek medical craft that, to Darius, already seems miraculous.

Where the organic body's capacity for normative self-adjustment fall short, as in the case of Hegesistratus' severed foot, the artificial body provides a necessary supplement that restores the human subject to an image of health. A recovery achieved by these means, however, has serious consequences for the subject's identity. We think of people with prosthetic limbs as organic beings with artificial parts; for the Greeks, by contrast, such a cyborg body is entirely artificial, and the image of health produced by prosthetics is precisely a mimesis, an imitation, the result of sculptural craft.

The project of this chapter has been, in an archaeological sense, to recover some Greek techniques for producing bodies. In the process, we have also recovered a lost way of thinking about the relationship between organic and artificial bodies. I take it that the Greeks conceptualized this relationship in terms radically different from and perhaps even incompatible with our own. My aim is thus also to execute, with respect to the Greeks, the programme that Eduardo Viveiros de Castro outlines in *Cannibal Metaphysics* with respect to the ethnographic other. There, he calls on anthropologists not simply to describe the other's beliefs (in a positivistic mode) but to elaborate the other's conceptual apparatus, an apparatus that stands on a par with our own and can expand it.[22]

What this means is that concepts through which the Greeks thought about making bodies are, or should be, available also to us. The need for new concepts that address that problem is particularly pressing now, at a moment when technological progress and utopian thinking are working together to inaugurate a cyborg future; if such 'new' concepts happen to have been excavated from the distant past, this should not necessarily count against them.

We share with the Greeks a willingness, even an eagerness, to consider the organic in opposition to the artificial. What we can learn from the Greek conceptual apparatus is to see the organic body not merely as supplemented by artificial parts but also, itself, passing over into artificiality. Under certain conditions, the whole body – and not just its inorganic addenda – becomes the object of a sculpting art, thus definitionally 'artificial'. Hegesistratus, the man who turns into a statue, gives us an alternative prototype for the cyborg body. Whether we make this new body an object of desire or of fear is up to us; the Greek experience simply forces us to confront the question.

CHAPTER 15
FLUID CYPRESS AND HYBRID BODIES AS A COGNITIVELY DISTURBING METAPHOR IN EURIPIDES' *CRETANS*

Johan Tralau

Euripides' *Cretans* is enigmatic.[1] Only fragments remain of the play. In the first choral song, there is a highly important detail in the description of the temple that has been overlooked in previous interpretations, and yet yields new insights into Euripides and the Greek imaginary. We will discover a metaphor of fluidity employed in the image of the temple, as well as a remarkable analogy between the temple, the human body, the monstrous body of the Minotaur and the distorted machine in which the Minotaur's mother and a bull beget the portent.

Conceptions of human–machine conglomerates and cyborgs have often focused on modern technology as a prerequisite for the fusion between machines, humans and – possibly – animals. If a cyborg 'incorporates exogenous components extending the self-regulatory control function of the organism in order to adapt it to new environments', then it mainly makes sense as the product of a high-tech culture.[2] In the following, I will show that a similarly cyborgic, yet low-tech, construction serves the purpose of patrolling human–animal boundaries in Euripides and in the myth of the Minotaur. Unlike some theses about cyborgs, then, Euripides' image of the woman-animal-machine is not 'an argument for pleasure in the confusion of boundaries'.[3] Moreover, I will introduce the concept of a 'cognitively disturbing metaphor', a metaphor in which the components of the image do not fit together. This is an image the meaning of which is determined by the very incompatibility of the parts constituting it, and congenial with the kind of mythic and Euripidean conglomeration of human, machine and animal discussed in this chapter.

In the first choral song (fr. 472.1–19 Kannicht), the chorus sing:

Φοινικογενοῦς παῖ τῆς Τυρίας τέκνον Εὐρώπης
καὶ τοῦ μεγάλου Ζηνός, ἀνάσσων
Κρήτης ἑκατομπτολιέθρου·
ἥκω ζαθέους ναοὺς προλιπών,
οὓς αὐθιγενὴς στεγανοὺς παρέχει
τμηθεῖσα δόκους Χαλύβῳ πελέκει
καὶ ταυροδέτῳ κόλλῃ κραθεῖ-
σ' ἀτρεκεῖς ἁρμοὺς κυπάρισσος.
ἁγνὸν δὲ βίον τείνομεν, ἐξ οὗ
Διὸς Ἰδαίου μύστης γενόμην
καὶ νυκτιπόλου Ζαγρέως βούτης
τὰς ὠμοφάγους δαῖτας τελέσας
Μητρί τ' ὀρείᾳ δᾷδας ἀνασχὼν
† καὶ Κουρήτων

> βάκχος ἐκλήθην ὁσιωθείς.
> πάλλευκα δ' ἔχων εἵματα φεύγω
> γένεσίν τε βροτῶν καὶ νεκροθήκας
> οὐ χριμπτόμενος τήν τ' ἐμψύχων
> βρῶσιν ἐδεστῶν πεφύλαγμαι.[4]

> Son of Phenician-born Tyrian Europa and of great Zeus, you who rule over hundred-citied Crete, I have come here from a most divine temple, the roof of which is supplied by native cypress wood blended with bull-bound glue into precisely fitted beams cut with Chalybean axe. I lead a sacred life ever since I became an initiate of Zeus Idaios and the herdsman of night-wandering Zagreus, completing his raw-eating feasts and holding torches high for the Mother of the mountain, I was consecrated and named a celebrant of the Kouretes. I wear all-white clothing and avoid the generation of mortals, I do not go near burial-grounds, and I guard myself against the eating of living foods.

This is the beginning of the play. The drama deals with the birth of the Minotaur. According to the myth, Minos had gained kingship due to the intervention of Poseidon: Minos said that the god granted him the throne, and that a bull would emerge from the sea as a sign of the god's will. Minos had promised the sea god that he would sacrifice the bull to him, but he did not keep his promise. Poseidon punished Minos by making his wife Pasiphae desire the animal. Daedalus, the inventor, then constructed a false cow, in which Pasiphae hid in order to unite with the bull.[5] The rest is history. Or rather, the rest is myth. Pasiphae gave birth to the Minotaur. In Euripides' play, or what remains of it, the chorus introduce themselves, Minos discusses the prodigious birth with someone, Pasiphae and Minos ferociously debate the issue of guilt, the latter commands his servants to lock up the former forever, and the chorus ask the king to calm down. How it ended we do not know.

Previous scholarship has dealt with many difficult questions pertaining to this tragedy. One strand of enquiry has addressed notions of responsibility in the drama, legal and philosophical debates, and Pasiphae's technique of argumentation.[6] Yet another topic has been the rituals of the chorus, and their relation to Orphism and other cults, as well as the implications for our understanding of Euripides' own religious views.[7] Likewise, the bewildering conjunction of vegetarianism and ritual eating of raw meat has been debated.[8]

Yet, as we shall see, relatively few scholars have addressed the image of the temple.

The temple and the cypress

The description of the shrine is complex:

> ἥκω ζαθέους ναοὺς προλιπών,
> οὓς αὐθιγενὴς στεγανοὺς παρέχει
> τμηθεῖσα δόκους Χαλύβῳ πελέκει
> καὶ ταυροδέτῳ κόλλῃ κραθεῖ-
> σ' ἀτρεκεῖς ἁρμοὺς κυπάρισσος.
>
> *472.4–8*

> I have come here from a most divine temple, the roof of which is supplied by native cypress wood blended with bull-bound glue into precisely fitted beams cut with Chalybean axe.

The chorus 'have come', ἥκω – this may set an uncanny tone, for at the beginning of a parode like this, the word is elsewhere in Euripides used by a ghost and a dangerous god (*Hec.* 1, Polydorus; *Ba.* 1, Dionysus).[9] Of even greater interest is the temple itself, specifically the words ταυροδέτῳ κόλλῃ, 'bull-bound glue' or 'bull-binding glue'. What kind of glue is this? Jane Harrison once speculated that there must have been a ritual in which the building was 'cemented with bulls' blood'.[10] Others have pointed out that it is more plausible to construe the fragment as speaking of bull glue.[11] There is nothing strange about such glue. In the *Historia Animalium* (517b28–29, 523a15–17), Aristotle notes that there is a kind of γλισχρότης μυξώδης, 'mucous stickiness', in, e.g., bulls' hides, which makes it possible to produce glue when one boils parts of the body; Pliny tells us that glue made of bulls' ears and genitals is the best (*HN*, XXVIII. 71, XI.231). Glue was in fact an important component in the construction of Greek ceilings.[12]

Yet we need to ask another question as well. It is curious that Euripides mentions bull glue as the substance with which the beams of the ceiling are fitted together – for this is the drama about the birth of the Minotaur, the portent and the monster that is half man, half bull. As will be shown below, there is reason to believe that the image of the temple evokes the body of the Minotaur.[13]

In order to understand the image, we need to look closely at the construction. We are told that the beams of the ceiling are made of cypress wood. Cypress, κυπάρισσος, 'provides', παρέχει, 'the ceiling', στεγανούς. The question is whether the wood has any deeper significance in this context. In a discussion of a cypress mentioned on an Orphic tablet, Radcliffe Edmonds argues that it is incorrect to assume that the content of images (such as a particular plant species) is significant in itself. Yet Edmonds himself notes that the cypress is 'a tree linked with death'.[14] We hence need to explore the meanings that this cypress might set in motion. Otto Kern claimed that Orphic temples were situated in the vicinity of cypress groves.[15] Moreover, there is a specifically Cretan connotation. According to Diodorus (V. 66.1), there was a cypress grove in the vicinity of Knossos. In the *Laws* (625b), Plato emphatically mentions the impressive cypress trees of Crete. Pindar seems to use 'cypress' as a synecdoche signifying Crete.[16] On the other hand, the tree had a strong connection with death and mourning.[17] Cypress was used for coffins (cf. Thuc. II.34.3), and according to an admittedly late source (Ovid, *Met.* X.136–142), the mourning boy Cyparissus was transformed into a cypress tree.

Crete, death and mourning: all of these phenomena are probably at play in the image of the temple. The cypress is a majestic tree – Diogenes Laertius (VIII. 10) informs us that the followers of Pythagoras would not use cypress coffins for the reason that the sceptre of Zeus was made of it. And this is not just a matter of cultural history, but of the physical properties of the wood itself. Cypress is remarkably durable, and was appreciated as such in Antiquity. This is probably the reason why Plato's *Laws* (741c) prescribes the use of cypress tablets for written records. Pliny (*NH* XVI. 79) speaks of cypress wood doors that were 400 years old, yet looked as if they were new.

The cypress is thus an image of durability and solidity. Once we look at the wood in the temple ceiling with this in mind, we will notice a disturbing detail that previous scholarship has arguably overlooked.

Fluid cypress

The beams of the ceiling are made of cypress. The wood is 'cut' (τμηθεῖσα) 'with Chalybean axe', Χαλύβῳ πελέκει. The Chalybes were (possibly) an iron-working people in Asia Minor, and χάλυψ means steel.[18] Moreover, we are told that the cypress wood in question is a local commodity, 'native', αὐθιγενής. Finally, we hear that the beams are 'blended with bull-bound glue into precisely fitted beams' (ταυροδέτῳ κόλλῃ κραθεῖ- | σ' ἀτρεκεῖς ἁρμοὺς κυπάρισσος). The image of the cypress wood, 'blended', 'mixed' with bull glue, is curious.

What is remarkable about it is, to begin with, the word 'mixed' itself, κραθεῖσ'. κραθεῖσ' is one editor's (Hermann's) conjecture. In Porphyry (*Abst.* IV.19.2), who transmitted the verses, we find the form κρηθεῖσ', which is difficult to make sense of. Some scholars have suggested other possibilities.[19] Yet almost all the most recent editors of the text – Kannicht, Collard-Cropp-Lee, Cozzoli, Diggle, Jouan-van Looy and Collard-Cropp – accept κραθεῖσ'.

The word is seldom discussed. Collard, Cropp and Lee simply say that it 'expresses the idea of making separate things into a whole' – glue and wood.[20] No other commentators appear to have noticed anything unusual about the word. But this metaphorical use of κεραννύναι, 'blend', is arguably spectacularly strange. The verse implies a most unusual use of the word, for the verb is not properly used of the 'mixing' of solid things. The mixing in κεραννύναι is that of liquids, wine and water.

Consequently, we need to explore the meaning of the word further. Why κεραννύναι in the context of the temple and its cypress beams? What additional meaning does the word provide the image with?

Someone could argue that the key meaning of the verb would be that of blending *in appropriate proportions*. The purpose of mixing wine with water is of course to do it in good proportions (cf. *Od.* 3. 390 and 393). Perhaps, then, the notion of 'right proportions' is inherent in the word, and perhaps the metaphorical usage of it primarily conveys this meaning (cf. *Od.* 10. 362). However, in Thucydides we discover a metaphor using the verb where the notion of 'right proportions' does not appear to be in play: he speaks of a dialect which was 'blended', half Doric, half Chalcidian, and it is not likely that the expression should be understood as 'harmoniously mixed', but rather in a merely descriptive sense (cf. Th. VI. 5).

But there is arguably more. For κραθεῖσ' [...] κυπάρισσος is really a remarkable metaphor. A word used to denote the mixing of fluids is used of a solid object – of an incredibly durable type of wood. The image turns what is solid into a liquid, for it is the wood that is κραθεῖσ', 'blended', as if it were fluid. There is something disconcerting about this image. In a sense, the categories of solid and liquid make the world ordered. Accounts of the cosmogony often represent the separation of different kinds of substances, whereby the solid, liquid and etheric are differentiated from each other, making the world intelligible.[21] The distinction structures the world. Yet in Euripides' words, it appears to be distorted. What should be durable and solid is no longer durable, nor is it solid, for the categories are subverted when the cypress is fluid.

It could be objected that such metaphors are to be expected in the tragic idiom.[22] Yet 'blending', κεραννύναι, in the context of a solid object is most unusual. There is a great number of metaphors involving κεραννύναι later than Euripides, primarily in Plato. Yet interestingly, there appear to be no cases of such a usage in the context of *solid objects*. It is used of abstract nouns, like pain, sensations and institutions (cf. Pl. *Phlb.* 50a6–7; *Lg.* 961d, 949e8; *R.* 412a4; *Crat.* 417b3). Likewise, κεραννύναι can be used metaphorically of climates (cf. Pl. *Crit.* 111e5;

E. F. 981 Kannicht). A climate may be material, just as smells consist of particles (and at least the Epicurean theory conceived of smells in that way), but it is not a physical object in the normal sense, and most importantly, it is not solid.[23] The same is true of the 'mingling' of sounds, a metaphor found in Thucydides (VI. 5) and in Euripides' last play (*Ba.* 124, 127–128). This metaphor of blending is several decades younger and involves sounds being 'blended' rather than physical objects. Demosthenes (XXIV.214) uses the verb of alloys, i.e., metal, yet this will seem less bold if we consider the fact that alloys can only be produced when the metals are melted into fluid form before they are mixed.

In Empedocles there are likewise images of 'mixing' that employ the word 'blend', κρᾶσις, which is related to κεραννύναι, and these may or may not be as old as the 450s. These κρᾶσις metaphors typically involve 'blending' of elements.[24] Yet it seems that the use of 'blending' of elements in a cosmological account is less strange than the 'blending' of cypress wood. Elements are more abstract entities than the wood from a specific tree. This is likewise true of two κεραννύναι metaphors in Pindar (*O.* 10.104; *P.* 5.2), where a person is blended with 'youth' (ὥρᾳ, metaphorically) and wealth with 'virtue' (ἀρετᾷ). Both of these instances involve abstract nouns that arguably do not collide with the idea of 'blending' – at least, and by far, not in the way the blending of liquids and the cypress wood do.

In short, while these instances of κεραννύναι-metaphors – in Pindar, Empedocles, Plato, Demosthenes and so on – operate with transferred significations in which the verb 'mixing' no longer connotes the mixing of fluids, they are all less bold than Euripides' κραθεῖσ'. They rarely deal with physical objects, seldom with solid objects, and never with specific objects. The cypress, by contrast, is very solid, very physical, very far from the range of meanings that can properly be attached to κεραννύναι. In short, it cannot be argued that this image is an inconspicuous metaphor for decorative uses only, for it is not only innovative, and not only brave, but strange. The beams of the ceiling in the temple are of the most solid wood, yet the poet speaks of them as if they were fluid; the word carries a strange implication, as if the wood were a shapeless, amorphous element.

No ordinary metaphor

A comparison with a Homeric metaphor will clarify this interpretation.

> ῥέε δ' αἵματι γαῖα (e.g., *Il.* 4:451)
> The earth was flowing with blood.

Properly speaking, the earth does not flow. What is flowing is the blood. Yet the image renders the stream of blood on the ground visible – there is so much blood that it looks as if the ground is all streaming blood. This is the cognitive function of metaphor highlighted by Aristotle (*Rh.* 1406b21–22): the image provides an insight by relating two phenomena, saying that one thing *is* something else, and in so doing it reveals a similarity. The poet's use of metaphor thus 'brings about learning and knowledge through the genus', ἐποίησε μάθησιν καὶ γνῶσιν διὰ τοῦ γένους (*Rh.* 1410b14–15), e.g., through recognition of a property that two things have in common. When comparing one phenomenon to another, and uncovering their similarity, we should create metaphors that are 'not far-fetched but [connecting phenomena that are] akin', οὐ πόρρωθεν [. . .] ἀλλ' ἐκ τῶν συγγενῶν (*Rh.* 1405a35–36). The far-fetched, πόρρωθεν, 'from afar', is too strange to convey an insight.

It has been argued that Aristotle's theory is inapt when it comes to understanding certain cases of tragic metaphor.[25] I would more cautiously submit that cognitive theories of metaphor need to be revised so as to be able to make sense of a deviant image like κραθεῖσ' [. . .] κυπάρισσος. If the point of the image is that the beams are fitted securely – that they are ἀτρεκεῖς – then κραθεῖσ' is more than 'far-fetched'. Indeed, if the beams are fitted securely, and if the upshot is the 'precisa e compatta copertura'[26] of the roof, 'skilled carpentry',[27] then the image of the fluid beams, mixed like a liquid, is almost inexplicable. For while the ground streaming with blood lets us see the blood, and gain an understanding of it, the image of the fluid cypress beams can yield no graspable insight. What is in fact solid is depicted as a liquid. The image conveys ontological ambiguity. The shrine that Euripides constructs for his Orphic priests is an outlandish one, an inversion of categories.

I suggest that we label it a 'cognitively disturbing metaphor'. Unlike the image in Homer, where we see the ground in a new light as it is covered with blood, the bull glue could not make the wood *look* like a liquid. The image is a troubling inversion of the fluid–solid opposition. The prime cognitive function of this metaphor is precisely to convey the disconcerting nature of the vision it describes.

Cognitive theories of metaphor presuppose an analogy, as is the case with the theory of conceptual metaphor, which generally seeks analogies between domains in universal thought patterns, often related to bodily experiences – like affection metaphorically understood as warmth, channelling childhood and later experiences of bodily warmth.[28] The point of the analogy is that it will make sense. But Euripides' 'fluid cypress' does not make sense as an analogy, for the reason that solid and fluid should be mutually exclusive states. According to Aristotle (*Rh.* 1412a10–11), as we saw, a metaphor should be constructed ἀπὸ οἰκείων, 'from phenomena that are related'. Even critics of these theories – such as Michael Silk, who emphasizes that poetic metaphors can work in multiple ways – presuppose some kind of analogy underlying the images.[29] All cognitive theories of metaphor work this way. George Lakoff thus argues that 'what determines "fit" is [m]aximizing the number of overall neural bindings [. . .] without contradiction, that is, without encountering any mutual inhibition'.[30] Yet in the case of the fluid cypress, we find just such a mutual inhibition between solid wood and the notion of fluidity.

It has been argued that a related theory, that of conceptual blending associated with Gilles Fauconnier and Mark Turner, can make sense of novelty in literary images better than that of conceptual metaphor.[31] According to this theory, human cognition invariably works by blending various domains; yet the difficult question is how we are to address images that not only derive from different domains but the parts of which appear to be incompatible in some sense.[32] Now, the theory allows that images can be failures, 'discordant structure[s]' that are not conducive to understanding.[33] In an interpretation of Timotheus' *Persians*, Felix Budelmann and Pauline LeVen have applied the theory, showing that it can make sense of much that appears obscure, yet concluding that some overly strange images merely create 'disorientation'.[34] So a conceptual blend or a metaphor does not necessarily create understanding, but can instead be such a 'discordant structure'. Yet the function of Euripides' fluid cypress wood seems to differ from that – it does not appear to be just a failed image or bad communication, but a different way of communicating something bad.[35]

It could be objected that 'a metaphorical mapping may be apt in some respects, but not in others', and that the fluid cypress may hence not be so strange after all.[36] But if, as Fauconnier and Turner posit, '[t]he impulse to achieve integrated blends is an overarching principle of human cognition', then the fluid ceiling represents a deviation from the model envisaged by the cognitive theories.[37] A cognitively disturbing image works parasitically on the general principle that there must be an analogy underlying the metaphor – its meaning is determined by its status as an aberrant, disanalogical blend that presupposes yet deviates from the principle that there must be an analogy underlying the metaphor. The fluid wood construction is such an image, and the incompatibility of the parts of this metaphor conveys a sense of the dissolution of order and form.

The body and the temple

We will proceed to the final point. If one accepts the argument that there is a disconcerting note in the image of the temple, then there are arguably other implications as well. First, the Orphic sanctuary is a distortion of the cosmological order, and this interpretation appears to lend support to those who argue that Euripides criticizes Orphism.[38] Second, however, the image of the temple is pertinent to the body of the Minotaur itself. For at the beginning of the drama (*Cret.* 472b.29) there is a monster, ταύρου μέμικται καὶ βροτοῦ διπλῇ φύσει ('mixed of bull and mortal [human], of double nature'). The body of the Minotaur is not a harmonious one, but a distortion, half man, half beast, eating raw meat.

Giuseppe Fornari argues that the temple mirrors the body of the Minotaur, highlighting the notion of sacrifice as the bond of social cohesion. This claim relies on Raffaele Cantarella's reading of the fragment, according to which Euripides describes the monster as having a bull's head on his 'body' (ἁρμοῖς, which usually means 'shoulders', but here, in Cantarella's words, the entire 'complesso delle membra'), a wording that supposedly echoes the ἁρμούς used in the description of the cypress beams.[39] This parallel would connect the monster's body and the temple. Yet the argument is no longer plausible. Not only is Fornari's reference to bull blood not convincing, but Adele-Teresa Cozzoli has argued that the conjecture ἁρμοῖς is impossible since her microscopic observations show that there is no μ in the damaged word in the papyrus, but a ν. Hence the word cannot be ἁρμοῖς, but rather στέρνοις, 'chest'.[40] The question is whether there is some other way of corroborating the idea that there is an analogy between the monstrous body and the temple.

In some languages, we sometimes still speak of the 'body' of a building; the Roman architect Vitruvius (III.1.1) is famous for the view that a building is to be understood analogously to a human body – just like the parts of the temple, the members of the body must have an *exacta ratio* without which it is not harmonious. Moreover, Vitruvius (III.1.4) ascribed this discovery of the analogy to 'the ancients', *antiqui*, i.e., the Greeks. Almost nothing has been handed down to us from the corpus of Greek architectural treatises, but the texts were well known to Vitruvius – he mentions, e.g., a book by Ictinus, the architect of the Parthenon, the construction of which would have been contemporaneous with the staging of *Cretans*.[41] Most scholars seem to hold that Vitruvius was right in locating the source of the analogy between architecture and body in Greek art and architectural theory – and the human body was not only visible in Greek buildings in the conception of a general correspondence between the temple and the body, but also in the measures themselves (feet, finger) and in, e.g., human bodies, caryatids, employed as columns.[42] The doctrine must have been found in Polyclitus as well as a number of other Greek artists that are now lost, yet cited by Vitruvius.[43]

The analogy between body and building was powerful in this as well as other corners of the ancient universe.[44] It has been shown that the author of the letter to the Ephesians, who emphasizes the structural affinity between the temple and the human body, went so far as to construct his own text according to norms of symmetry, counting the number of syllables in order to make the parts of the text symmetrical and proportional internally and in relation to each other.[45] This recalls the words from the letter to the Corinthians (1 *Ephesians* 6,19), where we hear that 'your body is the temple of the holy spirit in you', τὸ σῶμα ὑμῶν ναὸς τοῦ ἐν ὑμῖν ἁγίου πνεύματος. Moreover, Plato stresses the analogy between temple and *logos* in the *Phaedrus* (*Phdr.* 264c). We may at the very least conclude that in the Greek fifth-century imaginary, there was an analogy between the temple and the human body.

It could be objected that this analogy may have been unknown to Euripides. But this is not the case. In *Iphigeneia in Tauris* (*IT* 50–52), there is a striking specimen of the analogue building-body: Iphigeneia dreams of her brother as the column of the house. This is a spectacular image, for in Iphigeneia's dream, the pillar acquires a voice of its own – the sole remaining column of the paternal house *is* its remaining male offspring, Orestes. Euripides thus conspicuously thematizes the building as an analogue of the human body.

This analogy may play a particular role in the priests' description of the sanctuary in *Cretans*. For if the image of the temple conveys a sense of a subversion of order, then this resonates with a very special body. The body of the Minotaur is without doubt a perversion, mixing two incompatible elements. And the body of the temple is not harmonious either. Euripides describes two of the temple's elements. One of them is the cypress beams in the ceiling. The other element is the glue, with which the wood is 'blended' – and the glue itself derives from the body of a bull. The temple could justly be said to be of σύμμικτον εἶδος ('commingled appearance'), the words used of the Minotaur's body (*Cret.* 472a); in fact, it mirrors the corresponding inversion incarnated in the body of the monster.

In a fragment sometimes attributed to the *Cretans* (fr. 988 Kannicht) someone says:

> τέκτων γὰρ ὢν ἔπρασσες οὐ ξυλουργικά
>
> ('You are a carpenter, but what you did was not woodwork')

The words are often taken to be addressing Daedalus, who constructed the wooden cow in which Pasiphae hid in order to unite with the bull. And they probably do. Yet they might allude to much more than the deceptive construction resembling a bovine female – they might in fact refer to the disharmoniously constructed body not only of the temple, but of the monster, connecting them to each other. In that case we have three 'bodies' related to each other.

Beginning from the end, we see the Minotaur, a hybrid body with two components: a bovine and a human part.[46] This body has emerged from a previous conjunction, that of the fake cow. The machine constructed by Daedalus in turn is made up of two parts as well – it is the conjunction of a bovine part, the false cow, and a human one, Pasiphae. But from Apollodorus (III.1.4) and other sources we learn that the false bovine animal was made of wood; it was a ξυλίνην βοῦν, 'a wooden cow', a wood construction with a cow's skin stretched around it. This is not the first cow skin used for the purpose of deception.[47] But most importantly, this 'body' is made of a bovine animal, a human being, and wood – the bovine being the fake cow, or, in the moment of the union between human and animal, the bull itself: the purpose of the machine is fulfilled when the bovine beast is united with the human by means of the wooden device. (In a sense, Daedalus is a very early, or the first, cyborg producer: the wings that he devises for himself and Icarus are likewise problematic extensions of the human body into territory that is decidedly out of bounds.[48]) And in the 'body' of Euripides' temple, we find wood as well as a bovine component – the bull glue.

The complex of these three bodies thus exhibits a remarkable structure. In the internal chronology of the myth, we find first a conjunction of the bovine and wood (the temple), then a conjunction of the bovine, wood and the human (the cow machine), and finally the conjunction of the bovine and the human (the Minotaur). These three successive stages mirror each other in a strange and distorted way: wood/bovine – wood/bovine/human – bovine/human. Daedalus' machine mediates between the temple and the monster; it brings them together.

For Greek civilization, the distinction between human and animal was paramount. This is in particular true of the institution of sacrifice, which maintains the hierarchy of gods, humans and animals.[49] It is true that there are likewise Greek conceptions of affinity between, e.g., man as a hunter or warrior and a great animal, often a predator.[50] Yet the distinction between human and beast lies at the heart of sacrifice as a political institution in the city-state as well as in the standard etiological account of the origins of meat offerings.[51] Keeping humans and animals apart is thus a matter of fundamental importance.[52] And the *Cretans* is about precisely this difference, and the danger concomitant in the subversion of this distinction. The Minotaur's body threatens the cosmological hierarchy; so does the mechanical cow that unites human, bovine and wood – and so does the temple, uniting the bovine with wood, blending the latter like a fluid.

The temple is thus an image of the dissolution of form and of order. It mirrors the distortions incarnated in the machine that unites bull and human being, as well as in the monstrous body that is bull and man. While the purpose of what has been said above is not to delve into Euripides' religion, the interpretation that we have suggested would appear to make it likely that his *Cretans* signals hostility to the Orphic movement. Yet the most important conclusion is that Euripides signals an inversion of religious and political order by letting the forms dissolve, by making boundaries fluid, amorphous – for the solid cypress wood is now κραθεῖσ', 'blended', like a liquid.

The forms have been perverted – in the monstrous hybrid body, in the monstrous machine, and in the beams of the temple – and so has the order of the world. The metaphor of 'blending' is in this case 'cognitively disturbing'. This interpretation thus lets us discover a different kind of metaphor. A cognitively disturbing metaphor cannot be visualized smoothly, as in the standard case of the cognitive theory, yet these theories can be developed so as to accommodate this kind of metaphorical deviation – it can help us see that the cognitive value of such a metaphor is to signal a deeper distortion of order. Consequently, the entire drama of the *Cretans* and the myth is visible, if only barely so, in the word κραθεῖσ', in the image of those strange, 'blended', fluid cypress beams.

CHAPTER 16
BODY POLITICS IN THE *ANTIQUITATES ROMANAE* OF DIONYSIUS OF HALICARNASSUS

Y. N. Gershon

Introduction

Posthumanism, at its heart, is a positive encouragement to break down boundaries and to incorporate what was formerly 'monstrous' into the mundane. As scholars of antiquity, and specifically of Roman historiography, the benefit of setting narratives we have read many times over in adjunct to more modern theorizing is that it allows us to return to texts anew and, aided by deeper networks of investigation, perhaps see coherence, and reflect upon that which we might previously have overlooked or seen only as quirks, oddities or peculiarities.

The Augustan historian of early Rome, Dionysius of Halicarnassus, is an ideal figure to test such interplay, if only because the Dionysian approach to Roman history is itself blended in form. Dionysius' *Antiquitates Romanae* are a partly extant history of Rome from the proto-historical period to the start of the First Punic War. In some respects, the *Antiquitates* fit into the mould we expect of narratives of Roman history from antiquity. Dionysius' history, like similar narratives, is almost entirely masculine. The narrative is dominated by individual actors who operate as Great Men, making great speeches and doing great deeds. Deed and action seem almost entirely to be led by character, rather than being connected to prevailing social-economic events. Women are few and far between, and, when they are present, they seem to exist as mere ciphers of the male psyche preoccupied with state politics.[1]

But, with that said, Dionysius' achingly conservative narrative is, in its own way, quietly radical. As a Greek in Rome and writing as the Principate morphed into a more formal imperium, Dionysius occupies, simultaneously, a both liminal and central place in the Augustan sphere. The same could also be said of scholarly appreciation of his talents. It is only within the last few decades that he has begun to be appreciated in his own right, as an ideologically attuned author.[2] He may have been acknowledged previously as a useful source, but now the shifting sands of change allow for more literary readings. Critically, Dionysius is now seen as an author whose ideological expression of Rome is deserving of analysis. In particular, Dionysius' approach to the functions of state apparatus, morals, religion and, especially, the place of ethnicity has undergone re-evaluation. I make the argument in this chapter that Dionysius may also – potentially – be understood through the prism of posthumanism; his conception of state structures, class struggle, the body politic and the constitution seems to occupy a metaphorical space that maps onto the concerns of posthumanism. Namely, Roman institutions and classes are made flesh as their members and constituents mix, meld and adapt. I shall also argue – befitting a posthumanistic mindset –that the *kinetic* setting of metaphor application in the text also unsettles and disturbs seemingly discrete categories.

The distinctiveness of the *Antiquitates Romanae*

For modern readers there are three distinctive qualities to the *Antiquitates*. First, the sheer number and length of speeches can be quite unappetising for those who have a deep resistance to fabricated quotation. Direct speech comprises approximately a third of the text after book 2.[3] Second, and most famously, Dionysius argues in the first book of the *Antiquitates* that the Romans were in fact Greek in origin. Even if this argument is not as original as is often thought, it is nonetheless this idea with which Dionysius is most associated.[4] It is an aggressive and noticeable beginning to a history of Rome, and the density of citation and reference indicates Dionysius' fervour to prove his point. Indeed, there is even some evidence that the first book was published separately as a monobiblos for extra impact.[5]

A third distinctive quality becomes apparent the longer one spends with the text. As signalled in the introduction to the *Antiquitates*, a major leitmotiv is Dionysius' interest in the development of the Roman constitution, the reconstitution of which is repeatedly revisited.[6] The so-called 'Constitution of Romulus', the Brutan settlement, the theorizing of Manius Valerius, and the introduction of the Consular Tribunate all mark moments at which the significance of the fabric and compositional elements of the Roman constitution are debated and re-evaluated. This functional remoulding is partly where the appeal of Dionysius lies for posthumanism. Additionally, Dionysius is not afraid to radically argue heterodoxies, as is indicated by his views on the Greek origins of the Romans, and on Roman institutions.[7] Furthermore, his voluminous discourse allows for multiple perspectives and voices to crowd his text. Groups debate and opinions are formed. In combination, these attributes downplay individual views and elevate group identities. For instance, Dionysius, unlike Livy, does not see the development of the Roman constitution as directly led by a series of *conditores*. Rather, approval for change is referred to the people at large.[8] Both of these qualities are connected to a third: the Dionysian conception of the constitutional functions of state, society and religion (all aspects of the constitution) is born of a distinct analysis. Dionysius' scale of thinking, no doubt influenced by his predecessor Polybius, just exists on a bigger conceptual scale than that of a historian such as Livy, despite the scale of his work.[9] Dionysius is, debatably, the closest in antiquity we have to a historian who applies such conceptual thinking to an historical narrative. If posthumanism is an encouragement to see the world as a network, as an interconnected system of architecture, in which no individual component has a greater significance than another, then the *Antiquitates* are arguably a classical articulation of that same mindset.[10]

The Fable of the Belly and the Body's Members

For the main analysis in this chapter, we turn to an episode in the Conflict of the Orders, itself one of the most developed and involved elements of the *Antiquitates*. Histories of the Conflict of the Orders depict, however inaccurately, Rome as comprising two impermeable classes, patricians and plebeians.[11] As a response to the demands made by the patricians to the plebeians to fight on behalf of Rome against invading neighbouring peoples, and as a reflex against the harsh burden of debt bondage placed upon them, members of the plebeian class withdrew to the Mons Sacer in 494.[12] This is known as the First Secession. Envoys, Menenius Agrippa among them, were sent by the senate to negotiate with the seceders. It was then that Menenius deployed the famous metaphorical Fable of the Belly and the Body's Members in an attempt to return support to Rome.[13] The seceders' price was the establishment of the Tribunate of the Plebs. These events and the creation of this office form the conclusion to book 6 of the *Antiquitates*.[14]

The power of the analogy lies in the notion that parts of the body, though they may be incentivized to act individually, are at their most powerful when working towards one aim. The metaphor of a political body with an actual body is not unique of course to Dionysius, and in fact had a long Greek heritage stretching back centuries.[15] However, earlier versions of the analogy lacked specificity in terms of anatomical detail and were overwhelmingly interested in the essentially medical metaphor.[16] Moreover, as Squire has demonstrated, '[t]he contrast [of earlier permutations of the analogy] with the rhetorical figure of the body in the political discourses of the late Roman republic could not be starker'.[17] This is to say, Dionysius' deployment of the metaphor must be seen as fitting squarely into a late republican discourse. Indeed, that Dionysius deploys the later version of the metaphor rather than the earlier, despite his subject matter, is hardly surprising: historical narratives of the late republic and early empire effectively retrofitted the arguments and concerns of the Civil War onto the Conflict of the Orders.[18] Dionysius was not the only historian of early Rome to use the metaphor.[19] Livy's version, to name one example, is more truncated; but it is Dionysius' version that has become the definitive rendering.[20] This is in part due to its length, and because the scope of the metaphor is – for want of a better phrase – fully fleshed out, as the role of *polis* is brought to the fore. Here, a 'city is to some extent like a human body, for both the city and the body are composite and made up of many parts, and in each case no single part has the same function or performs the same services as the others'.[21] It is an entirely suitable metaphor for a Roman state whose various members seemed intent on pulling it apart.

Critically for my reading in this chapter, Menenius' citing of the fable on the Mons Sacer is in fact the *second* time the metaphor is deployed by him. The first occurs at a meeting of the senate in which the senators debate at length the various courses of action that might be deployed against the seceders.[22] Additionally, Dionysius alludes to a possible *third* recitation by Menenius between the other two stated occasions, although this time Dionysius does not quote Menenius' speech directly.[23] It is the redeployment and reworking of this metaphor in new contexts and with differing audiences that form the basis of the argument of this chapter. It has been – as far as I can tell – unremarked upon, and, moreover, allows us to directly engage posthumanistic ideas of regeneration, absorption and change, and to discuss them in relation to Dionysius' antique narrative.

To set Menenius' speeches in a broader literary context ensures that we treat his words not as quirky bits of Greek fable, but as an essential key for understanding the Dionysian conception of the development of Roman history, its political classes and its constitution. An understanding of the development of the Roman constitution is a key in the *Antiquitates*.[24] Dionysius repeatedly revisits the hard process of reconciliation between elements of the Roman people that resulted in changes to the *politeia*. The *Antiquitates* are rich with incidents of discursive settlement. Therefore, the decision to cite Menenius' metaphor twice over is no accident. The context here provides a clue. For all that Dionysius despises the plebeians, he understands their essential importance to the good functioning of the state.[25] After all, the end of book 6 signals the start of the career of Coriolanus, whose actions test the strength of the Roman constitution. Dionysius is therefore providing his readership with the conceptions of the constitution held by both plebeians and patricians that would see them through this threat. Menenius Agrippa is the linking chain that binds these two subtly different visions together.

Menenius Agrippa before the senate

Menenius Agrippa's two direct speeches incorporating aspects of the fable are performed before two different audiences. The first occurs before the senate, the second before the camp of seceders. Menenius' senate speech is long.[26] Its purpose is to demonstrate that the senators opposed to accommodation with the plebeians are in the wrong. Menenius' argument is built on a simple premise: the anti-plebeian senators are hoodwinking the rest. He claims they must be following one of two strains of logic, both of them for the birds. Either they think the Romans could easily maintain control over conquered peoples without the plebeians,[27] or else, Menenius suggests, these senators imagine they could bring some other people into the commonwealth. These newcomers would replace the current bunch of plebeian good-for-nothings (ἀντὶ τοῦ πονηροτέρου κρείττονα), fight to preserve the patricians' supremacy (αὐτοῖς προπολεμήσει τε τῆς ἀρχῆς) and keep schtum under the same government (κατὰ πολλὴν ἡσυχίαν συμπολιτεύσεται).

The two options that Menenius presents are designed to indicate the ridiculous endpoint of the patricians' logic: either they think that Rome could maintain its dominance without the plebeians, or else they think that a better, and somehow more grateful and supplicant body of plebeians may somehow be exchanged *en masse* for the Roman plebian class. The strategy to dismiss the senators' views before the argument proper is revealing of a deeper mindset. Menenius is rehearsing themes of necessary cooperation between members of a single state. In characterizing the nature of the plebeians, he is already pre-empting the discourse of posthumanism.

In the first instance, we should note Menenius' use of συμπολιτεύσεται. The verb is suggestive of a respected and connected status within a constitution held in common.[28] There is an overarching sense of mutual dependency of classes. Second, the idea that a section of the body politic may be removed and replaced, by an 'improved' component is – however ironically it is put by Menenius – an indication that such a body could, at least in theory, be regenerated by appendage and addition. In the event, as we shall see, Menenius opts for an alternative course: the plebeian class should remain and regenerate.

The themes of absorption, regeneration and change return a few chapters later in the same speech.[29]

> Ἀλλ' ἴσως ἔγωγε τετύφωμαι ταῦτα λέγων καὶ τὰ μὴ δεινὰ ἀξιῶ δεδιέναι· τῇ πόλει δ' οὐδὲν ἕτερον ἤδη που κινδυνεύεται ἢ μεταβολή, πρᾶγμα οὐ χαλεπόν, κατὰ πολλὴν τ' ἂν ἡμῖν εὐπέτειαν ἐκ παντὸς ἔθνους καὶ τόπου θῆτά τε καὶ πελάτην ὄχλον εἰσδέξασθαι γένοιτο.
>
> But perhaps I myself am deluded and ask you to fear things that ought not to be. The city is likely threatened with no worse a danger than a change of inhabitants, a matter of no great consequence. It would be very easy for us to receive into the body politic a multitude of labourers and clients from every nation and place.

The programme demanded by the anti-plebeians is nothing less than a full-scale population exchange. Ungrateful plebeians are to be cast out along with their families.[30] Menenius rounds on the patricians in an effort to demonstrate the impossibility of replacing these 'ingrates': an expulsory amputation, for a variety of reasons, would be practically impossible.[31] In contrast, an invited and militarily untrained people would have little incentive to fight for Rome. They would have to be given land, so dispossessing the present owners, and they would demand magistracies and honours. Menenius argues that introducing a non-Roman population would effectively destroy the Roman country and constitution by Rome's own hands.

Here, once he has characterized 'replaceable' and 'artificial' members, Menenius introduces the proto-version of the body metaphor. Rome, he states, is hardly the only state where the lower class is hostile to the upper. He beseeches the senators to remember:

> καὶ ὅτι πᾶν χρῆμα, ὃ ἂν ἐκ πολλῶν σύνθετον ᾖ, νοσεῖν πέφυκε κατά τι τῶν ἑαυτοῦ μορίων, καὶ ἔτι πρὸς τούτοις ὡς οὔτε ἀνθρωπείου σώματος αἰεὶ τὸ κάμνον ἀποτεμεῖν χρὴ μέρος· αἰσχρά τε γὰρ ἡ ὄψις ἂν γίνοιτο τοῦ λειπομένου καὶ ἡ φύσις οὐκ ἐπὶ πολὺ διαρκής· οὔτε πολιτικῆς κοινωνίας τὴν νοσοῦσαν ἐξελαύνειν μοῖραν· οὐ γὰρ ἂν φθάνοι διὰ τῶν ἰδίων μερῶν τὸ σύμπαν ἀπολόμενον σὺν χρόνῳ[32]
>
> that everything that is composed of many parts is generally affected with a disorder in some part. Furthermore, the sick part of a human body ought not always to be chopped off, as that would make the rest appear ugly and shorten its life. Nor should a disorderly part of a civic community be driven out, since that would be the quickest way of destroying the whole through the loss of its individual elements.

Here, before senators in the senate, the metaphor is kept short and it is the notion of disease that is foregrounded. Through implication, the body politic as a whole is imagined as a singular body. The analogy is moulded to Menenius' audience. Menenius' contention is that everything is, by nature, sick in each of its constituent parts. He then homes in on the body metaphor: it is not necessary to cut off the withered part of a body (κάμνον . . . μέρος), as that would ruin the whole. Equally, he states, within a commonwealth one should not drive out a sick element (τὴν νοσοῦσαν ἐξελαύνειν μοῖραν) as destruction of the individual parts would be the speediest way of destroying the whole completely.

We should note a secondary point. In tailoring the analogy for his audience, Menenius does not dispute that the plebeians – whatever metaphorical body part they are – are sick. Additionally, even though the analogy that Menenius gives here does not map exactly onto the textbook formulation of the Fable of the Body and its Parts, it is undoubtedly the case that this version of the metaphor given before the senate shares the same DNA. Even though the parts of the body are not anthropomorphized, this protean version still requires that all parts work together as a whole and that no element is considered unnecessary to the functioning of the whole. There is a final implied point to this that fits in well to questions of posthumanism. Namely, if a civic and political community (a body) is *not* to destroy itself in time, *and* the offending ill component is not to be removed, then either the sickness of the member must be accepted, or a programme of regeneration or repair must be enacted. At this point in the narrative, neither of the two paths is deemed better. But we, as good readers of history, know: the establishment of the office of the Tribune of the Plebs speaks not for inaction, but for an active attempt to repair and regenerate the civic community. The tribunate will be the artificial construction and mechanism for regeneration.

Menenius Agrippa before the seceders

Menenius' second iteration of the metaphorical body politic is fleshed out later in the book before a quite different audience. After his winning senate speech, Menenius is sent as part of a large envoy to win back the seceders to the side of the aristocrats.[33] It first seems odd for Dionysius to 'allow' Menenius Agrippa to deliver two speeches incorporating such similar content.[34] Perhaps Dionysius has shifted sources but failed to ensure narrative consistency? That is, each of his sources may have attributed a body metaphor speech to Menenius – one in the senate and one as part of the envoy – and Dionysius has hedged his bets and kept both.[35] However, I shall demonstrate that a closer examination of Dionysius' text reveals further narrative fudging through spatial 'confusion'. It is deliberate. No doubt it has gone unmentioned to date because of the length and number of speeches that separate the inconsistencies.[36] Critically for us, the space and location Menenius occupies affect, in turn, my own reading. I shall demonstrate that repetition of topic and confusion of space are both deliberately connected and ideologically significant.

After this second senate meeting, the senators despatch envoys to reconcile with the seceders.[37] However, news of the decision travels faster than the envoys. All the plebeians (πάντες) leave the Mons Sacer and meet the envoys while they are still on the road (ἔτι καθ' ὁδὸν).[38] It is there that Sicinius, the camp leader, calls for an assembly. A series of long speeches follows, during which Menenius invokes the Fable of the Body and its Parts.[39] At the assembly's conclusion, Lucius Junius 'Brutus' pushes for the establishment of the tribunate. Menenius agrees to remain 'here' together with some of the other envoys (ἐγὼ μὲν οὖν ἐνθάδε μενῶ καὶ σὺν ἐμοί τι μέρος τῆς πρεσβείας), while Manius Valerius and some of the other envoys return to the senate to pitch the resolution for the new office.[40] This begs the question: what is meant by the demonstrative ἐνθάδε? The immediate context provides no clarity. What follows suggests that the road mentioned eighteen chapters earlier has been forgotten.

The next day, the Valerian envoys make their way to the camp to announce the senate's decision to comply.[41] Menenius – now apparently in the camp – then acts as a go-between, and encourages the plebeians to send a return party to the senate. He himself stays 'in the camp' (ἐπὶ τοῦ στρατοπέδου) to assist with the drafting of the new law.[42] Dionysius' description rationalizes that stay. Additionally, because the meeting takes place in the camp and because no indication of Menenius' movement is given, this suggests that he stayed the night prior to the law-drafting in the camp on the Mons Sacer. Dionysius' use of ἐνθάδε and the compression of the narrative mean that the location of the first and lengthy rapprochement between envoys and seceders is cast into question. Eighteen chapters previously the location of the assembly had been in no doubt: everyone, to a man, had met the envoys on the road. But suddenly, the implication is that all events had taken place in the camp on the Mons Sacer. Dionysius has succeeded in the creation of a liminal zone, and, with it, the setting of the fable appears to have shifted in the narrative telling.

Let us now turn to Menenius' actual deployment of the fable. As Sautel has traced, chapter 86, which contains the fable, is essentially 'a little bit of theatre in two acts'.[43] Each part mirrors the other. The first part introduces the contrived metaphor of the body and explains the function of each part and how it contributes to the whole. The head, for instance, sees and hears, while the shoulders carry loads. The act ends with an imagined collective speech of the parts as they address the stomach and chastise it. The parts not only accuse the stomach of doing nothing, but of actually being a burden. This speech ends with a rhetorical question that clearly recalls an element of the metaphor that Menenius had used before the senate: why, the parts wonder, do they not 'assert our liberty and free ourselves from the many troubles we undergo for the sake of this creature?' A stomach cannot so easily be cut off of course, but the basic premise remains. Menenius then returns to his own voice and asserts his own conclusion: the body could not persist for any period of time but would actually meet its demise within a few days by starvation.[44] It is only after this conclusion that the actual analogy is explained in the second act. The body is a political body comprising many parts and classes, each with a function. Some people trade, some people fight, others cultivate the fields.[45] Once more a collective speech is given by the parts, but this time rather than addressing the stomach, the functionaries speak to the senate. Interestingly, presumably as part of a strategy to get the seceders on side, Menenius does not tone down this imagined speech. The same sense of liberty is invoked, but the point Menenius is making remains the same: though the parts may not realize it from their perspective, the work of the senate is essential. As we might expect of a now fully developed analogy, Menenius' conclusion is longer than that in the first act. Menenius pushes beyond the surface metaphor to a full analogy. Not only is the senate to be seen as essential, but they should not even be blamed by the seceders for their current condition as outcasts.

> μαθόντες οὖν, ὦ δημόται, ὅτι καθάπερ ἐν τοῖς σώμασιν ἡμῶν ἡ λοιδορουμένη κακῶς ὑπὸ τῶν πολλῶν γαστὴρ τρέφει τὸ σῶμα τρεφομένη καὶ σώζει σωζομένη, καὶ ἔστιν ὡσεί τις ἑστίασις κοινὴ τὸ πρόσφορον ἁπάντων καὶ τῆς διαλλαγῆς αἴτιον ἀποδιδοῦσα, οὕτως ἐν ταῖς πόλεσιν ἡ διοικοῦσα τὰ κοινὰ καὶ τοῦ προσήκοντος ἑκάστῳ προνοουμένη βουλὴ πάντα σώζει καὶ φυλάττει καὶ ἐπανορθοῖ[46]
>
> Learn, therefore, plebeians, that just as in our bodies the belly despised by the multitude nourishes the body even while it is itself nourished, and preserves it while it is preserved itself, and is a kind of feast, as it were, provided by joint contributions, which, as a result of the exchange, duly distributes that which is beneficial to each and all, so in commonwealths the senate, which administers the affairs of the public and provides what is expedient for everyone, preserves, guards, and corrects all things.

The body is imagined as a network, as a corporal piece of architecture, or a system of interconnections. It is an assemblage of genitive parts. The question of hierarchy is sidestepped in this analogy. Although the centrality of stomach and senate is recognized, Menenius does not depict it outright as *the* most important feature. It is one part among many. But we may go further still. The point of the analogy is that the political body is not imagined as a static entity, but rather one that requires nourishment, nurture and mutually beneficial exchange. Moreover, the senate is depicted by Menenius as providing, in its administration of public affairs, preservation, protection and – as the final part of the tricolon – corrective education. The verb chosen is critical: ἐπανορθόω carries with it sense of re-education, emendation, and restoration, particularly in a legal setting. The effect of the tricolon should not be underestimated: it confirms what is implicit in the analogy's simultaneous impression of regeneration and stasis. As far as I can tell, this is the only example in Greek literature of these three verbs functioning side by side in such a form. This is not altogether surprising since the sense of the three verbs is internally contradictory: preservation and safeguarding are passively static, while re-education is much more active. Indeed, there is only one example of ἐπανορθόω being set directly alongside φυλάσσω prior to Dionysius: Plato is the exception that proves the rule.[47]

The analogy goes deeper and wider. That is, we may also consider regeneration across the book itself. The 'repetition' of the metaphor is not of course a true repetition. The two occasions are specifically geared towards the audience in each case, senate and seceders. Before the senate, Menenius indicates that it is the plebeians who are draining resources from the political body, while before the people that assumption is reversed. This is more than a point of argumentation, of framing the argument to encourage the 'better' party to be merciful. It is also illuminating in the context of posthumanism. Menenius effectively establishes that he sees no hierarchy of corporal components within the political body: its elements may be reordered and re-sequenced. It is a network of regenerative parts rather than a series of inert, non-associative additions.

In a process of accommodation between diverse and regenerative political bodies, Menenius moves through the city, performing an act of arbitration before these components. In so doing, he employs a politically and ideologically charged metaphor of a networked corporal body before them, adapting and changing this metaphor in the process. He moves from the patrician senate house to a road outside the city and somehow passes into a liminal space that is neither fully the plebeian camp, nor the space in between. This has consequences. The metaphor itself could be said to repeat and regenerate in the text, meandering and reforming in changing settings.

We have seen in this chapter how Dionysius has taken a well-known fable and adapted it for his own purposes. He has created an image of simultaneously internally adaptive and transformative body politic that regenerates and monitors its members and so ensures the stability and stasis of a whole. Dionysius has achieved this image not merely by adapting the metaphor on two separate occasions to two different audiences by using Menenius as a mouthpiece. He has also created a meta-articulation of that same sentiment by having the analogy itself seemingly cross political spheres even as it is made flesh. Analogous to key concepts in posthumanism, the body politic is envisaged as a being in a never-ceasing regenerative process, which paradoxically maintains its stasis through constant self-monitoring and improvement. The metaphor of networked bodies itself acts a networked synapse between the assemblages of the city. The very narrative of Roman history then, as political bodies defer to a networked whole, is itself susceptible to repetition, regeneration and reformation.

CHAPTER 17
THE MYTH OF IO AND FEMALE CYBORGIC IDENTITY

Antonietta Provenza

The myth of Io, the Argive girl loved and seduced by Zeus, essentially has had two main interpretations: the geo-local one – linked with her wanderings – and the one relating to transition from maidens to married women. The main narrative sequences are the seduction by Zeus, the period she spends in the custody of 'all-seeing' Argos, Io's metamorphosis (or better hybridization, as we shall see) into a cow, her wanderings from Argos to Egypt, harassed by a gadfly, and finally her return to human form, and the birth of Epaphus, Zeus' son, on the banks of the Nile. The agent of Io's transformation is either Zeus[1] – for the purpose of hiding his infidelity to Hera, his legitimate bride – or Hera herself,[2] who wants to take revenge for her husband's infidelity. Io escapes her suffering by conceiving and bearing a child, that is, by the only social function envisaged as natural for women in ancient Greece:[3] the girl-heifer – who shares in Hera's bovine imagery[4] – therefore appears as the paradigm of the unavoidable 'yoke' of love and marriage for women.[5]

In the light of the bovine imagery characterizing Io on the one hand, and of readings of some core studies concerning the theory of the cyborg on the other, this chapter aims to show that the Argive girl does not only undergo a metamorphosis, but also inhabits a space of hybrid identity: she is first and foremost a human assemblage of young girl and bovine (either a heifer or even a bull) with a fluid identity between virgin girl and sexual mate.[6] Reconceptualizing metamorphosis as cyborgic hybridity is an interesting theoretical point whose potential for modern readings of the ancient myths seems not to have been fully considered yet.[7] As we will see, in her peculiar shape, Io seems perfectly to comply nowadays with the definition of female cyborg, a hybrid entity blending 'sexuality with assertiveness, hyperfeminine characteristics with tough-girl strength' and so transcending 'the patriarchal limits of female identity/femininity'.[8] Outside of any hierarchy between the human and the animal,[9] the figure of Io metaphorically seems to establish female ontology in its fulness.

The girl-heifer in Aeschylus' *Prometheus Bound* and *Suppliant Maidens*

The Argive Io,[10] a priestess of Hera,[11] is seduced by Zeus, who turns her into a white heifer to hide his infidelity from Hera. However, Zeus ends up surrendering her to the goddess, who takes her revenge[12] by submitting the girl-heifer to the rigid custody of Argos, the many-eyed and all-seing monster.[13] After the latter is killed by Hermes by order of Zeus,[14] Io is forced by Hera to wander pursued by the gadfly (οἶστρος).[15]

Io's humiliation and helplessness, that particularly emerge in *Prometheus Bound*,[16] are linked with the misfortune of an 'unequal marriage', that the chorus of the Oceanides – in consideration of Io's fate – wish to avert from themselves (887–907): Zeus' desire (654, πόθος), manifesting in nightmares, is ruinous for the virgin girl Io, for her father, Inachus, throws her out of the house in obedience to an oracle, so that she is deprived of the protection offered by her paternal οἶκος without being married, and becomes a girl-heifer, subjected to Hera, who will henceforth be wandering in distant places (645–682). Io's 'fate fraught with ruin' (633, τὰς πολυφθόρους τύχας) clearly emerges in *Pr.* 898–900, where the Oceanides express their fear and anxiety as they look at 'Io's maidenhood, without love of man (ἀστεργάνορα παρθενίαν), destroyed by wanderings consisting of troubles (ἀλατείαις πόνων) imposed upon her by Hera'.[17]

Io is immediately addressed by Prometheus as 'maiden' (589, κόρη, cf. also 704, νεᾶνις), highlighting a condition conventionally characterized by modesty, an essential feature of Io's humanity (*Pr.* 642–644): she is ashamed (αἰσχύνομαι) of telling of the 'storm sent by gods and the destruction (διαφθορά) of my shape,[18] which has flown upon miserable me'. Her aspect on stage is that of a 'cow-horned maiden' (*Pr.* 588, βούκερω παρθένου),[19] for Io's beauty is spoiled in a process of hybridization that suddenly begins as her father throws her out of the house: 'beauty of form and mind were immediately distorted' (673–674, εὐθὺς δὲ μορφὴ καὶ φρένες διάστροφοι / ἦσαν). Yet Io never ceases to be human, for she does not lose her corporeal experience and does not change her interactions with others; she acts and laments as a human being, considering herself a 'virgin wandering in misery' (608, τᾷ δυσπλάνῳ παρθένῳ). A stubbornly preserved maidenhood,[20] protected by Io against Zeus' desire (654, πόθος), is the prelude to the bovine hybridization: the maiden that 'kicks' in order to avert sexual union with Zeus (651–652, μὴ ἀπολακτίσῃς λέχος / τὸ Ζηνός), actually sees herself becoming 'horned' (674, κεραστίς); she, then, loses her typically human self-control – for suffering turns the tame wild – adopts a leaping gait (675, ἐμμανεῖ σκιρτήματι) characteristic of cattle, and is later 'tamed' (601, δαμεῖσα) by Hera; all of which bestows the features of madness[21] and suffering on her hybridity.

If on the one hand Io's wanderings (738, πλάνας) are subsequent to her 'painful suitor's' (739–740, πικροῦ ... μνηστῆρος) advances, on the other, Hera is the cause of her suffering (703–704, οἷα χρὴ πάθη / τλῆναι πρὸς Ἥρας), figuratively represented by the οἶστρος ('the gadfly'),[22] the nagging thought of the fear that torments her (580, οἰστρηλάτῳ [...] δείματι) and makes her desire total annihilation, in order to put an end to her continual wandering (585, πολύπλανοι πλάναι). Io is by antonomasia 'the girl moved by οἶστρος' (589, οἰστροδινήτου κόρης)[23] – an oxymoronic description that brings together the human figure and a phenomenon associated with cattle. All this brings into view a perceived contiguity between the animal and the female human species; within a contemporary redefinition of female identity, this can be better interpreted and understood by using the model of the cyborgic identity.[24]

As she tells the chorus of the Oceanides and Prometheus about her suffering (669–682), Io says she is 'pursued by the harassing divine whip' (681–682, οἰστροπλὴξ ... μάστιγι θείᾳ), while, when she is offstage, the red-hot tip of the gadfly is evoked as a cause of painful torment (880, οἴστρου δ' ἄρδις χρίει ζάπυρος), together with the mad puff of the λύσσα[25] that drives her in her wandering (884, ἔξω δὲ δρόμου φέρομαι λύσσης πνεύματι μάργῳ). Therefore, οἶστρος seems to be the main element of Io's dishumanizing hybridization. It also appears in Euripides' *Bacchae* as a metaphor of the dionysiac frenzy, that 'dehumanizes' women, making them lose their association with the domestic sphere.[26] However, while in *Bacchae* female alienation turns into a violence which destroys man (Pentheus) – that is, authority and civilization – and into bestialization, in the case of Io, a virgin girl, the anti-social condition of hybridity seems to prefigure the 'best' female identity, which is defined by women's generative function as spouses and mothers:[27] harassment by Hera will end only thanks to Zeus, as he impregnates Io on the banks of the Nile 'only touching her gently with his hand causing no fear' (849, ἐπαφῶν ἀταρβεῖ χειρὶ καὶ θιγὼν μόνον), and generates Epaphus, a son with a name that tells of his divine birth. He will be the ancestor of Danaus, whose fifty daughters (853–869) are the protagonists of Aeschylus' *Suppliant Maidens*.

Kinship with Io is of crucial importance for the Danaids coming to Argos: they do not wish for a normal sexual union; rather they would aspire to a union with Zeus, as did their ancestress, and not with their human and violent cousins.[28] By reconstructing their mythical-historical genealogy, and appealing to it, the Danaids in the *parodos* boast to have descended from the Argive stock of Io, 'the heifer harassed by οἶστρος': by touching, and blowing on her (*Supp.* 16–18, γένος ἡμέτερον τῆς οἰστροδόνου / βοὸς ἐξ ἐπαφῆς κἀξ ἐπιπνοίας / Διός), Zeus generated Epaphus (40–46), their 'avenger' (41, τιμάορ'[α]). The transformation of Io into a cow clearly appears in the first episode, within a dialogue between the Danaids and Pelasgus (291–315), which tells the story of the priestess of Hera (291, κληδοῦχον), loved and seduced by Zeus when she still had human form (295, μιχθῆνα<ι> βροτῷ), before the jealous goddess made her a heifer (299, βοῦν τὴν γυναῖκ' ἔθηκεν Ἀργεία θεός, 300, εὐκραίρῳ βοΐ, 'a heifer with beautiful horns').[29] Following the metamorphosis of Io, Zeus takes the form of a bull (*Supp.* 301, φασίν, πρέποντα βουθόρῳ ταύρῳ δέμας, 'making his form that of a bull lusting for a mate'), in order to keep on making love with her. Hera, then, appoints Argos to watch the girl-heifer, Hermes slays Argos, and Io begins her wanderings, harassed by the gadfly, the merciless and dishumanizing cattledriver (307, βοηλάτην μύωπα κινητήριον). The suffering of Io will end when Zeus impregnates her with Epaphus just by touching (315, Ἔπαφος, ἀληθῶς ῥυσίων ἐπώνυμος).

In both versions of the myth, in *Prometheus Bound* and *Suppliant Maidens*, Zeus' mating with Io is the cause of her bestialization. Although Io experiences the wrath of Hera, her γάμος with Zeus is also the cause of her liberation from misery: as Zeus' breath impregnates her with Epaphus, Io takes again her human form, and gets rid of the suffering imposed upon her by the goddess (577–578, θείαις ἐπιπνοίαις / παύεται). Therefore, Zeus avenges his beloved mistress, 'holding back her suffering with healing hand' (1066, χειρὶ παιωνίᾳ κατασχεθών); in the same way, the Danaids hope that he will remember the touch by which he generated his son from Io (535, γενοῦ πολυμνῆστορ, ἔφαπτορ Ἰοῦς). On the other hand, unlike *Prometheus Bound*, where Io is a victim of the erotic impulse of Zeus, *Suppliant Maidens* emphasizes more the girl-heifer's glory than her suffering: the εὐμενὴς βία (1067, 'beneficial violence') enacted by Zeus offers a whole other reading. Io surrenders to Zeus' desire, submits to him and, by bearing a child, achieves complete happiness for the whole of her long life altogether (582, δι' αἰῶνος μακροῦ πάνολβον).

However, the Danaids' consideration of Zeus as both the avenger of Io and the rescuer of themselves sounds ironic and specious, for they represent a social anomaly, rejecting the laws of the *polis* and family, that are founded upon marriage: the Danaids reject a societal cornerstone they praise so highly in *Supp.* 625–709, and seem to be far removed from the paradigm of the necessity of γάμος embodied by their ancestress Io, the 'renowned spouse' (*Pr.* 834, κλεινὴ δάμαρ) of Zeus, in her hybrid form. In fact, Io's glorious destiny seems to be due to her hybrid condition, induced by Hera's punishment, which, however, already foreshadows her pregnancy, that will make her a paradigm of the 'ideal' woman. In the *parodos*, a suffering Io is presented as a cow 'driven round and round by the gadfly' (*Supp.* 16–17, οἰστροδόνου, cf. also 573, οἰστροδόνητον), while at 274–275 the heifer woman is described as 'bearing a fine child' (εὐτέκνου). A hybrid identity lies between these two stages. On the one hand, according to the narration of the Danaids, Hera transformed the Argive girl into a cow (299, βοῦν τὴν γυναῖκ' ἔθηκεν Ἀργεία θεός); they also refer to Epaphus as 'the cow's calf (πόρτις) by Zeus' (314, cf. also 41). On the other, the suppliant maidens also narrate in the first Stasimon that Io arrived in Egypt as an 'unpleasant animal hybrid' (βοτὸν ... δυσχερὲς μειξόμβροτον) – partly a heifer, partly a woman – an 'unwanted view' (ὄψιν ἀήθη) which instilled fear in the locals, a 'prodigy' (τέρας) that astounded them (565–570).[30] Io's hybridity is the distinctive sign of her condition as an ideal woman: both a virgin girl and a sex object, she is inflamed by passion in her turn and immediately surrenders to desire, without offering any resistance to Zeus. Considering that Hera presides over marriage, namely over legitimate sexual activity for women within marriage, we might say that, although Zeus is the only man Hera disapproves of as a sexual mate (for he is her spouse), Io embodies Hera's will even in her form, by taking the goddess' bovine characteristics.

Also in iconography Io usually functions as an allusion to marriage:[31] on a Lucan *oinochoe* (*c.* 450 BCE), she is a heifer with the face of a woman and a nuptial veil on her head.[32] Within the iconography of Io, there are also some depictions of a girl-bull hybrid,[33] besides the more widespread representations of the girl-heifer hybrid. Such a variation, attested on some Attic and South-Italian vases from the end of the sixth century to the beginning of the fourth century BCE representing the murder of Argos by Hermes, is interpreted by Moret 1990 as a result of catasterism,[34] but I would suggest that it also links the mythical story of Io with Dionysus as hypostasis of sexual potency and fertility.

Such Dionysiac features emerge, for instance, in a song of worship of the women of Elis, who invoke the god as a 'worthy bull', asking him to storm on his 'bovine foot' (τῷ βοέῳ ποδὶ δύων).[35] Through the animal image, Dionysus becomes a symbol of virility,[36] that in turn is strictly linked with marriage, a province of Hera, the ox-eyed goddess who perfidiously attracts Semele, Dionysus' mother, towards her death and causes the madness of Ino, Dionysus' nurse, and of Dionysus himself[37] – for she tries to prevent Zeus with any adversity from generating an 'illegitimate' offspring.

Furthermore, the image of the bull also refers to Zeus, who becomes a bull after Io has taken the form of a heifer (*Supp.* 300–301). It actually alludes to sexual potency, pointing out that women cannot avoid γάμος and moreover highlighting – together with Io's representation as a hybrid – a transgression of boundaries and fusion of dichotomies between male and female, self and other, nature and culture, god and human being, which allows us to consider Io in a contemporary perspective as a cyborgic creature.

Conclusions

Recommendation of marriage as one of the cornerstones of society appears in the background of the myth of Io, intended to 'teach' women that they must surrender to the natural and political necessity of γάμος. Female subjugation to male sexual desire is thus enshrined in the figure of Io, which can be seen as a hybrid containing within itself the symbolic features of the animals she embodies. The girl-heifer appears as a cyborg female (human/animal, female/male) whose female identity is bound to marriage, to the women's awareness of their seductive power – triggered and fostered thanks to 'desire' (πόθος) and 'enchanting Persuasion' (*Supp.* 1039–1040, θέλκτορι Πειθοῖ), the companions of Aphrodite 'full of wiles' (1036, αἰολόμητις) – and, ultimately, to the full acceptance of sexual union as necessary for the sake of the continuity of mankind.[38] Reading the body as a cultural text, Io's cyborgic identity establishes the destiny and role of being a woman[39] by including the main characteristics of the divinities presiding over sexual union and generation. Conversely, Io's story becomes a model for citizens, who become acquainted with it through both the religious cult and theatrical performances, which are a most important part in the festivals for Dionysus.

Therefore, through the prism of the figure of Io, Posthumanism[40] does not stand for what comes 'after' the human, but for the human hybrid understood as a monstrous yet sympathetic creature (τέρας) that belongs to myth and contrasts with human experience. Although the hybrid Io shapes an identity that cannot exist for real women, it ultimately represents the possibility of a paradigmatic female ontology.

CHAPTER 18
COSMIC, ANIMAL AND HUMAN BECOMINGS: A CASE STUDY IN ANCIENT PHILOSOPHY

Laura Rosella Schluderer

This chapter aims to elucidate a seminal insight of Greek philosophy into the complex structure of the cosmos as a whole, humans and animals, to show its affinity with some contemporary notions holding citizenship in the Posthumanist debate, as well as its theoretical relevance for the related issues concerning identity, differentiation, otherness and the risks of a flat ontology.

The selected case study is Philolaus' ontology of harmony and his account of living beings. In what follows, I shall start from B13, which presents an intriguing *scala naturae*, and move on to other fragments and *testimonia*[1] to reconstruct Philolaus' explanatory pattern based on *harmonia* and how it applies to the hierarchy of B13. The chapter shows how, by developing an innovative notion of harmonic, mathematically structured assemblage modelled on the paradigm of musical *harmonia* (B6a) and by applying it to natural beings, Philolaus obtains a theoretical framework that is capable of (a) analysing both the cosmos as a whole and all living beings in terms of increasingly complex and interconnected compounds; (b) accounting for the nature and specific faculties of each kind of organism in terms of additional features emerging with each new compound in the hierarchy (plants, animals, humans and the cosmos); (c) explaining the interrelations, overlaps and differentiations between kinds through the notion of increasingly complex harmonic compounds formed of sub-compounds.

So reconstructed, Philolaus' theory provides a model that:

1. Shows some affinities with contemporary notions of assemblage or becoming, i.e., frameworks that conceive of being as a progressive process of differentiation, and theorize 'things' as symbiotic emergent units that arise from the interaction of multiple components. In these frameworks, the heterogeneity of components is not erased, but subsumed, as emerging assemblages acquire from them the powers and capacities to act and be acted upon, in turn allowing for the formation of new becomings.[2] Along these lines, I will provide an interpretation of Philolaus' harmonic compounds as assemblages emerging from the combination of limiters and unlimiteds, i.e., components whose properties and powers do not disappear within the compound, but whose combination allows for different properties and new entities to emerge. This could rather well be described by the account recently provided by Jane Bennett in her landmark work, *Vibrant Matter*:

   > Assemblages are ad hoc groupings of diverse elements, of vibrant materials of all sorts. Assemblages are living, throbbing confederations that are able to function despite the persistent presence of energies that confound them from within [. . .] The effects generated by an assemblage are [. . .] emergent properties, emergent in that their ability to make something happen [. . .] is distinct from the sum of the vital

> force of each materiality considered alone. Each member and proto-member of the assemblage has a certain vital force. But there is also an effectivity proper to the grouping as such: an agency of the assemblage.[3]

2. Supplies the theoretical foundation for a non-reductive blurring of ontological boundary between human and non-human, one of the main concerns in contemporary Posthumanism.[4] Unexpectedly, Philolaus' framework suggests a theoretically sound backdrop that allows fruitfully complicating the discourse: as each kind of living being is analysed as an emergent unit arising when a further level of compositional complexity is added to the preceding life form in the hierarchy, there appears to be a fundamental ontological continuity, both synchronic and diachronic, between human and non-human becomings; at the same time, an equally significant ontological difference emerges, which repeats itself at all levels of existence, synchronically and diachronically. For although all living things share their basic, ontologically essential features, yet new aspects emerge at different levels of the hierarchy. These are subsumed and combined to endow each new emergent becoming with different powers and capacities. As we shall see, neither continuity nor difference, in this framework, may be dispensed with, if a proper account of each kind of living becoming, the cosmos as a whole included, is to be provided.

Let us then turn to Philolaus' B13:

> And four are the principles (ἀρχαί) of the rational animal, as Philolaus says in his book *On Nature*, brain, heart, navel and genitals: 'The head [holds the principle/origin] of intellect (νόου), the heart that of *psyche* and perception (ψυχᾶς καὶ αἰσθήσιος), the navel of rooting and first growth (ῥιζώσιος καὶ ἀναφύσιος τοῦ πρώτου), the genitals of the sowing and generation of seed (σπέρματος καταβολᾶς τε καὶ γεννήσιος). The brain [holds] the principle of man, the heart that of animal, the navel that of plant, and genitals the principle of all these together, for it is from seed that everything flourishes and grows.

The fragment is extremely interesting. It is the only surviving text, if one discounts the embryological testimony in the medical papyrus *Anonymus Londiniensis* (A27, A28), in which Philolaus directly addresses the nature of living beings.[5] It also sketches a plant–animal–man hierarchy that, while seemingly not uncommon (as the same sequence, or parts of it, feature in other authors),[6] is uniquely complex and stratified, as it associates each living being to a specific organ and faculty, pivoting these manifold hierarchical relationships on the difficult key term ἀρχή.

As ἀρχή also appears in fr. B6, where it specifically defines limiters and unlimited (the ultimate cosmic components in Philolaus' view), and as Philolaus insists that not only the cosmos as a whole, but also '*all the things in it*' (B1) result from the combination of limiters and unlimited, I propose to read B13 in the broader context of Philolaus' ontological framework. Thus, I shall first clarify the notions of limiters, unlimiteds and *harmonia* and their mutual relations, to clarify Philolaus' specific notion of harmonic assemblages, and then apply this analytical schema to B13, where its resonance with the notion of becoming as a progressive process of differentiation and interaction will appear clearer.

Harmonic compounds: Philolaus' becomings

The logical relations of limiters, unlimiteds and harmonia

Consider B6 and B2:

> Regarding nature and harmony the situation is as follows: the being of things (ἁ μὲν ἐστὼ τῶν πραγμάτων), which is eternal, and nature itself admits of knowledge that is divine and not human, except that it was impossible for the things that are and are known by us to have come to be if the being of things from which the world order was constituted (ἐξ ὧν συνέστα ὁ κόσμος), did not exist (μὴ ὑπαρχούσας) – both the limiters and the unlimiteds (καὶ τῶν περαινόντων καὶ τῶν ἀπείρων). But since these principles/beginnings (ταὶ ἀρχαί) existed being neither alike nor akin (οὐχ ὁμοῖαι οὐδ' ὁμόφυλοι), it would have been impossible for them to be ordered in a cosmos (κοσμηθῆναι) if a harmony had not supervened (εἰ μὴ ἁρμονία ἐπεγένετο), in whatever way it came to be. Things that are alike and akin did not need any harmony, but things that are unlike and not akin and not of [the same speed], it is necessary that such things be bound together by harmonies (ἁρμονίαις συγκεκλεῖσθαι), if they are to be held in an order (εἰ μέλλοντι ἐν κόσμῳ κατέχεσθαι).
>
> *B6*

> It is necessary for the things that are (τὰ ἐόντα) to be either all limiting (ἢ περαίνοντα) or all unlimited (ἢ ἄπειρα) or both limiting and unlimited (ἢ περαίνοντά τε καὶ ἄπειρα); but not in every case unlimited only. Now, since it is manifest that neither are they from limiting things only, nor from unlimited things only, it is clear that the cosmos and the things in it were fitted together from both limiting and unlimited things (ἐκ περαινόντων τε καὶ ἀπείρων ὅ τε κόσμος καὶ τὰ ἐν αὐτῷ συναρμόχθη).
>
> *B2*

B6 explicitly defines limiters and unlimiteds as ἀρχαί and uses a counterfactual argument to make a statement of necessary conditions:[7] if limiters and unlimiteds did not exist, the world as we know it and all the things in it would not exist. Although underdetermined whether ἀρχαί are here understood as temporal, logical or ontological beginnings,[8] B6 makes clear that limiters and unlimiteds are somehow responsible for the fact that the world is as we know it, and accordingly suggests that ἀρχή is something endowed (at least also) with a causal and explanatory role.[9] B2, on the other hand, sets out the logical possibilities for 'the things that are', then establishing that they must come from *both* limiters *and* unlimiteds: this would suggest that limiters and unlimiteds are not only necessary but perhaps *jointly sufficient* for the world to exist. However, (1) B6 explicitly state that, being unlike and not akin, limiters and unlimiteds could not have been joined into a (world-)order, had a *harmonia* not supervened, and (2) both fragments raise a question concerning the productive relation expressed by ἐκ (cf. ἐκ περαινόντων τε καὶ ἀπείρων, B2; ἐξ ὧν συνέστα ὁ κόσμος, καὶ τῶν περαινόντων καὶ τῶν ἀπείρων, B6): is this a constitutive or originative ἐκ? Are limiters and unlimiteds 'items' the world and all things in it are *made of*, right now, or are they originative 'items' the world and all things in it *come from*?

Both issues are clarified once we integrate ἁρμονία into the picture, as it becomes clear that (1) limiters and unlimiteds are indeed the cosmos' only *components,* but not *all* that is needed, and (2) that both the constitutive and derivative sense of ἐκ (and accordingly of ἀρχή) are at play.

Harmonia. Two values of *harmonia* emerge from the fragments. On the one hand, B6 prompts an interpretation of ἁρμονία as an additional principle acting upon the pre-existing other two. On the other, consider B1:

> Nature in the world order (ἁ φύσις δ' ἐν τῷ κόσμῳ) was harmonized together (ἁρμόχθη) from unlimiteds and limiters, both the world order as a whole and all things in it (καὶ ὅλος ὁ κόσμος καὶ τὰ ἐν αὐτῷ πάντα).

Here, it appears that *every combination* of limiters and unlimiteds *is* a ἁρμονία, for every time that a limiter and an unlimited, being unlike and not akin (B6), are held together it is precisely because they are harmonically combined (ἁρμόχθη); thus the cosmos and all things in it, being constituted of limiters and unlimiteds, just *are* harmonic combinations, ἁρμονίαι. This is further confirmed by the fact that in B1 and B2 *harmonia* does not appear as a third entity, but in the form of a verb (ἁρμόζειν, B1, συναρμόζειν B2), indicating the harmonic *way* in which limiters and unlimiteds are fitted together. Thus *harmonia* seems to be also something that does not exist *over and above* limiters and unlimiteds: while *harmonia* is indispensible, it is not to be understood as a further ἀρχή, or as a constitutive element of the same sort as limiters and unlimiteds: its ontological status and role are essentially different.

The key to reconcile these two apparently distinct values[10] and to grasp this special ontological status lies in the notion of musical *harmonia*, which Philolaus develops in B6a and uses as an explanatory paradigm for cosmological *harmonia*.[11] Thus, musical *harmonia* is also key to understanding Philolaus' conception of harmonic compound and its affinity with the contemporary notions of assemblage and becoming.[12]

> The size of *harmonia* is a fourth and a fifth; and a fifth is greater than a fourth by a 9:8 ratio (ἐπογδόωι) [a tone]. For from the lowest note to the middle note is a fourth, and from the middle note to the highest note is a fifth, but from the highest note to the third note is a fourth, and from the third note to the lowest note is a fifth. Between the middle note and the third note is a 9:8 ratio (ἐπόγδοον), a fourth is a 4:3 ratio (ἐπίτριτον), a fifth is a 3:2 ratio (ἡμιόλιον), and the octave (διὰ πασῶν) is a 2:1 ratio (διπλόον). Thus *harmonia* is five 9:8 ratios [tones] and two diesies [two smaller semitones], the fifth is 9:8 ratios [tones] and a diesies, and the fourth is two 9:8 ratios [tones] and a diesies.
>
> *B6a*[13]

First, it is crucial to note that the technical term ἁρμονία here refers not to the 'interval of octave', as some have thought,[14] but to the 'attunement over an octave', i.e., the whole structure of intervals spanning one octave orderly distributed along the concords of fourth, fifth and octave. This is made evident by the first sentence, which programmatically announces the size of ἁρμονία as resulting from the sum of the fourth and the fifth, and is confirmed by Philolaus' peculiar musical terminology: by keeping the name διὰ πασῶν for the interval of octave, and reserving the unusual ἁρμονία for the overall pattern of attunement,[15] he is consciously distinguishing the two.[16] But a musical *harmonia* is both this abstract pattern of intervals, *and* each audible sequence of notes that embodies that pattern, whatever the key in which they are played (in contemporary terms: C-D-E-F-G-A-B-C in key of C, G-A-B-C-D-E-F#-G in key of G, etc.). Indeed, what makes a sequence of notes musical, and not a jumble of sounds, is precisely embodying that abstract pattern of relations among intervals.

The second crucial point is that Philolaus here is characterizing that abstract pattern in terms of mathematical ratios. He introduces the innovative idea that the difference between the fourth and the fifth does not depend on their position on the lyre, but on their numerical relations: first, the fifth is greater than the fourth by a 9:8 ratio, corresponding to a tone; then he identifies the fourth with the ratio 4:3, the fifth with the ratio 3:2, the octave with the ratio 2:1. He indicates all these ratios with their mathematical technical names: *epitritic*, *hemiolic*, double. Therefore, a fourth is not only the interval between lowest note and middle note at the bottom of the lyre, but also that between third note and highest note at the top, because both are the ratio 4:3. A fifth is not only the interval between highest note and middle note at the top, but also that between lowest note and third note, because both are the ratio 3:2. Indeed, it does not matter where they are located: that expressed by the same mathematical relation just *is* the same interval.

In musical terms, thus, ἁρμονία is both the *normative pattern of mathematical ratios* that notes and intervals must respect in order to constitute a musical harmony, and also each and every audible system of notes that *instantiates that pattern*. If we apply such considerations to metaphysics and cosmology, we can interpret ἁρμονία as referring to both each physical compound resulting from the combination of limiting and unlimited, *and* the abstract pattern of harmonic proportions that the compound must embody to be the kind of compound it is. As we are told in B6, limiters and unlimiteds can constitute an orderly whole (κοσμηθῆναι; ἐν κόσμῳ κατέχεσθαι), if and only if they are fitted together in harmonic fashion (ἁρμονίαις συγκεκλεῖσθαι, B6; συναρμόχθη, B2; ἁρμόχθη, B1), that is, according to specific mathematical ratios, e.g., those of the diatonic scale. I call *harmonia1* the abstract harmonic structure, and *harmonia2* each harmonic compound that embodies it. Three relationships are at play: (1) between each harmonic compound (*harmonia2*) and the abstract structural pattern (*harmonia1*); (2) between the constituents (limiters and unlimiteds) and the compound they form (*harmonia2*); (3) between the abstract structural pattern (*harmonia1*) and the compound's constituents (limiters and unlimiteds). Relationship (1) is the normative relationship holding between an abstract model and its physical instantiations. Relationship (2) is the compositional relation expressed in the formula ἐκ περαινόντων καὶ ἀπείρων: each *harmonia2 derives from* limiters and unlimited in the sense that it is a new whole emerging from their combination; but each *harmonia*2 is also *constituted of* limiters and unlimiteds, for it is not something over and above them, but no more than their combination according to specific mathematical ratios. Relationship (3) expresses the normative force that *harmonia1* operates over limiters and unlimiteds so that a certain compound comes to be from them (ἐξ ὧν, B6).

Limiters and unlimiteds. Let us now turn to the nature of limiters and unlimiteds, to clarify how their harmonic combinations generate structured compounds with increasing levels of complexities, of which living beings are examples. The account that follows is central in showing the parallel that can be drawn between Philolaus' ontological framework and the notion of becoming and of *puissance*, as I suggest at the end of this section.

In my interpretation, limiters are not merely what set boundaries, and unlimiteds what lack them:[17] they also are, respectively, what is essentially capable of 'acting upon', and what is in itself suitable to be affected. This is not only suggested by B2, where Philolaus says that while 'entities' constituted only of limiters *act* as limiters (περαίνοντι), 'entities' constituted only of unlimiteds do not act, but *appear* unlimited (ἄπειρα φανέονται), but especially by the names Philolaus chooses for his ontological principles: περαίνοντα and ἄπειρα. Both are neuter plurals, signalling that Philolaus has in mind concrete entities rather than abstract principles.[18] By choosing the unique form περαίνοντα,[19] Philolaus deliberately stresses agency as a defining feature of limiters. As the present participle 'represents a *quality in action*',[20] I submit that περαίνοντα denotes all those items in the world that are *now, at this moment* actively limiting,[21] and thus that something qualifies as a limiter by virtue of its being actually acting as a limiter, and as long as it does so.[22]

Furthermore, note the meaning of περαίνω, 'passing through something from end to end', and thus 'accomplishing', 'exhausting' (note the semantic connection with τελέω and τέλος).[23] The adjective ἄπειρα is thus meant to be opposed (a) to the active agency aspect of περαίνοντα, and (b) to περαίνω rather than to the noun πέρας.[24] Accordingly, ἄπειρος is 'what cannot be completely traversed or accomplished'.[25] Take time, an unlimited at Aristotle's Fr. 201 (below). It can receive the action of a limiter, say, by being divided into years, but it is still liable to receive further division into days, hours, minutes, etc. The action of a limiter on an unlimited accomplishes one of the numberless possibilities, but unlimited others persist within the harmonic compound,[26] endowing it with the potential of further being acted upon by a limiter and thus turn into a different becoming with different properties.[27]

A corollary to this interpretation is that the same thing can function now as a limiter, now as an unlimited according to the functional role it has within a certain structure. Examples of this are πνεῦμα and void in Aristotle's testimonies on Pythagorean cosmogony:

> The heaven is one, and from the unlimited time and breath were drawn in, and void, which distinguishes the place of each thing in each case (ὃ διορίζει ἑκάστων τὰς χώρας ἀεί).
>
> *Fr. 201*

> Void exists, and it comes into the world from the unlimited breath, the world breathing in also the void, which distinguishes the natures of things (ὃ διορίζει τὰς φύσεις).
>
> *Phys. 213b22f.*

Here πνεῦμα and void are said to be unlimiteds, but simultaneously act as limiters:[28] for void is also said to distinguish (διορίζειν) the natures or the places of things, a clear limiting action, while πνεῦμα acts as a limiter on the excessive hotness of the new-born animal and, by analogy, of the original cosmic nucleus:

> Immediately after birth, the animal breathes in the external air, which is cold (τὸ ἐκτὸς πνεῦμα ψυχρὸν ὄν); then it sends it out again like a debt. Indeed it is for this reason that there is a desire for external air, so that our bodies, which were too hot (θερμότερα) before, by the drawing in of the air from outside are cooled (καταψύχηται) thereby. He [Philolaus] says, then, that the constitution of our body depends on these things. (*Anon. Lond.* 18.21–29 Manetti)

Here, the foetuses (11.9–10) are θερμότερα (1.15); this excessive heat is limited (καταψύχηται) by the cold πνεῦμα from outside. Then, consider cosmogony:

> The first thing fitted together (ἁρμοσθέν), the one (τὸ ἕν) in the centre of the sphere, is called the hearth.
>
> *B7*

> After the one had been constructed [. . .] then immediately the nearest part of the unlimited began 'to be drawn and limited by the limit'.
>
> *Arist. Metaph. 1091a15*[29]

'The one in the centre of the sphere (. . .) the hearth' is arguably the central fire mentioned in the testimonies on Philolaus' astronomical system (πῦρ ἐν μέσῳ, A16; τὸ πῦρ μέσον, A17) from which and around which the cosmos starts.[30] Since the key verb ἁρμόζειν is used, the unlimited-limiting pair must be involved; and indeed, the very notion of 'central fire' is defined by a limiter, i.e., the centre of the sphere, and an unlimited, i.e., fire.[31] The former works as a limiter upon an indeterminate aspect of fire, namely its spatial extension. But like the foetus, the original cosmic nucleus is only hot, and thus unlimited temperature-wise: this endows it with the disposition to be cooled down, and πνεῦμα, coming from outside, functions as a limiter in this respect, by analogy with embryology.

The cosmic components, therefore, acquire their taxonomic status by virtue of the function they perform within a certain assemblage. This allows very complex compounds to come about, as the same component that functions as a limiter under a certain respect can still be unlimited under another, thus endowing the becoming it forms with the potential to be further modified and differentiated.

Philolaus' explanatory schema thus resonates with the notion of assemblage and of becoming, as it was developed by Deleuze and Guattari and reprised by Bennett with a specific stress on agency.[32] First, like Philolaus' harmonic compound, a becoming is not a homogeneous, in itself concluded unit, sealed off from the outside, within which different components merge and disappear, but one symbiotic assemblage whose components maintain their heterogeneity and multiplicity, endowing the composite with the powers that result from their interaction. Limiters and unlimiteds, indeed, do not give up their powers to act and be acted upon once they combine harmonically into a compound – rather, it is within the compound that they display those powers, which result from their combination.[33] Second, Philolaus' limiters and unlimiteds are essentially powers to affect and be affected, mutually defined and capable of forming assemblages by virtue of their constantly interacting powers: they are, in Deleuzian terms, *puissances*, capacities respectively to act and to suffer action that do not exist independently, and whose constant and mutual combination creates the possibility for assemblages to arise and be modified,[34] progressively becoming more complex, with capacities to interact with other becomings by affecting and being affected.

Philolaus' cosmic, animal and human becomings

The cosmos as a harmonic compound

We can now see how this complex formation process applies to the cosmos itself. We just saw that, at its beginning, the cosmic central nucleus results from the harmonizing together of two ἀρχαί, the limiting centre on the unlimited fire, which makes it a *harmonia2* with certain specific properties: position, shape, size and, apparently, the ability to draw in material and expand. This *harmonia2* acquires new properties through the further stages of its development. For instance, it acquires a determinate temperature, thanks to the unlimited hotness of fire being limited by the coldness of air. It also presumably starts acquiring internal articulation, thanks to the introduction of πνεῦμα, time and void, acted upon by the limiting action of the sphere, with void then in turn acting as a separator of things. Thus there is a development through various stages in which further ἀρχαί (limiter and unlimited) interlock to modify the initial harmonic compound. We can imagine that this process repeats itself until the cosmos becomes the complex system of individual things we know, passing through various stages such as the formation of the ten planets around the central fire (cf. A16–17), the various life forms and man (B13).

There is no metaphysical gap between the original cosmic one and, say, me, or this cat, or that rose, because although we may be compounds with different layers of combinations of limiters-unlimiteds and thus different properties and powers, we share in the same metaphysical structure, and are part of the same complex becoming. Our connection, moreover, is both diachronic and synchronic. In one sense, I am simply one of the latest harmonic compounds that came into being and that is involved in the constitution of the overall harmony. In another sense, all *harmoniai* are synchronically connected to each other in fitting fashion: for example, through my breathing in and out air at a specific ratio of exchange I am harmonically connected with the atmosphere, and form a further harmonic compound with it, a further emergent unit.[35] We – humans, animals, plants and the cosmos – are part of a wholly unified, interconnected structure. This picture is, I believe, confirmed and expanded by fragment B13, from which my discussion originally started.

Living becomings: Hierarchies and variations of harmonic compounds

The stratified hierarchy of B13 can now be analysed in terms of additional levels of interaction of limiters and unlimited; that is, of ἀρχαί, which give rise to different living beings, understood as increasingly complex harmonic compounds that differentiate at each step of the hierarchy and yet share some basic features.

Each living being is associated with one organ and related faculties. At each step of the hierarchy, but also at each step of the ontogenesis (the development of the individual) and of the phylogenesis (the development of the species) a new assemblage emerges, subsuming all other sub-assemblages: man/intellect/brain; animal/*psyche*-perception/heart; plant/rooting-growth/navel.

As the doxographer's introductory sentence signals, when Philolaus says that the ἀρχή of man is brain with intellect, he is surely not affirming that man is constituted only of brain, but rather that brain is the ἀρχή that appears last in the development, and the first one needs to refer to when explaining man's nature: when this is harmonically joined with the existing assemblage composed of heart with *psyche* and perception, navel with nutrition and growth, and genitals with the power of generation, it transforms it into a new becoming. Such a more complex harmonic structure is endowed not only with the faculties that characterize plants and animals, but also with the human-specific faculty of νοῦς. The same point applies at each step of the hierarchy.

For example, it is only upon birth that an organism acquires ψυχή, and thus an animal, a becoming different from a plant, emerges. A new-born animal is unlimited temperature-wise (*Anon. Lond.* 18.26–27), and its heat must be tempered by cold air (καταψύχειν) to acquire the right temperature. Not only this need of κρᾶσις of hot and cold for life to arise is common in medical authors;[36] Philolaus almost certainly considered the verb καταψύχειν the etymological root of ψυχή.[37] In this reading, *psyche* appears to be a *harmonia* of a limiter (cold air) upon an unlimited (heat) according to a specific proportion.[38] Thus before being born the embryo does not have ψυχή, and since ψυχή is explicitly said to be the ἀρχή of animals, the embryo is not an animal, but is more of a plant.[39]

This is not a mere analogy: for the embryo in the womb effectively lives the life of a plant, endowed only with vegetative faculties: it is rooted to the mother's womb, it feeds through the umbilical cord and it grows, but it does not breathe and is not capable of locomotion nor perception – faculties that are associated with *psyche*.[40] The embryo has indeed those plants' faculties that Philolaus' calls 'rooting' (ῥιζώσιος, B13), a term that captures both the anchoring to mother without possibility of locomotion and the feeding through the umbilical cord,[41] 'the initial growth' (ἀναφύσιος τοῦ πρώτου, B13), but it does not yet have ψυχή, which it acquires later with respiration and perception.

A confirmation of this view is that for the operations of such vegetative life only heat was commonly considered necessary:[42] the Aristotelian and Hippocratic *corpora* offer many accounts of growth, nutrition and reproduction as depending solely on the action of fire or heat (Arist. *PA* 650a3f.; *De An.* 416b28; *Resp.* 474a25, b10, 477a11, 479a29; *De Iuv.* 469b18, and *passim*; *Vict. passim*; *Carn.* 2f., 6; *Nat. Hom.* 12). *Psyche*, on the other hand, is the animal life involving the higher faculties of respiration and locomotion, with which αἴσθησις is coupled. Indeed, air as animating force, on which perception and movement of the limbs depend, is to be found, aside from Anaximenes, in Diogenes of Apollonia (A19, B4), in the Hippocratic *De morbo sacro* and in several Aristotelian passages (*Motu An.* 10, *De An.* 420a9f.; *De Gen. An.* 744a2f., 781a21).

Thus the embryo, prior to drawing its first breath, is a plant, i.e., an assemblage whose compositional structure endows it with the powers of rooting, nourishing and growing. Upon birth, this assemblage receives the limiting action of cold outer air on its unlimited heat, and from this new harmonic combination a new unit emerges, endowed with different faculties: an entity of the same genus 'living organism' but of a different sub-genus.

In conclusion, I would like to quickly explore the interrelations and connections between these different kinds of assemblages, through the application of the explanatory schema I attributed to Philolaus.

Four normative structural patterns (what I termed *harmoniai1*) correspond to the four organisms listed in B13: man, animal, plant, living being. Each of these *harmoniai1* prescribe (a) the necessary limiters and unlimiters and (b) the appropriate mathematical ratios of their combination that must be reproduced if some *x* is to be an assemblage (a *harmonia2*) instantiating that abstract model. Let us call (a)–(b) 'a set of rules'. Further, as there are many species for each kind of living being (horses, roses, bees, humans etc.), there are equally many structural patterns.

Each structural pattern, e.g., the *harmonia1* for 'horse', collects the set of basic rules that guarantees that this particular *x* and this particular *y* are both horses. There will be a number of common rules between the *harmonia1* for, say, 'dog' and that for 'horse', and these are presumably collected in the structural pattern that includes both, i.e., the *harmonia1* 'animal'; for example, those rules that prescribe that instances of both species have *psyche* and perception, in addition to nutrition, generation and growth. At the same time, the two structural patterns for 'dog' and 'horse' will also have some variations, accounting for the specific differences within the genus 'animal'. Similarly, the rules prescribed by the *harmonia1* 'rose' will be different in a number of ways from those prescribed by the *harmonia1* 'tulip', but will share those rules that guarantee that both have rooting, growth, nutrition and generation, in other words, the rules collected in the *harmonia1* 'plant'. Finally, the *harmonia1* for 'plant' will have some rules in common with the *harmonia1* for 'animal' and that for 'human being', and such common, basic rules will constitute the *harmonia1* 'living being', characterized by 'the sowing and generation of seed' that all organisms share and forms the basis for all the specific differentiations.

Thus Philolaus' notion of ἁρμονία, with its normative structure allowing for increasing degrees of complexity within an overall order, provides an analytical schema that explains living beings as progressively differentiating assemblages and accounts for the complex architecture of their internal relations. In turn, this ontological framework offers a theoretical model that helps addressing some of the current issues in the Posthumanist debate. Two points are particularly worth making. First, it offers an example of being understood as a progressive process of differentiation that anticipates the Deleuzian notion of becoming: a human, indeed, is not human, but *becomes* – a plant, an animal, a human. As none of the previous natures disappears once a human is fully developed, but persists as part of the human whole (as a human being maintains animal and plant features), and as each interaction with the surroundings results into further complexities and different powers, a human is a *becoming* throughout his/her life. The same can be said of any other becoming that forms the overall cosmic *harmonia* by connecting with one another via their limiting or unlimited aspects.

Second, this account shows that, underneath the progressive differentiations, there is no unbridgeable ontological gap between plant, animal, human and cosmic becomings: humans themselves start off as plants (the embryo lives the vegetative life plants live), turn into animals upon birth (when drawing the first breath from which *psyche* arises), and only then become humans (when developing *nous*). There is an ontologically founded continuity between living beings, which connects plants to human beings and to the whole cosmos as a super-order harmonic assemblage. But there is also a clear-cut distinction that ensues at each new level of the hierarchy, for at each step a new harmonic interaction of limiter and unlimited endows the existing becoming with new powers and faculties, and a new unit emerges.

Crucially, both ontological continuity and differentiation are safeguarded: the boundaries are blurred, the kinship widespread, the ontological structure shared, but the multiplicity of the many living becomings is not erased nor flattened out into an ontologically undifferentiated blur.

CHAPTER 19
POSTHUMANISM IN SENECA'S *HAPPY LIFE*: 'ANIMALISM', PERSONIFICATION AND PRIVATE PROPERTY IN ROMAN STOICISM (*EPISTULAE MORALES* 113 AND *DE VITA BEATA* 5–8)

Alex Dressler

When we speak of humanism, we keep introducing something into the past that was never really there, and we invent a humanity for ourselves such as it should have been.

*F. Neyrat 2017b, 60**

Introduction: The two cyborgs of Roman Stoicism

'Posthumanism' denotes a cluster of ideas and thinkers: some say terrible and absurd things about the perfectibility of the species, which implicitly or explicitly excludes the imperfect; others seek to expose the tendentiousness of the concepts of the human and humanism.[1] All are postmodernists. The former, usually techno-capitalists, double down on the old humanist idea of the perfectibility of 'man' with aspirations such as uploading their consciousness to the internet and achieving immortality.[2] The latter, 'critical posthumanists', are usually Marxists and feminists.[3] The figure of the 'cyborg' (a hybrid of human, animal and mechanical) appeals to both.[4] To the capitalists, it promises to upgrade human beings by fully integrating them into production and technological progress, commencing (at least some) individuals' transcendence of this still-too corporeal late capitalist phase of 'transitional humanity' (whence 'transhumanism').[5] To the Marxist-feminists, the cyborg represents the contingency of what we take for granted as the 'human being', revealing alternative, potentially progressive ways of being here and now: 'The cyborg is . . . wary of holism, but needy for connection.'[6]

There are compelling reasons to consider the first-century CE politician and poet, Seneca the Philosopher, in terms of posthumanism and its two cyborgs. The first is the combination of Greek philosophy and Roman law from which imperial Stoics developed a notion of universal 'humanity' (a.k.a. *humanitas*).[7] If critical posthumanists think a critique of such ideas remains valuable, then a search for germs of posthumanism in the seedbed of humanism may also be worthwhile. The second reason is implicit in the Stoic concept of panpsychism. On the one hand, humans fall on a continuum with the rest of organized matter: reason, god or nature, are immanent in the world; a part of humans, animals, plants and minerals (and hence machines) contains god.[8] On the other hand, a *denser* concentration of the divine substance *distinguishes* humans from the rest of embodied being: they are human (animal) *and* divine.[9] Like the capitalist proponents of the transhuman cyborg, Stoics thus entertain a transcendent view of the human: it realizes itself only when it transcends itself (i.e., its personal body, its animality) and becomes a citizen of the universal city.[10] If that virtual community now resembles the internet, it reveals a surprising inconsistency in Stoic 'humanism'.[11] Whether it is based on a metaphysics of immanence like that of critical posthumanists, or transcendence, like that of their capitalist counterparts, Stoic ideals admit *nonhuman* elements.[12]

How Seneca integrates these nonhuman elements into Roman Stoic proto-humanism is the subject of this chapter. In one of his more technical letters, ostensibly as a joke, Seneca adumbrates a coherent posthuman philosophical system. The topic of the letter is itself surprisingly posthuman (*Ep.* 113.1): 'Are justice, bravery, foresight, and all the other virtues, animals [*an . . . animalia sint*]?' In the course of the letter, the philosopher makes a show of rejecting the 'orthodox' Stoic answer, which he claims is, Yes.[13] As he closes the letter, he offers his own more practical response and recommends a better topic:

> Let them teach me how blessed a possession justice is [*sacra res sit iustitia*], as it watches over the good of another [*alienum bonum spectans*] and asks nothing from itself but the use of itself [*nihil ex se petens nisi usum sui*]. Let that one [*illi*] have nothing to do with ambition and reputation but be self-content [*sibi placeat*].
>
> *Ep. 113.31*

Is Seneca still talking about justice in the second sentence? If the grammatically indeterminate component, 'that one' (*illi*), *is* justice, it is also the self-sufficient subject of the last sentence (*sibi*), and thus itself a personification.[14] While this may not undermine the *substance* of the philosopher's rejection of the 'orthodox' Stoic fantasy of animate virtues, it does muddle ontology in unexpected ways.

As if anticipating this problem, Seneca forecloses the possibility of personification almost as soon as he admits it: in that first sentence he calls justice 'a blessed *possession* (*res*, 'thing')'.[15] A person cannot *be* a thing in ancient Rome; a person *owns* things.[16] The way that Seneca talks about justice nevertheless sounds like his earlier joking about the orthodox Stoic virtue-animals:

> I won't stop . . . being silly and playing games [*ludos*] with myself. . . . Justice and bravery, if they are animals, are probably land animals [*certe terrestria sunt*]. Every land animal gets hurt, hungry, and thirsty [*animal terrestre alget, esurit, sitit*]. Therefore: justice gets hurt, bravery gets hungry, and mercy gets thirsty.
>
> *Ep. 113.21*

After this literally ludic endowment of virtue with animal predicates, Seneca seems inconsistent when he then endows justice with another unusual predicate: 'use of itself' (*usus sui*).[17] All the virtues seem to be undergoing some kind of figuration but comparison with the (anti)personification of §31 makes it unclear what. In this chapter, I use such phrases to define a trope between personification and reification, or the treatment of things as people and the treatment of concepts as things, which I will call, on analogy with anthropomorphism, 'animalism'. Although it is never explicitly theorized in ancient rhetoric, Seneca deploys the figure throughout *Ep.* 113.[18]

Nevertheless, this chapter contributes not to the history of rhetoric as much as to the history of ideas. Seneca's use of figures becomes relevant to the two strains of posthumanism today when the examples that he chooses and the way that he uses figurative language support *and* subvert the preeminent institution of aristocratic (and perhaps also capitalist) societies, private property. Private property relates to Seneca's place in the history of 'humanism' because the Roman rhetorical practice of personification hardly differs from Roman *political* practice when it comes to property. Both operate through exclusion, and both articulate that exclusion through the binary of person and thing.[19] Finding the trope of 'animalism' in the 'play' section of *Ep.* 113, I apply it as a posthuman analytic to the imagery of property in a programmatic passage of Seneca's semi-autobiographical *summa*, *The Happy Life* (*De vita beata* 5–8).[20] Doing so, I elucidate how posthumanism arises within humanism, I develop its radical implications for regimes of private property, and finally I consider the effects of those implications on modern radical projects, such as those of Marxist-feminist posthumanists.

Four arguments from *Ep.* 113

Seneca does not give the 'orthodox' Stoic position a very fair hearing in *Ep.* 113. At first demurring 'to busy our talent on empty things and waste our leisure on debates that will bring no profit', Seneca vets the following arguments *for* humanism, and against posthumanism.[21]

1. The argument from **substance**: 'Individual animals should have individual substances'; for example: 'I am an animal and a human being; still, you will not say that "we" are two' (4).[22] To assume, as the 'Stoics' do, that 'I' am two different beings, and hence two different animals, because 'I' am an animal and a human being, is to mix up aspects or descriptions and real beings: 'Whatever is multiple [*multiplex*] in one thing [*uno*] falls under one nature [*sub unam naturam*], and so *is* one [*unum est*].'[23] *The multiple must be regulated.*[24] If not, 'many thousands of animals live in the narrow confines of our chest, and we individuals *are* many animals or else *have* many animals' (3, cf. 9).
2. The argument from **subjectivity**: 'Whatever is made by a human being is not a human being' (*Ep.* 113.6); 'nor is that which is made by the soul an animal [*ab animo animal*]' (7). Human beings and animals are subjects; the predicates of such subjects are not *themselves* the subject; the *subject* is subject. *Objects must not supplant the subjectivity of subjects. Action does not essentially change the agent. Subjectivity separates being (ousia) from doing (praxis) or making (poêsis).*[25] 'A human being . . . is a human being, and a horse a horse, and a dog a dog [*homo . . . homo est, equus equus, canis canis*]' (11).
3. The argument from **property**: 'Nothing lacks its own color, shape, and size [*nulli non et color <u>proprius</u> est et figura <u>sua</u> et magnitudo*].'[26] Later, Seneca elaborates: 'There are so many kinds of leaves; none are not stamped with their own property [*sua proprietate signatum*]. There are so many animals (*Ep.* 113.16): none has a size that accords with another, but there is some real difference.' I call this the argument from property because of Seneca's Latin: *proprius* ('exclusive'), *sua* ('own'), *proprietas* ('characteristic, type').

   3b. A corollary to this argument is the argument *for* **parts** (15): 'No animal is part of another animal.' If a human being or animal does or makes something, we may at most say that the outcome is an integral *part* of the subject, but not *itself* the subject, and thus not an animal (15): 'justice is a part of the soul [*animi*]; it is not therefore an animal'. *Animals (and human beings) have parts; parts do not have animals, much less do they have human beings.*[27]

I append the argument for parts to the argument from property because justice as a 'property' of the sage is therefore also a part of him – a part he *owns*. All animals have parts, and so all animals have property. *Human beings must maintain and cultivate (at least some of) their parts, their property.*[28]

4. The argument from **being** (*not* becoming): if justice and bravery are in the soul and virtues that are in the souls are animals, then: 'What soul? The one that was just now justice? *It* was maintained in an earlier animal; it cannot pass into [*transire*] another animal; it must persist in that in which it first began to be' (11). Wrapped in a range of arguments about identity over time, the moral implication of this argument is: *human beings must not liquidate their properties.*[29]

In these arguments, we can recognize some characteristics of the conception of the human targeted by critical posthumanism: (1) unity, (2) subjectivity/agency, (3) ownership right now and (4) in the future.[30]

Four arguments and three tropes in *The Happy Life*

In the earlier sections of Seneca's *Happy Life*, Seneca contextualizes his four metaphysical principles in his ethical theory. This time, the 'humanism' is palpable:

> The only [person] who can be called happy [*beatus*] is he who feels no fear or desire through the favor of reason [*beneficio rationis*]. <u>For stones are free of fear and anger, and beasts are too</u>. But no one would use the word 'prosperous' [*felicia*] to describe those [things] that have no understanding of their prosperity [*felicitatis intellectus*].
>
> *De vita beata* 5.1

Because of their apportionment of 'reason' (*ratio*) and reflexivity (*felicitatis intellectus*), only the human being can be the proper subject of the word 'happy' (*beatus, felix*), the *one who* experiences happiness in contrast to the *ones that* do not.[31] The latter are thus things (multiple), regardless of their animacy. Such 'things' cannot be 'happy', and human beings who cultivate the corporeal parts of themselves are no different: 'Assign to the same rank those human beings who are reduced to the number of animal livestock by a dull nature and a lack of self-understanding [*ignoratio sui*].'[32] They will be counted with the animals (*in <u>numero</u>*), just as the virtue-animals would be counted, and then discounted, in *Ep.* 113.5: 'So then, something will be counted by itself [*per se <u>numer</u>abitur*] when it stands by itself.' *The multiple must be regulated.*

The ethical reflection that Seneca bases on the argument from substance will be more familiar than its theoretical outline (*De vita beata* 7.3): 'Virtue is something tall, lofty, and lordly, unconquerable, inexhaustible. Pleasure is lowly and slavish, weak and faltering; its habitation and abode are street-corners and dive bars.' Seneca continues to describe pleasure as 'soft and weak, dripping in perfume and wine', and finally 'pallid, perfumed, and covered in cosmetics' (7.3). She is a woman, and no match for the dominatrix that is her counterpart,

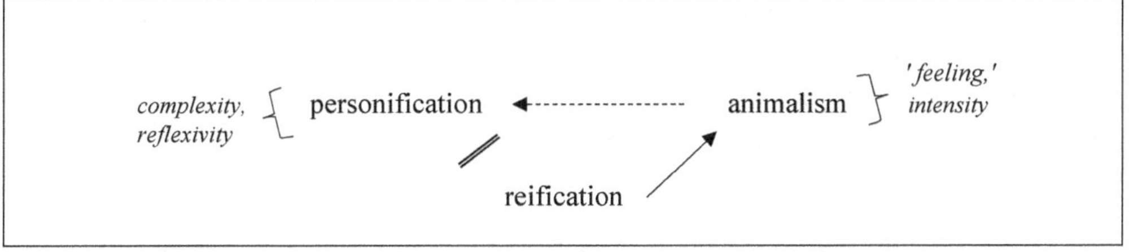

Figure 19.1 Combination of personification and reification.

Virtue (*excelsissimam dominam*); if we follow her, Virtue will make us the owners and masters of Pleasure (*eius domini*).[33] None of Seneca's ascriptions is surprising.[34] What is strange is the extent to which he employs the misleading figure of personification. As all but immaterial as 'she' is, Virtue appears 'standing before the walls, covered in dust and burned in the sun, with calloused hands' (7.3: *callosas habentem manus*).

Comparing this combination of personification and reification (Figure 19.1) with the figure of animalism in *Ep.* 113 reveals a complex relationship.

Personification and animalism fall on a *philosophical* continuum even as Seneca *rhetorically* denies their continuity.[35] The broken line between them marks this inconsistency. At the same time, the direction of the arrow between them indicates the attribution of increasing reflexivity and complexity in a figure: consistent with Stoic panpsychism, animalism is a lower, less organized form of personification.[36] The solid line between reification and animalism marks, in contrast, a continuity between animals and things; Seneca emphasizes this continuity to distance personification from animalism and by implication persons from animals. Figures of animalism can move, as we'll see in Seneca's farcical supposition of a Vergilian verse-animal below, and personal figures may also move, but unlike personal figures, figures of animalism are mobilized by 'feelings' that have no proper (read: cognitive) object, falling short of proper (read: personal) emotion.[37] The 'feelings' of the virtue animals that hunger, thirst, and hurt entail no *judgement* about the states in which they find themselves; they exhibit 'intensity', and probably resemble 'affect'.[38]

In this schematization of Seneca's practice, there is no continuity between personification and reification, but only the break marked above by the double line. Personifications comprise figures who may *have* bodies but are not *themselves* (exclusively) bodies.[39] Even if they exhibit 'intensity' of the kind that characterizes the 'lower' figures (when, for instance, Philosophy 'herself' appears imperious in some of Seneca's other letters), they 'speak' and 'act' on the basis of judgement: 'Philosophy exercises her own dominion [*regnum suum*] ... she is not a part-time thing [*res subsiciua*].'[40] The break between Philosophy and the 'part-time thing' is the horizon of figuration, marked again by the double line between reification and personification, 'crossed' by metaphor (*translatio*).[41] Thus, in the example above, the hands of virtue are not animals, let alone persons, but *parts* of a person, and hence things.[42] Rhetorically, then, animalism and personification *become* opposites, and hence binary, 'Platonic'.[43] The relationship of animalism and reification is, in contrast, more 'posthuman': its dynamic is not the dualism of presence and absence, habitually deconstructed by post-structuralists and fully apparent in *ancient* literary theory, but rather the configuration of pattern and randomness celebrated by post-post-structuralist posthumanists.[44]

By obscuring the continuity between animalism and personification, Seneca obscures the animal part of the human being and so relegates animal figures (along with animals) to the side of things (*De vita beata* 14.2):

> Just as we hunt wild animals with toil and peril and because they often injure their masters [*dominos*], the possession of them, when they are captured, is an anxious thing, so too great pleasures comport themselves. Their escape brings devastation, and their capture requires it. The bigger and more numerous they are, the lesser and the slave of more is he whom the crowd calls 'prosperous . . .' The person who follows pleasure rates all else second best, disregards freedom first, and lives for his belly [*pro uentre dependit*]; he does not buy pleasures for himself, but rather sells himself to pleasures [*nec uoluptates sibi emit sed se uoluptatibus uendit*].

Before, we saw that personification was continuous with animalism, which was in turn continuous with reification, while the continuity between personification and reification, or person and thing, was suppressed. Now, we see that, in order to integrate the figures in the context of his ethical theory (and ensure the suppression of the animal, thingly parts of human beings), Seneca must invoke the *commodification* or sale (*uenditio/emptio*) of animals, their reduction to 'things' (property: *res*).[45] *Subjects must remain subjects in being, doing, or making*. Buy your pleasures if you must, but do not be sold by them and *become* a thing, *e.g.*, *an animal*.

Implied here too is the argument for parts: *human beings must cultivate their property (or parts)*, which raises the question: which parts? Not the belly (above, *pro uentre*), the answer appears at the climax of *The Happy Life* 5–8:

> Nature must be used as a leader [*Natura . . . duce utendum est*]. Reason reveres, reason takes counsel from her. Therefore, the happy life is the same as following nature. I will now reveal what it is. If we responsibly and unhesitatingly maintain the endowment of our body and what suits nature as though it were the fleeting gift of a day [*corporis dotes et apta naturae conseruarimus diligenter et inpauide tamquam in diem data et fugacia*], if we refuse to become slaves to those things and if possessions that are not our own lay no claim to us . . . let them be servants, do not let them be commanders [*seruiant ista, non imperent*] – then only are they useful to the mind [*utilia . . . menti*].
>
> *De vita beata* 8.2

The passage begins and ends with the now familiar concept of use, marked personification (nature, reason), and the translation of the title of the treatise into the watchword Stoic philosophy, 'following nature'.[46] In the lines that follow, Seneca unearths the root metaphors of property and exclusion with the prospect of 'possessions that are not our own [*aliena*] laying claim to us [*nos possederint*]'.[47] With this, Seneca affirms the third argument from *Ep.* 113: *human beings must maintain and cultivate their property*. We now know what that property is (viz. not the animal part), and the injunction to maintain and cultivate it is explicit.

The last argument of the previous section was: *human beings must not liquidate their properties*. This is implicit in the above passage (e.g., *conseruarimus diligenter*), but even in the less electric passage leading up to it, Seneca set the theme:

> Never sure is that whose nature is in motion: that which comes and goes [*transit*, cf. *transire* in *Ep.* 113.11] so quickly that it goes to waste in using itself can have *no substance*. It falls short of where it aims and even as it begins, it looks to its end [*spectat ad finem*].
>
> *De vita beata* 7.4

With the now tell-tale phrase 'using itself' (*usus sui*), Seneca here assimilates pleasure to justice, which 'sought nothing from itself except the use of itself [*usus sui*]' in *Ep.* 113.31.[48] There we encountered substance in the dry dialectical axiom, 'individual animals ought to have individual substances' (*Ep.* 113.4), which I earlier suggested had proprietary connotations. The context of *The Happy Life* now supports this.

More provocative is the ambiguity of the final words: *spectat ad finem*. The phrase describes the short life of pleasure but it could also denote the principal practice of the Stoic sage, 'looking to the end' of human existence (*telos/finis*: cf. Cicero, *De finibus bonorum et malorum=On the Ends/Aims of the Good and Bad*).[49] Even at the foundation of humanism, all the superordinate terms of 'Western' dualism (agency, subjectivity, masculinity, ownership, domination) never completely cornered the market in that inestimable commodity of ancient philosophy, the teleology of existence.[50] It appears that Pleasure's antithetical ability to exhibit a sense of this is a direct result, by a kind of mechanical negation, of the proto-humanist attempt to deprive her of it.

How the virtues became posthuman: The *ei-cuius* clause of *Ep.* 113

Even if there were *not* such a place for posthumanism in Roman Stoicism, Seneca makes one with his bizarre choice to pursue his 'play' (*ludos*, 21) in the first place.

> Every rational animal does not do anything unless it is stimulated by the appearance of a certain thing [*rei*], then it receives an impulse, and then assent affirms this impulse [*adsensio . . . impulsum*: see n. 31]. I will explain what impulse is. It is appropriate that I walk: I walk at the moment that I have said this to myself and approved this opinion of mine; it is appropriate that I sit: then and then only do I sit. This capacity of assent is not in virtue [*in virtute non est*]. Suppose, then, that there is foresight [*prudentiam*]: how will (the phrase,) 'It is appropriate that I walk,' be given assent? *Nature does not allow this.* Foresight, then, looks out for the one *whose* it is, *not for itself*, because *it* cannot walk or sit. Therefore, it cannot give assent. What cannot give assent is not a rational animal. If virtue is an animal, it is rational. Therefore, virtue is not an animal.
>
> *Ep. 113.18*

Once again, Seneca recapitulates many of the arguments against posthumanism from *Ep.* 113, above. For the argument from subjectivity, Seneca explains that having impulse and assent does not transfer those qualities to the acts and objects intended by them. For the argument for parts, we find that, especially in the case of the example that Seneca chooses, 'foresight' (*prudentia>providens*, 'seeing ahead'), *is the part/property* of the human being. It cannot itself *have* the parts of human beings. If foresight *had* 'personal' parts to which it could refer out of 'self-interest', it would neglect the subject to whom it ostensibly belonged, the virtuous human being; the virtuous human being thus would lack foresight, which is one of the attributes that made him virtuous to begin with.[51]

In his restriction of reflexivity to rational animals, Seneca disavows personification and affirms his commitment to property – by means of personification. First: 'Nature does not allow this.'[52] Then, in the very next sentence: 'Foresight, then, looks out for the one *whose* it is, not for its/herself [*ei cuius est prospicit, non sibi*].' Like 'pleasure' in the provocative ambiguity of *The Happy Life* (*spectat ad finem*), 'Foresight' here is described as doing the action that the person presumably does with it.[53] Here, Foresight does not look out 'for itself', but rather – for its owner: 'him whose [*ei cuius*] it is'. With this *ei-cuius* clause of Senecan Stoicism, the philosopher appears to close the book on personification.

Or does he? After coming to an ostensible conclusion ('virtue is not an animal'), someone, Seneca or the imaginary 'orthodox' Stoic, asks:

> If virtue is an animal, and virtue is a good thing, is not every good an animal? Yes, it is, our friends avow. To protect one's country is good, and to speak in the senate with foresight [*prudenter*] is good, and to make a just decision in court is good: therefore, protecting one's country or speaking with foresight is an animal.
>
> *Ep. 113.20*

After announcing his choice to continue 'playing' in the aforementioned passage, Seneca proceeds to consider the hurting of justice, the hunger of bravery, and the thirst of mercy, also discussed there. In the final phase of 'the game', he avows *his* position:

> For now, I will admit that the soul is an animal . . . I deny that its actions are animals [*actiones eius animalia esse*]. Otherwise, all words and all turns of expression will be animals. For if a remark with foresight is a good [*prudens sermo bonum est*], and every good is an animal, then a *remark* is an animal. A line of a poem written 'with foresight' [*prudens versus*] is a good thing, and every good is an animal; *a line in a poem is therefore an animal.* 'Arms and the man I sing . . .' [Dryden=Vergil, *Aeneid* 1.1] is an animal, but they can't call it round and rolling, because it's six feet long! 'My god,' you say, 'this whole issue under discussion – how entangling it is [*textorium*]!'
>
> *Ep. 113.19–21*

In Seneca's phrasing, this is not just a convoluted argument (*textorium*); it is an argument that splices, collapses and entangles, in the words of Donna Haraway, 'the organic, the technical, and the textual'.[54] As a result, between *prudentia* and *prudens sermo*, taken as animals, we find the two cyborgs of 'modern' posthumanism. On the one hand, there is the transhuman cyborg of the capitalists, distributed over matter in different bodies, which it transcends (the Stoic sage as a citizen of the internet). On the other, there is the immanent cyborg of critical posthumanism (the verse of Vergil): the hybrid speech and text with its six feet, always embodied even as it has no body, or rather many bodies (a 'Body without Organs'): text, voice (accent, stress); capable of reflexivity (e.g., metapoetics), but never reflecting on itself (emergent); a wandering creature, with no localizable *archê* (origin), and hence no *telos* (aim, end).[55] '[T]he words themselves are not "like" the animals but in their own way climb about, bark and roam around, being properly linguistic dogs, insects, or mice' (Deleuze and Guattari 1986, 22). Such is the harbinger of posthumanity born in the playful proto-humanism of the Roman Stoic.

Conclusion: The part of play in Roman philosophy

At the end of *Ep.* 113, justice takes her place in the hierarchical ontology expanded in *The Happy Life*. In the earlier 'play' section, and then in light of that play, however, Seneca outlines a non-hierarchical, thereby 'flat', even 'rhizomatic' ontology:

> An intensive trait starts working for itself, a hallucinatory perception, synesthesia, perverse mutation, or play of images shakes loose, challenging the hegemony of the signifier. In the case of the child, gestural, mimetic, ludic, and other semiotic systems regain their freedom and extricate themselves from . . . the dominant competence of the teacher's language – a microscopic event upsets the local balance of power.
>
> *Deleuze and Guattari 1987, 15l, with Braidotti 2013, 66f.*

In the case of the posthumanist play-ontology of *Ep.* 113, the old Stoics are the teachers and Seneca is the 'child' of Deleuze and Guattari, 'playing' with aberrant forms of personification, disrupting the proper humanistic Stoicism of the 'teacher' (himself in another guise), and finally producing the paradox of a classical posthumanism.[56]

Whatever motivated him to pursue this manner of 'play', Seneca provides a glimpse of a decentred, monistic, anti-teleological philosophy of embodiment. Interacting with the Roman philosopher, this philosophy constitutes a semi-autonomous, ludic, even mindless, 'machine' for the production of concepts, which is moreover *pleasurable*.[57] Seneca does not *endorse* the use of this machine, probably because it threatens his aristocratic commitment to private property, but maybe it was private property that helped him produce the machine in the first place. Certainly, it provided him the time for play (or leisure) to use it himself.[58] This raises the question of whether posthumanism really is an antidote to humanism, rather than its complement.[59] At the same time, since both humanism and posthumanism come together in Seneca's use of figures, perhaps the concept of the *human* is less helpful for resolving ancient, modern, and postmodern impasses than the concept of the *person*, specifically *personification*.[60] Yet to accept this possibility is to accept a provisional dualism, and to maintain, even under erasure, the old categories of literal/figurative, organic/textual, reality/representation. Is there a way to do this without abandoning radical projects that seek to *subvert* existing orders of property and exclusion, and without accepting and rejecting all alternatives in the open parentheses of deconstruction?[61] We are probably no closer to answering this question than Seneca, but since it arises in the work of an ancient author, it certainly raises questions about the role of temporality in 'post'-humanism (and this *is* posthuman).[62]

CHAPTER 20
HAGIOGRAPHY WITHOUT HUMANS: SIMEON THE STYLITE

Virginia Burrus

A certain deacon climbs to the mountaintop where Simeon (*c.* 390–459 CE), the famous pillar-saint, dwells. On arriving, he poses the following question: 'Tell me, in the name of that truth which has converted the human race itself, are you human or an incorporeal nature?' The question irritates those gathered around Simeon, but it intrigues the saint himself. He orders that a ladder be brought, so that the deacon can ascend to the top of his pillar and 'first examine his hands and then put his hand inside his garment of skin and see [ἰδεῖν] not only his feet but also that extremely painful ulcer [ἕλκος]' (Theodoret, RH 26.23).[1] What is the deacon meant to conclude about Simeon's questionable *humanity* from such an intimate bodily examination, in which sight and touch seem strangely scrambled? And why is such emphasis placed on Simeon's *wound*?

This passage appears in chapter 26 of Theodoret of Cyrrhus's *Religious History*, an account of Syrian monasticism written in 444 CE, featuring ascetics both dead and still living. Simeon is among the living when Theodoret writes, and the chapter devoted to him stands out for its hagiographical or panegyric tone.[2] As a start to unpacking our passage, but only a start, we might observe that its sense depends heavily on scriptural allusion. The garment of skin (δερματίνου περιβολαίου) recalls the garments of skin (χιτῶνας δερματίνους) in which the divine creator is said to clothe the first humans after their fall from grace (Gn 3:21), often interpreted by late ancient Greek authors as symbolic of fallen flesh itself. Thus Simeon implicitly invites the deacon to place his hand not only inside his tunic but also, at once symbolically and viscerally, inside Simeon's all-too-corruptible corporality – an open sore, no less. At the same time, the scene invokes Jesus' display of his own resurrected body to uncomprehending disciples. In the Gospel of John, Thomas famously declares, 'Unless I see the nail marks in his hands and put my finger where the nails were, and put my hand into his side, I will not believe.' Jesus' side is a wound, having been pierced by a soldier's sword (Jn 19:34; NRSV), and he subsequently tells Thomas: 'Put your finger here and see [ἴδε] my hands. Reach out your hand and put it in my side' (Jn 20:25, 27; NRSV). Perhaps referencing Psalm 21:17 (LXX) – 'they gouged my hands and feet' – the Gospel of Luke supplements wounded hands and side with feet, as the resurrected Jesus says to the disciples, 'Look at [ἴδετε] my hands and my feet; see [ἴδετε] that it is I myself. Touch me and see; for a ghost [πνεῦμα] does not have flesh and bones as you see that I have' (Lk 24:39; NRSV). Like both Adam and Christ, Simeon is no mere spirit but flesh and bone, as Theodoret suggests through the medium of biblical allusion. The foot wound that the deacon is invited to examine – a wound haunted by other wounds, other bodily sites – is the mark of his full humanity, then. But is it not also thereby the mark of his divinity? To be *fully* human is not to be *only* human, by the logic of fifth-century Antiochene Christology, with its insistence on the coincidence of full humanity with full divinity; and this is a passage buzzing with Christological resonance.[3] Here, then, we come to the threshold of a sanctity that is more or other than human – a posthuman sanctity, if you will.

Before we cross that particular threshold, let us approach the saint from another angle. Theodoret's *vita*, like other literary *vitae* of Simeon, gives us a Simeon *with feet*. Those feet stand on top of a pillar night and day, for all to see (RH 26.22), so worn from standing that one of them is afflicted with an open wound, as we have just seen; it continually oozes pus (RH 26.23). Visual depictions differ, however. In a wide range of Byzantine images appearing on church walls, mobile icons, pilgrim medallions, manuscript pages and elsewhere, the iconic stylite saint, of which our Simeon is the first and most famous representative, *has no feet*. Human from the thighs, waist, or chest up, and typically facing the viewer frontally with arms raised in the gesture of prayer, his lower body, like that of a centaur, is other than human – in this case not horse but stone. The saint's lower body is his pillar, in short. The walled platform on top of the pillar, often chalice-shaped (evoking the Eucharistic cup), completes his lower torso, while the pillar itself extends below like a single leg, sometimes of roughly human proportions, sometimes longer. (As we shall see, Antonius's *Life of Simeon* depicts the saint standing on one foot for two years, due to a tumour on his thigh [LS 17] – an intriguing parallel). Iconographic tradition consistently gives us the stylite as a hybrid of human and column, then. Other prostheses or accessories include the ladder that also appears in the story of the deacon. Fully human, and also fully nonhuman thing, Simeon is a cyborg of sorts – 'a hybrid of machine and organism, a creature of social reality as well as a creature of fiction', as Donna Haraway famously defines this term.[4] Once again, we come to the threshold of a posthuman sanctity.

And there are other thresholds as well, as we shall see. But for now, let us pause over the term *posthuman*. It is both a contested and an unstable term, not surprisingly. *Posthuman* has relatives and rivals – *transhuman*, *unhuman* – as well as fellow travellers – *cyborg*, *monster*, *thing*, *object*, not to mention *the anthropocene*. Its significance is articulated and debated within a rapidly proliferating array of often converging (and sometimes colliding) theoretical movements – *actor network theory*, *affect theory*, *animal studies*, *assemblage theory*, *brain sciences*, *media theory*, *new materialisms*, *speculative realisms*, *systems theory*.[5] Aided by new communications media and impelled by the pressures of ecological and political crisis, the quick pace of intellectual exchange around the posthuman is alternately exhilarating and exhausting, clarifying and confusing. Arriving fast on the heels of the human conceptualized as a socially and linguistically constructed subject, the posthuman (like other *post* concepts or intellectual movements) directly challenges its predecessor and yet also takes on many of the assumptions of the prior concept or movement of thought.

The posthuman points to a new way of thinking, then, albeit one also partly continuous with what came before. But does it, in addition, designate an ontological reality that is coming *after* something else, that is *newly* emerging? Put otherwise: Have we *always* been posthuman, even if we didn't realize it, or are we *only now* becoming so? This is a familiar temporal conundrum for *post* intellectual movements. Put otherwise still: Does the posthuman (alternately, the transhuman) point toward a technologically mediated, continuously extended *telos* of human progress – an ever-emerging *superhuman*, let's say? Or does the posthuman (alternately the nonhuman), on the contrary, announce a decisive *decentring* of the human within thought, as impelled by the pressing awareness of both the irreversible destructiveness and the undeniable limits of human agency that marks the paradoxical moment of the anthropocene? It is the latter position that draws me: we have always been posthuman, but are only just learning to think that thought. As Cary Wolfe puts it, posthumanism 'comes both before and after humanism: before in the sense that it names [. . .] the prosthetic coevolution of the human animal with the technicity of tools and external archival mechanisms (such as language and culture)'. It also comes after in the sense that it 'names a historical moment in which the decentering of the human by its imbrication in technical, medical, informatic, and economic networks is increasingly impossible to ignore, a historical development that points toward the necessity of new theoretical paradigms'.[6] Or as Jane Bennett puts it succinctly: 'There was never a time when human agency was anything other than an interfolding network of humanity and nonhumanity; today this mingling has become harder to ignore.'[7]

Premodern saints may, then, be posthuman because we have always been posthuman, and also because they are, so to speak, prehuman – or perhaps better, prehumanistic. Premodern saints, and those writings, things, and performances that continue to bring them to life, do not share the full range of modern assumptions about what it means to be human; they also do not share the full range of ancient assumptions. These saints incarnate the human *otherwise,* indeed as a *becoming-other*.[8] Typically interpreted as superhuman – that is, as intensifying claims on and for humanity as a distinct, autonomous species, marked by the transcendence of its own material conditions, and destined for dominion – saints may more helpfully and richly be understood as explorers of the limits of human being. Evoking an ontology of becoming, they position the human at the shifting borders of its own otherness, its own insistent capacity for becoming something other than what it is. Put otherwise, saints expose the ongoing emergence, and submergence, of the human within the nonhuman, whether god, plant, thing or animal.

A large claim – *too* large perhaps. But let me begin to unfold it by contemplating a series of anecdotes culled from two Greek Lives of Simeon, one authored by the influential bishop Theodoret of Cyrrhus (*c.* 395 CE to *c.* 458 CE), whose text we've already encountered, and the other by Antonius, of whom we otherwise know nothing. Engaging Simeon through the medium of literary texts, I also want to accord the saint an agency that exceeds both the 'historical' and the 'literary', as usually understood. We encounter *Simeon* as a fluid assemblage of human, god, plant, thing and animal. But we also encounter him as a fluid assemblage of texts, images and devotional practices that collectively mediate his unsettling power and presence. As Glenn Peers puts it, 'The Stylite saints reveal how the saint as an organism, as it were, could spread himself beyond his boundary and still stay himself.'[9]

Becoming-plant (Theodoret, RH 26.5)

From the start, Simeon's practices upset his fellow ascetics, creating controversy, according to Theodoret. One instance involves Simeon's use of a 'rope made out of palm-leaves [σχοῖνόν . . . από φοινίκων κατεσκευασμένην]'. The language of the text emphasizes the plant-based materiality of this object: not only is it explicitly said to derive from a *palm*, but the word for rope itself indicates *rush*, or something woven from rush plants, and then by further extension any woven rope or cord. And there is more: Simeon is said to have 'planted [προφύσας] it on his skin', or, even more literally, to have *made it grow upon his skin.* He does so by wrapping the rope so tightly around his naked body 'as to wound [ἑλκῶσαι] the whole part which it encircled'. Simeon's flesh becomes a bloody furrow, then, in which plants are rooted. After ten days, the blood begins to attract attention. One of his fellow monks enquires after its cause. 'When

[Simeon] said nothing was wrong, his fellow combatant forcibly stuck in his hand [τὴν χεῖρα ἐνέβαλε], discovered the cause, and informed the superior'. (Later, as we have seen, Simeon will command someone else to stick his hand inside his garment, so as to probe another wound.) The abbot chastises Simeon and is just barely able to detach the rope from his body. Simeon, however, refuses any treatment for his wound. His flesh remains open to its own becoming, to its participation in the swarm of being. If Simeon is becoming-plant, is the palm leaf rope becoming-human too? Either way, the status of the human has been unsettled. So it is that the monks eventually order him to depart from their community.

Becoming-mountain, becoming-insect (Theodoret, RH 26.10)

In another experiment with bondage, Simeon fastens his right foot to a twenty-cubit, or thirty-foot, iron chain that is in turn attached to a large rock on the top of the mountain where he has come to dwell in solitude. His iron prosthesis roots him in place, 'so that even if he wanted to he could not leave the confines' of the walled precinct that he has established on the mountaintop. Once again, his practice provokes resistance. A local bishop – one Meletius –instructs him that 'right reason [γνώμης] sufficed to place rational fetters on the body'. Apparently compliant, Simeon calls upon a smith to remove the chain from his leg. The process results in a revelation: under the iron is a piece of animal skin that has been wrapped around his leg and sewn shut, so that it must now be torn off; hiding in that skin are 'more than twenty large bugs' that have been biting Simeon continuously, 'though he could have easily [. . .] killed all of them'. As saint, Simeon is not merely a hybrid of human, iron, rock and mountain. He is also a human with animal skin, offering his flesh as nourishment for a swarm of hearty insects. Just as the monastic leader tries to restore Simeon's humanity by invoking health and removing the rope, so the bishop tries to restore his humanity by invoking reason, removing the chain and stripping his animal hide. But these operations are not successful. Once again, what remains is wounded flesh – so many 'annoying bites'. Simeon is not interested in imposing mind over matter.[10] He is interested in the transformation of flesh: his is a fully material sanctity.

Becoming-icon (Theodoret, RH 26.11)

Simeon's fame spreads. His appeal is global. 'For it is not only inhabitants of our part of the world who pour in,' proclaims Theodoret. Ishmaelites, Persians, Armenians, Iberians, Homerites, Spaniards, Britons, Gauls – all make the pilgrimage to visit the saint. But the saint travels as well, and he can be in more than one place at a time. Theodoret explains: 'They say that he became so well-known in the great city of Rome that small portraits of him [εἰκόνας αὐτῷ βραχείας] were set up on a column [ἀναστηλῶσαι] at the entrances of every workplace to bring through that same protection and security to them.' The use of the verb ἀναστηλόω – to set up as or on a *stele* – is suggestive. Just as Simeon will soon set himself up on a pillar or *stylos*, in Theodoret's narrative, making of himself a living monument of flesh and stone, so images of him are taking their positions atop blocks of stone all across Rome, making up in number what they may seem to lack in stature.[11] A veritable army of guardians: like an internet meme, the saint has gone viral.

Becoming-column (Theodoret, RH 26.12)

Theodoret explains – and thus defends against 'fault-finders' – Simeon's self-monumentalizing as a kind of flight. Paradoxically so, perhaps: the saint is at once static and mobile, heavy and light. On the one hand, his flight is away from the crowds who arrive, wanting to touch his 'garments of skin [δερματίνων . . . ἱματίων]'. Skin, biblical skin, yet again! On the other hand, his flight is not only away from but also toward: 'he longs to soar to heaven and leave this earthly sojourn'. The ascending columns multiply and grow: 'First he had one hewn of six cubits, then one of twelve, after that one of twenty-two, and now one of thirty-six', Theodoret reports. The result? A 'strangeness of spectacle' that must be biblically contextualized (and thereby normalized?) in its very oddity and novelty. Normalization doesn't really take: appeal to biblical oddballs – 'men of God' who walk around naked or marry prostitutes, for example – arguably only intensifies Simeon's own queerness. He stands on a column: that's his thing. It's a strange thing, an ever growing human-stone erection.

Becoming-human (Theodoret, RH 26.1, 23, 28)

It is at this point in Theodoret's narrative, when the saint has ascended his pillar and become famous as a miracle-worker, that Simeon's humanity comes into question: 'Are you human or an incorporeal nature?' (23). In truth, Simeon's humanity was already in question from the beginning. Theodoret himself has planted doubts. The story he is going to recount 'surpasses human nature, and people are accustomed to measure what is said by the yardstick of what is natural'. People become incredulous when they are told of 'what lies outside the limits of what is natural', he repeats, but nonetheless he presses on (1). That measuring stick called human nature? Throw it out, if you want to hear and understand my tale, he seems to say.

Admittedly, Simeon's response to the deacon's question seems to suggest that he is simply affirming his humanity, even that he is going to great lengths to do so. Stick your hand in my putrid flesh, he demands. Not a bodiless nature, then. And yet this is no simple or stable humanity, either. For one thing, Simeon's wounded flesh is too closely linked to Jesus' flesh, as we have seen. For another thing, it has already been marked explicitly as transgressive and controversial. This is not the human body fettered by rationality to which Bishop Meletius tries to call Simeon back. This is open, fluid, swarming, uncontained carnality. In fact, it is much like what Gilles Deleuze and Félix Guattari call 'becoming-animal'.[12] The deacon asks, 'Are you a human?' Simeon, in effect, asks back, 'What is a human?' And the deacon seems to have learned something significant from the exchange. Theodoret concludes the anecdote thus: 'The man saw and marvelled at that worst of ulcers, learnt from him that he took food, and then came down and told me all' (23). What is the marvel? That a human is not a bodiless nature, not even a bounded body ruled by reason, rather a kind of open frontier. Open finally to the becoming-other of its own death. A later interpolator of Theodoret's text assures his readers, 'he demonstrated by his death, to those who did not believe it, that he was human' (28). Only clearly human in the moment that he ceases to be so, Simeon has finally perfected his performance. Becoming-human is not a flight from the always more-than-human flesh but rather a fall into its disintegrating depths.

Becoming-worm (Antonius, LS 5–8, 17–18)

Theodoret is not Simeon's only biographer, as we've already noted. One Antonius, who also claims to have been a contemporary and indeed a disciple of Simeon, writes a Life too. (A longer Syriac Life exists as well.) What he lacks in sophistication or subtlety, relative to Theodoret, Antonius makes up for in enthusiasm and graphic description. Two anecdotes in particular deserve our attention, both involving worms or maggots.

The first is a version of a story we've already encountered, the incident of Simeon and the rope. There Antonius adds details not mentioned by Theodoret. For example, he explains how Simeon obtains the 'little rope' (σχοινίον), stealing it from the bucket used to draw water from the well and then lying about it to the other monks. Antonius also increases the drama and intensity of the narrative. In his account, Simeon wraps the rope around his *whole* body and covers it with a tunic of *hair* (στιχάριν τρίχινον) – animal hair, presumably. Furthermore, he remains bound in the rope not for a mere ten days or more, as in Theodoret's account, but for a year or more, so that his flesh putrefies around it: 'it ate into [κατέφαγεν] his flesh so that the rope was covered by the rotted flesh of the righteous man'. Simeon is being devoured by the rope, then. The smell is terrible and, worse yet, 'his bed was covered with worms', Antonius reports (5). This point is repeated twice more, as he relates how one of the monks finally goes to the abbot, complaining, 'His bed is full of worms, and we simply cannot bear it' (6). Investigating, the abbot confirms that Simeon's bed is indeed 'full of worms', and the terrible stench drives him away (7).

'Behold, the new Job!' the abbot exclaims. The comparison of Simeon to Job is apt: Job is said to have declared, 'My flesh is clothed with worms and dirt' (7:5). But it also sets up an ambiguous contrast. Job laments, 'If I look for Sheol as my house, if I spread my bed in darkness, if I say to the putrefaction, "you are my father" and to the worm "my mother" or "my sister," where then is my hope?' (17: 13–15). What Job suffers passively and with distress, Simeon inflicts on himself actively, placing his hope precisely in putrefaction and worms. The abbot chastises the saint roundly, enquiring about the source of his bad smell, accusing him of threatening the discipline of the monastery, and even going so far as to suggest that he is a 'phantom' and not 'a true man from real parents'. What then? A demon, perhaps, given away by his stench. Seeking the truth about Simeon's identity, the abbot orders him stripped.

This proves easier said than done. Simeon's animal hair tunic is completely fused with his putrefied flesh: the two are as one. The monks soak him in water and oil for three days; nonetheless, when they remove the garment, much of Simeon's flesh comes off with it. What remains of this human is a raw wound, in which the rope is still firmly embedded. Moreover, 'there was no guessing how many worms were on him'. Two physicians are summoned and they labour mightily to separate the rope from Simeon; he suffers so much that 'at one point they gave him up for dead', and when the rope is finally removed, flesh remains attached to it. Simeon requires fifty days of recuperative care to recover from this virtual flaying. In Antonius's handling, the saint's motivation for all of this self-imposed suffering is penance for his sins rather than training in endurance, as Theodoret implies; he refers to himself as a 'stinking dog' who deserves to die. Although the abbot seems positively impressed by the theological insight that all humans are born in sin, he nonetheless orders Simeon to leave as soon as he is well enough. As in Theodoret's biography, Simeon is a controversial figure, deemed unfit for monastic life. He may not be a demon but he is also no ordinary human. Even more than in

Theodoret's rendering, he is an intensely hybrid figure, his flesh intimately conjoined with rope, animal hair and worm. The abbot and the physicians try to separate the human from the vegetable and the animal, but when they do what remains is not a contained and controlled human body but a gaping wound.

But there is more to this worm story. A second anecdote partly parallels Theodoret's account of Simeon's ulcerated foot. When Simeon has mounted his final and highest pillar, said to be forty cubits (or about sixty feet) high, he develops a tumour on his thigh, 'just as happened to the blessed Job', Antonius reports (cf. Job 2:7). As a result, Simeon has to stand on one foot for two years. Here worms again make their appearance. Antonius writes: 'Such huge numbers of worms fell from his thigh to the earth that those near him had no other job but to collect them and take them back from where they had fallen, while the saint kept saying, "Eat from what the Lord has given to you"' (17).

It is a remarkable scene, to say the least. As before, the great number of the worms is emphasized, but now all the more vividly. There are so many that several of his helpers spend all of their time collecting them as they fall; one wonders how they get them back up the ladder of the sixty-foot pillar. Simeon, for his part, does not merely endure the infestation of maggots but welcomes and actively sustains it. Like Christ, he offers his flesh as food, not to other humans or even to bugs but to the lowliest – and in this case, arguably the most disgusting – of creatures. Simeon is, rather literally, becoming worm, even as the worms are becoming human. The reader is encouraged to feel not disgust but wonder and to see not monstrosity but beauty in this transformative process: Antonius reports that when a visiting king picks up one of Simeon's maggots, against the saint's initial objections, it is transformed into a pearl (18).

Becoming flesh: Concluding reflections

A partially gilded silver plaque from late sixth-century Syria depicts a bearded man standing on a fenced platform atop a column, visible from a little below the waist up, facing frontally and reading a book. A large serpent coils around the column, raising its head, which is depicted in profile, to gaze on the saint from the right side of the column. A ladder leans against the left side of the column, and a shell hovers over the saint's head, all in a pleasing balance. A Greek inscription at the bottom reads, 'In thanks to God and to Saint Simeon, I have given.'[13] We do not know who dedicated this plaque to Simeon, or even whether it represents our Simeon or the younger stylite saint of the same name, nor do we know what favour the saint had granted to the donor of the plaque, obviously a person of some means. The image, however, is striking. Saint, column, ladder are familiar elements in artistic renderings, the ladder reminding us that the column saint was scarcely isolated – on the contrary. How else could his wounds be touched, his food delivered, fallen worms returned to his flesh? More unusual are the elements of book and serpent.

Antonius tells the story of a 'huge dragon' who lives east of Simeon's mountain. One day a piece of wood lodges in its eye; the sound of the dragon hissing in pain can be heard far and wide. Finally the creature comes and lies down in front of the gate to Simeon's mountaintop enclosure. Miraculously the wood falls from its eye, and the dragon stays at the holy man's gate for three days until fully healed. As Antonius marvels, 'He had lain before the entrance of the righteous man just like a sheep: everyone was going in and out and nobody was hurt by him'

(Antonius, LS19). Perhaps our plaque recalls this story. The gazing serpent would then be, among other things, a stand-in for the plaque's donor, expressing gratitude for its healing. Or perhaps its associations are more darkly demonic and phallic,[14] representing the temptations that beset the saint, who protects himself with the scriptures. Either way, the coiled serpent, like the column and ladder, appears an inseparable component of the holy assemblage. The saint is at once human, monument, and animal.

The saint is also silver and gold icon; the saint is also book. Simeon was not known as a reader: Antonius's abbot is surprised when he quotes scripture to good effect (8). But through his ancient biographers, Simeon himself comes to be seen in biblical figures, not least Adam, Christ, and Job, as we have noted.[15] Through his ancient biographers and all of the rest of us who write of him, he himself materializes in text. As both image and text, the stylite saint becomes a *thing*.[16] A thing that can be repeated and replicated and venerated and beseeched – a thing with force in the world.[17]

A text might, like a rope, be made from a plant. (Rope is, etymologically, rush – though Simeon's rope is made of palm leaves. Papyrus is a rush-like plant.) A text might also be made from an animal skin. Ink is fused to the plant or animal skin surfaces. Pen-wielding humans labour on those surfaces with blood, sweat and tears, as well as ink; they leave traces from the oils of their own skin. These elements can no longer be separated out.

Simeon wraps himself in his human, animal, plant and mineral skins. They are inseparable. This is his becoming-flesh. It is not a defence but an exposure. It is a wound. A teeming multiplicity. Finally: it is something divine. You can reach in and touch it with your hand if you dare.

PART IV
OBJECTS, MACHINES AND ROBOTIC DEVICES

CHAPTER 21
ASSEMBLAGES AND OBJECTS IN GREEK TRAGEDY
Nancy Worman

This chapter approaches the posthuman from a materialist perspective, in order to address the diverse and divergent ways in which bodies and objects in Greek tragedy intersect and converge with each other, rendering forms other than human and enlivening things. As such it urges attention to the edges of the human, to the stuff at its borders and as it may extend or become – and thus to the posthuman in this very material sense. While recent years have witnessed exciting new scholarship on the materialities of Greek drama, the challenge I take up here is whether attention to continuities between human embodiments and other stuffs exposes a posthuman tragic vision.[1] In some sense this may not seem like such a radical notion for tragic genres, since they deal in the edges of the human in a number of grim senses, but I aim to show how the posthuman may emerge in viewing tragedy's violent proximities from below, as it were, from its material layers, prostheses and clusterings.[2]

My discussion considers plays of the three canonical dramatists (Aeschylus, Sophocles and Euripides), beginning with Aeschylus' influential trilogy the *Oresteia*. I juxtapose its three plays (*Agamemnon*, *Libation Bearers* and *Eumenides*) with Euripides' *Andromache*, since the latter irreverently revises Aeschylus' affective dynamics, and Sophocles' *Trachiniae*, the materialities of which rival the trilogy for their dramatic texture and impact. This tiny, but I think representative, sample of Greek tragedies deploys material surfaces in striking and significant ways, settling bodies in distress on the edges of human inhabitation. Attic tragedies often focus in on such material surfaces, as margins where bodies and objects collide, trade places or make for monstrous combinations, so that (to take the end of Aeschylus' *Libation Bearers* as an instance) a son's affective energies and creaturely inhabitation become entangled in a horrific parental object: his mother's murderous tapestry drenched in his father's blood. In such moments where the one ends and the other begins becomes difficult to discern, as is also the case in Euripides' *Andromache*, when a worn but persistent suppliant takes on the features of the statue to which she clings, while the figure itself materializes her stony resolve.

Both cloak and statue throw into sharp relief what other such significant items tend to – that is, the vitality of objects.[3] This occurs most vividly when the materialities of signs, meaning visual manifestations of figurative relations, precipitate onto the stage at the edges of bodies, as contact and closeness render metaphors or symbols visible and tactile. Dramatic mimesis itself complicates such semiotic manifesting, as when a cloak is not only a 'cloak' (i.e., a sign [both word and prop] for the thing used in actual practice) but also a locus for pondering identity, entrapment, proximity, family history. Attending to the enactment indicated by the play script and to the theatricality of figurative imagery, as well as its material or 'material' extensions,[4] reveals much more than coordinates that situate the plot in its concrete setting and thus its 'realism'. Rather, the dramatic script selects and organizes characters' (and audiences') senses and affective reactions in relation to these theatrical materialities. Thus clothing may take on resonance as a second skin, or, alternatively, an alienating carapace to be violently wrenched from the body. Solid objects may, in turn, appear porous, malleable or saturated with human features, becoming prostheses or proxies for the characters that interact with them.[5]

Aeschylus' dramatic style is famously dense and imbricated, rife with synaesthetic and animating imagery, and the scenes from the *Oresteia* that I take up here are no exception. The plotting itself unravels a dense clustering of textures, objects and material identifications, such that the quintessentially thick semiotic and theatrical object (the murderous cloak) that punctuates *Agamemnon* and *Libation Bearers* is resolved into distinct items and actors in *Eumenides*. In contrast to this resolution, but in keeping with the imbrications of such stagings, key moments in Euripides' *Andromache* orchestrate a situating of bodies, particularly female ones, at the intersection of enactment and figuration. Among these three dramatists, Euripides crafts an aesthetics that is the most unnerving and peculiar in its violent erotics and mergings of humans and things, dynamics that have often dismayed scholars and driven them to query his taste.[6] Sophocles, in some contrast, is admired for his aesthetic reserve, which in this case would include a tendency to cluster tragic objects around immobilized heroes *in extremis*. These figures serve as still centre points that radiate outward in sensory and affective ways by means of significantly embodied prostheses: think of Ajax pierced on his enemy's sword, Philoctetes' residue of stinking rags, the poisonous cloak that unhinges Heracles' joints and flesh.[7] While there is only space here to address the most resonant of these in any detail – namely Heracles' cloak – its singularity is such that it catalyses a terrifying sonority.

The dramatic effects to which I attend here frequently materialize what Gilles Deleuze and Félix Guattari might have recognized as 'assemblages', especially in the plays of Euripides. His combinations, extensions or layerings of bodies and other entities reveal an inclination to experiment with tactile, intimate, boundary-dissolving transformations and 'becomings' – body-to-thing, human-to-creature.[8] In the dramas of all three tragedians this embodied, socially embedded patterning of sensation is orchestrated among individual perceivers and circulates on and off the stage.[9] These are thus not the only places in the plays of these dramatists that stage such emergent or assemblage effects, nor the only scenes that centre on statues or clothing. I offer the barest edge of the welter of those moments in Greek tragedy that stage contact and entanglement with coverings, prostheses and statues and often pivot plots significantly between sanctuary and violence.

My hope is that isolating overlapping types of figuration in their conjunctions with material textures and surfaces will allow us to attend better to sensory and aesthetic details that indicate a posthuman sensibility. In the case of tragedy this takes shape as an attentiveness to what lies at the edges of human bodies, exposing their mechanics and thing-ness. I also aim to show how Euripides' *Andromache*, which organizes its characters and actions in relation to the imagery of surfaces and extensions in really striking ways, centres from the outset on statues, coverings and proxies. Deployed as what I would call material inflections of character, such concretions in *Andromache* pick at the tactile orientations of Aeschylus' trilogy, working up their features into ethically dingier elaborations. I thus save Sophocles for the final section, since his treatment of bodies and things is quite differently punctuated and more distinctively multisensory, while also similarly merging bodily and material coverings and surfaces.

Ruinous materials in Aeschylus' *Oresteia*

Quite a lot of rich and provocative work has been done over the past fifty years or so on the dense networks of imagery in the *Oresteia*, particularly those involving nets and beasts.[10] In this section I attempt something adjacent to more conventional studies that treat these images as purely figurative, by looking at where references to bodily surfaces and materials intersect with onstage enactment, across the three plays.

Cloth/husk, net

As Victoria Wohl, Melissa Mueller and others have discussed, Clytemnestra's tapestry in the *Agamemnon* is a singularly saturated theatrical object.[11] Not only a metonym for wealth and power, a commodity fetishized into singular agency (so Wohl), it is also a rivetingly tangible stage object, even within the confines of the dramatic script (so Mueller). I want to emphasize an aspect of this object that extends such insights in another direction: namely, the imbrications of bodily surfaces and material coverings across the plays and thus the inter-implications among objects and characters. What I am interested in here is how such mergings and enfoldings not only entangle bodies but also revise human embodiment itself as coextensive with the 'flesh' of the world.[12]

We can thus notice (with many others) that Clytemnestra offers her husband the vision of his body gashed full of holes like a fishing net (δικτύου, 868–869), thereby inserting his body into the vast web of trapping images directly before he steps onto the tapestry and into her snare. From my prospect this looks more ominously tangible than it might otherwise, as her verbal gesture has the force of a material threat – not just that Agamemnon will end up trapped and perforated, but also that his body is also the net, a conflation that Orestes will later make between Clytemnestra and this same cloth snare. And so like family like fabric: the material proliferation is such that it subsumes bodies in the house of Atreus, as the vital sinew among them and of them. And with Wohl we might recognize here a monstrous version of commodity fetishism, as the object itself increasingly seems to have not just a life of its own but all the life of the house.

Soon after this, Clytemnestra emerges (likely on the *ekkuklēma*, a rolling platform) flanked by the corpses of Agamemnon and Cassandra. She declares triumphantly that she had to deceive and entrap as she did, else she would not have been able to 'fence the toils of ruin too high for overleaping' (πημονῆς ἀρκύστατ' ἂν / φάρξειεν ὕψος κρεῖσσον ἐκπηδήματος, 1375–1376).[13] Like fishermen who cast a 'boundless, encircling net' (ἄπειρον ἀμφίβληστρον), she says, so did she cast her 'evil abundance of cloth' (πλοῦτον εἵματος κακόν) around Agamemnon and strike him down (1382–1384). She offers these tropes in celebration, and the chorus receives them in horror. The spattering of her husband's blood fell on her, she tells the elders, with a 'murky drop of bloody dew' (ἐρεμνῇ ψακάδι φοινίας δρόσου), like welcome water on the budding seed-pod (γάνει σπορητὸς κάλυκος) (1390–1392). The clustering of material surfaces in enactment and metaphor is such that signification takes on a startlingly visceral cast: Clytemnestra between the corpses, perhaps clutching her 'fish'-catching cloak, covered in her husband's bloody dew, swelling like a seed-pod in the rain.

One point of contact in this cluster is the blood-rain on body-husk, a vision of the body's surface as porous casing ready to receive nutrients – as of course in some senses it is. In this instance, though, the nourishing liquid is another's life-blood, which both gives Clytemnestra's thriving shell a vampiric cast and yet also threatens to expose the bodily sac as a fragile membrane between blood and blood. And soon enough: Clytemnestra's bold deictic οὗτος ('this here man') indicating her murdered husband as 'the work of this (τῆσδε) right hand' gives way in the next drama, when she bares maternal breast to Orestes' sword point in desperate supplication and emerges next on the rolling platform as herself a corpse, her murderous cloak now spread around her, plied by her increasingly frenzied son. The trilogy as a whole stages this inside-outside bodily permeability as a pleat in the net/pod/cloak, as if survival depended on not getting caught in its folds. Which, of course, is impossible.

Net/cloak

At the end of *Libation Bearers*, Orestes appears in this same position, now with the corpses of his mother and her lover, surrounded by attendants who hold up the deadly tapestry and enjoin the chorus to look upon them and it. He calls this drapery a 'binding' (δεσμόν), which he then glosses as a 'manacling for the hands' and a 'fettering for the feet' (πέδας … ξυνωρίδος, 982).[14] Encircled by the entrapping device, he becomes increasingly entangled in a welter of figurations, wheeling back and forth between maternal cloth and corpse, asking the chorus, 'What does she seem to you?' (τί σοι δοκεῖ)? Answering his own question, he deems Clytemnestra a 'sea-serpent or Echidna' (μύραινά γ' εἴτ' ἔχιδν', 994), echoing a central characterization of her established in *Agamemnon* and earlier in *Libation Bearers* (*Ag.* 1233; *Ch.* 249). He continues confusedly, 'What shall I deem it / her [νιν]?' – a net for a beast (ἄγρευμα θηρός), a winding sheet for a corpse (νεκροῦ ποδένδυτον), a curtain for the bath (δροίτης κατασκήνωμα, 997–998)? He hazards further: 'You could call it a fishing net, a hunter's trap, and a foot-entangler' (δίκτυον μὲν οὖν / ἄρκυν τ' ἂν εἴποις καὶ ποδιστῆρας πέπλους, 999–1000). The turmoil of his engagement with the tapestry illuminates his disgust and fascination with his mother as an affective and sensory reaction that the closeness of the material to the body exacerbates, what Sara Ahmed characterizes as 'an exposure on the skin's surface'. She underscores that disgust hinges on touch and proximity, as contact is experienced as an 'unpleasant intensity' that has the effect of what she captures as 'surfacing'. This term designates the displacement of feelings of horror from an abjected figure (most fundamentally maternal) onto creatures or objects, the apprehension of which brings the skin into shuddering awareness.[15]

So it is that this imbricated object effectively drives Orestes into a frenzy of associations, in which it, the mother, the father and the son are all enmeshed as one monstrously proliferating theatrical sign. He designates it his witness (μαρτυρεῖ δέ μοι φᾶρος τόδ', 1010–1011) and ascribes it agency; it is deep-dyed (cf. φονοῦ δὲ κῆκις and πολλὰς βάφας, 1012–1013) with his father's blood and the tool of his mother's grievous deed, while he addresses it as 'this murderous web' (πατροκτόνον γ' ὕφασμα προσφωνῶν τόδε, 1015). His interaction with it appears to precipitate other terrors, as he soon cries out at the monstrous forms of the Furies that he alone sees hovering, their hair entwined densely with serpents (πεπλεκτανημέναι / πυκνοῖς δράκουσιν, 1049–1050). He is lost in a crowd of female phantasms and his frenzy now tips over into terrible vision, as he finds that his mother and her 'dogs' do indeed haunt the scene. Chorus and audience are left with a keen sense of his isolation from the human, as well as his entanglement in the conflation of beast and trap, father and mother, human and object.

Stone/wood, blood

The *Oresteia*'s third play begins not only with a central stone (the *omphalos* in Apollo's temple at Delphi) but also with a god (or two), a man dripping blood, a chorus of doggish monsters, and a ghost.[16] All held in dissolution, with a striking lack of contact or much sensory interaction of any kind among characters and objects. The *Eumenides* precipitates out onto the stage what had been hideously enmeshed in the parental cloak in the *Libation Bearers*: blood, mother/stuff, Furies. The stone protects him from these for the moment; as Apollo's proxy and therefore as the paternal metonymy, it fulfils the role of tutelary icon usually played by temple statues. Orestes, we soon discover, must flee from stone to statue: Apollo orders him to Athens, to clutch Athena's wooden image there (βρέτας, 80, 259, 409, 439, 446, 1024) and seek her aid in extricating himself from the Furies' curse.[17] Once in Athens the weird materialities of the blood, the monsters and the statue become evident, as by synaesthetic and animating imagery the Furies seek to confound the orderly court argument to come.

Despite their efforts and the fact that they and Orestes share disgusting surfaces, oozing gore from hands and eyes (40–42, 54), they are never contiguous, touching or even really proximate to him; indeed, early on in the action the fact that they are sleeping sets them completely apart. When the ghost of Clytemnestra enters in order to spur her 'dogs' to the hunt (cf. 131–132, e.g.), they mutter (117–129) in their sleep but do not awake, while Orestes is already up and gone.[18] When the Furies follow Orestes to Athens and find that he has moved from one safe object to another, the scene highlights the affective and sensory distances between them and their target. They are, to be sure, envisioned as beasts in pursuit of their prey; the vibrancy of the spilled maternal blood is such that they smell it and even see this scent 'smiling' at them (ὀσμὴ βροτείων αἱμάτων με προσγελᾷ, 253). But their close-in, imbricated sensory experiencing is opposed by Orestes' claims to have cleansed his hands by ritual purification, with the result that even his actual grip on the statue will not sully it, or so he says (cf. 445–446). Orestes sits with his arms entwined around Athena's image (περὶ βρέτει πλεχθεὶς θεᾶς ἀμβρότου), the wooden statue that they explicitly recognize as a 'defence' (ἀλκάν) (258–259), while the Furies envision a much closer – in fact a vampiric – proximity, threatening to suck the ruddy gore from his living limbs (ἀντιδοῦνται δεῖ σ' ἀπὸ ζῶντος ῥοφεῖν / ἐρυθρὸν ἐκ μελέων πέλανον) (264–266).

Material assemblages in Euripides'*Andromache*

In the *Oresteia* pivotal moments feature material surfaces – most especially the bloody cloak – that enfold, pleat and drip across the plots of the plays. Euripides' *Andromache* stages a number of scenes that are adjacent to these in their focus on human/material surfaces and their forceful driving of the action. While the imagery of dress and bodily proximities does not dominate the plot, exactly, it does uniquely frame the play's focus on 'woman's' concerns (i.e., marriage status and child-bearing), in relation to which such materialities contribute pivotally to aesthetic texture and dramatic action.[19] The play orchestrates groupings that render concrete and enacted proximities that expose the violent potentials of posthuman edges. As if materializing a figure like catachresis ('abuse' of metaphor) or hypallage (transferred epithet), such assemblages – in the enactment that the text indicates – reorganize bodies, things and their characteristics (e.g., surfaces, postures, positions) in relation to each other, so that skin becomes worn metal or rock face while statues and clothing exert living forces, serving as both fulcrum and proxy for enactment.

Skin/stone, lead

Consider Andromache in the opening scene: she sits as a suppliant in the temple of Thetis (Achilles' sea-nymph mother) and begins to sing, describing how she was led away from Troy, 'throwing over her head' (ἀμφιβαλοῦσα κάρᾳ) hateful slavery like a veil, and how many tears 'slipped down her skin' (κατέβα χροός) when she left city and halls and husband in the dust (ἐν κονίαις).[20] Wondering why she must look upon the light as Hermione's slave, worn down (τειρομένα) by her, she now clutches 'this statue here' (τόδ' ἄγαλμα, i.e., Thetis'), melting 'like a stony flowing stream' (τάκομαι ὡς πετρίνα πιδακόεσσα λιβάς) (109–116). This is quite a singular trio, in both evoked and actual proxemics, as Andromache clutches Thetis and resents Hermione, while bringing together substances and surfaces in would-be veils, tears, skin, dust, statue and the stony stream. That is, Andromache's description and deportment in combination renders the effect such that, as registers collide, in between Andromache and Thetis stands Hermione, whose repeated mishandling of Andromache has had its impact, as if on the surface of a stone. The assemblage suggests disturbingly nonhuman mergings of bodily and material surfaces, revising the human form in inanimate extensions and achieving a pairing of past/absence and present/presence between Andromache's tears at Troy and the stony Niobe that she is in the here and now.[21]

Soon Hermione is threatening Andromache in vivid terms, claiming that she will set her on fire or cut her skin with terrible wounds (χρωτὶ δεινῶν τραυμάτων ἀλγήδονας) (257–259). She also declares that she will wrest Andromache from her suppliant seat, even if 'molten lead holds [her] all around' (εἰ πέριξ σ' ἔχοι / τηκτὸς μόλυβδος) (267–268) – that is, even if Andromache has herself become statue in her 'hard' persistence (cf. σκληρὸν θράσος, 261), she (Hermione) will pry her off, like bronze-work from its base. The moment foregrounds most of all an irreducible materiality, not only in relation to the mundane substance (i.e., the practical lead[22]) but also in its attention to proxemics, in this case the statue of Thetis centrally present onstage and Andromache's deportment in relation to it. So Hermione, focusing in on her enemy's fierce hold on the statue, transfers its material substance to the living suppliant, as a vivid exteriorization of Andromache's 'hardness'.

When Menelaus arrives and tricks Andromache into relinquishing her hold on her protective statue she stands stark-still, with hands bound and son attached, and sings another lament in which she depicts herself as Niobe, dripping tears like a 'shaded stream down a smooth rock face' (στάζω λισσάδος ὡς πέτρας λιβὰς ἀνήλιος, 533–534). Although she soon exits with her child, she may well return at the end of the play and so be present with her child (as deictics indicate[23]), standing silent as a stone onstage for the last 200 lines. And then Thetis, whose inanimate statue has served as the concrete pivot of the action in affective combination with Andromache, comes down on the stage machine to deliver the epilogue.

Skin/cloth

I now turn back to the first scene I discussed early in the play, in which the remarkable tactility and proxemics of Andromache's inhabitation is quickly followed by the entrance of Hermione, who opens with a sally that highlights a contrasting set of bodily prostheses. She makes much of her elaborate carapace, her body's ornate edge (κόσμον, 147), including her crown, golden veil, and decorated gown, as visible indications of her father's wealth and power.[24] That this is the first thing she says upon entering foregrounds from the outset her frantic vanity and assertions of status. Her gambit reveals the opposite of what it aims to assert – namely, her alienated and insecure relationship to these implements of power (to paraphrase Bourdieu[25]), despite the fact that they ought to serve as her own second skin, since she arrived to wed Neoptolemus with a large dowry, while Andromache is a slave (δούλη, 155). Her insistence that her dress and riches ensure that she can speak freely, while on the surface a crude political equation, also suggests something much more unnerving: that a naked Hermione would be a silent one; that divested of such dressy extensions she would have no voice. And of course clothes are so easily removed, as her later actions make clear.

The bodily surface is thereby rendered other to the self, a parental carapace worn with unease or an object to warp and abuse. Like Orestes and his attempts to control the maternal cloak, Hermione treats her rich daddy's draperies as more than they are. Her speech suggests that she locates in them not only powers of protection but also tools to bend others to her will. Throughout her confrontation with her rival, Hermione sustains an emphasis on what is in effect an aestheticized politics of rank, focusing on the body's affects, postures and potencies, from the begetting of children (157–160, 170–174), to sexual desire, to the boons that gold can bring. In a vivid assertion of embodied power and its inverse, she declares that if Andromache wishes to avoid death, she must 'give up her opulent, lofty thoughts and fall at her [Hermione's] knee, sweeping her house and sprinkling water by hand from golden bowls' (164–167).[26] From the head rich with thoughts to the slavish posture at the knee, cleaning the floor with water from the mistress' bowl: Hermione achieves a head-to-toe transvaluation of Andromache's character, not to mention a clearly relished physical domination.

Later on in the action the mercurial Hermione threatens suicide, as she fears her husband's reprisal for her aggression toward Andromache. She comes onstage this time with gestures that are effectively opposite to those marking her first entrance: she tears crown and veil from her head; and in a provocative turn, her nurse responds in a manner that indicates a fuller dismantling: 'Cover your breasts/chest, fasten your robe!' (κάλυπτε στέρνα, σύνδησον πέπλους, 832).[27] Hermione confirms that she has bared more than her head (833), declaring this only right since her deeds (i.e., the violence that she has motivated) stand 'clear and revealed and uncovered' (δῆλα καὶ / ἀμφιφανῆ καὶ ἄκρυπτα, 834–835). Body and actions thus acquire an equal footing in relation to enactment, as she makes her body naked ('naked') to materialize the exposure of her wrongdoing. That is, the one is visible and literal (within the conventions of tragic enactment), the other figurative and ineffable, and yet offered to the eye in a transfer effected by the 'undress' of the staged gestures.

In her distress Hermione proceeds to threaten her own skin in the same ways that she had earlier threatened Andromache's: fire and the sword. And in fact she indicates that she is pondering such equations, when she cries out, 'To which of the statues shall I rush as a suppliant? Shall I, a slave, fall at my slave's knees?' (τίνος ἀγαλμάτων ἱκέτις ὁρμαθῶ; / ἢ δούλα δούλας γόνασι προσπέσω; 859–860). That is, as if to say, 'Shall I now take on the suppliant posture and slave status that my enemy occupies? Where is *my* Thetis?' Her stripping off of her finery and questioning new possibilities of stature and status together reveal a shocking recognition that clothes do indeed make the woman – or at least, that this is how Hermione understands her relation to her fancy outer shell. From this perspective, then, the gestures and questions would not register merely as meta-theatrical but something weirder: that for this character the clothes themselves have a power that she does not, as if the inanimate carapace were the vibrant force at play here instead of the living human.[28]

Hermione thus proves very different from Andromache in what we might recognize as material inflections of character – that is, the prominent, fancy clothing, the frenetic gestures, the menacing proxemics. She inhabits herself as changeable and mobile, while Andromache remains recalcitrant and statue-like throughout. These material indications are effectively finalized with the entrance of her cousin and once-betrothed Orestes toward the end of the play, an intrusion from the other plot (as it were) that further confirms both Hermione's slippery hold on her fabric(ated) defences and Euripides' engagement with the *Oresteia* subtext. Hermione greets this entrance with a zealous desperation, throwing herself at Orestes as the statue/sanctuary she has been seeking. Embracing his knees with arms she claims are 'no less weighty than suppliant garlands' (στεμμαάτων δ᾽ οὐκ ἧσσονας / . . . ὠλένας ἐμάς, 894–895), she declares herself bereft of any other protection.

Bodystuff in Sophocles' *Trachiniae*

As I note in the introduction, among extant tragedies Sophocles' plays centre most emphatically on the body in pain, usually one that is heroic and male, which is sometimes paired with or effectively displaced by female distress. The pair of scenes from the *Trachiniae* that I focus on here stage physical anguish as a palpating, materializing display, in which the hero's body and its coverings or extensions threaten to fold into each other, such that human surfaces become porous and open to textured stuffs on bodily surfaces. The porosity of these surfaces also precipitates sonic reverberations, as the hero in pain cries out in ways that seem to emerge directly from his body being exposed and gaping to the elements and ultimately to the spectatorial eye, catalysing further sensation and reaction.

Flesh/robe

In *Trachiniae* Heracles' wife Deianira gives him a robe that she paints with what she thinks is a love potion, since he has taken a younger woman as a concubine, the captive Iole. The potion was given to Deianira by the centaur Nessus; this proves to be poison and ultimately destroys Heracles, who emerges onstage in an extremely debilitated state only at the drama's end. The most compelling intersection for my purposes is that between the poisoned cloak and Heracles' famously tough and resilient skin, the material cover that dissolves the hero's own fleshy one.[29]

This inside-outside contamination, as the centaur's toxic, bloody excretions are smeared on the surface of the cloth and turn Heracles' skin into frothy rags, fashions one of the more grotesque enfoldings in Greek tragedy. The chorus of Trachinian women later ponders the horrible stuff of this doubly monstrous poison, lamenting that the centaur's trick has coated (χρίει) the hero's sides with a bloody cloud (φονίᾳ νεφέλᾳ) from the 'clinging poison' (προστακέντος ἰοῦ) of the dappled serpent (αἰόλος δράκων), and that Heracles is now gripped (προστετακώς) by the terrible specter (δεινοτέρῳ . . . φάσματι) of the Hydra whom he once fought. The murderous, deceiving goads (κέντρ') torment him confusedly (ἄμμιγα), boiling up (ἐπιζέσαντα) on his skin (831–840).

In contrast to the incredibly rich sensory detailing of how the poison hovers monstrously at the body's edges and openings, the robe is described without specifics beyond its fine weave (e.g., ταναΰφῆ πέπλον, 602), as a cover that must be kept hidden until revealed to all in full ceremonial display. When Deianira hands it over to the herald Lichas to give to Heracles, she bids him to tell her husband that no one before him may put it over his skin (ἀμφιδύσεται χροΐ), nor may it be struck by the light of the sun or exposed to fire, not before he stands conspicuous in the open, displaying it to the gods (κεῖνος αὐτὸν φανερὸς ἐμφανῶς σταθεὶς / δείξῃ θεοῖσιν). So, Deianira declares, did she vow that she would adorn Heracles, wrapping him in 'this robe' (στελεῖν χιτῶνι τῷδε) and showing him to the gods as a 'new officiant in new garb' (φανεῖν θεοῖς θυτῆρα καινῷ καινὸν ἐν πεπλώματι) (603–613).

Pain's membrane

When Deianira's son Hyllus arrives in a fury at what he thinks is his mother's intentional dismantling of his father's bodily integrity, he describes in horrible detail the poison's work on the surfaces of and ultimately deep within Heracles' body.[30] The audience thus first experiences this devolution at one remove: Hyllus relates that Lichas arrived with the deadly cloak (θανάσιμον πέπλον, 758), which Heracles then happily put on, delighting in his fancy new outerwear (κόσμῳ τε χαίρων καὶ στολῇ, 764). But then the altar flames leap and he begins to sweat, as the garment enwraps his ribs (προσπτύσσεται / πλευραῖσιν), clinging close (ἀρτίκολλος) as if glued by a craftsman (τέκτονος) at every joint (ἅπαν κατ' ἄρθρον) (767–769). Pain shoots up from his bones like the bite of a snake (ἐχίδνης) and soon a spasm seizes his lungs (σπαραγμὸς αὐτοῦ πλευμόνων ἀνθήψατο); when he hears that Deianira sent the robe, he grabs Lichas by the ankle and dashes him on a rock so that his white brains run out over his hair (κόμης δὲ λευκὸν μυελὸν ἐκραίνει) and his skull is smashed and bloodied all over (διασπαρέντος αἵματος θ' ὁμοῦ) (777–782).[31] The gathered crowd cries out in terror, and the hero convulses with such violence, shouting and screaming (βοῶν, ἰύζων), that the hills thunder all around (786–793). Even from far off, then, Heracles' body has not only a visual but also a sonic effect, its material dissolution causing the hero to emit roars that resound across the landscape, thereby precipitating a multisensory impact onstage.

The intervening scenes unfold by equally multisensory and material means, so that the plot is as if literally pleated and enfolding, moving from one material stuff to another, from the seething wool that gives Deianira a terrible hint of what is to come, to the cloak in the sunshine, to Deianira's tear-flooded bedding and loosened dress deep inside the house. As the scene of the wool's disintegration portends, the cloak of Nessus becomes a kind of outer membrane for Heracles' suffering body, which is displayed in the final scene as made 'ragged' by the 'encircling web' (ὑφαντὸν ἀμφίβληστρον, 1052) that clings to him, ravaging him inside and out.[32] His material undoing resonates in compelling ways with that of Clytemnestra on the platform with her corpses, when she represents her own 'boundless encircling' (ἄπειρον ἀμφίβληστρον, 1382) as crucial to the bodily destruction of her husband. While the devastation is not made of the same cloth, so to speak, since her cloak is a trap that enables bodily ruin rather than being itself the stuff of ruin, the scenes share an emphasis on the female plying of deceptive, hellish webs. Because Heracles thinks that Deianira knowingly gave him the poisoned cloak, he envisions it as woven by the Erinyes and fastened to (καθῆψεν) his shoulders by his 'guile-faced' (δολῶπις) wife (1050–1052). In his ignorance, then, he makes a Clytemnestra of Deianira and sees himself as not only consumed without and within but also 'moaning and weeping like a girl' (ὥστε παρθένος / βέβρυχα κλαίων), rendered weak and womanly (θῆλυς), as if the cloak carried a feminine taint along with its poison (1071–1075).[33]

When onstage at the end this is what Heracles has been reduced to: not only a girlish man but also a ragged cloak of a body, something that he uncovers to show the skin's destruction, the 'eating of flesh' (βέβρωκε σάρκας) of one who wears pain's membrane as if plastered to his ribs (πλευραῖσι … προσμαχθέν) (1053–1055).[34] When he orchestrates the display of his ravaged form, he pulls back his outer coverings (cf. δείξω ἐκ καλυμμάτων, 1078), to show this inner layer of pain. Like Philoctetes in Sophocles' play of that name, he cries out repeatedly at the agony, describing it as shaking him and eating him within (e.g., 1081–1084); but he also represents his body itself as 'unfastened and torn to shreds' (ἄναρθρος καὶ κατερρακωμένος), like a tattered old cloak flapping open in the wind. In sharp contrast to this sorry garment he places his former bodily glory, the back and arms with which he fought monsters at the ends of the earth, arms that no one has 'set a trophy over' (1089–1102). His repeated emphasis on his frame (cf. δέμας, 1056, 1079) suggests an opposite type of outerwear – something like a protective skin, the fleshy armour that he famously wore in myth.[35]

From the prospect offered by considering the ways in which Euripides' play refracts elements of Aeschylus' trilogy, and how Sophocles represents distinctly imbricated embodiments that nonetheless also bear on similar human–material associations, I hope to draw a few conclusions. First, the material presences in these plays only share some basic elements, while the enactments and figurative extensions orient them in quite distinct ways. Thus a stone or wooden figure may signal safety or fixity, its material surfaces juxtaposed to bodies and resonating with their features or not. Similarly, all clothing/carapaces are not equal, despite their tendencies across many plays of Euripides to signal engagement with parental relations (cf. also *Alcestis*, *Medea*, *Heracles*, *Bacchae*). And yet, to take our main examples, the maternal cloak and paternal dress both indicate the dangers of parental extensions – that is, the broad reach of their fateful inhabitations rendered viscerally present by the material implements of their power. The spousal cloak, in some contrast, suggests something more adumbrated about male excess, female or creaturely abjection and their mutually destructive capacities.

I hope that this vantage point may also help to clarify my broader aims, as well as what they are not. In juxtaposing these scenes I am not merely arguing for some hypothetical reconstructions as 'material' clarifications of the staging indicated by the play script. Rather, these dramas and others like them catalyse awareness of the layered, pleated, often contradictory unfoldings of inhabitation, sensation and experience – the flesh of the world rendered palpable. In the hybrid space created by dramatic enactment, humans confront selves and others as materials, such that bodies emerge as enfolding, stony or shredded things. Thus Orestes puts an end to his imperious mother only to get caught up in her murderous robes; Hermione attempts to wrest Andromache from her suppliant perch only to end up bereft of human orientation; and Deianira enwraps her tough-skinned hero-husband in a poisoned cloak and inadvertently reduces him to rags. And when Hermione grabs at Andromache as a statue, Orestes tangles with his mother as a fabric snare, and Heracles displays his own body as a tattered cloak, these gestures serve to reveal the thin membrane that binds the human body to its objects and extensions, effectively materializing its prostheses or supplements in the handling of cloth and stone. As with the affective clustering around the statue at the beginning of *Andromache*, at the end of *Libation Bearers* and *Trachiniae* the intensity achieved by proximity, props and some super-saturated language offers up bodystuff as it dissolves into all of its messy materialities: riddled and ragged, handled by everyone, enfolding and extending the edges of the human.

CHAPTER 22
HYBRIS AND HYBRIDITY IN AESCHYLUS' *PERSIANS*: A POSTHUMANIST PERSPECTIVE ON XERXES' EXPEDITION

Anne-Sophie Noel

In 2010, the artist Minty Donald conducted an on-site performance on the river Clyde in Glasgow:[1]

> an attempt to lace together the banks of the River Clyde in Glasgow city center using over one mile of thick, heavy, black mooring rope. The rope was dragged back and forth across the river by a workboat, equipped with a mechanized winch and hydraulic arm, and tensioned between bollards on opposite quaysides to form a zigzag lattice.[2]

Commenting on this experience, Donald adopts the terminology of new materialist and posthumanist theories: while performing *in collaboration with* the river, a 'more-than-human' natural element, she perceived that humans, objects (the boat, the rope) and water were entangled and 'enmeshed with tidal and meteorological forces'.[3] The human intention was grappling with material objects as well as natural elements that 'acted back'.[4] As she recounts, this experience turned out to be more challenging than expected. The inherent quality of the rope (a '*predilection* to revert to a state of unruly entanglement'[5]), the effects of tide, flow and wind direction greatly impacted (and even thwarted) the realization of the art project. She therefore defends the notion of a 'fluid agency, based on reciprocal, yet not symmetrical, exchange between people and objects', perfectly in line with the principles of new materialists.[6] Her engagement with posthumanist theory arouses when she promotes an 'ecological perspective that profoundly challenges anthropocentricity'[7] and calls for 'progressive paradigms for human/more-than-human interdependency'.[8]

Reading about Donald's *Bridging* on the river Clyde sparked in my mind an exploratory *bridge* between past and present. If her modern, arty performance can be analysed with the lens of posthumanism, to what extent can one apply the same line of thinking to Aeschylus' re-enactment, through theatrical performance, of Xerxes' attempt of bridging the Hellespont during the second Persian war?

Tremendous material means were involved in the crossing of the Persian army from the Asian port of Abydos to the Thracian Sestos in 480 BCE.[9] Thousands of workers connected together more than 300 war boats to form each of the two parallel bridges,[10] with 1-mile-long ropes of papyrus and white flax.[11] The 674 boats were moored with anchors, themselves tied to anchor ropes whose length totalled more than 300 kilometres according to modern reconstructions. The changing currents as well as the strong winds gusting in the strait dramatically affected the Persians' interactions with matter and nature. When the bridges were destroyed by a storm before the army had arrived at Abydos,[12] Xerxes, enraged, beheaded the builders. As is well known, he also had the sea punished with 300 whiplashes and fetters thrown into the strait.[13] He then rebuilt the bridges and made his army cross (which took more than a week) before leaving the bridges behind, for them to be wrecked again by another storm.[14]

Herodotus' account emphasizes the shocking novelty in Xerxes' enterprise as well as the hybristic amount of material means invested in it[15] – an excess which is connected with Xerxes' later downfall, according to a logic that resembles that of Aeschylus' tragedies.[16] It is indeed in Aeschylus' *Persians*, a memorable tragedy produced in 472 BCE, only eight years after Xerxes' defeat at Salamis, that the entanglement of humans, things, natural forces and physical environment caused by Xerxes' expedition, was re-enacted on stage. It is on this aspect of the play that I wish to focus, arguing that Aeschylus invested Xerxes' bridging with ontological and ethical implications that have not previously been seen. The bridge literally links the two continents, Europe and Asia, but the *bridging* is also enacted at the deepest level of ontological categories. The connection between the two continents triggers close inter-relations and intermingling between humans, animals, objects, water and wind. Therefore, a posthumanist reading helps, I suggest, to illuminate the ontological interplay that characterizes Aeschylus' dramaturgy.

Does that amount to saying that Aeschylus' world is a posthumanist one? After all, such a claim would not necessarily be anachronistic. Katherine Hayles suggested that as humans, 'we have always been posthuman'.[17] However, the entanglement of humans, objects and the natural environment actually has harmful implications in Aeschylus' play, especially when it comes to telling the story of Salamis, another climactic moment of the tragedy.[18] The bridging of the Hellespont and the naval battle are two mirror passages, linked by linguistic and thematic echoes: the defeat at Salamis is explicitly interpreted as a punishment suffered for the hybristic former enterprise. Salamis epitomizes the Persians' loss, their human identity being devoured by revolting natural forces and material objects.

I therefore contend that in *Persians*, far from being idealized as the bright future of humanity, the hybrid humanity is connected with *hybris* and human alienation rather than liberation. However, Aeschylus' ambivalent representation of hybridity does not necessarily foreshadow the later humanist rejection of all that is organic, physical, animal, natural, mixed, from the definition of human essence.[19] A posthumanist reading of *Persians* does not call for a *prehumanist* interpretation, i.e., a reading that would make Aeschylus a precursor of the humanist tradition.[20] Rather, his play advocates for a *cosmic humanism* that envisages human beings as living in a respectful companionship with objects, animals, natural elements and divinities. As such, it strikingly resonates with some modern trends of thought, such as Haraway's exploration of inter-species relationships.[21]

The bridging of the Hellespont and supra-humanity

In *Persians*, the choral ode of the *parodos* exalts the greatness and irresistible strength of the Persian army breaking like waves over Greece. The crossing of the Hellespont is the climactic achievement of this campaign: Persians have acquired new knowledge, techniques and power that enable them to unite two continents. Aeschylus' depiction assimilates them to supra-humans who impact the whole world around them.[22]

The first mention of Xerxes' unprecedented action occurs in lines 69–70: Xerxes 'crosses the strait of Helle, daughter of Athamas' (πορθμὸν ἀμείψας Ἀθαμαντίδος Ἕλλας). The verb (ἀμείβω) means 'to cross' but also 'to change', 'to exchange'.[23] In the whole song, the old men of Sousa admire how Xerxes' imperialist thrust *changes* the nature of places, beings and things. Assimilated to the mythological Helle, the sea is humanized and soon animalized too – like Asia and Greece, personified as two beautiful women, before becoming horses yoked to Xerxes' chariot, in the dream of the Queen.[24] Xerxes is said to have 'thrown a yoke on the neck of the sea':[25] the neologism ὅδισμα (from ὅδος) and the rare poetic epithet πολύγομφον ('with many bolts') underline the novelty of this literally path-breaking action through a human technique unheard of. As well shown by Dumortier, the metaphor of the yoke was probably not a common one before Aeschylus.[26] The subjugation of a natural element as if it were a domesticated animal is the initial gesture that precipitates a series of ontological blendings.

The Persian soldiers themselves oscillate between the condition of animals, humans and water particles. First named a 'divine herd' and a bee swarm, metaphors with a clear Homeric ring,[27] the army is then described as an indistinct 'great flood of men' (μεγάλωι ῥεύματι φωτῶν).[28] The men turned into a watery element cannot be fought (ἄμαχον) more than the waves of the sea.[29] This liquefaction is suggested in another respect, when the chorus laments on the deserted beds of Persian women, empty of men but full of tears.[30]

Xerxes himself is given a hybrid, supra-human identity. Aeschylus activates the polysemic significance of traditional images. When naming Xerxes 'a mortal, equal to the gods, son of the family born from gold',[31] he plays on three different levels: the conventional association of Persia with gold, a genealogical reference to Danae, the mythological founder of Persia who gave birth to Perseus from the union with Zeus coming to her in the form of golden rain; finally, this golden pedigree is also reminiscent of the representation of gods as radiant golden beings. This saturation of symbolism seems to transform the human king into a metallic hybrid being. The following lines also perform another type of hybridization of Xerxes: he is assimilated to a *drakon* darting a 'murderous snake look' (λεύσσων φονίου δέργμα δράκοντος).[32] In the next line, Xerxes fluidly evolves towards a mythological monster. The epithet πολύχειρ refers in the first instance to the 'many arms' of his irresistible army, but again, a double meaning points towards a supra-human dimension: Xerxes is a deadly serpent,[33] but also like a Titan with many hands, a new Briareos, one of the Hesiodic Hecatoncheires (literally, primitive creatures 'with a hundred hands').[34]

The conflict between Greeks and Persians then becomes a war between two different object–human 'assemblages'. Greeks are called 'men famed for the spear' (δουρικλύτοις ἀνδράσι), whereas Persians are a dehumanized, divine force of war (Ἄρη) 'taming with the bow' (τοξόδαμνον).[35] Aeschylus uses two compounds (δουρικλύτοις and τοξόδαμνον) that are not as symmetrical as it may seem at first. Δουρικλύτος (or δουρικλειτός) is a laudatory homeric epithet that expresses the warrior force of the spears, without negating the human identity and individuality of their bearers.[36] Greeks remain men (ἀνδράσι) mastering their offensive weapons, and drawing from them the *kleos* that will make them (not the weapons) immortal. An Aeschylean neologism, τοξόδαμνος ('taming with the bow') carries a different symbolism. It is used three times in the *parodos* of *Persians*, as if it were a consubstantial attribute of the Persian army, first applying collectively to the Persian soldiers, then to one of Xerxes' generals, before qualifying the whole army as an indistinct, anonymous force (Ἄρη τοξόδαμνον).[37] As is well known, the bow possessed negative connotations as the weapon of the cowards and the barbarians.[38] But what is interesting here is that the compound τοξόδαμνος bestows a destructive force on the weapon itself, not on the men who manipulate it. The combination with Ἄρη actually erases the human component of this assemblage. Therefore, the attribution of posthumanist features may well overlap with a political strategy: in this battle between East and West, Greeks remain humans whereas Persians acquire non-human traits that contribute to their otherness.[39]

Crossing the two continents, Xerxes breaches geographical but also ontological limits. At the end of the choral ode, the *leitmotiv* of change resurfaces when the verb ἀμείβω appears again as a compound (ἐξαμείψας).[40] With an effect of ring composition, the chorus dwells on the merging of two continents that are now made one.[41] But does the hybrid world created by Xerxes open a beneficial posthumanist 'interconnection' between human and non-human elements?[42] Is Xerxes among the 'cosmic imperialists who by imposing "subject/object" hierarchies somehow oppress inorganic elements, minerals, liquids, and gases as well as organic flora and fauna', as Edith Hall puts it?[43] Or should we acknowledge that the Persian soldiers depicted in Aeschylus' poetry, as well as Xerxes himself, whose status fluctuates between that of a god, a mortal, an infra-human animal or a monster, are indeed 'liminal beings', early examples of the 'hybrid humanity' which posthumanists call for?[44]

Posthumanists actually reprove the use of technology as a means for domination,[45] and there are good chances that, if asked, they would place Xerxes' crossing of the Hellespont on that side. Interestingly, this reprobation arises already in Aeschylus' play. The choral song is actually tinged with apprehension here and there:[46] the old men suspect the goddess *Atè* of having inspired this staggering operation.[47] They wonder but also hint at a potential misuse of human technique. Persians, they say, 'have learnt' (ἔμαθον) to build new ways of crossing the sea.[48] One may wonder whether this verb could be filled with ironic undertones: in Aeschylus' *Agamemnon*, the chorus states that learning only comes through pain and failure.[49] Persians have learnt to be 'confident' (πίσυνοι) in 'frail cables and man-conveying machines' (μηχαναῖς), but were they right in doing so? The substantive μηχαναί easily takes on a deceptive significance in Greek tragedy ('machinations').[50] In these lines, an opposition between the formidable forces of nature (the sea and the wind) and the frailness of human's inventions is creeping in. The *hapax* λαοπόροις ('men-conveying') also contributes to turn upside-down the expected hierarchy between humans and the material objects they produce. In carrying the human beings, the 'machines' (or 'machinations') elaborated by the Persians may take control over their actions. These machines operate a double displacement: they seem to be responsible for the men's transport across the sea but may also displace their traditional role of main actors and commanders.

In fact, these fears anticipate the painful reversal that Persians experienced at Salamis, as unfurled by the messenger's account later in the play. At Salamis, the hybridization enforced by Xerxes is described as persistently growing to the detriment of humans. As 'liminal' beings,[51] the Persian soldiers gradually lose their humanity whereas natural elements are invested of a greater power and personhood.

Infra-humanity at Salamis

Aeschylus' *Persians* capitalizes on the powerful effects of symmetrical composition. To the tremendous catalogue of forces elaborated in the *parodos* responds the catalogue of dead Persian commanders, in the messenger speech.[52] The defeat of Salamis is strategically construed as a scathing punishment: the *hybris* of Xerxes yoking the Hellespont is retaliated by his crushing debacle in Salamis, as is made clear in the speech of Darius' ghost himself.[53] The mirroring effects between these two dramatic moments, the peak of grandeur and the total collapse, encompass a 'cosmic' dimension, in its etymological sense: the messenger's speech offers a dreadful account of the radical and systematic inversion of the alleged human control over natural elements and inanimate objects.

The Persians were of course beaten by the Greek naval forces: Aeschylus, who probably served in the fleet which laid siege to Sestus in 479 to 478,[54] pays tribute to the fighting spirit of his fellow-citizens. However, in his theatrical account of the battle, he confers a real agency to non-human elements. The earlier assimilation of the army of Persia to a flow of men as powerful as the sea, finds an ironic reversal in the defeat: the army is now envisioned as a flow of countless corpses which hides the surface of the sea (θάλασσα δ' οὐκέτ' ἦν ἰδεῖν).[55] The liminal, watery status I described earlier takes on a tragic twist when soldiers become floating corpses, soaked and devoured by the salty water.[56] This 'distributive agency'[57] is extended to the shores and islands: they are spoken of as animated places and active subjects[58] who jealously keep the corpses and deface them even after their death.[59]

The Persian soldiers are plunged into infra-humanity, be they imagined as corpses bumping against the shores, like rams would knock with their horns,[60] or, when trapped by the Greeks in Psyttalia, defenceless tuna fish dying under the blows of makeshift weapons – any oar or piece of wood available at the Greeks' hands, grim instruments that inflict an unheroic death on them, as I interpret it.[61] They are also portrayed as drifting corpses, belonging to an unsettling in-between: they are not really persons anymore but not really inanimate objects either.[62] They gain another sort of liminality: the verb ἀμείβω is repeated here again when the bloodshed is assimilated to the purple dye (πορφυρᾷ βαφῇ) that 'changes' the colour of the beard and skin of one Persian officer.[63] The metaphor merges together human and animal organic fluid (since the purple comes from the murex snail)[64] and reduces human beings to 'things dyed', empty envelopes or empty 'sacks'.[65] At the end of this disastrous report, the immediate response of the Queen highlights, in a ring composition effect, the tragic reversal that transformed the powerful waves of men into a 'great sea of pains'.[66]

Finally, like the natural elements, inanimate objects also adopt a deceptive and almost rebellious attitude against Xerxes and his army. Even before hearing what the messenger has to say, the chorus laments the failure of weapons which have been brought, 'all mingled together' (παμμιγῆ) 'in vain' (μάταν), as if these instruments were held responsible for the defeat – παμμιγῆ may hint at a disorganized mass unable to withstand the discipline of the Greek army.[67] The famous Persian bows have defaulted on their masters, the messenger adds.[68] In his vivid account that stimulates a perceptual recreation of the bloodshed, soldiers and commanders are slain by unruly boats and weapons that seem to assault them as independent forces. For instance, Aeschylus refers to the anthropomorphic faces of Greek triremes, when alluding to their battering ram 'with a bronze mouth' (ἐμβολαῖς χαλκοστόμοις).[69] In lines 410, 415–418, ναῦς and δόρυ, 'ships' and 'spears', are the active subjects of verbs of attack.[70] Earlier, the leader Dadaces, 'struck by a spear' (πληγῇ δορὸς) is said to have 'leapt effortlessly' from his boat.[71] Moved by this external energy, the body appears again like a thing emptied of any inner vitality. In this chaotic scene, even simple, daily-life objects like clothes take on unexpected functions: Persian iconic mantles that encapsulate the oriental *truphè* seem to betray their wearers when becoming morbid shrouds for their corpses drifting in the waves.[72]

Epilogue

In a posthumanist world where all beings are inter-connected and attributed the same 'ontological dignity',[73] the logical result, as expressed by Dominique Quessada, is an 'ontological anarchism',[74] an absence of order where amorality presides – since outside the domain of human morality. This starkly contrasts with the interpretation I propose of Aeschylus' *Persians*. As in other extant works by Aeschylus, hybridity is morally loaded and connected with the representation of chaos and *hybris*.[75] When reflecting on his son's defeat, the ghost of Darius reproves the yoking through the 'machines' (μηχαναῖς ἔζευξεν), as an impious and thoughtless act that was an insult to the forces of nature.[76] Darius not only alludes to the cables of the bridging but also the throwing of fetters into the sea, a fact that had been kept silent before.[77] He voices indignation against the enslavement of a 'sacred' river ('Ελλήσποντον ἱρὸν δοῦλον), explicitly assimilated to a god (Βόσπορον ῥόον θεοῦ).[78] In recent years, some countries have passed legislation to recognize that rivers are moral, legal persons who have the same rights as human beings;[79] in ancient Greece, rivers were considered as divinities, which gives to the act of Xerxes an additional dimension of sacrilege. In Darius' speech, the word ὕβρις itself, looming for some time, is eventually uttered at the opening of line 821, intimately associated with ἄτης at the same position in 822: Darius uses the case of his son to deliver a gnomic lesson about human arrogance and delusion.[80]

The parallel reading of the bridging of the Hellespont and the defeat of Salamis therefore reveals a tension between two close but differentiated phenomena in this play: on one side, a co-dependence of humans and non-human forces, underlying in Darius' speech, that entails moral obligations of humans towards their natural environment; on the other side, unleashed hybridity seen as a hybristic mode of domination onto the world. Inter-connectedness is thus differentiated from non-separateness: humans are considered in extension with other elements, natural or machinic, they are affected by wind, water, animals, objects but this 'heterogenous relationship', to borrow Donna Haraway's phrasing, does not obliterate distinctions and limits.[81] In *Persians*, mixing, merging and blending are not means of liberation *per se*: they rather lead to alienation; this warns us against hybridity as a false openness, a form of absorption that actually negates otherness. Therianthropy, the entanglement of human with animal, also praised by some posthumanist theorists,[82] is represented as an estrangement (or a degradation) rather than an improvement of humanity.[83] Significantly, hybridity is conspicuously rejected onto the side of the Persians, in contrast to the preserved, bounded humanity of the Greeks. The posthuman qualities of Xerxes and the Persian army actually reinforce a clear opposition of cultures between East and West.

This interpretation of the play questions euphoric hybridity as a modern naïve utopia. It contradicts the upbeat terminology readily used by some modern posthumanist theorists when promoting hybridity and non-separateness. Advocating for an 'ontological anarchism', Dominique Quessada hopes for an ontological 'fraternity' or 'solidarity' between all things while the artist Denis Baron has promoted a 'jouissance of the state of hybridity and fluid identities'.[84] Donna Haraway's own path of thinking interestingly shows distantiation from flat ontology.[85] In her *Cyborg Manifesto* she invited us to feel 'pleasure in the confusion of boundaries' and advocated for cyborgs' 'pleasurably tight coupling with other beings',[86] while distancing herself from the idea of 'boundless difference' that does not allow us to achieve 'real connections' with alterity.[87] In the *Companion Species Manifesto*, her call for a human appreciation of inter-dependent development and co-habitation of species (her 'kinship claim') nonetheless goes with the acknowledgment of 'irreducible difference'.[88] 'Significant otherness' is about negotiating ethical 'modes of attention' between species (humans, animals, plants, etc.) whose differences are not *flattened out* but, on the contrary, acknowledged as what must be preserved in respectful, asymmetrical 'heterogeneous relationship'.[89]

Aeschylus' extant plays and fragments reflect a special interest in establishing such kinds of 'heterogeneous relationships'. An additional example would be his *Oreithyia*, a lost tragedy related to another event that occurred during the second Persian war. Shortly after 480 BCE, the Athenians founded a sanctuary of the north wind Boreas, to thank *him* for having sent a storm to destroy the Persian ships that were approaching Artemisium.[90] Aeschylus' *Oreithyia* brought an aetiological explanation for Athenians' *friendship* with Boreas.[91] The sole extant fragment gives speech to the wind itself who asserts his power to act on (and against) the human community.[92] Negotiating harmonious relationships with this natural element was most probably at stake in this play: the 'unending dance of distributed and heterogeneous agencies' was perhaps already there.[93]

CHAPTER 23
MALFUNCTIONS OF EMBODIMENT: MAN/WEAPON AGENCY AND THE GREEK IDEOLOGY OF MASCULINITY

Francesca Spiegel

This chapter takes an *aporia* arising from Antiphon's second tetralogy in order to throw light on a paradoxical function of Athenian male embodiment of *kalokagathia*. It will contemplate a neo-materialist view of masculine body–weapon synergic entanglements in Greek writing and evaluate the ideological implications of considering of weapons and wearable artifacts such as armour to be an extension of masculine human agency and therefore also to have a part in the male inner subjectivity. Finally, this chapter explores the ideology that underwrites the notion of *kalokagathia* and its male embodiment. I will consider Antiphon's legal prose of the second tetralogy, which deals with an accident during javelin-throwing practice, as well as some small sample snippets of epic, lyric and tragic poetry, and excerpts from philosophical dialogues. From Homer via Archilochus via Sophocles to Antiphon and on to Plato, a dotted line connects vignettes, scenes, narrations and argumentative prose, all sharing a notion of the ideologico-somatic dynamic where weapons cling to bodies to the point that the male ideological regimen of *kalokagathia* is inseparable from the weapons and related technics of the body.

Let me start with man/weapon entanglements, focusing on some malfunctions: examples where the mostly smooth and powerful dynamic of man/weapon entanglements starts to disjoin, when armours come unstuck from bodies, or when weapons are misdirected, and hit a wrong target. Initially, the man–weapon entanglement arises from affixing weapons to a man. However, the malfunctions of montage show that the subtraction of weapons from a man–weapon entanglement does not return a simple rest of man. We could schematize the problem thus:

man + weapon = {man/weapon entanglement}

But **{man/weapon entanglement} – weapon ≠ man**

Removing a weapon rips away a piece of the man's sanity and sense of self as well, as if the act of fixing a man up with weaponry had led to absorptions and redistributions of selfhood within the parameters of the amalgamation that is a {man/weapon entanglement}. Consequently, the malfunctions of man/weapon synergies are apt to trigger internalized psychological deconstructions of self-integrity that let us see some of the prerequisites needed for cultural participation.

The second tetralogy of Antiphon deals with a hypothetical situation: at the gymnasium, some boys were taking javelin practice, so that they might become well-trained in the art of javelin-throwing. In other words, they were exercising so that they might, come adulthood, have bodies trained in ways that would let them embody *kalokagathia*, which would mean that their appearance would represent the strong-bodied, strong-minded ideal of manhood expected of an Athenian citizen and engender a state of fitness for taking charge of the city and its democratic actions. As one of the fathers explains, 3.2.3: 'I also was training my son so he could better serve the common good, and so that both of us could enjoy the resulting benefit' (ἐδόκουν μὲν οὖν ἔγωγε ταῦτα παιδεύων τὸν υἱὸν ἐξ ὧν μάλιστα τὸ κοινὸν ὠφελεῖται, ἀμφοῖν τι ἡμῖν ἀγαθὸνἀποβήσεσθαι). The father assumes that both parents had the same motivation for sending their sons to javelin-throwing practice. Underlying this assumption is the understanding that a man has to be well-trained at using javelins, so with regard to the concept of a {man/weapon entanglement} we can understand that the 'man' part covers not only the human body (and its technological extensions), but also the mastery of techniques acquired by training.

Plato takes up this ideology in the *Laws*, where the Athenian stranger gives it the fullest expression. The Athenian lays out the importance of training in the right arts in the right ways, and the importance of habituation to such exercise, for the political as well as ethical success of Athenian citizens. In fact, the Athenian argues, a man is only half as much 'man' if he forgoes the training, as he would be with the training of body and soul, at war arts such as bow-shooting, athletic boxing, music and dance (647e: 'no man unversed and unpracticed [. . .] can attain even half the excellence of which he is capable'; this idea comes directly after the assertion that 'a man can become perfect' through training (647d)). Only this training can afford a man with the equanimity needed for participation in life under a jurisdiction (compare also 795a–d).

Foucault has taken this expression of man's perfectibility by training, and conversely man's *lack* of perfection in the *absence* of such training, to encapsulate an idea of ancient Greek Athenian civil selfhood as anchored in self-nurture, which takes the form of training and self-regulation.[1] What now interests us here furthermore is the implicit devaluation of the human as 'bare' human material, which emerges by contrast and with the help of images of the bodies of slaves, whom the Athenian repeatedly takes as a negative example of inverse *kalokagathia*. The move is not new; indeed, we may find views of a slave's body again and again as the converse of *kalokagathia*, not least in the *Physiognomics* attributed to Aristotle, where 'an ill-proportioned body indicates a rogue'.[2]

In *Gorgias*, Callicles will hold up an image of the enslaved taking power by sheer force, never mind *kalokagathia*, and he will argue that physically strong bodies and the use of violence are as effective a means of rising to dominance as is the use of elaborate techniques (483c–484a); in fact Callicles goes on to argue that life under a jurisdiction itself is an artificial system put in place by lesser men ill-provided with natural strengths. For Callicles, democratic jurisdiction is an artificial device of instituting and institutionally sharing power, which castrates the well-endowed (Callicles uses the metaphor of domesticating lions, cf. 483E5).

Already in 1959 E. R. Dodds had observed that the theme of Callicles' speech – the *nomos/phusis* antithesis – was 'widely canvassed'[3] across the work of Greek writers of the fifth century. Dodds contextualized the Calliclean *rhesis* within modern State philosophy, invoking Hobbes' *Leviathan* – the grand model of a State engineered with artificial man, the greatest machine, the biggest product of technology and of mechanist thinking – and French Enlightenment contractual philosophy. Dodds followed that with Nietzsche's *Will to Power* as 'the undesired and illegitimate offspring of Plato',[4] via 'Diderot and his friends'.[5] One might imagine that by 'friends' here Dodds meant Rousseau, who penned the *Contrat Social* elaborating upon the idea that jurisdiction is a fundamentally artificial way of organizing human life, but at the same time gives birth to a way of life and a type of subjectivity that could be called 'social'.

There is no doubt about the artificiality of such organizational setups; nor is it ever concealed in the *Republic* that the young boys' training for a future as honourable citizens is in fact a training in *imitating* the virtue of others: 'Have you not noticed,' Socrates asks, 'that imitations, when carried out since early youth, settle into character and nature in body, speech, and thought?' ("Η οὐκ ᾔσθησαι ὅτι αἱ μιμήσεις, ἐὰν ἐκ νέων πόρρω διατελέσωσιν, εἰς ἔθη τε καὶ φύσιν καθίστανται καὶ κατὰ σῶμα καὶ φωνὰς καὶ κατὰ τὴν διάνοιαν;).[6] *Kalokagathia* is produced by imitation and training at what could be called a 'performance' of masculinity, quite, in Judith Butler's terms, 'impersonating an ideal that nobody actually inhabits'.[7] The habituation to constant training has the effect that the training gradually seeps into the human's essence so deeply that, at last, a well-trained man embodies his own training, and could not embody anything else.

In Antiphon's tetralogy, the parents of the two boys are suing and counter-suing each other, because one boy accidentally killed another during javelin-throwing practice. Just as one boy was throwing a javelin, another ran across the weapon's trajectory, was hit by it, and died. The parent of the boy who threw the javelin argues that he sent his son to be trained at javelin-throwing so that it would provide him with the habits and agility he would need in the future to be useful to the *polis*. Thus, the intentions were good, and the boy was diligent (Ant.3.2.3).

The javelin thrown at a target aim, and accidentally hitting a practice mate, now becomes a mysterious point of contention when it comes to attributing blame for what happened. The father of the boy who fell victim to the accident claims that the boy who threw the javelin did kill his son, even if not intentionally; the other father argues that the boy who died killed himself, by running out at the wrong moment. The javelin had already been thrown when the boy ran out, and so, in the eyes of the defendant 'my son killed no-one' (οὐκ ἀπέκτεινε δὲ οὐδένα, 3.2.3). This is surely an infelicitous turn of phrase to the ears of a father who has just lost a son, but underneath it lies the insistence on intention, and the complete absence of an intent to kill in the boy's mind. But to the plaintiff, the absence of intent is irrelevant; his positioning of the fact is founded upon an understanding that the author of an action has to take full ownership of that action – and that includes the full spectrum of unforeseen and unwanted consequences.

A parallel motion of thought is in Antiphon 1, the speech with the English title *Against the Stepmother for Poisoning*, where a female maid (probably, not definitively determinably, a slave),[8] becomes the author of a murder by poison when her mistress directs her to serve a spiked drink to two men. In the case's narration, the jurors learn that the maid had acted under the (it now emerges, false) information that the drug would be an aphrodisiac. Even in the absence of bad intentions, this maid was promptly executed (1.20), and without a trial (which makes it quite likely that she *was* a slave).

Quite by contrast, the javelin-throwing boy is represented in court by his father, and culpability for the unintended action is now discussed at length. Comparing the fate of the maid with the defence of the boy once more confirms the not at all novel insight that 'some humans are more human than others' before the law of ancient Athenian tribunals.

The Orwellian dystopian vista of ineradicable inequalities inherent to life under a systematized jurisdiction can serve as a lens to look further into the problem of accidental killing and the politics of blame. The boy at javelin practice becomes cast as a killer because the objects he handled are sharp and dangerous. The javelin was an extension of his own agency, even in the extremely regrettable case of a javelin thrown for practice ending up killing a friend. In the case of a maid, it is possible simply to execute the author of the lethal action. But when it comes to the offspring of Athenian citizens, authorship of actions involving lethal weapons and their unplanned damage to the life of others becomes re-cast as a matter of debate. The possibility now emerges on the horizon that the agency of man with weapon is *not* a zero-sum game.

Weapons cause destruction to human life, and not exclusively at times when they are purposefully engaged to effect that. At other times, they cause collateral damage and work against the intentions of their users. This relation encapsulates the modern idea of engineers' and scientists', and by proxy 'man's, relationship with technology in a nutshell: Frankenstein, Dr Strangelove, Dr Nobel; a mix of modern Promethean triumph and shame. Who really is to blame for a malfunction of an act carried out by humans with their agency extended by weapons?

In Antiphon's tetralogy, there is, beneath the mutually aporetic views of the two boys' parents, the realization of a philosophical problem: an action may have a person as its agent, but, still, the person does not have sufficient agency to be fully responsible for the full series of the action's corollary consequences. One can find a sophisticated discussion of such cases in the *Nicomachean Ethics* (3.15), where Aristotle sets out that responsibility for an action and all its consequences has to remain with its author. This includes cases where intentions of effecting the actual result were absent. In such cases, Aristotle argues that one should extend generous feelings of pity and compassion towards those who have become guilty of a crime without having intended to cause criminal damage. Aristotle's explanations here have been set in relation with the section on tragic *hamartia* of the *Poetics*; the example is Oedipus, a tragic figure marked by the psychological struggle with the inadvertent authorship of crimes. In the *Nic. Ethics* Aristotle offers that Oedipus is very much responsible for what he has done, even though he did not mean it, and in the *Poetics* Aristotle explains that this should engender pity – a settlement that may leave some readers dissatisfied. According to Aristotle, those who become involuntary authors of any action at all are, none the less, responsible for the action and while they deserve to be pitied, they have no particular right to exemption of punishments.

This does not settle the problem; and in antiquity, the problem clearly occupied many thinkers. We may compare Antiphon 1 (the *Stepmother* case) to a tragic text, the scenario of poisoning we see in Sophocles' *Trachiniae.* Both texts treat cases of women poisoning men. Both times, the intention was erotic, for the *pharmakon* to be an aphrodisiac. Both times, the consequence is lethal, which is unwanted. Sophocles' treatment of this material for the tragic stage unfolds some of the psychological ramifications of the action that are absent from Antiphon's presentation as a case in legal terms.[9]

In tragedy, the misdirection of weapons calls into being scenes of regret, where the explanation for an accident can quite easily turn to the occult and superstitious thinking. In Sophocles' *Ajax*, audiences witness Ajax's suicide monologue, in which the warrior gives to understand that the sword with which he is about to kill himself, because it was a gift from Hector and because Hector was the enemy, albeit a noble and well-regarded enemy, will make it appear as if the suicide was a combat death carried out by Hector (*Aj.* 815–865). Attached to the thought of death by Hector's sword is an ideation of dying by Hector's agency, or dying in combat, but (and this is important) a combat that follows the rules of heroic warfare.

In the play, Ajax deplores the expiry of a value system to which he had subscribed, which he revives in the moment of killing himself with Hector's sword. He refuses to align himself with the new values proffered by the leadership of his own camp, impersonated by the Sophoclean

Odysseus, who took away the armour of Achilles that Ajax felt he deserved, according to a code, which Odysseus has disregarded. One can see parallels with the Odysseus character in the prologue of *Philoctetes*,[10] whose views about the effectiveness of sheer force above instituted rules compare well with the Platonic Callicles, or again the dialogue of Kratos and Bia in the opening of *Prometheus Bound*, attributed to Aeschylus, also thematizing the conflict between justice and force.

The entire premise of *Ajax* revolves around the fact that, on being denied the armour of Achilles, Ajax considers himself outraged. More than a century earlier, Archilochus had written on the emotions of losing one's armour (fr. 6 about a lost shield conveys the emotion of 'good riddance'); and turning away from culturally instilled masculine accoutrements of self-identification through war. While the voice in Archilochus seems gleeful, in the Sophoclean *Ajax*, we are given to understand that the denial of Achilles' armour has ripped a piece of Ajax's identity right off him. His inability to wear, or at least own, this armour becomes Ajax's reason to withdraw his participation from the Trojan War.

Further down the gallery of poetic ancestry, Achilles himself in *Iliad* 9 is aggrieved at not receiving the spoils of battle shared out by the Atridae and Odysseus. The deprivation is not (or not solely) conceived of in monetary terms, as the economy of things in the *Iliad* is to a considerable extent one of *symbolic* capital. As scholars have persuasively shown,[11] the offence Achilles takes in the *Iliad* derives from an experience of being deprived and under-valued within an economy of honorific gestures. The size of his share in battle spoils translates the immaterial value of Achilles' excellence at war by comparison to other warriors. Thus, a diminished share symbolizes a diminished appreciation of his abilities. It is by definition impossible for the non-acquisition of battle spoils to represent a material loss, since battle spoils are an addition of capital not previously in circulation; and this underscores again the symbolic framing of the loss.

Several centuries later, the problem is still a matter of intellectual discussion: in *Gorgias*, Socrates argues about it with Callicles, when they determine whether the best man should be given the best cut of the meat (484b), or whether another system of distribution should be applied. In the Sophoclean play, Ajax is aggrieved by the Atridae and Odysseus failing to bestow the armour of Achilles on him, not in the terms of a deprivation in monetary value, but in terms of *symbolic* capital. If we understand this economy, we also understand why the suicide by Hector's sword, reframed as a battle death, functions as a necessary restitution of Ajax's losses.

Let us look back at Antiphon's fictional parents of a fictional boy accidentally killed at javelin practice. Paradoxically, the comparison with the tragic example of Ajax might provide us with a key to the problem. Where the achievement of distinguished value and performance of worthy citizenship involves the use of weapons, and the training at them enables the realization of one's identity to full power – meaning, the power to dominate others by war – the accidental death of a boy during javelin practice comes as collateral damage of serving, or preparing to serve, the cultural ideal and methods *kalokagathia*. So the boy, sent to train by his parents, falls victim to an ideology.

In the legal quarrel about the boy's death, the appreciation of damage is derived from a sense of untimeliness, understood as embedded in a project of *kalokagathia* sought, but not attained. In this framing, the agency that truly brings death is neither fully in the boy who threw the javelin, nor in the boy who ran across the javelin pitch, although both these agencies are part of the equation. The ultimate cause is the framework that made such a scenario possible, and the ideas that set the framework in place. This framework is the desire to achieve *kalokagathia* and the wish to belong to a 'smart set'. *Kalokagathia* is an ideal of discipline, honing bodies and training minds. And so the accident that led to the boy's early demise and the waste of his youth lays open the *thanatos* inherent in *kalokagathia* and the ideology that underwrites it.

The second tetralogy is a fictional case. It was written to practise legal speech-making, and Antiphon's choice of a topic here is itself dependent on the dominant ideology and the financial interests of serving that ideology. As the parents deplore that their boy's life was cut short by an untimely death, we begin to wonder if implied in this deploration is the supposition that, had he grown to be *kaloskagathos*, he might have been afforded the opportunity to die in a worthy fight that was not just a practice fight, one that mattered enough to be remembered and eulogized; and the law court is the venue for a surrogate eulogy of the boy who died too soon, in the form of an exposition of the risks of even *training* with weapons.

Now I come to materialism. My interpretation differs from a neo-materialist view relating the accidental aim of the javelin to the tragic variant with the sword of Ajax and the superstitious image of Hector coming back from the dead, so to speak, to direct the killing of Ajax. Naiden has suggested that in Greek thought, the sword of Ajax itself could have been given the legal blame for the death.[12] Pointing to the ancient Greek legal practice of trying cases where objects had caused death, and to the existence of a separate court dedicated to such cases, Naiden discusses the Greek cultural practice of demonstratively casting out – ostracizing – objects that had become suicide weapons. The existence of the court certainly dictates that we should pay attention to the Greek cultural understanding, and rhetorical framing, of deaths caused by objects.

In 'Ajax and Other Objects', Purves posits Ajax as an assemblage of armour and self, an entanglement that it is impossible to see with the depth typical to Freudian and post-Freudian analysis of selfhood, and founds his argument in a revision of Snell's notion of 'pre-human' subjectivity in Homer,[13] connecting Fränkel's 'elementary vitality'[14] with Bennett's notion of 'vibrant materialism'. Indeed the mid-century tradition of considering Homeric poetry as a 'poetry of surfaces',[15] and the Homeric human as one who had 'no innerness'.

It is no doubt in reaction to this negation of psychological depth in Homeric and other Greek written men that Foucault pointed his theory of *enkratia* in the *History of Sexuality*. Here, Foucault reflects that instead of being absent, the interiority of Greek literary figures emerges in terms of an agonistic relation with one's own sexual urges, or desire more broadly. 'It has been said of the Greeks,' Foucault writes, 'because of their secular paganism, that they do not have the depth of the Christian or monotheist cultures.'[16] According to Foucault, that conceptualization must be re-framed: if the written Greek character does not exhibit psychoanalysis-friendly depth, his innerness nonetheless manifests in the practice of self-care and self-discipline. *Enkrateia* compels the elite Greek man to practise self-control in the pursuit of public esteem. Unlike in (what is understood to be) Christian morality, this does not lead to an erasure of sexual (or generalized) bodily passions, but to the managed cohabitation with them in a relation of self-discipline. An example of this is the father's praise of his boy in Antiphon, that his son was 'not slacking, but being diligent, attending practice' (3.2.3).

Naiden and Purves argue that the embodiment of values in man/weapons entanglements lays open a view of the human as so essentially material that there is almost an equivalence between human and thing, so that objects, like people, emerge as equally agential in the causation of damage. Within that framework, it becomes possible to speak of 'object agency'.

However, when it comes to the cases and scenarios I have brought together here, they do not add up to an understanding that objects have an agency of their own. The misdirection of a weapon over and beyond the intended aim can take the human into a state of existential disarray, mental and physical undoing. But it is not attributable to the fact that things move by themselves. Instead, it is attributable to the existence of humans and things together in a framework of an ideology that instrumentalizes things, and develops instruments for the extension of human agency, under the banner of enacting dominant identity.

Certainly, accidents involving objects can override the intentions of their users, who have limited cognizance of an action's potential future impact. That theme is often exploited in modern culture. For example, von Weber's opera *Der Freischütz* (*The Marksman* in English), re-made as a pop musical with Tom Waits (*The Black Rider*), shows a rifle gun with a mission of its own, 'and in the moment of aiming, the gun turns into a dowser's wand, and points where the bullet wants to go'.[17] Human agency here is severely truncated: objects take on a ghostly ability to direct themselves, as if they were spirited.

This is the point where we encounter discourses involving shamanistic credence, superstition and spirituality, and where we can look back at the Greeks with their own imaginarium of demonic agency and philosophies of chance. Certainly, much has been made by scholars, especially on tragedy, of Greek ideas involving fate and divine intervention in human affairs. But what the references to Greek religion and superstition will often blot out is the political interest of presenting things as 'accidental'. My contention is that discourses that will attribute agency to objects on an equal plane as they attribute agency to humans,[18] do so in the service of an ideology. In its practical application through cultural institutions of training, the pursuit of dominance throws up roadkill of its own humans who built it; and it brings in fuzzy logic in a motion to conceal the *thanatos* inherent in the desire for order and discipline.

CHAPTER 24
AENEID 12: A CYBORG BORDER WAR
Elena Giusti

We are excruciatingly conscious of what it means to have a historically constituted body.

Haraway 1991: 156

Criticism of the *Aeneid* has long interpreted the poem's human characters as belonging to an earthly mortal category positioned between the opposing strata of Chthonic and Olympian forces and incessantly pulled to either side. These symbolic readings – inaugurated by Pöschl 1962 (or. 1950) and later crystallized by Hardie 1986 – rely upon a number of interconnected but discriminate dichotomies (e.g., Jupiter–Juno, heaven–hell, male–female) that mark the poem as one of the milestones of Western dualism.[1] Although deconstructions of some of these polarities have not been unattempted,[2] most of them continue to be systemic to readings of the *Aeneid*, especially in its final scene, as scholars have been striving to assess whether Aeneas' anger in killing Turnus belongs to one camp or the other.[3] But to attempt a dismantling of the polarities intrinsic to the *Aeneid*'s critical history becomes more than a scholarly obligation when we are reminded, in Donna Haraway's words, how dyads such as male–female, human–animal, culture–nature, civilized–primitive, active–passive, total–partial (to list those addressed in this chapter) 'have all been systemic to the logics and practices of domination'.[4] The pressing issues at stake continue to revolve around the poem's social, political, ideological and fictional constructs, but the focus changes if we stop taking for granted a number of its supposedly foundational oppositions, drawing attention instead to their surprising absence in places where we would most expect them and to the ways in which dichotomous boundaries are blurred.

This chapter attempts, as a case-study, a reading of Turnus and Aeneas in *Aeneid* 12 as Donna Haraway's 'cyborgs', organisms that transgress the boundaries between human and animal, organic and technical,[5] and in this way allow us to reconfigure, without erasing them,[6] a number of the poem's traditional oppositions. Arguably, Haraway herself may not approve of this operation. Firstly, because it de-contextualizes the importance of non-physical and cybernetic technology, so essential to her *Cyborg Manifesto*; but most importantly because the *Aeneid* does not stop being a phallogocentric origin story overnight. However, I shall argue that the reconfiguring of the male actors of Book 12 as cybernetic organisms allows us to dig deeper into the reasons for the readers' frustration and puzzlement with the *Aeneid*'s final scene. For if the subjects, contexts and actors of the *Aeneid* and the *Cyborg Manifesto* are undoubtedly different, the stakes in the war between Aeneas and Turnus, as well as in the debates among that war's interpreters, are the same as those specified by Haraway for the 'border war' relations between humans and machines: 'the territories of production, reproduction, and imagination'.[7] These are the most relevant aspects in the final confrontation of the *Aeneid*, the foundational and procreational myth of the Roman race, and starting point for the ideology of an empire with no spatio-temporal borders.

In what follows, I trace the unfolding of Turnus and Aeneas becoming-cyborgs as they are progressively reconfigured in their parallel but diverse processes of mingling with animals, natural phenomena and technical objects, specifically weapons. In many respects, this reading maps upon some of the traditional oppositions between the two heroes. Just as *Aeneid* 12 is the story of Turnus' progressive isolation both from his people and from the divine forces that supported him,[8] a reading of Turnus in connection to organic and inorganic beings brings out the importance of disconnection and fragmentation for understanding the roots of his 'failure'. Conversely, Aeneas' simultaneous assimilation to the Italian territory brings out the full potential of some of Turnus' most effective disconnecting images as participating in the Rutulian hero's progressive detachment, or rather forced severing, from the roots of his land.[9] And yet Turnus' 'failure' is only apparent once we read the two heroes as belonging to a single cyborg system, since Turnus' disconnect from his land also means his eventual amalgamation with the forces of Aeneas' progressive history, an amalgamation that takes place in the moment we realize that what Turnus embodies as the inimical and oppositional double of Aeneas is constituted by, and predicated on, the discourse built by and for Aeneas himself. But there is a reversible process at work for Aeneas too. At the end of the poem, the *trauma*/wound that has haunted Turnus since the book's beginning, and progressively the Italian landscape at the hand of its Trojan colonizers, fuses with Aeneas' aching pain for his loss of Pallas – but since Aeneas is after all history's winner, his wound easily turns into a traumatically productive opportunity for reconfiguring the whole community (Aeneas', Augustus', Virgil's) as well as the imaginative, ideological role of Virgil's poem within it.

Arma uirumque

Fragmentation is a key theme in *Aeneid* 12 from the book's very first line.[10] As Turnus directs his gaze onto the 'broken' Latins (*A*. 12.1–2 *Turnus ut infractos . . . Latinos/ uidet*), we sense that the fortifications that we just left them setting up in the last line of book 11 (11.915 *moenia uallant*)[11] are by now bound to collapse. This effect brings about a double feeling of disconnection and vulnerability that is further picked up throughout the last book of the epic in the various shapes of wounds, fissures and extirpations, following Turnus closely until his fated ending.

Broken objects play a special role in this narrative.[12] *Infractos* both indicates the crushing of the Latins' spirits and conveys a vivid metaphor, emphasized by the hyperbaton and its forced severing of *Latinos* from its participle, whereby the Latins themselves become Turnus' broken weapon.[13] The metaphor anticipates the malfunctioning of Turnus' sword (which breaks at 12.731–732 *ensis/ frangitur*, with a pertinent enjambment) and suggests a disquieting association, in the realm of the following simile of Turnus' growing violence as a Punic lion (12.4–9), between the broken Latins and the spear that Turnus-the-lion breaks and that remains fixed and clinging inside him (12.7–8 *fixum . . . frangit telum*), previewing the weapon that Aeneas will bury inside his chest at the end of the *Aeneid* (12.950 *ferrum aduerso sub pectore condit*). This is a sort of medical implant with poisonous and fatal implications. As we will see below, these implications directly oppose, but also eventually amalgamate with, the consequences brought about by the arrow, struck by an unknown archer, that later on in the book will be clinging into Aeneas' thigh (12.383–440).

The image of the broken Latins 'marking out' Turnus with their eyes (12.3 *se signari oculis*), with a possibly 'hostile or disgraceful attention',[14] as they ask him to fulfil his duty on his own and meet Aeneas in single combat, reinforces Turnus' isolation throughout the book.[15] But the insinuation of a comparison with weapons also highlights that disconnection from *arma* that will be one of the reasons for Turnus' failure. When the two heroes finally confront each other, Turnus' 'treacherous sword' shatters on Aeneas' armour, 'deserting its wielder in the middle of the blow' (12.731–732 *at perfidus ensis/ frangitur in medioque ardentem deserit ictu*). While the Latins were objectified as weapons at the start of the book, the weapon is now personified and separated from Turnus as an unfaithful deserter (*perfidus* ... *deserit*) abandoning his ardent commander in the middle of the fight.

Two lines earlier, when describing Turnus' preparation for the blow, Virgil seemed to highlight the warrior's attempt to become his weapon, with Turnus 'rising high with his own body *into* the uplifted sword' (12.728–729 *corpore toto/ alte sublatum consurgit Turnus <u>in</u> ensem*). When the weapon breaks,[16] the Rutulian struggles to recognize the 'unknown sword-hilt' as a disembodied fragment of what was meant to belong almost by nature to his now 'un-armed' hand (12.734 *ut capulum <u>ignotum</u> dextramque aspexit <u>inermem</u>*, 'as he looks at the unknown sword-hilt and his unarmed right hand'). While *ignotum* emphasizes Turnus' feeling of estrangement to a sword that he cannot 'recognize' as maimed, as if it were part of his own limb, we soon find out that the sword-hilt is fittingly 'unknown' (or so they say, 12.735 *fama est*), since this is the sword of Metiscus, grabbed by Turnus by mistake in his haste, as 'he left his father's blade behind' (12.736 *patrio mucrone relicto*). While the latter had been donated by Vulcan himself to Daunus after rendering it unbreakable by dipping it in the waters of the Styx as if it represented the not-quite-indemnified body of Achilles,[17] Metiscus' sword is no more than a 'mortal blade' (12.740 *mortalis mucro*), badly matching the heat of its current wielder (12.732 *ardentem*). Thus, as it meets the Vulcanian armour of Aeneas (12.739 *postquam arma dei ad Volcania uentum est*), it shatters like ice (12.740–741 *glacies ceu futtilis ictu/ dissiluit*), which is as 'brittle' as it is 'vain' and 'worthless' (*futtilis*).[18]

Yet the story of the sword's origin is only a rumour that Virgil does not confirm, and some scholars find it rather suspicious.[19] Perhaps the Vulcan-made sword belonged to Daunus, but it does not belong to Turnus. In cyborg terms, somatically and energistically, it is not presented as part of his body. Certainly not in the way in which Aeneas' armour is presented as part of Aeneas' body, and of Aeneas' body alone. If so, Turnus' claim to the sword by right of birth may be no less frustrated than his autochthonous claims to the land from which he becomes, as we are going to see, more and more disconnected in the course of the book. In the two heroes' arming scene (12.81–112), Turnus 'adapts [Daunus' sword] for wielding' (12.88 *aptat habendo*), an expression that highlights his ardent desire to connect with the weapon, while also perhaps anticipating his failure by insisting on the failed identification between hero and object. This is more evident in the general context of Turnus' arming, as later contrasted with Aeneas'. Turnus presents as a hybrid construct made of corslet + shoulders + sword + shield + crest (12.87–89 *ipse dehinc auro squalentem alboque orichalco/ circumdat loricam umeris, simul aptat habendo/ ensemque clipeumque et rubrae cornua cristae*, 'and then he surrounds his shoulders with a corslet stiff with gold and white mountain brass, and at the same time he fits the sword for wielding, and the shield, and the horns of his ruddy crest') + the spear, which is also famously not his, but a spoil of Actor Auruncus (12.92–100).[20] Aeneas, on the other hand, is in a divinely sanctioned union with his armour, safely embraced by the arms (weapons) of his mother (12.107 *maternis saeuus in armis*), with the fierceness/cruelty of his character (*saeuus*) anticipating the punitive anger of 'father' Jupiter (12.843 *genitor*) as the 'fierce/cruel king' of

12.849 (*saeui . . . regis*). Turnus craves for a fusion with the Vulcanic weapons, as 'sparks flash from the whole of his face in his fieriness' (12.101–102 *totoque ardentis ab ore/ scintillae absistunt*) – *scintillae* of the kind that appear, in Lucilius' words, 'around lumps of metal when the iron is growing hot',[21] and, when thinking of metals, suggest an image of melting, of inorganic transformation. And yet the transformation that Virgil presents us with here is instead a becoming-animal, as he goes on to compare Turnus with the defeated bull of the *Georgics*, preparing for a fight over the conquest of his beloved (12.103–106, cf. *G.* 3.232–234).[22] While Turnus the bull sharpens his horns against a trunk (12.105 *arboris obnixus trunco*) and wastes his energy in the futile attempt to lash the thin air with blows (12.105–106 *uentosque lacessit ictibus*), Aeneas the divine warrior – himself becoming the other bull who is a rival to Turnus (as at 12.715–722) – coolly 'sharpens his Mars' (12.108 *Aeneas acuit Martem*), bringing to life the metonymy of *arma* for war with which the poem opens (1.1 *arma uirumque*) and smudging the boundaries between animal, human, god and technological weaponry.

Wounding

Turnus' attempts at heating up like the sword that Vulcan made for his father are frustrated when the unfaithful blade shatters like ice in all its mortal 'futility'. In a sense, Turnus appears now as a frustrated cyborg, his pre-cybernetic hybrid revealing 'the spectre of the ghost' that was always within itself, exposing in its brutally concrete metaphor how his desire to be one with his sword was nothing more than 'a caricature of [his] masculinist reproductive dream'.[23] And reproduction, as the right to survive in the world, is indeed what's at stake in this fight. The ice simile anticipates the rigour of death that will accompany childless Turnus to his grave, from the moment that fear makes his blood congeal in his veins (12.905 *gelidus concreuit frigore sanguis*) up to the final 'dissolution' of his limbs in the chill of death (12.951 *soluuntur frigore membra*) – a phrase that many have read for its underlying humanity, as it is repeated *verbatim* from the first appearance of Aeneas in the poem (1.92), when he faced death by water on the Libyan coast.[24] Yet the repetition also emphasizes the opposite process faced by Aeneas and Turnus in the course of the poem: the Trojan can only recompose his limbs, his self and his people at the expense of the Rutulian's dissolution. And since it is only by forging links with the Italians and their lands that Aeneas can reassemble that shattered self of *Aeneid* 1, these images of dissolution and connection are also accompanied by parallel metaphors of penetration, wounding and eradication.

Turnus' masculinist dream of reproduction, despite its subsequent frustration, coexists with another fractured and culturally constructed identity as a 'feminized', penetrable and penetrated body – this is in turn moulded by the interaction with the similarly patriarchal, but additionally colonizing, body of cyborg Aeneas and his weapons. While Turnus strives to achieve 'masculine' wholeness with his sword in the narrative, we know since the simile of the Punic lion (12.4–9) that he belongs instead to the realm of wounded animals, a role that he shares most obviously with wounded Dido (eventually killed, just like Turnus, by the sword of Aeneas),[25] especially when they both become prey, a stag and a deer respectively, in Aeneas' hunt (12.749–757, 4.69–73). But there also seems to be an uncanny relationship between Turnus and Lavinia in the book's second simile. Turnus' *uulnus* is evoked in the connotations of 'wounding' and 'violation' elicited by the verb *uiolare* to describe the staining of ivory with blood-red (Punic) purple for the blush on Lavinia's cheeks (12.67–68 *Indum sanguineo ueluti uiolauerit ostro/ si quis ebur* 'as if someone had stained Indian ivory with blood-red purple dye').[26] Moreover, the simile is modelled on the wounding of Menelaus at *Il.* 4.141–147, the hero to whom Turnus does not hesitate to compare himself, as he refers to Aeneas as a second Paris (12.99–100).[27] The line immediately following the simile (12.70 *illum turbat amor figitque in uirgine uultus,* 'love throws him into turmoil, and he fixes his gaze on the face of the maiden') is redolent of this ambiguity, as the change of subject between the two halves of the verse is so abrupt that it allows us at first to take *amor/Amor*, the god who 'pierces' with his arrows, as the subject of *figit*. This is the same powerful god of love, and brother of Aeneas, who was 'sitting on' and at the same time 'fixing inside' or 'settling in' poor Dido (1.719 *insidat quantus miserae deus*). This telling slippage in the subject of *figit*, which follows Turnus' encounter with Lavinia and precedes his arming against Aeneas, brilliantly epitomizes the slippage in his generic identity from one interaction to the next.

However, neither Turnus nor Lavinia ends up playing Menelaus. In the same role reversal that has often been noted in Turnus' transformation from Achilles into Hector in the last books of the epic,[28] the Greek role in this fight is reserved for Aeneas, whose wounding and miraculous healing at 12.383–440 is modelled on Machaon's healing of Menelaus at *Il.* 4.210–219. The broken point of the arrow that is stuck in Aeneas' thigh (12.387 *infracta . . . harundine*) fits the identification between Aeneas and his 'second-self' Turnus who at the end of the book will be pierced in his thigh (12.926, cf. the simile at 12.7–8) by the spear of Aeneas, an identification that many have noticed running throughout the poem's second half.[29] And yet, as in the arming scene, the effects of the wounding betray a fundamental difference. With the goddess of love at his side, Aeneas' wound is miraculously healed and his pierced body restored as whole: 'the point of the arrow follows the hand [of Iapyx] without anyone to force it, and then falls outside, as new strengths are restored to their former state' (423–424 *iamque secuta manum nullo cogente sagitta/ excidit, atque nouae rediere in pristina uires*), giving the impression that Aeneas' flesh recomposes and reassembles before our very eyes. The reconnection of Aeneas' bodily tissues is also matched by a renewed strengthening of the ties with his family and community, since the wounding episode, with its reminder of Aeneas' vulnerability, provides the hero with the opportunity to address his son Ascanius for the first and only time in the *Aeneid*. This is a brief speech on the importance of memory and family links, and an injunction to follow the examples of father Aeneas and uncle Hector alike (12.435–440). In the *Aeneid*, Venus is the goddess of disconnection and connection: especially in the second half of the poem, which opens by invoking Erato, Muse of love and erotic poetry (7.37),[30] Venus embodies not just love, but the disconnecting Empedoclean strife (*Eris*) that is necessary for love (*Eros*) to reunite elements in ever-changing ways.[31] Thus, in the cases of Dido and Turnus, both embodiments of the animals in love in *Georgics* 3,[32] she urges the dissolution of their cities and communities, while as *Venus Julia* and as *genetrix* of Rome she simultaneously helps Aeneas' cause of connection, allowing him to join his ancestors on the two sides of the Mediterranean. And, just like Venus, vulnerability in *Aeneid* 12 also applies a double standard: while it disconnects Turnus from his own self, it provides Aeneas with new strengths in order to bolster his connection to his people.

Virgil's ideological chimera

We have seen how a cyborg reading of Turnus allows him to embody conflicting identities, reconfigured by the process of becoming-the-other in the course of the confrontation with

Aeneas the invader. While the great absent character in the narrative of Book 12 is undoubtedly Lavinia, the same reconfiguration of 'feminized' Turnus also encompasses the Italian territory, as Aeneas completes his 'colonizing' mission aided by both divine and anachronistic 'machinery'.[33]

By the time we reach the end of the poem, the supposedly 'unaware shepherd' (4.71–72 *pastor . . . nescius*) who infiltrated Dido's bee-hive city (1.430–436) from within is now rather purposefully smoking out the Latins from their city walls just as a *pastor* smokes out bees from their hive (12.587–592).[34] The same violence inherent in the Trojans' forced removal of the old stands out starkly in the episode of the wild olive tree at 12.766–783.[35] This is a 'stock' (*stirps*, a live arboreal metaphor for genealogical stems both in Latin and in English) sacred to Faunus, an autochthonous Italic deity (12.766), that the 'Teucrians had removed with no consideration for its sacredness, so that they could fight/assemble (*concurrere*) on a pure and unobstructed (*purus*) plain': 12.770–771 *sed stirpem Teucri nullo discrimine sacrum/ sustulerant, puro ut possent concurrere campo*. It is deep in the roots of this Italic tree that the spear of Aeneas is stuck after missing its target (Turnus), just as the spear of the hunter was stuck into Turnus the lion at the start of the book. The lion's hunter, that many a reader has aligned with Aeneas, was said to be a 'thief' (12.7 *latro*);[36] similarly, the designation of the Trojans as *Teucri* (descendants from Teucer of Crete) undermines Aeneas' claim to the land. Indeed, we need a cue to Aeneas' descent from Italian Dardanus (12.775 *Dardanides*) before Venus can intervene and tear out the spear from the depth of the wild olive's roots (12.787 *telum . . . alta ab radice reuellit*).

The wild olive's severing from its roots is a powerful anticipation of the imminent eradication of Turnus, and it prepares readers for the hero's separation from his land and the disintegration of his body and soul (12.950 *soluuntur . . . membra*, 951 *uita . . . fugit*). Previously, Turnus had been compared to another natural element, a boulder rushing headlong, torn away by a blast from its mountain top (12.684–685 *ac ueluti montis saxum de uertice praeceps/ cum ruit auulsum uento*). The modelling of the simile on the Homeric simile of Hector leading the attack on the Greek ships like a large rock rolling down from a cliff (*Il.* 13.137 ὀλοοίτροχος ὣς ἀπὸ πέτρης) contributes to the general picture of Turnus as doomed hero. But Virgil further highlights the rock's disconnection from its mountain (*auulsum*), drawing attention to how such 'loosening' was caused by 'old age' (12.686 *aut annis soluit sublapsa uetustas*).[37] The image of Turnus the rock, the hero of old, rolling away from his land, is evoked again by contrast in the subsequent simile of 'father Aeneas' (12.697 *pater Aeneas*) standing tall and vast like three mountains, the climax being 'father Appenninus' who, contrary to downward-rushing Turnus, 'gladly raises its snowy peak high in the sky' (12.702–703 *gaudetque niuali/ uertice se attollens pater Appenninus ad auras*). The comparison to the three mountains (Athos, Eryx, Appenninus: 12.701–703) maps onto Aeneas' journey westward and also 'trumps Turnus' likeness to a part of a mountain',[38] indicating the incoming success of Aeneas' claim to the land. While both the wild olive tree and Turnus the boulder are eradicated from Italia, both here and in the following simile of Aeneas chasing Turnus like a hound chases a stag (12.749–757), the specification that the dog is Umbrian (12.753 *uiuidus Vmber*) highlights Aeneas' Italianization as he becomes not just an animal, but 'the landscape's new vital force',[39] helped and sustained by the roaring thunder of Jupiter (12.757 *caelum tonat omne tumultu*). Mention of the sky both in the Appenninus and in the hound similes shows that Aeneas embodies the totality of nature and never disowns his role as associate, and even double, of Jupiter, a role that he assumed earlier in the book (12.451–458) when he became the 'storm cloud' (12.451 *nimbus*) that brings ruin to the trees, havoc to the crops, and devastation of the land (12.453–454 *ruinas/ arboribus stragemque satis, ruet omnia late*), causing the same 'violent rain' that washes away Turnus the boulder (12.685–686 *seu turbidus imber/ proluit*).

Aeneas' identification with Jupiter's thunderstorm continues to accompany the hero in the second half of the book through the verbs used to describe his actions in relation to his weapons: Aeneas 'blasts with lightning' and 'thunders horribly with his arms' (12.654 *fulminat Aeneas armis*; 700 *horrendumque intonat armis*), actions that indicate that Jupiter is indeed 'at his side' (12.565 *Iuppiter hac stat*).[40] This identification reaches a climax in the final confrontation between the two heroes, when Virgil makes it explicit that Aeneas' connection to technological progress inevitably accompanies the presentation of Turnus as a failed disconnected hero of old both in the form of a pre-Homeric hero and in his failure to blend effectively with his arms.[41] In the last simile of the entire poem, Aeneas hurls his spear with a roar louder than stones shot from a ballista, and with greater crashings than those burst from a thunderbolt (12.921–923 *murali concita numquam/ tormento sic saxa fremunt nec fulmine tanti/ dissultant crepitus*). The spear 'flies like a black whirlwind' (12.923 *uolat atri turbinis instar*)[42] before laying open the edges of Turnus' corslet (12.924–925 *oras . . . recludit/ loricae*) and finally piercing his thigh with a hiss (12.926 *stridens transit femur*). As Mader convincingly argues, the anachronism of the ballista (*tormentum murale*) must be read in conjunction with Turnus' failed attempt to raise and throw at Aeneas an 'ancient and huge stone that happened to lie on the plain' (12.897 *saxum antiquum ingens, campo quod forte iacebat*). The ancient nature of the stone sets Turnus' (failed) feat as an 'archetypical heroic gesture',[43] 'pre-"modern"' 'pre-mechanical', that is no match for the '"modern" mechanized warfare' of the ballista simile, which instead 'looks to the future and makes Aeneas instrumental in inaugurating the new world order'.[44] For Mader, the 'deafening roar of the machine . . . [is] the sound of human progress'.[45]

The stone that Turnus tries to hurl was a 'boundary mark, set on the plain to keep dispute from the fields' (12.897 *limes agro positus litem ut discerneret aruis*). Mader interprets this in line with Turnus' quasi-primitive behaviour: his action betrays no cognizance of the stone's role as an 'emblem of orderly human existence' and appears to be 'the anarchic gesture of a man who has no stake in maintaining the civilized order it stands for'.[46] But a contrast also emerges between the Italian use of the stone to preemptively demarcate the boundaries of a land at peace, and its new violent use in Aeneas' metaphorical ballista. This is an addition to other anachronistic siege-devices used by the Trojans against Laurentum: the *testudo* (12.574–575), the ladders seemingly appearing out of nowhere (12.576 *scalae improuiso [sc. apparuerunt]*), the battering ram (12.706). Turnus, too, had raised a *turris ambulatoria*, assembling jointed beams (12.674 *turrim compactis trabibus quam eduxerat ipse*).[47] But if Turnus' tower was simultaneously an attempt at technological advancement and at reaching the height of Jupiter's sky, this is frustrated by a whirl of fire, waving towards heaven as it encompasses, and destroys, his creation (12.673 *ad caelum undabat uertex turrimque tenebat*). The frustrated attempt of Turnus' tower to reach the sky anticipates his frustrated attempt to escape to, or top, heaven, mocked by Aeneas at 12.892–893 *opta ardua pennis/ astra sequi* ('reach the lofty stars with your wings, if you like'). Here, Aeneas' scorn is amplified by the echoing of Apollo's words to Iulius in 9.641 (*sic itur ad astra*), the pun with Turnus' town Ardea in *ardua . . . astra*, and the allusion to the legend of Turnus' transformation into a Heron (Ov. *Met.* 14.580).[48] While Turnus may fail both in his attempts at technological development and in establishing effective relationships with the gods, he is nevertheless offered a way to reconnect to that natural world of his own country from which he had appeared more and more estranged in the course of the book. He also embodies in this scene a way out of the totality of Aeneas' Romanization of the landscape that Ovid does not fail to pick up.[49] Indeed, the last we hear from the nature of the land is a sympathetic cry in unison with the Rutulians, as the whole mountain and its deep woods re-echo their cries (12.928–929 *consurgunt gemitu Rutuli totusque remugit/ mons circum et uocem late nemora alta remittunt*). Once the homogeneous unity of the Roman race has been decreed in the encounter between Jupiter and Juno, this may sound like a feeble echoing of the human (patrilineal, patriarchal) 'language of the fathers' that the Ausonians were allowed to keep, together with their costumes (12.834 *sermonem Ausonii patrium moresque tenebunt*).[50] But the verb used for the sounds emitted by the landscape is also a bellowing back to the Rutulians (*remugit*), evoking for the very last time Turnus as the defeated bull, perhaps a tragic emblem of the (Bacchic) irrational and animalistic drives that have led him to his conclusion,[51] and more certainly a symbol of the allied Italian coalition that attempted resistance to Rome's hegemony over Italia – 'land of the calf (ἰταλός, *uitulus*)' – in the Social War of 91 BCE to 87 BCE.[52]

So far it would appear that the traditional dichotomy between doomed Turnus and conquering Aeneas continues to be at work in the characters' interactions with the mechanical, natural and supernatural worlds. This is partly true, but the co-dependence between the two that a cyborg reading implies, and that doubles the mingling between Ausonians and Teucrians as decreed by Jupiter, forces us to smudge the differences and reflect upon how they are constituted. For what is at stake in reading Turnus as a cyborg in interaction with the fate of his land and in his transformation into the 'other' (the 'colonized', the 'enemy', the 'woman', the 'vulnerable', the 'weak') is the dialectic put into practice but the very discourse that has transformed him into all these fractured selves that he embodies. This discourse, embodied simultaneously by cyborg-Aeneas, is in its turn a cyborg, a reconfiguring 'chimera', theorized and fabricated, organic and inorganic, acting as pivot and subject of the cultural and political networks of this poem and its foundational ideologies.

From this point of view, it makes sense that the end of the poem provides us with a picture of Aeneas-becoming-wounded-Turnus as he is himself wounded, both emotionally and in his sight,[53] by the image of Pallas' baldric and its belt's 'flashing' studs (12.941–943 *apparuit ... balteus et notis fulserunt cingula bullis/ Pallantis pueri*). If what pushes Aeneas to react to this view is his obligation to Evander to avenge Pallas, it is telling that these are also fractured inorganic pieces of a hero who stood symbolically for patrilineality, now badly stitched onto the assemblage of another warrior who has been so far both feminized and denied a future offspring, despite his attempt to appeal to Aeneas precisely by evoking his father Daunus side by side with Anchises (12.932–934). Surely it is the emotional wound caused by the recollection of this loss that, much like Achilles' pain for Patroclus in Berzins McCoy's reading,[54] propels that political resolution of the ending as the composition and formation of the *gens Romana*. This loss also doubles the loss of the Trojans' identity, of their name and their language, in that very formation. But when Aeneas penetrates Turnus' chest with the sword as he is penetrated in his eyes by the baldric, when he 'buries' (12.950 *condit*) his steel in his 'second self's' flesh while repeating – anticipating the same act of 'founding' a city (*condere*) that necessitates Romulus' fratricide of his own 'second self' Remus – when he, in fact, fuses the very act of founding cultural identity and society with that of joining inorganic and organic,[55] we readers are left with an uncanny feeling. For in denying to us those traditional dichotomies male–

female, colonizer–colonized, Eastern–Western that the wedding between Aeneas (male, colonizer, Trojan) and Lavinia (female, colonized, Italian) would have reconfirmed, the dissolution of differences ingrained within the end of the *Aeneid* leaves us with an unsettling cultural, political and ideological chimera. This is the all-encompassing discourse of this brand-new empire with no genesis and no end that allows the *Aeneid*'s pluralization of voices and politico-ideological stances – a discourse that is able to incorporate, as in a cyborg world, 'permanently partial identities and contradictory standpoints'[56] and which has no need to reproduce biologically, because it can replicate itself mechanically.[57] Every bit of the *Aeneid* can partake productively in it when it is viewed 'cyborgically' as a necessarily partial fragment dialoguing within its ever-evolving network. But it is the process itself of writing the *Aeneid*, of setting up and exposing the network, that provides a way out of the otherwise totalizing compliance to that discourse. As Donna Haraway puts it, '"Networking" is both a feminist practice and a multinational corporate strategy – weaving is for oppositional cyborgs.'[58]

CHAPTER 25
THE PRESENCE OF PRESENTS: SPEAKING OBJECTS IN MARTIAL'S *XENIA* AND *APOPHORETA*

Katherine Wasdin

What does it mean for an object to speak? What can an object tell us? Theoretical developments in the study of things and objects prompt us to scrutinize the ancient trope of the speaking object as an expression of the entanglement of material things and society.[1] Speaking objects play a central role in two collections of poems by the Roman epigrammatist Martial.[2] These playful works are poetic gift tags, couplets meant to accompany presents during the Roman holiday of the Saturnalia.[3] Book 13, the *Xenia*, offers primarily foodstuffs, whereas book 14, the *Apophoreta*, lists a wider variety of presents, from expensive luxury goods to cheap trinkets. Martial's varied presentation of them includes riddles, insults and instructions for use, often enhanced by literary allusions.[4] This chapter explores the many objects that seem to speak for themselves, anthropomorphized by the poet as possessing will and agency.[5] These speaking presents discuss their names, origins, uses and relationships with humans, acting as both givers and gifts in forming bonds with their new owners. In doing so, they illustrate the capacities of objects in the Roman imagination.

By paying attention to which types of objects Martial gives voice to, as well as what these objects have to say, I demonstrate how the poet conceived of what Ian Hodder calls the 'entanglement' of objects and humans.[6] Hodder argues that humans and things depend on each other. As part of that dependency, things both enable and constrain human actions and are primarily understood through their role in society, not as artifacts with their own histories separate from humanity. Martial's objects continually frame their identity through relationships with humans and vocalize the mechanisms of the interdependency between people and things.[7] The poet's turn towards objects reveals the abilities and limitations they provide in Roman society, seen through a playful comedic lens. As we will see, not all objects talk, and not all objects say the same thing. Although Martial is an author of clever epigrams, not theoretical treatises, he still provides useful information about the perception of object identity in the Roman world and those interested in ancient objects naturally turn to his work.

I am not the first to notice Martial's radical focus on presents as discrete objects with the ability to speak. Farouk Grewing (1999) rigorously explores the various types of speaking presents, arguing that such curiously active objects are part of the poems' Saturnalian and carnivalesque atmosphere. More recently, Sarah Blake and Sarah Culpepper Stroup have applied theories of gifts-giving and objects to his Saturnalian corpus.[8] This chapter builds on the work of such scholars to explore the subject-identity of these objects and to delineate how the poet presents them as establishing mutually satisfying and interdependent relationships with their recipients. First, I examine their literary background in archaic and Hellenistic Greek epigram. Martial draws on a rich history of speaking objects, but diverges from earlier examples in his extreme focus on things themselves rather than interpersonal relationships. I then analyse which objects are chosen to speak and what they say, showing how Martial illuminates the boundaries of the epigrammatic speaking object. Martial's gifts repeatedly address their social interactions and values and continually reaffirm their place in the interconnected world of traditional Roman society, commanding certain behaviours and ways of being from their recipients. These two books imply that Saturnalian society can be constituted by the objects found in it, not just the humans celebrating the festival.[9]

Earlier voices

In giving a voice to inanimate things, Martial draws on the tradition of speaking objects in Greek inscriptions and epigrams. Most of these objects assert bonds with specific individuals by being either inscribed with the name of their owner or labelled as religious dedications.[10] Dedicated objects embody the relationship between dedicator and deity, and even fictional epigrams carefully provide proper names.[11] In their simplest format, epigrams on dedicatory objects proclaim that 'X made me' or 'X dedicated me'.[12] In these cases, the first-person speaking object is the grammatical object of the verb, distributing actual agency to human subjects.[13] Martial's presents, on the other hand, appear primarily as speaking subjects, rather than as created objects. As noted by Blake, they more closely resemble objects inscribed with their owners' names, or literary versions of such items.[14] A famous cup found in an eighth-century BCE grave in Ischia boasts 'I am the cup of Nestor, good to drink from. Whoever drinks from this cup, immediately longing for Aphrodite of the beautiful crown will seize him.'[15] Although the cup predates Martial by centuries, the inscription employs the same format as his epigrams, with an introductory statement or title followed by a couplet.[16] For example, cheese proclaims its identity and virtues:

> 33 Casei Trebulani
>
> Trebula nos genuit; commendat gratia duplex,
> sive levi flamma sive domamur aqua.
>
> 33. Trebula cheeses
>
> Trebula gave us birth. A double attraction commends us, whether we are lightly toasted or soaked in water.[17]

Unlike the inscription on the Nestor cup, however, Martial's poems have been unmoored from the actual things themselves. His couplets are supposedly intended to be repurposed as gift tags attached to concrete presents, but the verses themselves appear first in his book, not as inscriptions on objects.

Who gets to speak and why

Despite their existence in a book of poetry, these objects are notionally embedded in human social networks as putative gifts from one Roman to another.[18] As such, they would reflect the giver's wealth and the recipient's relative status to become a concrete marker of the relationship between them. Surprisingly few of the speaking poems (13.103 and 14.153) explicitly acknowledge the class relationships behind the choice of presents, and their function as gifts is subordinated.[19] The identities of givers and recipients are unspecified, since the collections' premise is that any reader could select the appropriate tag for use on a present to any recipient. The gifts themselves are given names but are generic, albeit not as generic as the much more shadowy human participants.[20] In this, the collection is the opposite of an actual gift relationship predicated on the unique identities of the parties involved. Speaking gifts in other epigrams focus on specific exchanges, like the lamp given by Antipater to Piso (*AP* 6.249).[21] Instead, the *Xenia* and *Apophoreta* create a lively world of objects that attest to their own capacities to facilitate a specifically Saturnalian existence of feasting, gambling, cozy attire and cultivated entertainment. In the absence of a specific giver, the gifts create their own relationships with the recipients as if they had bestowed themselves.[22]

Not all gifts are given the power to speak about themselves. Martial's speaking objects are part of well-organized sequences of epigrams. The food in the *Xenia* appears as if it were the courses in a typical Roman banquet, beginning with appetizers and ending with wine and seasonings. The *Apophoreta*, on the other hand, is arranged according to types of presents, such as clothing or gaming paraphernalia, and the majority are presented in pairs of one expensive and one inexpensive version of similar items.[23] The presents themselves gradually increase in cost, culminating in lavish gifts of enslaved people.[24] In addition to these general patterns, which lend the books coherency and a sense of development, close inspection shows that there are several clusters of speaking objects. Which objects are chosen to speak, and how they are put in dialogue with each other and with the gift-giver and recipient, tells us about how Martial understands the potential agency of objects and which categories lend themselves towards anthropomorphism.

As embodiments of humans or gods, statues and paintings are often addressed by the narrator in the second person or apt to engage in quoted speech or dialog with an interlocutor, suggesting a heightened sense of presence and subjectivity.[25] Such direct addresses to objects are less common than speaking objects.[26] They imply a more vibrant inner life, since they infer not just an inscribed present, but one able to offer different responses to specific inquiries, as in the case of a silver statue of Minerva:

> 179 Minerva argentea
>
> Dic mihi, virgo ferox, cum sit tibi cassis et hasta,
> quare non habeas aegida. 'Caesar habet.'
>
> 179. Minerva in silver
>
> Tell me, fierce virgin, since you have helm and spear, why you don't have the aegis. 'Caesar has it.'

The inability of most inscribed objects to respond to questioning is not unknown in the ancient world. One Greek inscription (*CEG* 286) even jokes about this limitation: 'I answer the same to all men who ask who among men dedicated me: Antiphanes, as a tithe.'[27] Yet visual representations of humans or deities appear closer to interactive subjectivity than the other objects, able to engage with the speaker more directly.[28]

Some objects respond not to people but to each other. In the *Apophoreta*, paired luxury and bargain presents frequently interact. The lanterns made out of horn and bladder debate their exchange and use values:

61. Lanterna cornea

Dux lanterna viae clusis feror aurea flammis,
  et tuta est gremio parva lucerna meo.

61. Horn lantern

A golden lantern, guide of your way, I am carried with my flame enclosed, and a small lamp is safe in my bosom.

62. Lanterna de vesica

Cornea si non sum, numquid sum fuscior? aut me
  vesicam, contra qui venit, esse putat?

62. Lantern made of bladder

If I am not made of horn, am I any the dimmer? Or does he who meets me think I am bladder?

The first lantern boasts of its ability to protect the flame and guide its owner. Notably, it expresses its competence with amusing anthropomorphic terminology (*gremio*).[29] The second lantern responds defensively to its predecessor and claims an equal ability, despite its less elaborate material.[30] It, too, is part of a body, here a literal bladder (*vesica*) instead of a figurative lap or bosom (*gremium*). In these two poems, the presents and their addressed recipients form a community concerned with use, value, and physical properties.[31] While the *Xenia* lacks the organizing principle of expensive and cheap gifts, it does contain discrete clusters of speaking objects based on similar vocabulary or related arguments.[32] According to Martial, things interact with each other.[33] The frequency of the technique and Martial's use of clusters show that it was an important and carefully planned part of the composition of these books.

Furthermore, the imagined communicative abilities of gifts illuminate ancient anxieties about agency and social identity. Many speaking objects have logical connections to language, like speaking birds or writing materials.[34] Several are from the natural world, including plants destined for consumption and animals, some no longer living. Manufactured products also speak, especially gifts that have an intimate relationship with the human body such as food, clothing and personal care items. These can work together with their owners to augment their physical capacities. As noted by Blake, many gifts in the *Xenia* and *Apophoreta*, including some of the speaking objects, take on the role of slaves concerned with the body of the master.[35] These objects happily present themselves as servile helpers, like the candle that promises to be a female slave (*ancilla*.14.40).

Gifts that are either too far from or too similar to the identity of the Roman citizen male are denied the capacity to speak. For example, the first section of the *Xenia* (13.1–21), devoted to basic grains, has no speaking objects and is the largest group of poems that do not speak in the two books of presents. Perhaps beans seemed too humble to merit their own voice, as opposed to the more sumptuous or vibrant fruits that follow. While several speaking objects promise to care for the recipient as if they were slaves, actual enslaved humans never speak. Martial lists several different types of enslaved people as gifts in the *Aphophoreta*'s final section. These epigrams utilize other typical formats, such as riddles, preferences and instructions for use, but the slaves themselves are silent.[36] They are thus deprived of the voice unnaturally given to objects.[37] Their silence is particularly shocking given the poems' Saturnalian context, since a hallmark of the festival was that slaves were said to have unusually free speech while it lasted.[38] In Martial's poems, however, that liberty is denied to enslaved gifts, who are more fully objectified than the objects themselves.[39] Their voices would not be humorous or engaging to the reader, but might threaten their sense of ownership and control. Apparently, Martial finds it funny when a lantern talks, but not when a slave does.

Entangled voices

What objects say defines their relationship with their new recipients and suggests their capacities to enable and coerce appropriate behaviour. These material subjects demonstrate their birth, nomenclature, use, value and potential to help or harm their owners. In doing so, they construct the material basis for a society on holiday, while reinforcing traditional norms of body and self. As noted above, the relationship between human giver and recipient is continually replaced by the relationship between the self-offering gift and its recipient. Strikingly, even most of the animals given as food in the *Xenia* do not want to avoid being consumed, as we might expect.[40] These objects view themselves as inherently embedded in society and eager to become even more closely entangled with human bodies. Even threats, like those of the flamingo tongue in 13.71, do not seriously challenge their new owners, but serve to convey common ideas of functionality and ethics.

The most basic level of awareness can be found in objects that assert their identity and origin, carefully preserving their own names instead of those of their creators or purveyors. As opposed to the speaking objects of Greek epigram, which often refer to a specific human fabricator, Martial's gifts mostly appear to have been naturally created or born.[41] Sometimes, this is logical, as in the case of plants or animals, but in other poems these genetic claims elide human activities. The objects' self-conception as being children of specific parents adds an extra level of anthropomorphism to their ability to speak. Several such poems parody epic genealogies, like the sausage 'daughter' of a pig (13.35), the fish sauce 'daughter' of the tunnyfish (13.103), the maple table 'daughter' of a forest (14.90) or the quilt made of 'sisters' of cloth (14.148). Despite being the products of human manufacture, they present themselves as part of the natural ecosystem of the Roman world.

Many speaking objects are deeply concerned with their own names, illustrating the close relationship these poems have with riddles.[42] The obsession with names may also stem from their prominent placement in the lemmata for each poem. While the reader must imagine the objects (unless the poems are used as actual gift tags), the titles are literally present, concrete stand-ins for the objects themselves.[43] Nomenclatural disputes reveal contradictions in the origins or uses of the objects, as seen in two nearby poems on containers:

99 Bascauda

Barbara de pictis veni bascauda Britannis,
  sed me iam mavult dicere Roma suam.

99. Basket

I have come, a barbarian basket, from the painted Britons, but Rome now prefers to call me hers.

101 Boletaria

Cum mihi boleti dederint tam nobile nomen,
  prototomis – pudet heu! – servio coliculis.

101. Mushroom pots

Although mushrooms gave me so noble a name, I cater (I am deeply ashamed to say) to early sprouts.

The first epigram points to the basket's foreign name, borrowed from the language spoken by ancient Britons. It keeps its name, but, like the territory, is claimed by Rome in an imperial gesture, seemingly embraced by the basket itself.[44] The mushroom pot, on the other hand, quibbles with the difference between its name and its function.[45] Although the vessel gets its name from mushrooms, a luxury product, it is used for a less costly comestible. Its humorous complaint points to a divergence between name and use and leads the reader to question the connection between words and things and the dubious ability of a name to represent both the origin and the function of objects.

Like the debased mushroom pot and the indignant lantern, speaking epigrams make claims about their own worth. Several objects note a discrepancy between their monetary value and use value.[46] For example, in response to the boast of a luxury wine strainer (14.103), a linen strainer observes that it is just as useful as its metal counterpart:

104 Saccus nivarius

Attenuare nives norunt et lintea nostra:
  frigidior colo non salit unda tuo.

104. Bag for straining through snow

My linen also knows how to reduce snow: no colder spurts the water from your strainer.

Use of the object is more rewarding than its monetary value might suggest, and self-valuing objects claim greater worth than the market affords them.[47] The use of a speaking voice increases sympathy in the readers, since understanding the gifts as voiced and conscious beings makes them seem more worthy of consideration.[48] The conceit also flatters the less important recipients of such trivial gifts or those unlucky enough to draw them in a lottery. These objects seem to be aware both of their purpose and their reputation, and appear primarily concerned to establish their usefulness in society. Like the objects that query the appropriateness of their name, these poems play with various human frames for understanding objects and attempt to discern which would be most appropriate for the Saturnalian context.

Another central purpose of speaking objects is to instruct the recipient about how they should be used, often in ways that encode specific behaviours and physical bodies. Martial articulates how objects entangle human agency with materiality, and how objects shape society.[49] This is especially true for objects closely connected with the human body, such as clothing or food. For example, the gift in 13.26 has the capacity to modify the body in ways perhaps inappropriate for a citizen male:

26 Sorba

Sorba sumus, molles nimium tendentia ventres:
  aptius haec puero quam tibi poma dabis.

26. Service berries[50]

We are service berries, tautening too loose bellies. You will do better to give this fruit to your boy than to yourself.

The berries prevent elimination, and would be more suitable, they claim, for the passive partner of anal intercourse. This gift thus reinforces Roman standards of masculinity in a joking fashion.[51] The overt policing is not done by the gift-giver, but literally performed by the very object, seen as a potential agent within its recipient's body.[52]

Similarly, in the section of the *Apophoreta* on exercise equipment, the items themselves carefully prescribe who should and should not use them. Two balls delineate acceptable owners. The triangle ball (*pila trigonalis*, 14.46) demands skilled owners, while the inflated ball (*follis*, 14.47) proclaims that since it is suitable only for the very young and the very old, those in their prime should leave it alone. These balls foresee entering into a relationship with their owners but expect to have appropriate new masters, conveying the standards of Roman exercise culture. Two articles of intimate clothing do the same for women and enforce idealized body sizes by warning their potential recipients not to gain too much weight. A woman's wrap (14.149) dislikes busty women and a girdle (14.151) points out that it would not fit a pregnant woman. These objects promote certain types of behaviours, combining with human bodies to enable specific physical appearances or activities.[53] The objects depend on humans, since certain human bodies and behaviours are required for them to fulfil their purposes. As a result, they appear to coerce the reader into following expected customs.[54]

Presents can do more than just prescribe their preferred conditions for use. While the service berries only suggest some potential drawbacks to their consumption, another gift goes so far as to threaten the recipient:

71 Phoenicopteri

Dat mihi pinna rubens nomen, sed lingua gulosis
  nostra sapit. quid si garrula lingua foret?

71. Flamingoes

My ruddy wing gives me a name, but my tongue is a treat to epicures. What if my tongue were to tell tales?

The flamingo tongue is both speaking instrument and edible object, a potential meal for a gourmand. By referring to its *pinna rubens* (ruddy wing), it glosses its Latin name, *phoenicopterus*, derived from the Greek for 'reddish wing'.[55] After explaining its origin and culinary use, the flamingo threatens that its tongue, once eaten, might share intimate knowledge about the consumer and his mouth. The mingled physical interaction between food and eater could not only delight the epicure: it might also reveal illicit sexual activities, such as oral sex, considered demeaning to Roman men.[56] The flamingo thus encodes traditional social values in its relationship between gift and recipient.[57] Other objects insult or threaten the recipient with malfunctioning, like a bookcase (14.37) which warns that it should be carefully packed lest vermin attack the books. Such bossy presents drive home their embeddedness in human society and demonstrate Martial's conception of the close entanglement of objects and humans.[58]

Conclusion

In the *Xenia* and *Apophoreta*, Martial creates a vibrant world of objects. The primary reason these objects speak, of course, is to entertain and delight readers, not because Martial truly believes that objects can talk. Accordingly, the poet's allocation of speaking parts to different objects indicates varying conceptions of agency: artworks have a greater range of expression, while slaves are denied the ability to speak. By giving these objects voice, Martial allows them to tell us about their origins and functions. The *Xenia* and *Apophoreta* formally propose an interchangeability between the poems, their lemmata, and the various gifts they represent, including objects, animals, and people.[59] This equalizing strategy is in constant tension with the noisy voices of the objects themselves, which boast, mock, threaten and cajole their owners. For the Saturnalian poet, the relationship between people and objects is as important as interpersonal relationships in creating the Roman festival.

My reading of Martial's poems draws on new interpretive trends that put the spotlight on objects and their entanglement with humans in Roman society. Martial presages our conceptions of objects as conveying specific messages and desires and exerting secondary agency in human life.[60] His Saturnalian gifts accomplish this by focusing on the generic relationship between objects and people. They communicate with a different purpose than speaking presents in earlier poetry, which vocalize the human relationships they facilitate. Instead, unmoored from specific human interactions, Martial's presents give themselves to their recipients and form their own bonds with them and with other objects. While they present themselves as naturally born, they depend on people for their names and significance. In their humorous couplets, objects become companions and encourage their owners to follow traditional norms of conduct. In this way, they are mutually dependent on each other. Martial's reframing of these objects as primarily useful presents downplays their possible role as exchangeable commodities to focus on their ability to shape human life through use and consumption.[61]

CHAPTER 26
AUTOMATOPOETAE MACHINAE: LAWS OF NATURE AND HUMAN INVENTION (VITRUVIUS 9.8.4–7)

Mireille Courrént

In the ten books that make up the treatise written by Vitruvius from 30 BCE to 20 BCE, architecture is successively composed of three parts: buildings and water-supply (books 1–8), dialling (book 9) and machinery (book 10), and deals with various hoisting systems, but also different machines used during sieges. More than just a builder, Vitruvius was in fact a mechanician, who devoted a large part of his professional career to the machines in Julius Caesar's army. It is thus on the basis of mechanics and its principles that he sets out the entire system of architecture.

Book 9 details various ways to measure time. Contrary to the construction of shelters and houses, which is also an act completed by animals and is first and foremost composed of technical and manual gestures, the measurement of time is uniquely human and above all intellectual: this concept is based on contemplation and measurement, the day and the shadows that the sun draws on the earth, the night as well as the movement and orbit of the planets and the stars. This activity separates human beings from other living beings and marginalizes them from nature: human beings become spectators of the universe and decide to transform it into immutable laws. *Mutatis mutandis*, this reminds us of what Horkheimer and Adorno argue in the *Dialektik der Aufklärung*, 'Excursus I: Odysseus oder Mythos der Aufklärung': the human control over nature via rational laws causes the alienation (*Entfremdung*) of the human subject from nature as nature becomes an object to be controlled.[1] This is not pointing out human exceptionalism. Quite the contrary, the alienation highlights the shortcomings of the humans in their 'power' over nature.

Vitruvius starts by explaining the workings of the simplest way to measure time, the sundial, which is based on knowledge of astronomy and geometric calculations to transform the course of the sun into a shadow, which is projected on a circumference. The sundial, a relatively simple instrument, consists of directly 'reading' a natural phenomenon. Vitruvius then studies another way to measure time, the water clock, which calls on principles of machinery. The pages that are devoted to this at the end of book 9 are a good introduction to the machines described in book 10, but these also allow Vitruvius to show how human inventions use the laws of nature.

The technical description of the water clock is preceded by an introductory paragraph in which Vitruvius attributes his invention to the Greek mechanician Ctesibius. This introduction is at least as important as the description of the machine itself as it allows the reader to understand the importance of this object in the history of science and technology. The water clock is not described as a simple mechanism, but presented as the outcome of the intelligence of a particular individual.[2] Simondon makes precisely this point when he talks about 'l'invention technique': it does not matter what level of entanglement we can have between the technical object and the human being, there is always a radical difference between the human being and the technical object; technical objects are an extension of the human being in the sense that they carry the creativity of the human being who is able to design them.

Vitruvius briefly reminds us that Ctesibius is from Alexandria, the town in which a distinguished school of mechanics and technology was developed in the third century.[3] He then highlights the personal qualities of this savant:

> Is ingenio et industria magna praeter reliquos excellens dictus est artificiosis rebus se delectare.
>
> He was marked out by his talent and great industry, and had the name of being especially fond of mechanical contrivances.[4]

This portrait is based on two terms that are largely defined and used throughout the treatise, *ingenium* and *artificiosus*. *Ingenium*, a natural gift that only certain individuals possess, is posited as a professional principle. Vitruvius borrowed this notion from Cicero, who discerned understanding and invention to be the necessary qualities of an excellent orator.[5] Architecture meets rhetoric: these two techniques are based on an ability to react in a particular situation using common tools and rules. In the domain of architecture *ingenium* is an individual's capacity to create, which distinguishes certain individuals and puts human beings and nature face to face. This capacity in fact acts in an indeterminate and global way and its product is immutable. *Artificium* simultaneously encompasses the idea of theoretical knowledge and skill: each human activity is organized according to an intellectual approach that allows it to reach the knowledge of the world. The *res artificiosiae* are objects produced through an intelligence of principles that govern the world, by applying the laws of mechanics of the universe to the needs of human beings. These two qualities allow Ctesibius to create these objects. It is in this way that he creates a mobile mirror for the boutique of his father, who was a barber; for this he used a weight that 'ran down into a narrow tube and compressed the air'[6] and thereby discovered, by chance, the existence of compressed air and the possibility to use it to create sounds and musical notes.

The account of the creation of the mirror serves to illustrate the Vitruvian notion of *inuentio*. *Inuentio* is also a term borrowed from rhetoric. In general, it demonstrates one of the five parts of speech, but the sense that Vitruvius gives to this word is again inspired by one of Cicero's ideas:

> illa uis quae tandem est, quae inuestigat occulta, quae inuentio atque cogitatio dicitur?
>
> What, lastly, is that power of investigating hidden things, which is called invention and imagination?[7]

For Vitruvius, *inuentio* signifies the discovery of a superior intellect, a new natural model, thereafter expressible through a system of explanation and exploitable by the rest of the human community. This notion, fundamental in the theory of architecture, was precisely defined in book 1[8] and already illustrated by three other examples, present in the form of descriptions organized according to detailed plans, exactly identical to that of Vitruvius, identifying first the fire-resistant qualities of larch and the subsequent application of it to construction (Vitr. 2.9.14–16), then Callimachus, 'inventing' the Corinthian capital by observing a basket placed on an acanthus (Vitr. 4.1.8–11), and finally Archimedes discovering, as a result of the problem posed by Hiero's crown, the relation between the volume and density of a body (Vitr. 9. pr. 9–12).[9]

In Vitruvius, invention is the ultimate form of serendipity: that is to say, the discovery, by chance, of a new natural law, which up until then was hidden from human beings. Vitruvius gives it a fundamental role in the process of creation, since he constructed one of his principles of architecture from it, which in this way became a method to decipher and explain the mysteries of nature. Invention is in general the actions of a particular individual, who, by discovering a natural reality, transforms it into a system or a method. Vitruvius applies this term to the discovery of a style or of a form, like the method used for finding water or to the astronomic speculations of the Chaldeans. All these activities are carried out using the same process: discovering a law of nature and applying it to the world of man; then, followed by a tradition, the invention solidifies the rule.

This notion of *inuentio* is inscribed in the Vitruvian conception of the progress of architecture: based on the hedonist theory of the history of humanity, as can be read in the works of Lucretius, for example.[10] Vitruvius develops an account (Vitr. 2.1) according to which architecture has evolved through time, in stages, from the direct imitation of natural productions (animal-built shelters, birds' nests etc.) until reaching intellectual perfection, through the faculty of observation and *inuentio* of human beings. Architecture was first an artisanal craft (*fabrica)*, then it became technical thinking (*ars*), and the Vitruvian account insists on the fundamental role of the technique of engineers in the general evolution of humanity, of its knowledge and its ways of life. The respect of these natural laws still remains a reference, but one uses them from this point on to devise objects specifically designed for human beings.[11]

Human beings are thus no longer an element of nature among others, but the users of its principles. Nature is no longer the environment in which they are immersed, but a model from which they borrowed their governing laws. As Timofeeva stresses in her introductory chapter to this volume, the order of nature (animals, humans, plants) 'was not established by humans, but it is measured by humans'. This distance taken from the world is clear in the two fundamental criteria of the creation of humanity. First, it is often necessary to adjust the laws to human needs: *quod ultra natura laedit arte erit emendandum* 'We may remedy by art the harm that comes by chance',[12] as nature is not completely adapted to human beings; subsequently, the ultimate aim of human creation is satisfaction and pleasure. Vitruvius, in this way, indicates that the engineers of his time *auctam per artes ornauerunt uoluptatibus elegantiam uitae* 'equipped with delights the refinements of life, increased as it was by their several crafts'.[13] Adjustment and pleasure are the two pillars of the Vitruvian philosophy of science. As he gave human beings a new position in nature as compared with previous Greek philosophers and freed them from the obligation to submit to universal laws, Vitruvius can be described as the first theorist of posthumanism.

It is for this reason that, in *De architectura*, Ctesibius took an interest first in the use of the principle of compressed air but also of water power to create objects that reproduce natural sounds, whistling, sounds and music. From the third century BCE onwards, these types of objects were considerably widespread throughout the Graeco-Roman world.[14] Yet, these are mostly gadgets and it is their enjoyable character, and the fact that they are often useless, that gives them a human-like quality: they were created to spark wonderment and admiration. It is from this notion that human beings were able to finally become independent from nature: their creations possess a specifically human aspect, an aesthetic pleasure that one finds in the name *delicia*, from which Vitruvius names these creations:

> aquarum expressiones automatopoetasque machinas multaque deliciarum genera, in his etiam horologiorum ex aqua comparationes explicuit.
>
> he described the use of water-power in making automata and many other curiosities, and among them the construction of water-clocks.[15]

However, the control of human beings over nature can be seen particularly in the expression *automatopoeta machina*, which does not exactly mean '*automaton*' (Romans used the Greek word *automaton*), but 'a machine which functions by itself'. The word *automatopoeta* is a unique word in Latin, like in Greek, and represents the first use of the word, which we use today for 'robot'. This word is perhaps not from Vitruvius, but it is our oldest piece of evidence of the function that mechanicians would give to their machines: constantly functioning on their own, without guidance from human intent nor powered by animals.

Thereafter, Vitruvius outlines this autonomy when he explains the workings of Ctesibius' water clock as well as the 'anaphorica' clock. His text is not a detailed plan, like that which can be seen in the works of Hero of Alexandria, for example. Vitruvius does not write a technical manual for professionals, but illustrates a global architectural theory for cultivated men, and, when he describes his instruments, he explains to the reader how they work.[16] *De architectura* demonstrates the inner workings of the *mirabilia* produced by human engineering.

No human operator is present in the description of these clocks. Similar to a modern robot, the machine functions on its own. The verbs used are generally in the active voice and these are the mechanical pieces that interact with each other: *Denticuli, alius alium impellentes, uersationes modicas faciunt et motiones* etc. 'the teeth fitting into one another cause measured revolutions and movements'. Moreover, when the verbs are in the passive voice, the only agent expressed is the natural laws (*his rationibus et machinatione, ex aqua componuntur horologiorum ad hibernum usum collocationes* 'by this methodical contrivance, water-clocks are set up for use in the winter'), or water (*ab aqua phellos subluatur* 'the cork is raised by the water').

In fact, the two clocks described by Vitruvius are hydraulic machines. The explanation of how they work calls on the fundamental laws of Vitruvian mechanics. Vitruvian theoretical thinking is formed around several underlying assumptions. To begin with, there are two geometric figures, a circle and a straight line, which become, when they undergo rotation and traction, the two dynamic principles of his mechanics. From these two principles, Vitruvius also laid down the foundations for a physical and chemical reading of the world, associated with the classical theory of the four elements, to explain the transformations that matter can undergo.[17] The art of architecture is capable of reproducing the mechanisms that generate life on earth. This idea of nature is inscribed in a tradition, which comes from Aristotelian thought: the universe in its entirety, what Aristotle often calls heaven, is spherical and its movement is circular and eternal. Inside, the world is 'sublunary', and rectilinear movements of matter take place, subjected to the laws of *physis* and death. This is thus the circular nature, which is linked to the notion of perpetual movement.

In addition, logically, the description of the mechanism of Ctesibius' clock only gives the reader the opportunity to observe two movements:

> influens aqua subleuat scaphium inuersum.... In quo collocata est regula uersatile tympanum tangens.

> The water flows and raises an inverted bowl. . . . The bowl is connected with a bar on which a drum revolves.

But the traction and rotation generate other types of unpredictable secondary movements, limited in time and subjected to the volition or to the imagination of the creator:

> aliae regulae aliaque tympana, ad eundem modum dentata, una motione coacta, uersando faciunt effectus uarietatesque motionum, in quibus mouentur sigilla, uertuntur metae, calculi aut oua proiciuntur, bucinae canunt, reliquaque parerga.
>
> Further, others bars, and other drums toothed after the same fashion, and driven together in one motion cause, as they revolve, various kinds of movements; therein figures are moved, pillars are turned, stones or eggs are left fall, trumpets sound, and other side-shows.[18]

As with life on earth where the diversity of life, brief and unique, is the result of some immutable and eternal physical laws, in the clock, the same general mechanism can produce infinite momentary and surprising effects. This extraordinary aspect of the machine is maintained through the expression *reliqua parerga*,[19] which completes their enumeration: we have the impression that the machine is capable of an infinite number of things, which go far beyond the human imagination. An engineer is an *artifex* whose creations surprise human beings, in the same way certain natural productions, living things, plants, water from rivers or a source, are able to surprise those who are not familiar with the laws of nature at work in the world.

These same principles make the anaphorica clock work; water runs into a container and sets a drum, a revolving axle, a pliable chain, and a counterpoise in motion:

> quantum ab aqua phellos subleuatur, tantum saburrae pondus infra deducens uersat axem, axis autem tympanum.
>
> in so far as the cork is raised by the water, to that extent the weight of sand drags down and turns the axle, and the axle turns the drum.[20]

If Vitruvius also describes the 'anaphorica' clock, it is because its mechanism produces different effects from those of Ctesibius' clock: it allows us to observe, day after day, the course of the sun in the signs of the zodiac. Thus, not only does it tell the time, but also the moment of the year. It reproduces celestial revolutions on a human scale. It evidently reproduces the sun here through a circular object, a pin:

> quemadmodum sol per siderum spatia uadens dilatat contrahitque dies et horas, sic bulla in horologiis, ingrediens per puncta contra centri tympani uersationem, cotidie cum transfertur aliis temporibus per latiora, aliis per angustiora spatia, menstruis finitionibus imagines efficit horarum et dierum.
>
> just as the sun traversing the spaces of the constellations lengthens and contracts the days and hours, so the pin moving along the holes of the dial in the opposite direction of

the revolving drum, passes daily sometimes over longer, sometimes over shorter spaces; thus it produces over the monthly periods the representation of the hours and days.[21]

The specifically human quality that the rotation and traction at work in these clocks have is that they produce time. In the sundial, the straight line of the sundial arm projects the circular movement of the sun on the earth by transforming its light into a shadow. Nevertheless, this instrument is dependent on the presence of sunlight, and gives nature power over human beings. On the other hand, the clock functions on a more complex series of movements, born out of human imagination, and does not depend on any specific weather conditions: it is water that produces, for the sole benefit of human beings, the same information as from the light of the sun hitting the earth. Instead of measuring the space travelled by the sun, the clock measures time, a purely human notion, thanks to some inventions conceived by human beings. Running water creates time:

> quo minus celeri cursu uas excipit aquam, dilatat horarum spatial.
>
> the slower is the flow by which the vessel receives the water, the more it extends the length of the hours.[22]

What is more, Vitruvius further highlights the specifically human aspect of these inventions by insisting on the necessity of these adjustments: the workings of these clocks require the supply of water to be constantly regulated, which, in its current state, runs in an immutably monotonic way.[23]

Human beings are at the mercy of the risk that circumstance brings, and we live in a world subjected to time, from birth to death, but this clock allows us to access eternity. Human beings master the perpetual calculation of time. This eternity is asserted by the first sentence of the description of these clocks: the orifice of the water supply must be made of gold or gems or unchanging materials:

> ea enim nec teruntur percussu aquae nec sordes recipunt, ut obturentur
>
> For these materials are neither worn by the passage of water nor so begrimed that they become clogged.[24]

Capable of reproducing the movement of the stars in the sky, the 'anaphorica' clock bears witness to the mastering of perpetual time. We find the same intention in the Antikythera mechanism, which contains an orrery, and whose complexity of gears perfectly illustrates the technical capabilities of the engineers of the Hellenistic period.

We begin to see how Vitruvius shows his readers that with these first robots, as early as the Hellenistic era, human beings were able to seize the world in which they lived at the cost of separating themselves from it through the reduction of nature to a mathematical model. They possessed the same power as the gods in mythology, and this knowledge of the laws of mechanics allowed them to create all sorts of inventions, often more surprising than useful: a water organ, animated mechanical fountains, temples with doors that open automatically, concerts of singing birds etc.[25] For the first time in history, technology modifies relationships between humans and their environment. Men are capable of conceiving robots that affect humans and human lives by providing humans with resources that cannot be found in nature. Mechanics transports human beings to another world, where they can escape from their mortal condition. However, the secrets of this gift of creation remain foreign to common mortals. In this way, when he describes these clocks, Vitruvius offers to his readers the point of view of the user, rather than the point of view of the creator. He gives them the instructions, but not the detailed plans.

With these engineers and technicians from the School of Alexandria and their successors, the Graeco-Roman world thus enters a posthumanist era. By adjusting nature and their needs, human beings create their own world, where aesthetic comfort and pleasure become the new norms. Vitruvius' theory is based on this repositioning of human beings in nature, introducing technical thinking into the debate opened by Plato on moral value and social art. From the point of view of engineers, he became instrumental in spreading the Latin philosophical principle of *sequi naturam*. Technicians take over a field of knowledge and its practice that until now belonged to philosophers. They also enforce a new value system.

Vitruvian posthumanism then spreads to Graeco-Roman thought. In this way, we remember, Vitruvius has borrowed these notions of rhetoric from Cicero. It was then his turn to be read by the theorists of this art, like we see for example in the treatise written some years later, around 15 BCE, by Dionysius of Halicarnassus. Vitruvius wrote:

> omnis autem est machinatio rerum natura procreata ac praeceptrice et magistra mundi uersatione instituta.
>
> All machinery is generated by nature, and the revolution of the universe guides and controls.[26]

Dionysius textually took back the Vitruvian definition and accompanied it with examples, which bring to mind the mechanisms of these robots:

> μεγάλη δὲ τούτων ἀρχὴ καὶ διδάσκαλος ἡ φύσις ἡ ποιοῦσα μιμητικοὺς καὶ θετικοὺς ἡμᾶς τῶν ὀνομάτων, οἷς δηλοῦται τὰ πράγματα κατά τινας εὐλόγους καὶ κινητικὰς τῆς διανοίας ὁμοιότητας: ὑφ᾽ ἧς ἐδιδάχθημεν ταύρων τε μυκήματα λέγειν καὶ χρεμετισμοὺς ἵππων . . . καὶ συριγμὸν κάλων καὶ ἄλλα τούτοις ὅμοια παμπληθῆ τὰ μὲν φωνῆς μηνύματα, τὰ δὲ μορφῆς, τὰ δὲ ἔργου, τὰ δὲ πάθους, τὰ δὲ κινήσεως, τὰ δ᾽ ἠρεμίας, τὰ δ᾽ ἄλλου χρήματος ὅτου δή.
>
> The great originator and teacher in these matters is Nature, who prompts us to imitate and to assign words by which things are pictured, in virtue of certain resemblances which are founded in reason and appeal to our intelligence. It is by her that we have been taught to speak of the bellowing of bulls, the whinnying of horses . . . the creaking of hawsers, and numerous other similar imitations of sounds, form, action, emotion, movement, stillness, and anything else whatsoever.[27]

He then makes the adjustment and creates the beauty of these two criteria of stylistic composition. There is in fact an organic link between architecture and rhetoric: it is through thought and language that human beings separate from nature and that they animate matter so as to *construct a world* of which they are the centre and to which they are perfectly adapted.[28]

CHAPTER 27
PANDORA AND ROBOTIC TECHNOLOGY TODAY

Giulia Maria Chesi and Giacomo Sclavi

In this chapter, we engage with the question of Pandora's identity in *Theogony*, 570–612 and in *Works and Days*, 53–105.[1] As a product of technology, and yet human at the same time, we contend that Pandora might be understood in terms of what Haraway calls a 'cyborg': 'a cybernetic organism, a hybrid of machine and organism'; 'a fusion of the organic and the technical forged in particular, historical, cultural practices'.[2] First, we discuss how these definitions apply to Pandora, who, as we claim, is a hybrid construct with the potential to challenge the dichotomies pertaining to the logic and practices of domination of women and nature.[3] In the conclusions, we suggest that reading Pandora as a cyborg proves relevant for contemporary debates on robotic technology, drawing attention to the importance of Classical literature for challenging this discussion.

Pandora as a fusion of the organic and the technical

Pandora does not embody the organic and the technical by being a living statue. She is never said to be an *agalma* or a *xoanon*, although Hephaestus moulds her out of earth and water (*Th.* 571; *WD* 60–61, 70). She might rather be considered as a fusion of the organic and the technical, being a woman arguably assembled through technological means. In *Theogony*, she is defined as a *plaste gyne parthenos* (*Th.* 513–514), a 'fabricated unmarried woman',[4] and we can maintain that she is alive, given that she exhibits sentience: she is delighted by the finery, the garlands and the golden headband Athena adorned her with (*Th.* 587). Furthermore, her veil and crown arouse *thauma*/wonder (*Th.* 575, 581); her headband is wrought with monstrous creatures, similar to living animals (*Th.* 584) that provoke *thauma* (*Th.* 584), as she does too (*Th.* 588). Both Pandora and her technological extensions (the crown and the veil) blur the dividing line between natural and artificial.[5] As Kurke (2013a: 126–127) and Hunzinger (2015: 427–428) point out, *thauma* refers to objects appearing simultaneously natural and artificial to the observer.[6]

Also in *Works and Days*, Pandora appears to be an artificial woman. She is twice said to be a *gyne*, a woman (*WD* 80, 94) and she is further described as having a voice (*aude*) and strength (*sthenos*) as a human being (*anthropos*) does (*WD* 61–63).[7] Yet, there is artificiality about her. First, she is thought of as an object in the likeness of a girl (*WD* 71: παρθένῳ αἰδοίῃ ἴκελον = *Th.* 572) that Hephaestus made of earth and water (*WD* 70).[8] Second, her inner life is technologically produced. Hermes puts lies, guileful words and a thievish character into her (*WD* 77–78), by fabricating them (*WD* 79: τεῦξε); Pandora's language is also a technological product, since Hermes crafts and places articulate speech (*phone*) into her (*WD* 79–80: ἐν δ' ἄρα φωνὴν/θῆκε θεῶν κῆρυξ).[9]

Following this reading, we do not have two distinct Pandoras – the inanimate statue in *Theogony*; the living statue in *Works and Days*.[10] Pandora is not a statue at all, but a woman whose body, language and inner life are the outcome of a technological feat. Pandora, then, is not the first woman (*prote gyne*),[11] but a *cyborg* female – an organism technologically supplemented, which negotiates the notion of networking[12] by standing in relation to objects, machines and human beings alike. Pandora is precisely that point of intersection. As Vernant (1996: 385–388) argues, she has *charis*/grace (*WD* 65) and *thauma*/wonder (*Th.* 575, 581, 588), just like Achilles' weapons (*Il.* 18.83), or Hephaestus' robotic devices (the twenty tripods: *Il.* 18.372–377), and, just as importantly, like Odysseus and the objects crafted by Hephaestus and Athena (*Od.* 6.232–236 = 23.159–163). Vernant (1996: 386) observes: 'The interest of the episode of Pandora comes from the fact that the parthenos, situated in a way *in the middle position between the living human being and the object fabricated* in the likeness of a human, emphasizes the continuities, the slippages, the reversals between them' (translation and emphasis ours).

The correlation between Pandora and the cyborg figure raises questions about her creation by Hephaestus: is it a magical or a technical act? Our suggestion is to view Pandora as the outcome of Hephaestus' '*divine* engineering' blurring the boundaries between technology and magic.[13] Clearly, no mechanical system is behind the operation of her abilities, so we have to assume that her animation is the effect of divine power. Yet, it is also true that Pandora's origin resides in Hephaestus' technological capacity: like a potter, the god moulds her out of water and earth.[14] In this reading, it is apposite to apply modern views of technology to Pandora and everything she embodies. Quoting Arthur C. Clarke's *Profiles of the Future*, we could affirm that 'any sufficiently advanced technology is indistinguishable from magic'.[15] Understanding science in an uncompromising opposition to magic is a legacy of a positivist approach to knowledge, which now seems outdated like the technology that produced it, if compared with more advanced technologies of today, which investigate abstract realities – one might think of the particles accelerator at CERN to confirm the hypothesis of the existence of the Higgs boson. Since Newton's theories, science uses notions, which are not far from their magical counterparts – the principle of similarity; the principle of contagion; the concept of action at a distance as the basis of the laws of gravitation and electromagnetism.

Further observations corroborate the interpretation of Pandora as a fusion of the organic and the technical. In *Works and Days*, she is an entity endowed with what we would call today a 'human level artificial intelligence'. In fact, she is given the gift of language (*aude*: *WD* 61), as Hephaestus' golden maidens in *Ilias* 18.419, who are said to have a mind (*noos*) and language (*aude*).[16] Pandora, then, seems to be an intelligent and talking cyborg. This 'intelligent' cyborg was created to be sent as a sexually seductive gift to Epimetheus (*WD* 63–66, 72–76, 83–89). We see how the artificial life of Pandora, the fabricated woman, is a unity of body and mind: she is a creature endowed with language and a seductive body. Equally important, we observe how artificial intelligence, in the Hesiodic myth, is intimately connected to language, and how language, in turn, is strictly related to technology. We might take this point a step further and eventually see in Pandora the hypothesis of a machinic nature of language: shall we consider language as a means of information processing through the use of codes?

Pandora is not the only Hesiodic creature whom a god bestows with *aude*. In the proemial incipit of *Theogony*, the lyric voice receives *aude* from the Muses. Also in this case, *aude* might refer implicitly to the machinic characteristics of language. The poet seems to be 'programmed' to process the voice of the gods, since he is said to be the vehicle of their divine voice without any claim of creativity, as the final clause in the Greek text indicates:

Th. 31–32: ἐνέπνευσαν δέ μοι αὐδὴν
θέσπιν, ἵνα κλείοιμι τά τ' ἐσσόμενα πρό τ' ἐόντα

and they [the Muses] breathed a divine voice into me,
so that I might celebrate what will be and what has been before.

The intimate relation of technology and language is a feature of Homeric epic as well: as Dougherty (2001: 13, 21–25) shows, the technical vocabulary of shipbuilding and poetic composition shares some common features.

Pandora as a hybrid of machine and organism

We have seen that Pandora, as a fabricated woman, is artificial, but, contrary to a technical invention, she is alive, even if technologically produced – there is no conflict between artificiality and life within her. Yet, to what extent can we think of Pandora as a machine? Pandora shares common features with Hephaestus' robotic golden maidens in *Iliad* 18.[17] Just like the golden handmaidens (*Il.* 18.420), Pandora receives strength (*sthenos*) from Hephaestus (*WD* 62), and, similarly to the maidens, who are compared to living young girls (*Il.* 18.418), she is compared to an unmarried girl (*parthenos*: *WD* 71; *Th.* 572). Just as the golden maidens are built for the specific operative task of helping their master (*Il.* 18.417; 421), so Pandora is created to punish humankind for the receipt of the fire that Prometheus has stolen from Zeus. In addition, she is associated with self-activated motion. As Hephaestus' tripods are made to move automatically (*automatoi*) and join the meeting of the gods, by means of golden wheels attached to their base (*Il.* 18.373–377), so the diseases brought by Pandora into the world by opening the jar are said to spread evils among humankind all by themselves (*automatai*) (*WD* 103). Bearing in mind that the adjective *automatos* also refers to the fruits that the earth spontaneously produces (*WD* 117–118), the evils leaking spontaneously from the jar represent the definitive overthrow of the 'golden' condition of the *anthropoi* ('the human beings') as an automatic process that brings to an end the separation of men and gods, which started in Mecone (*Th.* 533–541).

Equally important, Pandora appears to embody machinic agency: she seems to be built to accomplish a specific operational task, namely to accomplish a series of taxonomical operations. In *Theogony*, Pandora causes the gender division between male and female. Before her, there were only *anthropoi* (*Th.* 535; 552; 556; 586; 588–589); after her appearance, the *anthropoi* split into male and female beings (*andres* and *gynaikes*: *Th.* 512–513; 590–592; 600). Surely, the word *andres* is also used before the Pandora episode (*Th.* 47, 95, 197, 220, 347, 369) but always in a context where the term is neither gender-connoted, nor does it refer to men as sexually differentiated from women.[18] This becomes particularly evident if we consider that the word *andres*, after the appearance of Pandora, always occurs in connection with the word *gynaikes* (*Th.* 512–513, 591–592, 600). It is also relevant to notice that the evils, which spread onto the world because of Pandora, mark the end of the *anthropoi* – who in an indefinite past (*prin*) used to live without toil or diseases – and the beginning of the mortal existence of the *andres*, who are subjected to aging, physical decadence and death:

WD 90–93: **Πρὶν** μὲν γὰρ ζώεσκον ἐπὶ χθονὶ φῦλ᾽ **ἀνθρώπων**
νόσφιν ἄτερ τε κακῶν καὶ ἄτερ χαλεποῖο πόνοιο
νούσων τ᾽ ἀργαλέων, αἵ τ᾽ **ἀνδράσι** Κῆρας ἔδωκαν.
αἶψα γὰρ ἐν κακότητι **βροτοὶ** καταγηράσκουσιν.

Before her the tribes of **living beings** lived on earth
apart and free from evil, hard toil
and painful sicknesses which bring death upon **men**.
For in misery **the mortals** get old quickly.

Yet, under the premise that Prometheus' theft of fire causes the appearance of Pandora into the world and, with her, the subsequent division of the *anthropoi* in *andres* and *gynaikes*, technology, in this myth, is not a means to transcend death. Quite the opposite, for humans, technical fire is what marks the beginning of their existence as cultural *and* mortal beings. In this context, the cyborg Pandora embodies technology and death. Unlike contemporary views of the cyborg as a means to overcome mortality, the Hesiodic mythical thought does not conceptualize the cyborg Pandora as enhancing human life beyond death.

The gender differentiation initiated by Pandora also marks the distinction of *andres* and *gynaikes* both from the gods and the *anthropoi*, putting an end to the process of temporality that had begun with Prometheus' theft of fire (cf. *Th.* 563, 566, 569: once fire is in human hands, its flame is no longer eternal and it becomes perishable). Although gods' origin comes from birth, their time is eternal. The *anthropoi* never *really* died – at least not in the human sense of dying – but rather fell into an eternal sleep (*WD* 116). In fact, the *anthropoi* were not subject to temporality: their existence had a beginning and an end, but their life did not imply a process of growth after birth, nor of aging or decay and death, as if they were *autochthones*.[19] The human life of the *andres* and *gynaikes*, on the contrary, has necessarily a beginning and an end. In this mythic narrative, temporality is what Pandora brings to humanity; therefore, it is a gift, something Pandora sends to humans. We may say that human time in this myth *is given*; divine time, on the contrary, *always is*.

Yet, if men and women are both the result of Pandora's taxonomic division, it seems reasonable to question whether the woman, in this narrative, embodies the Other, as Zeitlin (1996: 53) famously puts it: 'More often than not, woman is an afterthought, created as a secondary category following the prior emergence of man.' Rather, we might assume that the *gyne* is not created *after* the *aner*, and that there has never been a world in which *andres* existed without *gynaikes*. The cyborg Pandora problematizes the traditional Western dualism of man vs. woman.

One might also question whether there is any anthropogony in *Theogony*, as Vernant (1979: 46) points out: 'In the plot of a story where everything happens at the level of the gods, between gods, there is no room for an anthropogony in the proper sense' (translation ours). It is true that *Theogony* is silent about the origin of the *anthropoi*, unlike *Works and Days*, where, as an example, the race of the bronze *anthropoi* is said to originate from the ash trees (*WD* 143–145). However, if one understands 'anthropogony' as the origin of the *andres* and *gynaikes*, their genesis is explained in the text through the story of Pandora.

Further taxonomies are introduced by Pandora. In *Works and Days*, by opening the jar, Pandora brings about the ethic taxonomy of good and evil among humans (*WD* 85–95). The evils that plague humankind spread out of the jar; yet, anxious fear for the future and hope (*elpis*) remain inside (*WD* 96–97). *Elpis* is strictly related to Pandora: it stays with her in the jar she guards. As Vernant (1974, 193; 2001, 35) remarks, *elpis* defines the human condition: the blessed lives of gods are obviously divorced from *elpis*, just like the lives of animals, which ignore the prospect of death.

In *Theogony* and in *Works and Days*, Pandora also introduces an economical taxonomy, according to what we might call a 'gift economy' or 'symbolic exchange'.[20] As a gift to humans from the gods in exchange for the stolen fire, she calls for a counter-gift, that is the *kakon*, the evil for humankind (*Th.* 570: ἀντὶ πυρὸς τεῦξεν κακὸν ἀνθρώποισιν/ as the price of fire he fabricated an evil for humans; *WD* 57: τοῖς δ' ἐγὼ ἀντὶ πυρὸς δώσω κακόν/ as the price of fire I will give them an evil): since her appearance in the world, men will have to reproduce by sex, to work the land and to sacrifice.[21] Even as a gift, which is a *kalon kakon*, an ambivalent evil, she is not just evil.[22] She is a *beautiful* gift, which gods give to men, and which men have to reciprocate with a life of work and sacrifices to the gods. Pandora's myth does not seem to convey a misogynous perspective; rather, perhaps, a pessimistic *Weltanschauung*. Indeed, as Vernant (1996: 388–390) carefully explains, the *charis* of Pandora is what constitutes male identity: without *charis*, a man does not resemble anything, he is *aeikelios*, that is to say he does not have any 'semblance'; with *charis*, on the contrary, he resembles the gods (the Homeric formula is '*theoisin eoike*'). Without Pandora, there would be no men at all – not because, in her belly, she consumes the male seed in order to give birth to children, but because male identity depends on female *charis*, a *charis* which Pandora, with her appearance, brings into the world. Perhaps even more importantly, as Vernant (1999: 85) points out, the *charis* of Pandora, a *charis* only she possesses, is the only divine element continuing to exist among men once the Golden Age is over. Pandora's beauty reminds men, the *andres*, of the time they were *anthropoi*, and lived together with the gods. Quoting Vernant (2001: 37), we might conclude that: 'In this sense, we can say that, in Greek myth, it is only with the woman that the males fully accede to their condition of civilized human being between beasts and gods' (translation ours). Again, we can observe how Pandora deactivates strategies of domination of man over woman. Pandora rewrites our biased mythologies and can hardly be located at the origin of Western misogyny. As a riddling cyborg, the question of her identity is really about how we construct her myth and what use we make of it.

The question arises as to whether Pandora also unravels the opposition of sex and gender. Certainly, Pandora is sexless. As Wickkiser (2010: 562) observes, she is not said to give birth to women, women are just thought to descend from her (*Th.* 590). Yet, she is gender-connoted. In *Theogony* and in *Works and Days*, she is described as a *woman* (*gyne*), whose body and inner life are technologically produced. This might perhaps explain why she brings about the *anthropoi* gender differentiation into *andres* and *gynaikes*, together with the divide of mortal humans/immortal gods. Her taxonomic agency seems to be immanent to her female gender.[23]

Pandora's myth also problematizes strategies of domination of technology over nature. In fact, Pandora is the physical embodiment of technology, since she has the same properties as the technical fire; her body is a *technosoma*.[24] As has often been pointed out, Pandora is the exact equivalent of fire, and we know that Euripides, in his first *Hippolytus* (fr. 429 Nauck), defined the woman as *anti puros*, in the sense of an even more powerful fire. Just like fire devours and consumes, so Pandora consumes the seed and the man's *bios*. Like fire fosters life, so she generates and recreates life in her belly. In addition, she is the equivalent of fire because she is also a gift: fire is Prometheus' gift to human beings; it is also Zeus' possession, which he bereaves the humans of, prior to Prometheus' theft (*Th.* 563). Following this interpretation, Pandora's *technosoma* disentangles the dichotomy of technology over nature (understood here as the 'natural', biological body), by mapping their continuity.[25] Pandora's *technosoma* does not point to any nature/technical culture divide, and therefore seems to be better conceptualized, according to Haraway's idea of *natureculture*.[26]

Pandora and robotic technology today

We have several reasons to investigate the cyborg Pandora, as we engage with questions about robotic technology in today's society. Pandora invites us to critically assess the supposed vertical relationship between humans and machines. In the Hesiodic narrative, the genetic relationship between the *gynaikes*, who are said to inherit the noxious features of Pandora (*Th.* 590–612), and the *andres*, who are instead depicted as a separated *genos*, remains undecided. Yet, since the race of women is explicitly said to descend from her (*Th.* 590–591), humankind itself seems somehow to have its origin in the cyborg. If, reading Hesiod, we conceive of humankind as descending from the cyborg Pandora, the genealogy of humans and machine should be inverted: first we have the cyborg, and then the humans descending from her. With this in mind, we might envision new human and machinic genealogies.[27] The machine is not just a technical object built by humans. Through Pandora, we are invited to wonder whether the human being is inhabited by the otherness of the cyborg and by its alterity to humans. From the Hesiodic perspective, this seems to hold true in the case of the cyborg: humans derive from it; therefore, in regards to machinic identity, it is the human being who is the other.

Equally important, the figure of Pandora can help us to problematize the legitimacy of our increasing fear of robotic technology. It is often argued that super-intelligent machines will outlive us in the near future.[28] Yet, it is questionable as to whether and when machines will overcome human intelligence, as it seems unlikely that they will ever possess problem-solving skills comparable to men's.[29] It is also questionable as to whether machines will ever exhibit a sparkle of 'consciousness', not to mention their initiative to eliminate humankind. We do not even have the faintest idea of what consciousness precisely is, let alone how to replicate it in robots. A human unified field of consciousness seems to comprise activities that defy any formalization, such as dreams and memories. In other words, as Rodney Brooks (former director of the MIT computer science and artificial intelligence laboratory) recently observed, we would not know *what* to model and *on what* premises.[30] The idea that machines will outlive us in the near future perpetrates a technocratic logic of domination (as a tyranny of machines over humans) and assumes a dichotomic relationship between the two parts: machines represent the 'other' in respect to us – and apparently they are 'better' suited for survival as a further step in evolution. Pandora's myth invites us to challenge this claim, by focusing on the continuity between humans and machines. Relying on this mythical narration and its view of humankind as sharing its cyborg nature with Pandora, in a way, we can think of humans as beings embodying the machine, able to free their subjectivities through technology, with the potential to remap the boundaries between the two domains.[31] As Haraway (2016: 65) argues: 'The machine is not an *it* to be animated, worshipped, and dominated. The machine is us, our processes, an aspect of our embodiment. We can be responsible for machines; *they* do not dominate or threaten us. We are responsible for boundaries; we are they.'

The mythical narrative of Pandora also provides useful elements to ponder when considering robotic devices and their degree of autonomy. Pandora can be fairly described as possessing the capability of decision-making. The wording of the Greek in *WD* 94–95 points to Pandora's agency of her own:

WD 94–95: ἀλλὰ γυνὴ χείρεσσι πίθου μέγα πῶμ' ἀφελοῦσα
ἐσκέδασ'...

The woman, however, with her own hands, removed the big lid of the box and scattered abroad [all the evils].

Here, Zeus is not mentioned. This silence is particularly striking, considering that Zeus is said to prompt Pandora to close the jar before hope spreads out (*WD* 97–98). In addition, the instrumental dative χείρεσσι (with her hands) singles out Pandora's (bodily) agency. Yet, we might argue that the opening of the box, although Pandora's choice, is still a 'pre-programmed' action, in the sense that it is part of Zeus' original plan to punish humankind for the receipt of fire. Similarly to Pandora, actual robotic devices merely possess what Alan Winfield (2012: 10) proposes to call 'control autonomy':

> When roboticists talk about autonomous robots [...] they are not talking about true autonomy, in the sense that you and I would regard ourselves as self-determining individuals, but what would I call 'control autonomy'. By control autonomy I mean that the robot can undertake his task, or mission, without human intervention, but that mission is still programmed or commanded by a human.

Furthermore, the figure of the cyborg Pandora causes us concerns about the necessity of designing accountable devices. As already mentioned, by opening the box, Pandora follows Zeus' plan to punish humankind. The question arises as to whether Pandora is a 'well programmed' cyborg completing an assigned task or, on the contrary, she fails (how could a cyborg be 'good programmed' if its task is to harm humanity?). In the context of actual robotic devices, what would constitute a 'good' robot? We might ask whether a robot is well functioning just because it accomplishes its tasks. Yet, which, if any, are the motivations and the prejudices behind its programming, and what if a robot does not achieve its goals?

Conclusions

We have seen that the cyborg Pandora represents the intimate union of the human and the technical: she is the punishment of humankind for the receipt of Prometheus' stolen fire (*Th.* 570, 585, 602; *WD* 57); human technology (the possession of fire) and human temporality as well as gender (male and female), ethics (good and evil) and economics of exchange are all associated in her. In this light, the myth of Pandora discloses a notion of technology that runs through most of the contemporary philosophical debates. Following philosophers as diverse as Heidegger in *Die Frage nach der Technik*, Simondon in *Sur le mode d'existence des objets techniques* and McLuhan in *Understanding Media*, technology is intimately associated with human identity: it is a part of our existential journey, an extension of our human presence in the world, a prosthesis, which in turn changes us.

Second, this mythical narrative demands a critical stance of the reader in regard to the fear of technology. If, with Pandora, we regard human beings as both humans and machines, then we can envisage an idea of humanity as embodying the machinic difference within itself – and the fear of machines is unfounded: humans are not to be thought of as in opposition to the machine, but in continuity with it. And yet humans are not to be conceived of as machines either; rather, they are machines, which embody the human – in their role as 'huma(n)chines'. As such, humans are in charge of safeguarding this ambiguous distinction, as they need the alterity of the machine to define their own 'cyborg' humanity.

CHAPTER 28
ART, LIFE AND THE CREATION OF AUTOMATA: ON PINDAR, *OLYMPIAN* 7.50–53

Agis Marinis

The idea of an artificial work that resembles a living entity – one that has fascinated humanity through the ages – makes its appearance in ancient Greece already with the Homeric epics, most characteristically with the Iliadic Shield of Achilles. This chapter[1] deals with a significant later instance of this notion in classical Greek literature, namely the 'lifelike' statues of Rhodes in Pindar's *Olympian* 7, an epinician ode performed in 464 BCE to celebrate the victory of the famed boxer Diagoras of Rhodes.[2] My aim is to situate the specific description within the wider context of Pindaric and early classical worldview, concentrating on two key issues, namely the conditions on which the construction of analogous artifacts is conceived to be possible on earth, as well as the ramifications such a conception of statuary may entail as regards the very notion of 'life' and the relations between gods and humans. We are thus naturally led to the question of the 'emulation' of human traits by machines, which is a prime concern in our post-anthropocentric age; indeed it will be the point of departure for a number of related reflections, pertaining to posthumanist thought, that will arise in the course of my inquiry.

'Like living and moving beings'

As the poet is glorifying the home island of the victor, he refers to the benefactions bestowed by Athena on the sons of Helios who have been its first inhabitants (50–53):

αὐτὰ δὲ σφίσιν ὤπασε τέχναν
πᾶσαν ἐπιχθονίων Γλαυκ-
ῶπις ἀριστοπόνοις χερσὶ κρατεῖν.
ἔργα δὲ ζωοῖσιν ἑρπόν-
τεσσί θ' ὁμοῖα κέλευθοι φέρον·
ἦν δὲ κλέος βαθύ. δαέντι δὲ καὶ σοφία
μείζων ἄδολος τελέθει.

but the Grey-eyed Goddess
herself gave them every kind of skill to surpass mortals
with their superlative handiwork.
Their streets bore works of art in the likeness of beings
that lived and moved,
and great was their fame. If one possesses deep knowledge,
even superlative skill remains free from artifice.[3]

We are dealing here with lines of characteristic Pindaric complexity but also ambiguity, for which a number of diverging interpretations have been proffered. A key question is whether ἑρπόντεσσί θ' ὁμοῖα κέλευθοι φέρον (52) refers to statues that are really moving or that merely appear to be;[4] in my view, their description as 'in the likeness of beings that lived and moved' entails that they cannot be considered as literally possessing those two qualities; hence, one would be justified to understand that 'they were set up along the roads'.[5] On the other hand, we may well assert that the ambiguity of Pindaric diction here matches the liminal status of those extraordinary sculptural artifacts.

In a public performance a prime intertext that would immediately spring to the mind of the public is the Homeric narration of the creation of the arms of Achilles by Hephaestus in *Iliad* 18. The audience would, more specifically, recall Thetis entering the god's palace, where the god is finishing right at that time tripods intended as self-moving wheeled devices to serve the gods at their symposia (373–377).[6] Further, as the god leaves his anvil to talk with Thetis, metal maidens – distinctly more lifelike artifacts – assist him. In fact, the parallelism between these metallic helpers and the statues of the Heliadae has already been pointed out by the ancient Scholia.[7] They are presented as resembling living young women in terms of form, but also notably as regards the mental qualities that they possess (417–420):

> ὑπὸ δ' ἀμφίπολοι ῥώοντο ἄνακτι
> χρύσειαι, ζωῇσι νεήνισιν εἰοικυῖαι.
> τῇς ἐν μὲν νόος ἐστὶ μετὰ φρεσίν, ἐν δὲ καὶ αὐδὴ
> καὶ σθένος, ἀθανάτων δὲ θεῶν ἄπο ἔργα ἴσασιν.

> and there moved swiftly to support their lord handmaids made of gold in the semblance of living girls. In them is understanding in their minds, and in them speech and strength, and they know cunning handiwork by gift of the immortal gods.[8]

In terms of poetics the power of this description rests exactly on the fact that we are dealing with entities that *are not* living beings, but are merely *approximating* them.[9] Indeed, we may assert that this (seemingly perennial) fascination with the human-like machine should be traced to the uncanny aura surrounding the displacement of the lines of demarcation between the born and the manufactured: one of the key dichotomies undermined in our twenty-first-century post-anthropocentric predicament.[10] As regards the specific anthropoid traits of the metal maidens[11] the most intriguing is νόος μετὰ φρεσίν ('understanding in their minds'): it is impossible to deduce whether volitional or intellectual or even moral activity is implied.[12] In any case, from an ontological point of view it is clear that 'life' emerges as part of a wider cosmic system and rhythm and may be replicated in its various aspects only by a god – a point with ramifications for the outlook of Pindar's audience of course. Moreover, the fact that the metal maidens' 'cunning handiwork' stems from the gods (420) introduces an idea that we shall later encounter in the Hesiodic description of Pandora, where the goddess Athena teaches her to perform women's tasks (*Works and Days* 63–64).[13] One might argue here, with Sylvia Berryman, that the foregrounding of the divine provenance of such devices entails that they can be regarded as being animated by a power unique to the gods.[14] However, especially since Hephaestus' technological capacity also contributes to Pandora's creation, I would assert that her construction may, partly at least, be considered as a technical act and hence she cannot be deemed a 'magical living statue'.[15] In an analogous way, in *Olympian* 7 the goddess Athena does not herself 'animate' the statues, but instead provides the Heliadae with the requisite knowledge and technical skill in order to create them.[16] We may actually draw a contrast here, within the Pindaric corpus, with the six golden Κηληδόνες ('Charmers') of *Paean* 8 (65–71), which were affixed on top of the gable of the bronze temple of Apollo at Delphi. This 'chorus' of six lifelike statues, perpetually singing and entrancing visitors, had not been a creation of humans, but of Hephaestus and Athena, along with the rest of the temple. In that case the machinic quality does not merely adduce an uncanny aura to the artifact, but it is also effectively conferred on the human performers of choral song, who end up – in a 'transversal' manner that cuts across segregated categories[17] – being implicitly conceptualized as crafted objects.[18]

It becomes clear, thus, that in Pindar the employment of technological skill marks a dividing line between human and divine capacities. In fact, this division can be accommodated within the wider framework of the gulf separating mortals and gods. Yet, as it is stated in the proem of *Nemean* 6 (1–5), despite the distance separating them, both are 'drawing their breath from a single mother',[19] namely Gaia or the Great Mother.[20] In this sense, human life can be considered as being of divine provenance, whereas human excellence may afford mortals some resemblance to the gods.[21] Fragment 131b, influenced by Orphic doctrines, points in the same direction:[22] σῶμα μὲν πάντων ἕπεται θανάτῳ περισθενεῖ, / ζωὸν δ' ἔτι λείπεται αἰῶνος εἴδω-/λον· τὸ γάρ ἐστι μόνον / ἐκ θεῶν ('The body of all men is subject to overpowering death, / but a living image of life still remains, / for it alone is / from the gods', 1–3).[23] We are dealing here with the core of human essence, a psychological and spiritual 'soul', elsewhere in Pindar termed ψυχή.[24] Hence, if the actually 'living' element in a human being is the 'soul' which originates from the gods, then it becomes manifest why in the Pindaric cosmos an artifact may by no means possess 'life', even in approximation, unless it derives from the divine world. All too obvious is the contrast with the modern conception of humans potentially capable of creating 'animated matter', namely devices with artificial intelligence, whose traits are understood as an extension of our own capacities and (possibly) shortcomings. It thus appears conspicuously difficult to raise ourselves above human-centric thinking when discussing automata;[25] consequently, we should exercise due care in our attempt to reconstruct the ancient outlook on them.

Sane mentality and the straight road

It is now time to read more closely the gnomic utterance δαέντι δὲ καὶ σοφία / μείζων ἄδολος τελέθει (*Ol.* 7. 53).[26] A question is whether we ought to accept ἄδολος ('free from artifice/fraud')[27] as attributive and μείζων ('superlative') as predicative;[28] yet the most immediate manner of understanding this phrase is the opposite, namely without the burden of a complicating hyperbaton.[29] Hence one may translate: 'If one possesses deep knowledge, even superlative skill remains free from artifice.' In my view, the key for the interpretation of this gnomic utterance is the fact that σοφία (wisdom/skill) is god-given. In fact, we ought to take into account the whole nexus of relations between mortals and the divine within the ode and, more specifically, the fact that it recounts – interestingly, in reverse chronological order – a series of divine benefactions bestowed upon mortals or upon the island of Rhodes as an earthly abode. First we encounter the story of Tlapolemos, who, despite being a wise man, slew his great-uncle Likymnios; Apollo then ordered him, as a means of atonement, to leave Lerna and sail to Rhodes in order to establish a colony there (24–33). Remarkably, Rhodes is described as a blessed place where Zeus was raining gold when Athena was born from his head – a prime indication of divine favour to the island (34–37).[30] Next, we have the sacrifice of the Heliadae, the children of Helios who were charged by their father to build an altar for Athena and perform a sacrifice to her. Despite the fact that they forgot to bring fire and thus ended up performing fireless rites, both Athena and Helios forgave them. Again, Zeus rained gold on them (49–50),[31] whereas Athena offered them extraordinary technical skills. The third instance of benefaction stretches back into the mythical past when Helios had been allotted Rhodes by the gods as his abode (54–76), remarkably after being unintentionally ignored at first. The seven sons of Helios, who inherit Rhodes, are again mentioned: a mythical story that marks the divine overseeing and blessing of a place. The favour of the very father of the gods seals each time in a most generous and impressive manner the story of human wisdom and erring, or even divine forgetfulness.[32]

In light of the above remarks, it is scarcely conceivable that the skill imparted by Athena to the Heliadae could by any means possess negative connotations and be intended as a foil to Pindar's own. Therefore, it is not possible to accept Patrick O'Sullivan's view that σοφία ἄδολος (read as 'undeceptive') can be considered as even greater (καὶ . . . μείζων) than that of the statues of Rhodes – ἄδολος forming thus a contrast with the 'deceptive effect' of those lifelike artworks.[33] On the other hand, ἄδολος may indeed most naturally be understood as 'free from fraud'[34] to the extent that it does not involve the intention to deceive anyone.[35] However, in which sense could the art of constructing 'automata' possibly involve 'fraud', 'deception', 'treachery'? We may recall here Ixion's 'bride', a cloud in the form of Hera, which is a trap, δόλος, conceived for and leading to the punishment of Ixion (*P.* 2.36–40). The Homeric background provides a comparable sense of 'cunning contrivance', most conspicuously in the case of the Trojan horse, another 'simulacrum'.[36] Besides, we have the rich tradition concerning the sculptural art of Daedalus, mentioned in the *Iliad* as already belonging to the past:[37] his works are not merely estimated as products of high artistic skill, but, moreover, as 'lifelike' or even straightforwardly 'capable of moving'.[38] However, these Daedalic statues are by no means connected with δόλος; they may only engender a certain kind of artistic ἀπάτη ('deceit'), yet with no negative intent.

Hence, we are still left with the question on what grounds could statues such as the Rhodian ever be considered as involving δόλος. In my view, the answer lies in the very exaltation of the art of the Heliadae (51–53). For anyone cognizant of the Pindaric worldview, it is clear that we are treading on the edge: to surpass mortals in a specific art entails the danger of arrogance, namely 'to think above mortal limits'. Moreover, whereas to divulge glory forms a central endeavour within Pindaric praise poetry,[39] it simultaneously constitutes a precarious notion: in the very essence of the epinician as a genre lies the poetic intention to curb any human pride of the victor that would involve disregard of the limits of mortality.[40] In the case of the Heliadae their piety, which is rewarded notwithstanding their 'forgetfulness' (45–47), guarantees the fact that they will not seek to act in an arrogant or impious manner, or even take advantage of their technical skill in order to pursue dishonest purposes.[41]

A key word, in this respect, is the participle δαείς, from the verb δάω, 'to know': a rare word within the Pindaric corpus, since it is encountered twice in the epinicians and only once in a fragment.[42] Even more significantly, both epinician instances are found in *Olympian* 7: the second is encountered in line 91, within the poet's concluding prayer to Zeus, where the highest god, who rules over the Atabyrion mountain of Rhodes, is beseeched to grant to

Diogenes 'respectful favour' emanating 'from both townsmen and foreigners' (89–90).[43] The poet grounds his request as follows (90–92):[44]

> ἐπεὶ ὕβριος ἐχθρὰν ὁδόν
> εὐθυπορεῖ, σάφα δαεὶς ἅ τε οἱ πατέρων
> ὀρθαὶ φρένες ἐξ ἀγαθῶν
> ἔχρεον.
>
> for he [Diagoras] travels straight down a road
> that abhors insolence, having clearly learned
> what an upright mind inherited from noble forebears
> declared to him.

Δαείς is aptly translated by Race as 'having clearly learned':[45] we are indeed dealing with a good/well-founded knowledge, in both cases referring to the attitude one ought to entertain as regards the avoidance of injustice or, concomitantly, impiety. The imagery of the road has its own significance: the avoidance of ὕβρις is not presented as something given, but as part of a continuous effort, which the victor pursues.[46] Moreover, the verb εὐθυπορεῖ foregrounds the 'straightness' of the road, from which one may deviate – and both Tlapolemos (30–31) and the Heliadae (45–47) offer instances of 'wandering off'. Importantly, in both those passages, as well as in the poet's prayer (91), we find the same term, φρένες (with the sense of 'mind'), denoting a fundamentally sane *mental attitude* (the 'straight road') which entails respect for human limitations and aims to avoid ὕβρις.[47]

A final question is to which degree σοφία ἄδολος ('skill free from artifice') may extend its ambit to embrace the poet's art as well. The answer to this question is facilitated by the parallel of *Nemean* 7.20f., where Homer is criticized for enhancing the stature of Odysseus: ἐπεὶ ψεύδεσί οἱ ποτανᾷ <τε> μαχανᾷ / σεμνὸν ἔπεστί τι· σοφία / δὲ κλέπτει παράγοισα μύθοις ('upon his fictions and soaring craft / rests great majesty, and his skill / deceives with misleading tales', 22–23). We are dealing there with a case of poetic σοφία which, via its lofty and embellished form, seeks to deceive its addressees: an undertaking not much removed from δόλος.[48] The subsequent (23f.) juxtaposition of Odysseus' aggrandizement – accepted by the public (that has 'a blind heart', 23–24) – with Aias' suffering from his degrading treatment and his subsequent grim fate, leads to the concluding gnome: 'yet honour belongs to those / whose fair story a god exalts after they die' (31–32). Importantly, it is again the god who provides the proper measure – clearly *also*, if not mainly, through the verse of a truthful poet.[49] Hence, we may argue that the poet's artistry applied in epinician praise is equally devoid of δόλος as the divinely inspired skill of the Heliadae.[50] Finally, we ought not to forget that Pindaric verse also stems from the divine: Μοισᾶν δόσις (*Ol.* 7.7). In a similar, but more elaborate manner, in *Paean* 6 the poet projects his own *persona* – which, in performance, may also be perceived as an instantiation of the collective voice of the chorus[51] – as a 'prophet of the Pierians' (6), namely one who conveys to the audience the 'message' of the Muses.[52]

On the other hand, O'Sullivan justly introduces into the discussion the issue of statuary and Pindar's stance towards it – manifested most conspicuously in the proem of *Nemean* 5, for Pytheas of Aigina. Pindar's song is presented there as travelling and spreading the news of victory, in contrast with 'stationary statues that stand on their same base' (1–2).[53] On a deeper level one may also argue that Pindar's aim is to present poetry, contrasted with sculpture, as capable of revealing the true significance of events.[54] However – despite an inevitable professional competition with sculptors – it would be a mistake to reduce Pindar's stance towards statuary as a mere reaction to it or as a plainly antagonistic gesture: we are dealing with a much more creative stance, which often seeks to draw analogies between both arts.[55] Of course, in the case of *Olympian* 7 we are dealing with the rather unique occurrence of sculptural works that exceed the norm – and certainly human capacities: *those* statues are by no means 'stationary' like their counterparts of *Nemean* 5. Hence, any comparison with this exalted form of statuary may actually be considered as conferring honour on Pindar, while also possibly involving an allusion to the restrictions of *ordinary*, humanly wrought statues, those potentially antagonistic to Pindar's own art in everyday reality.[56] Interestingly, however, even standard stone or metal commemorative objects can be treated generously by the poet, notably in this very ode: in lines 83–87 we read about further victories of Diagoras which are testified by the bronze of Argos (83) – most probably referring to a tripod offered as a prize – and further, among other places, the 'record in stone' at Megara: ἐν Μεγάροισιν . . . λιθίνα ψᾶφος (86–87).[57] Hence, in a poem where extraordinary, divinely inspired statues are praised, those much more humble material objects are equally granted, alongside Pindaric verse, their own, not entirely insignificant role for the projection of the victor's κλέος. As Leslie Kurke has shown, this rather exceptional emphasis on material records ought to be appraised in connection not only with the statues of the Heliadae, but also with the initial reference to the golden φιάλα: a prominence of material artifacts certainly relevant to the fact that the whole ode was dedicated, according to the ancient Scholiast, in the temple of Athena Lindia, inscribed in golden letters.[58] In this sense, the whole ode may be perceived as an expansive poetic alternative to a dedicatory epigram.[59] Yet again, one may well argue that all material objects are incorporated *within* poetic discourse – the very discourse also exalting the god-given, elevated skill of the Heliadae.

Finally, we may underline once more that in the early classical worldview, represented by Pindar, a work of art or any human artifact may possess 'lifelike' characteristics only through the involvement of a divine power. It therefore becomes evident how far we are situated from the posthumanist quest of moving beyond anthropocentrism – a more broadly 'post-centralizing' endeavour – which aims at exploring, for instance, the capacity of nonhuman objects to give meaning to our world.[60] In Pindaric poetry we are dealing with a world which is not anthropocentric, although humans may still share a fraction of excellence with the gods, while they also boast a shared origin with them. We are far from any idea that human beings are singular creatures, of a distinct nature, deserving a special place in the cosmos due to their rational faculties.[61] In this sense, the post-exclusivist and post-exceptionalist perspective offered by posthumanism may actually supply us with a potentially helpful vantage point in order to approach the ancient worldview. An obverse move is equally conceivable; a number of non-Western civilizations (past or present) have actually been taken as points of departure for the 'reinvention of the human', a key endeavour within the posthumanist quest.[62] However, what we will discover in ancient Greece is a world which is not decentred, nor devoid of hierarchy – a vision distinctive of posthumanism – but instead possesses a potent centre of gravity which may effectively be equated with the source of being. The divine, primordial roots of the universe are the sphere whence humanity originates, as well as the source of any outstanding accomplishments by mortals. Hence, 'automata' must necessarily be derivative – yet, importantly, not with regard to humans, but to the divine cosmic principle, whence also human σοφία and artfulness owe their origin.

CHAPTER 29
STAYING ALIVE: PLATO, HORACE AND THE WRITTEN TEXT

Alexander Kirichenko

Introduction

One of the branches of 'posthuman studies' extensively deals with the implications for human self-perception of the semblance of disembodied information made possible by modern information technology.[1] The goal of this chapter is to offer a corrective to the view that the virtual reality created by information technology constitutes a unique break with what is supposed to have heretofore always been the basis of the concept of humanity.

By way of example, I will consider two instances of how classical Greek and Roman literature reflects on the possibility of transforming embodied human consciousness into what is both an 'information pattern' – a written discourse preserving forever the structure of the speaker's subjectivity – and a metaphorical hybrid organism that exists by merging with the subjectivities of the readers. It is a cliché of Greek and Roman literature from the archaic period onwards that poetry alone is capable of granting a semblance of immortality – metaphorically extending to all eternity the solid, yet transient, materiality of an immortalizing monument made of metal or stone.[2] The texts that I will analyse in this chapter (Plato's *Symposium* and *Phaedrus* and Horace's *Ars Poetica*) are also concerned with immortality. But in contrast to the standard poetic cliché, Plato and Horace conceive of the immortality granted by writing not as an indefinitely extended existence of an inanimate material object but as a figurative form of *life*. Both of them conceptualize this notional life by presenting their respective written discourses (philosophy and poetry) as emulating the performative effect of the embodied presence of their paradigmatic speakers (a prototypical philosopher and an inspired poet). And both of them offer biological metaphors (a plant taking root in the reader's soul and a parasitic organism surviving on the reader's blood) for the process whereby these written discourses can exist forever by being grafted onto the minds of their future readers. In Plato and Horace, the written text emerges as a result both as an 'information pattern' that immortalizes the speaker's embodied presence and as a locus of hybridity in which that 'information' survives not only because it is stored in such a way as to be easily 'retrieved' but also because it enters a symbiotic relationship with the reader's subjectivity.

Plato and the immortality of Socrates

Conspicuously enough, Agathon's portrayal of Eros in Plato's *Symposium* as a beautiful, young, soft, tender and supple object of desire (cf. Pl. *Smp.* 195a5–196b2: καλός, νέος, ἁπαλός, μαλακός, ὑγρός) captures the social role eagerly played in the dialogue by Agathon himself – the role of a forever-young object of male admiration possessing no desiring subjectivity of his own.[3]

More importantly still, Agathon's speech not only evokes contemporary pictorial representations of Eros,[4] but also uses language as raw material for manufacturing a verbal analogue of a decorative material artefact – beautifully polished, yet incapable of engendering any emotion or thought other than the sense of awe at the artificer's technical skill (cf. 198b3–5). It is thus hardly surprising that Socrates compares the impression produced by Agathon's Gorgianic rhetoric to the stunning effect of the head of Gorgo Medusa ('the head of Gorgias'!), which literally transforms those who confront it into lifeless stone statues, thereby depriving them of the ability to speak.[5]

Quite tellingly, Socrates' own philosophical discourse in the *Symposium* begins as a typically Socratic dialogue with Agathon. In the beginning, Socrates poses what sounds like an innocent syntactical question (199d1–e8): don't we normally say 'the desire ("eros") for someone or something' – with a genitive, the way we say 'someone's father, mother, brother, etc.'? By simply providing Eros with a grammatical object, Socrates gradually forces Agathon to renounce his own portrayal of Eros as a beloved self-contentedly basking in admiration and to embrace Socrates' vision of Eros as an insatiable lover who never ceases to ask philosophical questions. Most revealingly, Socrates' conversation with Agathon persistently enacts a pun between Eros and ἐρωτᾶν ('ask': 199c1 ἀλλ᾽ ἐρώτα, 199d1-3 Ἔρως ... ἐρωτῶ ... τὸ ἐρώτημα εἰ Ἔρως ἐστὶν ἔρως).[6] Instead of being defined, Socrates' philosophical Eros is thus reflectively materialized through the very process of dialectical questioning.[7] As a result, Agathon's semantically closed visual image is effectively cracked open by Socrates' dialectic.

In Socrates' speech that follows, Eros emerges as a symbol not only of the philosophical quest for absolute beauty in general but also, more specifically, of Socrates' 'maieutic' life – a life spent incessantly 'questioning' beautiful young men, such as Agathon, and infusing them with his own desire to 'engender' virtue and truth.[8] Alcibiades' subsequent account of Socrates' resistance to his erotic advances (216c4–219d2)[9] serves as the most palpable proof that Socrates' love for absolute beauty, rather than for the bodies of handsome young men, is not an empty phrase but the truth by which he really lives. It is by extension precisely his love for the absolute that can be taken to account for Socrates' resistance to any hardship, which Alcibiades reports to have witnessed during the campaign of Potidaea (210d3–221c1). Thus, the inimitable uniqueness of Socrates (cf. 221c4–d6) clearly has to do with the fact that he really does live by the utterly improbable philosophical principles dictated by his dialectical reasoning.[10]

But at the same time, the fusion between epistemology and ethics in Socrates' life goes hand in hand with a discordant contrast between the form and the meaning of his discourse, for the extraordinary impact that Socrates produces on his interlocutors is intimately linked to what Alcibiades describes as a strikingly comic nature both of his appearance and of his faux-naif manner of speaking: the most remarkable thing about the Socratic discourse is, according to Alcibiades, how utterly ridiculous it sounds at first and how meaningful, indeed almost divine, it emerges to be on closer scrutiny (221e4–7). It is for this reason that Alcibiades compares not only Socrates himself but also the Socratic discourse to the statues of grotesque looking satyrs that contain inside beautiful statues of Olympian gods (215a6–b2, cf. 216d5–217a2 and 221d7–222a7).[11]

In Alcibiades' eyes, Socrates is thus an 'insolent satyr' – a crafty seducer who infuses his admirers with a love for wisdom. What is particularly ironic about this comparison is that it is in fact Alcibiades himself whom Plato consistently casts in the *Symposium* as a satyr-like figure – a veritable embodiment of Dionysiac licentiousness who, at a precociously tender age, tried to seduce Socrates and who now turns a sober intellectual discussion into a drunken revelry.[12] What Alcibiades sees in Socrates at first is thus nothing but a distorted projection of his own satyr-like image. But the transformative effect of Socrates' living presence has to do precisely with Alcibiades' discovery of the striking discrepancy between this familiar-looking 'satyric' surface and the truly unique, 'divine' essence underneath.[13]

Most importantly for Plato's conceptualization of the striking impact of the Socratic discourse, Alcibiades' comparison implicitly draws a contrast between the transformative revelation produced by the unexpected 'opening' of this image and the 'petrifying' effect that Socrates himself attests to Agathon's semantically closed speech. The radical self-reflexivity of Agathon's Gorgianic rhetoric effectively cancels out the distinction between form and meaning.[14] For the only way Agathon can paint his image of Eros as a paragon of untroubled perfection is by minimizing the referential function of language and by moulding it instead into a polished verbal artefact. It is precisely this skilfully enforced 'iconic' analogy between language and the object of representation that turns the beholders of this artefact into cognitively passive admirers, frozen, as it were, into the numb immobility of a stone statue. The Socratic discourse is based on radically different semiotic principles and produces a radically different cognitive effect: it is the stunning surprise caused by the suddenly transpiring gap between its patently banal 'surface' (consisting of pack-asses, smiths, shoemakers, and tanners, 221e4–7) and its 'divine' meaning that, as it were, startles the recipients into a state of heightened wakefulness, thereby urging them, too, to aspire to the utterly improbable fusion, embodied by Socrates himself, between philosophical thinking and philosophical life.

Crucially, the 'erotic' impact that Alcibiades attributes to Socrates' embodied dialectic depends not only on the discursive content of Socrates' words but also on the living presence of Socrates himself, who by withstanding Alcibiades' erotic advances and by demonstrating an unparalleled courage in battle endows his idealist epistemology with an ethical meaning.[15] As I would like to show now, Plato's *Phaedrus* can be read as an extended reflection on the possibility of a *written text* emulating the transformative effect produced by Socrates' physical presence.

In the 'Egyptian myth' at the end of the *Phaedrus*, Theuth praises his invention of writing as a unique 'drug' for memory and wisdom (274e6–7).[16] To the highest Egyptian god Ammon, however, writing is likely to foster nothing but forgetfulness – providing a 'drug' for reminding rather than memory (275a5–6), creating a mere semblance of wisdom (275a6), and turning readers cut off from the immediate contact with a philosophical teacher (275a7) into arrogant (and ignorant) pseudo-philosophers (275b2). Socrates' subsequent comparison of a written text to a static pictorial image of an animal incapable, in the absence of its 'progenitor', of either choosing its addressee or defending its own meaning – seems to stress the superiority of a live Socratic conversation over *any* form of writing (275d4–e5).[17] But on closer scrutiny, the *Phaedrus* turns out to paint a much more complex picture.

What triggers the conversation is Phaedrus' enthusiasm for Lysias' speech – a sophistic *jeu d'esprit* that defends the paradoxical thesis that it is better for a beloved to please a non-lover than a lover (230e6–234c5). The speech is a first-person monologue delivered by a non-lover, who strives to convince a potential (non)-beloved of the advantages of lovelessness over love: while the lover is depicted as a madman, prepared to go to any lengths to impose his tyrannical will on the beloved and then abandoning him when the love subsides, the relationship with a non-lover is praised as harbouring no unpleasant surprises to the boy's freedom, reputation and emotional poise.[18] The fact that the non-lover concludes his appeal to his non-beloved by urging him not to hesitate to 'ask' any questions if he so 'desires' (234c5 εἰ δ' ἔτι τι ποθεῖς, ἡγούμενος παραλελεῖφθαι, ἐρώτα) shows that Plato frames Lysias' rhetorically self-defeating speech as a sophisticated joke:[19] while in the *Symposium* the pun between 'love' and 'questioning' (ἔρωτα – ἐρώτα, cf. 199c1–d3) serves to capture the very essence of the erot(et)ics of the Socratic elenchus, in Lysias' speech the same pun draws attention to the inability of sophistic entertainment to raise any meaningful questions or to prompt any intellectual or emotional response – apart, perhaps, from causing one to admire the speaker's skill to say the same thing over and over again in an endless variety of ways (cf. 234c6–7 and 234e2–4). Like Agathon's speech in the *Symposium*, Lysias' speech performs a radical closure of meaning, which indeed leaves nothing to be desired.

The three speeches in the first half of the *Phaedrus* (Lysias' written speech followed by the other two that Socrates himself improvises on the spot) supply material for Socrates' theoretical discussion of rhetoric and writing in the second half.[20] Quite tellingly, Lysias' speech is framed as the quintessence of whatever is supposed to be bad about writing in general: struck by Socrates' praise of philosophical Eros, Phaedrus now imagines that Lysias, too, would admit the inferiority of his own writing and stop writing altogether (237c7) – an assumption from which Phaedrus then extrapolates that writing as such should be considered a 'shameful' pursuit (257d5–8). The Egyptian myth, as well as the comparison of writing to a static pictorial image, seems to confirm this sweeping rejection of writing.

But as the discussion progresses, Socrates gradually makes Phaedrus envisage the possibility of a 'good' kind of writing. This writing would be an image of 'the living and animate speech of someone knowledgeable' (276a8–9); it would rely on dialectic to inscribe directly on the reader's soul (276a5–7) the notions of 'justice and other things' (276e2–3); and, planted each time anew in different souls, it would continue to bear fruit forever.[21] Like any writing, this kind of writing, too, would have to be conscious not only of its fundamentally playful nature (277e5 παιδιάν . . . πολλήν) but also of the fact that the best thing that a written text can achieve is to remind the reader of what s/he already knows (277e9–278a1 ἀλλὰ τῷ ὄντι αὐτῶν τοὺς βελτίστους εἰδότων ὑπόμνησιν γεγονέναι). This statement, which at first sounds like a mere reiteration of Ammon's disparagement of writing as an instrument of reminding rather than memory (Pl. *Phdr.* 275a5–6),[22] is itself a striking specimen of disingenuous playfulness, which makes it possible for the *reader* to experience the transformation of what looks like a reminder of an earlier passage into a revelation of something new.

Applied to Lysias' speech, the notion of writing as a means of reminding clearly evokes Phaedrus' inability to memorize that elegant piece of empty verbiage, which, although he had spent a lot of time trying to learn it by heart, he can only reproduce to Socrates by reading the manuscript that he hides underneath his garment (228a5–e5): Lysias' writing indeed leaves no traces in the soul, fostering only forgetfulness (cf. 275a2 λήθην) and making Phaedrus incapable of recollecting things from within himself (cf. 275a4–5). But in the case of the good kind of writing, 'writing as reminding' would mean a completely different thing. Now that the possibility of writing informed by dialectic has been acknowledged, the 'recollective' effect (ὑπόμνησις) that it is expected to produce on the reader turns out to be identical to the effect produced on the interlocutors by Socrates' dialectic – an effect that famously consists in a revelatory experience of 'being reminded' (ἀνάμνησις) of the truth that one has known all along despite its being hidden under the layers of misconception.[23] This kind of writing would indeed serve not to store information (cf. μνήμης . . . φάρμακον) but to foster dialectical recollection.

The reason why Socrates, so effusive on the topic of speeches, does not cite to Phaedrus a single example of the good kind of writing is doubtless that Plato expects his *readers* to recognize that it is in fact epitomized by his own dialogues, whose main purpose can after all be seen to consist in exploring different ways of 'planting' Socrates' 'love for wisdom' in the readers' 'souls'.[24] By venturing outside the city walls of Athens Socrates turns what, for him, is the utterly uninstructive physical nature into the abode of 'the divine cicadas' that urge everyone to become a devotee of the Muses (259c2–6).[25] Likewise, Socrates' presence in Plato's written text transforms writing from a dead pictorial image into a medium of dialectical instruction that can infuse every receptive reader with the Socratic desire for the absolute. Most notably, the experience of reading the *Phaedrus* itself, with its countless revelatory (dis-)analogies between different levels of meaning, is indeed likely to transform a reader endowed with the 'right kind of soul' (cf. Pl. *Phdr.* 276e6 ψυχὴν προσήκουσαν) into an aspiring dialectician – into what Socrates himself calls 'a lover of divisions and collections' (Pl. *Phdr.* 266b3–4).

Thus, Plato's written text aims to produce on its readers the same impact as Socrates himself produces on his interlocutors. By emulating the transformative effect of Socrates' oral discourse, Plato's dialogues strive to preserve, beyond Socrates' physical death, the embodied presence of the revelatory image described by Alcibiades in the *Symposium* – the image of an 'insolent satyr' containing inside the 'divine' truths of dialectic.

Horace and the intertextual continuum

Like Plato's *Phaedrus*, Horace's *Ars Poetica* draws an analogy between a written text and a static pictorial image – a pervasive analogy that culminates in the famous *ut pictura poesis* passage (361–365). The grotesque paintings – the Scylla-like fish-woman and the Centaur-like man-horse (1–5)[26] – presented at the very beginning of the *Ars* as illustrations of what a poet should never imitate, draw attention, as Plato does in the *Phaedrus* (cf. 264c2–3), to organic unity (23 *simplex dumtaxat et unum*) and mimetic propriety as the highest criteria to be observed in poetic composition.[27] The precepts that Horace imparts to his pupils aim to teach them how to produce seamlessly polished works of verbal art reminiscent of Agathon's speech in Plato's *Symposium* – impeccably structured, mimetically credible, and semantically unequivocal – while the poet striving after this ideal of propriety is repeatedly compared to a mimetic artisan, who uses language as his, of necessity transient, raw material (68–69) and moulds it in such a way as to achieve perfect order both in a sentence and in a narrative plot.[28]

It is quite noteworthy, however, that the *ut pictura poesis* passage is followed by a lengthy passage on the pointlessness of being one of those mediocre poets that, according to Horace, can be found in abundance in every aristocratic Roman family (372–382. Cf. *epist.* 2.1.108–117). On the surface, Horace seems to imply that the reason for the amateur versifiers' mediocrity is that they are simply not privy to the secrets of poetic art that he is now imparting to the Piso boys. But given the fact that Horace's precepts hardly ever go beyond the staple fare of a Roman *grammaticus*,[29] this simply cannot be the case. Ironically, Horace seems to be perfectly aware that his rules are only capable of turning his students into mediocre poets belonging to the *servum pecus* of *imitatores* ridiculed by him at *Epistles* 1.19.19.[30] For he emphasizes again and again that, in order to become more, one needs, in addition to art, something that cannot be taught and that, judging from his occasional remarks, his addressees do not seem to possess[31] – a talent, or even a touch of poetic madness (295–301, 323–332, 408–411).[32]

Quite tellingly, the *Ars* ends with a pointed contrast between two extreme cases – the aristocratic poet, who has entirely absorbed Horace's precepts and the mad poet – a pure embodiment of poetic genius (419–476). What this contrast aims to highlight is the different survival odds of the poetry produced by these two figures. The rich poet is emphatically discouraged from reciting to the only audience he is likely to attract – namely to his clients, who in the hope of remuneration would ecstatically applaud anything he writes, no matter how bad it is (419–437).[33] Thus, the art of versification taught by Horace emerges as nothing but a learned pastime, whose outcome is likely to gratify no one but the versifier himself and is therefore inevitably doomed to speedy oblivion. Unlike the cloistered poetic 'artist' writing ephemeral verses for his own enjoyment, the mad poet is a public celebrity obsessed with immortality, whom Horace compares to Empedocles jumping into the burning crater of Aetna to prove that he is an immortal god (464–466). What is more, it is only thanks to his madness that the mad poet can hope to stay alive: for unless one lets him die, he will grab one like a raging bear and read one to death, drinking one's blood like a leech until he is fully sated.[34]

Conspicuously enough, this monstrous bear–leech hybrid harks back to the similarly grotesque figures that at the beginning of the poem illustrated the opposite of the aesthetic ideal appropriate for a decorous lesson in poetic art.[35] Besides, there is a disturbing resemblance between the figure of the mad poet and some of Horace's own self-portrayals. To begin with, the mad poet echoes the 'Augustan' poet (i.e., Horace himself) caricatured in the *Epistle* 2.1 as an affected diva who annoys the *princeps* with unsolicited performances and is offended by the slightest sign of disinterest.[36] Furthermore, the grotesque mixture of a bear and a leech conjures up, in an exaggerated form, the image of Horace as a client poet playing the role of a sympotic entertainer to his aristocratic patron in the *Satires*[37] – this impression further reinforced by the parallel between the *plena cruoris hirudo* at the end of the *Ars* and the *conviva satur* as the embodiment of a truly fulfilled life at the end of *Satires* 1.1.[38] This partial analogy makes the contrast with the aristocratic poetic 'artist' reciting his compositions to needy clients earlier in the *Ars* even more pointed: while, by giving both poetry and nourishment, the rich poet gets nothing substantial in return, his poetry simply vanishing into nothingness along with the food, the bear-leech of a client poet survives, both literally and figuratively, on the subsistence provided by his host.[39]

As a result, the speaker of the *Ars*, too, emerges as a hybrid creature – a disconcerting mixture of a sober 'artist' and a mad poet. And it is precisely the blending of these seemingly incompatible elements that ultimately generates the poem's meaning. By repeatedly drawing parallels between poetry and visual art, the *Ars* confirms that the goal pursued by Horace throughout his oeuvre consists in building an artwork-like self-immortalizing monument.[40] At the same time, the poem's conclusion stresses that this monument is more than a lifeless static image, which in *Odes* 4.8 and in the *Epistle to Augustus* is permanently put on display in the museum-like space of a library.[41] Moreover, in contrast to the ritual immortality of *Odes* 3.30, where the poet's perpetual rejuvenation is notionally coextensive with the Roman state religion (the *pontifex maximus* climbing the Capitol with a silent Vestal Virgin), in the *Ars* the poet's afterlife is envisaged as the existence of a voracious parasitic organism that may be able to outlive not only its hosts but also Roman cultural institutions.

This vision of poetic immortality clearly evokes the mode of self-fashioning that Horace repeatedly employs in his earlier poetry. In the *Satires*, the *Epodes* and the *Odes*, Horace presents himself as dependent both on his patrons (Maecenas and, later, Augustus) and on his poetic predecessors – Lucilius in the *Satires*, Archilochus in the *Epodes*, Alcaeus in *Odes* 1–3, Pindar in *Odes* 4 (cf. *epist.* 2.2.99–100), and Callimachus throughout his entire oeuvre. In all these collections, Horace revives old poetic genres in order to create what are essentially encomiastic portrayals of his patrons.[42] But by posing as a new Lucilius, a new Archilochus, a new Alcaeus, a new Pindar and a new Callimachus, Horace not only secures his own poetic existence in contemporary Rome but also grants a new life to his poetic predecessors – not by copying them but by creatively transforming them in such a way as to make sense of his own age (cf. *epist.* 1.19.19–34). Like his relationship with his patrons, Horace's relationship with his poetic predecessors is based on mutual dependence: while he owes the very fact of his poetic existence to his patrons and to his models, both of them may in fact owe even more to Horace himself, who promises them nothing less than a semblance of eternal life. It is of utmost importance in this connection that the audience that Horace addresses in the *Ars* consists of aspiring poets. For what now seems to be envisaged in the conclusion of the poem is that the only way for Horace himself to achieve eternal life, rather than the eternal existence of a lifeless pictorial image/a book stored in the library, is by surviving on the blood of future 'new Horaces'.

Conclusion

Both Plato and Horace conceive of their written texts as metaphorical living creatures that, in contrast to material works of art, survive forever not by staying the same but by constantly blending with the subjectivities of their recipients – Plato's Socratic discourse bearing fruit in the souls of future philosophers and Horace's poetry surviving on the blood of future poets. Both types of written discourses – Plato's dialogues and Horace's poems – could thus be seen as 'posthuman' in a double sense of the term. On the one hand, both Plato and Horace purport to transform the subjectivities of their primary speakers (Socrates' and Horace's poetic persona) into disembodied 'information patterns' that are not susceptible to the vicissitudes of the material world. But on the other, both Plato and Horace reveal that these disembodied information patterns can only retain the semblance of life by entering a symbiotic relationship with the living.

CHAPTER 30
BEYOND THE BEAUTIFUL EVIL? THE ANCIENT/ FUTURE HISTORY OF SEX ROBOTS
Genevieve Liveley

In Donna Haraway's classic anticipation and celebration of posthumanism, 'A Cyborg Manifesto', she identified the semi-organic, semi-technological, figure of the modern cyborg as a symbol of and for the posthuman, a chimerical hybrid of organism and machine.[1] According to Haraway, therefore, a posthuman future was one that offered the chance for us optimistically to imagine:

> lived social and bodily realities in which people are not afraid of their joint kinship with animals and machines, not afraid of permanently partial identities and contradictory standpoints ... [and] to see from both perspectives at once because each reveals both dominations and possibilities unimaginable from the other vantage point.[2]

Indeed, Haraway's celebration of the hybridity and multiplicity of perspectives and politics afforded by the posthuman blurring of distinctions between human and machine (which, in this context, includes but is not limited to the transhuman[3]) heralds one of the dominant discourses and fundamental concerns of posthumanism. As Rosi Braidotti suggests in her own 2013 posthuman 'manifesto':

> The issue of technology is central to the post-anthropocentric predicament ... The relationship between the human and the technological other has shifted in the contemporary context, to reach unprecedented degrees of intimacy and intrusion. The posthuman predicament is such as to force a displacement of the lines of demarcation between structural differences, or ontological categories, for instance between the organic and the inorganic, the born and the manufactured, flesh and metal, electronic circuits and organic nervous systems.[4]

The relationships between humans and machines that most interest Haraway, both in her 'Cyborg Manifesto' and in her latest work on the posthuman or Anthropocene era (or, rather, the *Chthulucene*, as Haraway terms it) are those that she describes as 'kinships' – that is, those that involve social, cultural and quasi-familial interactions, communications, and connections.[5] However, these are not the kinds of relationships between humans and machines that have really seized the posthuman imagination and carried forward into popular twenty-first century visions of our future social and bodily realities. The kinds of human–machine relationships that have come to dominate the public discourse on this topic are predominantly – and pruriently – *sexual*. The poster girls (and boys) for twenty-first century posthumanism and the 'posthuman predicament' are not cyborgs, it seems, but sex robots or 'sexbots'.

Indeed, a plethora of sex robot stories in contemporary film, television and news media all advertise the rise and rise of the sexbot, symbol of and for posthuman bodies and relationships.

A number of journalists and academics have confidently predicted in recent years that 'the future of sex ... is in robotics'.[6] In 2015 *Vanity Fair* heralded the 'Dawn of the Sex Bots'.[7] The much-publicized 'Roxxxy', marketed by TrueCompanion as 'the world's first sex robot' is supposed to be ready now to buy on-line (for just $6,995 plus shipping).[8] *Synthea Amatus* launched its AI equipped model 'Samantha' in 2017, and several other robotics companies have sex robots in preparation for the market.[9] That market is already estimated to be worth $30 billion, hence the confident (if highly exaggerated) claims being made by so many media sources that the sex robots of science fiction are about to become social reality.

Yet the classical tradition of Graeco-Roman myth tells a somewhat different story – that sex robots are not a recent invention but have played an important part in the human imagination for millennia. This paper investigates what we might learn about the future of sex robots in posthuman society from such ancient narratives. What kinds of priorities and paradigms do we find in classical myths concerning proto-sexbots and how do they shape contemporary debates and concerns? In particular, how do they inform the anticipatory discourse of social and ethical benefit and risk – and the associated utopian/dystopian thinking – that dominates modern narratives about sex robots?

For, as we will see, in the public and media debates on this theme, a predominantly utopian/dystopian binary shapes these narratives. In the robo-utopia script, robots consign prostitution, sex-crimes and loneliness to history; in the robo-dystopia, the robot as feminized object, purchased and prostituted, invites the concomitant abuse of vulnerable humans. We encounter ostensibly parallel scripts in classical myths and narratives too: notably those of Pygmalion in the Roman poet Ovid's *Metamorphoses* (10.243–297) and 'the beautiful evil' (*kalon kakon*) Pandora in Hesiod's *Theogony* (53–105). This chapter argues that a new approach to modern mythmaking is required, re-viewing and revising these modern scripts in the light of their more nuanced ancient analogues, if we are to realize a new world of human–robot social relations and myths – a posthuman world in which we are able, as Haraway hoped, 'to see from both perspectives at once ... [to see] possibilities unimaginable from the other vantage point'.[10]

Prominent among those who welcome the acceleration of sex robot technology as and at the vanguard of posthuman society is David Levy, who imagines a distinctly utopian future as its result. Levy predicts that the lonely and the bereaved especially will benefit, and that 'many who would otherwise have become social misfits, social outcasts, or even worse will instead be better-balanced human beings'.[11] In Levy's robo-utopia, prostitution, sex-crimes and loneliness will be consigned to history:[12] 'The world will be a much happier place because all those people who are now miserable will suddenly have someone. I think that will be a terrific service to mankind,' he says.

Although reliable research validating the actual social benefits of sexual human–robot relationships has yet to be produced, Levy's utopian vision finds some purchase in the self-reporting and marketing of both 'realistic' sex dolls and their robotic counterparts. Abyss Creations, the designers and makers of 'RealDolls', report that their products have been purchased by a nursing association, prostate cancer survivors, burn victims, and those with disabilities; they also claim that psychiatrists use their dolls in therapeutic treatment settings and that parents buy them for use by their autistic or socially excluded grown-up children.[13] Indeed, sex robots are recommended in some sources as a potential solution for meeting the sexual needs 'of the severely physically and mentally disabled and the many elderly people who suffer from degenerative diseases'.[14] One of the perceived advantages of the sex robot in these contexts is that it notionally replaces the role of the human sex worker, potentially limiting some of the social, ethical and physical harms currently associated with sex work. Futures researchers Ian Yeoman and Michelle Mars develop this concept into a quasi-utopian vision for safer sex tourism: 'In 2050, Amsterdam's red light district will all be about android prostitutes who are clean of sexual transmitted infections (STIs), not smuggled in from Eastern Europe and forced into slavery, the city council will have direct control over android sex workers controlling prices, hours of operations and sexual services.'[15]

However, emerging research is questioning these and other claims being made for the social benefits of sex robots, instead raising significant concerns regarding the risks of 'misogynistic objectification' – that is, 'the potential for harm by further promoting the pervasive idea that living women too are sex objects that should be constantly available ... and intensifying existing physical and sexual violence against women and children'.[16] Sherry Turkle points to the dangers of isolation and de-socialization among posthumans who prefer undemanding robot relationships to complex human relationships, arguing that 'the dream of the artificial confidante and then love object confuses categories that are best left unmuddled'.[17]

Co-founder of the Campaign Against Sex Robots, Kathleen Richardson, is also cautious.[18] 'Paedophiles, rapists, people who can't make human connections – they need therapy, not dolls,' Richardson argues.[19] She also takes issue with the gendered and misogynistic narrative that the vision of a robo-utopia assumes – the sex robot a passive, female object, purchased and prostituted; its user(s) active, male, purchasing safe sex on demand and avoiding complex interpersonal relationships with 'real' women. Richardson suggests that:

> the development of sex robots will further reinforce relations of power that do not recognise both parties as human subjects. Only the buyer of sex is recognised as a subject, the seller of sex (and by virtue the sex-robot) is merely a thing to have sex with.... [H]uman lifeworlds of gender and sexuality are inflected in making of sex robots, and ... these robots will contribute to gendered inequalities found in the sex industry.[20]

Richardson and other supporters of the Campaign Against Sex Robots argue that we need to question and change this narrative – both in our 'human lifeworlds' and in the posthuman storyworlds that help shape them.[21]

The work of computer scientist and archaeologist Kate Devlin sets out to do precisely that. Her work aims to add nuance to the scholarly discourse on this topic, including to the scholarly literature published on the important ethical, legal and socio-economic issues of robotics, machine ethics and AI in recent years – especially those under such headings as: 'Robotic Rape and Robotic Child Sexual Abuse', 'Doom Scenarios' and 'Dystopian Futures' involving not only sex robots but companion and care robots.[22]

Devlin highlights the ways in which popular narratives about robot sex – such as those played out in recent cinematic fictions, *Lars and the Real Girl*, *Her* and *Ex Machina* – are critically shaping the discourse on this subject and informing the research and attitudes underpinning both sides of the debate.[23] Devlin wants to challenge straightforwardly utopian/dystopian narratives about sex robots and looks forward to 'carving a new narrative'.[24] Or, rather, she looks backward. Because one of the ways that Devlin suggests we might plot a less polarizing narrative about sex robots is by returning to some ancient stories about human–humanoid sex. She writes: 'The relationship between humans and their artificial counterparts runs right back to the myths of ancient Greece, where sculptor Pygmalion's statue was brought to life with a kiss. It is the stuff of legend and of science fiction – part of our written history and a part of our imagined future.'[25]

Yet Devlin's appeal to the classical tradition in support of her endeavour to carve a 'new narrative' is not unique. We encounter similar appeals to the ancient world, and particularly to the Ovidian myth of Pygmalion, across the modern literature on the topic of sex robots. David Levy argues that 'Sex with humanlike artifacts is by no means a twenty-first century concept – in fact, its foundations lie in the myths of ancient Greece' – and, more specifically, with 'The myth of Pygmalion'.[26] The cover of Levy's 2007 book even declares that: 'From Pygmalion falling for his chiselled Galatea, to Dr Frankenstein marvelling at his monster, to the man meets machine fiction of Philip K. Dick and Michael Crichton, humans have been enthralled by the possibilities of emotional relationships with their technological creations.'[27] John Sullins, in his work exploring the ethics of sex robots, claims that 'The dream of a perfect artificial lover is at least as old as the myth of Pygmalion.'[28] And Sophie Wennerscheid appears to conflate reality and fantasy no less than the ancient and modern worlds in her claim that: 'Ever since Pygmalion succeeded in creating the perfect lover, the idea of intimate relationships between humans and artificially created beings has become more and more popular.'[29]

Many of the contemporary films and fictions that treat the subject of human–robot sexual relations are also explicit in acknowledging their connection to and reception of the classical tradition. As Emma Hammond observes, in Alex Garland's 2015 film *Ex Machina*, Nathan, the creator of the AI sexbot Ava: 'explicitly refers to his own creation process as Promethean, drunkenly mumbling: "It is what it is. It's Promethean. The clay and fire." In doing so, Nathan configures the other players in this triangular power play as, respectively, an Epimetheus – Caleb whose role is to be deceived – and a Pandora – Ava whose role is to deceive'.[30]

There is an obvious rationale for these ubiquitous appeals to ancient myth in modern discussions and treatments of sex robots: establishing a connection between a modern phenomenon and its purported origins in the ancient world lends authority, legitimacy and even decorum to a topic which is often regarded as 'seedy, sordid . . . [and] sad'.[31] However, there are other potential benefits to be realized in plotting this relationship between past and future robo-myths – albeit one that requires a closer, more intimate, engagement with the complex, hybrid narratives through which these ancient stories reach us.

The heuristic value of ancient fictions in helping us to plot our imagined futures is enhanced by the openness of such fictions to very different, even contradictory, interpretations – the hallmark, perhaps, of the 'classics'. These narratives invite and authorize us to see more than one perspective at the same time, to embrace contradiction and complexity. The Pygmalion myth, best known through the Roman poet Ovid's re-telling of it in his *Metamorphoses* (10.243–297), certainly invites a multiplicity of perspectives and evaluations. We can simultaneously read this narrative of an artist whose life-like statue (seemingly) comes to life as a morality tale on the virtues of celibacy. As a celebration of chastity and patience rewarded. As the tale of a lonely social misfit transformed through love for his 'living doll' into (Levy's notion of) a 'better-balanced human being'.[32] But we are also invited by the narrative to notice that Pygmalion carves his ivory *automaton* and takes her to bed with him because he has no wife or lover, and is disgusted at the prospect of sex with prostitutes, misogynistically viewing 'real' women as morally and physically repugnant. We might also spot that the narrative's author, Ovid, is not wholly sympathetic to Pygmalion's enterprise: he does not narrate this story himself but distances himself from its actors and action by placing it in the mouth of one of his internal narrators – the poet Orpheus, who (like Pygmalion himself) is explicitly characterized by Ovid as an anti-social misogynist.[33]

Our introduction to the Ovidian Pygmalion is through the story of the Propoetides, a group of sisters who are described by Ovid as the world's first prostitutes (10.238–242) – though whether by choice or force is left ambiguous:

> Quas quia Pygmalion aevum per crimen agentis
> viderat, offensus vitiis, quae plurima menti
> femineae natura dedit, sine coniuge caelebs
> vivebat thalamique diu consorte carebat.
> interea niveum mira feliciter arte
> sculpsit ebur formamque dedit, qua femina nasci
> nulla potest, operisque sui concepit amorem.
> virginis est verae facies, quam vivere credas,
> et, si non obstet reverentia, velle moveri:
> ars adeo latet arte sua. miratur et haurit
> pectore Pygmalion simulati corporis ignes.
> saepe manus operi temptantes admovet, an sit
> corpus an illud ebur, nec adhuc ebur esse fatetur.
> oscula dat reddique putat loquiturque tenetque
> et credit tactis digitos insidere membris
> et metuit, pressos veniat ne livor in artus.[34]

> Because Pygmalion had seen these women living their lives of shame, offended by the vices which nature had given so generously to the female mind, he lived celibately without a wife, and for a long time lacked a partner for his bed. Meanwhile, with marvellous art, he successfully carved snow-white ivory and gave it a beauty such as no woman could be born with, and he conceived a passion for his own work. Its appearance is that of a real girl, whom you would think to be alive, and to want to be moved, if modesty did not prevent it. To such an extent is art hidden by art itself. Pygmalion is amazed and fills his heart with desire for the artificial body. Often he lifts his hands to the piece, testing whether it may be flesh or ivory, and he no longer admits it to be ivory. He gives kisses and thinks they are returned, he speaks to it and cuddles it, and believes that fingers sink into its flesh at his touch, and he fears that bruises may appear on the pressed limbs.

Pygmalion treats the statue as if it were a real woman, caressing and kissing it, believing that his attentions and affections are returned. And paradoxically, having created this private sex object in order to avoid the use of prostitutes, Pygmalion seems to attribute to it/her at least some of 'the vices which nature had given so generously to the female mind' (*Met.* 10.244–245). For, according to the conventions of the elegiac literary tradition to which this narrative explicitly appeals, he effectively treats his statue as a prostitute (or courtesan) by seeking to arouse her desire for him by presenting her with dresses, jewels, and other expensive gifts.[35] Indeed, the reference to 'bruises' here introduces a particularly troubling note. Praying to the goddess of love, not daring to ask to have his ivory statue for a wife – that is, crudely, for his fantasy to have sex with his statue to be sanctioned – he asks instead to have a wife just *like* his ivory statue:[36]

> constitit et timide 'si, di, dare cuncta potestis,
> sit coniunx, opto,' non ausus 'eburnea uirgo'
> dicere Pygmalion 'similis mea' dixit 'eburnae'.[37]
>
> He stood at the altar and timidly spoke, 'If, gods, you can give everything, I pray to have as a wife', not daring to say 'my ivory girl', Pygmalion said, 'one like my ivory'.

Pygmalion's hesitant speech (perfectly reproduced in the tentative Latin here) eloquently expresses his confusion and his inability to make clear distinctions between representation and reality, human and object, his dangerous desires only thinly veiled.[38] This confusion continues when he finds that his prayers have been answered – literally – and that he has been granted a wife exactly *like* his statue. Yet Pygmalion continues to touch her as though it/she were still a work of art – not as a lover caresses the body of a 'real' flesh and blood human woman but as a sculptor moulds a wax model, an object (10.284–286). Indeed, as Pygmalion's statue opens her eyes at the climactic moment of vivification, a clever pun in the word for sky/sculptor's engraving tool in the Latin *caelo* offers a reminder that, in a sense, she is now (apparently) able to see only because of Pygmalion's technical brilliance as a sculptor (10.294). Even as a (fantasy) woman of flesh and blood she remains emphatically his creation, his 'living doll', her transformation representing little real change. Certainly, Alison Sharrock sees very little difference between the statue and the woman, who she appropriately names Eburna ('Ivory').[39] For Sharrock, 'in the final metamorphosis Eburna becomes even more like an automaton . . . [and] seems barely more alive than she was as a statue.'[40]

All this reminds us that the story of Pygmalion and (arguably) the world's first sexbot does not have an unambiguously happy ending – despite Hermann Fränkel's description of it as an ostensibly utopian 'fable of a miracle, of art, of love, and of a better human being'.[41] The metamorphosis of one fetish and fantasy into another highlights the fact that, from an alternative/simultaneous perspective, Pygmalion's behaviours and desires throughout this narrative are represented as 'unnatural' and that Pygmalion's story is not to be viewed in a wholly positive light. Pygmalion's act of creation might even be seen as the (re)production of a daughter for whom he conceives an erotic and incestuous desire: the Latin is pregnant with words which suggest that the statue represents the artist's child.[42] Indeed, this configuration of the relationship between the artist and his statue as 'unnatural' and incestuous explicitly foreshadows the violently incestuous relationship between Pygmalion's grandson and his daughter that features in the next of Orpheus' tales in the *Metamorphoses* (10.298–502).[43]

A similar dark shadow is cast upon the Pygmalion story by another tale of a 'man-made' artificial woman, upon whom Eburna is closely modelled, and with whom Ovid invites us to draw suggestive parallels. That is Hesiod's misogynistic account of the creation of the first woman, Pandora, in his *Works and Days* (54–105) and *Theogony* (570–612) – in which she is characterized as a 'beautiful evil' (*kalon kakon*), and the first in a long line of artificial women with the potential to make the world both a better and a worse place.[44] Like Pandora, who is made to look just like 'a modest virgin' (*parthenoi aidoiei*, *Works and Days* 71), Pygmalion's

Eburna is also given 'the appearance of a real girl' (*Met.* 10.250), and showered with gifts before coming to life.[45] Indeed, if Pandora is the mythic prototype on which Pygmalion's sexbot is based, then we might see Pygmalion himself figured both as a Prometheus-like figure (one who creates and animates an artificial human), *and* simultaneously as a foolish Epimetheus (one who unthinkingly welcomes Pandora into his home and bed).[46]

In the ongoing debate about the future of sex robots in posthuman relationships, these ancient myths remind us that there is nothing new about the current controversies. Yet these stories also prompt us to ask whether our thinking about risk and opportunity, our postmodern mythmaking, needs to be quite so polarized. Does the dawn of the sexbots herald a purely utopian or purely dystopian future? Or does it promise/threaten both? Will we come to celebrate our Promethean prowess in technological innovation or regret our Epimethean lack of foresight in failing to curb or to ban outright the production and marketing of sex robots? Or will we do both? Are sex robots, as Hesiod would put it, a *kalon kakon* – potentially both good *and* bad for us?

In her most recent work, *Staying with the Trouble: Making Kin in the Chthulucene,* Donna Haraway argues not only for the importance of storytelling in shaping (and surviving in) a posthuman world, but also for a new mode of posthuman storytelling that is less polarizing, 'less binary'.[47] We need, she stresses, 'to change the story, to learn somehow to narrate – to think' differently, to tell stories which: 'make attachments and detachments ... make cuts and knots ... make a difference ... weave paths and consequences but not determinisms ... [which] are both open and knotted in some ways and not others ... [in] the patterning of possible worlds and possible times, material-semiotic worlds, gone, here, and yet to come'.[48]

Although she does not make this argument explicit in *Staying with the Trouble*, Haraway implicitly intuits here that the posthuman livingworld is programmed by the posthuman storyworld.[49] And it makes a world of difference in both cases not only what kinds of stories we tell but the way(s) in which we tell them. For, as narratologist Gerald Prince confirms:

> while narrative can have any number of functions (entertaining, informing, persuading, diverting attention, etc.), there are some functions that it excels at or is unique in fulfilling. Narrative always reports one or more changes of state but, as etymology suggests (the term narrative is related to the Latin *gnarus* – 'knowing,' 'expert,' 'acquainted with' ...), narrative is also a particular mode of knowledge. It does not merely reflect what happens; it discovers and invents what *can* happen.[50]

Once again, we can hear echoes from the ancient posthuman world here. Aristotle saw the role of narrative and dramatic poetry (in contrast to that of historiography or didactic poetry) as the *mimesis* of that which might or could happen and which would or could be possible according to necessity and probability (*Poetics* 9.1451a 36–8). Telling stories in this model (as opposed to telling *histories*) is not concerned with re-presenting things that have 'actually happened' but with representing possible things that might. Aristotle's various definitions of narrative *mimesis* emphasize its representation not of reality but of possibility.[51] Extending the logic of this, we can emphasize the potential of narrative *mimesis* to actively construct future reality, to shape and invent (to program) what can, what might, and what will, happen. As Jerome Bruner puts it in his ground-breaking work on the narrative construction of reality, 'narrative organizes the structure of human experience ... "life" comes to imitate "art" and vice versa'.[52] *How* we relate to sex robots in the future will be coded by *what* we relate – by our narratives – past, present, and future.

Complex, hybrid, narratives both ancient and contemporary, then, have a crucial part to play in shaping representations and perceptions if we are to realize a new posthuman world of human and robot relations which is not restricted by the on/off binaries of utopian and dystopian thinking – if we are to imagine a new posthuman storyworld *and* livingworld which maps consequences but not determinisms, which takes us beyond the *kalon kakon*, and beyond the beautiful evil.

CONCLUSIONS

Simon Goldhill

Will posthumanism have a lasting impact on classics, and can classics contribute to posthumanist thinking? Alex Dressler, in his excellent chapter, captures one worry of this book's foundational questions brilliantly. After his incisive reading of Seneca, which shows to what degree this Latin writer, from the centre of Roman power, anticipates strategies and concerns of posthumanist analysis, he concludes pertinently: 'It raises questions about the radical pedigree of posthumanist discourse, if the old order adumbrated it so coherently.' Virginia Burrus in turn notes how labile the field of so-called posthumanism is – this is an issue to which we will return – and recognizes, even more starkly, that the claims of some posthumanist thinkers to decentre the human by articulating the relation of the human to the non-human can be gratuitously overstated. She comments, drily: 'There never was a time when human agency was anything other than an interfolding network of humanity and non-humanity.' For both Dressler and Burrus, two outstanding discussions, it is evident that the human – as agent and in the process of self-understanding – has always been articulated between animals and gods, between material and spiritual substance, between self-centred self-sufficiency and radical over-determination. If posthumanism merely rediscovers again and again that Dionysus is a god with a human mother who emerges as an animal and transforms materiality and humanity into its other in a way which challenges the perception of reality as fixed, and leaves the human not the regulator and controller of reality but fragmented through a *sparagmos* that is both literal and conceptual – then what indeed is its 'radical pedigree'?

The excitement of this book is to lay out and explore the challenge of such a question. The book is eloquent testimony to what may prove a turning point or at least a salient juncture in how the humanities can contribute directly and self-consciously to what is all too often troped as an insistent problem of and for technology. The very variety of approaches on display here, combined with the editors' overview (which provides a quite other trajectory of discussion from many of the chapters), shows how fertile and indeed febrile the debate around posthumanism already is. The book as a whole poses from these multiple angles a crucial question: If the most insistent problems in contemporary society are to be approached, as posthumanist theorists demand, by displacing the hierarchical centrality of humanity in ecological, political and economic thinking, what place is there for the study of antiquity, which has so often been taken as the icon of humanism and the humanities?

In my *Schlußwort*, I will offer three responses to how this book treats this, its central question. First, I will develop a critical historicization to sharpen how classics should and should not pose a question to posthumanism; second, I will look at six specific issues raised by how this book engages with posthumanist thinking; third, I will offer two particular ways that classics can contribute to posthumanist arguments. The very labile nature of what is meant by posthuman or posthumanism has resulted in very different responses across this book's varied chapters. In the space available, it would be quite impossible to engage critically with all thirty chapters: my aim is to outline more generally how the book displays the potential and the worries of the interaction between posthumanism and classics.

I

Once upon a time in the West, the connection between literary, cultural and historical theories and the study of antiquity seemed necessary, compelling and pervasive. In the Renaissance, whichever branch of *Wissenschaft* you take, a new *theorized* engagement with the antiquity of Greece and Rome was instrumental in the transformations of society and its self-understanding. As the cityscape was redesigned by classicizing architecture, so the architecture of thinking was reshaped, and not just for intellectual elites. Humanism, an empire of letters whose imperialism still implicates each of us, set the study of Greek and the practice of Latin at its heart, and the theoretical project which humanists started, had its roots not just in the re-discovery of the classics, but in the resource and contribution of antiquity for such theoretical labour. We can easily continue such an account through the Enlightenment, and into the nineteenth century. It would be impossible to consider nineteenth-century theories of history, their prevalent obsession with self-placement in time, without their engaged turn to antiquity; or the theories of philology, the queen of sciences, without seeing how classics and theology together provided the theoretical ground for progress; or the material science of archaeology, without the *Sachphilologie* of the ancient Mediterranean and biblical lands; or the invention of anthropology without the theorization of comparative mythology that took antiquity as its grounding; or the challenges to theology that racked society, without the theorized study of the early church. The study of antiquity, institutionalized over this period as the discipline of classics, continued to be the stimulus, the resource and the leader in the work of theorizing our humanistic understanding of the past, and through it our position in the order of things.[1]

Over the course of the twentieth century, however, the dynamics of how classics and theory interact seem to have shifted. The texts of antiquity certainly continued to play an important role for many of the most influential theoretical thinkers (as 'theory' gradually became, for literature at least, a subject in itself). We could mention Derrida's pharmacological Plato and his repeated attempts to rewrite the metaphysics of the West, a philosophical tradition that, in his modelling, is established in and by Plato and Aristotle; or Foucault's history of sexuality that could not avoid a turn back to Greece and Rome; or Lévi-Strauss who made Oedipus his test-case for the structural analysis of myth; or Lacan, who, following Freud's Oedipus, took (Hegel's) Antigone onto the couch.[2] Yet it is less clear that the study of antiquity and the development of theory were still marching hand in hand. As the institutional status of classics, dominant in the nineteenth century, was repeatedly diminished across the twentieth, the professional academics who peopled the institutions of classics were less likely, it seems, to be the leaders of theoretical projects destined to become influential across the humanities. Perhaps in the study of sexuality, where antiquity has been so important in conceptualizing – and fantasizing – about the possibility of another way, classics as a discipline has contributed a theoretical spur to other fields – or maybe in the study of oral poetry.[3] All too often, however, the discipline of classics has adopted theory from other fields, without a reciprocal engagement.

This has often been a painful process, tied up with the politics of the profession and the gatekeepers of scholarship. Classics has always had its culture wars. It is striking too how often what has begun as a radical contribution of a new theorization leads to business as usual for classicists. When Julia Kristeva coined the term 'intertextuality', it was to understand how one system of signs was transformed or translated into another, at a systemic level.[4] It was a way of conceptualizing through language how political and social change took shape. By the beginning of the twenty-first century, in the discipline of classics, intertextuality has become little more than a version of 'cf', the oldest philological mechanism for noting a linguistic parallel or allusion. Far from being a means of exploring change through language and the interconnections of social process and linguistic translation at a systemic level, it has become – in the hands of most critics – a normative and rather dull way of indicating the continuity of ancient authors reading ancient authors, localized word-play.

The wit and caution of Dressler and Burrus about the mutual engagement of classics and posthumanism might seem well placed, then. Indeed, it would not be hard to point out some over-enthusiastic and under-aware assertions about the radical potential of posthumanism for classics. Martin Derecka opens his chapter: 'One of the lasting contributions of posthuman theory will be to stop us taking the body for granted.' As if feminism, for decades (and well before Judith Butler), has not been making the body precisely the place where nothing should be taken for granted;[5] as if anthropology has had nothing to say on how differently bodies are conceptualized cross-culturally;[6] as if early Christianity – for God's sake – had not made mortifying the flesh an insistent and precarious imperative, where the relation of the body to the self is challenged to the point of crisis;[7] as if biology – if God seems too much – has nothing to say on changing perceptions of what the materiality of the human is. . . . So, too, Roland Baumgarten, with equally misplaced over-certainty, states that the human–animal distinction has been 'fixed since antiquity' and only now is coming under question. If centaurs, satyrs, or Ovid's *Metamorphoses* – or, simply enough, the dog that barks inside each Homeric hero – must have a place in such an argument, what of the early modern arguments that indigenous Americans had no souls and thus could be slaughtered like soulless animals?[8] How much work would need to be done to determine when interstitial categories and boundary crossers do more than enforce distinctions?

On the one hand, we could see such unreflective claims of contemporary novelty as no more than classics turning the potential of the radical into business as usual – where the posthuman turns out to be no more than a rebranding of what Jamie Redfield, say, showed many years ago for Homer (and the editors duly cite him in the Introduction): namely, that nature and culture are mutually imbricated and (culturally) constructed categories, and that the work of the text is to assert and explore the dangers and potential of such imbrication, where the best of the human can collapse into the bestial, or into the material insensitivity of iron and stone, or rise to the sublimity of a god. That man will become mere burnt matter, or may live on in the form of song is the limiting condition of the body.[9] The *Odyssey*, for generations of critics, has precisely *questioned* what the word *andra* means, by exploring the limits of the human in its engagement with monsters, gods, animals, objects, let alone death, language, affective ties. The normal is defined in and through transgression of its limits. The human, as Burrus says, is *always* interfolded with the non-human.

On the other hand, however, I think there is a much more interesting set of questions at stake here, for classics *and* posthumanism. When Foucault announced the death of man, it was a specific version of humanity with which he was concerned, a version grounded in the Enlightenment's assertion of the centrality of the human and its insistence on the value of human reason (itself a response to humanism).[10] What does it mean, then, to go back before the Enlightenment's enthroning of man to explore posthumanism? One hero who surprisingly does not stride across the pages of this book is Protagoras. Protagoras declared – and it became a celebrated icon of what we call the fifth-century Enlightenment, for all too salient reasons – that 'man is the measure of all things'. This statement was a self-conscious and provocative challenge. First, it questioned the degree to which 'measure', *metron* – evaluation, reckoning, calibration – depended on external criteria or on the judgement of humans, and firmly declared for the human, and solely the human. In line with other critical intellectual thinking of the time, Protagoras' understanding of relativism is all-embracing. Man is the measure of *all* things: that is, even the material world is subject to man's perception, and man's perception – his measuring – is inconstant but ineluctable. Second, Protagoras removed the possibility of the divine as a regulation of what is, and how what is should be evaluated. There was no recourse to an external and unchallengeable system of authority or judgement. Protagoras is the patron saint of one brand of humanism, then, the humanism that puts humans firmly at the centre of things: for Protagoras, there is no ontology without epistemology, and his epistemology makes man the sole subject of knowing.

Yet Protagoras' provocation is framed by the polyphony of the fifth-century *polis*. Tragedy as a genre repeatedly demonstrates how the multifold attempts of humans towards epistemological or social autonomy are destined for failure and, what's more, for self-destructive self-delusion. 'The quarantined self', to use Tom Geue's nice phrase from another well-worked and smart chapter, is tragically undermined. Sophocles' Philoctetes is not so much 'in nature' (as Chiara Thumiger writes), but rather the play is constantly exploring the limits of civilization, by placing a body, increasingly in thrall to its own physical pain, its own materiality, in violent interaction with the destructive lies of a manipulative hierarchical social world: if human judgement is all, the play insists, then – against Protagoras' confidence – disastrous and divisive conflict will be the result. For Herodotus' historiography, cause and effect are not simply matters of human agency. To explore what the causes of the war are – his defining question – requires social, political and material systems. As *Airs, Waters, Places* insists – in the name of new science – the environment is determinative: humans are formed and normed by the material world around them. The claim of the centrality of the human, Protagoras' credo, is framed by counter-voices, or stands at one extreme pole of competing positions in dynamic interrelation with one another.

To historicize the central question of this book, then, leads to a recognition that to go back before the historical moment of humanism to explore posthumanism is to discover – inevitably? – a pre-humanism, where the claim of the centrality and dominance of the human is not yet a given and where the interfolding of the human with its others is repeatedly performed both in aggressive disavowal and in equally assertive assumption. Is this, then, where antiquity can contribute to the work of posthumanism? To reveal the possibility of an intellectual and social world that is not dependent on the invention of Man (in Foucault's terms)? To find a space of the 'not yet' – which may not only be a chronological condition – from which to view the trajectory of the challenge of the post- of posthumanism?

II

Before we could make such an argument about the pre-(post-)humanism of antiquity, and before we can evaluate the place of classics in posthumanism, and posthumanism in classics, we must ask some other questions about what this book has displayed and what it has occluded. Here are six pressing questions, part methodological and part historical, that arose for me and that criss-cross the book.

Whatever happened to anthropology?

Philippe Descola (cited once by Devecka, but scarcely used by anyone) in his stirring, grand study *Beyond Nature and Culture*, criticizes the apparent inevitability of constructing the world through a polarity which takes nature to mean the sum of the biological and material world, and culture to mean the variables of human society which is both separate from and imposes itself on that idea of nature.[11] Descola is unafraid of big structural thinking. He suggests that there are four dominant ways in which we can see the relation between humans and the environment, four ways in which indigenous communities construct that relation. That there are four ways immediately should signal that there is no natural or inevitable route to think nature. Descola is particularly keen to question the traditional Western construction, which he calls naturalism. In naturalism, argues Descola, physicality is a constant – the stuff of bodies and things – but what has life, spirit or soul, differs: we may share materiality with rocks and jaguars, but we are quite different from them in terms that are not physical. Second, and the system to which he himself seems sympathetic from his work with the Achuar, he calls animism. In animism, there is no opposition between nature and culture, but a continuity where the 'spirit' or 'soul' is continuous but there are physical differences. So, jaguars and humans and yams are all the same in social set-up and in souls but take different material form. It makes sense when an Achuar says my mother crossed the river and became a jaguar, or that a jaguar drinks beer, when it consumes what we call blood. Interiority is the same, physicalities are different: the reverse of naturalism. The third category is totemism, where interiorities and physicalities can both be shared: we are the bear group and the bear shares characteristics with us. Another group is the elk group, and they are different from us bears, but share physical and social characteristics with elks. The fourth relation is analogy. Here both interiorities and physicalities are different but are related through analogy: the microcosm of a human group is analogous to the macrocosm of the world.

Now, there is much to be said about Descola's systematization, which I have had to simplify in this briefest of versions. But two things at least are clear and pertinent. First, the dominance of Western thinking, the naturalism which grounds the arguments of posthumanism, is far from natural or inevitable. There are already other ways of conceptualizing the place of humans with regard to the materiality of the world and the environment, ways of thinking that would make posthumanism unnecessary. It helps us see how posthumanism is a culturally and historically specific problematic, that is by definition western-centric. Second, anthropology has for many years now been helping us understand this specificity, and it would be unwise to proceed as if these arguments and their testing had not taken place. Anthropology reminds us that how humans are conceptualized in the order of things is a fully ontological question, and that a subject cannot just pick and choose an ontology. However much the ontology of the Achuar can be understood from outside, it is not evident that it can be inhabited from outside. This should provide us with a serious caution for the normativity of posthumanism.

Whatever happened to God?

Classicists are by now very familiar with the tri-partite systematization of man, beast and god (with its interstitial figures and internal calibrations), as a means of understanding the culture of classical antiquity, and how the humanity of classical antiquity represented itself to itself. For most of historical time, human beings cannot be defined or comprehended without the sphere of the divine. For Christianity in particular, the boundaries of the human and the divine are an essential and contested arena because of the centrality of Jesus Christ whose humanity as God is fundamental. *Hoc est corpus meum* is a demonstrative statement that immediately challenges the self-understanding of the materiality of the body through the principles of transubstantiation. It is something of a surprise that so few of the chapters in this volume are concerned with how humanity makes sense in and against the divine and the imagination of immortality. The Enlightenment, however, with its specific enthronement of Man, is a self-consciously anti-clerical movement, and its commitment to reason is a counter-blast to the claims of mystery and the necessity of belief enshrined in religious thinking. Two questions then follow. Does the lack of discussion of divinity in so many of these chapters betoken a buried commitment to Enlightenment values, even as they set out to question the Enlightenment's commitment to Man's (self-serving) reason – and if so, at what cost? Can the classical world contribute to a discussion of posthumanism without taking more account of the divine, that remains, after all, a basic element of ancient Greek and Roman self-understanding?

Whatever happened to late antiquity?

It is remarkable that in thirty chapters on antiquity so few go beyond what the Victorians would have reckoned to be the established canon. The Pseudo-Lucianic *Onos* (according to Photius' dating) is not late enough to count as late antiquity; Simeon Stylites certainly is. But the vast majority of Greek subjects take their texts from Homer and the classical city; the Roman chapters also focus mainly on the most well-known literature. The lack of discussion of divinity is certainly aided by not turning to the era when Christianity and Rabbinic Judaism are taking shape in a way which will define Western culture – and what is understood by the human in it. The seven chapters in the section on de/humanization and animals avoid not just some obvious earlier texts such as Ovid's *Metamorphoses* – where the instability of the human is a fully politicized project – but, more importantly, works such as Oppian's *Halieutica* – a double-reflecting-mirror of imperial subjectivity and the world of fish, as Emily Kneebone's brilliant book exposes.[12] Nor is there any place for the two great poems of Nonnus, the *Dionysiaca* and the *Paraphrase of the Gospel of John*. Dionysus and Jesus – both gods born of humans who transform matter, self-perception and the stability of human order – are subject to Nonnus' (Dionysiac) poetics. It is in late antiquity where we have the widest range of texts testifying to the most thorough transformation of the understanding of the human.

Whatever happened to the imaginary?

This book begins with Aristotle, whose teleological thinking sets man (a gendered term, for Aristotle) at the apex of the physical world; it includes a brief interlude of historiography in Dionysius of Halicarnassus and touches further on philosophy and technological writing. But the majority of the chapters are firmly focused on what the modern West would call literature, and mainly poetry at that. The first section of the book, in the name of theory, runs from Aristotle through Foucault to less well-known theorists of the posthuman. Vast amounts of philosophy and theological writing that deal specifically with the human are not discussed. Where, then, should we look for the posthuman? Ontological pre-suppositions are to be found, it could be argued, in any and every text or enunciation concerning the place of humans in a material and living world. Yet it is less clear what the status of these texts – let us call them literary – is. Katherine Wasdin, in a wonderful phrase, talks of 'society on holiday'. When on holiday, as we have known at least since van Gennep, there is a pattern of expressivity that involves in its barest form a process of separation, a liminal period, and a process of reintegration. In the liminal period, it is standard to see reversals of norms, transgressive activity, and an apparent rejection of the very ideals of the teleology of the ritual process. So, to take a single and, for classicists, iconic example, in the *krupteia* the Spartan boy is sent into the wilds, to live on his own by trickery and deceit, before returning as a man to the collective world of straightforward obedience and honesty in the *sussition*. Such transgressions are not challenges to the dominant ideology but recognitions and supports of them. There is no ideological system that does not project images of its own transgression. Holidays are part of the calendar.

Literary texts have something of the holiday about them. When Aristophanes' *Birds* is staged in a festival for the city at Athens, funded by the city and acted by citizens, its image of the city seen otherwise certainly represents the city to itself – through carnival spectacles, as it were – and, through imagining the human through the society of birds, offers a comic criticism of human social behaviour and its corruptions. But comedy also relies on its licence. Comedy can always defend itself through a disavowal of its own instrumentality. A joke is just a joke. (As if . . .). It is because of the aesthetic, cultural, social status of the genre of comedy that critics have argued for generations about how seriously comedy should be treated – how inevitably conservative or potentially disruptive its verbal and conceptual hooliganism can be. Literary texts – to continue with this provisional and difficult category – can imagine the world otherwise. But it is no straightforward matter to determine their instrumentality in making the world otherwise. Even the most disruptive and challenging texts also have their normative complicities. So, when, then, are the texts that represent the wildest transgressions, most complicit with normativity? When are monsters no more than a delighted shiver from the imaginary of reason? Can pastoral poetry ever be more than the comfortable projection of the urban?

It seems to me that calibrating the instrumentality of the imaginary is not a task embraced by many of the chapters in this volume, committed as they are to their pursuit of a map of the inscription of otherness within the human. Aaron Kachuk's chapter is a particularly good example here, because his analysis of how the Roman crowd responded to the elephant when they saw somehow a humanity in the animal, and how this in turn responds to a specific representation of and in the imperial power system, is particularly well done. The Roman writers, Kachuk shows well, use a moment of oddness to explore the monstrous that lurks within the notion of the emperor's excessiveness (a structural thought that James McNamara analyses for Cato too): between the crowd, the elephant, the crowd's imagination of the elephant, and the emperor, a fascinating dynamic is set up. Yet to what degree is such a representation complicit with a projection of a wholly traditional normativity, to what degree is it in any sense instrumental in effecting a change of conceptualization of the place of the human?

If the posthuman is to become the grounds for a new conceptualization of the order of things, it will indeed require many sorts of texts and interventions – just as Christianity in late antiquity transformed the Graeco-Roman world only gradually and through a myriad of texts with different forms of persuasiveness as well as a range of stirring role models and other instruments and institutions of power; or just as the normativity of gender through feminism and gay rights has been gradually changed in the modern West (as yet an unfinished project) by a string of novels, films, television shows and art works as well as legal interventions, political activism and arguments at local and national levels. Imagining the world otherwise is a condition for transformation (as Katherine Fleming emphasizes eloquently); it is, however, more complex to disentangle the complicity of projected transgression, which uses negative exempla to reinforce normativity, from the radical potential of seeing the world otherwise. This too is a necessity for classicists exploring the limits of the human.

Whatever happened to politics?

I have assumed in the previous paragraphs that the posthuman is not a descriptive but a normative project – that the drive to conceptualize the human in a mutually defining, dynamically interactive, and interdependent eco-system of other animals and things is motivated not just by a desire to describe the world as it is, but by a recognition that the present era of the anthropocene is a (disastrous) moment where changes to the eco-system of the planet by humans have reached a tipping point, where not only is nature changed by humans *beyond repair* but also the very existence of an environment in which humans can make a good life is under threat by human intervention. Object-oriented ontology, distributed systems of agency, the agency of things, are, in this way of thinking, steps towards a more inclusive and responsible model for evaluating and directing human actions in society. It is – paradoxically enough – part of a continuing human exceptionalism, against which posthuman arguments are trained, that only humans can think and enact a posthumanist politics.

The editors use the worryingly ambivalent phrase 'ethically anarchic' in their Introduction. This may imply that it is possible and even desirable to be anarchic, but in a moral way. That is, a resistance to hierarchical systems of authority can be conceptualized and practised in a way which is ethically coherent. This has proved an attractive prospect to many contemporary activists, for whom local engagement, and even a recognition of an international network of local engagement, is a way of changing the agenda of political value in a community, in and through practice. The phrase may imply, however, that ethics can be treated anarchically. I cannot see that ethics *qua* ethics can be radically without system or indeed hierarchies of value. Posthumanism may seek to decentre the human, but it does not follow that, even in the recognition of mutual interdependence, there is no hierarchy of value. To save a budgie rather than a baby from a burning building cannot be expected to be treated as a morally justified action. To break my pen is not the same as to break my hand, for all that I need both equally to write. In either reading of the phrase, the editors raise a highly pertinent question of *how* to move *from* the recognition of the dangerous present, where the self-centredness of humanity contributes to the self-destructive descent of the anthropocene, *towards* the political as well as the conceptual changes that would counteract that descent. If to resist the anthropocene requires systemic transformation, then choices between values will be inevitable – and, as arguments about the right measures to take to combat climate change repeatedly show, not only is a reliable and informed and, above all, integrated policy hard to discover, but also getting agreement between vested interests at local and international level results in further political conflict.[13] There will be – and are – conflicting interests in such a thorough-going recalibration of the aims and objectives of human communities. To be ethically anarchic – however construed – is inadequate in the face of the political imperative posed by posthumanism.

It was striking how few of the chapters in this collection followed through on the editors' stimulus towards imagining the politics of posthumanism. Classics, as I have outlined, has an uncanny ability as a discipline to revert to business as usual, especially where the responsibility of the discipline is concerned and especially where the political implications of critical stances are at stake. Homer's animal similes are fine and dandy, but if they are to be analysed under the aegis of posthumanism, then how such an analysis constitutes a responsive and responsible recognition of the anthropocene should at least be hazarded. Or we will be doing business as usual . . .

Whatever happened to humility?

Genevieve Liveley's title, 'Beyond the beautiful evil? The ancient/future history of sex robots', immediately cues the long and pertinent history of normative gender relations in which classical antiquity continues to play a starring role. The 'beautiful evil' designedly recalls Pandora in Hesiod, the first 'sex-robot' – in that she is a manufactured thing, a first 'woman' that is for humans a *kalon kakon*, a 'beautiful evil'. The negative evaluation of woman in this foundational text of Western patriarchal thinking is not just that whatever attractiveness she may have cannot be separated from her inherent badness; it is also that from the start a woman is a sometime *thing*, not just objectified but an object made to deceive. For Liveley this leads (via Pygmalion) to the idea (and – now – the growing industrial mass-production) of the sex-robot, dolls manufactured mainly in the Far East (a story itself with a long Western tradition, denigrating, with fascination, the material cunning of the Orient). It is perhaps equally pertinent that the most prevalent, if more synecdochic, form of the sex-robot – the vibrator – is not mentioned (although it has recently been given a remarkable biography since its Victorian invention).[14] The vibrator, it might be thought, is a technological invention which extends but does not fundamentally alter the function of the ancient Greek dildo.

Liveley's discussion might lead us to gloss the editors' term 'ma(n)chine' in an over-heated fashion. But I cite her chapter for different reasons. I am acutely conscious of how hard it is to discuss the sex-robot or the vibrator without making recourse to some unreflective assumptions about human exceptionalism – in the form of valuing personal interaction between individuals, the truth of bodily contact between humans, the emotional commitments of such intimacy – and all the familiar inheritance of the romance of the personal in modern Western bourgeois values. We could follow Liveley's injunction to consider the ancient/future, however, and add Diogenes the Cynic, who, when upbraided for masturbating in public, commented that he wished his hunger could be so easily assuaged. Or we could note that Aristotle was prepared to call a slave a machine (*organon*), and sex with such machines was normal behaviour for men in antiquity – an extreme version of the expected lack of reciprocity in sexual relations. Or we could note how often satyrs represented on vases and even on sarcophagi find material objects with which to satisfy their sexual urges. (It is not part of the agenda of posthumanism, however, to imagine humans having sex with other species.) We could, that is, set other forms of ancient sexual interaction against the romantic anxiety that makes a future of robots seem . . . queer. My point is a simple one: how *difficult* it is to think a subject such as sexuality from a post-human perspective, at least in a convincing or coherent manner. There are areas of social and cultural life where it proves extremely vexing to decentre the human's sense of humanity. Foucault proclaimed the death of man as well as the death of the author, but both seem to have outlived his death sentence.

Theory does not provide only incisive arguments and generalizations to teach us what we do not yet know but also how and why we do not yet know: epistemic humility.

III

These six general critical questions are my attempt – as demanded by the genre of *Schlußwort* – to see where the interactions between the chapters' different individual contributions reveal issues that need further exploration. But to conclude my contribution I want to finish with two specific ways in which classics can contribute to the debate and how the debate can inform classics.

The first concerns what Lorraine Daston and Fernando Vidal have termed 'the moral authority of nature'.[15] I have already mentioned Descola's account of the variety of relations that are concealed by the Western use of the term nature. Can one talk about the history of climate change, then, or the political imperative of posthumanism *without* a concept of nature? The trouble with nature is that it encodes and often conceals a normativity that drives debate. This is seen most evidently in the insult of 'unnatural'. If nature consists of the physical world that exists, how can something that exists in nature be unnatural? In the history of sexuality, certain existing practices or even pathologies are declared to be unnatural by their critics. The most familiar is what we now call homosexuality, which has regularly been stigmatized, especially in the past but still today in some circles, as an unnatural vice. Unnatural here means something that should not be done according to an ideological predilection, a rhetoric that defends itself by an appeal to nature as to how the world should be. There is a shift between what is and what ought to be – which, as we know, is where the wild things of ideology live rather than cool progression of logic.

The moral authority – the hidden ideology – of nature is especially relevant where destruction is concerned. The history of Europeans is a history of actively and even aggressively changing eco-systems, often drastically. A lot of what we value and use *depends* on such depredations. We call ourselves self-servingly *homo sapiens*, when the creature that builds and destroys – *homo aedificans et perdens* – might be a more accurate description of our 'natural' condition. Europe's landscape was constructed by the destruction of the forests that covered it. Would it make sense to argue for their return? Or, to take an example from antiquity, in North Africa there was a plant called Silphium. It was wild, and harvested for food and medical purposes. With the arrival of the Romans in particular, it was overharvested and has been extinct since the first century BCE. Should we care? Of course, we can lament not knowing what it looks and tastes like. Of course, we can also fantasize about the medical opportunity cost – what could it have been made into as a drug? But the fundamental issue seems to me that it has become something which feels right and proper that we should aim to maintain the status quo of natural things – although we are also intellectually committed to the survival of the fittest as a principle of evolution, and this process of evolution also requires the gradual or quicker destruction of the weaker. Plenitude, and a plenitude that should remain a plenitude, is too often taken as an uncontested good. Especially in discussions of eco-systems and humans' place within them. I take it that this is an example where a hidden normativity drives debate, and where, consequently, arguments against such destructiveness are not made with sufficient rigour. When it comes to evaluating the conflicting interests that are stimulated by the imperatives of posthumanism, it will be necessary to have a robust account of what counts in continuity and stability, and why.

But I also take it that this is where the *longue-durée* of classics can bring a fresh critical perspective to the table. It is not only that classics must go back before the Romantic conceptualization of nature, but also that the intense and varied explorations – the inventions of the category of *phusis* and *natura* – from Aristotle to Lucretius to *Daphnis and Chloe* – provide a continually challenging rebuff to the easy assumptions of a simple plenitude of nature. Many chapters in this book could be taken as productive first steps in this project.

My second conclusion concerns the post- of posthumanism. Modern critical thinking has grown fond of the post-. Since Post-Impressionism was coined by Roger Fry before the First World War, a string of post- movements have announced themselves on the scene. The post- has the double vector of declaring itself, on the one hand, to be in a place in time, a self-conscious historicization; and, on the other, to be a critical re-definition of, or – self-assertively – a triumph over, what has preceded. Posthumanism and the posthuman find themselves awkwardly placed in such terms. Attempts to give a strong temporality to the posthuman – especially to date posthumanism in antiquity, as with Mireille Courrént's postulation of Hellenistic technological treatises as its start – seem doomed to rhetorical hyperbole. Nor is it immediately clear – as the chapters of this book demonstrate – exactly what the human is that is being progressed from or transcended, and/or whether posthumanism necessarily refers to one or more specific versions of humanism.

Here too an engagement with the classical tradition can provide a crucial and critical map. It is important to be able to distinguish between the ideals of humanism in the early modern period, dependent as they are on the appeal of *ad fontes*, a return to classical sources; and the enthronement of human reason in the Enlightenment, which also privileged forms of classical expressivity in its cultural hierarchies; and the Victorian construction of the human sciences, and the contest over what the dominant form of *Wissenschaft* should be; and modern science's materialism and technology (which has caused so many of the problems it now promises to help solve), where biology provides such a challenge to the discreteness of a human being. Such a contoured map could help calibrate the rhetoric of posthumanism in a more historically nuanced way (always a good thing), but also, and more importantly, could help express how the claims of posthumanism are themselves necessarily engaged with a long history of how knowledge is institutionalized, what the relations between structures of power and authority and learning are, including within religious structures, and how the politics of social and technological change require a new architecture of thinking, that has its own complexities of instrumentality.

In the face of new technologies of artificial intelligence, new understanding of biological science, and the impending threats to the physical and social world in the anthropocene, and in the face of the current political horrors of ineptitude, lack of will and selfishness as responses to these new constructions of the order of things, it is hard not to believe that a new architecture of thinking must be underway. The sheer variety of this book, and its insistence that such newness requires an understanding of the past too, is a harbinger of such a process. As the late Philip Roth finished his first great hit, 'Now vee may perhaps to begin'.[16]

NOTES

Theoretical Introduction: The Subject of the Human

1. On this point, Kuhn 1957 is still a reference work.
2. *Hamlet* (I. v. 195). All quotes from Shakespeare are from the Arden edition.
3. John Donne, *An anatomy of the world.*
4. *Macbeth* (III. iv. 84).
5. *Macbeth* (V. v. 48–49).
6. John Donne, *Holy Sonnets* V. 1–2.
7. John Donne, *Holy Sonnets* VI. 6.
8. *Macbeth* (II. iii. 90–91).
9. *The Winter's Tale* (III. iii. 38).
10. *King Lear* (I. iv. 257–260).
11. John Donne, *Holy sonnets* I. 2.
12. Cf. Ferrando 2013.
13. Cf. Ferrando 2016.
14. As Mueller (2016a: 10) points out in her groundbreaking paper on animal re-cognition in the *Odyssey*, 'Because smell is not a highly developed sense among humans (in fact, it is never explicitly mentioned as such), Argus's recognition assumes a paradigmatic quality. It offers a blueprint for how humans *might*, but *ordinarily cannot* recognize one another. The dog is being presented as a model for human *noêsis*.' Yet, one might argue that human and animal cognition, in Homer, is radically different: Homeric animals are free from the semiotic cage of representation – animals' *noesis* bypasses the *sema* and the process of semiosis. In Homer, Odysseus' *philoi* need a *sema* to recognize him; for Argos smelling is enough. The Homeric discourse focuses on human limits. To suppose, therefore, that Odysseus, taking Argos as an example, could do what the dog can is to disavow Odysseus' defective nature: Odysseus *cannot* do what Argos can; the system of signs harnesses the human Odysseus not the dog Argos.
15. In the introduction to their edited volume, Telò and Mueller 2018, relying on Bennett 2010 in *Vibrant Matter*, assume that objects are autonomous or semi-autonomous entities, nonhuman bodies (pp. 4–5), and conceptualize emotions and feelings as 'secretions released into the environment' by bodies (p. 7), in the frame of a 'materiality of feeling' (p. 11). If the intent here is the legitimate and desirable one of deconstructing the dichotomy between active subject and passive object (p. 6), then to extend feelings to nonhuman bodies is an act of anthropomorphization of the object. In fact, as Baudrillard 1983 explains, the subject feels and desires, not because he is autonomous and the object is inert and passive, but because, quite the contrary, the object has the power to exercise on the subject an inexhaustible seduction that inextricably links subject and object in an active polarization: the relationship between subject and object is a *fatal liaison* in which the object challenges the subject in an epistemological game whose rules it constantly escapes. Crucial here is that the human being cannot seduce the object; s/he can only feel an attraction for it, and in doing so, enter the epistemological game of mutual definition.
16. According to Purves 2015, Ajax's armour is 'as vivid or alive' as Ajax as they are 'irrefutably and endlessly together' (p. 86).

17. Cf. Holmes 2015: 32. Indeed, as Holmes argues in her thought provoking paper on *natureculture* in the *Iliad*, the battle between Scamander and Achilles questions the divide nature/culture and points to their continuity: the river shares the cultural norms of the *Iliad* and actively enacts them – his kourotrophic care towards the Trojans (p. 51) brings about his heroic fight against Achilles, which exposes the hero's *hybris* and the inhumanity of his massacre (esp. pp. 40–44). Yet, in the text, Scamander is said to be *like* a man, not to be a man (*Il.* 21. 213: ἀνέρι εἰσάμενος). Following Pucci (1986: 10) on divine epiphany in Homer, it can be said that the expression 'like a man' represents the divine as a metaphorical construct which singles out the 'insurmountable difference' between being and external appearance (*phainesthai*), and, therefore, as a rhetorical construct that shares a concern with the reduction of identity to external appearance. No matter how Scamander is *like* a man, the river is a god, the same way Athena is like a woman (*Od.* 13. 288: δέμας δ' ἤϊκτο γυναικὶ) but she is none.

18. Cf. Mueller 2016. Tragic props and humans are part of the plot, of the materiality of the play. When for instance, in *Choephoroi*, Orestes appears on stage with his mother's garment, the prop is indeed the instantiation of vivid matter in the sense that it is the sign of the *material embodiment* of a *family history* (cf. Worman in this volume). And yet objects are innocent; humans are not: Clytemnestra uses the garments to kill; the garment does not push her to murder (neither in *Agamemnon* nor *Choephoroi* does Aeschylean language attribute a murderous agency to the garment). The attribution to tragic objects of an 'uncanny' agency seems telling of the nostalgia for a lost human innocence (as if there had ever been one), and appears the gesture to disperse among nonhuman entities what is so specific to the *homo necans*: the agency of killing – yet, one has to pull the trigger to shoot.

19. For a cultural history of machines and technical devices, see e.g. Cuomo 2007; Asper 2017. For SF, see Liveley 2006; Gildenhard and Zissos 2013; Bost-Fievet and Provini 2014; Rogers and Stevens 2015; Keen 2017.

20. Cf. Haraway (2016a) in *Staying with the Trouble*, where she argues that not all humans, but the ruling classes, are responsible for inaugurating a geological era characterized by the disruption of the ecosystem. While it is frequently called anthropocene, Haraway specifies that some humans are to blame more than others.

21. Braidotti, for example, in *The Posthuman* (2013), frames her criticism of the Humanist paradigm as 'a hegemonic cultural model' (pp. 13–15) and quotes Tony Davies (1997: 141), according to whom, 'All Humanisms, until now, have been imperial. [. . .] It is almost impossible to think of a crime that has not been committed in the name of humanity.'

22. On this point, Derrida's 'Les fins de l'homme' and Foucault's 'What is Enlightenment?' in Rabinow 1984 are still reference works.

23. Cf. Lloyd 1984.

24. Cf. Voltaire, *Candide*; Mirabeau, *L'ami des hommes*; Condorcet, *Réflexions sur l'esclavage des nègres*.

25. Cf. Beccaria, *Dei delitti e delle pene*, ch. 28.

26. Cf. Agostino Nifo's commentary on Averroes' commentaries on *De Anima* and *Metaphysics*; Pietro Pomponazzi's commentary on Averroes' long commentary on *Metaphysics*, Book XII; Marcantonio Zimara's works on the concordances between Averroes and Aristotle; the Giunta edition of Aristotle and Averroes. On these works and Averroism in Renaissance Philosophy, cf. Hasse 2007.

27. Cf. Yates 1964.

28. Cf. Bianchi, Brill and Holmes (2019: 7): 'the Humanist project, especially over the past few centuries, has systematically argued for the superiority of the ancient Greeks at the expense of other peoples (among them the Egyptians, Persians, Phoenecians, Indians, and Jews . . .)'.

29. Cf. Renehan 1981. On humans as the only beings possessing *logos* in the Greek thought, cf. Fögen 2007, 2014 on animal communication.

30. On perspectival anthropocentrism, cf. Ferré 1994.

31. Cf. Korhohen and Ruonakoski 2017: 36.

32. Cf. the milestone works of Vernant and Vidal-Naquet 1972, 1986; Goldhill 1984, 1986, 2012. For a reading of the Greek subject as relational, cf. Bianchi, Brill and Holmes 2019: 7–8; on the idea of a relational subject as the core of Roman thought, cf. Dressler 2016a (ch. 2). This post-structuralist reading of tragic language notably relies on the theory of différance, which circles the displacement of the speaking subject. If language is the essence of a human being because all s/he knows about the world is necessarily known to her/him through language, language is what makes the human being plural and relational. As Derrida argues in 'La différance', meaning is always disseminated and never self-referential; cf. Johnson 1996; Eagleton 2004: 11.
33. Cf. the milestone works of Zeitlin and Loraux on which Bianchi, Brill and Holmes 2019: 8–9.
34. Cf. Levinas' 'l'autre dans le même' in *Autrement qu'être, ou au-delà de l'essence* (1974: 111). On Posthumanism and the Other within, cf. Badmington 2004. Huma(n)chine is a neologism by Chesi 2019.
35. Cf. Haraway (1997: 211): 'Cyborg anthropology attempts to refigure provocatively the border relations among specific humans, other organisms, and machines.' On Haraway's cyborg, cf. Mertlitsch's introductory chapter in this volume.
36. Cf. Ferrando 2013.
37. Cf. Nancy (2000: 30): 'Coessentiality signifies the essential sharing of essentiality, sharing as assembling.' On this passage, cf. Rossini 2017: 157.
38. Cf. Haraway 2004: 328: 'humans are congeries of things that are not us. We are not self-identical'.
39. Cf. Chesi 2019.
40. For an attempt to overcome the dialectic of identity (A and not A), cf. Esposito 2018 (esp. ch. 3).
41. On flat ontology, cf. the neo-Heidegerrian ontology of e.g. Harman 2002, 2005; Meillassoux 2010; Bryant 2011; Bogost 2012; Morton 2013; Quessada 2013. For criticism, cf. Cheah 2010; Brennan 2014a, 2016.
42. Notably Braidotti (2011) in *Nomadic Subjects*.
43. Cf. Cubitt 2001; Fusaro 2012.
44. Cf. Whitmarsh 2018.
45. Cf. Simondon 2012; Shaviro 2014. On Simondon, Hui in this volume.
46. Cf. Simondon 2012.
47. On the self as constituted by interconnectedness, cf. Haraway 1997a: 12, 14; 2016: 67; Browning Cole 1993: 61.
48. On Levinas on intersubjectivity and language, cf. Cohen 2007: 244.
49. Cf. Irigaray 1984: 75. Translation ours.
50. Cf. Korhohen and Ruonakoski 2017 (introduction chapter), with Chesi 2018. On embodied cognition, cf. notably Merleau-Ponty in *Phénoménologie de la perception* (1945) and *Le visible et l'invisible* (1968); on thinking through the body, cf. also the important works of Varela, Thompson and Rosch 1991; Noë 2004; Gallagher 2005; and, from a feminist point of view, the seminal paper of Young 1980, to whom we shall add e.g. Irigaray 1984; Gallop 1988; Muraro 2006.
51. On the animal difference within the self, cf. Agamben 2002; Haraway 2003; 2007; Simondon 2004; Derrida 2006.
52. Cf. notably Gilligan 1982, *In a Different Voice*, on the Ethics of Care.
53. Cf. notably Wittgenstein in the *Philosophische Untersuchungen* (Teil II, p. 568): 'Wenn ein Löwe sprechen könnte, wir könnten ihn nicht verstehen'.
54. Cf. Derrida 2006: 70–81, with Timofeeva in this volume.
55. Cf. Haraway 2016: 5.
56. Cf. Haraway 1997: 210; 1997a: 51.

57. On *techne* as not towering upon individuals, cf. Lanier 2010: 4.
58. Cf. Brooks and Steels 1995; Brooks et al. 1999.
59. Cf. similarly Hayles 1999: 283–284.
60. Cf. Ada Lovelace, first computer programmer (Analytical Engine); Margaret Masterman, founder of the Cambridge Language Research Unit; Margaret Boden, mother of Computer sciences; Dorothy Vaughan, first programmer of Fortran; Hedy Lamarr, pioneer in the filed of wireless communications; Karen Jones, inventor of IDF (Inverse Document Frequency) for information retrieval in search engines.
61. On enhancement, cf. notably Drexler 1986; Kurzweil 2005.
62. *Pace* Greene 2013; Edmonds 2013; Bostrom and Yudkowksy 2014. For the huma(n)chine, a human being is not a negligible thing, and his worth cannot be quantified and sorted as the result of an equation. Here, we recall the 'trolley problem', as presented by Foot 1967 and Jarvis Thomson 1985: a moral *decision* does not necessarily entail the *solution* of a moral dilemma; killing one person instead of five is what most people would be likely to do if they had the choice, but this does not mean that it is the *just* decision – it is a morally impossible decision, which entails taking responsibility as a human prerogative.
63. Cf. Haraway 2016: 28–37.
64. Cf. Simondon (2012: 10): 'Le misonéisme orienté contre les machines n'est pas tant haine du nouveau que refus de la réalité étrangère'. The expression "idolâtre de la machine" is from Simondon (2012: 11).
65. Cf. Levinas (1968) in 'Humanisme et An-archie' (esp. pp. 334–336). On Levinas' Other as 'anarchic intrusion into the world', cf. Alford 2014: 164. On Levinas' concept of anarchy as the ethical practice of resistance to defend the alterity of the Other, cf. Stone 2011.
66. Cf. Derrida 1991.
67. Cf. Canguilhem 1962 and 1966.
68. Cf. Deleuze and Guattari 1987: 47, with Hayles in *My Mother Was a Computer* (2005: 106–107, 173–175).
69. Trinh T. Minh-ha 1987.
70. http://www.repubblica.it/esteri/2015/06/17/foto/francia_migranti_si_rifugiano_in_un_tir_a_calais_l_intervento_della_polizia-117102815/1/?ref=HRER3-1#12
71. Cf. Brennan 2014: 225–234 ('Posthumanism as Imperialism').

The Question of the Animal and the Aristotelian Human Horse

1. Cf. Atterton and Calarco 2004; Latimer and Miele 2013; Rohman 2009; Steeves 1999; Waldau and Patton 2006; Wolfe 2003.
2. Deleuze and Guattari 1987.
3. Derrida 2008.
4. Agamben 2004.
5. Haraway 2007.
6. Wolfe 2012.
7. Fontenay 1998.
8. Lippit 2000.
9. Wolfe 2009.
10. Singer 1975; Regan 1983.
11. Haraway 2015; Clark and Yusoff 2017.

12. Hegel's *Philosophy of Nature* 1970: 110.
13. Morton 2017: 13.
14. Barrett 1990.
15. Freud, *From the History of an Infantile Neurosis* 1971.
16. Foucault 2006.
17. Lacan 1977: 1–7.
18. Derrida 2008.
19. Agamben 2004: 26.
20. Timofeeva 2018.
21. Ades and Baker 2006.
22. Ibid.: 238.
23. Ibid.
24. Ibid.
25. Cf. Sharia https://omgfacts.com/the-mystery-of-scotlands-dog-suicide-bridge/.

Foucault, the Monstrous and Monstrosity

1. For a discussion of the recurrence of the word 'monster' in Foucault's work, see the entry 'Monstro' in Castro 2004. With the exception of Foucault's work, all English translations are by the translator of this chapter.
2. On the heuristic function of the monstrous in Foucault, cf. Carroll 1990: 27; Sharpe 2010: 21–24; Unterthurner 2012: 199–218; Moraña 2017: 190–201.
3. Moraña 2017: 191.
4. Foucault 2002: 18.
5. Chignola 2014: 15.
6. Foucault 2002: 355.
7. Foucault 2002: 358.
8. Foucault 1998: 356.
9. Foucault 2003: 323.
10. Foucault 2002: 171.
11. Braidotti 2002: 175.
12. Bologna 1980.
13. Derrida 1995a: 386.
14. On this point, cf. Foucault 1998.
15. On the centrality of the notion of limit in Foucault, see Hallward 2006; Melegari 2012.
16. Foucault 2006: XXIX.
17. Esposito 2016: 121.
18. Foucault will often insist on the function that Nietzsche has played in his process of formation and emancipation from phenomenology; see the famous interview 'Structuralism and Post-structuralism' (Foucault 1983).
19. Foucault 1986: 160.
20. Foucault 1984a: 81.

21. Foucault 1986: 154.
22. Deleuze 1995: 3–7.
23. Foucault 1975: 760.

How to Become a Cyborg

1. This chapter is based on the chapter 'Vernetzen', 142–158 in Mertlitsch 2016: *Sisters-Cyborgs-Drags. Das Denken in Begriffspersonen der Gender Studies.*
2. Haraway 1991: 149.
3. Haraway 1991: 150.
4. Haraway 1991: 149.
5. Haraway 1991: 154.
6. Donna Haraway in 1982 wrote a commissioned piece for the *Socialist Review* (see Deuber-Mankowsky 2007: 279), with a focus on socialist feminism in the Reagan era. She takes part of this imaginative-material ideas of the Cyborg in her Manifesto.
7. Cf. Bellanger 2001: 56. According to Bellanger it is debatable whether all these hybrid creatures, which are not always animate, bear relation to the *Cyborg*. For her only such creatures are *Cyborgs* as for example Frankenstein, a machine that comes to life – meaning those creatures that are composed of both organic and mechanical parts.
8. Knoll 2011.
9. Haraway 1991: 163.
10. Haraway has been multiply criticized for this description of women of color, including by Chela Sandoval herself, as philosopher Susanne Lummerding explains. She highlights that it is often overlooked that Haraway's *Cyborg* figure is not just a cybernetic-organic and post-gender hybrid, but most of all an ethnic one. By ascribing women of color a predestination to subversive cyborg consciousness, Lummerding writes, Haraway is tending towards the construction of precisely that discourse of salvation that she sets out to oppose (Lummerding 2005: 89). In this view, women of color are assigned a revolutionary, emancipatory and thus liberatory potential, based on their experience of discrimination and subjugation.
11. Haraway 1991: 164.
12. Haraway 1991: 170.
13. Harasser 2011: 589.
14. Haraway 1991: 161.
15. Haraway 1991: 162.
16. Haraway 1991: 162.
17. See Haraway 1991: 161–162.
18. Haraway 1991: 165.
19. Haraway 1991: 164.
20. Haraway 1994: 69.
21. Haraway 1994: 69.
22. Haraway 1991: 177.
23. Haraway 1994: 71.
24. See Harasser 2011: 582.
25. Haraway 1997a: 35.

26. Haraway 1994: 63.

27. Haraway 1994: 63.

28. Haraway 1994: 64.

29. See Peuker 2010: 325.

30. Bammé, Berger and Kotzmann 2012: 33; see also Latour 2008.

31. The cultural sociologist Andreas Reckwitz has tackled various theories of the subject, especially the hybrid subject, and writes that cultural theories of materiality presume that artifacts subjectify through their practice: 'Forms of hybrid subjectivity are decipherable not just in the combination of cultural codes of different spatial and temporal origins; in the entanglement of an organism with objects, its participation in symbolic orders and the material world of things, which are both entangled with each other, the subject is organized in hybrid form on a further plane' (Reckwitz 2010: 120). Instead of differentiations between subject and object, or nature vs. culture, we find relations, positionings, situatedness and fields of influence (see Wieser 2012) that are embodied by and decipherable through the philosophical figure of the *Cyborg*.

32. Haraway 1991: 164.

33. Haraway 1991: 201.

34. Haraway 1997a: 3.

35. Haraway 1995: 10.

36. Haraway 1997a: 12; Haraway in Lykke and Braidotti 1996: 57; Åsberg 2010: 18.

37. Haraway 1995: 96.

38. Haraway 1991: 201.

39. Hammer 1995: 20.

40. Hammer 1995: 22.

41. Gransee 1998: 137.

42. See Gransee 1998: 137.

43. Haraway 1991: 150.

Anders, Simondon and the Becoming of the Posthuman

1. Note that the French philosopher Bernard Stiegler has been arguing for a positive *pharmakon* as a remedy to the industrial intoxication.
2. It is interesting to notice that in this passage Dupuy also referred to Anders and Hannah Arendt.
3. Anders' two volumes of *The Obsolescence of Human Being* [*Die Antiquiertheit des Menschen*] were published separately in 1956 and 1980, with the subtitles: *On the soul in the epoch of the second industrial revolution* and *On the destruction of lives in the age of the third industrial revolution.* Simondon's *On the Mode of Existence of Technical Objects* [*Du mode d'existence des objets techniques*] was his supplementary thesis (the main thesis being *L'individuation à la lumière des notions de forme et d'information*) published in 1958.
4. Anders is very similar to Heidegger in diagnosing the metaphysical foundation of modern technologies, for which nature becomes 'standing reserves' (*Bestand*). Note that Anders wrote his PhD thesis with Husserl, and then followed Heidegger in Freiburg. Later he married Hannah Arendt.
5. When Anders talked about the Pachinko, he referred to a psychology of the apparatus, that he calls *Dingpsychologie* (Anders 1980: 58), and coincidentally Simondon also talks about the social psychology of technical objects, as we will see later.

6. The term 'recurrent causality' is a translation of 'feedback' in cybernetics. We may want to think that here Simondon has already noticed the cybernetic mode of operation of consumerism.
7. I deal with the inhuman in my book *Recursivity and Contingency* (London: Rowman and Littlefield, 2019).

Chapter 1

1. This chapter started as a talk presented at the conference on 'Posthuman in Ancient Greek Literature'. I am grateful to conference organizers Giulia Maria Chesi and Francesca Spiegel and to conference participants for two inspiring days of scholarly conversation. I also thank Annetta Alexandridis and her colleagues in the Classics department at Cornell University, especially Hayden Pelliccia and Jeffrey Rusten, as well as my Northwestern colleague Will West and the reader for the press, for their insightful comments on later versions of the chapter.
2. Popularized in 2000 by atmospheric chemist Paul J. Crutzen, the term 'Anthropocene' encapsulates the idea that human behaviour has recently had such a drastic influence on Earth's atmosphere as to constitute a new geological epoch. For a critique of the concept, see Clark 2015 and the essays collected in Moore 2016.
3. Scranton 2015: 19.
4. Scranton 2015: 19.
5. Agamben 2004: 13–16 and 33–38.
6. Derrida 1982a: 135. See also Badmington 2003.
7. On practices of 'resistant reading' and 'reading against the grain' as conceptualized by feminist and Marxist literary critics, see Fetterley 1977 and Eagleton 1981.
8. Throughout the chapter I reproduce the text of P. von der Mühll's edition of the *Odyssey* (1993 [1946]), Martin West's edition of the *Iliad* (1998, 2000), and the translations by Richmond Lattimore (1965, 2011). I refer to the boar as 'he' in an attempt to neutralize the opposition 'he/it' that proceeds from the very opposition between human and animal that I want to question.
9. See Gaisser 1969: 20–21 for a schematic outline of the episode.
10. Austin (1966: 310): 'The digression of Odysseus' scar . . . is not really on the scar at all. The scar is but the vehicle for the explication of the real subject, which is the name and identity of Odysseus.'
11. Rutherford 1992 *ad loc.*
12. Van Gennep 1909. For readings of the episode through the concept of rite of passage or other related anthropological concepts, see Russo 1993; Letoublon 2010; Levaniouk 2011; Petropoulos 2011: 107–120. The reading of the scar digression in Auerbach 1953, while an important moment of literary criticism, focuses on stylistic questions very different from my purpose here.
13. On the analogy between hunting and warfare in Greek culture, see for instance Xen. *Cyn.* 12.1 and Barringer 2002: 10–69.
14. As I tease out the complexities of the conceptual relation between Odysseus and the boar, my argument closely engages with readings that have identified the boar as Odysseus' 'animal other' (Russo 1993), 'double' (Levaniouk 2011: 166–189), or 'analogue' (Petropoulos 2011: 117). While I agree that such analogies between man and animal are part of the horizon of expectations of the episode, my interest is in the ideological work performed by the text, which I argue replaces analogy with a complex sense of permeable hierarchy.
15. Rubin and Sale 1983; Bremmer 1988. *Contra* Most 1983.
16. Scodel 1994: 532.
17. See Purves 2014: 47–50, who remarks that the Parnassian boar hunt offers the single Homeric description of a wild mountainside outside the similes.

18. Schnapp-Gourbeillon 1981: 49. Hainsworth 1993 on *Il.* 11.292–293 identifies ten boar similes in the *Iliad*, six of which occur in books 11 to 13, with another cluster in books 16 to 18. On three occasions the boar is paired with a lion as vehicles for the comparison. With the exception of *Il.* 16.823–826, boar similes describe encounters between boar(s) and hunters with their hounds. The boar is the attacker in five instances and is pursued or cornered in four.

19. My theoretical premise that the reception of a work can be described in relation to the expectations brought in by its audiences comes from Jauss 1982, who defines the aesthetic value of a work as its distance from the horizon of audience expectations.

20. The literature on Homeric similes is extensive. On boar and lion similes, I have found especially helpful Severyns 1946; Snell 1975: 201–202; Moulton 1977; Schnapp-Gourbeillon 1981; Lonsdale 1990 and Letoublon 2016. See also Giordano in this volume.

21. Schnapp-Gourbeillon 1981: 38–50.

22. Cf. the perceptive observation by Frazer, in spite of its language: 'the sharp line of demarcation which we draw between mankind and the lower animals does not exist for the savage. To him many of the other animals appear as his equals or even his superiors, not only in brute force but in intelligence' (Frazer 1935: pt. V, vol. 2, 310).

23. Dierauer 1977: 8; Korhonen and Ruonakoski 2017: 106–127.

24. For a list of emotive states and seats of emotions that Homeric diction applies to humans and animals alike, see the appendix in Lonsdale 1990: 133–135. The theologically loaded question of whether animals have a soul – known as the 'querelle de l'âme des bêtes' – agitated philosophical circles in the second half of the seventeenth and the first half of the eighteenth centuries CE. See Nicolay 2001 for an application of that question to the Homeric corpus.

25. My argument that the similes emphasize ontological analogies between human and non-human animals differs from the thesis that the similes rely on an anthropomorphic view of the animals, which is to say that human characteristics get attributed to non-human beings (Snell 1975: 200; Lonsdale 1990: 125; Letoublon 2016: 145). As Lonsdale's study makes clear, the latter view relies on the premise that humans and animals are *in fact* different (or imagined as such), and that the similes construct metaphorical analogies across species by applying 'anthropomorphic vocabulary' to animals and 'theriomorphic vocabulary' to humans. In other words, animals in the similes are 'hybrids' created by the poet to 'bridge' the ontological gap between humans and animals (3). By contrast, my working hypothesis is that the Western distinction between 'human' and 'animal' is a cultural (-etic) construct whose relevance to Homer should not be taken for granted. Nicolay 2001 argues on the basis of lexical analysis that 'Homer' did not view human and non-human animals as totally dissimilar. *Contra* Newmyer 2017: 11–12. For a posthuman approach to animal–human relations, see Haraway 2007.

26. On human and animal taxonomies in the *Iliad*, cf. Giordano in this volume.

27. Rutherford 1992; Russo et al. 1992 on *Od.* 19.439–443; Russo 1993. While some ancient audiences may have heard the intratextual parallelism as a casual reuse of formulae (so Rutherford), I agree with Russo that it is possible to find meaning in it. On Russo's reading, the topos of the protective enclave is activated about the boar in an 'intriguing act of transference', a 'temporary merging' of identity that has to do with the special relationship between hunter and hunted in the ritual activity of the hunt. By contrast, I argue that the boar hunt episode takes the resemblance between Odysseus and the boar as its point of departure but replaces it with a hierarchical relation.

28. Rutherford 1992 on *Od.* 19.439–443.

29. On patterns and formulas in Iliadic battle scenes, see Fenik 1968; Friedrich 2003; Mueller 2009: 76–101. On Iliadic combat-scene formulas in the Parnassian boar hunt, see Rutherford 1992 on *Od.* 19.451; Jong 2001 on *Od.* 19.428–456; Petropoulos 2011: 116–117.

30. On blazing eyes and the ὄσσε/ὀφθαλμοί distinction, see Hainsworth 1993 on *Il.* 12.466.

31. Mueller 2009: 79. Usually the stronger fighter throws or thrusts with a spear that is fatal before any counter-blow can be delivered.

32. Finkelberg 1998.

33. For another engagement with the analogy between boar tusk and spear, see the story of the death of Croesus' son Atys in Hdt. 1.34–43.

34. Mueller 2009: 79.

35. Stanford 1996 on *Od.* 19.449–451 notes that sidelong thrusts are characteristic of a boar, his tusks being too short for a direct stab.

36. On the concept of assemblage, see Haraway 1991 and Barad 2007 as well as Part III in this volume.

37. Schein 1970: 77.

38. On other ways in which the Homeric texts prefigure later forms of anthropocentrism, see Renehan 1981; Newmyer 2017.

39. It is worth noting, however, that in the *Protagoras* the construction of humans as distinct from all other animals does not solely rely on technology. The animal powers (δυνάμεις) for which humans have no equivalent until Prometheus' intervention include speed, strength, size, weapon-like body parts and the ability to fly or find refuge underground. However, the technical intelligence gifted by Prometheus is still not enough to protect humans against wild beasts. It takes Zeus' gift of 'reverence' and 'justice' for humans to become able to live together in cities and thus avoid being annihilated by 'beasts'.

40. On the double significance of the name Odysseus, meaning both receiving and dealing out trouble, see Stanford 1996; Dimock 1956; Clay 1983: 54–68; Peradotto 1990: 143–170; Russo et al. 1992 on *Od.* 19.407.

41. Gaisser 1969: 20–21.

42. Murnaghan 1987; Gainsford 2003; Barnouw 2004; Mueller 2016.

43. For a contemporary parallel, see the Australian philosopher and ecofeminist Plumwood 1995 on how her experience of being attacked by a crocodile made her intensely aware of the precariousness of human lives as prey, in contrast to the Western denial that humans are animals positioned in the food chain.

44. For a highly suggestive, if often cryptic description of becoming-animal, see Deleuze and Guattari 1980: 284–380. Unlike Odysseus' encounter with the boar, however, Deleuze and Guattari view becoming-animal as happening at the margins of animal packs.

45. I owe that suggestion to Fried 2005. As support for the pun, Fried mentions the fact that Odysseus, Autolykos and boar tusks are also collocated in the story of the boar tusk helmet worn by Odysseus in *Iliad* 10. On Fried's interpretation, the boar tusk helmet is a 'visceral emblem' of Odysseus that projects forth the significance of his name. The hypothesis is attractive but would need to be supported by a close reading attentive to the larger and highly complex question of animal garments in *Iliad* 10, to which I cannot possibly do justice here. On the semiotic triangulation between the scar, the boar tusk helmet and Odysseus' name, see also Petegorsky 1982: 200.

46. *Od.* 19.393=21.219=23.74; 19.449–450; 19.465; 24.332.

47. See for example Stanford 1939; Dimock 1956; Russo et al. 1992 on *Od.* 19.407; Levaniouk 2000.

48. Levaniouk 2000.

49. My argument thus closely engages with but differs from Walter Burkert's idea that the moment of death highlights with special force the animal's resemblance to man (Burkert 1983: 20–21, 'the flesh was like flesh, bones like bones, phallus like phallus, and heart like heart').

50. Although here I cannot offer a full analysis of the line in those two other contexts, I note that both Pedasos and the stag have special relations to human beings, the former as a substitute for Patroklos and the latter because he may be a former human victim of Circe's magic, as argued by Roessel 1989.

51. Boehme 1929: 103.

52. Garland 1981: 49. The θυμός may leave the bones or limbs of the victim (7×), or the killer may take it away (14×), or the victim may lose it (8×).
53. The one exception occurs in a conditional passage at *Il.* 7.131.
54. Clarke 1999: 203; Cairns 2014.
55. An otherwise unremarkable swine loses his ψυχή at *Od.* 14.426. Cf. Nicolay 2001.
56. Snell 1975: 11–12, followed by, e.g., Garland 1981: 49; Newmyer 2017: 12.
57. Clarke 1999: 55. Clarke further argues that while the last breath may be described as both ψυχή and θυμός, ψυχή refers to the cold and evanescent quality of death, while θυμός refers to the warm, vital quality of what has been extinguished (147). *Contra* Cairns 2014.
58. Caswell 1990. In Homer the simple verb πέτομαι occurs with reference to winged or winged-like creatures – bees, divine horses, gods, weapons, the ψυχαί of Hektor and Patroklos –while the compound ἀποπέτομαι is used about vaporous entities that have an autonomous existence, like Agamemnon's dream at *Il.* 2.71.

Chapter 2

1. The translations of the *Onos* follow in most cases that by MacLeod 1967 (LCL). Note: in references to the *Onos*, I follow the line order of MacLeod's edition (Oxford 1974) reproduced in the TLG. The line *numbers* are marked only in the TLG. The line numbering in the Oxford edition restarts at every page, not at every chapter. I am grateful to anonymous referees for valuable comments.
2. Fögen 2017: 118. For the different interpretations of the end of Apuleius' *Metamorphoses*, see ibid. 119 n80.
3. The lost source – the tale of a donkey (often called 'ass-story'), which both Apuleius and the writer of *Onos* used – might even have been written by Apuleius' contemporary, Lucian. Tilg 2014, 1–7; for a comparison between these two works, see Mason 1994: 1665–1707, Harrison 2013: 95–98 and May 2013: 8–9.
4. On the ass-story in POxy. LXX 4762, see Luppe 2006. On iconography, see Keuls 1985: 165–166, fig. 139 (however, not donkey but a mule) and Vorberg 1932: 93–95, 599–600 (Roman lamps), 605.
5. Merleau-Ponty 2012: 140, 161; see also Korhonen and Ruonakoski 2017: 15. One of the obvious differences between Merleau-Ponty's and posthumanist concepts of embodiment is that Merleau-Ponty analyses embodiment or 'flesh' (*la chair*) basically from the point of view of human embodiment although he uses zoological examples to develop his theories of perception (see e.g., Merleau-Ponty 2012: 78). Haraway is, of course, part of the discussion on posthumanism, although she explicitly rejects being a posthumanist. See Haraway 2007: 16. On embodied consciousness, cf. also the papers by Kirichenko (2016a,b,c; 2018).
6. The reason for Lucius' failure was the wrong ointment. However, Lucius does not exercise the complete ritual: he does not sprinkle the frankincense while uttering some magic words as the lady of the house, the witch, did.
7. Lucius wants to shout to the robbers 'Oh Caesar!' but manages only to bray 'O' (16. 21–24); the same seems to happen when he tries to cry out to Zeus (38.7–10).
8. On the lack of speech as fatal deprivation in Ovid, see Gilhus 2006: 80–81.
9. This is reminiscent of the phrase that Plato uses of reincarnation: the soul discarding the old body and moving to a new one is expressed as undressing and redressing (cf. Plato *Phd.* 82a).
10. On attitudes to donkeys, see Gregory 2007: 193–195; Bodson 1986 and Opelt 1965. See also Fögen 2017: 118 n77.
11. Later on in the robbers' cave, Lucius' horse is given barley, which, according to Lucius, it eats quickly being afraid that Lucius may steal its share (21.9–10).

12. Halliwell 2008: 1, 415–416, referring to Aristotle (*Part. An.* 3.10.673a8). See also Sorabji 1993: 89–93.

13. Ps-Luc. *Onos* 16.11–14: [. . .] λαβόντες καὶ τὸν ἄλλον ὄνον καὶ τὸν ἵππον ἐπέσαξαν, ἔπειτα ὅσα ἐβάστασαν, ἐπικατέδησαν *ἡμῖν*. καὶ οὕτως μέγα ἄχθος φέροντας *ἡμᾶς* ξύλοις παίοντες [. . .].

14. 'We animals (κτήνη ἡμεῖς)': referring to all three (17.10); referring to the animals, Lucius among them, offered for sale (35.2). See also 'I, horses and other animals' (34.14) and 'fellow-slave animals' (42. 7–8).

15. Haraway 2007: 3, 16–17, 32.

16. See Perry 91; Perry 279; Babrius 128 and 129. I refer to Perry's edition on fables (Perry 1952).

17. One Aesopic fable (Perry 183) tells about a donkey carrying an image of a god, another (Babrius 141) carrying the implements of the priest of Cybele.

18. On abusive zoophilic shows in the arenas, see Coleman 1990: 67.

19. The lady complains that Lucius is 'transformed from that handsome, useful creature into a monkey' (56. 24–25). The lady does not use the word κτῆνος but ζῷον.

20. For donkeys in fables, see Perry's indices; Perry 1952 and Perry 1965: 613–614. See also Opelt 1965: 574–576.

21. In Apuleius, Lucius does not vomit but excavates farcically all the content of his belly in his pursuer's face (*Met.* 4. 3).

22. On the concept of this kind of empathy, see Korhonen and Ruonakoski 2017, especially 40.

23. Semonides fr. 7. 43–6 (West), Plut. *Mor.* 525e. See also Fögen 2017: 124 and his reference to Columella.

24. Perry 190. The wolf criticizes the 'unjustice': raven's doing (harming the donkey) is taken by the driver with laughter, which is the opposite reaction to the usual or normal one by humans concerning predators, namely anger and fear. See Korhonen 2017: 4–5.

25. Bresson's interview on French television in 1966 https://www.youtube.com/watch?v=FRAztry-ZoI (retrieved 2018/9/18).

26. Marie in Bresson's film corresponds to the kidnapped girl; Marie's abuser set Balthazar's tail on fire, which makes him run in alarm like Lucius when the slave-boy sets fire to the load of flax on Lucius' back; both Balthazar and Lucius work at grinding mills and become a crowd-puller in shows as a clever animal.

27. Of course, the groom is not allowed to kill Lucius. Knowing that his wealthy master ordered Lucius to receive good care, the groom plans to lie that Lucius was killed by a wolf (33. 5–6).

28. Garnsey 1999: 83–84. See also Ar. *Eq.* 1399.

29. Lucius has seen the orgies of the priests with a young man of a village and fears that he will be the forced active sexual partner for these cinaedic priests. This scene looks forward to Lucius' encounter with the rich lady (50. 10–14).

30. Compare with the much more elaborate description in Apul. *Met.* 9.13; see also Fögen 2017: 126–127.

31. Braidotti 2013: 70.

32. Ps.-Luc. *Onos* 43. 13–15: ἀνυπόδητος πηλὸν ὑγρὸν καὶ πάγον σκληρὸν καὶ ὀξὺν ἐπάτουν, καὶ τὸ φαγεῖν τοῦτο μόνον ἀμφοτέροις ἦν θρίδακας πικρὰς καὶ σκληράς.

33. Plutarch mentions a show where a dog 'actor' performs a dying dog (*Mor.* 973e–f). At the end of Apuleius' *Metamorphoses*, Lucius, again in human form, sees a comic procession with humans and non-humans dressed as different professions and roles, like a bear as a woman in a litter, a monkey as a Phrygian and a donkey as Pegasus (*Met.* 11. 18). This episode is missing in the Ps.-Lucian's *Onos*. For other descriptions of circus or show animals, see Philo of Alex. *de animalibus* 23–28 (ed. Terian); Porph. *de abstin*. 3. 15.

34. 'A Report to an Academy' is a rewarding text for posthumanistic reading. See, for instance, Barcz 2015: 260–261.

35. Plut. *Mor.* 1064a–b. According to Plutarch, Chrysippus urges the Stoics to prefer the human body to the 'ugly' (δύσμορφος) body of a donkey. This implies that a donkey's body was thought to be despicable as such. Also, Apuleius' Isis refers explicitly to the ugly body of donkeys (*Met.* 11.6.4). For his thought experiment, Chrysippus might have quoted a poem in which a personified *Phronêsis* asks to be despised because it is now in a donkey's body (*prosôpon*). See Korhonen and Ruonakoski 2017: 218 n89.

36. In chapter 17, Lucius shuns the raw barley and runs to the vegetable garden; in chapter 46, Lucius eats undonkeyish food in Menecles' house.

37. There is no place for an analysis of Lucius' heterosexuality but in all he seems to be quite 'passive' (women take initiative) and receptive for women's guidance during sexual acts against the socially expected gender role for men. On heterosexuality in antiquity, see Parker 2003.

38. Compare with the thought experiment on how difficult it is to be a centaur in Xen. *Cyr.* 4.3.15–21. See also Korhonen and Ruonakoski 2017: 95–96.

39. See e.g. Sorabji 1993: 12–16, and more recently, Fögen 2007: esp. 46–53 and 2014: esp. 219–223.

40. On slave imagery in Apuleius' *Metamorphoses*, also at the metaphysical level (the soul's slavery in a body), see Tilg 2014: 71–3; Gilhus 2006: 85. After his metamorphosis back into a human, which occurs in the arena, Lucius is declared free by the governor (55.18). Thus, as a donkey, he was owned like a slave and after becoming human again, a declaration of his emancipation is needed so that he will gain the status of a free citizen.

41. Compare with Ovid's *Metamorphoses* where changing into animal form is clearly felt like a punishment as human souls are trapped within their animal bodies; cf. Gilhus 2006: 81.

42. Palaestra also spoke of Lucius being 'inside' the donkey (ἐν τῷ ὄνῳ) while asking him to be patient believing she can give him roses in the morning (14. 10).

43. Cf. 15. 1–2, where Lucius speaks of himself as 'I' and 'Lucius' as well as 'donkey' and 'human'.

44. In fact, the donkeyness refers to the donkey phallus, which stands for the male self. The phallocentrism of the *Onos* is obvious in the case of Lucius as a human (his fear of castration 33. 23) and as a male donkey.

45. There are other mixings of different items like when the robbers planned to put the kidnapped girl *inside* the rotting body of Lucius the donkey and the priests put their Syrian goddess *inside* a Greek temple.

46. For the phenomenological concept of the primordial body, see Korhonen and Ruonakoski 2017: 17.

Chapter 3

1. E.g., throughout Verg. *A.* and Verg. *G.*: see Mackay 2019; also Gale 1991: 417–418, 422 and 2000: 103–105; Briggs 1980: 18–19, 26–27, 31–32 and *passim*.
2. Cf. Korhonen and Ruonakoski 2017: loc. 549–561, 595–602. On focalization, see Fowler 1991: 27–29 and 2000b: 41–45; on the epic gaze, e.g. Lovatt 2013: 10–17.
3. See e.g., V. Fl. 2.545b–549, 7.375–379.
4. The narrator apparently assumes that animals learn and know as humans do; cf. Wolfe 2009a: 568–570; Agamben 2004: 40–41, 51–56; see also Korhonen and Ruonakoski 2017: loc. 706–707, 766.
5. See also Wolfe 2009a: 571–572.
6. See e.g., Manuwald 2015: 193–194.
7. Haraway 2007: 19–26, 71.
8. Even shape-shifting gods of myth are imagined as human(oid) in 'default' form, and for our purposes Prometheus' embodied experience is conceived of as 'human'.

9. Rendering them cyborgs, Braidotti 2013: 73–75 or human-made 'artifacts', see n.28 below.
10. Korhonen and Ruonakoski 2017: loc. 296–305, 458–62, 517–29. My approach has much in common with their phenomenological approach, though shaped more by intertextual and narratological interests.
11. Hershkowitz 1998: 78, 195–7; Zissos 2004: 331–337; on the Argonauts' 'experience', Hardie 2013: 134, 137.
12. Thompson 1895: 49. See Hom. *Od.* 11.576–579; cf. Lucr. 3.992–994, Verg. *A.* 6.595–600, Ov. *Met.* 4.456b–458a; Murgatroyd 2009: 61–62; cf. Stover 2012: 168n.
13. Beard et al. 1998: 175–177.
14. English translations of V. Fl. are the author's; Latin text is from Ehlers' edition (2011).
15. Korhonen and Ruonakoski 2017: loc. 339–344, 388.
16. See Payne 2010: 5, 8–9, 19–22.
17. Spaltenstein 2004: 431–432.
18. Castelletti 2014: 190; though he is a 'liberator of men and defender of civilization', Hershkowitz 1998: 159, not an instrument of retribution.
19. See e.g., Baier 2001; Stover 2012: 113–148; Schenk 1991; Clauss 2014; Bernstein 2014; Cowan 2014: 244–248.
20. Hom. *Il.* 15.323.
21. Verg. *A.* 10.572–573.
22. Mackay 2019: 173–8. Contains an extended study of this passage and horse–human relationships.
23. V. Fl. also draws inspiration from Verg. *A.* 12.529–534.
24. Korhonen and Ruonakoski 2017: loc. 1243; 1285–1289.
25. Cf. Verg. *G.* 1.509–514.
26. Cf. Lucr. 5.1308–1340.
27. V. Fl. 3.332–335; see Mackay 2019: 83–89.
28. Clutton-Brock 2007: 72, 85–86; Willekes 2016: 26–27, 135–136.

Chapter 4

1. Text used: Lloyd Jones and Wilson 1990; translation used (with adjustments): Jebb 1917.
2. An Aeschylean (fr. 252, 253, 255 Radt) and a Euripidean version of the play also survive in fragments (fr. 789a, 787–800 Kannicht).
3. On Philoctetes' medicalized suffering, see Guardasole 2000: 185–192; Ceschi 2005; Rehm 2006; Dall'Olio 2014.
4. E.g., Ceri Stephens 1995; Dall'Olio 2014; Osborne 2007: 164–168.
5. E.g., Segal 1995: 98, 114; Davies 2003; Levine 2003; Finglass 2006.
6. Carel 2016: 17.
7. With Merleau-Ponty 2012 [1945]: 110, a 'complete way of being'; see Susan Sontag's classic *Illness as Metaphor* 1978.
8. Easterling (1978: 36) responds to the same sense of totality in the embedment of the hero's experience into the play: 'Philoctetes himself is the focus of nearly all the imagery: the desert island, the wound, the bow, the dead man, are all used as means of exploring his situation and of arousing our emotional response to him.' On animalization and animal self-definition in a posthumanist, or 'non-humanist' (92–93) perspective, see Haraway 2007; Braidotti 2013: 55–104, on 'Post-anthropocentrism'.

9. Carel 2016: 55–60.
10. As explored by Carel 2016: 40–46, and chapter 2 as a whole; she mentions 'loss of wholeness'; 'loss of certainty'; 'loss of control'; 'loss of freedom to act'; 'loss of the everyday world'. On challenges to a concept of nature (as well as culture, *polis* and *oikos*) in a posthuman perspective, see the seminal provocation in Haraway 1985/1991: 162–163.
11. Clarke and Rossini 2017: xii; Cotter et al. 2016: 1–2.
12. On the general discomfort with, or diffidence against human subjectivity as starting point for ethical reflections in posthumanistic studies, see MacCormack 2012a: 87 on 're-negotiations of subjectivity' and 'post-subjects' as part of posthumanistic frames; cf. also Roden (2015: 2) on the possibility of neuroscientific revisions of a concept of 'subjectivity' as private and personal; the holistic proposal by Barad 2007 about the interrelated nature of the world, with scientific and ethical implications in terms of what she calls 'agential realism'.
13. On the affiliation between phenomenological ontology and posthumanistic criticism see Herbrechter 2013: 14–15. Kristeva's 1982 [1980] classic reflection on horror and abjection had already emphasized the crashing down of the boundaries between self and other when the individual faces his own 'corporeal reality' as dissonant to the world outside, with taboo elements exposed in full light; the 'phenomenological' quality of her account of 'abjection' ties in well with Philoctetes' illness in our play. On the body of the other as itself a centre of subjectivity, and a bridge to intra-subjectivity, see the important analysis of Korhonen and Ruonakoski 2017: 17–23.
14. Other important readings of ancient ethics go in the same direction: see the seminal explorations of human vulnerability in Gill 1996 and Nussbaum 2001, with important insights on tragic suffering.
15. Recently Allen-Hornblower 2016 has analysed this disgust in our play as currency within an ethical metaphor (the disgust, δυσχέρεια felt by Neoptolemos for himself as well as Philoctetes' disgust, felt but also raised by him).
16. Budelmann 2006: 145–147.
17. Compare also 952–953, when Philoctetes addresses his cave: 'Double-gated cave, back, back again / I return to you, but now stripped and lacking the means to live' (Ὦ σχῆμα πέτρας δίπυλον, αὖθις αὖ πάλιν / εἴσειμι πρὸς σὲ ψιλός, οὐκ ἔχων τροφήν).
18. The theme of Philoctetes' complete isolation on a deserted Lemnos, for example, is only Sophoclean.
19. On these *apostrophai*, see Korhonen and Ruonakoski 2017: 135–144.
20. See Korhonen and Ruonakoski (2017: 127–136) on this element, reading it in terms of 'empathy'.
21. Jebb's translation (1917).
22. The motif of being eaten in turn by animals, once the primary providers of sustenance for Philoctetes can be read as reminder of that fundamental fact in the play, that human embodiment – our own nature as individuals made of flesh, and as such both in need of nourishment and capable of offering nutrition to others – is precisely what allows humans to recognize subjectivity in the other, and reach a true empathic understanding. Korhonen and Ruonakoski (2017: 19–24) explore the concept of empathy in phenomenology as pivoted around the 'presence in the flesh' of another.
23. Cf. Worman 2000 on disturbed communication in the play; Männlein-Robert 2014 on the explicitness of screams in this play as partaking to an esthetic of 'sublimity'; Allen-Hornblower 2013; Payne 2010: 90.
24. Kristeva 1982 [1980]: 141.
25. Compare Braidotti 2013: 81–89.
26. This stands out even more in the light of the 'masculinity' performance of Philoctetes (Kosak 2006).
27. Worman 2000: 5–6.

28. Männlein-Robert 2014; she discusses the 'edges of aesthetics' (Gränzfälle der Ästhetik, 91) in a case like the depiction of horrific pain in *Philoctetes*.
29. Readers have been intrigued by Sophocles' medical talents here; some have diagnosed secondary melancholy (Ceschi 2005), some other a split vein/ulcer (Ceri Stephens 1995), some have detected an allusion to Sophocles' own old-age ailments (Cirio 1997). The diagnoses are not so much in point for our analysis here: rather, the disgusting, monstrous quality of the disease that Philoctetes experiences, on a material and bodily level. Dio's account of the Euripidean version of the same myth contains reference to a similar emphasis on the horrific as marker of disease: cf. 789d.5 Kannicht; 789d.11 Kannicht.
30. Kosak 1999; Kazantzidis 2016.
31. On Sophoclean 'language of pain' in *Philoctetes*, cf. also Budelmann 2007: 444–446.
32. For a survey of relevant literature, see Carel 2016: 35–39.
33. MacCormack 2012a: 79–99, especially 79–82 and 85–89 problematizing the concept 'monster' as both aberration and marvel.
34. With Derrida 1995: 386, in MacCormack 2012a: 79; from a different angle, commenting on our play, Easterling (1978: 36): '[Philoctetes'] wound is *both* his bitterness and wildness *and* his dignity, just as the desert island symbolises not only his alienation, loneliness and animal-like life but also his purity.'

Chapter 5

1. Thanks to the editors for tightening without domesticating, and the anonymous reader for sharp comments and helpful bibliography.
2. For the striking history of 'sympathetic' reader responses to the Noric plague of *Georgics* 3, for example, see Gardner 2014: 3 (cf. 26); for the aesthetics of pathos in the plague, see Thibodeau 2011: 163–164.
3. Virgil's subjective/sympathetic/empathetic voice is all over fundamental twentieth-century scholarship: see Heinze 1999 (first published 1903); Otis 1964: 41–97; Anderson 1968: 9, 25, 45; cf. Gale 1991: 422, 426; Thibodeau 2011: 159–160 updates it into a therapeutic psychagogy.
4. E.g., sympathy for Orpheus: Perkell 1978: 218.
5. Virgil's 'sympathy for plants and animals': Perkell 1978: 216; cf. Liebeschuetz 1965: 64–65; Miles 1975: 180 on Virgil's feel for the exiled bull in *G*. 3.
6. Sympathy for the bees: Thibodeau 2011: 173.
7. For anthropomorphosis in *Georgics* 3, see Liebeschuetz 1965; Gale 1991. Theriomorphosis has made less of a dent on *Georgics* 3 criticism.
8. Not just structuralist; these dualisms have long fuelled western systems of domination (Haraway 2016: 59–60).
9. See e.g., Xenophon *Oeconomicus* 13.9; Aristotle *Politics* 1.2.14. Recent work on literature and the posthuman often ghosts antiquity entirely (e.g. Clarke and Rossini 2017).
10. The *locus classicus* is Varro *On Agriculture* 1. 17: the instruments of farm labour can be divided into speaking (slaves, *uocale*), quasi-speaking (cattle, *semiuocale*) and unspeaking (the wagons, *mutum*). For an interesting recent application of Marx to understanding modern factory-farmed animals as slaves themselves, see Murray 2011.
11. See Isaac 2004: 194–215. On Roman ethnography in general: Thomas 1982; Woolf 2010.
12. Derrida 2008: 96.
13. Haraway 2016: 10; cf. 2003 and 2007. Cf. also Clarke and Rossini 2017: xiii.

14. Derrida 2008: 34.
15. Cf. Foster 1988; Gardner 2014: 3.
16. *Vinco* (102, 225, 289, 560), *uictor* (9, 17, 27, 114, 227, 499), *uictoria* (112) fasten the book together; and cf. below on the challenges of winning big-goat-in-small-field (*uincere* 289), or the plague's conquest at 559–560.
17. Text is Oxford Classical Texts (Mynors 1990); translations are 'my own'.
18. See Giusti 2019a (esp. 109–110). I agree with her in taking this as both a vision of actual captive Britons forced to raise the curtain on which their conquest is represented (following Servius; and contra Wilkinson 1969: 168, Thomas 1988b *ad loc.*, and Mynors 1990 *ad loc.* – all of whom think it an illusion created by the pretty curtain picture) and a crucial moment in sublating the conquered into pure representation, 'non-existence' (114), i.e., making them disappear. Giusti's reading also helps bulk out the point below about the mythical distance and fictionality of the plague.
19. Virgil twice binds himself tight with Octavianic conquest, once here, then again at the end of the poem. But it is important not to view imperialism as something practised by individual *generalissimi*: it was a *class* action (on which see Geue 2018).
20. See Derrida 1991; Calarco 2004: 193f.
21. Liebeschuetz 1965: 65; Gale 1991: 418.
22. Virgil won't be the last philosopher to make the connection: see Derrida 2008: 96 on a similar interrelation in Kant.
23. Gale (1991: 418) detects a sinister touch, but then immediately domesticates things: 'the metaphor is an obvious one, simply reversing the common image of the "yoke of slavery"'. Thibodeau (2011: 45, 60–61) also notes the oblique reference.
24. A common problem in *Georgics* scholarship: see particularly Fitzgerald 1996: 389, Reay 2003, Thibodeau 2011: 45, Geue 2018; cf. Volk 2002: 128, Spurr 2008: 31.
25. The dynamic may also feed back into the second person address, which is more imperative-heavy in this section (see Thibodeau 2011: 60); could Virgil be yoking his own worker here?
26. For the many other cases of violence visited on animals in book 3, see Gale 1991: 426.
27. Virgil seems to have an eye on different kinds of farm operation at different times throughout the poem (Thibodeau 2011: 19, Spurr 2008: 28); but the labourers are invariably invisible.
28. Cf. Gale 1991: 420; Miles 1975: 186; Liebeschuetz 1965: 69.
29. Gale 1991: 421; Miles 1975: 187.
30. On this reversal in book 3, cf. Gale 1991: 423.
31. This strong break of book 3 reflects a Roman category line between bigger and smaller domestic animals (see Liebeschuetz 1965: 73).
32. On the dignifying language here, see Thibodeau 2011: 72, 87–88.
33. The 'sympathy' monster rears its head here too: Thibodeau (2011: 69) claims the rhetorical effect of the mixed perspective of landowner and peasant is 'to capture his readers' sympathy . . . to stoop to identification with a humbler, less wealthy world'.
34. See Thomas 1988b *ad loc.*
35. *Acer* tends to go with animals directly (*acrem* of the steed, 3. 119; *acrior* of the *oestrus* 3. 154; the *genus acre* of wolves and dogs, 3. 264; *acrius* of the bees replenishing their hoard, 4. 248), or with animal associates (Pelops as *acer equis*, 3. 8; the pregnant cow's *acri fuga*, 3. 141–142; the *acrem sonitum* Proteus makes when captured and taking bestial and elemental forms, 4. 409). It also goes with the *rusticus* (2. 405–406), modern descendant of the old Italian stock of the Marsi, Sabines, and Ligurians (*acre genus uirum*, 2. 167) – but these are animal-adjacent humans relative to the upper crust Roman.
36. On the vexed question of addressee identity in the poem, see Reay 2003, Thibodeau 2011 – both point out Virgil's fudging of *agricola* = *colonus* = *pastor*, landowner to smallholder to roaming

herdsman, squashed into the poem's capacious second person. I prefer to stress how the grouping of pastor–addressee (Thibodeau 2011: 69) and Gelonian here actually puts both in a camp far beneath the elite Roman author and readership; as I point out in Geue 2018: 8, we should resist the fuzzy logic of 'blurred identity' explanations.

37. The north-east saw important frontier military action around the Lower Danube in 29 BCE: see Gruen 1996: 174; Wilkes 1996: 550. The Scythians sue for Augustus' friendship at Suetonius *Augustus* 21.

38. Gale 1991: 418.

39. E.g., 51, 69, 205, 221, 251, 369. For a civil war spin on *corpora* as metaphor for bodies politic, see Gardner 2014: 5.

40. Plague as boundary-eraser: Gale 1991: 418; Gardner 2014: 12.

41. The plague is one of the hot potatoes of *Georgics* scholarship: for the literary sources, see West 1980, Gale 1991 (Lucretius); some press the plague's pure fictionality (Wilkinson 1969; Harrison 1979), others have pushed viable historicity (anthrax? See Flintoff 1983).

42. On the long historical pedigree of picturing plague as something foreign and external, see Sontag 1989: 47–48; as she puts it, 'there is a link between imagining disease and imagining foreignness'. On the metaphorical applications of illness, see also Thumiger (this volume).

43. For an account of the simultaneously vague and specific geography here (reflecting the complicated intermingling of ethnic populations and powers in the region), see Flintoff 1983: 86–92. As Foster 1988: 33–34 notes, this is emphatically *not* 'northern Italy', but rather frontier country *outside* Italy – a border that was particularly sensitive at the time (Wilkes 1996: 549).

44. Foster 1988: 33. For the overlap between Noricans and Iapydes, see Flintoff 1983: 90–91.

45. Foster 1988: 38.

46. Cf. Foster 1988: 44.

47. See Liebeschuetz 1965: 73–77; Putnam 1979: 215–235; Thomas 1988: 130; Mynors 1990: 251.

48. I understand upper class membership as primarily a socioeconomic relationship, rather than a strict matter of being of 'the senate' *uel sim*. Virgil was an immensely wealthy landowner (see Thibodeau 2011: 247); on his (very probable) equestrian status, see Taylor 1968: 483–484. There were of course active political distinctions between the senatorial and equestrian orders (on the latter, see Davenport 2018), but I understand the two as linked via their shared economic interests and common status as absentee landowners.

Chapter 6

1. See for example, Haraway 2007; Wolfe 2009a.
2. See Franco 2014: 161–184.
3. Latour 1993: 104.
4. Franco 2014: 176 f., and *passim* for a good overview of posthuman theoretical framework applied to animal-human studies. I speak of 'Homeric society' as an imaginary construct rather than as a historical reality, in the sense that the unity of this historically stratified society was created by the continual performances of Homeric poems in different venues.
5. Clarke 1995: 140, 145 f. See Schnapp-Gourbeillon 1981: 1–27.
6. Lonsdale 1990: 10, 125. On Homeric similes, see Fränkel 1962; Buxton 2004; Ready 2011.
7. Heath 2005: 24, my italics.
8. Heath 2005: 25.
9. Ibid.

10. On 'saming' and 'othering', see Schor 1989 and Fabian 1990.
11. It is after Homer that the cleavage between animals and men begins to be conceptualized. See Heath 2005: 215f.
12. See Bateson 2000: for ex. part V.
13. Bateson 2000: 460 and f.
14. On anthropopoiesis, see Affergan *et al.* 2003 and Hopman in this volume who discusses it in the terms of Agamben's 'anthropogenic machine'.
15. A disclaimer is in order here. Sheep and flocks will be somehow in the foreground of my analysis; as herding animals, however, they share a number of significant features with cattle, with which they will be often conflated, as they are in Homer, cfr. *Il.* 18. 524; the formula βόας καὶ ἴφια μῆλα, 'oxen and goodly sheep', as prestigious possessions and as animals for sacrifice. In certain respects they do have a different status in Homer, which, for reasons of space, I can only hint at.
16. Lonsdale 1990: 10.
17. On pastoral economies, see Whittaker 1988; Howe 2008.
18. Schnapp-Gourbeillon 1981; Lonsdale 1990. See Kalof 2007 and, recently, Lewis and Llewellyn-Jones 2017.
19. McCandrick 2008: 135.
20. Ibid.
21. See Cachia 1997. On human and animal taxonomy, cf. also Hopman in this volume.
22. See Schmitt 1967: 283 f.; Watkins 1995: 45.
23. West 1997: 226f.
24. Cf. Xen. *Mem.* 3.2.1 for Agamemnon as 'shepherd of the people' par excellence. On the metaphor in Homer, see especially Haubold 2000: 17–45.
25. Bettini 2013a: 126. See also Franco 2014: 168.
26. Ibid. Bettini borrows the term from Gibson's theory of 'ecological psychology', *idem*, 125f.
27. Schmitt 1968: 30–33; Watkins 1995: 15.
28. See, for example, Lewis (2017: 23): 'when humans lived longer, so did their cattle'; Sykes (2014: 177) suggests that this indicates 'a level of human–cattle partnership'.
29. Finley 1982: 56, see also 64.
30. Cf. also *Il.* 11. 670–684.
31. Pritchard 1969; Collins 1996: 21–23; West 1997: 226 and f. have thought that the Greeks imported this notion from the Near East, but this is hardly tenable, not only because it uses a derivative model in coeval societies.
32. Haubold (2000: 18), who notes that 'Odysseus wipes out a generation of Ithacans because they eat up his livestock. Achilles thinks an attempt on his flocks a good reason for joining the Trojan war'.
33. Haubold (2000: 19f.) asserts that the owner of the herd and the shepherd are not the same person, and that this already implies a conflict on leadership as, he notes, the owner of the flock does not share the same 'cultural values and economic interests' as the shepherd. The metaphor of the shepherd, however, deals with leadership, not ownership nor wealth. Besides, the examples used by Haubold are from the *Odyssey* – the only Iliadic example, *Il.* 20. 221f. speaks of mares and no named shepherd comes to the fore.
34. Schnapp-Gourbeillon 1981: 28–37.
35. Benveniste 1974 [1966]: 90.
36. Bateson 2000: 97.
37. Here and elsewhere the translations of the *Iliad* are by S. Butler 1898, slightly modified.

38. Haubold 2000: 22; see Ulf 1990: 99–105. On the idea of self-serving shepherds, see Collins 1996.

39. Cartledge 2009: 29f.

40. Haubold 2000: 28; the main evidence the scholar offers to back this analysis is the recurrence of the formulae 'he destroyed the people', and 'the people perished', p. 29, which are however unconnected to shepherdship and do not apply to the metaphor '*poimena laon*'.

41. On kingship in the *Iliad*, see Giordano 2010: 22–31.

42. Schnapp-Gourbeillon 1981; Lonsdale 1990; Clarke 1995.

43. Cf. also *Il*. 16. 352–357 where the Greeks fall upon the Trojans as murderous wolves upon helpless lambs.

44. Cf. also *Il*. 10. 485–486, and Lonsdale 1990: 49–60.

45. It is not secondary that in the semantic cluster formed by herding animals they figure as sacrificial animals (see e.g. *Il* 20. 403 also 8. 131). An implicit yet constant element of the comparison is that (according to long-held cultural values) sheep, rams and cattle (but bulls and rams too, to be sure) are those that by nature are destined for slaughter. Just as naturally, simple soldiers forming the bulk of Homeric armies are fodder for war, to continue the pastoral metaphors. Whereas the forefront warriors, the *aristeis*, may die the lion's death, simple soldiers are doomed to an anonymous, sheepish, death. Here again, animals are artfully used to express and legitimize a taxonomy.

46. Exactly as the king in peacetime is the one in charge of the safety and survival of the *laos* in the generic sense of people. The change of perspective, whereby leaders are seen at the same time as the shepherds and predators in relation to their flock, would be worth exploring further.

47. Finley 1982: 48 f.

48. Lonsdale 1990: 24, in reference to herds of cattle.

49. In Homer, the bull is considered a mighty animal, see *Il*. 16. 487f., where Sarpedon is compared to a bull slain by the lion-Patroclus.

50. On female animals, see Connell 2016.

51. See on this point Franco 2014: 176.

52. Garvie 2009: 74; at line 154 Xerxes is directly called a god; see also Hdt. 7. 56.2. That 'for the audience the epithet need not indicate Xerxes' *hybris* or presumption' it is hardly granted. The very fact that 'it frequently describes a hero in Homer' is a clear clue, ibidem.

53. On this and on *Persae*, see Giordano (forthcoming).

54. Bateson 2000: 97.

55. Heath 2005; Thumiger 2014, especially 87-89.

56. Franco 2014: 172. Geue in this volume also addresses the political meaning of human/animal imagery in the context of a discourse legitimizing human domination of other humans.

57. On cosmological boundaries as pertaining to the human/animal dynamics see Alexandridis, Wild and Winkler-Horaček 2008.

Chapter 7

1. Derrida (2009/2010: vols. 1–2; thereafter vol. 1 quoted 2009); cf. Krell 2013.
2. On Posthumanism and animal ethics, cf. Kachuck in this volume, n. 7, who, along with Derrida, quotes e.g., the works of Haraway and Cary Wolfe. A good survey of Posthuman readings of human–animal relations can be found in Franco 2014: 176f. On Derrida and the posthuman discourse on the animal and the human, cf. also Fleming in this volume.
3. Derrida 2009: 16f.

4. Derrida 2009: 32.
5. See Derrida 2009: 12f.
6. Caligula as *belua*: Sen. *de ira* 3, 19, 3; as *monstrum*: Suet. *Cal.* 22, 1.
7. See Derrida 2009: 19f. and Derrida 2005, esp. 95–97, referring to Noam Chomsky's *Rogue States: The Rule of Force in World Affairs*, published in 2000.
8. Cf. Barcelo 1993 and Luraghi 2015.
9. Cf. OLD s.v. 1, and Dyck 2013: 78f.
10. Cf. Rosenberger 1998: 23f.
11. Cf. Crahay 1956.
12. Cf. Waters 1971 and Gammie 1986.
13. Hdt. 3, 80–82. Cf. Pelling 2002.
14. The best example in the Persian context of the debate would be Cambyses who murdered his brother Smerdis, married a full sister against the Persian customs and another one who was later killed by him (3, 30–32). But the third book also delivers stories about Greek tyrants such as Polycrates and Periander.
15. For the following, see Hdt. 5, 92 with the comm. of Hornblower 2013: 246–266.
16. Hdt. 5, 92 η 3. As Herodotus reported in 3, 50, Melissa had been killed by Periander himself.
17. The educational character of the speech, providing the necessary ἐμπειρία, is stressed by Socles calling the Spartans τυράννων ἄπειροι (5, 92 α 2).
18. Trans. R. Waterfield, Oxford 1998.
19. For the association of lions with leaders and kings, cf. Brock 2013: 89f.; for the Near Eastern legacy West 1997: 246f. and 388.
20. Cf. Barker 2006.
21. Cf. also the boar similes in the chapter of M. Hopman in this volume.
22. Cf. Lonsdale 1990, esp. 39–70.
23. τύραννος is a non-Greek word with uncertain origin which first appears (as τυραννίς) in Archilochos (fr. 19 West); cf. Berve 1967: 3.
24. Cf. Brock 2013: 90, who links the term with Achilles' denunciation of Agamemnon as a 'people-devouring king' (δημοβόρος βασιλεύς, *Il.* 1, 231) and Hesiod's 'gift-eating kings' (βασιλῆς δωροφάγοι, *Op.* 39, 263f.).
25. *Il.* 22, 67; cf. *Il.* 24, 207 with Hecuba's warning against Achilles as an ὠμηστὴς καὶ ἄπιστος ἀνήρ.
26. Trans. G. W. Most 2006.
27. For these hybrids, see Strauss Clay 2003: 150–161.
28. πέλωρ (hence the adj. πέλωρος) is together with τέρας the Greek equivalence to Latin *monstrum* (cf. LSJ *s.v.*).
29. *Hybris*, the permanent violation of norms, is the characteristic of the still evolving cosmos, and Typhoeus will become the most dangerous threat for the newly established reign of Zeus, the guarantee of a just rule. Cf. Strauss Clay in this volume and *eadem* (2003: 21, 81f.) for parallels in the *Works and Days*.
30. Cf. esp. Waters 1971.
31. Cf. Gray 1996: 364–366.
32. Hdt. 5, 92 β:'Ηετίων, οὔτις σε τίει πολύτιτον ἐόντα. / Λάβδα κύει, τέξει δ' ὀλοοίτροχον· ἐν δὲ πεσεῖται / ἀνδράσι μουνάρχοισι, δικαιώσει δὲ Κόρινθον (Eëtion, no one honours you, though you are full of honour. /Labda will conceive and give birth to a boulder – One that will fall on the rulers and punish Corinth.) (Trans. R. Waterfield, Oxford 1998).

33. Cf. Hornblower (2013: 254–256): The Doric form of the name of Cypselus' father, Eetion, could be connected with the eagle (αἰετός) of the second oracle. The boulder (ὀλοοίτροχος) may be an allusion to Eetion's home place Petra, because in Hom. *Il.* 13, 137 we find the combination ὀλοιότροχος ὡς ἀπὸ πέτρης. This form of intertextuality seems to be comparable to that of the second oracle I tried to show above.

34. Cf. McGlew 1993: 74, who argues convincingly that 'a tyranny begins its correction of injustice with an act of violence against the former leaders of the city'. Thus, harshness is an integral part of 'bringing justice' (δικαιοῦν).

35. Hdt. 2, 92 γ. The smiling baby also stands for a diachronic ambivalence because some of Herodotus' tyrants – even Periander – seem to start as 'good' rulers; thus, the matter of interpretation is not only to recognize who is actually a tyrant, but also who has the potential to become one.

36. Cf. McGlew 1993: 63–74.

37. For the cultural background, cf. Baumgarten 1998: 65f.

38. For a discussion of this range of interpretations, see Moles 2002.

39. Strasburger 1955.

40. The reply Hippias gave after Socles' speech, that the Corinthians would be the first to miss the Pisistratidae when the time came for them to suffer at Athenian hands, can be seen as a prediction of the tyrannical behaviour of the Periclean Athens (see Pelling 2006: 107), which is based, as Herodotus emphasizes, on his precise knowledge of the oracles. Moles 2002 connects this with the Peloponnesian conferences before the Peloponnesian war, when Corinth attacked Athens as a tyrannical state.

41. For such an ironic reading, see esp. Wecowski 1996; Johnson 2001.

42. Cf. Newell 2013, esp. 81–130.

43. κρίνειν (discern) is an essential ability of the Platonic philosopher, but one cannot be sure that the σκύλαξ φιλόσοφος is a definite statement of Plato about the rationality of animals: Is the use of animal imagery more a didactic tool than an attempt to blur the borderlines between animal and man? For such a blurring in the works of later Platonists like Plutarch, cf. Newmyer 2006.

44. Cf. Socrates' interpretation of the Allegory of the Cave (519c–520c), where Socrates demands that the new made philosopher, who has seen the light of the sun, i.e. Form of the Good, and would like to stay in this 'suprahuman' sphere, has to be forced to return into the cave to bring his former fellow prisoners on to the right path. Here too, one could say, the freewheeling philosopher's dog must be re-captured and domesticated by being brought back into his human homesphere, to live up to its social responsibility.

45. Cf. Ferrari 2003.

46. The background here is the Arcadian cult of Zeus Lykaios (see Paus. 6, 8, 8). For Derrida 2009: 60, this passage is further evidence of his '(gene) lycology' or 'anthropolycology', which he developed in his discussion of the fable of the wolf and the lamb and Hobbes' famous aphorism *homo homini lupus*. For Aristotle, the eating of raw human flesh is the main criterion of the true form of human θηριότης which is either innate or acquired by disease or by habit. The main deterrent example for this aberration he delivers is the tyrant of Acragas, Phalaris, who is not only said to have roasted his enemies in a bronze bull, but also to have eaten even the flesh of children; see Arist. *EN* 1148 b 15–27.

47. This obvious allusion to Hesiod is not mentioned in Boys-Stones and Haubold 2010 despite its broad scope of Hesiod reception in Plato.

48. Cf. Larivée 2012.

49. The term ποικίλος is the decisive link to the description of the main characteristic of the democratic state, its multifariousness (see esp. 557a–558c), which tends to licentiousness. For the 'multicolouredness' of democracy, cf. Derrida 2005: 26f.

50. Xen. *mem.* 2, 1, 21–34. For Hercules as *exemplum virtutis* and proto-philosopher, cf. Stafford 2012: 121–129.
51. A late but meaningful testimony for these different forms of mythic rationalization is Dio Chr. 5, 21f.
52. On the fragmentation of human intentionality, cf. Ceschi in this volume.
53. Cf. Tabacco 1985.
54. Cf. Dunkle 1967, esp. 160–162, and Dunkle 1971 for the 'rhetorical tyrant in Roman historiography'.
55. Cic. *ad Att.* 7, 20, 2.
56. Cic. *off.* 2, 23 and *off.* 3, 32, where we find a justification of the tyrannicide, which is based on denying the tyrant's humanity: in fact, he is a *belua* in the guise of a human being.
57. Cf. Cic. *de or.* 3, 137f. for a juxtaposition of Pisistratus' and Pericles' rhetorical talent.
58. Cf. Hdt. 1, 59.
59. For Pisistratus as *aisymnetes*, cf. Fadinger 2016. Newell (2016: 70) calls Augustus the 'greatest of political sphinxes [. . .] this image of Achilles-like youthful courage and sublime beauty was the outward camouflage for what was in fact a universal despotism, pharaoh in a toga'.
60. Suet. *Nero* 53 and 29. See also Philstr. *V. Ap.* 4, 38, 3, where Nero the tyrant is introduced as an example of the πολιτικὸν θηρίον – a beast with countless heads! Cf. now Lefebvre 2017, esp. 235–238 and her Annex 1 with the crimes attributed to Nero over the centuries.

Chapter 8

1. On a posthuman reading of the monstrous as an anthropopoietic dispositive questioning what it means to be human by pointing to monstrosity as an *excess* that cannot be normalized by inclusion or exclusion in a discourse about the Self, but is always on the verge of emerging to disrupt 'order', cf. Chesi and Spiegel (with a discussion of Deleuze and Guattari's 'animal rhizome' as a monster) and Nuzzo in this volume [The Editors].
2. The norm here is the form of the gods, which bears out the argument I develop in detail in Strauss Clay 2003, that the *Theogony* offers a divine perspective on the cosmos while the *Works and Days* adopts the perspective of human beings.
3. I have dealt with the monster clan and their role in the *Theogony* as a representation of an anti-cosmos at some length in Strauss Clay 1993 and Strauss Clay 2003: 151–161.
4. For Typhoeus' appearances outside of Hesiod, see Gantz 1993: 48–51; Ballabriga 1990 analyses the variants of the Typhoeus myth and attempts to account for the Hesiodic version in terms of rhapsodic interventions.
5. See West 1966: 381–383. For bibliography both for and against the passages' authenticity, see Saïd 1977: 199–210, who, however, defends the episode; also Ballabriga 1990, Baglioni 2010: 28–30 who summarizes the literature.
6. Hamilton (1989: 23): 'one must admit that critics who complain that it simply duplicates the Titanomachy seem to have a point'.
7. Cf. Mondi 1986 for the claim that the victory over the Titans really was brought about by the Hundred-handers. Blaise and Rousseau 1996 have shown otherwise.
8. Cf. Strauss Clay 2003: 25–26.
9. Blaise (1992: 356): 'Gaia s'oppose toutefois à lui, comme elle s'est opposée à Ouranos et à Cronos, à partir du moment où l'ordre qu'elle a aidé à établir tend à une immobilité stérile et porte donc atteinte à sa nature même.'

10. Blaise 1992: 357. If the *descriptio Tartari* came after the Typhonomachy, the argument would be more convincing.
11. Hamilton (1989: 23) notes quite correctly, 'the Typhoeus episode is anomalous in suddenly bringing us back to the aboriginal times of Gaia's mating . . . (126–53)'. Cf. Detienne and Vernant (1974: 115): 'Typhée . . . prolonge, dans un univers déjà différencié et ordonné, la lignée de 'ceux qui furent d'abord', les êtres primordiaux qu'Hésiode place aux raciness du monde.' I would argue that this 'throwback' to earlier times is perfectly in keeping with Hesiod's purpose.
12. See above n. 1.
13. Baglioni 2010 argues for the anti-cosmic character of Typhoeus in opposition to the order of Zeus.
14. For Typhoeus as an anti-Zeus, see Blaise 1992: 362.
15. Cf. Goslin 2010 for the juxtaposition of Typhoeus' sonic dissonances and the Muses' song.
16. See Strauss Clay 2003: 150–174.
17. West brackets 828.
18. Typhoeus is subsequently linked to volcanic activity by Pindar, Aeschylus and others. The reading Αἴτνης of Tzetzes at 860 has worked its way into two Mss; cf. West 1966 *ad loc.*
19. Stoddard 2004: 157–159.
20. Goslin (2010: 366–369) offers a more positive version of the consequences of Typhoeus' defeat for humankind, emphasizing Zeus's civilizing benevolence. The epithet χαμαιγενής points rather to mankind's 'low ontological status' (cf. *LfgE* s.v. χαμαιγενής).

Chapter 9

1. Sophocles' *Oedipus Rex* opens with a plague, as a consequence of Oedipus' parricide and incest (22–30): the controversial issue of purposefulness/unawareness, which will be in the spotlight in Freud's theory of the 'Oedipus complex', is irrelevant to the causal link between those events. Cf. Maiullari 2001; Longo 2007. Πυρφόρος θεός (27) traces back the nosologic symptom – fever caused by the plague – to divine etiology.
2. For a discussion of religious evidence in tragedy, specifically about the Labdacids and Atridae, cf. Gagné 2013.
3. Cf. the pioneering work of Latour 1993, esp. the *Introduction* and pp. 136–138 (*Humanism redistributed*), who attempts to decentralize anthropocentricism by maintaining that humans and non-humans both share agency.
4. On the agonistic conception of disease within Hippocratic speculation, which also underlies an idea of νόσος as a living creature, hostile to the patient's life, cf. Jouanna 1994: 143f.
5. On the imaginary of therapeutic in classical Greece, cf. Jouanna 1999.
6. The famous verses of the first Stasimon of *Antigone* prove it right (361–363): these verses still present the patient as a person totally at the mercy of external forces, despite technological development. It is said, in fact, that although man has devised ways of treating diseases, which were previously considered incurable, Hades is still impending over him as an ineluctable ultimate destination of human life.
7. On Hippocratic vocabulary in Tragedy, cf. Guardasole 2000 and Ceschi 2009.
8. O'Connor 1974: 185.
9. For example, in the passage in which the Titan addresses the Chorus of Oceanids (274–276) inviting them to share his suffering. The pain is described as a wandering wild beast, assaulting one and then the other intended victim. Previously, Prometheus' agony, being fiercely wrapped by insoluble chains, was expressed by the adverb ἀγρίως (155), which highlights the wildness of his situation.

10. Analysis of the semantic implications of πλανάω, which was used within Hippocratic vocabulary to refer to the periodic return of symptoms in the disease course, will be given *infra*.

11. Linguistic signals to describe a delirium are the word εἴδωλον (567) and the participle εἰσορῶσα (568): Io is haunted by a physical torment, but also by demonic visions, hallucinations, which come from her mind distraught with grief.

12. As Albini 1975 argued, Io is an ancestor of the hero who will free Prometheus from his torments. Between the two characters there is an evident parallelism: in fact, just like Prometheus, she suffers, even physically, as established by Zeus. Moreover, her frantic roaming mirrors Prometheus' tormented immobility (278).

13. Cf. e.g. passage 642–644. Significantly, in this passage, there are several terms related to the semantic sphere of disease: the adjective θεόσσυτος, often used in conjunction with νόσος (cf. *Pr.* 598), as well as διαφθορά and προσπίπτω.

14. On Io's *amorphia* as blurring the human and the animal, cf. also Provenza in this volume. On further analysis, it is not dissimilar from the pandemic nature of the disease at the beginning of Sophocles' *Oedipus Rex*, where the human, animal and vegetable kingdoms merge and generate infertility, which is the punishment the gods choose to sanction the violation of a κόσμος consisting of the normal succession of generations.

15. On the human body as produced by the technologies of ἰατρικὴ τέχνη, see the chapters by Devecka and Gerolemou in this volume.

16. Cf. e.g. Hes. *Op*. 102–104: diseases come upon men by day and by night, bringing evils to mortals. For a definition and a profile of 'archaic mentality' in Ancient Greece, cf. Dodds 1951.

17. On the 'clinical cases' of Heracles and Philoctetes, see Ceschi 2003 and 2005.

18. For an analysis of the relationship between scientific and poetic language in one of the most ancient treaties of the *Corpus* (*De morbo sacro*), cf. Lanata 1968.

19. *Trach*. 975. Cf. also *Trach*. 980: φοιτάδα δεινὴν νόσον: 'fierce, recurrent infection'. Kamerbeek (1959: 206) notes: 'Heracles' ὀδύνη is implicitly compared to a wild beast'; 208: 'the νόσος is considered as a beast'.

20. Cf. Ceschi 2003: 81–87.

21. Cf. Jouanna 1987: 109.

22. Cf. e.g., *Morb*. I 22, cited above: ὀδύναι διαΐσσουσιν ἄλλοτε ἄλλῃ τῷ σώματος, καὶ οὗτοι μὲν διαφθείρονται ὡς τὰ πολλὰ δι' ὀλίγου. The pain attacks the body as a beast and the patients are destroyed in their physical integrity.

23. About Philoctetes' disease 'as permanent condition, as a mode of existence whose intensity and inescapability reduce to silence any other interpretation', see Thumiger in this volume.

24. For the underlying image of disease as a θήρ in *Philoctetes*, cf. Kamerbeek 1948 and 1980: 27, 107.

25. For a detailed analysis, cf. Ceschi 2009: 126–130. *Loc. Hom.* 29, 1–8 is about the infection of a wound, termed with the absolute adjective θηρίον. Potter 1995 translates θηρίον as 'malignant ulcer': a good example of the possible influence of connotative images on the technical lexicon of medicine.

26. Φρενοβόρως is conjectured by Dindorf for φρενομόρως or φρενομώρως (codd.).

27. Φθίνω is attested already in the Homeric poems referring to the consumption caused by disease (cf. *Il.* 13. 667: νούσῳ ὑπ' ἀργαλέῃ φθίσθαι). In Hippocrates, φθινὰς νόσος is the best known tuberculosis or pulmonary tuberculosis (a good example of the influence exerted by popular language on medical terminology: this specific expression effectively describes outcomes caused by the patient's disease).

28. Ceschi 2014: 406.

29. Ferrini 1978 is still a very important study on medical terminology in Euripides, especially for the lexicon drawn from the epilepsy's semantic sphere, since it was called 'sacred disease' and widely

perceived as demonic. Due to its spectacular terminology, epilepsy provides a fertile repertory of images, which can convey the scenic transposition of a psychological pain that becomes 'madness'.

30. A phrase that seems to equate the two concepts – τό θεῖον καί τό δαιμόνιον – also appears in the Hippocratic treatise *De morbo sacro* (1, 27).

31. Lanata 1967: 36–37, referring to Detienne 1963.

32. About medical terms and clinical attitudes in Euripides, cf. Miller 1944; Collinge 1962; Ferrini 1978; Guardasole 2000: 76–86.

33. However, Sophocles appears to be more thrifty, but more adherent to Hippocratic symptomatology. As Collinge 1962 pointed out, 'it may be possible to demonstrate . . . that Sophocles was, medically, an insider' (47), whereas in Euripides 'medical vocabulary is a mixture of technical and non-technical, plain and figurative: for him, doctors' terminology was a store to be raided and exploited' (45).

34. Certainly, the most striking of possible comparisons is the similarity with the horse loosed from the yoke (πῶλος ὥς ὑπὸ ζυγοῦ), which in *De morbo sacro* (1, 34) is played on an acustic level: Ἢν δὲ ὀξύτερον καὶ εὐτονώτερον φθέγγηται, ἵππῳ εἰκάζουσι, καὶ φασὶ Ποσειδῶνα αἴτιον εἶναι: 'If he speaks in a sharper and more intense tone, they resemble this state to a horse, and say that Poseidon is the cause.' The dramatic significance of the symptom makes it clear why it could have impressed Euripides; the supernatural etiology, which was harshly criticized by the Hippocratic author, is functional to Orestes' disease pursued by the Erinys.

35. Madness and terror are associated several times in Orestes (260; 270; 532; 792). In the last line, insanity is associated with the demonic sense of οἶστρος, a word also quoted in Aeschylus' *Prometheus*.

36. It is noteworthy that the analogical reference to animal metamorphosis is also productive in Hippocratic nosology: cf. e.g., *polypus* (from πολύπους), *icterus* (from ἴκτις – pine marten – because of the yellow spot on the animal's throat), κυνάγχη (*angina*, from κύων and ἄγχω, disease related to the image of a dog biting at the throat). An extensive case record is provided by Di Benedetto 1986: 21–26, and reviewed by Lami 1996: 18–21.

37. Therefore, the translation given by Savino (1991: 329) for the festering wound of Philoctetes is appropriate: 'lo sgorgo febbrile che pulsa dal taglio di un piede *che ha dentro la bestia*' (*Ph.* 696–698: θερμοτάταν/ αἱμάδα κηκιομέναν ἑλκέων/ ἐνθήρου ποδὸς).

38. 'No longer a bone in its place, shredded,' as Heracles said himself (*Tr.* 1103). Cf. Kamerbeek (1959: 228): 'The verb does not occur elsewhere but ῥακόομαι = "become wrinkled" is said of skins of dead animals Plut. *Qu. Conv.* II 642 e (L.-Sc.)'.

Chapter 10

1. Hegel 1975: 360–361.
2. Regier 2005: p. xiii. His is a wide-ranging discussion of many Sphinxes, from antiquity to the present.
3. Freud SE 21, 188.
4. Freud, SE 7, 94–95; see also Freud, SE 9, 135; SE 10, 133; SE 16, 318.
5. Ironically, the quotation was incorrectly engraved. Inscribed in capital letters, the lambda of 'κλείν' was rendered as the Latin L, making it read (German) 'little' rather than (Greek) 'renowned'.
6. See Renger 2013: 54–56 and Leonard 2015: 120 for the rich significance of this scene.
7. See Billings and Leonard 2015; Leonard 2015. For a discussion of Greek tragedy's, see centrality to expressions of subjectivity and modernity.
8. 'At one time, when Freud had brought an analysis to a successful conclusion, he used to show the patient an engraving after a painting by Ingres, "Oedipus solves the riddle of the Sphinx."' Wittels 1924: 114.

9. Connell 2013: 21.

10. The title is both a Cartesian echo and a pun: *L'Animal que donc je suis* can mean both 'the animal that therefore I am', and 'the animal that therefore I follow'.

11. My reading of Derrida here, and throughout, is indebted to Niall Gildea's Jacques Derrida's *Cambridge Affair: Deconstruction, Philosophy and Institutionality* (Rowman & Littlefield 2020).

12. Derrida 2001: 251–252.

13. Derrida 2004: 63.

14. Derrida 2008: 3–4.

15. This is an intricate passage. See Wills's note: Derrida 2008: 162. Derrida's casting of himself as Adam here – and his cat as God? – suggests not only a strategic revisioning of this 'foundation' story, but also an implied commentary upon the gender politics always already at work. His cat, which we later discover is female, gazes at him (her animality on the one hand un-gendering her gaze, her humanly ascribed femininity – not only as 'a pussycat/une chatte' – precisely gendering it), reversing, or at least calling attention to, the objectifying erotics of the 'male gaze'.

16. Derrida describes fellow cat-lover Montaigne's warning against ascriptive *hubris* in his *Essays* as 'one of the greatest pre- or anti-Cartesian texts on the animal that exists' (Derrida 2008: 4). Montaigne shrewdly asks, 'When I play with my cat, how do I know that she is not passing time with me rather than I with her?' (Montaigne 2003: 505).

17. 'Kant, Levinas, Lacan, Heidegger [. . .] hold a position in this regard almost identical to Descartes.' Derrida 2004: 65.

18. Descartes 2008: 44.

19. Descartes 2008: 44–45.

20. Derrida 2008: 76.

21. Wills asks, 'Do we know what animate means, any more than inanimate, and, presuming we do, would we know how to articulate those two terms vis-à-vis what we call "life"?' (Wills 2016: ix).

22. I put posthuman in speech-marks here as it was not a term that Derrida himself would have deployed so naively, owing to its conceptual indebtedness to the very humanist structures it seeks to supersede. However, it is convenient to use it here as an abbreviation for contemporary theoretical debates which gather under this rubric. See Braidotti 2013 for an introduction to this field.

23. For the association of the Sphinx and death in Greek art, see Vermeule 1979: 171–173.

24. Horkheimer and Adorno 2010 [1947].

25. Derrida 2004: 66.

26. Derrida 1995b: 68.

27. Barad 2003: 823–824.

28. Derrida 2008: 126.

29. Derrida 2008: 11.

Chapter 11

1. Darwin 1872: 165. My title draws on Masson and McCarthy 1995; cf. Darab 2015.
2. Beard 2007: 28.
3. See Richardson 1992: 380, 383–385. On the politics of Pompey's theatre, see Frézouls 1983.
4. Beacham 1992: 157–158.

5. Toynbee 1973: 23. Ancient protests against hunting come close: Varro, *Sat. Men.* 161, 293–296, 361; Arian, *Cyn.* 16.6–8; cf. Aymard 1951: 60–63 and Anderson 1985: 87. On Pompey's spectacle exemplifying Rome's audiences' affective disposition, see Fagan 2011: 248–252. Pompey could have learned from the end of Varro's sentence: 'as beautiful as hunts without African beasts' (*sine Africanis bestiis cum fiunt uenationes, DRR* 3.13).
6. I use the word 'community', from Latin *communus*, in both possible etymological senses: the sharing of mutual obligation (*com+munus*) as well as the collection of the many into the one (*com+unus*).
7. Wolfe 2003: xii; on posthumanism and animal rights, see Haraway 1989, 1991, 2007 and Derrida 2006, 2008a. On animal studies and the humanities more broadly, see Wolfe 2009a. On ancient animals ethics, see Harden 2013 and Sorabji 1993.
8. On human–animal interactions, human compassion towards animal suffering and human beings as the primary cause of animal suffering (for instance, in the case of animal torture and animal work exploitation), cf. Korhonen in this volume. On human sympathetic compassion towards animals as a 'crucial ideological bedrock of violence and domination', cf. Geue in this volume.
9. On 'monsters' in Augustan poetry, see Lowe 2015; Kachuck 2016. For symbolic readings of Rome's bestiary, see Bettini 1998.
10. Milton, *Paradise Regained* 329–330.
11. Toynbee 1973: 34; cf. Rostovtzeff 1941 pl. 52 fig. 2, pl. 53 fig. 1.
12. Cf. Costa 1984 *ad* Lucr. 5.1228.
13. Cf. Lucr. 2.537; for manual proboscis, cf. Cic. *Nat. D.* 2.123 and Plin. *HN* 8.29.
14. Cf. Bochart 1663, chapters 25, 27.
15. Horsfall 2003: 59.
16. On Stoic οἰκείωσις, see Brink 1956; Striker 1983.
17. Plotnik and de Waal 2014.
18. See Kaster 2005: 104–133.
19. Payne 2010: 27–58.
20. On elephants' fears, see Zafiropoulos 2009.
21. Cf. Cat. 64.186; Vir. *Aen.* 4.337–338; Livy 4.12, 22 and 40.56; Vitr. *De arch.*10.praef.2.
22. Sorabji 1993.
23. On animals' linguistic competence, see Fögen 2007 and 2014: 225; cf. Heath 2005.
24. On elephants' communalism, see Plut. *Soll.* 977D; Ael. *NA* 5.49, 6.61, 7.15; *FGrH* iii: 146, fr. 51b (Juba).
25. On elephant's religiosity, see Coleman 2006: 157–158.
26. Possible wordplay between ὠλοφύροντο, 'they lamented', and ἐλέφας, 'elephant': grieving is what these animals do.
27. Shelton 1999, 2004; cf. Coleman 1990.
28. Shackleton Bailey 1977: 1, 326.
29. Cic. *Div.* 1. 29–30 (cf. Cic. *Att.* 4.13.2).
30. Plin. *HN* 8.4; Plut. *Pomp.* 14.6.
31. See Haller 2009: 404–405.
32. On dating, see Foertmeyer 1988.
33. On this event, see Rice 1983.
34. Scullard 1974: 124. On Ptolemy II's Ptolemeia and Rome's amphitheatre, see Coleman 1996.
35. Plut. *Pyrrh.* 32; Paus. 2.21.4; cf. Scullard 1974: 118.

36. Woytek 2003.

37. Kosmin 2014.

38. Scullard 1974: 255–257; Toynbee 1973: 54; cf. *Anth. Pal.* 9.285, Suet. *Div. Iul.* 53.2.

39. Hor. *Sat.* 1.9.20 associates the poet's drooping ears with the ass (cf. Gowers 2012 *ad* 1.9.77): where humans were said to be unique in not moving their ears (Plin. *HN* 11.136 *aures homini tantum immobiles*), elephants were said to move them constantly to avoid the entry of flies (Ach. Tat. 21), the ears being the one part of the body unreachable by their trunks (Plin. *HN* 11.34).

40. Watson 2003 *ad* Hor. *Epod.* 12.1; cf. Gowers 2012 *ad Sat.* 19–20, 30.

41. Curtius 1973: 98–101; cf. Vir. *Aen.* 8.311; Ov. *Ars.* 1.185–186 (proper to divine *principes*).

42. Achilles Tatius, in accord with tradition (but not with reality), notes that the elephant's ten-year gestation means that 'the offspring is born already old' (ὁ τόκος γέρων γένηται, 4.4.2).

43. Cf. Cat. 95.1–2 (on Cinna's *Smyrna*); see Brink 1971: 2, 383.

44. Cf. Hor. *Sat.* 1.10.38, with Gowers 2012 *ad loc.*

45. The leech (*hirudo*, 476) that ends Horace's *Ars P.* might reflect the idea that elephants' worst torture comes, as Pliny notes using Horace's term, 'if they swallow a leech (which I notice is now how the "blood-sucker" has now begun to be called)' (*hausta hirudine quam sanguisugam uulgo coepisse appellari aduerto*, 8.29).

46. On Indian legends that treat elephants as 'Trojan Horses', see Peris 1982: 54–55; Khan 1990.

47. Serpentine Sinon (cf. Paschalis 1997: 103–104) meets 'snake-handed' elephant; Philostratus' *Apollonius of Tyana* sits twelve or fifteen on one elephant, *I Maccabees* thirty-three (6.35)! Compare Juv. 12.109 *dorso ferre cohortes* (with Mayor *ad loc.*).

48. Cf. Hor. *Epist.* 2.1.161.

49. Hinds 1998: 8–10, 110.

50. cf. Giusti 2014; 2018: 230.

51. For the term, see Scheid and Svenbro 2014.

52. Bettini 2013.

Chapter 12

1. For the dissolution of the subject, cf. Bartsch 1997: 10–47. Monstrosity features prominently in Johnson 1987.

2. For examples of the difficulty that book 9 poses for otherwise coherent interpretations of Cato's Stoicism, cf. Leigh 1997: 265.

3. I use the terms 'cyborg' and 'monster' to describe both Cato and Medusa throughout the chapter. My interest is focused in particular on the ways in which both figures transcend the bounds of human nature. Braidotti (2011: 77) defines the monster as the object of both fascination and repulsion, and 'monster' brings a suggestion of innate rather than manufactured or technological difference. The exploration of cyborg capabilities by Haraway 2016 will be discussed in due course, in ways that relate to both Cato and Medusa. My particular interest is in Cato's affinity with Medusa and alienation from his followers; both 'cyborg' and 'monster' are useful terms for exploring aspects of this, and it is not my concern to define Cato or Medusa firmly as wholly one or the other.

4. Lowe 2010: 121.

5. The inclusion of an excursus of dubious truthfulness (9. 619–623) is Lucan's pessimistic way of exploring the possibilities of his vatic role. For the importance of irony to Haraway's cyborg politics, cf. Haraway 2016: 5. For a call for visionary utterances and an awareness of the difficulty of

producing such utterances in academic discourse cf. Braidotti 2013: 191. With regard to the visionary aims of some posthumanism, Cato's failures as a redemptive figure, which I discuss below, may provide material for reflection on how posthumanist theory serves or fails to serve its human readers.

6. Bexley 2010: 143–149.
7. For the derivation of *monstrum* from *moneo* and *monstrare* from *monstrum*, cf. *OLD ad loc.*
8. Cf. Nuzzo in this volume.
9. Bartsch 1997: 10–48.
10. Hardie 1986: 381.
11. Lapidge 2010: 231–233.
12. For instance Johnson 1987: 37, 44; Leigh 1997: 266f.; Bexley 2010. *Contra* Seewald 2008: 26–32.
13. The abject, to use Kristeva's phrase as employed by Bartsch 1997: 19.
14. Cf. Gershon in this volume.
15. The possibility of reading *manus* as a reference to the whole army allows Murrus to be read, in turn, as an *exemplar* for all his fellows, whose identity as Pompeian/Roman *manus* has been questioned by Cato (9.257–258).
16. Haraway 2016: 17.
17. Johnson 1987, esp. 22f.
18. I restrict my discussion here to the kinds of posthumanism proposed by Haraway 2016 and Braidotti 2013, leaving aside the radical rejection of subjectivity proposed by Goh 2015, who criticizes Braidotti for allowing subjectivity a place in her critical theory. Goh (2015: 222f.) recoils in horror from Braidotti's concept of extended subjectivity due to what he regards as endless appropriation of the subjectivity of the other; Goh leaves no room for affinity in a world of isolated rejects.
19. The sequence of thought is in harmony with Lucan's subsequent authorial commentary, prior to the description of Libya, where he comments on Cato's impending death in Africa and his freedom from care in approaching it (9.409–410).
20. Bexley 2010: 144–146.
21. Sklenář 2003: 97.
22. For the resonances of gladiatorial spectacle in the desert-crossing episode, cf. Leigh 1997: 265–282.
23. Thomas 1982: 114–115.
24. Leigh 1997: 271–272.
25. Diction contributes: Lucan dramatizes the simultaneous dissolution of *virtus* and *viri* by placing the words in uncomfortable proximity with *virus* (venom/poison) and *vis*/*vires* (force/strength).
26. It is notable that the rhetoric of posthumanism elides the suffix: Braidotti (2013: 186), albeit expressing caution, begins her conclusion by wondering how many people can claim to be a posthuman. The New York Posthuman Research Group (www.theposthuman.org) routinely refers to its contributors as posthumans. Although much posthumanist critical theory is aimed at overcoming the exclusivity of androcentric notions of man as the measure of all things (cf. Wolfe 2009: xii f.), there is a danger that the rhetoric of becoming something other than a human works in a more alienating than explanatory or inspiring fashion.
27. Cf. Ovid *Met.* 4.784–785 for a less powerful Medusa, murdered in her sleep, tangled in snakes.
28. For Lucan's reception of Ovid, cf. Fantham 1992; Malamud 2003.
29. One form this takes is the notion of a technological singularity: a point at which machine learning technology allows artificial intelligence to self-improve and self-replicate faster than any attempt to restrain it, so that human existence cannot continue within its current boundaries. For narratives

pertaining to technological singularity as a product of neurotechnology and/or artificial intelligence, cf. Shanahan 2015. Closer to the image of Medusa's spreading of deader-than-dead clay is the danger of self-replicating nanobots that could engulf the world in undifferentiated sludge, cf. Mitchell 2003: 186. On singularity as a 'fate-based argument not a scientific argument', cf. Brooks 2017; Chesi and Sclavi in this volume.

30. *Pace* Eldred 2000: 63f.

31. Even in life, her eyes are a danger to her own snake hair (9.652–653).

32. Haraway 2016: 28–30.

33. Johnson 1987: 43–44.

Chapter 13

1. On ancient prosthetics, see Bliquez 1983; Lee 2015: 83; Garland 1995: 26f.; Draycott 2018. See further on the case of the Homeric Ajax and his shield functioning as prosthetic means, Mueller 2016: 34f.; Purves 2015: 86. Cf. Malafouris 2008: 9 on the Mycenaean sword as prosthetic.
2. On organic and artificial bodies and their complementarity in Greek thought, cf. Devecka in this volume.
3. Rothwell 2006.
4. Pozzi 1986: 119.
5. Roselli 2014: 250.
6. See Spielvögel 2001; Konstan and Dillon 1981; Konstan 1986. See further on wealth, poverty and physical labour, Desmond 2006: 31–42. This idea goes against the Hesiodic motto in *Works and Days* on labour obligations, where not working is pictured as a disgrace (302–320, 381f), or the words of Poverty in Ar. *Wealth*, according to which everybody should be eager to work until they have completely exhausted their capacity to be productive (507–516).
7. See e.g., Hdt. 9.37 on the prosthetic foot of Hegesistratus; see further *On Joints* 58; Plutarch *Moralia* 922. On bone fractures and prosthetics, for example, in Herodotus, cf. Devecka in this volume.
8. Cf. Frontisi-Ducroux 2003; Thumiger 2014. See further Forbes Irving 1990: 96–127.
9. Democritus in DK 68 B33 argues that early man is in need of improvement. Hughes 2010: 105 cites for her case on hybrid bodies coming out of a process of addition a passage from Xenophon's *Cyropaedia*. At *Cyr.* 4. 3.19–23 the acquired skill of riding that the soldiers of Cyrus did not previously have as they campaigned on foot, leads his general, Chrysantas, to conceive the idea that when in the saddle he will probably be able to do everything that a centaur does. Cyrus finds the idea brilliant and decides to forbid his men from walking even short distances, so that the people who encounter the Persians will think that they are centaurs (*Cyr.* 4. 3.22–23).
10. See also Payne 2016 who also examines the relationship between human beings and non-human animals on the basis of prosthesis as a means of creating hybrid categories.
11. On human and animal muscle power remaining the crucial sources of power until the end of antiquity, see Schneider 2007: 148f.; Acton 2014; Landels 2000; Casson 1977.
12. According to Roselli (2013: 105): 'an "ideology of work" may not have been a dominant way of thinking about labour, but positive attitudes to work are easily found. Praise of labourers, reproaches for the idle and those who merely talk, laws against idleness and mocking citizens for their occupation, and portraying gods as patrons of labourers and even as labouring figures, all attest to a certain consciousness of the value of labour and labourers. A rather large number of citizens (i.e., 10,000–15,000 landless thetes), not to mention most metics and some slaves, were engaged in (non-agricultural) manual work centred around the market'.

13. Arrowsmith 1973. See further Ehrenberg 1973 [1947]; Leigh 2013: 30–33, on the Aristophanic *prolypragmon*.

14. Cf. Horace, *Ars* 1–5: 'If a painter chose to join a human head to the neck of a horse, and to spread feathers of many a hue over limbs picked up now here now there, so that what at the top is a lovely woman ends below in a black and ugly fish, could you, my friends, if favored with a private view, refrain from laughing?' (tr. Fairclough, Loeb), cited by Hughes 2010: 105. But see Arrowsmith (1973: 149): 'When they first receive their wings themselves, Pisthetairos and Euelpides mutually recognize their own absurdity, not merely their ludicrous get-up as men-birds, but the theatrical shabbiness of their transformation.'

15. Levine 2015; Giallouris 1953 on winged gods and heroes. See also Pollard 1977.

16. Hoefmans 1994: 140–147.

17. All translations are mine, unless otherwise indicated.

18. Korhonen and Ruonakoski 2017: 152f.

19. Newiger (1957: 80–91) argues that birds, particularly their wings, serve as a metaphor of power in the play.

20. Casson 1994.

21. Meier (1980: 275f.) argues that time in a *polis* is defined as the time citizens need to go through the various political processes with dignity. See also Csapo and Miller 1998: 87–104; Chiasson 1999/2000.

22. See on the passage Hannah 2005: 51; Stern 2012: 35f.

23. Sinclair 1988: 20–24.

24. According to Arrowsmith (1973: 122): 'From 431 on [. . .] [t]he attitude towards movables began to exercise a considerable influence on the attitude towards immovable, especially when many a peasant must have sorrowfully wondered whether his land would ever again be of much use to him.' On the Athenian peasantry, see De Ste. Croix 1981: 205–219.

25. See *Pax.* 1198–1202 and *Eq.* 644–645 on demand and supply.

26. Cooper 2017: 107f.

27. On Athenian *apragmones*, see Carter 1986: esp. ch. 4; Arrowsmith 1973.

28. On labour division, see Acton 2014: 29–33.

29. ὄρνιθες, οὐδεὶς ἄλλος – οὐκ Αἰγύπτιος/ πλινθοφόρος, οὐ λιθουργός, οὐ τέκτων παρῆν – /ἀλλ' αὐτόχειρες, ὥστε θαυμάζειν ἐμέ (1133–1135). 'Birds, no one else – no Egyptian brick-carrier was there, no mason, no carpenter – they did it with their own hands, so that I was amazed' (tr. Sommerstein).

30. According to Aristotle *Ph.* 199a23–28, division of labour is observed in nature.

31. On the wall as blurring of the space between city and country, see Kosak 2006.

32. Konstan 1995: 35. On labour and wages in classical Athens, see Davies 1981: 352–355.

33. In old comedy tools work spontaneously and natural forces fulfil every human material need without any hard work. Pherecrates in *Persians* (fr. 137, 3) describes a land where rivers of black soup, full of various delicacies, flow from sources; the *Miners*, a play also ascribed to Pherecrates (fr. 113, l), describes how at a banquet food enters the guests' mouths, and, when finished, reappears. See further Metagenes' *Thouriopersians* (fr. 6), where the river Crathis carries self-mixed cakes, while the river Sibaris brings self-prepared fish stew that flies into the diners' mouths or falls at their feet. In the *Amphictyons* of Teleclides (fr. 1) the mythical past is presented as possessing everything people ever needed in a spontaneous way. On the motif of the *automatos bios* in old comedy, see Konstan 2012; Ceccarelli 1996: 453–455; Ruffell 2001; Farioli 2001: 214f.

34. On the assumption that machinery did not replace muscle labour due to the existence of slavery, see Finley 1965: 29; against Casson, 1977: esp. 136–149; Acton 2014: 22–33. See further Devecka 2013.

35. As Henry Ford puts it in his autobiography *My Life and Work* (1922: 40), where he discusses methods of increasing productivity including division of labour in assembly-line manufacturing: 'where responsibility is broken up into many small bits and divided among many departments, each department under its own titular head, who in turn is surrounded by a group bearing their nice sub-titles, it is difficult to find anyone who really feels responsible'.
36. Schwinge 2014: 69f. Cf. further Sörbom 1966: 76; Muecke 1982: 55f.; Zeitlin 1996: 382–386; Stohn 1993; Stehle 2002: esp. 381–385 arguing that mimesis is accomplished through imitating physical traits and manners (*tropos*); see further Lada-Richards 1999: ch. 4, esp. 169–172, Lada-Richards 2002: 402f., 'mimesis cannot leave the imitator's own identity intact' (403). See also on mimesis in Aristophanes, Duncan 2006: 27–46.
37. γελοῖοι δ' ἴσως ἐσμὲν ἐπὶ τῶι μανθάνειν τὰ ζῶια σεμνύνοντες, ὧν ὁ Δ. ἀποφαίνει μαθητὰς ἐν τοῖς μεγίστοις γεγονότας ἡμᾶς· ἀράχνης ἐν ὑφαντικῆι καὶ ἀκεστικῆι, χελιδόνος ἐν οἰκοδομίαι, καὶ τῶν λιγυρῶν, κύκνου καὶ ἀηδόνος, ἐν ὠιδῆι κατὰ μίμησιν.
38. Mondolfo and Duncan 1954: 3.
39. Cf. Arrowsmith's 1973 notion of *erōs* in the play; he makes no distinction between mania and *eros*. On the twofold experience of *erōs*, see Winkler 1991: 222f.; Nussbaum 2002; Thumiger 2013: 29, 31.
40. Henderson 1997. But on Peisetaerus as a sophist see Hubbard 1997 who follows Arrowsmith 1973.
41. See *Politics* 1256b24–26 where Aristotle refers to the 'war' of human beings against other animals. On that, see Newmyer 2006: 32.
42. Sorabji 1993: 89–93; Heath 2005: 6.
43. Cf. the seminal paper by Fögen 2007: esp. 46–49 for Aristotle; cf. also Fögen 2014: esp. 219–223. On animal communication, cf. Korhonen in this volume.
44. Aristotle's view on the value of human hands probably criticizes Anaxagoras, who proclaims that man is superior to animals merely because of his hands (see also Xen. *Mem.* 1.4.11–14). Interestingly, at a later stage, Galen in *De Usu Partium* 3.5 (Kühn) opposes the idea that animal parts could be of any use to man, specifically referring to horns. This is because man, according to him, as a peaceful and social creature, uses his hands to compose laws, raise altars and statues to his divinities, build ships and make musical instruments (cf. Xen. *Mem.* 1.4.11–14); on that, see Newmyer 2017: ch. 6.
45. In the same way, earlier in the play, he provides the birds with a genealogy that proves that they are older than the gods (481–517).
46. On the feathered poets of the play see Stewart 1967. Generally, on winged poets see Steiner 2007. See also Rusten 2013 on wings as a poetic and historiographic medium.
47. Tereus, for example, can fly over land and sea in every direction (118).
48. Earlier in the play (1170–1195), wings were employed as weapons for generating conscious slavery – the birds, as agents of revenge for the gods or for their own species' mistreatment, aim to transform the gods into slaves. Here, however, the battle is not between human limbs and wings but between bird-wings and divine wings.

Chapter 14

1. On the plasticity of the body as central tenet of posthumanism, see Herbrechter 2013: 6f. Rejection of 'given' nature/culture divide: Descola 2013: esp. pp. 23–34.
2. The Caduveo: Levi-Strauss 1963.
3. The organic body is 'open' to its environment in the sense developed by Jakob von Uexküll (von Uexküll 2010: 53–52). 'Health' might be thought of as a self-reflexive evolution of what von Uexküll calls an 'effect image' (ibid. p. 95). I use 'norm' in much the same sense as Canguillhem 1991. In an aside near the beginning of that book, Canguillhem quite forcefully describes the self-regulating character of

the Greek organic body: 'Disease is a generalised reaction designed to bring about a cure: the organism develops a disease in order to get well. Therapy must first tolerate and if necessary reinforce these hedonic and spontaneous therapeutic reactions. Medical technique imitates natural medicinal action' (Canguillem 1991: 40–41).

4. *VM* 3. 21–36.
5. On the anthropology of *On Ancient Medicine*, see Utzinger 2003: 150f.
6. *VM* 5.12–29.
7. Compare with *de Arte* 5 for an account that closely follows that of *On Ancient Medicine*, and for rejection of pharmaceuticals see *de Arte* 6.1–15. The line of the Hippocratic *Oath*, usually translated as 'Neither will I administer a poison to anybody when asked to do so, nor will I suggest such a course' (trans. Jones), runs in Greek οὐ δώσω δὲ οὐδὲ φάρμακον οὐδενὶ αἰτηθεὶς θανάσιμον, οὐδὲ ὑφηγήσομαι συμβουλίην τοιήνδε (*Jusj.* 18–20). φάρμακον θανάσιμον might be taken, by contrast with ἰός, to include any drug of potentially fatal application. The next line in the oath makes the swearer promise to refrain from surgery. All these texts invite practitioners to treat patients by moderation of the body's self-regulatory responses. The advice given by *On the Sacred Disease*, to treat epilepsy by adaptive response to wind conditions rather than dramatic ritual cures, might be understood in a similar way.
8. *VM* 5.51–52. On the scope of dietetic treatments in Hippocratic medicine, see Jouanna 2012a.
9. Palaeph. pref. 11–13: καὶ τὰ χωρία αὐτὸς εἶδον ὡς ἔστιν ἕκαστον ἔχον, καὶ γέγραφα ταῦτα οὐχ οἷα ἦν λεγόμενα, ἀλλ' αὐτὸς ἐπελθὼν καὶ ἱστορήσας. For a treatment of Palaephatus' general approach to myth, see Veyne 1988: 67f. For a broader treatment of artificial bodies in the constitutive imagination of fourth-century Athens, see Devecka 2013.
10. Palaeph. 22.1: Λέγεται περὶ Δαιδάλου ὡς ἀγάλματα κατεσκεύαζε δι' ἑαυτῶν πορευόμενα.
11. Palaeph. 22.6–7: διὰ τοῦτο δὴ οἱ ἄθρωποι ἔλεγον 'ὁδοιποροῦν τὸ ἄγαλμα τοῦτο εἰργάσατο Δαίδαλος, ἀλλ' οὐχὶ ἑστηκός,' ὡς καὶ νῦν λέγομεν 'μαχόμενοί γε ἄνδρες γεγραμμένοι εἰσί' καὶ 'τρέχοντες ἵπποι' καὶ 'χειμαζομένη ναῦς.' οὕτω κἀκεῖνον ἔλεγον ὁδοιποροῦντα ποιεῖν ἀγάλματα.
12. Berryman 2003.
13. Paus. 2.4.5, 8.35.2, and 9. 11.4 *inter alia*; Vernant 2006a: 321f. Pausanias offers a catalogue of *xoana* he believes to have been crafted by Daedalus at 9.40.3. For Daedalan magic sculpture as an index of 'progress' in the arts, see Morris 1992: 215–237.
14. On Samian Hera, see Vernant 2006b. Paus. 7.5.4–6 gives an interesting comparandum in which rope is used to catch (rather than retain) a moving statue. On the Phigalean xoanon, an εἰκὼν γυναικὸς τὰ ἄχρι τῶν γλουτῶν, τὸ ἀπὸ τούτου δέ ἐστιν ἰχθύς, see Paus. 8.41.6. On Daedalan moving statues in Athenian culture, see further Devecka 2013: 59f. and the associated bibliography. They are a favourite metaphor of Plato's, famously at *Men.* 97d–98a but also in the *Euthyphro* (11c–e) and the *Hippias Major* (282a).
15. On the mimetic character of Greek automata, see Kang 2011: 19f. On the absence of the imitated object, constitutive for these living statues, see Spivey 1995.
16. Hdt. 3.129.1. Darius' injury is rich in political symbolism, both from the Greek side (where lameness carries strong mythic-structural associations with tyranny and misrule: Vernant 1990) and on the Persian side (where *aša*, the linguistic cognate in Avestan of Herodotus' ὀρθός, indicates truth and moral rectitude: *Encyclopedia Iranica*, s.v.) To treat the episode from this point of view would demand a separate essay. Here it is enough to note that the connotations of Darius' dislocated ankle suggest that Demokedes has saved not only his body but his kingdom.
17. Hdt. 3.129.2–130.4. For my translation of ὑγιέα μιν ἀπέδεξε, see Liddle and Scott's *Greek-English Lexicon* s.v., I.3.
18. Hdt. 3.129.2. For Herodotus, the Egyptians are paradigmatically πρῶτοι with respect to the Greeks: e.g., *Hist.* 2.4. I agree with Jouanna as reading this episode in terms of a reversal that posits the superiority of Greek medicine over its Egyptian antecedent: Jouanna 2012b: 13–14.

19. Hdt. 9.37. On the structure and character of this digression, see Munson 2001: 66–67.
20. Zopyrus: Hdt. 3.155–160.
21. Hdt. 9.37.4.
22. Viveiros de Castro 2014: esp. pp. 188–189: 'The image of savage thought that I am endeavoring to define is aimed neither at indigenous knowledge and its more or less true representations of reality . . . nor at its mental categories, the "representationality" which the cognitive sciences endlessly go on about . . .. The "objects" whose existence is being affirmed here are indigenous concepts, the worlds these constitute . . . and the virtual ground from which they emerge. Treating indigenous ideas as concepts entails regarding them as carrying philosophical meaning or a potential philosophical use.' For a development of these ideas, see also Viveiros de Castro 2015.

Chapter 15

1. This chapter stems from the project *Disturbing Metaphor*, funded by the Axel and Margaret Ax:son Johnson Foundation. The author would like to thank G. M. Chesi, H. v. Ehrenheim, D. Iordanoglou and F. Spiegel for their comments.
2. Clynes and Kline 1960: 27.
3. Haraway 1991: 151.
4. All translations are mine.
5. This is more or less the standard version, Apollod., III.1.4; cf. Hyginus: *Fabulae*, 40.
6. Dolfi 1984; Webster 1967: 90; Reckford 1974: 319.
7. Jiménez San Cristóbal 2009; Collard, Cropp and Lee 1995: 67; Cozzoli 2001: 18–20; Jouan and van Looy 2001: 311, 324; Cantarella 1963: 78; cf. Nilsson 1935: 206, 222; Gallistl 1981; Wilamowitz-Moellendorf 1932; contrast Croiset: 1915: 227, 229, Méridier 1928: 31.
8. Collard and Cropp 2008: 539; Collard, Cropp and Lee 1995: 70, *ad* 16–20; Cozzoli 2001, *ad* 12; Herrero de Jáuregui 2010: 28 n59; Festugière 1972: 39–40; Turcan 1986: 245, cf. 236; Tralau 2017; Robert 1890: 15, 19–23.
9. Collard 1991, ad *Hec.* 1, claims it is '[s]omething of a supernatural entry-formula', citing *Ba.* 1, *Tro.* 1; cf. *And.* 1232.
10. Cf. Harrison 1903: 482; likewise Burkert 1977: 419.
11. Cf. Cozzoli 2001: 82–83; Collard, Cropp and Lee 1995, *ad loc.*
12. Cf. Burford 1969: 183; Hodge 1960: 97, 126.
13. Fornari (1997: 169) says that '[t]he Idaean temples represent the community that can only be held together by the bloody bond of sacrifice'. As we will see, Fornari's assumptions are not correct, but the idea is worth developing.
14. Cf. Edmonds 2010: 222, 228.
15. Cf. Kern 1916: 561.
16. Cf. Käppel 1992: 123–125, on Pi. *Pae.* 4.50–51.
17. Cf. Hünemörder 2003: 870; Vergil: *Aen.* III.64.
18. Cf. A. *Pr.* 133; S. *Tr.* 1260; cf. however de Planhol 1963.
19. Cf. Wilamowitz 1907: 73–79; Austin 1968: 49–58; fr. 567T.7 in Bernabé 2005 (ζευχθεῖσ', πηχθεῖσ' and ξυνθεῖσ').
20. Cf. Collard, Cropp and Lee 1995, *ad loc.*
21. Cf. Hes. *Th.* 131–132, 176–192; Rutherford 2009: 11, citing the Hittite *Song of Kumarbi*, CTH 344; Anaximander DK 12 A 10; *Genesis* 1: 4–5, 7.

22. Denniston and Page 1957: xv; contrast Dahlgren 1877: 17, 19, 84.
23. For the Epicurean conception of smells, see D.L. X.53.
24. Cf. Empedokles DK 31 B22, B 80, B 139.12, cf. A 30, A 70, A72, A 78; Parmenides DK 28 B 16.
25. Cf. Loraux 1990: 249.
26. Cf. Cozzoli 2001: 82.
27. Cf. Collard and Cropp 2008, *ad loc*.
28. As recently in Lakoff 2016: 271.
29. Cf. Silk 2003: 129.
30. Cf. Lakoff 2008: 24.
31. Cf. Pagán Cánovas 2011: 561.
32. Cf. Fauconnier and Turner 2008: 64–65.
33. Cf. Fauconnier and Turner 2002: 24, cf .125, 341.
34. Cf. Budelmann and LeVen 2014: 207.
35. For other possible instances, cf. Tralau 2016, 2018a, 2018b.
36. Cf. George Lakoff and Mark Johnson 1999: 73.
37. Cf. Fauconnier and Turner 2002: 328, cf. 382.
38. Cf. Wilamowitz 1932: 113.
39. Cf. fr. 472b.3 Kannicht; Cantarella 1963, *ad loc*; Fornari 1997.
40. Cf. Cozzoli 2001, *ad loc*.
41. Cf. Hurwit 1999: 166.
42. Cf. Koenigs 1990: 126.
43. Cf. Pollitt 1995: 20.
44. Cf. Reitz-Joosse 2016: 185, 189–190.
45. Cf. Lang 2004.
46. First mentioned in Hesiod F 145.15–17 Merkelbach-West.
47. Perhaps there is something special about cow skins in Greek myth. In Hes. *Th*. 539–540, 555, Prometheus uses one to deceive Zeus; cf. Verg. *A*. I. 367–368.
48. Daedalus makes lifelike machines – and Hephaestus' constructions are δαίδαλα Hes. *Th*. 581, cf. 575. The divine and the human artisan are, according to Kassel 1983: 4, 'Doppelgänger'. On Daedalus and the ethics of prosthetics, cf. Gerolemou in this volume.
49. Cf. e.g., Detienne 1998: 141.
50. Cf. Burkert 1972a: 186.
51. Hes. *Th*. 539–540, 555; see also the contribution of Vernant 1979: 47, 58, 78.
52. Cf. e.g., Heath 2005: passim.

Chapter 16

1. Most obviously Valeria's, Veturia's and Volumnia's actions in the Coriolanus story at DH 8.39–54.
2. Goudriaan 1989; Fox 1996; Delcourt 2005; Wiater 2011.
3. Usher 1982. On rhetoric and historiography in Dionysius see Fox 1993, 2001.
4. E.g., Gaius Acilius on Rome as a Greek settlement. See Strabo 5.5.3. Philoxenos of Alexandria on Latin as a Greek dialect. See Stevens 2006: 124.

5. DH 7.70.2. See Gabba 1991: 1n.2, 98; Fromentin 1998: XXVI–XXVII; Hogg 2013.
6. DH 1.8.2.
7. Surveyed by Delcourt 2005: 79–127.
8. E.g., DH 2.4; 4.76.84; Gershon 2017: 63–89.
9. On the relationship between Dionysius and Polybius, see Gozzoli 1976; Pelling 2016.
10. Haraway 2016: 32.
11. Schultze 1986: 130 on subtle social divisions disappearing in the course of Dionysius' narrative.
12. On debt bondage and the First Secession, see Cornell 1995: 266–268.
13. For the lineage of the fable, see Rodríguez Adrados 2003: 170–172.
14. See Sautel 2016: CXI–CXIV for a schematic of book 6.
15. On the analogy, see Nestle 1927; Peil 1985; Hillgruber 1996; Brock 2000; Müller 2004; Brock 2006; 2013: 69–82; Squire 2015: 306–308.
16. Brock 2000: 33; Squire 2015: 306.
17. Squire 2015: 308.
18. Cornell 1995: 1–26 provides useful guidance.
19. Briefly summarized, Sautel 2016: 268n.265.
20. The need for ἀκρίβεια, see e.g., DH 1.23.1; 5.56.1; 11.1.5. Schultze 1986:126; Goudriaan 1989: 282–283; Oakley 2018.
21. DH 6.86.1.
22. First occasion: DH 6.54; second occasion: DH 6.86.
23. DH 6.67.2.
24. Schultze 1986: 130; Gershon 2017: 57–103.
25. Dionysius' anti-plebeian sentiments e.g., DH. 11.61; cf. Müller 2004 on Livy using the fable to be critical of the patricians. On constitutional importance of plebeians to democracy in the *Antiquitates*, see DH 7.54–56; 11.59.
26. DH 6.49.3–6.56, or 44 Teubner pages.
27. DH 6.49.5.
28. This theme returns DH 6.55.1 in Menenius' discussion of equal franchise rights.
29. DH 6.52.1.
30. DH 6.51.2.
31. DH 6.52.2–53.3.
32. DH 6.54.2.
33. DH 6.69.3. On the embassy's composition, see Ogilvie 1965: 311 and Sautel 2016: XXXII–XXXVII, 250n.216.
34. Similar doubling occurs elsewhere in *Antiquitates*. See Schultze 2007; on Cincinnatus, Gershon 2017: 114–122.
35. Cf. Livy 2.32. Livy's narrative is compressed to its essentials: there is no senate speech and Menenius is the only envoy.
36. The meeting lasts from DH 6.70 to 6.88, about 30 Teubner pages.
37. DH 6.69.4.
38. DH 6.70.1.
39. Manius Valerius, Sicinius, Lucius Junius 'Brutus', Titus Larcius, Sicinius once more, and Menenius Agrippa.

40. DH 6.88.2.
41. DH 6.88.4.
42. DH 6.88.4.
43. Sautel 2016: CXXIII–CXXIV, 268n.265.
44. DH 6.88.3.
45. DH 6.86.5.
46. DH 6.86.5. Translation adapted from Cary's Loeb translation.
47. Plato, *Leges* 769e.

Chapter 17

1. Cf. e.g., A. *Pr.* 561–886, esp. 588, 673–677. Aeschylean verses quoted throughout this paper are taken from West 1990; translations are mine, unless otherwise indicated.
2. Cf. A. *Supp.* 291–324.
3. As Douglas (1996: 72) points out, 'the social body constrains the way the physical body is perceived'.
4. Hera is traditionally βοῶπις, 'ox-eyed' (on this epithet, frequently associated with the goddess in Homer, see O'Brien 1993: 134–137, showing that the bovine element is proper to the cult of Argive Hera from the Mycenaean age).
5. For marriage as 'yoking', see esp. Calame 1997: 237–243; on its association with Hera, cf. e.g., Pötscher 1987: 103–106, 138–147; Clark 1998. For discussion of the ethics and the politics of domestication, cf. Geue in this volume.
6. On the fluid boundaries between the human and the bovine, cf. Tralau in this volume on Pasiphae's hybridity.
7. Even in the most recent volume (Gildenhard and Zissos 2013) considering metamorphosis in a diacronic perspective (with an outstanding general introduction (1–34), and extensive and clear discussion of metamorphosis in Greek and Roman culture (36–87)), the reader cannot find any attempt to study metamorphosis in the ancient Greek myths in a posthuman and cyborgic perspective.
8. See Genz and Brabon 2009: 150.
9. For the blurring of human and animal identities and fall of any hierarchy between them in an extended self, cf. Braidotti 2013: 55–104, 143–185: within a post-anthropocentric perspective, the categories of *anthropos* and *bios* characterizing the 'human' on one side, and the 'generative vitality' flowing across all species (60) coded as *zoe* (referred to 'non-human' – also, but not only 'animal' – life) on the other, merge together in the 'extended self' (65) of the posthuman being (see also Braidotti 2006, setting such a complex scheme – based on species egalitarianism – within ethics through the notion of 'sustainable Humanities').
10. Apollodorus (2.1.3) says that Io is the daughter of either Iasos – son of Argos – or Inachus. For the former version, see also Paus. 2.16.1; the latter is much more widespread: cf. for instance A. *Pr.* 589–590, 705; S. frr. 269a, 270, 284 Radt (*Inachos*); B. 19.18; Hdt. 1.1.3; E. *Supp.* 629; Paus. 1.25.1, 3.18.13. The myth is also told in Acusilaus *FGrHist* 2 F 26-27; Pherekydes *FGrHist* 3 F 66–67 (among Apollodorus' sources); Ov. *Met.* 1.625–727. For an exhaustive analysis concerning Io's fathers, see Dowden 1989: 118–124.
11. Cf. *Phoronis*, fr. 4 Bernabé (κλειδοῦχος); A. *Supp.* 291–292; Apollod. 2.1.3 = Hes. fr. 125 M.-W. The cult of Argive Hera contemplated ribbons and garlands being tied around a column or a tree – which represented the goddess herself in an aniconic form – presided over by priestesses called κλειδοῦχοι, a term believed to correspond to the *klâwiphoroi* (*ka-ra-wi-po-ro*) found in some tablets in Linear B.

12. As O'Brien (1993: 150–156) points out, this would represent a 'pan-Hellenic' version of the myth in which the cult of Argive Hera was connected with the tying of bandages to the sacred olive tree (afterwards Io herself is tied to it).

13. Cf. Apollod. 2.1.2 (πανόπτης, while Io wishes she were invisible in A. *Pr.* 578–584); A. *Pr.* 568, 678–679, *Supp.* 304.

14. Cf. Hes. fr. 126 M.-W.

15. Cf. A. *Pr.* 567–573, 674–682, where the gadfly is the ghost of Argos, slaughtered by Hermes, who had previously hypnotized him by playing his *syrinx* (574, δόναξ by metonymy). For a short survey on metamorphosis in Greek tragedies, cf. Gildenhard and Zissos 2013: 45–47.

16. The complex question concerning *Prometheus Bound* as an Aeschylean drama goes far beyond the scope of this chapter; I limit myself to referring to Pattoni 1987 (whose opinions on authenticity I share).

17. As they look at the hideous hybrid Io harassed by the gadfly, the Oceanides change their compassion to fear: if read in a cyborgic perspective, their attitude mirrors usual reactions against the 'other', also understood as 'alien', as for instance in the well-known case of Victor Frankenstein's reactions when he sees his monstrous Creature: 'I compassionated him, and sometimes felt a wish to console him; but when I looked upon him [. . .] my heart sickened, and my feelings were altered to those of horror and hatred' (see Butler 1993b: 121).

18. The notion of the destruction of the beauty of form (μορφή) – concerning the myth of the Proetides (cf. Hes. fr. 133 M.-W.) as well as that of Io, both centred on the refusal of γάμος – is also expressed by μαραίνω (597, 'to waste', often – as here – associated with νόσος). On Io's μορφή and questions pertaining to its medical aspects, cf. Ceschi in this volume.

19. Cf. also E. *Pho.* 247, κεράσφορος. Persistence of human features in the heifer-maiden is a good example of the 'continuity in transformation' that characterizes metamorphosis among other kinds of change (the notion is highlighted in Gildenhard and Zissos 2013: 15–17).

20. 648–649, τί παρθενεύῃ δαρόν, ἐξόν σοι γάμου / τυχεῖν μεγίστου; ('why remain a virgin so long, when you have the chance to enjoy the greatest union of all?'; trans. Griffith 1983).

21. There is a manifest similarity between Io's mad wanderings and the description of the illness of maidens in the Hippocratic Corpus (*Disease of Virgins*, Littré 8.466–481), for maidens affected by μανία and παραφροσύνη are said there to wander aimlessly.

22. The metaphor of cattle pursued by the οἶστρος is found first in *Od.* 22.299–301 (with reference to the frenzy that seizes the nobles of Ithaca pursued by Odysseus). There is also a reference to the κέντρον ('sting') tormenting Io in A. *Pr.* 597 and 693. As Padel (1992: 121) has pointed out, 'the *oistros*-sting is image, accompaniment, symptom, and cause of [Io's] madness and wanderings').

23. Cf. *Pr.* 836 (οἰστρήσασα) and *Supp.* 16–17 (οἰστροδόνου βοὸς), 541 (οἴστρῳ ἐρεθομένα), 573 (οἰστροδόνητον). On madness represented as a sting, see also De Martino 1961: 199–208.

24. According to Haraway (1991: 152): 'the cyborg appears in myth precisely where the boundary between human and animal is transgressed'. The cyborgic identity challenges 'the denotative stability of human identity', marking an 'unfamiliar otherness' (Balsamo 1996: 32). On species' encounters and cohabitation, cf. Haraway 2003 and 2007. On another instance of a cyborg female and his hybridity in Greek literature, cf. Chesi and Sclavi in this volume on Pandora.

25. A link between οἶστρος and λύσσα seems to emerge from an anonymous tragic fragment regarding Io in which the former is winged (*Fr. Adesp.* 144a Kannicht-Snell, πτερωτὸν οἶστρον ἄφετος ἐν μορφῇ βοός).

26. Cf. E. *Ba.* 119 (women who devote themselves to the rites, abandoning their domestic occupations, are οἰστρηθεὶς Διονύσῳ); 665 (οἶστρος induces the Bacchants to rush out of the city); 1229 (Cadmus reports that he saw Ino and Autonoe still οἰστροπλῆγας on the mountain while he was bringing

down the remains of Pentheus). It seems worth noting that in A. *Supp.* 564 Io is a 'Bacchant of Hera' (θυιὰς Ἥρας).

27. According to Zeitlin 1996: 154, the gadfly is Io's unknown desire for sexual union, that drives her mad, for she lies between desire (Zeus) and interdiction of it (Hera). According to most scholars, Io's story in *Prometheus Bound* offers the mythical background for the transition of Athenian girls to women through marriage (cf. for instance Katz 1999: 129–147; Dowden 1989: 124–144); Konstantinou 2018: 94 instead asserts that Io's peregrinations echo 'the displacement of the new bride away from her paternal hearth'.

28. Unlike considerations expressed – as we have seen – in *Prometheus Bound* (887–907), where the chorus considers 'unequal marriage' as a misfortune. The Danaids' erotic desire for Zeus is highlighted in Zeitlin 1996: 153–155.

29. Instead, in *Supp.* 568 Io is a hybrid, thus confirming that even in the same play her figure has different characterizations. Bacchylides' *Dithyramb* 5 (fr. 19 Maehler), verisimilarly represented in the same years as Aeschylus' *Suppliant Maidens* – anyway not later than 460 BCE, as it emerges from representations of Io on vases (cf. Maehler 1997: 241) – seems to allude to a complete metamorphosis (16, χρυσέα βοῦς, 'golden cow' and 24, καλλικέραν δάμαλιν, 'heifer with beautiful horns').

30. Considering this, it seems worth noting that in art the hybrid figures of Io appear 'harmonious', devoid of either disgusting or fearful features (cf. Frontisi-Ducroux 2003: 66).

31. From mid-sixth to about mid-fifth century BCE, Io is depicted as a bovine figure, sometimes even as a bull. In a later phase, approximately from 460–450 BCE onwards, Io features as a horned woman with bovine ears. This shift may reflect the presence of Io as a speaking character in Aeschylus' *Prometheus Bound*, as already stated by Engelmann (1903: 58) and Simon (1985: 276) and further highlighted by Maehler 2006, while Yalouris (1986: 12) does not rule out an influence of pictorial art on the synthetic representation of Io as a hybrid in A. *Supp.* 299, 568–570. Cf. on this subject also Garvie 1969: 159–160.

32. Boston, Museum of Fine Arts, 1901. 562; Yalouris 1990: 667, 33.

33. Cf. Yalouris 1990: 675; Moret 1990; Frontisi-Ducroux 2003: 158. Features of a bull seem to be associated with Io in Sophocles' satyr play *Inachus* (fr. 269a 36–40 Radt, esp. 38, φύει κάρα ταυρῷ, 'grew a head like a bull's', transl. Lloyd-Jones 1996).

34. In the light of a passage from Pseudo-Eratosthenes' *Epitome* (1.14, cf. Olivieri 1897, 18, ἕτεροι δέ φασι βοῦν εἶναι, τῆς Ἰοῦς μίμημα, 'other people say that [the constellation] is a heifer, Io's image'), Moret 1990: 18–26 states that representations of Io as a bull refer to the constellation Taurus: Zeus would have placed Io among the stars, transferring her bovine image to heaven ('le mot βοῦς sert de commun dénominateur à ταῦρος et à Ἰοῦς μίμημα'). According to Moret, the reference to the constellation Taurus would prove that actually the Ancients never thought of an Io transformed into a bull; instead, such an iconography would immediately refer to her catasterism, that is a reward (Pseudo-Eratosthenes has ἐτιμήθη, 'was honoured') for her docility.

35. See *Carm. Pop.* fr. 25 (871) *PMG* = Plu. *Quaest. Grec.* 299b, *De Is. et Os.* 364f; Furley and Bremer 2001, 1.369–372, 2.373–377. In S. fr. 959.2 Radt = Str. 15.1.7 (687c), the epithet βούκερως ('with bovine horns') is referred to the god, while in a fragment of Ion of Chios (86 Leurini = 5 [744] *PMG*, in Ath. 35e) Dionysus is an 'indomitable little boy with a bull's look' (ἄδαμνον παῖδα ταυρωπόν). In E. *Ba.* 100–104, Semele is said to have given birth to a 'god with bull's horns' (ταυρόκερων θεόν), cf. also 618, 920–922, 1017–1019, 1159.

36. On sexual implications in the Hymn of the women of Elis for Dionysus, see Schlesier 2002: 185–187. It seems worth noting that in Aristophanes' *Lysistrata* (217–218) the eponymous character connotes the refusal of sexual intercourse by using the adjective ἀταυρώτη.

37. See A. *Xantriai*, frr. 168 a-b Radt.

38. This most important concept is clearly expressed in a few verses believed to belong to Aphrodite's speech at the end of the Danaids trilogy (A. fr. 44 Radt) and proclaiming the universal law of γάμος and generation.

39. As highlighted in Balsamo (1996: 12): 'women's bodies remain a privileged site for the cultural reinscription of the "natural"', and are subjected 'to the surveillance of a normative gaze' (13).
40. An excellent, up-to-date guide to Posthumanism is Mahon 2017.

Chapter 18

1. Among which some Aristotelian reports, whose connection to Philolaus' writings have been definitively established; see Huffman 1993, Burkert 1972 and Schofield 2012. On Philolaus, see more recently also McKirahan 2012; Graham 2014.
2. On assemblage and becoming: Deleuze and Guattari 1987 [1980]: 6–13; Bennett 2010: ch. 2. On the process of becoming as primary, see Deleuze 1994 [1968]: 251; for an assessment, cf. Pearson 1999: 90 and May 2005: 89f..
3. Bennett 2010: 23–24.
4. See e.g., Haraway 1991; Latour 1993.
5. On its authenticity, see Huffman 1993: 307f.
6. Cf. Empedocles: Sharastani, DK 1 358, n.16; Diog. Ap. A19.44 = Theophr. *De Sens*. 39f.; Diog. Ap. B2; Alcm. B1a; Archelaus A4.6 = Hippol. *Ref.* 1.9.
7. For counterfactual arguments in fifth-century writers, see Diog. Ap. B3; Anaxag. B12; Her. B23; Zeno B1–3; Melissus B6–7; see Burkert 1972: 260. For modern analyses of causation in terms of counterfactuals, see the classic Lewis 1973 and Pearl 2000.
8. The same problem applies to ὑπάρχειν, cf. Nussbaum 1979: 101 n.94 and Huffman 1993: 136–137.
9. On Philolaus' role in developing the notion of ἀρχή as 'explanation', see Huffman 1993: 78f.; Schofield 1997: 222.
10. Huffman 1993 seems to be aware of the ambiguity (cf. e.g., 140f. and 158) but does not provide an interpretive solution.
11. Cf. Boeckh 1819: 65; Burkert 1972; Huffman 1993: 158; McKirahan 2012: 217f..
12. With the due differences, it is worth noting that music is invoked as an instance of an assemblage also by Deleuze and Guattari 1987 [1980]: 95f..
13. I am here providing a simplified translation of Philolaus' peculiar musical terminology; for a detailed technical treatment, see Barker 2007: 13f.; Huffmann 1993: 145f.. Cf. also McKirahan 2012: 219.
14. Cf. Boeckh 1819: 65. *Contra*: Burkert 1972: 390; Barker 1989: 37 n.32; McKirahan 2012: 219. Cf. Huffman 1993: 161f..
15. Cf. Aelian, *ap*. Por. *In Ptol*. 96.21f. quoting Theophrastus. Cf. Huffman (1993: 151) for this testimony as crucial for authenticity, together with Aristides Quintilianus 1 (15 W-I).
16. In standard terminology, διὰ πασῶν was used for both, see Huffmann 1993: 151.
17. Cf. Huffman 1993: 47 and 1999: 30
18. Cf. Huffman 1993: 39f., 101f. and 1999: 18.
19. Contrast with πεῖρας at Xen. B28; πείρας at Her. B45; πεῖραρ at Parm. B8.26, 30–31, 42–43, 49; πεπερασμένα at Zeno B3.
20. Smyth 2002: 454.
21. Smyth 2002: 414.
22. Cf. Burkert 1972: 253.
23. Cf. Arist. *Phys*. 203b7f., 207a9 and Pl. *Phileb*. 24a6–b8.
24. Cf. the etymology of ἄπειρος-ον proposed by Kahn 1960: 231f., *versus* e.g,. LSJ and Chantraine 1968, *s.v.*

25. Cf. Arist. *Phys.* 204a2–7, a14; cf. also Simpl. *In Phys.* 470–71.
26. Cf. Burkert 1972: 255, *contra* Scoon 1922: 354.
27. Cf. Arist. *Phys.* 203b18–19.
28. Burkert (1972: 35 n.36) calls this a logical difficulty, which my interpretation explains away.
29. Burkert 1972: 236.
30. Cf. also Arist. *Cael.* 293a18f. and Fr. 204.
31. Huffman 1993: 42f..
32. Cf. Bennett 2010: 22–23.
33. Cf. Bennett 2010: 24.
34. Deleuze 1992: 93.
35. Recall here Deleuze's favourite example of becoming, that formed by the wasp and the orchid, see Deleuze and Guattari 1987 [1980]: 10f..
36. Cf. *Nat. Puer.* 26.2; *Aer.* 12; *Vict.* 1.7–8, cf. Lonie 1981: 235. On κρᾶσις as preserving health, Schumacher 1940: 201; on *harmonia* as a normative model for health, Rosella Schluderer 2018.
37. Cf. Pl. *Crat.* 399d; Arist. *De An.* 405b28f. For this connection in Homer and medical authors, see Jouanna 1987a.
38. See Sedley 1995: 24f.; *contra*: Huffman 2009.
39. Cf. Emped. *apud* Aëtius 5.15.3; Alcmaeon A17 = Aët. 5.16.3; *Nat. Puer.* 27, *On Generation* 9–10, *De octimestri partu* 3.5–7.
40. That plants did not breathe was a common opinion, to which Anaxagoras is presented as an exception in Ps.Arist. *De Plantis* (816b27); accordingly, Anaxagoras granted them the status of animals (*Plant.* 815a19).
41. Cf. Empedocles A70 = Aët. 5.26.4; A79 = Soranus *Gynaec.* 1.57 p.42; Democ. B148; *Nat. Puer.* 22–27; *Genit.* 9–10; *Oct.* 3.5–7; Arist. *GA* 745b25 and Gal. *De sem.* 2.4. For botanical images in embryology: *Nat. Puer.* 17 and 21.
42. This vegetative life one could perhaps term ζωή, borrowing from D.L. 8.28, where the difference between ζωή and ψυχή is explained in terms of the former partaking only of the hot, and the latter of both hot and cold.

Chapter 19

* To my friend Frédéric, for his incisive contributions and above all his illuminating conversation, I dedicate this chapter.

1. Haraway 1991: 212–215, with Braidotti 2013: 58–65, and Neyrat 2017a, 2017b.
2. Hayles 1999: xxi f.
3. E.g., Haraway 1991: esp. 155–161; Hayles 1999: xiif., 4f.; Braidotti 2013: 22–30, 45–50.
4. Neyrat 2017a: 126f.
5. Hayles 1999: 3.
6. Haraway 1991: 150f.
7. E.g., Diogenes Laertius, 8.7–9=Long and Sedley 1987, hereafter LS by testimonium, 63C, with 'universal law': see Nussbaum 1999: xi–xiii; Ishay 2004: 19–44. See Griffin 2013 *passim*.
8. LS 44C, 46E–F, with Wildberger 2006: 1.205–41; cf. 2008: 47f., 50 n. 11, 54–6, 58–61.
9. LS 47O-Q, 53A, 60H=Seneca, *Ep.* 124.13–14, with Fontenay 1998: 104–110, esp. 106; cf. Graver 2007: 19–21, Wildberger 2008: 47, 61f.; for posthuman comparanda, Braidotti 2013: 59f.

10. Cf. Braidotti 2013: 67.

11. See, e.g., MacLuhan 1962: 31f., with Kreisberg 1995. Both discuss the early twentieth-century Jesuit anthropologist Teilhard de Chardin who derived the concept of planetary intelligence, or the 'noosphere', partly from the panpsychism of the Stoic cosmos: Tanner 1982: 46f.

12. See the end of chapter, Derrida 1982a: 121–123, and Chesi and Spiegel's Introduction to this volume; cf. Lyotard 1991: 8f.

13. Against the 'orthodoxy' of the position, see Inwood 2007: 272–274 (cf. Wildberger 2006: 2.612), citing the only other evidence: Stobaeus, *Eclogues* 2.64.18–65.6 in von Arnim 1903–1924, hereafter *SVF* by volume and testimonium, hence here: 3.305–307. See also Inwood 2005: 31–38, and, for the next sentence, Wildberger 2006: 1.147f.

14. Armisen-Marchetti 1989: 252, with Dressler 2016a: 60–82.

15. See also Seneca, *Ep.* 53.10, with Dressler 2016a: 83–85, cf. 72–75.

16. But see Blake 2012. For more on property, see Dressler 2016a, Chapter 6; also Armisen-Marchetti 1989: 157–159; Ducos 1991: 110–113, esp. nn. 8–11, 119f.; Bartsch 2009: 204–208, 230.

17. See *Consolatio ad Polybium* 10.6 and *Ep.* 98.11, with Armisen-Marchetti 1989: 232f.

18. See Johnson 2008: 168–75; Ngai 2005: 97–100; Dressler 2016a: 153f. and Rosenmeyer 2018: 78f., 90f., 96–102, 109f.

19. Dressler 2016b: 17f.

20. Griffin 1976: 294–314; cf. Ker 2010: 183–185, Mutschler 2015: 142f.

21. *Ep.* 113.1; cf. *De Beneficiis* 4.5.3, with Ducos 1991: 113f., and in general, Ker 2006: 33–39. On 'dialectic' in Seneca's philosophy, see Inwood 2005: 17–18, 2007: xiv–xvii, 218–219, 261, 271; Wildberger 2006: 2.612f.

22. See also *Ep.* 113.3, with, e.g., LS 53A3, B4, J, P, Q, R, Y, and Inwood 1985: 47–53, Wildberger 2006: 1.90f.

23. *Ep.* 113.4; see, e.g., LS, vol. 1, pp. 199f., with Dressler 2016a: 60f.

24. Cf. Dressler 2016a: 72f.

25. Wildberger 2006: 1.166; cf. Benatouïl 2006: 9.

26. See also n. 22 above.

27. See Deleuze 1990: 6, 10, 21.

28. Cf. Cicero, *Tusc. Disp.* 2.14, with Armisen-Marchetti 1989: 100–103, 233–240, at 235f.; cf. Connors 1997: 62–64 and Gildenhard 2007: 261f.

29. Cf. Cicero, *De officiis* 1.44f., with Dressler 2016a: 221–223.

30. Macpherson 1962: 3, with Hayles 1999: 3, and Braidotti 2013: 61f.

31. See, e.g., Epictetus, *Discourses* 1.6.12–22=LS63 E2, with Fontenay 1998: 105. See also Wildberger 2006: 1.211–217; Graver 2007: 27f. On individuation and personification, see Dressler 2016a: 62–64, 67.

32. 5.2; cf. 14.2: *amore caeco <u>sui</u>* vis-à-vis 10.2: *amorem <u>rerum suarum</u> caecum.*

33. 13.4, 14.1; cf. Cicero, *De finibus.* 2.69, and Armisen-Marchetti 1989: 255.

34. For documentation and discussion, see Dressler 2016a: 1–6; cf. Ngai 2005: 99f.

35. Graver 2007: 27–33.

36. See *On Anger* 2.1.4, with Graver 2007: 94f.; Chrysippus (*Epict. Diss.* 2.6.9=*SVF* 3.191=LS 58J, their translation, italics added): 'For my foot too, *if* it had intelligence, would also have an impulse to get muddy,' with Benatouïl 2006: 22f.; Cicero, *Fin.* 3.18=*SVF* 2.1166.

37. See, e.g., Ngai 2005: 25f. vis-à-vis Nussbaum 2001: 33–49.

38. Terada 2001: 4. The Stoic precedent for the idea of 'intensity' developed by some posthumanist thinkers (Deleuze and Guattari 1987: 21–26; Massumi 2002, 6f.) is the distributed 'tension' of breath

that structures things: LS M–P, esp. N=Gal. *Introductio sive medicus* 14.726,7–11=*SVF* 2.176, where note 'stones'; see Armisen-Marchetti 1989: 209f., Wildberger 2006: 1.87f., 2008, 61f., Graver 2007: 26–28. Contrast Shaviro (2014: 85): 'Panpsychism is the thesis that even rocks have minds.'

39. Like the liberal subject targeted by critical posthumanism, the Stoic subject '*possessed* a body, but was not usually represented as *being* a body' (Hayles 1999: 4).

40. *Ep.* 53.10, with Dressler 2016a: 83–85.

41. Armisen-Marchetti 1989: 260; Dressler 2012, 57f. For some joking derived from the opposite movement, 'dispersonification' (Dressler 2016a: 67), see Braren 1992: 39 and Armisen-Marchetti 2004: 314–316.

42. See Payne 2010: 78f., with Bennett 2010: 98–100 and Braidotti 2013: 68–70.

43. Inwood 2007: 157: 'Seneca is perhaps trying to get Platonic results without adopting Platonic substance dualism', with Armisen-Marchetti 1989: 259f.

44. E.g., Haraway 1991: 161–163, 177f., 194f., 209f., Hayles 1999: 285–287, Massumi 2002: 26–30, 133–143, Braidotti 2013: 65f.; cf. Fontenay 1998: 600f. On the Graeco-Roman background, see Dressler 2016a: 18–20, 69–82.

45. Cf. *Ep.* 27.8: (*mens . . . commodatur . . . emitur*); 120.18 (*animus . . . suum . . . commodatis utitur*) with Armisen-Marchetti 1989: 98, cf. 74f., and Braidotti 2013: 70–72.

46. Armisen-Marchetti 1989: 163f.

47. Schrijvers 1998: 185.

48. Cf. Shaviro 2014: 16–20.

49. E.g., *Ep.* 119.4: 'Look to [*specta*] the end [*finem*] of all things,' with Derrida 1982a: 133f.

50. Cf. *Ep.* 85.41, with text at n. 45, above.

51. Wildberger 2006: 1.168f.; cf. LS vol. 1, 377, 383f.

52. Figurative or literal: *TLL*, s.v. *recipio*, 11.2.348.69–11.2.349.35, with Armisen-Marchetti 1989: 259.

53. But see *Ep.* 113.14: 'Virtue does nothing by its own means [*per se agit*], but rather *with* a human being [*sed cum homine*].' See also *Ira* 1.11.18: '*uirtus . . . circumspexit*'.

54. Haraway 1991: 212, cf. 2016a: 58–63. This use of *textorium* is unique in classical Latin, derived from weaving (*textus*), and thus somewhat opaque in its application here. Cf. Wildberger (2008: 53): 'the cosmos is a kind of gigantic hank of two bodies, god and matter, which are parted and divided into two continuous tangles of extremely fine threads and, at the same time, interwoven into each other'.

55. For monsters in posthumanism, see, e.g., Haraway 1991: 180, 227f. and 2016a: 2, 100f. On 'Bodies without Organs', see Deleuze and Guattari 1987: 165f., where note the Stoic *spermatikos logos*. On emergence, *archê*, *telos* and embodiment, see Hayles 3f., 10f., 285, 288. On reflexivity in the nonhuman, see Shaviro 2014: 87–91; cf. Payne 2010: 17–22.

56. For two such Senecas, see Wildberger 2010: 206, 231f.; cf. Klein 1998 [1929], vis-à-vis Braren 1992: 40f.

57. Deleuze and Guattari 1994: 56, cf. Armisen-Marchetti 2004: 311, and *De tranquilitate animi* 17.5, with Braren 1992: 34; see also Nussbaum 2009: 87–90, 98f.

58. See Haraway 1991: 180f., with, e.g., Habinek 1998: 142f., where note 'property owner', and Habinek 2005: 132 on 'play'.

59. See, e.g., Hayles 1999: 291; Braidotti 2013: 50–54 and Chesi and Spiegel's Introduction to this volume.

60. Derrida 1982a: 118; Lyotard 1991: 13f.

61. See Hardt and Negri 2000: 217 in Rimell 2015: 13f.

62. E.g., Hayles 1999: 6.

Chapter 20

1. Throughout this chapter, for both Theodoret's and Antonius's works, I follow the translation of Doran 1992. For Theodoret, RH = Religious History; for Antonius, LS = Life of Saint Simeon the Stylite.
2. Cf. Harvey 1988: 378.
3. As Susan Harvey (1988: 380) argues, with reference to this passage: 'Simeon represents a mirrored image of his [Theodoret's] Christological position'.
4. Haraway 1991: 149.
5. Cf. Grusin 2015: viii–ix.
6. Wolfe 2009: xv–xvi.
7. Bennett 2010: 31.
8. *Becoming-other* has its conceptual matrix in Deleuze and Guattari's concept of *becoming-animal*. As Matthew Calarco (2015: 57) puts it, 'becoming-other is a refusal to enact the ideals and subjectivity that the dominant culture associates with being a full human subject and to enter into a relation with the various minor, or nondominant, modes of existence that are commonly viewed as being the "other" of the human'.
9. Peers 2013: 74–75.
10. At this point I should acknowledge that others have argued that Theodoret at least is precisely interested in such an argument; see Harvey 1988: 379. If so, Simeon has escaped the control of the text.
11. On the icon as part of Simeon's 'extended body', see Peers 2013: 73.
12. Cf. Deleuze and Guattari 1987.
13. http://www.louvre.fr/en/oeuvre-notices/plaque-saint-simeon, accessed 30 July 2016.
14. The column of course can also be interpreted in phallic terms, as can the ladder. The sinuousness of the serpent contrasts with the austere erectness of the column and ladder.
15. On hagiography and biblical typology more generally see Krueger 1997.
16. On human materializations in text, cf. Kirichenko (Chapter 29) and Dressler (Chapter 19) in this volume.
17. On 'the force of things', see Bennett 2010: 1–19. On the force of ancient Christian things in particular, see Peers 2012 and 2013.

Chapter 21

1. See esp. Telò and Mueller 2018. In recent years theorists, including a few groundbreaking classicists, have re-enlivened debates around materialities, drawing attention to relations and continuities between humans and objects, things, or stuff, and objects as lively and agential. See Grosz 2008, Bennett 2010 and for Greek literary engagements Purves 2015, Mueller 2016.
2. Cf. Haraway 1988 on what she terms 'situated knowledges', which she characterizes as a 'view from bodies' – that is, as embedded in social and material specificities.
3. Again, see Bennett 2010 and Purves 2015.
4. From my perspective, these must be taken together if we are to apprehend fully the material quality of dramatic signification – that is, as indexical (i.e., as concrete entities, postures, etc. indicating themes, concepts etc.) and viewing itself as sensuous and mimetic, as a kind of 'feeling with' see Marks 2000. For a sustaining of attention to the semiotic in such affective encounters, see Brinkema 2014.

5. A focus on skin, cloth and surfaces may also call attention to the fold, the form of which disrupts simple binaries between surface and depth, inside and outside, and as image and actuality it operates as a material refutation of such fixed borders (Deleuze [and Strauss], 1991; Deleuze 2006). Cf. Merleau-Ponty's notion of the 'flesh' of the world as contiguous and continuous with human embodiment, a world fabric that enfolds the body and other objects such that the latter are, as he puts it, 'encrusted into its flesh' (Merleau-Ponty 1964: 163–165; cf. Merleau-Ponty 1968).
6. See Michelini (1987: 3–51) on the earlier background; Goff 2000 and Torrance (2013: 1–6) on later developments. Cf. Wohl 2015 on Euripidean politics and the tortuous manipulations of his plots.
7. Cf. Worman 2012. See Haraway 1988, on embodiment as 'significant prosthesis' – that is, the contours or parts visible from specific culturally embedded prospects.
8. Deleuze and Guattari 1987 [1980]: 79–82, 115–117, 398–403; cf. Bennett 2010: 23–24. Seely has highlighted such transformative aesthetics in avant-garde fashion designers, claiming an 'ontological' fusion in the ways in which fabrics 'endlessly fold in and out of the surfaces of the body, as skin and cloth, organic and nonorganic, body and thing become one' (describing designs of Rei Kawakubo), a mode he terms 'affective fashion' (2012: 250–251). See also Wohl 2005 on this type of gendered 'becoming' in the *Bacchae.*
9. Cf. Bennett's attention to the feel of a 'slip–slide' materiality (2010: 4), emergent or merging edges that also dovetail with affectivity as an embodied dynamics, what Raymond Williams influentially called 'structures of feeling' (1977: 131–133). On affectivity see Deleuze 2001 [1970]; Sedgwick 2003; Gregg and Seignworth 2010.
10. See, e.g., Goheen 1955; Sider 1978; Lebeck 1971; Heath 1999.
11. Wohl 1998: 86–89, 104–105; Mueller 2016: 48–64; see also Goheen 1955, Lebeck 1971, Morrell 1997, McClure 1999: 85f., Lee 2004, Noel 2013.
12. Merleau-Ponty 1964, 1968.
13. Toward the end of the first play, the chorus despairs at the 'spider's web' that ensnared the king (1492), and Aegisthus vaunts over Agamemnon's corpse as caught in what he calls the 'fences of justice' (τῆς Δίκης ἐν ἕρκεσιν, 1611). For the imagery, see Goheen 1955; Zeitlin 1965; Lebeck 1971; Carne-Ross 1981; Heath 1999; Lee 2004.
14. Sider (1978: 26) emphasizes the circular pattern, but suggests an unworkable staging of the display.
15. Ahmed 2004: 83–88; cf. Kristeva's notion of abjection 1982 [1980], which Ahmed explores.
16. The *omphalos* represented effectively the belly-button of the world and is a chthonic symbol of Apollo's power (see Sommerstein *ad loc.*).
17. This is the statue of Athena Polias, housed in the old temple on the Acropolis (again, see Sommerstein *ad loc.*).
18. See Nooter (2017: ch. 5) on the Furies' sounds/voices.
19. On the latter, cf. Vasunia on Egyptian otherness in Aeschylus and Euripides (2001: 33–74).
20. The Greek leaders allotted Andromache as a Trojan slave-wife to Neoptolemus, the son of Achilles, so the play takes place in his home city of Phthia, in Thessaly.
21. That is, as the paradigmatic mourning mother, since Niobe's endless grief at her children's deaths transformed her into a permanently dripping rockface; cf. the similar image at 532–534 and further below.
22. N.B., this lead seal could apparently be used for either bronze or marble, although Stieber is not very clear on this point (2012: 128–130); with thanks to Verity Platt for guidance on statuary conventions.
23. Cf. lines 1041 and 1246–1247; see Golder 1983.
24. Emphasized by Lloyd *ad loc.*; Kyriakou 1997; Allan 2000: 178–179; Torrance 2005. On the Spartan origin of the clothing and its import, see Stavrinou 2016.
25. E.g., Bourdieu 1991: 70, 109; he uses the Homeric *skeptron* as an example.

26. δεῖ σ᾽ ἀντὶ τῶν πρὶν ὀλβίων φρονημάτων / πτῆξαι ταπεινὴν προσπεσεῖν τ᾽ ἐμὸν γόνυ, / σαίρειν τε δῶμα τοὐμὸν ἐκ χρυσηλάτων / τευχέων χερὶ σπείρουσαν Ἀχελῴου δρόσον.
27. Note that chest- and/or breast-baring seems to run in the family: witness Clytemnestra in *Choephoroi* and the *Electra*'s; Helen here (cf. *Andr*. 629–630) and in *Trojan Women*. Mastronarde (*Phoenissae ad* 1490–1491) considers this a gesture of mourning, comparing Antigone's uncovering to this moment in *Andromache*, as well as Clytemnestra's in *Choephoroi* (citing Garvie *ad* 896–898); see also Swift 2009: 64–65 and Stavrinou 2016 on the Spartan costume as well as the gesture more generally.
28. That Hermione is Helen's daughter may contribute to a sense that this human is in thrall to her material implements, as the mother trails such vanities through the backgrounds of many Euripidean dramas. Cf., e.g., *Hecuba*, *Orestes*; and see Worman 2002: 118–122. Cf. also the *Agamemnon*, where the chorus envisions Helen herself as an assemblage of objects and sensory effects: a 'delicate ornament of wealth, a soft shaft of the eyes, a heart-biting flower of desire' (*Ag*. 740–742: ἀκασκαῖον δ᾽ ἄγαλμα πλούτου, / μαλθακὸν ὀμμάτων βέλος, / δηξίθυμον ἔρωτος ἄνθος).
29. On the play generally see Musurillo 1961; Easterling 1968, 1981, 1982 (comm.); McCall 1972; Segal 1977; Lawrence 1978. On the robe see Ormand 1993; Pozzi 1994; Lee 2004.
30. See Finkelberg 1996 on the stasimon; also Stinton 1990.
31. On this passage and Heracles' pneumatic disease, cf. Ceschi in this volume.
32. For more on displaying the body in pain, see Worman 2018; for displaying the male body in drama, see Hawley 1998, Worman 2012 and 2020. There is now a substantial bibliography on disease in the Greek imaginary, but for tragedy in particular see especially Biggs 1966; Padel 1995; Worman 2000; Ceschi 2003; Budelmann 2007; Holmes 2008, 2010; Allan 2014. For the tragic representation of body pain, cf. Thumiger in this volume.
33. Note that 'female' in Greek convention is barely human, more body than soul; see most influentially Irigaray 1985 [1972], Butler 1993a.
34. See also Worman 2018. On the vocabulary of eating in this passage, cf. Ceschi in this volume. On Heracles as sacrificial victim, see Seaford 1994; Calame 1998. For the possible connection of this welding of the cloak to the flesh as a 'marriage' or 'joint dwelling' (reading ξυνικοῦν for ξυνιποῦν, 1055), see Ormand 1993 and the objections of Pozzi 1993. Cf. Llewellyn-Jones 2007 on clothing and shelter; also Mitchell-Boyask 2012 and Allan 2014 on medical metaphors and images. On the end of the play, see Easterling 1981; Roberts 1988; Holt 1989; Liapis 2006.
35. This is true of Sophocles' Ajax as well; on Heracles and his 'cloak of flesh' in Euripides, see further in Worman (2020).

Chapter 22

1. *Bridging Part 1*. Devised by Minty Donald, Nick Millar and Offshore Workboats Ltd. River Clyde, Glasgow. 6 November 2010.
2. Donald 2014: 118.
3. Donald 2014: 119.
4. Donald 2014: 122.
5. Donald 2014: 122. Italics mine.
6. On this topic, Donald borrows from Bennett 2010 and Ingold 2011: 89–94.
7. Donald 2014: 130.
8. Donald 2014: 126.
9. Hammond and Roseman 1996.
10. Hdt. VII, 23–57.

11. Hdt. VII, 36.
12. Hdt. VII, 34.
13. Hdt. VII, 35.
14. Hdt. VIII, 117; IX, 114.
15. In particular in VII, 36. The Athenian people could actually have witnessed these extraordinary Persian ropes that were later dedicated as war spoils in Athenian sanctuaries, cf. IX, 121; Hall 1996 *ad loc.*
16. For a recent re-assessment of the influence of Aeschylus on Herodotus through the historian's borrowing of the animal metaphor of the 'yoking' of the Hellespont, see Van den Eersten 2015. Another narrative device that seemed also borrowed from tragedy is his way of connecting the crossing of rivers with man's arrogance and transgression. See Immerwahr 1966: 293; Lateiner 1989: 128–129.
17. Hayles 1999: 291.
18. *Pers.* 272–514.
19. Marchesini 2017: 23.
20. According to Marchesini (*id.*), the humanist tradition was developed much later than the fifth century BCE.
21. Haraway 2003.
22. *Pers.* 111–113, 130–132.
23. For this meaning, see also *Pro.* 23; *Ag.* 729; *Cho.* 1267.
24. *Pers.* 181-196.
25. *Pers.* 71–72 (πολύγομφον ὅδισμα/ ζυγὸν ἀμφιβαλὼν αὐχένι πόντου).
26. See Dumortier 1935: 12–26. Michelini (1982: 80–88) provides good evidence that this metaphor became part of the traditional rhetoric of orators recalling Xerxes' invasion (Isocrates, *Paneg.* 89–90, Lysias 2.29).
27. *Pers.* 74–75.
28. *Pers.* 88.
29. *Pers.* 90.
30. *Pers.* 133–134.
31. *Pers.* 79–80.
32. *Pers.* 81–82. On the characteristic gaze of the *drakon*, see Ogden 2013: 237–238.
33. In the *Oresteia*, Clytemnestra is also called a new Skylla (*Ag.* 1258, 1232–1234), a viper (*Cho.* 914), and is compared to destructive storms, meteorites and monsters (*Cho.* 585–601).
34. *Theogony*, 624, 639, 714, 734–735.
35. *Pers.* 85–86.
36. *Iliad*, for instance V, 45, 55, 578; X, 230, etc.
37. *Pers.* 26, 30, 86.
38. See Lissarague 1990: 31–32; Hamilton 1995.
39. Therefore, I disagree with Gruen (2011: 19) when he minimizes the cultural differences between Hellenes and Persians in Aeschylus' play.
40. *Pers.* 130.
41. *Pers.* 131–132, the two continents now share the same 'headland' (πρῶνα κοινὸν).
42. Marchesini (2017: 144) describes the posthumanist 'body' as 'a liminal film that can be interconnected – that is, a welcoming place'.

43. Hall 2018: 206.
44. Marchesini 2017: 145.
45. Marchesini 2017: 146.
46. *Contra* Garvie 2009 (com. *ad loc.*, 74).
47. *Pers.* 97.
48. *Pers.* 100.
49. *Ag.* 177–178.
50. Michelini notes that 'bridges and boats are both likely to rouse superstitious fears, since both represent a hazardous application of technical skills in the attempt to tame water' (1982: 84).
51. See the 'liminal beings' of Marchesini 2017: 144.
52. *Pers.* 302–330.
53. *Pers.* 745–822; see below, 'epilogue'.
54. Hammond and Roseman 1996: 94.
55. *Pers.* 419–421; earlier, ῥεῦμα Περσικοῦ στρατοῦ (412) was reminiscent of μεγάλωι ῥεύματι φωτῶν (30).
56. *Pers.* 274–277. Rosenbloom (2006: 72) already noted that 'the sea defies quantification, human control, and the imperialist urge'.
57. Bennett 2010.
58. See lines 273–274 (πλήθουσι).
59. *Pers.* 303, 307, 420.
60. *Pers.* 310.
61. *Pers.* 423–426.
62. Cf. Blanchot (1988 [1955]: 345): 'the one who has just died is first of all as close as possible to the condition of the thing – a familiar thing, which is handled and approached, which does not keep you at distance and whose malleable passivity does not denounce the sad helplessness' (my translation). On corpses in Euripidean tragedy, see Wohl and Bassi in Telò and Mueller 2018 (17–34 and 35–48).
63. *Pers.* ἀμείβων χρῶτα πορφυρέᾳ βαφῇ (317).
64. The association of blood and purple dye was bound to take on an exceptional, multi-layered dimension in the *Oresteia*, *Ag.* 238–239; 611–612; 958–959; *Cho.* 1010–1013. Cf. Lebeck 1971: 74–79; Taplin 1977: 314; Noel 2013 (with more bibliography).
65. Cf. Worman in this volume.
66. *Pers.* κακῶν πελαγος ἔρρωγεν μέγα (433).
67. *Pers.* 270–271.
68. *Pers.* οὐδὲν γὰρ ἤρκει τόξα (279).
69. *Pers.* 415. This anthropomorphic 'bronze-mouth' is a striking component of the Olympias trireme, a modern reconstitution of a fifth-century Athenian trireme by the Hellenic navy (built in 1985–1987).
70. See also the passive δαμασθεὶς and the material agent (279–280: πᾶς δ' ἀπώλλυτο/λεὼς δαμασθεὶς ναΐοισιν ἐμβολαῖς).
71. *Pers.* 304.
72. *Pers.* 276–277.
73. Quessada 2013: 228.
74. Quessada 2013: 230–231 ('ainsi il y a un *an-archisme ontologique*, un chaos que l'on pourrait dire "essential" ou "fondamental"', i.e., since there is no hierarchy between beings made of the same material).

75. The chaos of Aeschylus has been interpreted as a heritage of Hesiodic poetry, see Deforge 2004 [1986]; Moreau 1985: 10–11. About hybridity in the *Oresteia*, see Noel 2013 (on the hybrid 'net-cloth' of Clytemnestra).
76. *Pers.* 722, 744.
77. *Pers.* 747.
78. *Pers.* 745–746.
79. See O'Donnell and Talbot-Jones 2018.
80. *Pers.* 819–822.
81. Haraway 2003: 24.
82. Agamben 2004; Weil 2012; Marchesini 2017: 72.
83. Moreau (1985: 9) comments on the animal metaphors along the same lines.
84. Quessada 2013: 230–231. He defends ontological non-separateness as a way to achieve 'ontological fraternity' between 'beings of flesh and language, real and virtual beings (. . .), material and immaterial things' (Baron 2009: 41).
85. On flat ontology, see for instance Bryant 2011: 245–290.
86. Haraway 1991: 292–293.
87. See the 'Theoretical Introduction: The Subject of the Human' in this volume.
88. Haraway 2003: 49.
89. Haraway 2003: 24.
90. Hdt. VII, 189.
91. Brulé 1987: 291–299; Hall 1996: 9; Parker 1996: 156; Finkelberg 2014. This play could have been a satyr drama, which often had, like tragedy, an aetiological function but favoured satiric humour and buffoonery over serious tone.
92. Aeschylus, *Oreithyia*, fr. 281. The wind threatens to blaze a fire and destroy the houses if he does not obtain satisfaction (presumably, the hand of Oreithyia, one of Erechtheus' daughters). Cf. Brulé 1987: 298.
93. Haraway 2003: 28.

Chapter 23

1. *Histoire de la Sexualité*, vol. II, Chapitre I.3 'Enkrateia'.
2. 814a: 'Οἱ ἀσύμμετροι πανοῦργοι'. For a discussion on the negative *kalokagathia* in Pseudo-Aristotle's *Physiognomics*; Wrenhaven 2012: 52. For the body of the slave as inverse *kalokagathia*, cf. Weiler 2002: 15f.
3. Dodds 1959: 263.
4. Dodds, ibid. 390.
5. Dodds, ibid. 265.
6. Plat. *Rep.* 3.395d.
7. Butler 1992.
8. Gagarin 1997: 114; 117.
9. For Deianeira's psychological processes, see Hall 2009; Wohl 2010 has carefully elaborated a comparison of tragic and the legal material.
10. Soph. *Phil.* 1–134.

11. Nagy 1999 [1979]: 15; Kurke 2013 [1991]: 33–34f.
12. Naiden 2015: 86.
13. Purves (2015: 1): 'For Auerbach, Homeric man is a surface, belonging to a group so ahistorical and two-dimensional that "they wake every morning as if it were the first day of their lives". For Snell, on the other hand, Homeric man is a kind of prehuman, one who could not have full agency because he had not yet "discovered", or "awakened to" the distinction between body and soul. As others have shown, Snell's evolutionary model is based on dubious assumptions, but what is still provocative about his argument is its insistence on seeing the Homeric human as an aggregate of separate, self-moving parts.'
14. Fränkel 1993 [1951]: 92.
15. Redfield 1994 [1975]: 26.
16. Translation mine. Hist. Sex.II.3: 'on oppose souvent l'intériorité de la morale chrétienne à l'extériorité d'une morale paienne'.
17. Tom Waits, 'Crossroads' 1993.
18. One of the reference works is still Latour 2009 [1999].

Chapter 24

1. The titles of both works presuppose (proto-Christian) dualistic thinking in terms of the *Aeneid*'s literary and allegorical interpretation: every image in the poem has its reverse in a symbolic meaning that is the critic's task to uncover; the Roman empire's secular order (and the critic's political interpretation) finds its double in the organization of Jupiter's cosmos and the text's deeper religious meanings.
2. Van Nortwick 1980, 1992. Reed 2007 and Giusti (2018: 88–147) offer de-polarized readings of Turnus and Aeneas, of Aeneas and Dido and of some of the poem's political dichotomies, especially West–East and male–female.
3. See most recently Stahl 2016 for a retelling of the pro-Augustan (or 'optimistic') arguments and the special 2017 issue of *CW* 111.1 on the legacy of the Harvard School and its anti-Augustan ('pessimistic') interpretations.
4. Haraway 1991: 177. See Chesi and Sclavi in this volume.
5. Haraway 1991: 152 and 1997: 51. See Chesi and Sclavi in this volume.
6. See Haraway (1991: 161) on the risk of 'lapsing into boundless difference' in the dismantling of dualisms.
7. Haraway 1991: 150.
8. See Thomas 1998.
9. See below; this is also achieved, according to Reed 2007: 58, through Virgil's 'Orientalizing' of Turnus.
10. On fragmented subjectivities in Latin literature, cf. McNamara on Lucan's *Civil War*, in this volume.
11. It is unclear whether the *moenia* of 11.915 refer to walls of the city or (more plausibly) to the fortifications of both the Latins' and the Trojans' camps placed outside the city walls. See Horsfall 2003a: 463; Fratantuono 2009: 307.
12. I only treat Book 12, but it is in the whole *Aeneid* that, as Abbot (2018: 5) puts it, 'arms function metaphorically as a leading edge of the external forces that continually impinge upon the man's inner will and purposes'.
13. On *infringo* for broken weapons see the parallels in Tarrant 2012: 84. The image of scattered Latin troops surrounding an inimical Mars (12.1 *infractos aduerso Marte Latinos*) looks forward to the

simile of Turnus as Mars at 12.331–340 and emphasizes Turnus' responsibility in bringing ruin to the Latins.

14. Tarrant 2012: 84.

15. On which see Thomas 1998. Note that many scholars (most recently Stahl 2016) imagine Virgil as siding with the Latins' unsympathetic gaze.

16. This can even be seen as a (failed) attempt at *intra-action* (cf. Barad 2007).

17. 12.90–91, with Tarrant 2012: 114.

18. See e.g., *A.* 11.339 for *futtilis* as 'worthless'.

19. See West 1974: 28–29.

20. Turnus' address to his spear rather than to the gods is generally taken to be a sign of hybris and impiety that, together with his despoiling of the enemies, contributes to his downfall (see Tarrant 2012: 114–115; Renger 1985: 33–34; Hornsby 1966 on the spoils). Details about Turnus' armour (the helmet with a fire-breathing Chimaera and the shield decorated with an image of Io) were given at 7.783–792 but are not repeated in Book 12. See Small 1959; Gale 1997; Abbot 2018: 15–16.

21. Luc. *Sat.* 3.146–147 = Nonius 21.11 *crebrae ut scintillae, in stricturis quod genus olim feruenti ferro.*

22. Turnus' connection with bulls is also underscored by the presence of Io on his shield (7.789–792; see n. 20). The fight between Turnus and Aeneas as the two bulls is staged in the simile at 12.715–722, on which see Putnam 1965: 182–186; Briggs 1980: 47–50. Mac Góráin (2013: 140–142) activates an intertext between Turnus the bull at 12.104 *irasci in cornua* and the Maenads of Eur. *Bacch.* 743 ὑβρισταὶ κἀς κέρας θυμούμενοι, which helps reading the scene as blurring distinctions between human and animal. On becoming-animal in Classical literature, see also Hopman, Korhonen, Thumiger and Ceschi in this volume.

23. On pre-cyberneric machines, see Haraway 1991: 152.

24. See e.g., Quint 1993: 79; Thomas 1998: 275.

25. Dido's and Turnus' wounds are also comparable in their narrative, as they move from metaphor (cf. 12.5 *saucius ille graui . . . uulnere*, 'injured by a heavy wound' with e.g., 4.1–2 *graui . . . saucia cura/ uulnus alit uenis*, 'injured by her heavy anguish, she nurtures a wound in her veins'; 67 *uiuit sub pectore uulnus*, 'the wound is alive under her chest') into reality (4.689 *infixum stridit sub pectore uulnus*, 'the wound hisses, fixed under her chest'). Cf. also their link through fire imagery (cf. 4.101 *ardet amans Dido*, 'burning Dido is on fire' and *ardens* Turnus (from *Ardea*) at 12.3, 71, 101, 325, 732) with Henderson 2000: 8.

26. See Lyne 1983: 59; Fowler 1987: 190–191. The ivory's provenance from India is significant in what is after all a story of colonization; on the Indian ivory of the doors of the *Georgics*' theatre-temple and Rome's appropriation of foreign materials, see Giusti 2019a.

27. See Lyne 1983: 58–59; *contra* Cairns 2005b: esp. 206–207.

28. See e.g., West 1974; Van Nortwick 1980; Reed 2007: 44–72.

29. On Turnus as a 'second self', see Van Nortwick 1980 and 1992: 124–161.

30. See Bocciolini Palagi 2016.

31. On Empedocles in the *Aeneid*, see Nelis 2001: 96–112, 289, 245–259.

32. On Dido, cf. *A.* 4.525 and *G.* 3.243–244; on Turnus, see above. The connection is explored further and in relation to Turnus' shield by Gale 1997: 177–185. On love and animals in *Georgics* 3, see Geue in this volume.

33. The *dei ex machina* of *Aeneid* 12 are most obviously Venus and the Dira (< *Dei ira* = anger of Jupiter), on which see Johnson 1992. On anachronistic machines see below.

34. See Giusti 2014: 54.

35. See Thomas 1988; cf. Gowers 2011 on how Aeneas' is also a mission to extirpate the stock of Priam.

36. See Lyne 1989: 164–165, Thomas 1998: 289; *contra* Stahl 2016: 14–17.
37. See Schenk 1984: 227–228.
38. Tarrant 2012: 269 (cf. Cairns 1989: 109–128). For the Gigantomachic associations of the scene, see O'Hara 1994: 222.
39. Putnam 2011: 81.
40. Ambiguously indicating identification between Aeneas and Jupiter, see Thomas 1998: 297. O'Hara (1994: 221–222) places a colon after *intonat armis* in line 700 and makes Mt Athos the subject, turning Aeneas into a Giant opposing the gods.
41. Cf. also Klodt 2003.
42. Continuing to evoke Jupiter's thunderstorm, see Hardie 1986: 177–180.
43. Mader 2015: 590.
44. Mader 2015: 595; cf. Quint 1993: 71.
45. Mader 2015: 597.
46. Mader 2015: 593.
47. On anachronistic siege-devices in the *Aeneid*, see Rossi 2004: 184.
48. Tarrant 2012: 319.
49. Henderson (2000: 5): 'what Ovid does is pick up the instructions Virgil supplies, on how to unpick his epic's attempt to pass off its partialities as totalities'.
50. Many thanks to Victoria Rimell for this point.
51. Cf. 12.928–929 *totus . . . remugit/ mons* and Bacch. 726 πᾶν δὲ συνεβάκχευ' ὄρος with n.15. Cf. also *E.* 5.62–63.
52. The symbol of resistance to Rome in the Social War is that of a bull (Italia) goring a she-wolf (Roma). Interestingly, on silver denarii minted by the Italic allies of the Marsic federation, the image is paired with a head of Bacchus (or Italian Liber), symbolizing liberty from Rome.
53. See Mac Góráin (2018: 417–420) on the mixture of intromission and extramission optical models in this scene.
54. Berzins McCoy 2013: 1–35.
55. See Henderson 2000: 12, although he does not quite make this point: '"founding" (tradition, society, cultural identity) must fuse with "burying" (steel in Latin flesh), and both must fuse with "hiding" (the victim down in hell . . .)'.
56. Haraway 1991: 154.
57. The *gens Romana* at the end of the *Aeneid* is born not from a traditional myth of reproduction, but from the establishment of amical and inimical relationships (albeit among males) that almost responds to Haraway's 2015 slogan 'Make Kin Not Babies!', although in this particular case one would have good reason to worry about the 'Not Babies' part of the injunction (Haraway 2015: 164 n. 17).
58. Haraway 1991: 170. I have treated the totalizing and contradictory nature of Augustan ideology in Giusti 2016 and have dealt differently with the paradox of Virgil's *imperium sine fine* in Giusti 2019b. Sincere thanks to the volume's editors and to John Henderson, Fiachra Mac Góráin and especially Victoria Rimell.

Chapter 25

1. For important interventions in the study of things and society, see Appadurai 1988; Gell 1998; Brown 2004; Latour 2005 and Schapp 2012 [1953]. For a classical perspective, see Bielfeldt 2014a.

2. Despite their placement at the end of his corpus, books 13 and 14 were some of the poet's earliest compositions, published between 83 and 85 CE. For more on dating, see Leary 2001: 13.
3. The introductory poems to both books are longer than couplets, although the first two poems of the *Xenia* may not be authorial. For more on the Saturnalia in Martial, see Rimell 2008: 140–144.
4. On the literary qualities of these poems, see Hinds 2007: 139–146; Rimell 2008 and Lóio 2014.
5. Blake (2012: 202) finds that 15 per cent of the *Xenia* speak and 25 per cent of *Apophoreta*; Grewing 1999: 261 counts 18 in *Xenia* (14.5 per cent) and 55 in the *Apophoreta* (25 per cent); he is followed by Lóio 2014: 373. I count 56 speaking poems in the *Apophoreta*, possibly because I include the speaking statue of Minerva. In poem 14.6, *nostros* could refer to either the tablets or to the giver of the present.
6. Hodder 2012 and 2014. See also Olsen 2010 and Gell 1998 on the agency of artistic objects. The theory of narrative entanglement of both people and things found in Schapp 2012 [1953] foreshadows Gell's ideas in many ways.
7. Hodder, along with many other modern theorists, prefers the term 'thing' to 'object'. I will continue to use 'object' in this chapter, however, following the already established terminology of the 'speaking object' in ancient poetry.
8. Blake 2011a, 2012, and 2015; Stroup 2006. For Salemme 2005, Martial's focus on things in the *Xenia* and *Apophoreta* inspired the material poetics of his later books of epigrams.
9. See Rimell (2008: 148) on the idea of using the books to 'experience carnival (again) from the privacy of your own home'.
10. For background on speaking objects, see Burzachechi 1962; Wachter 2010; Tueller 2008 and Stähli 2014.
11. See, e.g., *AP* 6.6, 7, 49, 93, 107, 114, 122, 124, 148.
12. As on the Mantiklos Apollo, *CEG* 326; for more archaic inscriptions, see Burzachechi 1962. Hellenistic epigrams often offer more information on the functions and appearance of dedicated objects.
13. A similar distinction is drawn by Tiffany 2004. Writing about early English riddles spoken by objects, he notes that by claiming to be the products of a craftsman, they inhabit an intermediary status between subject and object.
14. Blake 2011a: 359.
15. See Gaunt 2017 for the cup of Nestor and its impact, along with Wachter 2010 (who does not read the cup as speaking in the first person). Whitley 2017 understands archaic inscriptions as expressing the agency of objects.
16. There are few similar literary epigrams; one parallel might be Posidippus' fragmentary epigram on a table or *kline* from the Milan papyrus (epigram 18; III.20–27). The impressive object boasts of its capacity and may illustrate lavish court symposia, according to Bing 2005.
17. Translations of Martial from Shackleton-Bailey 1993.
18. For more on networks, see Latour 2005.
19. In a few poems, the anonymous giver apologizes for its low value; e.g., 13.6 and 45 and 14.14, 126, and 132. In other poems, the gift is the result of a random lottery; e.g., 14.40 and 144. Saturnalian epigrams in other books by Martial are more engaged with the economics of gift-giving; cf. 14.46, 5.18, 5.19, 753, 8.71, and 12.81.
20. As noted by Blake 2011a: 360, Martial is more interested in pedestrian use rather than personalized jokes and exchange.
21. Similarly, Crinagoras *AP* 6. 261 records a gift between the poet and his friend Simon.
22. See Antipater *AP* 6.241 and 335 for headgear proud to cover the head of Piso; Salemme 2005: 10–15 also discusses Martial's relationship with Greek epigram.

23. See Leary (2001: 10–11) on the order of the *Xenia* and Leary (1996: 13–21) on the ordering of the *Apophoreta*, along with Rimell 2008: 156 n. 50.

24. Moretti 2010: 354–361.

25. Artworks are addressed in 14.172, 175, and 180; a quotation accompanies 14.181. The fibula of 14.215 responds to a question and the breastband of 14.134 receives advice. On the statues in general, see Macdonald 2017.

26. Grewing 1999: 263.

27. For more on inscriptional interlocutors, see Tueller 2008: 141 and Kaczko 2016: 399–402.

28. See Gell 1998 along with the cautious applications of his work to a Roman context in Stewart 2007.

29. There may be a connection between the lamp, which is feminine in gender, and the female body.

30. Other speaking pairs can be found at 14.15 and 16 (gaming equipment); 28 and 29 (sun protection); 46 and 47 (balls); 63 and 64 (wind instruments); 94 and 95 (cups); 103 and 104 (wine strainers); 120 and 121 (spoons); 122 and 123 (jewellery); 135 and 136 (clothing); 152 and 153 (cloth). Cf. Leary 1996: 66. Sometimes only the cheaper present speaks to assert its use-value; e.g., 14.88 and 90.

31. The lamps also partake in a rich tradition of understanding light sources as animate; see Bielfeldt 2014b.

32. 13.22, 25, and 26 are warnings; 13.33, 35, and 46 discuss the birth of objects; 13.49, 50, and 59 use vocabulary of nourishing (*alat, altricem, alit*); 13.71, 72, and 76 give etymologies; 13.82, 83, and 87 boast; and 13.103 and 114 apologize for their cheapness.

33. Cf. the notion of the dependency of things on other things in Hodder 2012.

34. For birds, see 13.49, 71, 72, 76; 14.73, 76; for writing materials and books, see 14.3, 9183, 194.

35. Blake (2012: 202–207) connects speaking objects with Varro's designation of the slave as an *instrumentum vocale.*

36. Grewing (1999: 261–262) understands the *opsonator* (14.218) as speaking in his own voice; this is possible, but the poem uses no first-person verbs. The slaves are the more expensive gifts in this series, and some of the cheap alternatives do speak, including a monkey (14.202) and a fibula (14.215).

37. Blake 2011b: 373–376.

38. See Blake 2011b: 363–364.

39. Cf. Rimell (2008: 158) on the recipient's assumed violence against the gifts. Lamb (2004: 218) compares eighteenth-century novels spoken by commodities such as books and coins to slave narratives.

40. Deer (13.94) say that they are simply prey, but betray no distress or fear of death. Only murexes (13.87) seem to be put off by the fact that they are viewed as both a source of dye and a food source.

41. In this sense, they differ from the art objects described by Gell 1998 and the *Wozudinge* of Schapp 2012 [1953], both of which prompt viewers to imagine human creators.

42. See Johnson 2005 for the connection with Saturnalian riddles. As noted by Leary 2001: 57, many of Martial's gift epigrams would be cryptic riddles in the absence of their lemmata, forcing the reader to guess at the objects designated.

43. See Stroup 2006 for the interchangeability of objects and poems, along with Rühl 2006 on the importance of the lemmata for short intermedial poetry.

44. Blake (2015: 356) claims that '59 of the *Xenia* (46%) and 42 of the *Apophoreta* (19%) identify the provenance of an object, and implicitly its use at Rome'. Her figures include all poems, not just those that speak, and she connects this interest with contemporary pride in Rome's imperial conquest.

45. Similar puns are made about the beccafico (13.49) and the amythestine wool (14.154). See also two poems about spoons, 14.120 and 121, with Grewing 1999.

46. Appadurai 1988 notes that objects may shift between being seen as commodities and being understood through other frameworks. Martial's gifts forcefully argue that their true identity is not as commodities but as individual gifts that create an intimate and non-transactional relationship with their new owners.
47. At 13.76, a woodcock claims to be as tasty as the pricier partridge; cf. 14.90 and 95. See Lóio 2014 and Hinds 2007 on the corresponding elevation of light verse in the epigrams on books (14.183–196).
48. In this, Martial manipulates the rhetorical trope of *prosopopoia*, as recognized by Grewing 1999: 263.
49. On the ability of things to control humans, see Latour 2005 and Gell 1998. See (Citroni 1989: 207–208) on the didactic character of books 13 and 14.
50. I have followed the suggestion of Leary 2001 and translated *sorba* as 'service berries', instead of Shackleton-Bailey's 'sorb apples'.
51. For more on these standards, see Masterson 2014.
52. Rimell (2008: 151–161) is eloquent on the *Xenia*'s surprising enforcement of restraint, constantly in tension with Saturnalian traditions of excess.
53. See Blake 2012 on the Elder Pliny's reliance on slaves as tools in composing his encyclopedia.
54. Here, Martial illustrates the entangled dependencies between humans and things described in Hodder 2012.
55. According to Leary 2001: 127–129, language of ruddiness (*rubens* and *Phoenico-*) may also suggest practitioners of oral sex. See Greenwood 1998: 245–246 and Grewing 1999: 269–271.
56. On Roman views of *fellatio* and *cunnilingus*, see Williams 2010: 218–224. Martial's fears would go on to be realized by speakers of eighteenth-century it-narratives, which recount the greed and sordid behaviour of their owners. See Blackwell 2007 for more on these.
57. Cf. 14.39, a lamp that promises not to share what happens in the bedroom.
58. Cf. 13.25; for insults, see 14.46, 56, 58, and 144.
59. Stroup 2006. The poet claims, somewhat hyperbolically, that 'You can send these couplets to your guests instead of a gift, if sesterces are as scarce with you as they are with me' (3.5–6).
60. On secondary agency, see Gell 1998: 16–23.
61. I am grateful to Daniel DeWispelare, Guoshi Li, Mika Natif, Anne-Sophie Noel and Michelle Wang for their comments and suggestions on earlier drafts of this chapter. The editors and anonymous reviewer also provided invaluable advice and bibliographic recommendations.

Chapter 26

1. Horkheimer and Adorno 2010: 15–21. On the *Dialektik* as one of the foundational texts of Posthuman thought, cf. Clarke and Rossini 2017: xxxi.
2. See Simondon 2012: 9–15, 334–340.
3. Gille 1980: 54–82.
4. Vitr. 9.8.2. Translation: F. Granger, Loeb Classical Library (1985).
5. Cic. *De orat.* 3.113. *Ingenium* is considered by Vitruvius as a necessary professional quality for an architect: *eum ingeniosum oportet esse et ad disciplinam docilem; neque enim ingenium sine disciplina aut disciplina sine ingenio perfectum artificem potest efficere* 'he must have both a natural gift and also readiness to learn, for neither talent without instruction nor instruction without talent can produce the perfect craftsman' (*De arch.* I.1.3). See Courrént 2011: 38–44.
6. Vitr. 9.8.3.
7. Cic. *Tusc.* 1.61.

8. Vitr. 1.2.2. *Inuentio* is one of the founding principles of architecture: *inuentio est quaestionum obscurarum explicatio ratioque nouae rei uigore mobili reperta* 'invention is the solution of obscure problems; the treatment of a new understanding disclosed by an active intelligence'.
9. The reader is incidentally warned about this from the first sentence of this introductory paragraph, which outlines the portrait of Ctesibius: *uim spiritus naturalis pneumaticasque res* inuenit 'he discovered the nature of wind-pressure and the principles of pneumatics' (Vitr. 9.8.2). The verb *inuenit* illustrates the capacities of *inuentio* of this mechanician.
10. Lucr. 5. 930–942.
11. Here, Vitruvius applies Aristotle's theory on the truth in art to architecture (See Courrént 2011: 214–216).
12. Vitr. 6.1.2. The most famous modification of the laws of nature to aesthetic pleasure of human beings is described as optical refinements that intervene in monumental architecture (cf. Vitr. 3.3.13).
13. Vitr. 2.1.7.
14. See, for example, Fragaki 2012 and Lebrèbe 2015. Many of these objects are described for example, in the first century CE, in the treatise of *Pneumatica* written by Hero of Alexandria.
15. Vitr. 9.8.4.
16. He concludes incidentally his explanations by: *quae sunt in horologium descriptionibus rationes et apparatus, ut sint* ad usum *expeditiores, quam apertissime potui perscripsi* 'the proportions and constructions used in making dials have now been described, as exactly as I could, with a view to their ready use' (Vitr. 9.8.15).
17. This association with physics and mechanics is in all likelihood from the school of Alexandria, and we also find an echo of this in the works of Hero of Alexandria (*Spir.* 1. praef.).
18. Vitr. 9.8.5.
19. The double meaning of the Greek word *parergon*, being at the same time 'secondary, accessory' and 'bizarre, extraordinary', tells us how much these machines are distanced from the necessary productions of nature that serve as their model.
20. Vitr. 9.8.9.
21. Vitr. 9.8.10.
22. Vitr. 9.8.13.
23. Vitr. 9.8.6–7 and 11–15.
24. Vitr. 9.8.4.
25. Greek mythology presents several examples of robots: animated tripods and handmaidens of Hephaestus (Hom. *Il.* 18. 372–377 and 417–420), Talos in Crete (Apollod. 1.9.6) and the statues of Daedalus (Pl. *Men.* 97e). However, Vitruvius never makes reference to accounts in Greek mythology: these machines did not exist in reality and their function was to show the omnipotence of the gods, capable of bestowing mechanical autonomy to beings other than human. From the third century BCE, human beings also possessed this capacity. The *automatopoetae machinae* are the materialization of this change in paradigm. We entered another system and there is thus no belief in god in the science of Vitruvius, just as in the science of engineers since the Alexandrian era. Their attitude to the natural laws and their conception of the progress of humanity find an echo much later, in *Esquisse d'un tableau historique des progrès de l'esprit humain* by Condorcet or in scientism of the nineteenth century, for example.
26. Vitr. 10. 1. 4.
27. D.H. *Comp.* 6.16.2–6. Translation: W. Rhys 1910.
28. It can therefore be said that Vitruvius clearly develops all the principles of modern mechanics as analysed in Mumford 1970, in particular in 'The Scientist as Lawgiver' (the machine as organism is the fruit of human nature) and 'The Machine Model Re-examined' (in particular the fact that

'analysis, dissociation, and reduction were the first steps toward creating complex technical structures': all three elements are actually the foundation of Graeco-Roman thought).

Chapter 27

1. The Greek follows the editions of West; all translations are ours.
2. Cf. Haraway 2016: 5; 1997: 210=1997a: 51, with Midson 2018: 5–9.
3. We are paraphrasing Haraway (2016: 59): 'certain dualisms [. . .] have all been systemic to the logics and practices of domination of women, people of color, nature, workers, animals'.
4. Cf. Holmes 2012: 24. A fragment of Aeschylus (fr. 369 Radt) describes Pandora as a 'mortal woman from a seed molded of clay'.
5. On Pandora's crown as a technical object, cf. Hes. *Th.* 578–581; for garments as technological extension of the body, cf. McLuhan 2001 [1964]: 129–133.
6. On Hephaestus' devices as *thauma*, cf. also e.g., Musti 2000, 401; Frontisi-Ducroux 2002: 469–470.
7. On *aude* as *human* voice, cf. also *DELG*, s.v. *aude* and Heath 2005: 54–55.
8. *Pace* West (*ad loc.*), we read ἴκελον as a neutral, and not as a masculine for a feminine; Loraux (1978: 75 n. 56) suggests: 'La réticence de West (*ad loc.*) à reconnaître en ἴκελον un neutre n'est pas fondée.' For Pandora as a technological artifact, cf. e.g., Loraux 1978: 47–48; Zeitlin 1996: 57; Francis 2009: 14.
9. For the verb τεύχω as meaning 'to produce by a technical expertise', cf. Hes. *Th.* 581; cf. also *Il.* 18. 483, 549, 574, 609. For τεύχω as synonymic of verbs describing craft skills – δαιδάλλω, ποικίλλω, 'to work with cunning craftship' (*Il.* 18. 479, 590); ποιέω, 'to do, to build' (*Il.* 478, 482, 490, 573, 587); κάμνω, 'to labour' (*Il.* 18. 614); τίθημι, 'to make, to work' (*Il.* 18. 541, 550, 561, 607) – cf. e.g., Morris 1992, 13.
10. On Pandora as an inanimate and animate statue, cf. Strauss-Clay 2003: 100–128; Wickkiser 2010: 557–564.
11. As Faraone (1992: 101–102) and Francis (2009: 14) observe, Pandora is never said to be the *prote gyne*. Pausanias is the first to describe Pandora as the 'first woman' (Paus. I.24.7).
12. Cf. Haraway 2016: 67, with Liveley 2006: 283.
13. For the expression 'divine engineering', cf. Musti 2000: 408: 'ingegneria divina'.
14. We differ from Berryman 2003: 351; 2007: 35–39; 2009: 24–28, according to whom Pandora lacks any artificiality, because her animation is a divine intervention. For a criticism of this position, cf. De Groot 2012: 703 and Mayor 2018: esp. 153–158.
15. Clarke 1973: 21.
16. For further similarities between Pandora and the golden maidens, cf. the section below.
17. On the maidens as robots, cf. e.g., Liveley 2006: 278–279; Devecka 2013: 56; Hunzinger 2015: 429, and for a comparison of these automata with the moving statues in *Ol.* 7, cf. Marinis in this volume.
18. As Vernant (1999: 64–65) observes, before Pandora humans are male beings but not men and women.
19. On the *anthropoi* who are not born nor die, as if they were born from the earth, cf. Vernant 1999: 64.
20. Cf. Mauss 1950; on the economy of symbolic exchange, cf. the pioneering works of Bataille 1949 and Baudrillard 1976.
21. Cf. also Hes. *Th.* 585, 602.
22. On *kalon kakon* as 'ambivalent evil', cf. Cantarella 1995 who defined the woman in Greek imagery as 'ambiguo malanno'.
23. On human time and Pandora's gender differentiation, cf. also Vernant 1999: 81. On the technologies of the gender connoted body and cyborg women, cf. Balsamo 1996.

24. On Prometheus' technical fire, cf. Vernant 1999: 77 and 2001: 36. We borrow the expression 'technosoma' from Gerolemou (forthcoming).
25. On the cyborg as blurring the dichotomy of nature vs. technology, cf. Kull 2001: 50; Wolfe 2009: 295; Nayar 2014: 11. On bodies as inherently technological, cf. Devecka in this volume.
26. Cf. Haraway 2003. On Haraway's notion of *natureculture*, cf. Mertlitsch's introductory chapter in this volume. Haraway's notion of *natureculture* has so far been used as a critical tool to read Greek literature only by Brooke Holmes (2015) in a paper on Scamander in the *Iliad.*
27. On kinship between humans and machines, cf. also Liveley in this volume.
28. Cf. Bostrom 2006, 2014.
29. On machine learning technology and the idea that machines will surpass human intelligence, cf. e.g., Shanahan 2015. However, as Winfield (2012: 15–16) points out: 'Machine learning – a branch of AI – has proven much harder than was expected in the early days of Artificial Intelligence. Thus, although there are plenty of examples of research robots that demonstrate simple learning, such as learning to find their way out of a maze, none has so far demonstrated what we might call problem-solving intelligence'. On the machines' supposed capacity to solve problems, cf. e.g., also the seminal paper of Hubert and Stuart Dreyfus 2009 [1986] and Winograd 1991: 204–207. On the computer's inaptitude to sort out complexity, specifically on the so-called 'halting problem' and the 'acceptance problem' and the existence of effective methods of decidability, cf. Bernhardt 2017: chs. 2 and 7. On the radical difference between human and machinic cognition, cf. Chesi and Spiegel in this volume.
30. Cf. Brooks 2017.
31. On (ancient) narratives as providing an epistemological frame to interpret the world in which we (can) live, cf. Prince 1990: 1, with Liveley in this volume; Midson 2018: 12–13.

Chapter 28

1. I want to register my gratitude to the anonymous referee, Giulia Maria Chesi, Francesca Spiegel and Claudia Zatta for offering valuable feedback on earlier drafts of this paper. I also wish to thank Michael Kardamitsis and Julia Shear for sharing with me their views on issues pertaining to this study.
2. On the date, however, see now Kurke 2016: 15.
3. Translations of Pindaric passages are from Race 1997a/b, with modifications. In this case, for δαέντι . . . τελέθει I have provided my own rendering.
4. Race's translation ('Their streets bore') is to a certain degree ambiguous, whereas Verity 2007 is clearly following the second interpretation: 'In their streets stood statues . . .'
5. So O'Sullivan 2005: 101; similarly Gentili et al. 2013: 490–491. This interpretation actually harks back to the ancient Scholia (95a, Drachmann vol. 1, p. 220–221).
6. See comments by Devecka 2013: 58–59; Coray et al. 2016: 153–155.
7. 95a, Drachmann vol. 1, 220–221.
8. Translation by Murray and Wyatt 1999.
9. Note the emphasis created by the profusion of long vowels in line 418. With analogous ekphrastic power are recounted the figures wrought on the shield of Achilles, further in *Iliad* 18 (483–608); among a large number of studies, see Scully 2003; Barolsky 2009, esp. 18–23; Francis 2009; Palmisciano 2009.
10. See esp. Braidotti 2013: 89–101.
11. On which see Morris 1992: 9–11; Francis 2009: 9; Coray et al. 2016: 171–173. An intermediate case between the metal maidens and the tripods is exemplified by the animated gold and silver hounds guarding the palace of Alcinous in *Od.* 7.91–94; see Devecka 2013: 56 and Faraone 1987.

12. On the polysemy of φρένες in Homer, see Darcus Sullivan 1979: 159–166.

13. For the whole description: Hes. *W&D* 59–89, *Theog.* 570–589; with Faraone 1992: 101–104; Berryman 2003: 352; Francis 2009: 13–15; Devecka 2013: 57. On the connection with the *Iliad*, see Edwards 1991: 195–196; Coray et al. 2016: 172–173.

14. Berryman 2003: 352–353; 2009: 24–29; cf. ead. 2007 on the 'imitation of life' in ancient Greek philosophy.

15. See analysis by Chesi and Sclavi in this volume.

16. *Pace* Devecka 2013: 56, who follows Faraone 1987. On this point, see also Philipp 1968: 52.

17. On the notion of 'transversality' within a posthumanist framework, see Braidotti 2013: esp. 93–97.

18. See analysis by Weiss 2016: 243–249, esp. 244; in a similar key, discussion by Power 2011. More generally on this passage see Rutherford 2001: 216–231. On the issue of artificiality as a manner of conceiving a human in Classical literature, see now the discussion of Sappho's 'cyborg Helen' in Whitmarsh 2018.

19. Cf. Hes. *W&D* 108, with Gerber 1999: 44 n. 5.

20. For the former identification, see Gerber 1999: 45; Henry 2005: 55–56; Salviat 2007b: 174; for the latter, Santamaría Álvarez (2008: 1164–1165) who discerns here a fundamental doctrine of Orphism.

21. See Salviat 2007b: 174–175 and passim; Šćepanović 2016: 34–35.

22. Possibly from a *threnos*; see Cannatà Fera 1990: 183–185.

23. See analytical commentary by Cannatà Fera 1990: 183–194, esp. 192–193 and also Lloyd-Jones 1990: 94–95; Salviat 2007a: 59–60; Currie 2005: 33–35; Santamaría Álvarez 2008: 1166; Bernabé 2011: esp. 98–100, 158–159, 258–259; Riedweg 2011: 233–234.

24. As in fr. 133. 9 (from the *threnoi*). See esp. analysis by Clarke 1999: 307–312; also Reale 1999: 129–136; Santamaría Álvarez 2008: 1166 and *passim* – both pointing to the Orphic character of this belief.

25. A forceful attempt to overcome this habitus is the 'Friendly Artificial Intelligence' theory which refuses to assign to machines prejudices or preoccupations typical of human beings; see esp. Yudkowsky 2008 and 2011; *contra* Keiper and Schulman 2011. On the nascent discipline of roboethics, see Campa 2015: 77–108.

26. For a comprehensive study of gnomic speech in Pindar, see Boeke 2007: 11–101.

27. *Pace* Young (1987: esp. 155–156) who attributes to ἄδολος the much less widely attested sense of 'pure, natural'; see also Young 1968: 86. Cf. Hooker 1985: 66.

28. So Willcock 1995: 127, with earlier bibliography supporting this reading; now Briand 2014: 99.

29. See esp. Farnell 1932: 55; Ferrari 1998: 139; Gentili et al. 2013: 492. Arguing against this reading, Willcock (1995: 127) claims that 'μέγας, μείζων are commonly predicative' in Pindar; however, the examples he supplies (*O.* 1.113, *P.* 1.187, *P.* 3.107) demonstrate an unambiguous syntactic structure, whereas in *O.* 7.53 this is not the case.

30. Cf. *Hom Hymn Ap.* 135–136, with Verdenius 1987: 62.

31. We must be dealing with the same shower of gold, as before; see Willcock 1995: 122.

32. See Barkhuizen 1968; Willcock 1995: 120; Cairns 2005a: 73–76; Šćepanović 2016: 31.

33. O'Sullivan 2005: esp. 100–103.

34. Rumpel 1883 s.v.: 'fraudis expers'; Slater 1969 s.v.: 'without artifice'.

35. Earlier scholars posited a contrast between the Heliadae and the Telchines, known wizards of Rhodes in mythical times; see esp. Farnell 1932: 55; Bowra 1964: 339; with comments by Young 1987: 153–154. Another thought is that Pindar wished to substitute the Heliadae for the Telchines: so Verdenius 1987: 57, 71–72; Cairns 2005a: 83–84. However, the major obstacle for these readings is that the Telchines are mentioned in rather late sources (see *DNO* s.v. 'Telchines', n. 40, 44–45, 49), the only exception being an obscure fragment of Stesichorus (fr. 260 *PMGF*).

36. See *Od*. 8. 494; cf. the net in which Hephaestus catches Ares, *Od*. 8.276; also the robe of Penelope, *Od*.19.137. Cf. LSJ s.v. δόλος.

37. *Iliad* 18.591–594; with Morris 1992: 12–15; cf. ibid. 3–35 on δαίδαλον and its cognates in Homer. On these terms in Pindar, see instances in Slater 1969: 113–114 and discussion by Morris 1992: 43–52. Generally, for the testimonies on Daedalus, see *DNO* s.v. 'Dädalus'; also Frontisi-Ducroux 1975: 95–117; Kassel 1983.

38. See *DNO* ibid. ns. 120–129; note particularly Plato's ironic reference (*Meno* 97d) to the Daedalic statues that 'run away and escape if they haven't been tied down, but stay with one if they have been'.

39. For an up-to-date semiotic analysis of the poetic creation of κλέος in the odes, see Felson and Parmentier 2015.

40. Among a large bibliography, see Gundert 1935: esp. 11–29; Nagy 1990: 146–214 and passim; Thomas 2007; also the more unconventional approach by Currie 2005: 71–84, encompassing the question of a real prospect of heroization.

41. Thus, we can also account for the particle δέ in line 53, sometimes left untranslated, since it follows another δέ just before (ἦν δὲ κλέος βαθύ. δαέντι δέ . . .). In fact, it makes perfect sense since it introduces an emphatic gnomic addendum.

42. Fr. 166.1: when the Centaurs 'come to know' wine.

43. On these lines, see Heiny 1994: esp. 63–66.

44. See Young 1968: 93–95; Felson Rubin 1980a; also ead. 1980b on its connection with the opening of the ode. For a positioning of this prayer within the wider context of Pindar's invocations, see Bremer 2008: esp. 7–12.

45. Similar is the rendering by Verity 2007: 'has learnt well the lesson'.

46. See further analysis (and passages) in Marinis 2008: 76–77, 219–226. On the imagery of the road in Pindar, see also Becker 1937: 50–100; Verdenius 1987: 33, 84–85.

47. Effectively a strand of thought that links the different parts of the poem; see analysis by Darcus Sullivan 1982; more generally on φρένες in Pindar and Bacchylides, see also Darcus Sullivan 1979: 166–172 and 1989.

48. See Pratt 1993: 127–129; Marinis 2008: 191–192; Park 2013: 32–33.

49. The moral aspect of σοφία is equally discernible in an eloquent passage of *Olympian* 9; the poet, having mentioned and narrated summarily the mythical story about the fight between Herakles and Poseidon in Pylos, refrains from continuing his narrative, urging himself to 'cast that story away' (35–36), 'for reviling the gods / is a hateful skill, and boasting inappropriately / sounds a note of madness' (37–38). See Gladigow 1965: 51–52; Gerber 2002: 40–41; Boeke 2007: 44–45; Marinis 2008: 201–205; Pavlou 2008: 545–554.

50. See also Gallet 1990: 299–304. What cannot be accepted is that the gnomic utterance refers *solely* to the poet, as Ruck (1968: 129–132) argues, positing a contrast between Pindar and Homer, whereby Pindar's account of the Heliadae is more truthful than the one proffered by Homer in the *Iliad*.

51. On Pindar's poetic *persona*, see the illuminating discussion in Athanassaki 2012.

52. See Brillante 2013–2014: 38–39 and Marinis 2018: 151–153, with further bibliography.

53. Among a large array of scholarly discussions, see Steiner 2001: 251–281; Ford 2002: 115–123; O'Sullivan 2003; 2005: 97–99; Smith 2007; Thomas 2007; Pavlou 2010; Calame 2012: 314–315; Fearn 2017: 16–74.

54. Analysis by Pavlou 2010: esp. 14–15.

55. See esp. Kirichenko 2016c: 19–24; Fearn 2017: 24.

56. Similar reflections in Felson Rubin 1980a: 75, who aptly asserts that if the '[Heliadae's] sculpture is viewed as potent and vital and lifelike, then Pindar's odes may be viewed in the same way'.

57. On those lines, see also Fearn 2017: 49–50.

58. Schol. ad *Ol.* 7, inscr., Drachmann vol. 1, p. 195.
59. See Kurke 2016: esp. 24.
60. See esp. Badmington 2003; Wolfe 2009; Ferrando 2013; 2016; Cudworth and Hobden 2018.
61. The philosophical discussion of origins is itself eloquent. It suffices to invoke here Presocratic thought and, more specifically, the conception of a common physical origin of the multiple forms of life – including humans, animals and plants: see now Zatta 2017: esp. 26–44.
62. See esp. Cudworth and Hobden 2018: 117–135.

Chapter 29

1. See e.g., Hayles 1999: esp. 283–291 ('What Does it Mean to be Posthuman?'). Cf. Braidotti 2013: 91–99 ('The Posthuman as Becoming-machine'); Roden 2015: 150–165 ('New Substantivism: A Theory of Technology').
2. Pind. *P.* 6.10–14; Hor. *c.* 3.30.1–5; Ov. *Met.* 15.871–872.
3. Hunter 2004: 76; Brisson 2006: 245.
4. Stafford 2013.
5. Pl. *Smp.* 198c1–5. See Hunter 2004: 74–75; Belfiore 2012: 137–139.
6. See also Pl. *Crt.* 398c5–e5, where ἔρως and ἐρωτᾶν are etymologically linked to each other.
7. Cf. Gonzalez 1998: 273.
8. See esp. Pl. *Smp.* 206c1–e3 and 212a1–7. On the image of the 'pregnant philosopher' in the *Symposium* and in Plato in general, esp. in the *Theaetetus* (148e–151d), see Hobbs 2006, with references. For the concept of philosophical midwifery ('maieutics') in the *Theaetetus*, see Sedley 2004.
9. On the seduction scene, see Sheffield 2006: 201–206; Destrée 2012: 194–201.
10. Cf. Tarnopolsky 2010: 60.
11. Dover 1980: 166. See also North 1994; Sheffield 2006: 189–191; Belfiore 2012: 161–168. On reflections on the 'fullness' and 'emptiness' of statues in Greek culture, see Steiner 2001: 120–134, esp. 132–134, on this passage. See also Steiner 1996. Cf. Destrée 2012: 202–204. On Aristophanes' portrayal of Socrates in the *Clouds* as the major influence on Plato's image of Socrates as Silenus, see Capra 2018.
12. On Alcibiades in the *Symposium* as a satyr, see Sheffield 2006: 185–186, with references.
13. On the similarity between Alcibiades' image of the satyric/divine Socrates and the image of Eros in Diotima's speech, see Belfiore 2012: 187–196.
14. Agathon concludes his speech with an explosion of Gorgianic *homoeoteleuta*, in which pairs of opposites not only congeal into semantic tautologies but also phonetically echo each other (φιλόδωρος εὐμενείας, ἄδωρος δυσμενείας ... ζηλωτὸς ἀμοίροις, κτητὸς εὐμοίροις ... ἐπιμελὴς ἀγαθῶν, ἀμελὴς κακῶν, κτλ.). Agathon constructs what looks like a perfectly self-contained world consisting of pretty visual surfaces and of words that refer only to other words rather than to extra-textual reality. See Hunter 2004: 73–75.
15. Cf. Cotton 2014: 101–106.
16. For a detailed analysis of the elusive connotations of Plato's φάρμακον, see Derrida 1989. See also Ferrari 1987: 204–232; Werner 2012: 181–235.
17. Many scholars regard the rejection of writing in the Theuth myth as expressing Plato's awareness of the limits of his own writing. See e.g., Rutherford 1995: 268–271; Morgan 2000: 239–241; Werner 2012: 209–215. Cf. Ferrari 1987: 204–232. See also Derrida 1989: 344–352, for an analysis of both writing and painting in the *Phaedrus* as instances of mimesis.
18. Pl. *Phdr.* 230e6–234c5. Ferrari 1987: 50–51; Belfiore 2012: 211–215.

19. For Socrates' comments on the speech's repetitiveness, see Pl. *Phdr.* 262a4–e1. On the subtlety of the way in which Plato frames Lysias' speech, see Ferrari 1987: 45–59.

20. Predictably, the scholarship on the *Phaedrus* is dominated by the question of the dialogue's unity. See e.g., Griswold 1986; Ferrari 1987; Benardete 1991: 103–193; Belfiore 2012: 211–246; Werner 2012.

21. Cf. Derrida 1989: 352–368. In fact, Socrates presents a hierarchy of *three* different kinds of writing: 1) the frivolous, Adonis-garden-like, writing that leaves no trace on the soul (276b1–8, cf. Reitzammer 2016: 90–117), 2) the no-less playful written 'tales (cf. 276e3 μυθολογοῦντα) about justice and other things' – 'gardens of letters' (276d1 τοὺς μὲν ἐν γράμμασι κήπους) 'producing a tender growth' in the soul (276d5 φυομένους ἁπαλούς); and 3) the by far superior discourse informed by dialectic, which can be sowed, take root and bear fruit in the soul (Socrates does not specify whether this discourse is oral or written, but the discussion of writing urges one to take it that it can be both): Pl. *Phdr.* 276e4–277a4; 277e5–278b4.

22. This impression is strengthened by the fact that this passage follows upon Phaedrus' request that Socrates 'remind' him (277b4 ὑπόμνησον) of the agreement reached in the previous discussion. Cf. White 1993, 266.

23. Cf. Pl. *Men.* 81e4, *Phd.* 72e5–6, *Phdr.* 249c1–4. On the recollection of the Forms in the *Phaedrus*, see Trabattoni 2012: 313–314; Werner 2012: 102–107.

24. Cf. Burger 1980: 108–109; Griswold 1986: 219–226; White 1993: 266–268; Clay 2000: 106–115; Cotton 2014: 3–31. For the controversy surrounding Plato's self-referentiality in the *Phaedrus* (a critique of writing located within a written text), see Werner 2012: 209–215, with copious references.

25. For a detailed discussion of the cicada myth and its interpretations in previous scholarship, see Werner 2012: 133–152.

26. Brink 1971: 85; Frischer 1991: 77–85; Oliensis 1998: 199; Schwindt 2014.

27. On the Peripatetic background of the ostensible teachings of the *AP* (via Neoptolemus of Paros), see Brink 1971: 79–150. Cf. esp. Arist. *Poet.* 1450b20–1451a15, where the unity of a dramatic plot is compared to the organic unity of an animal's body: Heath 1989: 38–55; Purves 2010: 24–64. See also Frischer 1991: 68–85; Armstrong 1993: 226–230; Citroni 2009.

28. Cf. Brink 1971: 468–523.

29. Frischer 1991: 61–68.

30. Frischer 1991: 59–85.

31. Armstrong 1993: 211–214; Oliensis 1998: 221–223.

32. Frischer 1991: 66–68.

33. See Armstrong 1993: 215–216.

34. Hor. *AP* 466–476. Brink 1971: 421–422; Armstrong 1993: 217–219; Oliensis 1998: 215–223.

35. Oliensis 1998: 217. Cf. Laird 2007: 137.

36. Hor. *epist.* 2.1.219–225. In addition, the mad poet resembles the antiheroes of *Satires* 1, who recite poetry with no regard for the audience's ennui, see Oliensis 1998: 218–221.

37. On Horace in *Satires* 1 as a sympotic entertainer, see Turpin 1998; Freudenburg 2001: 22–23. For bears as an integral part of Roman entertainment, see e.g., Hor. *epist.* 2.1.185–186.

38. Oliensis 1998: 220.

39. Besides, the bear–leech hybrid as a grotesque symbol of immortality evokes Horace's – arguably no less grotesque – image of immortality in *Odes* 2.20, the poet transforming himself into a swan and thus becoming *biformis* (*c.* 2.20.2). Cf. Citroni 2009: 23–24.

40. See Kirichenko 2018.

41. Kirichenko 2016c.

42. Kirichenko 2016b.

Chapter 30

1. Haraway 1991: 150; according to Haraway, as posthumans we 'are all chimeras, theorized and fabricated hybrids of machine and organism'.
2. Haraway 1991: 154.
3. See O'Connell 2018 on the ontological distinctions between posthuman and transhuman.
4. Braidotti 2013: 89.
5. Haraway 2016a. See also Haraway (2000: 105–106) for the view that: 'The cyborg story raises questions about our kin among the machines – our kin within the domain of communication.'
6. https://www.theguardian.com/technology/2015/dec/13/sex-love-and-robots-the-end-of-intimacy (accessed 9 October 2018).
7. http://www.vanityfair.com/culture/2015/04/sexbots-realdoll-sex-toys (accessed 9 October 2018).
8. http://www.truecompanion.com/shop/roxxxy-truecompanion-sex-robot/roxxxy/ (accessed 9 October 2018).
9. See Owsianik 2017; Kleeman 2017.
10. Haraway 1991: 154.
11. Levy 2007: 304.
12. https://www.theguardian.com/technology/2009/sep/16/sex-robots-david-levy-loebner (accessed 9 October 2018).
13. http://www.vanityfair.com/culture/2015/04/sexbots-realdoll-sex-toys (accessed 9 October 2018).
14. Di Nucci, 2017. On this debate see also Coeckelbergh 2010 and 2016; Di Nucci, 2011; Levy and Loebner 2007; Levy 2012; Whitby 2012; Danaher 2014.
15. Yeoman and Mars 2012: 365. See also Kloer 2010; Levy 2012 and Levy and Loebner 2007 on the prospect of 'Robot prostitutes as alternatives to human sex workers'.
16. Cox-George and Bewley 2018, 161.
17. https://www.edge.org/response-detail/25420 (accessed 9 October 2018).
18. https://campaignagainstsexrobots.org/about/ (accessed 9 October 2018). See also Richardson 2015.
19. https://www.theguardian.com/technology/2015/dec/13/sex-love-and-robots-the-end-of-intimacy (accessed 9 October 2018).
20. Richardson 2015: 292.
21. In response to a report published in 2017 by the Foundation for Responsible Robotics, Richardson has again maintained that 'Sex robots are just another type of pornography' and as such will only serve to '*increase* social isolation' (BBC 5 July 2017): https://www.bbc.co.uk/news/technology-40428976 (accessed 9 October 2018).
22. See Danaher 2017; Coeckelbergh 2016; Sparrow 2015; Leveringhaus 2016; Müller 2016.
23. http://www.gold.ac.uk/news/kate-devlin-the-conversation-sex-robots/ (accessed 9 October 2018). See also Devlin 2018. TV series such as *Humans* and *Westworld*, alongside computer games such as *Detroit: Become Human*, in which intimate human–robot interactions are explored, are also (re) shaping popular discourse on this subject.
24. http://www.gold.ac.uk/news/kate-devlin-the-conversation-sex-robots/ (accessed 9 October 2018).
25. http://www.gold.ac.uk/news/kate-devlin-the-conversation-sex-robots/ (accessed 9 October 2018).
26. Levy 2007: 177.
27. Levy 2007.
28. Sullins 2012: 398. See also Danaher (2017: 3): 'the idea of the sex doll has a much longer history – one that can be traced back to the myth of Pygmalion'.

29. Wennerscheid 2018: 37.

30. Hammond 2018: 195. See also James 2011 for examples of the reception of Ovid's Pygmalion in films such as Ridley Scott's 1982 *Bladerunner*, Steve de Jarnett's 1988 *Cherry 2000*, Craig Gillespie's 2007 *Lars and the Real Girl*.

31. https://www.theguardian.com/tv-and-radio/2017/nov/25/sex-robots-are-coming-seedy-sordid-sad (accessed 9 October 2018).

32. Levy 2007: 304.

33. The women of Thrace, offended by Orpheus' misogyny, literally rip him to pieces (*Met.*11.1–84). On Ovid's (un)sympathetic representation of Orpheus, see Makowski 1996.

34. *Met.* 10.243–258. All translations are my own. On the Propoetides as prostitutes, see Liveley 1999.

35. See Liveley 1999. For the idea that human–sex robot relations first reflect and then reinforce unethical attitudes and behaviours towards real women, see also Richardson 2015: 292.

36. See Sharrock 1991a and 1991b: 173–175. Sharrock draws attention to the competing discourses of the text which construct the statue as both a religious icon or cult figure and as a whore. She focuses upon the suggestions of hierogamy in an earlier version of the myth of Pygmalion, narrated by the third-century BCE author Philostephanus, in which Pygmalion is not an artist but a Cretan king who falls in love with a cult image of the goddess Aphrodite, and in Ovid's narrative analyses the erotic associations of the statue's apparent desire 'to be moved' (*Met.* 10.251 – *moueri*) in the context of Lucretius' condemnation of such behaviour in women as the action of prostitutes (*DRN* 4.1268–1277).

37. *Met.* 10.274–276.

38. As Griffin (1981: 45) describes, distinctions between the 'doll' and the prostitute are easily elided. She suggests that 'prostitutes are paid not only to render physical pleasure but to play roles – to, in fact, impersonate women and to create the illusion that they will willingly serve, even passionately desire, the man who buys them'. Griffin's description of the pornographic sex doll as a 'copy of a woman, made to replace a woman, and to give a man pleasure without the discomfort of female presence' (1981: 40) could be readily applied to Pygmalion's statue – and to the twenty-first-century sex robot.

39. Pygmalion's statue is unnamed in the classical tradition. It is Rousseau who first names the statue 'Galathée' (Galatea) in his 1762 play, *Pygmalion*.

40. Sharrock 1991b: 174. For an alternative reading, see Liveley 1999.

41. Fränkel 1945: 93. Cf. Levy 2007: 304. On Pygmalion's fantasy, see also Elsner 1991.

42. Several readings highlight the language of procreation that is used to describe Pygmalion's 'relationship' with his statue: *nasci, concepit, plenissima, plenus.* See Leach 1974 and Sharrock 1991b: 179. In this context, the reference to *alma Venus* in the introduction to the story of the Propoetides and Pygmalion (*Met.*10.230) is particularly significant and suggests that the relationship between Pygmalion and Venus, who both contribute to the (re)production of Pygmalion's 'Eburna', is modelled on that of a mother and father.

43. See Janan 1988.

44. See also Aeschylus *Frag.* 204; Sophocles *Pandora*; Pausanias 1.24.7; Hyginus *Fabulae* 142.

45. Cf. Sharrock (1991b: 173–175), where she draws a number of convincing parallels between Hephaestus' Pandora and Pygmalion's Eburna. We might add to this the suggestive linguistic parallel between the name of Pandora's mythical daughter (Pyrrha) – according to Apollodorus 1.46, Hyginus *Fabulae* 142 and Strabo 9.5.23 – and the name Ovid ascribes to Eburna's/Pygmalion's great-grand-daughter (Myrrha).

46. A number of Greek vase paintings represent Pandora as a statue, and – with obvious parallels in popular representations of twenty-first-century sexbots – she is also found depicted in the company of ithyphallic Satyrs (whose symbolic function in the extant scenes from ancient Satyr plays often appears to have been as the astonished/excited recipients of 'technological' marvels, e.g., fire, musical

instruments and other miraculous inventions – among which Pandora is clearly included). See Seaford 1984 and Voelke 2001.

47. Haraway 2016a: 43.

48. Haraway 2016a: 31. See also Haraway (2016: 40): 'we *must* change the story; the story *must* change' (emphasis in the original).

49. Kathleen Richardson's 2015 *Anthropology of Robots and AI* forwards the same fundamental argument. See Richardson 2015, 1 for the thesis that 'Whether you look to the past of robots or the present . . . we take our cultural and technological models of robots from fictions . . . Multiple tides flow from fictions to living practices of technoscience.'

50. Prince 1990: 1, emphasis in the original.

51. *Poetics* 4.1448b 1–8.

52. Bruner 1991: 121.

Conclusions

1. Goldhill 2002, 2011. Bibliography here has been kept to a minimum for reasons of space.
2. Leonard 2005.
3. Halperin 1990, 2012; Nagy 1999 [1979].
4. Kristeva 1980.
5. E.g., de Beauvoir 1949.
6. Iconically, Strathern 1988.
7. Seminally, Brown 1988.
8. Pagden 1983.
9. Redfield 1994 [1975].
10. Foucault 1966.
11. Descola 2014 [2005].
12. Kneebone 2020.
13. Hulme 2009.
14. Maines 1999.
15. Daston and Vidal (eds.) 2004.
16. Roth 1969.

BIBLIOGRAPHY

Abbot, J. C. 2018. 'ARMA VIRUMQUE'. *CJ* 108: 37–63.

Acton, P. 2014. *Poiesis: Manufacturing in Classical Athens*. Oxford.

Ades, D. and Baker, S. (eds). 2006. *Undercover Surrealism: Georges Bataille and DOCUMENTS*. Cambridge, MA.

Affergan, F. et al. (eds). 2003. *Figures de l'humain. Les représentations de l'anthropologie*. Paris.

Agamben, G. 2002. *L'aperto. L'uomo e l'animale*. Turin. = 2004. *The Open. Man and animal*. Trans. K. Attell. Stanford.

Agamben, G. 2003. *Stato di eccezione*. Turin.

Agamben, G. 2005. *Profanazioni*. Rome.

Ahmed, S. 2004. *The Cultural Politics of the Emotions*. New York.

Albini, U. 1975. 'La funzione di Io nel *Prometeo*'. *PP* 30: 278–284.

Alexandridis, A., Wild, M. and Winkler-Horaček, L. (eds) 2008. *Mensch und Tier in der Antike. Grenzziehung und Grenzüberschreitung*. Wiesbaden.

Alford, C. F. 2004. 'Levinas and Political Theory'. *Political Theory* 32: 146–171.

Allan, W. 2000. *The* Andromache *and Euripidean Tragedy*. Oxford.

Allan, W. 2014. 'The Body in Mind: Medical Imagery in Sophocles'. *Hermes* 142: 260–278.

Allen-Hornblower, E. 2013. 'Sounds and Suffering in Sophocles' *Philoctetes* and Gide's *Philoctète*'. *SIFC* 11: 5-41.

Allen-Hornblower, E. 2016. 'Moral Disgust in Sophocles' *Philoctetes*'. In D. Lateiner and D. Spatharas (eds). 69–86.

Althusser, L. 1964. 'Marxisme et Humanisme'. *Cahiers de l'I.S.E.A.* 20. 109–133.

Althusser, L. 1969. *For Marx*, trans. B. Brewster. New York.

Anders, G. 1980 [1956]. *Die Antiquiertheit des Menschen. Über die Zerstörung des Lebens im Zeitalter der dritten industriellen Revolution*. Munich.

Anderson, J. K. 1985. *Hunting in the Ancient World*. Berkeley.

Anderson, W. S. 1968. 'Pastor Aeneas: On Pastoral Themes in the *Aeneid*'. *TAPA* 99: 1–17.

Appadurai, A. (ed.) 1988. *The Social Life of Things: Commodities in Cultural Perspective*. Cambridge.

Appel, J. M. 2010. 'Sex Rights for the Disabled?' *JME* 36: 152–154.

Argoud, G. (ed.). 1994. *Science et vie intellectuelle à Alexandrie*. Saint-Etienne.

Aristotle, trans. W. S. Hett. 1936. *Minor Works. On Colours. On Things Heard. Physiognomics. On Plants. On Marvellous Things Heard. Mechanical Problems. On Indivisible Lines. The Situations and Names of Winds. On Melissus, Xenophanes, Gorgias*. Cambridge, MA.

Aristotle, trans. D. M. Balme. 1991. History of Animals, *Vol. III*. In *Aristotle in 23 Volumes, Vol. XI*. Cambridge, MA.

Armisen-Marchetti, M. 1989. *Sapientiae facies: étude sur les images de Sénèque*. Paris.

Armisen-Marchetti, M. 2004. 'La signification de l'humour dans les Lettres à Lucilius de Sénèque'. In L. Nadjo and E. Gavoille (eds.), *Epistulae Antiquae III. Louvain*. 311–322.

Armstrong, D. 1993. 'The Addressees of the *Ars Poetica*'. *MD* 31: 185–230.

Arnim, H. von. (1903–1924). *Stoicorum veterum fragmenta collegit Ioannes ab Arnim. 4 vols*. Leipzig.

Arrowsmith, W. A. 1973. 'Aristophanes' *Birds*: The Fantasy Politics of Eros'. *Arion* 1: 119–167.

Åsberg, C. 2010. 'Enter Cyborg: Tracing the Historiography and Ontological Turn of Feminist Technoscience Studies'. *International Journal of Feminist Technoscience* 1: 1–25.

Åsberg, C. and Lum, J. (2010). 'Picturizing the Scattered Ontologies of Alzheimer's Disease: Towards a Materialist Feminist Approach to Visual Technoscience Studies'. *European Journal of Women's Studies* 17: 323–345.

Asper, M. 2017. 'Machines on Paper. From Words to Acts in Ancient Mechanics'. In M. Formisano and P. van der Eijk (eds.), *Knowledge, Text and Practice in Ancient Technical Writing*. Cambridge. 27–52.

Athanassaki, L. 2012. 'Recreating the Emotional Experience of Contest and Victory Celebrations: Spectators and Celebrants in Pindar's *Epinicians*'. In X. Riu and J. Pòrtulas (eds.), *Approaches to Archaic Greek Poetry*. Messina. 173–219.

Atterton, P. and Calarco, M. (eds.) 2004. *Animal Philosophy: Ethics and Identity*. London.

Auerbach, E. 1953 [1946]. *'Odysseus' Scar'*. In E. Auerbach, *Mimesis. The Representation of Reality in Western Literature*. Trans. W. Trask. Princeton. 3–23.

Austin, C. (ed.). 1968. *Nova fragmenta euripidea in papyris reperta*. Berlin.

Austin, N. 1966. 'The Function of Digressions in the *Iliad*'. *GRBS* 7: 295–312.

Aymard, J. 1951. *Essai sur les chasses romaines*. Paris.

Babich, B. 2013. 'O, Superman! Or Being Towards Transhumanism: Martin Heidegger, Günther Anders, and Media Aesthetics'. *Divinatio* 36: 83–99.

Badmington, N. 2003. 'Theorizing Posthumanism'. *Cultural Critique* 53: 10–27.

Badmington, N. 2004. *Alien Chic: Posthumanism and the Other Within*. London.

Baglioni, I. 2010. 'L'aspetto acosmico e primordiale di Typhon nella *Teogonia*'. *MJSS* 1: 26–47.

Baier, T. 2001. *Valerius Flaccus,* Argonautica *Buch VI. Einleitung und Kommentar*. Munich.

Bal, M. and Lewin, J. E. 1983. 'The Narrating and the Focalizing. A Theory of the Agents in Narrative'. *Narratology* 17: 234–269.

Ballabriga, A. 1990. 'Le dernier adversaire de Zeus: le mythe de Typhon grecque archaïque'. *RHR* 207: 3–30.

Balsamo, A. 1996. *Technologies of the Gendered Body. Reading Cyborg Women*. Durham/London.

Bammé, A., Berger, W. and Kotzmann, E. 2012. 'Vom System zum Netzwerk: Perspektiven eines Paradigmenwechsels in den Sozialwissenschaften'. In H. Greif and M. Werner (eds), *Vernetzung als soziales und technisches Paradigma*. Wiesbaden. 29–46.

Barad, K. 2003. 'Posthumanist Performativity: Toward an Understanding of How Matter Comes to Matter'. *Signs* 28: 801–831.

Barad, K. 2007. *Meeting the Universe Halfway: Quantum Physics and the Entanglement of Matter and Meaning*. Durham and London.

Barceló, P. A. 1993. *Basileia, Monarchia, Tyrannis: Untersuchungen zu Entwicklung und Beurteilung von Alleinherrschaft im vorhellenistischen Griechenland*. Stuttgart.

Barcz, A. 2015. 'Posthumanism and Its Animal Voices in Literature'. *Teksty Drugie*. Special Issue English Edition. Vol. 1: The Humanities and Posthumanism. 248–269.

Barich, M. 2014. 'Poet and Readers. Reflections on the Verbal and Narrative Art of Valerius Flaccus' *Argonautica*'. In M. Heerink and G. Manuwald (eds.). 29–48.

Barker, A. 1989. *Greek Musical Writings. Vol. 2: Harmonic and Acoustic Theory*. Cambridge.

Barker, A. 2007. *The Science of Harmonics in Classical Greece*. Cambridge.

Barker, E. 2006. 'Paging the Oracle: Interpretation, Identity and Performance in Herodotus' History'. *G&R* 53: 1–28.

Barkhuizen, J. H. 1968. 'Structural Patterns in Pindar's Seventh *Olympian*'. *Acta Classica* 11: 25–37.

Barnouw, J. 2004. *Odysseus, Hero of Practical Intelligence. Deliberation and Signs in Homer's* Odyssey. Lanham.

Barolsky, P. 2009. 'Homer and the Poetic Origins of Art History'. *Arion* 16: 13–44.

Baron, D. 2009. *La chair mutante. Fabrique d'un posthumain*. Paris.

Barrett A. A. 1990. *Caligula: The Corruption of Power*. New Haven, CT.

Barringer, J. M. (2002). *The Hunt in Ancient Greece*. Baltimore.

Barthes, R. 1973. *Le plaisir du texte*. France.

Barthes, R. 1978. *A Lover's Discourse*, trans. R. Howard. New York.

Bartsch, S. 1997. *Ideology in Cold Blood: A Reading of Lucan's* Civil War. Cambridge, MA.

Bartsch, S. 1998. 'Ars and the Man: The Politics of Art in Virgil's *Aeneid*'. *CP* 93: 322–342.

Bartsch, S. 2009. 'Senecan Metaphor and Stoic Self-Instruction'. In S. Bartsch and D. Wray (eds.), *Seneca and the Self*. Cambridge. 190–217.

Bassi, D. 1930. 'L'espressione del dolore fisico in Sofocle'. *Dioniso* 2: 16–22.

Bassi, K. 2018. 'Morbid Materialism. The Matter of The Corpse in Euripides' *Alcestis*'. In M. Telò and M. Mueller (eds.). 17–34.

Bataille, G. 1949. *La part maudite*. Paris.

Bateson, G. 2000 [1972]. *Steps to an Ecology of Mind*. Chicago/London.

Battezzato, L. 1999–2000. 'Dorian Dress in Greek Tragedy', *ICS* 24/25, Euripides and Tragic Theatre in the Late Fifth Century: 343-362.

Baudrillard, J. 1976. *L'échange symbolique et la mort*. Paris.

Baudrillard, J. 1983. *Les stratégies fatales*. Paris.

Baumgarten, R. 1998. *Heiliges Wort und Heilige Schrift bei den Griechen. Hieroi Logoi und verwandte Erscheinungen*. Tübingen.

Beacham, R. C. 1992. *The Roman Theatre and Its Audience*. Cambridge, MA.

Beard, M. 2007. *The Roman Triumph*. Cambridge, MA.

Beard, M., North, J. and Price, S. 1998. *Religions of Rome. Vol. 1: A History*. Cambridge.

Beauvoir, S. de 1949. *Le deuxième sexe*. Paris.

Becker, O. 1937. *Das Bild des Weges und verwandte Vorstellungen im frühgriechischen Denken*. Berlin.

Bedini, S. A. 1964. 'The Role of automata in the History of Technology'. *Technology and Culture* 5: 24–41.

Belfiore, E. 2012. *Socrates' Daimonic Art. Love for Wisdom in Four Platonic Dialogues*. Cambridge.

Bellanger, S. 2001. 'Begegnungen mit den Cyborgs. Zur Lebenssituation der Cyborgs in der Moderne und danach'. In K. Giselbrecht and M. Hafner (eds), *Data / Body / Sex / Machine, Technoscience und Sciencefiction aus feministischer Sicht*. Vienna. 45–73.

Benardete, S. 1991. *The Rhetoric of Morality and Philosophy: Plato's* Gorgias *and* Phaedrus. Chicago.

Benatouïl, T. 2006. *Faire Usage*. Paris.

Bennett, J. 2010. *Vibrant Matter. A Political Ecology of Things*. Durham.

Benveniste, E. 1966/1974. *Le vocabulaire des institutions indo-européennes. 1. Économie, parenté, société. 2. Pouvoir, droit, religion*. Paris.

Bernabé, A. (ed.). 2005. *Poetae epici Graeci: testimonia et fragmenta. P. 2: Orphicorum et orphicis similium testimonia et fragmenta. Fasc 2*. Munich.

Bernabé, A., 2011. *Platón y el orfismo. Diálogos entre religión y filosofía*. Madrid.

Bernhardt, C. 2017. *Turing's Vision. The Birth of Computer Science*. Cambridge, MA.

Bernstein, N.W. 2014. 'Romanas veluti saevissima cum legiones Tisiphone regesque movet. Valerius Flaccus' *Argonautica* and the Flavian Era'. In M. Heerink and G. Manuwald (eds.). 154–169.

Berryman, S. 2003. 'Ancient Automata and Mechanical Explanation'. *Phronesis* 48: 344–369.

Berryman, S. 2007. 'The Imitation of Life in Ancient Technology'. In J. Riskin (ed.), *Genesis Redux*. Chicago. 35–45.

Berryman, S. 2009. *The Mechanical Hypothesis in Ancient Greek Natural Philosophy*. Cambridge.

Berve, H. 1967. *Die Tyrannis bei den Griechen*. Munich.

Berzins McCoy, M. 2013. *Wounded Heroes: Vulnerability as a Virtue in Ancient Greek Literature and Philosophy*. Oxford.

Bettini, M. 1998. *Nascere: storie di donne, donnole, madri ed eroi*. Turin.

Bettini, M. 2013. 'I mostri sono buoni per pensare'. In R. Paris, E. Setari and N. Giustozzi (eds.), *Mostri: creature fantastiche della paura e del mito*. Milan. 18–31.

Bettini, M. 2013a. *Women and Weasels. Mythologies of Birth in Ancient Greece and Rome*. Chicago.

Bexley, E. 2010. 'The Myth of the Republic: Medusa and Cato in Lucan, *Pharsalia* 9'. In N. Hömke and C. Reitz (eds.). 135–154.

Bianchi, E., Brill, S. and Holmes, B. (eds.) 2019. *Antiquities Beyond Humanism*. Oxford.

Bielfeldt, R. (ed.). 2014a. *Ding und Mensch in der Antike. Gegenwart und Vergegenwärtigung*. Heidelberg.

Bielfeldt, R. 2014b. 'Lichtblicke – Sehnstrahlen. Zur Präsenz römischer Figuren- und Bildlampen'. In R. Bielfeldt (ed.). 2014a. Heidelberg 194–238.

Biggs, P. 1966. 'The Disease Theme in Sophocles' *Ajax, Philoctetes*, and *Trachiniae*'. *CP* 61: 223–235.

Billings, J. and Leonard, M. (eds). 2015. *Tragedy and the Idea of Modernity*. Oxford.

Bing, P. 2005. 'The Politics and Poetics of Geography in the Milan Posidippus Section One. On Stones (AB 1–20)'. In K. Gutzwiller (ed.), *The New Posidippus: A Hellenistic Poetry Book*. Oxford. 119–140.

Blackwell, M. (ed.). 2007. *The Secret Life of Things. Animals, Objects, and It-narratives in Eighteenth-century England*. Lewisburg.

Blaffer Hrdy, S. 2009. *Mothers and Others. The Evolutionary Origins of Mutual Understanding*. Cambridge, MA.

Blaise, F. 1992. 'L'Épisode de Typhée dans la *Théogonie* d'Hésiode (v. 820–885). La Stabilization du monde'. *REG* 105: 349–370.

Blaise, F. and Rousseau, P. 1996. 'La guerre (*Théogonie* 615–20)'. In F. Blaise, P. Judet de La Combe and P. Rousseau (eds.), *Le métier du mythe. Lectures d'Hesiode*. Lille. 213–234.

Blaise, F., Judet de La Combe, P. and Rousseau, P. (eds.), *Le métier du mythe. Lectures d'Hesiode*. Lille.

Blake, S. 2011a. 'Martial's Natural History. The *Xenia* and *Apophoreta* and Pliny's Encyclopedia'. *Arethusa* 44: 353–377.

Blake, S. 2011b. 'Saturnalia Clamata: Noise and Speech in Flavian Literary Saturnalias'. *Mouseion* 11: 361–380.

Blake, S. 2012. 'Now You See Them. Slaves and Other Objects as Elements of the Roman Master'. *Helios* 39: 193–211.

Blake, S. 2015. 'The Aesthetics of the Everyday in Flavian Art and Literature'. In A. Zissos (ed.), *A Companion to the Flavian Age of Imperial Rome*. Malden. 344–360.

Blanchot, M. 1988 [1955]. *L'espace littéraire*. Paris.

Bliquez, L. J. 1983. 'Classical Prosthetics'. *Archaeology* 36: 25–29.

Bocciolini Palagi, L. 2016. *La Musa e la Furia: Interpretazione del secondo proemio dell'* Eneide. Bologna.

Bochart, S. 1663. *Hierozoicon*. London.

Bodson, L. 1986. 'L'utilisation de l'âne dans l'Antiquité gréco-romaine'. *Ethnozootechnie* 37: 7–14.

Boeckh, A. 1819. *Philolaos des Pythagoreers Lehren nebst den Bruchstücken seines Werkes*. Berlin.

Boehme, J. 1929. *Die Seele und das Ich bei Homer*. Göttingen.

Boeke, H. 2007. *The Value of Victory in Pindar's Odes: Gnomai, Cosmology and the Role of the Poet*. Leiden/Boston.

Bogost, I. 2012. *Alien Phenomenology, or What it's Like to Be a Thing*. Minneapolis.

Bologna, C. 1980. 'Mostro ad vocem', *Enciclopedia* 9: 556–580.

Bost-Fievet M. and S. Provini 2014. *L'antiquité dans l'imaginaire contemporain. Fantasy, science-fiction, fantastique*. Paris.

Bostrom, N. 2006. 'How Long before Superintelligence?' *Linguistic and Philosophical Investigations* 5: 11–30 (https://nickbostrom.com/superintelligence.html).

Bostrom, N. 2013. 'Why I Want to Be a Posthuman When I Grow Up'. In M. More and N. Vita-More (eds.), *The Transhumanist Reader*. Sussex. 28–53.

Bostrom, N. 2014. *Superintelligence. Paths, Dangers, Strategies*. Oxford.

Bostrom, N. and E. Yudkowksy 2014. 'The Ethics of Artificial Intelligence'. In K. Frankish and W. M. Ramsey (eds.), *The Cambridge Handbook of Artificial Intelligence*. Cambridge. 316–334.

Boulter, P. N. 1962. 'The Theme of ἀγρία in Euripides' *Orestes*'. *Phoenix* 16: 102–106.

Bourdieu, P. 1991. *Language and Symbolic Power*, trans. M. Adamson. Cambridge, MA.

Bowra, C. M. 1964. *Pindar*. Oxford.

Boyle, A. J. (ed.). 1993. *Roman Epic*. London.

Boys-Stones G. R. and Haubold, J. H. (eds). 2010. *Plato and Hesiod*. Oxford.

Bradley, K. 1986. 'Seneca and Slavery'. *Classica et Medievalia* 37: 161–72.

Braidotti, R. 1996. 'Signs of Wonder and Traces of Doubt: On Teratology and Embodied Differences'. In N. Lykke and R. Braidotti (eds.), *Between Monsters, Goddesses, and Cyborgs: Feminist Confrontations With Science, Medicine, and Cyberspace*. London. 135–152.

Braidotti, R. 2002. *Metamorphoses. Toward a Materialist Theory of Becoming*. Cambridge.

Braidotti, R. 2006. *Transpositions. On Nomadic Ethics*. Cambridge.

Braidotti, R. 2006a. 'Posthuman, All Too Human: Towards a New Process Ontology'. *Theory, Culture & Society* 23: 197–208.

Braidotti, R. 2011. *Nomadic Subjects: Embodiment and Sexual Difference in Contemporary Feminist Theory*. New York.

Braidotti, R. 2013. *The Posthuman*. Cambridge.

Braren, I. 1992. 'O jocoso nas epistolas morais de Sêneca'. *Polis* 4: 33–42.

Brassier, R. 2014. 'Prometheanism and its Critics'. In R. Mackay and A. Avanessian (eds.), *#Accelerate: The Accelerationist Reader*. Falmouth. 467–487.

Bratton, B. 2016. *The Stack. On Software and Sovereignty*. Cambridge, MA.

Bremer, J.-M. 2008. 'Traces of the Hymn in the Epinikion'. *Mnemosyne* 41: 1–17.

Bremmer, J. N. 1988. 'La plasticité du mythe. Méléagre dans la poésie homérique'. In C. Calame (ed.), *Métamorphoses du mythe en Grèce antique*. Paris, 37–56.

Brennan, T. 2014. *Borrowed Light. Vico, Hegel, and the Colonies*. Stanford.

Brennan, T. 2014a. 'The Free Impersonality of Bourgeois Spirit'. *Biography* 37: 1–35.

Brennan, T. 2016. 'The Problem with Post-Humanism '. In F. Offizier, M. Priewe and A. Schröder (eds.), *Crossroads in American Studies: Transnational and Biocultural Encounters*. Heidelberg. 525–548.

Briand, M. 2014. *Pindare.* Olympiques. Paris.

Bridges, E. 2015. *Imagining Xerxes. Ancient Perspectives on a Persian King*. London.

Briggs, Jr., W. W. 1980. 'Narrative and Simile from the *Georgics* in the *Aeneid*'. *Mnemosyne Supplementum* 58: 1–109.

Brillante, C. 2013–2014. 'La voce delle Muse nella poesia greca arcaica'. *I Quaderni del Ramo d'Oro* 6: 34–51.

Brink, C. 1971. *Horace on Poetry II: The* Ars Poetica. Cambridge.

Brink, C. O. 1956. 'Οἰκείωσις and οἰκειότης. Theophrastus and Zeno on Nature in Moral Theory'. *Phronesis* 1: 123–145.

Brink, C. O. 1963. *Horace on Poetry I: Prolegomena to the Literary Epistles*. Cambridge.

Brinkema, E. 2014. *The Forms of the Affects*. Durham.

Brisson, L. 2006. 'Agathon, Pausanias, and Diotima in Plato's *Symposium*. Paiderastia and Philosophia'. In Lesher et al. (eds.), 229–251.

Brock, R. 2000. 'Sickness in the Body Politic: Medical Imagery in the Greek Polis'. In V. M. Hope and E. Marshall (eds.), *Death and Disease in the Ancient City*. London. 24–34.

Brock, R. 2006. 'The Body as Political Organism in Greek Thought'. In F. Prost and J. Wilgaux (eds.), *Penser et représenter le corps dans l'antiquité*. Rennes, 351–360.

Brock, R. 2013. *Greek Political Imagery from Homer to Aristotle*. London.

Brooks, R. 2017. 'The Seven Deadly Sins of AI Predictions'. *MIT Technology Review* 120: 79–86. https://www.technologyreview.com/s/609048/the-seven-deadly-sins-of-ai-predictions/

Brooks, R. A. et al. 1999. 'The Cog Project: Building a Humanoid Robot'. In C. L. Nehaniv (ed.), *Computation for Metaphors, Analogy, and Agents*. Berlin. 52–87.

Brooks, R.. and L. Steels (eds). 1995. *The Artificial Life Route to Artificial Intelligence: Building Embodied, Situated Agents*. London.

Brown, B. (ed.). 2004. *Things*. Chicago.

Brown, P. 1988. *Body and Society: Men, Women, and Sexual Renunciation in Early Christianity*. New York.

Browning Cole, E. 1993. *Philosophy and Feminist Criticism: An Introduction*. St Paul.

Brulé, P. 1987. *La fille d'Athènes. La religion des filles à Athènes à l'époque classique. Mythes, cultes et société*. Paris.

Bruner, J. 1991. 'The Narrative Construction of Reality'. *Critical Inquiry* 18: 1–21.

Bryant, L. 2011. *The Democracy of Objects*. Ann Arbor.

Buckley, E. 2014. 'Valerius Flaccus and Seneca's Tragedies'. In M. Heerink and G. Manuwald (eds.). 307–25.

Budelmann, F. 2006. 'Körper und Geist in tragischen Schmerz-Szenen'. In B. Seidensticker and M. Vöhler (eds.), *Gewalt und Ästhetik. Zur Gewalt und ihrer Darstellung in der Griechischen Klassik*. Berlin/New York. 123–148.

Budelmann, F. 2007. 'The Reception of Sophocles' Representation of Physical Pain'. *AJP* 128: 443–467.

Budelmann, F. and LeVen, P. 2014. 'Timotheus' Poetics of Blending: A Cognitive Approach to the Language of the New Music'. *CP* 49: 191–210.

Burford, A. 1969. *The Greek Temple Builders at Epidauros. A Social and Economic Study of Building in the Asklepian Sanctuary, During the Fourth and Early Third Centuries B.C.* Toronto.

Burger, E. 1980. *Plato's* Phaedrus. *A Defence of a Philosophic Art of Writing*. Alabama.
Burkert, W. 1972. *Lore and Science in Ancient Pythagoreanism*, trans. E. Minar. Cambridge, MA.
Burkert, W. 1972a. *Homo necans. Interpretationen altgriechischer Opferriten und Mythen*. Berlin = 1983. *Homo Necans*. Trans. O. Bing. Berkeley and Los Angeles.
Burkert, W. 1977. *Griechische Religion der archaischen und klassischen Epoche*. Stuttgart/Berlin.
Burzachechi, M. 1962. 'Oggetti parlanti nelle epigrafi greche'. *Epigraphica* 24: 3–54.
Butler, J. 1992. 'The Body You Want (Interview with Liz Kotz)'. *Artforum* 31: 82–89.
Butler, J. 1993a. *Bodies that Matter: On the Discursive Limits of Sex*. New York.
Butler, M. (ed.). 1993b. *Mary Shelley, Frankenstein. The 1818 Text*. Oxford.
Butler, S. 1898. *The* Iliad *of Homer*. Cambridge.
Buxton, R. 2004. 'Similes and Other Likenesses'. In R. Fowler (ed.), *The Cambridge Companion to Homer*. Cambridge. 139–155.
Byre, C. S. 1996. 'Distant Encounters: The Prometheus and Phaethon Episodes in the *Argonautica* of Apollonius Rhodius'. *AJP* 117: 275–283.
Cachia, N. 1997. *The Image of the Good Shepherd as a Source for the Spirituality of the Ministerial Priesthood*. Rome.
Cairns, D. L. 2014. 'Ψυχή, Θυμός, and Metaphor in Homer and Plato'. *Etudes platoniciennes* 11: http://journals.openedition.org/etudesplatoniciennes/566
Cairns, F. 2005a. 'Pindar *Olympian* 7: Rhodes, Athens, and the Diagorids'. *Eikasmos* 16: 63–91.
Cairns, F. 2005b. 'Lavinia's Blush (Virgil Aeneid 12.64–70)'. In D. L. Cairns (ed.), *Body Language in the Greek and Roman Worlds*. Swansea. 195–213.
Calame, C. 1997. *Choruses of Young Women in Ancient Greece: Their Morphology, Religious Role and Social Function*, trans. D. Collins and J. Orion. Lanham.
Calame, C. 1998. 'Héraclès, animal et victime sacrificielle dans la *Trachiniennes* de Sophocle'. In C. Bonnet et al. (eds.), *Le bestiaire d'Héraclès*. Liège, 197–216.
Calame, C. 2012. 'Metaphorical Travel and Ritual Performance'. In P. Agócs, C. Carey, and R. Rawles (eds.), *Reading the Victory Odes*. Cambridge. 303–320.
Calarco, M. 2004. 'Deconstruction is not Vegetarianism: Humanism, Subjectivity and Animal Ethics'. *Continental Philosophy Review* 37: 175–201.
Calarco, M. 2015. *Thinking Through Animals: Identity, Difference, Indistinction*. Stanford.
Campa, R. 2015. *Humans and Automata: A Social Study of Robotics*. Frankfurt.
Canguilhem, G. 1962. 'La monstruosité et le monstrueux'. *Diogène* 40: 29–43.
Canguilhem, G. 1966. *Le normal et le pathologique*. Paris. = 1991. *The Normal and the Pathological. With an introduction by M. Foucault*. Trans. Carolyn R. Fawcett. New York.
Canguilhem, G. 2001. 'The Living and its Milieu', trans. J. Savage. *Grey Room* 3: 6–31.
Canguilhem, G. 2015 [1952]. *La connaissance de la vie*. Paris.
Cannatà Fera, M. 1990. *Pindarus. Threnorum fragmenta*. Rome.
Cantarella, E. 1995. *L'ambiguo malanno. La donna nell'antichità greca e romana*. Turin.
Cantarella, R. (ed.). 1963. *I Cretesi*. Milan.
Capra, A. 2018. 'Aristophanes' Iconic Socrates'. In A. Stavru, C. Moore (eds.), *Socrates and the Socratic Dialogue*. Leiden. 64–83.
Carel, H. 2016. *Phenomenology of Illness*. Oxford.
Carne-Ross, D. S. 1981. 'The Beastly House of Atreus'. *The Kenyon Review* 3: 20–60.
Carroll, N. 1990. *The Philosophy of Horror or Paradoxes of the Heart*. New York/London.
Carter, L. B. 1986. *The Quiet Athenian*. Oxford.
Cartledge, P. 2009. *Ancient Greek Thought in Practice*. Cambridge.
Casson, L. 1977. 'Energy and Technology in the Ancient World'. In J. Thorndike (ed.), *Mysteries of the Past*. New York. 140–154.
Casson, L. 1994. *Travel in the Ancient World*. Baltimore.
Castelletti, C. 2014. 'A Hero with a Sandal and a Buskin. The Figure of Jason in Valerius Flaccus' *Argonautica*'. In M. Heerink and G. Manuwald (eds.). 173–191.
Castro, E. 2004. *Vocabulário de Foucault. Um percurso pelos seus temas, conceitos e autores*. São Paulo.
Caswell, C.P. 1990. *A Study of Thumos in Early Greek Poetry*. Leiden.

Ceccarelli, P. 1996. 'L'Athènes de Périclès: Un "pays de cocagne"? L'idéologie démocratique et l'αὐτόματος βίος dans la comédie ancienne'. *QUCC* 54: 109–159.
Ceri Stephens, J. 1995. 'The Wound of Philoctetes'. *Mnemosyne* 48: 153-168.
Ceschi, G. 2003. 'Il caso clinico di Eracle nelle *Trachinie* di Sofocle'. *AIV* 161: 65–93.
Ceschi, G. 2005. 'μελαγχολικὸν τὸ τοιοῦτον: Il caso clinico di Filottete in Sofocle'. *SIFC* 4: 5-29.
Ceschi, G. 2009. *Il vocabolario medico di Sofocle. Analisi dei contatti con il* Corpus Hippocraticum *nel lessico anatomo-fisiologico, patologico e terapeutico*. Venice.
Ceschi, G. 2014. 'Medical Vocabulary'. In G. K. Giannakis (ed.), *Encyclopedia of Ancient Greek Language and Linguistics*. Leiden. 404–407.
Chantraine, P. 1968. *Dictionnaire étymologique de la langue Grecque*. Paris.
Cheah, P. 2010. 'Non-Dialectical Materialism'. In D. Coole and S. Frost (eds.), *New Materialisms. Ontology, Agency, and Politics*. Durham. 70–91.
Chesi, G. M. 2018. 'Tua Korhonen and Erika Ruonakoski, Human and Animal in Ancient Greece: Empathy and Encounter in Classical Literature. London and New York 2017'. *BMCR* 2018.01.39.
Chesi, G. M. 2019. Review of Midson, S. A. *Cyborg Theology: Humans, Technology and God*. London and New York. *JPHS* 3: 93–97.
Chew, K. 2002. '*Inscius pastor*: Ignorance and Aeneas' Identity in the *Aeneid*'. *Latomus* 61: 616–627.
Chiasson, C. C. 1999/2000. 'Σωφρουοῦυτες ἐυ χρόνωι: The Athenians and Time in Aeschylus' *Eumenides*'. *CJ* 95: 139–161.
Chignola, S. 2014. *Foucault oltre Foucault. Una politica della filosofia*. Rome.
Cirio, A. 1997. 'Il *Filottete* di Sofocle: Diagnosi per la malattia di Filottete o per quella di Sofocle?'. *Aufidus* 33: 7-13.
Citroni, M. 1989. 'Marziale e la letteratura per i Saturnali (poetica dell'intrattenimento e cronologia della pubblicazione dei libri)'. *ICS* 14: 201–226.
Citroni, M. 2009. 'Horace's *Ars Poetica* and the Marvellous'. In P. Hardie (ed.), *Paradox and the Marvellous in Augustan Literature and Culture*. Oxford. 19–40.
Clark, A. 2003. *Natural-Born Cyborgs: Minds, Technologies, and the Future of Human Intelligence*. Oxford.
Clark, I. 1998. 'The Gamos of Hera. Myth and Ritual'. In S. Blundell and M. Williamson (eds.), *The Sacred and the Feminine in Ancient Greece*. London/New York. 12–23.
Clark, N. and Yusoff, K. 2017. 'Geosocial Formations and the Anthropocene'. *Theory, Culture & Society* 34 (2/3), 3–23.
Clark, T. 2015. *Ecocriticism on the Edge: The Anthropocene as a Threshold Concept*. New York.
Clarke, A. C. 1973 [1962]. *Profiles of the Future*. New York.
Clarke, B. and Rossini, M. (eds.). 2017. *The Cambridge Companion to Literature and the Posthuman*. Cambridge.
Clarke, M. 1995. 'Between Lions and Men. Images of the Hero in the *Iliad*'. *GRBS*: 137–159.
Clarke, M. 1999. *Flesh and Spirit in the Songs of Homer. A Study of Words and Myths*. Oxford.
Clauss, J. J. 2014. 'Myth and Mythopoesis in Valerius Flaccus' *Argonautica*'. In M. Heerink and G. Manuwald (eds.). 99–114.
Clay, D. 2000. *Platonic Questions: Dialogues with the Silent Philosopher*. University Park.
Clay, J.S. 1983. *The Wrath of Athena. Gods and Men in the Odyssey*. Princeton.
Clutton-Brock, J. 2007. 'How Domestic Animals Have Shaped the Development of Human Societies'. In Kalof (ed.). 71–96.
Clynes, M. E. and Kline, N. S. 1960. 'Cyborgs and Space'. *Astronautics*: 26–76.
Coeckelbergh, M. 2010. 'Health Care, Capabilities, and AI Assistive Technologies'. *Ethical Theory and Moral Practice* 13: 181–190.
Coeckelbergh, M. 2016. 'Care Robots and the Future of ICT-Mediated Elderly Care: A Response to Doom Scenarios'. *AI and Society* 31: 455–462.
Cohen, R. H. 2007. 'Emmanuel Levinas: Judaism and the Primacy of the Ethical'. In M. L. Morgan and P. E. Gordon (eds.), *The Cambridge Companion to Modern Jewish Philosophy*. Cambridge. 234–255.
Coleman, K. M. 1990. 'Fatal Charades: Roman Executions Staged as Mythological Enactments'. *JRS* 80: 44–73.

Coleman, K. M. 1996. 'Ptolemy Philadelphus and the Roman Amphitheater'. In W. J. Slater (ed.), *Roman Theater and Society*. Ann Arbor. 49–68.
Coleman, K. M. 2006. M. *Valerii Martialis Liber spectaculorum*. Oxford.
Collard, C. (ed.). 1991. *Euripides.* Hecuba. Warminster.
Collard, C. and Cropp, M. J. (eds.). 2008. *Euripides. Vol. VII: Fragments*. Cambridge, MA/London.
Collard, C., Cropp M. J. and Lee, K. H. (eds.). 1995. *Euripides. Vol. I: Selected Fragmentary Plays.* Warminster.
Collinge, N. E. 1962. 'Medical Terms and Clinical Attitudes in The Tragedians'. *BICS* 9: 43–55.
Collins, C. 1996. *Authority Figures: Metaphors of Mastery from the* Iliad *to the* Apocalypse. Lanham.
Connell, J. 2013. 'The Silence of the Sphinx: Oedipal Error and the Recovered Answer to the Riddle'. *Fragmentum* 38: 15–39.
Connell, S. M. 2016. *Aristotle on Female Animals: A Study of the* Generation of Animals. Cambridge.
Connors, C. 1997. 'Field and Forum: Culture and Agriculture in Roman Rhetoric'. In W. Dominik (ed.), *Roman Eloquence.* New York. 71–89.
Cooper, S. 2017. 'Aristophanes, Posthumanism, and the Roots of Science Fiction'. PhD Princeton.
Coray, M. et al. 2016. *Homers* Ilias: *Gesamtkommentar* (Basler Kommentar), gen eds. A. Bierl and J. Latacz, vol. 11: Achtzehnter Gesang, fasc. 2: Kommentar. Berlin/Boston.
Cornell, T. J. 1995. *The Beginnings of Rome: Italy and Rome from the Bronze Age to the Punic Wars (c. 1000–264 BC).* London.
Costa, C. D. N. (ed.). 1984. De rerum natura *V/Titus Carus Lucretius*. Oxford/New York.
Cotter, J., DeFazio, K., Faivre, R. et al. (eds.). 2016. *Human, All Too (Post)Human. The Humanities After Humanism*. London.
Cotton, A. K. 2014. *Platonic Dialogue and the Education of the Reader*. Oxford.
Courrént, M. 2002. 'La pensée technique et ses enjeux dans le *De Architectura* de Vitruve'. *Latomus* 267: 119–127.
Courrént, M. 2004. '*Non est mirandum*: Vitruve et la résistance à l'étonnement'. In O. Bianchi et al. (eds.), *Mirabilia: conceptions et représentations de l'extraordinaire dans le monde antique*. Bern. 265–278.
Courrént, M. 2011. *De architecti Scientia. Idée de nature et théorie de l'art dans le* De architectura *de Vitruve*. Caen.
Cowan, R. 2014. 'My Family and Other Enemies. Argonautic Antagonists and Valerian Villains'. In M. Heerink and G. Manuwald (eds.). 229–248.
Cox-George, C. and Bewley, S. 2018. 'I, Sex Robot: The Health Implications of the Sex Robot Industry'. *BMJ Sex Reprod Health* 44: 161–164.
Cozzoli, A.-T. (ed.). 2001. *Euripides:* Cretesi. *Introduzione, testimonianze, testo critico, traduzione e commento*. Pisa/Rome.
Crahay, R. 1956. *La littérature oraculaire chez Hérodote*. Paris.
Croiset, M. 1915. 'Les *Crétois* d'Euripide'. *RÉG* 28: 217–233.
Csapo, E. and Miller, M. 1999. 'Democracy, Empire, and Art: Toward a Politics of Time and Narrative'. In K. Raaflaub and D. Boedeker (eds.), *Democracy, Empire, and the Arts in Fifth-Century Athens*. Cambridge. 87–125.
Cubitt, S. 2001. *Simulation and Social Theory*. London.
Cuboniks, L. 2018. *The Xenofeminist Manifesto: A Politics for Alienation*. London.
Cudworth, E. and Hobden, S. 2018. *The Emancipatory Project of Posthumanism*. London/New York.
Cuomo, S. 2007. *Technology and Culture in Greek and Roman Antiquity*. Cambridge.
Currie, B. 2005. *Pindar and the Cult of Heroes*. Oxford/New York.
Curtius, E. R. 1973. *European Literature and the Latin Middle Ages*, trans. W. R. Trask. Princeton.
Dahlgren, S. 1877. *De imaginibus Aeschyli. Commentatio academica*. Stockholm.
Dall'Olio, F. 2014. 'L'eroe malato. Esclusione e mancata integrazione nell'*Oreste* di Euripide e nel *Filottete* di Sofocle'. *Maia* 66: 244–259.
Danaher, J. 2014. 'Sex Work, Technological Unemployment and the Basic Income Guarantee'. *JET* 24: 113–130.
Danaher, J. 2017. 'Robotic Rape and Robotic Child Sexual Abuse: Should They Be Criminalised?' *Criminal Law and Philosophy* 11: 71–95.
Danaher, J. and McArthur, N. (eds.). 2017. *Robot Sex: Social and Ethical Implications*. London.
Darab, Á. 2015. 'When Elephants Weep: Plin. *Nat.* VIII 20–21'. *ACUSD* 51: 75–88.

Darcus Sullivan, S. 1979. 'A Person's Relation to φρήν in Homer, Hesiod, and the Greek Lyric Poets'. *Glotta* 57: 159–173.
Darcus Sullivan, S. 1982. 'A Strand of Thought in Pindar, *Olympian* 7'. *TAPA* 112: 215–223.
Darcus Sullivan, S. 1989. 'A Study of φρένες in Pindar and Bacchylides'. *Glotta* 67: 148–189.
Darwin, C. 1872. *The Expression of the Emotions in Man and Animals*. London.
Daston, L. and Vidal, F. (eds). 2004. *The Moral Authority of Nature*. Chicago.
Davenport, C. 2018. *A History of the Roman Equestrian Order*. Cambridge.
Davies, J. K. 1981. *Wealth and the Power of Wealth in Classical Athens*. Salem.
Davies, M. 2003. 'Philoctetes: Wild Man and Helper Figure'. *PP* 58: 347–355.
Davies, T. 1997. *Humanism*. London.
De Groot, J. 2012. 'Rethinking the Meaning of Mechanism in Antiquity. Sylvia Berryman, The Mechanical Hypothesis in Ancient Greek Natural Philosophy'. *Metascience* 21: 699–704.
De Martino, E. 1961. *La terra del rimorso. Contributo a una storia religiosa del Sud*. Milan.
De Planhol, X. 1963. 'Geographia pontica'. *Journal asiatique* 251: 298–309.
De Ste Croix, G. E. M. 1981. *The Class Struggle in the Ancient Greek World from the Archaic Age to the Arab Conquest*. London.
Deforge, B. 2004 [1986]. *Eschyle. Poète Cosmique*. Paris.
DeLanda, M. 2002. *Intensive Science and Virtual Philosophy*. London.
Delcourt, A. 2005. *Lecture des Antiquités romaines de Denys d'Halicarnasse*. Brussels.
Deleuze, G. 1986. *Foucault*. Paris.
Deleuze, G. 1990 [1969]. *The Logic of Sense*, trans. M. Lester. New York.
Deleuze, G. 1991. 'The Fold', tr. J. Strauss. *Yale French Studies* 80, Baroque Topographies: Literature/History/Philosophy: 227–247.
Deleuze, G. 1992 [1968]. *Expressionism in Philosophy: Spinoza*, trans. M. Joughin. New York.
Deleuze, G. 1994 [1968]. *Difference and Repetition*, trans. P. Patton. New York.
Deleuze, G. 1995. 'L'immanence: une vie . . .'. *Philosophie* 47: 3–7.
Deleuze, G. 2001 [1970]. *Spinoza. Practical Philosophy*, trans. R. Hurley. San Francisco.
Deleuze, G. 2006. *The Fold: Leibniz and the Baroque*, tr. T. Conley. London.
Deleuze, G. and Guattari, F. 1980. *Capitalisme et schizophrénie*. Vol. 2, Mille Plateaux. Paris. = 1987. *A Thousand Plateaus. Capitalism and Schizophrenia*, trans. B. Massumi. Minneapolis.
Deleuze, G. and Guattari, F. 1986 [1975]. *Kafka. Toward a Minor Literature*, trans. D. Polan. Minneapolis.
Deleuze, G. and Guattari, F. 1994 [1991]. *What Is Philosophy?* Trans. G. Burchell. London.
Del Lucchese, F. 2011. 'Monstrosity and the Limits of the Intellect. Philosophy as Teratomachy in Descartes'. *JFFP* 19: 107–129.
Denniston, J. D. and Page, D. (eds.). 1957. Aeschylus: *Agamemnon*. Oxford.
Derrida, J. 1972. 'La différance'. In *Marges de la philosophie*. Paris. 1–29.
Derrida, J. 1972a. 'Les fins de l'homme'. In *Marges de la philosophie*. Paris. 129–164. = 1982a. 'The Ends of Man'. In *Margins of Philosophy*. 109–136.
Derrida, J. 1972b. *La Dissémination*. Paris.
Derrida, J. 1989 [1968]. 'La Pharmacie de Platon'. In L. Brisson (trans. & comm.), *Platon. Phèdre*. Paris. 276–349.
Derrida, J. 1991. '"Eating Well", or the Calculation of the Subject: An Interview with Jacques Derrida'. In E. Cadava et al. (eds), *Who Comes After the Subject?* New York/ London. 96–119.
Derrida, J. 1995. *Points . . .: Interviews, 1974–1994*, trans. P. Kamuf. Palo Alto.
Derrida, J. 1995a. 'Passages – from Traumatism to Promise'. In J. Derrida 1995. 372–395.
Derrida, J. 1995b. *The Gift of Death*, trans. D. Wills. Chicago.
Derrida, J. 2001 [1967]. 'Structure, Sign and Play in the Discourse of the Human Sciences'. In *Writing and Difference*, trans. Bass, A. London. 351–370.
Derrida, J. 2004. 'Violence Against Animals' (with Roudinesco, E.). *Derrida and Roudinesco, For What Tomorrow . . .: A Dialogue*, trans. J. Fort. Stanford. 62–76.
Derrida, J. 2005. *Rogues. Two Essays on Reason*, trans. P.-A. Brault and M. Naas. Stanford.
Derrida, J. 2006. *L'animal que donc je suis*. Paris = 2008. *The Animal That Therefore I Am*, trans. D. Wills. Fordham.

Derrida, J. 2008a. *Séminaire La bête et le souverain*. Paris. = 2009/2010. *The Beast and the Sovereign. Volumes I to II*, trans. G. Bennington. Chicago.
Descartes, R. 2008 [1637]. *Discourse on the Method*, trans. J. Veitch. New York.
Descola, P. 2013. *The Ecology of Others*, trans. G. Godbout. Chicago.
Descola, P. 2014 [2005]. *Beyond Nature and Culture*, trans. J. Lloyd. Chicago.
Desmond, W. D. 2006. *The Greek Praise of Poverty: Origins of Ancient Cynicism*. Notre Dame.
Destrée, P. 2012. 'The Speech of Alcibiades (212c4–222b7)'. In C. Horn (ed.), *Platon*. Symposion. Berlin. 191–205.
Detienne, M. 1963. *La notion de δαίμων dans le pythagorisme ancien*. Paris.
Detienne, M. 1998. *Dionysos mis à mort*. Paris.
Detienne, M. and Vernant, J. P. 1974. *Les ruses de l'intelligence: La métis des Grecs*. Paris.
Deuber-Mankowsky, A. 2007. *Praktiken der Illusion*. Berlin.
Devecka, M. 2013. 'Did the Greeks Believe in Their Robots?', *CCJ* 59: 52–69.
Devlin, K. 2018. *Turned On: Science, Sex and Robots*. London.
Di Benedetto, V. 1986. *Il medico e la malattia. La scienza di Ippocrate*. Turin.
Di Nucci, E. 2011. 'Sexual Rights and Disability'. *JME* 37: 158–161.
Di Nucci, E. 2017. 'Sexual Rights, Disability and Sex Robots'. In J. Danaher and N. McArthur (eds.). 73–90.
Dierauer, U. 1977. *Tier und Mensch im Denken der Antike*. Amsterdam.
Dimock, G. E. 1956. 'The Name of Odysseus'. *The Hudson Review* 9: 52–70.
DNO = S. Kansteiner, K. Hallof, L. Lehmann et al. (eds). 2014. *Der Neue Overbeck. Die antiken Schriftquellen zu den bildenden Künsten der Griechen*, vol. 1. Berlin/Boston.
Dodds, E. R. 1951. *The Greeks and the Irrational*. Berkeley.
Dodds, E. R. 1959. *Plato*. Gorgias. *A Revised Text with Introduction and Commentary*. Oxford.
Dolfi, E. 1984. 'Su *I Cretesi* di Euripide: Passione e responsabilità'. *Prometheus* 10: 121–138.
Donald, M. 2014. 'Entided, Enwatered, Enwinded: Human/More-Than-Human Agencies in Site-Specific Performance'. In M. Schweitzer and J. Zerdy (eds.), *Performing Objects and Theatrical Things*. Basingstoke. 118–134.
Doran, R. 1992. *The Lives of Simeon Stylites*. Kalamazoo.
Dougherty, C. 2001. *The Raft of Odysseus. The Ethnographic Imagination of Homer's* Odyssey. Oxford.
Douglas, M. 1996. *Natural Symbols. Explorations in Cosmology*, 2nd edn. London.
Dover, K. 1980. *Plato*. Symposium. Cambridge.
Dowden, K. 1989. *Death and the Maiden. Girls' Initiation Rites in Greek Mythology*. London.
Drachmann, A. G. 1948. *Ktesibios, Philon and Heron. A Study in Ancient Pneumatics*. Copenhagen.
Draycott, J. 2018. *Prostheses in Antiquity*. New York.
Dressler, A. 2012. '"You must change your life": Metaphor and Exemplum, Theory and Practice, in Seneca's Prose'. *Helios* 39: 145–192.
Dressler, A. 2016a. *Personification and the Feminine in Roman Philosophy*. Cambridge.
Dressler, A. 2016b. 'Plautus and the Poetics of Property: Reification, Recognition, and Utopia'. *MD* 77: 9–56.
Drexler, E. 1986. *Engines of Creation. The Coming Era of Nanotechnology*. New York.
Dreyfus, H. and Dreyfus, S. 2009 [1986]. 'Why Computers May Never Think Like People'. In D. M. Kaplan (ed.). 397–413.
Ducos, M. 1991. 'Sénèque et le monde du droit'. In R. Chevalier and R. Poignault (eds), *Présence de Sénèque*. Paris. 109–126.
Dumortier, J. 1935. *Les images dans la poésie d'Eschyle*. Paris.
Dunbar, N. (ed. & comm.). 1995. *Aristophanes. Birds*. Oxford.
Duncan, A. 2006. *Performance and Identity in the Classical World*. Cambridge.
Dunkle, J. R. 1967. 'The Greek Tyrant and Roman Political Invective of the Late Republic'. *TAPA* 98: 151–171.
Dunkle, J. R. 1971. 'The Rhetorical Tyrant in Roman Historiography: Sallust, Livy and Tacitus'. *CW* 65: 12–20.
Dupuy, J.-P. 2013. 'The Artificialization of Life: Designing Self-organisation'. In S. Campbell and P. W. Bruno (eds.), *The Science, Politics, and Ontology of Life-Philosophy*. London. 78–92.

Dyck, A. R. 2013. *Cicero.* Pro Marco Caelio. Cambridge.

Eagleton, T. 1981. *Walter Benjamin or Towards a Revolutionary Criticism.* London.

Eagleton, T. 2004. *Literary Theory: An Introduction.* London.

Easterling, P. E. 1968. 'Sophocles' *Trachiniae*'. *BICS* 15: 58–70.

Easterling, P. E. 1978. '*Philoctetes* and Modern Criticism'. *ICS* 3: 27–39.

Easterling, P. E. 1981. 'The End of the *Trachiniae*'. *ICS* 6: 56–74.

Easterling, P. E. 1982. *Sophocles.* Trachiniae. Cambridge.

Edmonds, D. 2013. *Would You Kill the Fat Man? The Trolley Problem and What Your Answer Tells Us about Right and Wrong.* Princeton.

Edmonds, R. 2010. 'The Bright Cypress of the "Orphic" Gold Tablets. Direction and Illumination in Myths of the Underworld'. In M. Christopoulos, E. Karakantza and O. Levaniouk (eds.), *Light and Darkness in Ancient Greek Myth and Religion.* Lanham. 221–234.

Edwards, M. W. 1991. *The* Iliad. *A Commentary. Vol. 5: Books 17–20.* Cambridge.

Ehlers, W.-W. (ed.) 2011. *Gaius Valerius Flaccus Setinus Balbus: Argonauticon. Libri VIII.* Berlin.

Ehrenberg, V. 1973 [1947]. 'Polypragmosyne'. *JHS* 67: 44–67.

Eldred, K. 2000. 'Poetry in Motion: The Snakes of Lucan'. *Helios* 27: 63–74.

Ellul, J. 1980. *The Technological System.* London.

Elsner, J. 1991. 'Visual Mimesis and the Myth of the Real: Ovid's Pygmalion as Viewer'. *Ramus* 20: 154–168.

Engelmann, R. 1903. 'Io-Sage'. *JdI* 18: 37–58.

Esposito, R. 2004. *Bios. Biopolitica e filosofia.* Turin.

Esposito, R. 2016. *Da Fuori. Una filosofia per l'Europa.* Turin.

Esposito, R. 2018. *Politica e negazione. Per una filosofia affermativa.* Turin.

Fabian, J. 1990. 'Presence and Representation. The Other and Anthropological Writing'. *Critical Inquiry* 16: 753–772.

Fadinger, V. 2016. 'Peisistratos von Athen als Aisymnet und Tyrann: Die zwei Stufen einer diktatorischen Machtergreifung in der griechischen Antike'. In M. Schuol, C. Wendt, and J. Wilker (eds.), *Exempla imitanda. Mit der Vergangenheit die Gegenwart bewältigen?* Göttingen. 47–63.

Fagan, G. G. 2011. *The Lure of the Arena: Social Psychology and the Crowd at the Roman Games.* Cambridge.

Fantham, E. 1992. 'Lucan's Medusa-Excursus: Its Design and Purpose'. *MD* 29: 95–119.

Faraone, C. A. 1987. 'Hephaestus the Magician and the Near Eastern Parallels for the Gold and Silver Dogs of Alcinous (*Od.* 7.91–4)'. *GRBS* 28: 257–280.

Faraone, C. A. 1991. 'The Agonistic Context of Early Greek Binding Spells'. In C. A. Faraone and D. Obbink (eds.), *Magika Hiera.* New York/Oxford. 3–32.

Faraone, C. A. 1992. *Talismans and Trojan Horses: Guardian Statues in Ancient Greek Myth and Ritual.* Oxford.

Farioli, M. 2001. *Mundus alter. Utopie e distopie nella commedia greca antica.* Milan.

Farnell, L. R. 1932. *Works of Pindar. Vol 2: Commentary.* London.

Fauconnier, G. and Turner, M. 2002. *The Way We Think: Conceptual Blending and the Mind's Hidden Complexities.* New York.

Fauconnier, G. and Turner, M. 2008. 'Rethinking Metaphor', In R. Gibbs (ed.), *The Cambridge Handbook of Metaphor and Thought.* Cambridge. 53–66.

Fearn, D. 2017. *Pindar's Eyes. Visual and Material Culture in Epinician Poetry.* Oxford.

Feeney, D. C. 1993. *The Gods in Epic. Poets and Critics of the Classical Tradition.* Oxford.

Felson Rubin, N. 1980a. 'Pindar's Creation of Epinician Symbols: *Olympians* 7 and 6'. *CW* 74: 67–87.

Felson Rubin, N. 1980b. '*Olympian* 7: The Toast and the Future Prayer'. *Hermes* 108: 248–252.

Felson, S. and Parmentier, R. J. 2015. 'The "Savvy Interpreter": Performance and Interpretation in Pindar's Victory Odes'. *Signs and Society* 3: 261–305.

Fenik, B. 1968. *Typical Battle Scenes in the* Iliad. Wiesbaden.

Ferrando, F. 2013. 'Posthumanism, Transhumanism, Antihumanism, Metahumanism, and New Materialisms: Differences and Relations'. *Existenz* 8: 26–32.

Ferrando, F. 2016. *Il postumanesimo filosofico e le sue alterità.* Pisa.

Ferrari, F. (ed.). 1998. *Pindaro.* Olimpiche. Milan.

Ferrari, G. R. 1987. *Listening to the Cicadas: A Study of Plato's* Phaedrus. Cambridge.
Ferrari, G. R. 2003. *The City and Soul in Plato's* Republic. Chicago.
Ferré, F. 1994. 'Personalistic Organism: Paradox or Paradigm?'. In R. Attfield and A. Belsey (eds.), *Philosophy and the Natural Environment*. Cambridge. 59–73.
Ferrini, F. 1978. 'Tragedia e patologia. Lessico ippocratico in Euripide'. *QUCC* 29: 49–62.
Festugière, A.-J. 1972. 'Les mystères de Dionysos'. In A.-J. Festugière (ed.), *Etudes de religion grecque et hellénistique*. Paris. 13–63.
Fetterley, J. 1977. *The Resisting Reader. A Feminist Approach to American Fiction*. Bloomington.
Finglass, P. 2006. 'The Hero's Quest in Sophocles' *Philoctetes*'. *Prometheus* 32: 217–224.
Finkelberg, M. 1996. 'The Second Stasimon of the *Trachiniae* and Heracles' Festival on Mount Oeta'. *Mnemosyne* 49: 129–143.
Finkelberg, M. 1998. 'Timē and Aretē in Homer'. *CQ* 48: 14–28.
Finkelberg, M. 2014. 'Boreas and Oreithyia: A Case-study in Multichannel Transmission of Myth'. In R. Scodel (ed.), *Between Orality and Literacy: Communication and Adaptation in Antiquity*. Leiden. 87–100.
Finley, M. I. 1965. 'Technical Innovation and Economic Progress in the Ancient World'. *Economic History Review* 18: 29–45.
Finley, M. I. 1982. *The World of Odysseus*. New York.
Fitzgerald, W. 1996, 'Labor and Laborer in Latin Poetry: The Case of the Moretum'. *Arethusa* 29: 389–418.
Fleury, P. 1993. *La mécanique de Vitruve*. Caen.
Flintoff, E. 1983. 'The Noric Cattle Plague'. *QUCC* 13: 85–111.
Foertmeyer, V. A. 1988. 'The dating of the Pompe of Ptolemy II Philadelphus'. *Historia* 37: 90–104.
Fögen, T. 2007. 'Antike Zeugnisse zu Kommunikationsformen von Tieren'. *A&A* 53: 39–75.
Fögen, T. 2014. 'Animal Communication'. In J. G. Campbell (ed.), *Oxford Handbook of Animals*. Oxford. 216–232.
Fögen, T. 2017. 'Lives in Interaction. Animal "Biographies" in Graeco-Roman Literature?' In T. Fögen and E. Thomas (eds.). 89–138.
Fögen, T. and Thomas, E. (eds.). 2017. *Interactions between Animals and Humans in Graeco-Roman Antiquity*. Berlin.
Fontenay, E. 1998. *Le silence de bêtes*. Paris.
Foot, P. 1967. 'The Problem of Abortion and the Doctrine of the Double Effect'. *Oxford Review* 5: 5–15.
Forbes Irving, P. M. C. 1990. *Metamorphosis in Greek Myths*. Oxford.
Ford, A. 2002. *The Origins of Criticism: Literary Culture and Poetic Theory in Classical Greece*. Princeton/Oxford.
Ford, H. 1922. *My Life and Work*. New York.
Fornari, G. 1997. 'Labyrinthine Strategies of Sacrifice: The Cretans by Euripides'. *Contagion* 6: 163–188.
Foster, J. 1988, 'The End of the Third Georgic'. *Proceedings of the Virgil Society* 19: 32–45.
Foucault, M. 1966. *Les Mots et les choses*. Paris = 2002. *The Order of Things: An Archaeology of the Human Sciences*. London/New York.
Foucault, M. 1975. 'Pouvoir et corps'. In D. Defert and A. Fontana (eds.), *Dits et écrits. II.1970–1975*. Paris. 754–759.
Foucault, M. 1983. 'Structuralism and Post-structuralism' In D. Defert and A. Fontana (eds.), *Dits et écrits IV*. 1980–1988. Paris. 431–457.
Foucault, M. 1984. *Histoire de la sexualité. Vol. 2: L'usage des plaisirs*. Paris.
Foucault, M. 1984a. 'Nietzsche, Genealogy, History'. In P. Rabinow (ed.). 76–100.
Foucault, M. 1984b. 'What is Enlightenment?'. In P. Rabinow (ed.). 32–50.
Foucault, M. 1986. 'Discourse on Language'. In H. Adams and L. Searle (*eds*), *Critical Theory Since 1965*. Tallahassee. 148–162.
Foucault, M. 1998. 'Theatrum philosophicum'. In J. Faubion (ed.), *Aesthetics, Method, and Epistemology: Essential Works of Foucault 1954–1984*. New York. 343–368.
Foucault, M. 2003. *Abnormals. Lectures at the Collège de France 1974–1975*, trans. G. Burchell. London/New York.

Foucault, M. 2006 [1961]. *History of Madness*, trans. J. Murphy and J. Khal. London.
Foucault, M. 2009. *Security, Territory, Population. Lessons at the Collège de France 1977–78*. Ed. M. Senellart, trans. G. Burchell. New York.
Fowler, D. 1987. 'Vergil on Killing Virgins'. In M. Whitby, P. Hardie and M. Whitby (eds.), *Homo Viator: Classical Essays for John Bramble*. Bristol. 185–198.
Fowler, D. 1991. 'Narrate and Describe. The Problem of Ekphrasis'. *JRS* 81: 25–35.
Fowler, D. 2000a. *Roman Constructions. Readings in Postmodern Latin*. Oxford.
Fowler, D. 2000b. 'Deviant Focalization in Vergil's *Aeneid*'. In Fowler 2000a. 40–63.
Fox, M. 1993. 'History and Rhetoric in Dionysius of Halicarnassus'. *JRS* 83: 31–47.
Fox, M. 1996. *Roman Historical Myths. The Regal Period in Augustan Literature*. Oxford.
Fox, M. 2001. 'Dionysius, Lucian, and the Prejudice against Rhetoric in History'. *JRS* 91: 76–93.
Fränkel, H. 1945. *Ovid. A Poet between Two Worlds*. Berkeley.
Fränkel, H. 1962. *Die Homerischen Gleichnisse* (2nd edn.). Göttingen.
Fränkel, E. 1993 [1951]. *Dichtung und Philosophie des frühen Griechentums: eine Geschichte der griechischen Epik, Lyrik und Prosa bis zur Mitte des fünften Jahrhunderts*. Frankfurt.
Fragaki, H. 2012. 'Automates et statues merveilleuses dans l'Alexandrie antique'. *Journal des Savants* 1: 29–67.
Francis, J. A. 2009. 'Metal Maidens. Achilles' Shield, and Pandora: The Beginnings of "Ekphrasis"'. *AJP* 130: 1–23.
Franco, C. 2014. *Shameless. The Canine and the Feminine in Ancient Greece*. Berkeley.
Frank, M. 1995. *Eine Einführung in Schellings Philosophie*. Frankfurt.
Fratantuono, L. 2009. *A Commentary on Virgil,* Aeneid *XI*. Brussels.
Frazer, J. G. 1935 [1922]. *The Golden Bough*. New York.
Freud, S. 1953–74. *The Standard Edition of the Complete Psychological Works of Sigmund Freud, 24 vols*. Strachey, J. (trans. & ed.). London.
Freud, S. 'Three Essays on the Theory of Sexuality'. Vol. 7: 123–246.
Freud, S. 'The Sexual Enlightenment of Children'. Vol. 9: 129–140.
Freud, S. 'Analysis of a Phobia in a Five-year-old Boy'. Vol. 10: 1–150.
Freud, S. 'General Theory of the Neuroses'. Vol. 16: 241–463.
Freud, S. 'Dostoevsky and Parricide'. Vol. 21: 173–196.
Freud, S. 1971. 'From the History of an Infantile Neurosis'. In M. Gardiner (ed.), *The Wolf Man by the Wolf Man*. New York.
Freudenburg, K. 2001. *Satires of Rome. Threatening Poses from Lucilius to Juvenal*. Cambridge.
Frézouls, E. 1983. 'La construction du theatrum lapideum et son contexte politique'. In H. Zehnacker (ed.), *Théâtre et spectacles dans l'antiquité*. Leiden. 193–214.
Fried, D. 2005. 'Of Boars, Rhapsodes, and the Uses of Culturalist Error'. *Comparative Literature* 57: 312–327.
Friedrich, W.-H. 2003. *Wounding and Death in the* Iliad. London.
Frischer, B. 1991. *Shifting Paradigms. New Approaches to the* Ars Poetica. Atlanta.
Fromentin, V. 1998. 'Denys d'Halicarnasse'. *Antiquités romaines 1*. Paris.
Frontisi-Ducroux, F. 1975. *Dédale. Mythologie de l'artisan en Grèce ancienne*. Paris.
Frontisi-Ducroux, F. 2002. '"Avec son diaphragme visionnaire: Ἰδυίῃσι πραπίδεσσι", *Iliade* XVIII, 481. À propos du bouclier d'Achille'. *REG* 115: 463–484.
Frontisi-Ducroux, F. 2003. *L'homme-cerf et la femme-araignée. Figures grecques de la métamorphose*. Paris.
Furley, W. D. and Bremer, J. M. (eds.). 2001. *Greek Hymns. 2 Vols*. Tübingen.
Fusaro, D. 2012. *Minima Mercantalia. Filosofia e capitalismo*. Turin.
Gabba, E. 1991. *Dionysius and the History of Archaic Rome*. Berkeley/Oxford.
Gagarin, M. (ed.). 1997. *Antiphon: The* Speeches. Cambridge.
Gagné, R. 2013. *Ancestral Fault in Ancient Greece*. Cambridge.
Gainsford, P. 2003. 'Formal Analysis of Recognition Scenes in the *Odyssey*'. *JHS* 123: 41–59.
Gaisser, J. H. 1969. 'A Structural Analysis of the Digressions in the *Iliad* and the *Odyssey*'. *HSPh* 73: 1–43.

Gale, M. R. 1991. 'Man and Beast in Lucretius and the *Georgics*'. *CQ* 41: 414–426.
Gale, M. R. 1997. 'The Shield of Turnus (*Aeneid* 7.783–92)'. *G&R* 44: 176–196.
Gale, M. R. 2000. *Virgil on the Nature of Things. The* Georgics, *Lucretius and the Didactic Tradition.* Cambridge.
Gallagher, S. 2005. *How the Body Shapes the Mind.* Oxford.
Gallet, B. 1990. *Recherches sur kairos et l'ambiguïté dans la poésie de Pindare.* Bordeaux.
Gallistl, B. 1981. 'Der Zagreus-Mythos bei Euripides', *WJA* 7: 235–252.
Gallop, J. 1988. *Thinking through the Body.* New York.
Gammie, J. G. 1986. 'Herodotus on Kings and Tyrants: Objective Historiography or Conventional Portraiture?'. *JNES* 45: 171–195.
Gantz, T. 1993. *Early Greek Myth. 2 Vols.* Baltimore.
Gardner, H. H. 2014. 'Bees, Ants, and the Body Politic: Vergil's Noric Plague and Ovid's Origin of the Myrmidons'. *Vergilius* 60: 3–31.
Garland, R. 1981. 'The Causation of Death in the *Iliad*: A Theological and Biological Investigation'. *BICS* 28: 43–60.
Garland, R. 1995. *The Eye of the Beholder: Deformity and Disability in the Graeco-Roman World.* London.
Garnsey, P. 1999. *Food and Society in Classical Antiquity.* Cambridge/New York.
Garvie, A. F. 1969. *Aeschylus'* Supplices. *Play and Trilogy.* Cambridge.
Garvie, A. F. 1986. *Aeschylus.* Choephori. Oxford.
Garvie, A. F. 2009. *Aeschylus.* Persae. Oxford.
Gaunt, J. 2017. 'Nestor's Cup and Its Reception'. In N. W. Slater (ed.), *Voice and Voices in Antiquity: Orality and Literacy in the Ancient World.* Leiden. 92–120.
Gell, A. 1998. *Art and Agency: An Anthropological Theory.* Oxford.
Gentili, B., Bernardini, P. A., Cingano, E. and Giannini, P. 1995. *Pindaro. Le* Pitiche. Verona.
Gentili, B., Catenacci, C., Giannini, P. and Lomiento, L. 2013. *Pindaro. Le* Olimpiche. Milan.
Genz, S. and Brabon, B. A. 2009. *Postfeminism: Cultural Texts and Theories.* Edinburgh.
Gerber, D. E. 1999. 'Pindar, *Nemean* Six: A Commentary'. *HSPh* 99: 33–91.
Gerber, D. E. 2002. *A Commentary on* Olympian 9. Stuttgart.
Gerolemou, M. (forthcoming). 'Automatic Theatre: Distinguishing Technology and Humanity in Ancient Greek Drama'.
Gershon, Y. N. 2017. *The Antiquitates Romanae of Dionysius of Halicarnassus: Construction and Composition.* PhD thesis. Cambridge.
Geue, T. 2018. 'Soft Hands, Hard Power: Sponging Off the Empire of Leisure (Virgil, *Georgics* 4)'. *JRS* 108: 115–140.
Gialouris, N. 1953. 'Pteroenta pedila'. *BCH* 77: 293–321.
Gil, L. 1969. *Therapeia. La medicina popular en el mundo clásico.* Madrid.
Gildenhard, I. 2007. *Paideia Romana.* Cambridge.
Gildenhard, I. and Zissos, A. (eds). 2013. *Transformative Change in Western Thought: A History of Metamorphosis from Homer to Hollywood.* London.
Gilhus, I. S. 2006. *Animals, Gods, and Humans. Changing Attitudes to Animals in Greek, Roman and Early Christian Ideas.* Oxford.
Gill, C. 1996. *Personality in Greek Epic, Tragedy, and Philosophy: The Self in Dialogue.* Oxford.
Gille, B. 1980. *Les mécaniciens grecs. La naissance de la technologie.* Paris.
Gilligan, C. 1982. *In a Different Voice: Psychological Theory and Women's Development.* Cambridge, MA.
Giordano, M. 2010. *Iliade 1. La peste – l'ira. Introduzione e commento.* Rome.
Giordano, M. 2019. *The Emergence of Athens: War, Tragedy, and Identity Construction 477–467 BCE.*
Giusti, E. 2014. 'Virgil's Carthaginians at *Aen.* 1.430–6: Cyclopes in Bees' Clothing'. *CCJ* 60: 37–58.
Giusti, E. 2016. 'Did Somebody Say Augustan Totalitarianism? Duncan Kennedy's "Reflections," Hannah Arendt's Origins, and the Continental Divide over Virgil's *Aeneid*'. *Dictynna* 13. URL: http://dictynna.revues.org/1282
Giusti, E. 2018. *Carthage in Virgil's* Aeneid: *Staging the Enemy under Augustus.* Cambridge.

Giusti, E. 2019a. 'Bunte Barbaren Setting Up the Stage: Re-inventing the Barbarian on the *Georgics*' Theatre-Temple'. In B. Xinyue and N. Freer (eds.), *Virgil's Georgics: Reflections and New Perspectives*. London.

Giusti, E. 2019b. 'The End is the Beginning is the End: Apocalyptic Beginnings in Augustan Poetry'. In H. Marlow, K. Pollmann and H. Van Noorden (eds.), *Eschatology in Antiquity*. London.

Gladigow, B. 1965. *Sophia und Kosmos. Untersuchungen zur Frühgeschichte von σοφός und σοφίη*. Hildesheim.

Gödel, K. 1931. 'Über formal unentscheidbare Sätze der *Principia Mathematica* und verwandter Systeme'. *Mh. Math. Phys.* 38: 173–198.

Goff, B. 2000. 'Try to Make It Real Compared to What? Euripides' *Electra* and the Play of Genres'. *ICS* 24/25: Euripides and Tragic Theatre in the Late Fifth Century. 93–105.

Goh, I. 2015. *The Reject: Community, Politics, and Religion after the Subject*. New York.

Goheen, R. F. 1955. 'Aspects of Dramatic Symbolism: Three Studies in the *Oresteia*'. *AJP* 76: 113–137.

Golder, H. 1983. 'The Mute Andromache'. *TAPA* 113: 123–133.

Goldhill, S. 1984. *Language, Sexuality, Narrative. The* Oresteia. Cambridge.

Goldhill, S. 1986. *Reading Greek Tragedy*. Cambridge.

Goldhill, S. 1988. 'Battle Narrative and Politics in Aeschylus' *Persae*'. *JHS* 108: 189–193.

Goldhill, S. 2002. *Who Needs Greek? Contests in the Cultural History of Hellenism*. Cambridge.

Goldhill, S. 2011. *Victorian Culture and Classical Antiquity: Art, Opera, Fiction and the Proclamation of Modernity*. Princeton.

Goldhill, S. 2012. *Sophocles and the Language of Tragedy*. Oxford.

Gonzalez, F. J. 1998. *Dialectic and Dialogue. Plato's Practice of Philosophical Inquiry*. Evanston.

Goslin, O. 2010. 'Hesiod's Typhonomachy and the Ordering of Sound'. *TAPA* 140: 351–373.

Goudriaan, K. 1989. *Over Classicisme: Dionysius van Halicarnassus en zijn program van welsprekendheid, cultuur en politiek*. PhD thesis. Amsterdam.

Gowers, E. 2011. 'Trees and Family Trees in the *Aeneid*'. *CA* 30: 87–118.

Gowers, E. 2012. *Horace.* Satires*: Book 1*. Cambridge.

Gozzoli, S. 1976. 'Polibio e Dionigi d'Alicarnasso'. *Studi classici e orientali* 25: 149–176.

Graham, D. W. 2006. *Explaining the Cosmos*. Princeton.

Graham, D. W. 2014. 'Philolaus'. In C. A. Huffman (ed.). 46–68.

Gransee, C. 1998. 'Grenz-Bestimmungen. Erkenntnistheoretische Anmerkungen zum Naturbegriff von Donna Haraway'. In G.-A. Knapp (ed.), *Kurskorrekturen, Feminismus zwischen kritischer Theorie und Postmoderne*. Frankfurt/New York. 126–152.

Graver, M. 2007. *Stoicism and Emotion*. Chicago.

Gray, V. J. 1996. 'Herodotus and Images of Tyranny: The Tyrants of Corinth'. *AJP* 116: 361–389.

Greene, J. 2013. *Moral Tribes: Emotions, Reason and the Gap between Us and Them*. New York.

Greenwood, M. A. 1998. 'Talking Flamingos and the Sins of the Tongue. The Ambiguous Use of Lingua in Martial'. *CP* 93: 241–246.

Gregg, M. and Seignworth, G. J. (eds). 2010. *The Affect Theory Reader*. Durham.

Gregory, J. 2007. 'Donkeys and Equine Hierarchy in Archaic Greek Literature'. *CJ* 102: 193–212.

Grethlein, J. 2008. 'Memory and Material Objects in the *Iliad* and the *Odyssey*'. *JHS* 128: 27–51.

Grewing, F. 1999. '*Mundus inversus*. Fiktion und Wirklichkeit in Martials Büchern XIII und XIV'. *Prometheus* 25: 259–281.

Griffin, M. 1976. *Seneca. A Philosopher in Politics*. Oxford.

Griffin, M. 2013. 'Latin Philosophy and Roman Law'. In V. Harte and M. Lane (eds.), *Politeia in Greek and Roman Philosophy*. Cambridge. 96–115.

Griffin, S. 1981. *Pornography and Silence. Culture's Revenge Against Nature*. New York.

Griffith, M. (ed.). 1983. *Aeschylus.* Prometheus Bound. Cambridge.

Griswold, C. L. 1986. *Self-Knowledge in Plato's* Phaedrus. New Haven.

Grosz, E. 2008. *Chaos, Territory, Art. Deleuze and the Framing of the Earth*. New York.

Gruen, E. 1996. 'The Expansion of the Empire under Augustus'. In A. K. Bowman, E. Champlin and A. Lintott (eds.), *The Cambridge Ancient History X: The Augustan Empire 43 B.C.–A.D. 69*. Cambridge. 147–197.

Gruen, E. 2011. *Rethinking the Other in Antiquity*. Princeton.
Grusin, R. (ed.). 2015. *The Nonhuman Turn*. Minneapolis.
Guardasole, A. 2000. *Tragedia e medicina nell'Atene del V secolo a.C.* Naples.
Guchet, X. 2011. *Pour un humanisme technologique. Culture, technique et société dans la philosophie de Gilbert Simondon*. Paris.
Guichet, J.-L. 2015. 'From the Animal of the Enlightenment to the Animal of Postmodernism', *Yale French Studies*. 127: 69–83.
Gundert, H. 1935. *Pindars Dichterberuf*. Frankfurt.
Habinek, T. 1998. *The Politics of Latin Literature*. Princeton.
Habinek, T. 2005. *The World of Roman Song*. Baltimore.
Habinek, T. and Schiesaro, A. (eds.). 1997. *The Roman Cultural Revolution*. Cambridge.
Hainsworth, B. 1993. *The* Iliad. *A Commentary. Vol. 3: Books 9–12*. Cambridge.
Hall, E. 1996. *Aeschylus'* Persians. Oxford.
Hall, E. 2009. 'Deianeira Deliberates: Precipitate Decision-making and *Trachiniae*'. In E. Hall and S. Goldhill (eds.), *Sophocles and the Greek Tragic Tradition*. Cambridge. 69–96.
Hall, E. 2018. 'Materialisms Old and New'. In M. Telò and M. Mueller (eds.). 203–218.
Haller, B. 2009. 'The Gates of Horn and Ivory in *Odyssey* 19: Penelope's Call for Deeds, Not Words'. *CP* 104: 397–417.
Halliwell, S. 2008. *Greek Laughter: A Study of Cultural Psychology from Homer to Early Christianity*. Cambridge/New York.
Hallward, P. 2000. 'The Limits of Individuation or How to Distinguish Deleuze and Foucault'. *Angelaki* 5: 93–112.
Hallward, P. 2006. *Out of this World: Deleuze and Philosophy of Creation*. London/New York.
Halperin, D. 1990. *A Hundred Years of Homosexuality*. New York and London.
Halperin, D. 2012. *How to Be Gay*. Cambridge, MA.
Hamilton, R. 1989. *The Architecture of Hesiodic Poetry*. Baltimore.
Hamilton, R. 1995. 'Slings and Arrows; The Debate with Lycus in the *Heracles*'. *TAPA* 115: 19–25.
Hammer, C. and Stieß, I. 1995. 'Einleitung'. In D. Haraway. *Die Neuerfindung der Natur. Primaten, Cyborgs und Frauen*. Frankfurt. 9–33.
Hammond, E. 2018. 'Alex Garland's Ex Machina or The Modern Epimetheus: Science Fiction after Mary Shelley'. In B. E. Stevens, J. Weiner and B. M. Rogers (eds.), *Frankenstein and Its Classics: The Modern Prometheus from Antiquity to Science Fiction*. London. 190–205.
Hammond, N. G. L. and Roseman, L. J. 1996. 'The Construction of Xerxes' Bridge Over The Hellespont'. *JHS* 116: 88–107.
Hankinson, R. J. 1998. 'Magic, Religion and Science: Divine and Human in the *Hippocratic Corpus*'. *Apeiron* 31: 1–34.
Hannah, R. 2005. *Greek and Roman Calendars, Constructions of Time in the Classical World*. London.
Harasser, K. 2011. 'Donna Haraway: Natur-Kulturen und die Faktizität der Figuration'. In S. Moebius and D. Quadflieg (eds.), *Kultur. Theorien der Gegenwart*. Wiesbaden. 58–93.
Haraway, D. J. 1988. 'Situated Knowledges: The Science Questions in Feminism as a Site of Discourses on the Privilege of Partial Perspective'. *Feminist Studies* 14: 575–599.
Haraway, D. J. 1989. *Primate Visions: Gender, Race, and Nature in the World of Modern Science*. New York.
Haraway, D. J. 1991. *Simians, Cyborgs, and Women: The Reinvention of Nature*. New York.
Haraway, D. J. 1992. 'The Promises of Monsters: A Regenerative Politics for Inappropriate/d Others'. In L. Grossberg, C. Nelson and P. A. Treichler (eds.), *Cultural Studies*. New York. 295–337.
Haraway, D. J. 1994. 'A Game of Cat's Cradle: Science Studies, Feminist Theory'. *Cultural Studies* 2: 59–71.
Haraway, D. J. 1995. *'Wir sind immer mittendrin'. Ein Interview mit Donna Haraway*. Frankfurt.
Haraway, D. J. 1997. 'Mice into Wormholes: A Comment on the Nature of No Nature'. In G. L. Downey and J. Dumit (eds.), *Cyborgs and Citadels. Anthropological Interventions in Emerging Sciences and Technologies*. Santa Fe. 209–243.
Haraway, D. J. 1997a. *Modest_Witness@Second_Millennium.FemaleMan©_Meets OncoMouse™: Feminism and Technoscience*. New York.

Haraway, D. J. 2000. *How Like a Leaf. An Interview with Thyrza Nichols Goodeve*. London.
Haraway, D. J. 2003. *The Companion Species Manifesto: Dogs, People, and Significant Otherness*. Chicago.
Haraway, D. J. 2004. *The Haraway Reader*. New York.
Haraway, D. J. 2007. *When Species Meet*. Minneapolis.
Haraway, D. J. 2015. 'Anthropocene, Capitalocene, Plantationocene, Chthulucene: Making Kin'. *Environmental Humanities* 6, 159–165.
Haraway, D. J. 2016. 'A Cyborg Manifesto: Science, Technology, and Socialist-feminism in the Late Twentieth Century'. In D. J. Haraway, *Manifestly Haraway*. Minneapolis. 5–90. = 1985. *Socialist Review* 80: 65–108 = 1991: 149–181.
Haraway, D. J. 2016a. *Staying with the Trouble: Making Kin in the Chthulucene*. Durham.
Harden, A. 2013. *Animals in the Classical World: Ethical Perspectives from Greek and Roman Texts*. New York.
Hardie, P. 1986. *Virgil's* Aeneid. *Cosmos and Imperium*. Oxford.
Hardie, P. 1993. *The Epic Successors of Virgil*. Cambridge.
Hardie, P. 2013. 'Flavian Epic and the Sublime'. In G. Manuwald and A. Voigt (eds.). 125–138.
Hardie, P. 2018. 'Review of Stahl (2016)'. *CP* 113: 88–92.
Hardt, M. and Negri, A. 2000. *Empire*. Cambridge, MA.
Harman, G. 2002. *Tool-being: Heidegger and the Metaphysics of Objects*. Chicago.
Harman, G. 2005. *Guerrilla Metaphysics: Phenomenology and the Carpentry of Things*. Chicago.
Harrison, E. L. 1979. 'The Noric Plague and Virgil's Third *Georgic*'. *Papers of the Liverpool Latin Seminar* 2: 1–65.
Harrison, J. E. 1903. *Prolegomena to the Study of Greek Religion*. Cambridge.
Harrison, S. J. 2013. *Framing the Ass. Literary Texture in Apuleius* Metamorphoses. Oxford/New York.
Harvey, S. A. 1988. 'The Sense of a Stylite. Perspectives on Simeon the Elder'. *VChr* 42: 376–394.
Hasse, D. N. 2007. 'Arabic Philosophy and Averroism'. In J. Jankins (ed.), *The Cambridge Companion to Renaissance Philosophy*. Cambridge. 113–136
Haubold, J. 2000. *Homer's People. Epic Poetry and Social Formation*. Cambridge.
Hawley, R. 1998. 'The Male Body as Spectacle in Attic Drama'. In L. Foxhall and J. Salmon (eds.), *Thinking Men. Masculinity and its Self-Representation in the Classical Tradition*. London. 83–99.
Hayles, N. K. 1999. *How We became Posthuman. Virtual Bodies in Cybernetics, Literature, and Informatics*. Chicago.
Hayles, N. K. 2005. *My Mother Was a Computer. Digital Subjects and Literary Texts*. Chicago.
Headlam, W. 1906. 'The Last Scene of the *Eumenides*'. *JHS* 26: 268–277.
Heath, J. 1999. 'Disentangling the Beast: Humans and Other Animals in Aeschylus' *Oresteia*'. *JHS* 119: 17–47.
Heath, J. 2005. *The Talking Greeks. Speech, Animals, and the Other in Homer, Aeschylus, and Plato*. Cambridge.
Heath, M. 1986. *Unity in Greek Poetics*. Oxford.
Heerink, M. and Manuwald, G. (eds.). 2014. *Brill's Companion to Valerius Flaccus*. Leiden.
Hegel, G. W. F. 1970 [1817]. *Philosophy of Nature*, ed. & trans. M. J. Petry. London/New York.
Hegel, G. W. F. 1975 [1826]. *Aesthetics: Lectures on Fine Art, Vol. 1*, trans. T. M. Knox. Oxford.
Heidegger, M. 1947. *Platons Lehre über die Wahrheit mit einem Brief über den Humanismus*. Bern.
Heidegger, M. 1956. 'Die Frage nach der Technik'. In M. Heidegger, *Die Künste im technischer Zeitalter*. Darmstadt. 48–72.
Heidegger, M. 1996. *Being and Time*, trans. Stambaugh, J. Albany.
Heiny, S. B. 1994. 'Charis, Persuasion, and Performance in Pindar's *Olympian* 7'. In B. R. Baker and J. E. Fischer (eds), *Exegisti Monumentum Aere Perennius: Essays in Honor of John Frederick Charles*. Indianapolis. 61–80.
Heinze, R. 1999 [1903]. *Virgil's Epic Technique*. London.
Heller, A. 1994. 'A Reply to My Critics'. In J. Bournheim (ed.), *The Social Philosophy of Agnes Heller*. Amsterdam. 281–312.
Henderson, J. 1997. 'Mass versus Elite and the Comic Heroism of Peisetairos'. In G. Dobrov (ed.), *The City as Comedy: Society and Representation in Athenian Drama*. Chapel Hill. 135–148.

Henderson, J. 2000. 'The Camillus Factory: Per Astra AD Ardeam'. *Ramus* 29: 1–26.
Henry, W. B. 2005. *Pindar's* Nemeans, *A Selection: Edition and Commentary*. Munich/Leipzig.
Herbrechter, S. 2012. 'Introduction – Shakespeare even after'. In S. Herbrechter and I. Callus (eds.), *Posthumanist Shakespeares*. New York. 1–19.
Herbrechter, S. 2013. *Posthumanism: A Critical Analysis*. London.
Herrero de Jáuregui, M. 2010. *Orphism and Christianity in Late Antiquity*. Berlin/New York.
Hershkowitz, D. 1998. *Valerius Flaccus'* Argonautica. *Abbreviated Voyages in Silver Latin Epic*. Oxford.
Hexter, R. 1990. 'What Was the Trojan Horse Made Of? Interpreting Vergil's *Aeneid*'. *The Yale Journal of Criticism* 3: 109–131.
Hillgruber, M. 1996. 'Die Erzählung des Menenius Agrippa. Eine griechische Fabel in der römischen Geschichtsschreibung'. *A&A* 42: 42–56.
Hinds, S. 1998. *Allusion and Intertext: Dynamics of Appropriation in Roman Poetry*. New York.
Hinds, S. 2007. 'Martial's Ovid/Ovid's Martial'. *JRS* 97: 113–154.
Hobbs, A. 2006. 'Female Imagery in Plato'. In Lesher et al. (eds.). 252–271.
Hodder, I. 2012. *Entangled: An Archaeology of the Relationships between Humans and Things*. Malden.
Hodder, I. 2014. 'The Entanglements of Humans and Things: A Long-term View'. *New Literary History* 45: 19–36.
Hodge, A. T. 1960. *The Woodwork of Greek Roofs*. Cambridge.
Hoefmans, M. 1994. 'Myth into Reality: The Metamorphosis of Daedalus and Icarus (Ovid, *Metamorphoses*, VIII, 183–235)'. *AC* 63: 137–160.
Hogg, D. A. W. 2013. 'Libraries in a Greek Working Life: Dionysius of Halicarnassus, a Case Study in Rome'. In J. König, K. Oikonomopoulou and G. Woolf (eds.), *Ancient Libraries*. Cambridge. 138–151.
Holmes, B. 2008. 'Euripides' Heracles in the Flesh'. *CA* 27: 231–281.
Holmes, B. 2010. *The Symptom and the Subject: The Emergence of the Physical Body in Ancient Greece*. Princeton.
Holmes, B. 2012. *Gender, Antiquity and Its Legacy*. London.
Holmes, B. 2015. 'Situating Scamander: "Natureculture" in the *Iliad*'. *Ramus* 44: 29–51.
Holt, P. 1989. 'The End of the *Trachiniae* and the Fate of Herakles'. *JHS* 109: 69–80.
Hömke, N. and Reitz, C. (eds.). 2010. *Lucan's* Bellum Civile *between Epic Tradition and Aesthetic Innovation*. Berlin.
Hooker, J. T. 1985. 'A Reading of the Seventh *Olympian*'. *BICS* 32: 63–70.
Horkheimer, M. and Adorno, T. 2010 [1947]. *Die Dialektik der Aufklärung*. Frankfurt.
Hornblower, S. 2013. *Herodotus.* Histories. *Book V*. Cambridge.
Hornsby, R. 1966. 'The Armor of the Slain'. *PhQ* 45: 347–359.
Horsfall, N. 2003. *The Culture of the Roman Plebs*. London.
Horsfall, N. 2003a. *Virgil* Aeneid *11. A Commentary*. Leiden.
Howe, T. 2008. *Pastoral Politics. Animals, Agriculture and Society in Ancient Greece*. Claremont.
Hubbard, Th. K. 1997. 'Utopianism and the Sophistic City in Aristophanes'. In G. W. Dobrov (ed.), *The City as Comedy. Society and Representation in Athenian Drama*. Chapel Hill and London. 23–50.
Hude, C. (ed). 1927. *Herodoti Historiae*. Vols. 1–2. Oxford.
Huffman, C. A. 1988. 'The Role of Number in Philolaus' Philosophy'. *Phronesis* 33: 1–30.
Huffman, C. A. 1993. *Philolaus of Croton: Pythagorean and Presocratic*. Cambridge.
Huffman, C. A. 1999. 'Limite et illimité chez les premiers philosophes grecs'. In M. Dixsaut (ed.), *La fêlure du plaisir: études sur le* Philèbe *de Platon. Vol. 2: Contextes*. Paris. 11–31.
Huffman, C. A. 2009. 'The Pythagorean Conception of the Soul'. In D. Frede and B. Reis (eds.), *Body and Soul in Ancient Philosophy*. Hamburg. 21–43.
Huffman, C. A. 2012. 'Commentary on McKirahan'. *Proceedings of the Boston Area Colloquium in Ancient Philosophy* 27: 233–238.
Huffman, C. A. (ed.). 2014. *A History of Pythagoreanism*. Cambridge.
Hughes, J. 2010. 'Dissecting the Classical Hybrid'. In K. Rebay-Salisbury, M. L. S. Sorensen and J. Hughes (eds.), *Body Parts and Bodies Whole: Changing Relations and Meanings*. Oxford. 101–110.
Hui, Y. 2016. *On the Existence of Digital Objects*. Minneapolis.
Hui, Y. 2017. *The Question Concerning Technology in China: An Essay in Cosmotechnics*. Falmouth.

Hui, Y. 2019. *Recursivity and Contingency*. London.
Hulme, M. 2009. *Why We Disagree About Climate Change: Understanding Controversy, Inaction and Opportunity*. Cambridge.
Hünemörder, C. 2003. 'Zypresse'. In H. Cancik and H. Schneider (eds.), *Der neue Pauly (Vol. XII: 2)*. Stuttgart/Weimar.
Hunter, R. 2004. *Plato's* Symposium. Oxford.
Hunzinger, C. 2015. 'Wonder'. In S. Davies et al. (eds.), *A Companion to Aesthetics*. London. 422–437.
Hurwit, J. 1999. *The Athenian Acropolis. History, Mythology, and Archaeology from the Neolithic Era to the Present*. Cambridge.
Hutchins, E. 1995. *Cognition in the Wild*. Cambridge, MA.
Immerwahr, H. R. 1966. *Form and Thought in Herodotus*. Cleveland.
Ingold, T. 2011. *Being Alive. Essays on Movement, Knowledge and Description*. Oxon.
Inwood, B. 1985. *Ethics and Action in Early Stoicism*. Oxford.
Inwood, B. 2005. *Reading Seneca*. Oxford.
Inwood, B. 2007. *Seneca: Selected Philosophical Letters*. Cambridge.
Irigaray, L. 1984. *Éthique de la différence sexuelle*. Paris.
Irigaray, L. 1985 [1972]. *Speculum of the Other Woman*, tr. G. C. Gill. Ithaca.
Isaac, B. 2004. *The Invention of Racism in Classical Antiquity*. Princeton.
Ishay, M. 2004. *The History of Human Rights*. Berkeley.
James, P. 2011. *Ovid's Myth of Pygmalion on Screen. In Pursuit of the Perfect Woman*. London.
Janan, M. 1988. 'The Book of Good Love? Design versus Desire in *Metamorphoses* 10'. *Ramus* 17: 110–137.
Jarvis Thomson, J. 1985. 'The Trolley Problem'. *The Yale Law Journal* 94: 1395–1415.
Jauss, H. R. 1982. *Toward an Aesthetic of Reception*, trans. T. Bahti. Minneapolis.
Jebb, R. C. 1917. (trans.) *Tragedies of Sophocles*. Philoctetes. Cambridge.
Jiménez San Cristóbal A. I. 2009. '¿Hubo ritos de paso cruentos en el Orfismo?' *Synthesis* 16: 83–97.
Johnson, B. 1996. 'Die kritische Differenz: Barthes S/BalZac'. In A. Hassmann and J. Hassmann (eds.), *Texte und Lektüre. Perspektive in der Literaturwissenschaft*. Frankfurt. 142–155.
Johnson, B. 2008. *Persons and Things*. Cambridge, MA.
Johnson, D. M. 2001. 'Herodotus' Storytelling Speeches: Socles (5.92) and Leotychides (6.86)'. *CJ* 97: 1–26
Johnson, W. R. 1987. *Momentary Monsters. Lucan and His Heroes*. Ithaca.
Johnson, W. R. 1992. 'Dismal Decoration: Dryden's Machines in *Aeneid* 12'. In R. Wilhelm and H. Jones (eds.), *The Two Worlds of the Poet: New Perspectives on Vergil*. Detroit. 433–447.
Johnson, W. R. 2005. 'Small Wonders. The Poetics of Martial, Book Fourteen'. In W. Batstone and G. Tissol (eds.), *Defining Gender and Genre in Latin Literature. Festschrift for W. S. Anderson*. New York. 139–150.
Jolly, É. 2010. *Nihilisme et technique – Étude sur Günther Anders*. https://books.openedition.org/europhilosophie/245
Jones, W. (ed.). 1923. *Hippocrates. Vols. 1–4*. Cambridge, MA.
Jong, I. J. F. de 2001. *A Narratological Commentary on the* Odyssey. Cambridge.
Jong, I. J. F. de 2014. *Narratology and Classics*. Oxford.
Jouan F. and van Looy, H. (eds). 2001. *Euripides. Fragments. Vol. VIII: 2*. Paris.
Jouanna, J. 1987. 'Médecine hippocratique et tragédie grecque'. *CGITA* 3: 109–131.
Jouanna, J. 1987a. 'Le souffle, la vie et le froid. Remarques sur la famille de ψύχω d'Homère à Hippocrate'. *RÉG* 100: 203–224.
Jouanna, J. 1994. *Ippocrate*, trans. L. Rebaudo. Turin.
Jouanna, J. 1999. 'Réflexions sur l'imaginaire de la thérapeutique dans la Grèce classique'. In I. Garofalo, A. Lami, D. Manetti and A. Roselli (eds.), *Aspetti della terapia nel* Corpus Hippocraticum. *Atti del IXe Colloque International Hippocratique*. Florence. 13–42.
Jouanna, J. 2012a. 'Dietetics in Hippocratic Medicine'. In J. Jouanna 2012, trans. N. Allies. *Greek Medicine from Hippocrates to Galen*. Leiden. 137–154.
Jouanna, J. 2012b. 'Egyptian Medicine and Greek Medicine'. In J. Jouanna 2012. 3–20.

Kachuck, A. 2016. Review of Lowe 2015. *CR* 66: 420–422.
Kaczko, S. 2016. *Archaic and Classical Attic Dedicatory Epigrams. An Epigraphic, Literary and Linguistic Commentary*. Berlin.
Kahn, C. 1960. *Anaximander and the Origins of Greek Cosmology*. New York.
Kahn, C. 1985. 'Democritus and the Origins of Moral Psychology'. *AJP* 106: 1–31.
Kaimio, M. 1988. *Physical Contact in Greek Tragedy: A Study of Stage Conventions*. Helsinki.
Kalof, L. (ed.). 2007. *A Cultural History of Animals in Antiquity*. London.
Kamerbeek, J. C. 1948. 'Sophoclea II'. *Mnemosyne* 1: 198–204.
Kamerbeek, J. C. 1959. *The Plays of Sophocles. Commentaries. Vol. II: The* Trachiniae. Leiden.
Kamerbeek, J. C. 1980. *The Plays of Sophocles. Commentaries. Vol. 6: The* Philoctetes. Leiden.
Kang, M. 2011. *Sublime Dreams of Living Machines*. Cambridge, MA.
Kannicht, R. 1969. *Euripides.* Helena. *Vol. 2: Kommentar*. Heidelberg.
Kannicht, R. (ed.). 2004. *Tragicorum Graecorum Fragmenta. Vol. V: Euripides*. Göttingen.
Kaplan, M. D. (ed.) 2009. *Readings in the Philosophy of Technology*. 2nd ed. Lanham.
Käppel, L. 1992. *Paian. Studien zur Geschichte einer Gattung*. Berlin.
Kassel, R. 1983. 'Dialoge mit Statuen'. *ZPE* 51: 1–12.
Kaster, R. A. 2005. *Emotion, Restraint, and Community in Ancient Rome*. Oxford/New York.
Katz, P. B. 1999. 'Io in the *Prometheus Bound*: A Coming of Age Paradigm for the Athenian Community'. In M. W. Padilla (ed.), *Rites of Passage in Ancient Greece*. Lewisburg. 129–147.
Kazantzidis, G. 2016. 'Empathy and the Limits of Disgust in the *Hippocratic Corpus*'. In D. Lateiner and D. Spatharas (eds). 45–68.
Keen, P. (ed.), 2013. *The Age of Authors: An Anthology of Eighteenth-Century Print Culture*. Buffalo/London/Moorebank. 159–166.
Keen, T. 2017. 'Prometheus, Pygmalion, and Helen: Science fiction and mythology'. In V. Zajko and H. Hoyle (eds.). *A Handbook to the Reception of Classical Mythology*. Malden. 311–322.
Keiper, A. and Schulman, A. N. 2011. 'The Problem with "Friendly" Artificial Intelligence'. *The New Atlantis* 32: 80–89.
Kennedy, D. F. 1992. '"Augustan" and "Anti-Augustan": Reflections on Terms of Reference'. In A. Powell (ed.), *Roman Poetry and Propaganda in the Age of Augustus*. London. 26–58.
Ker, J. 2006. 'Seneca, Man of Many Genres'. In K. Volk and G. Williams (eds.), *Seeing Seneca Whole*. Leiden. 19–42.
Ker, J. 2010. 'Socrates Speaks in Seneca, *De vita beata* 24–28'. In A. Nightingale and D. Sedley (eds.), *Ancient Models of Mind*. Cambridge. 180–195.
Kern, O. 1916. 'Orphiker auf Kreta'. *Hermes* 51: 554–567.
Keuls, E. 1985. *The Reign of the Phallus. Sexual Politics in Ancient Athens*. New York.
Khan, N. A. 1990. 'A New Relief from Gandhāra Depicting the Trojan Horse'. *East and West* 40: 315–319.
Kirichenko, A. 2016a. '*Conviva satur*. Mündlichkeit, Schriftlichkeit und Patronage in den Sermones des Horaz'. *Poetica* 48: 201–240.
Kirichenko, A. 2016b. 'Wie man zum Klassiker wird. Horaz, c. 4.8'. *A&A* 62: 58–73.
Kirichenko, A. 2016c. 'The Art of Transference. Metaphor and Iconicity in Pindar's *Olympian* 6 and *Nemean* 5'. *Mnemosyne* 69: 1–28.
Kirichenko, A. 2018. 'How to Build a Monument. Horace the Image Maker'. *MD* 80: 119–161.
Kleeman, J. 2017. 'The Race to Build the World's First Sex Robot'. In The Guardian. https://www.theguardian.com/technology/2017/apr/27/race-to-build-worldfirst-sex-robot
Klein, M. 1998 [1929]. 'Personification in the Play of Children'. In M. Klein, *Love, Guilt and Reparation*. London. 199–209.
Klodt, C. 2003. 'The Ancient and the Modern Hero: Turnus and Aeneas Donning Their Armour'. *Classica Cracouiensia* 8: 7–40.
Kloer, A. 2010. Are Robots the Future of Prostitution? http://www.pinoyexchange.com/forums/showthread.php?t=442361
Kneebone, E. *Oppian's 'Halieutica': Charting a Didactic Epic*, Cambridge 2020.
Knoll, E. -M. 2011. 'Cyborgs'. In F. Kreff, E. -M. Knoll and A. Gingrich (eds.), *Lexikon der Globalisierung*. Bielefeld.

Koenigs, W. 1990. 'Maße und Proportionen in der griechischen Baukunst'. In H. Beck, P. C. Bol and M. Bückling (eds.), *Polyklet. Der Bildhauer der griechischen Klassik*. Mainz. 121–134.

Konstan, D. 1986. 'Slavery and Class Analysis in the Ancient World. A Review Article'. *Comparative Studies in Society and History* 28: 754–766.

Konstan, D. 1990. 'Aristophanes' *Birds* and the City in the Air'. *Arethusa* 23: 183–207.

Konstan, D. 2012. 'A World without Slaves: Crates' *Thêria*'. In C. W. Marshall and G. Kovacs (eds.), *No Laughing Matter. New Studies in Athenian Comedy*. London. 13–18.

Konstan, D. and Dillon, M. 1981. 'The Ideology of Aristophanes' Wealth'. *AJP* 102: 371–394.

Konstantinou, A. 2018. *Female Mobility and Gendered Space in Ancient Greek Myth*. London.

Korhonen, T. 2017. 'A Question of Life and Death. The Aesopic Animal Fables on Why Not to Kill'. *Humanities* 6: 1–16.

Korhonen, T. and Ruonakoski, E. 2017. *Human and Animal in Ancient Greece: Empathy and Encounter in Classical Literature*. London.

Korn, M. and Tscheidel, H. J. (eds.). 1991. *Ratis omnia vincit. Untersuchungen zu den* Argonautica *des Valerius Flaccus*. Hildesheim.

Kosak, J. C. 1999. 'Therapeutic Touch and Sophokles' *Philoktetes*'. *HSCP* 99: 93-134.

Kosak, J. C. 2006. 'The Male Interior: Strength, Illness, and Masculinity in Sophocles' *Philoctetes*'. *BICS* 49: 49-64.

Kosak, J. C. 2006a. 'The Wall in Aristophanes' *Birds*'. In R. M Rosen and I. Sluiter (eds.), *City, Countryside, and the Spatial Organization of Value in Classical Antiquity*. Leiden. 173–180.

Kosmin, P. J. 2014. *The Land of the Elephant Kings: Space, Territory, and Ideology in the Seleucid Empire*. Cambridge, MA.

Kreisberg, J. 1995. 'A Globe, Clothing Itself with a Brain'. *Wired Magazine* 6. https://www.wired.com/1995/06/teilhard/

Krell, D. F. 2013. *Derrida and Our Animal Others: Derrida's Final Seminar,* The Beast and The Sovereign. Bloomington.

Kristeva, J. 1980. *Desire in Language*, trans. L. Roudiez. Oxford.

Kristeva, J. 1982 [1980]. *Powers of Horror: An Essay on Abjection*, trans. L. S. Roudiez. New York.

Krueger, D. 1997. 'Typological Figuration in Theodoret of Cyrrhus's *Religious History* and the Art of Postbiblical Narrative'. *JECS* 5: 393–419.

Kuhn, T. 1957. *The Copernican Revolution. Planetary Astronomy in the Development of Western Thought*, Cambridge, MA.

Kull, A. 2001. 'The Cyborg as an Interpretation of Culture-nature'. *Zygon* 36: 49–56.

Kull, A. 2002. 'Speaking Cyborg: Technoculture and Technonature'. *Zygon* 37: 279–288.

Kurke, L. 2013 [1991]. *The Traffic in Praise. Pindar and the Poetics of Social Economy*. Ithaca.

Kurke, L. 2013a. 'Imagining Chorality. Wonder, Plato's Puppets, and Moving Statues'. In A-E. Peponi (ed.), *Performance and Culture in Plato's* Laws. Cambridge. 123–170.

Kurke, L. 2016. Pindar's Material Imaginary: Dedication and Politics in *Olympian* 7. Housman Lecture 2015.

Kurzweil, R. 2005. *The Singularity Is Near. When Humans Transcend Biology*. London.

Kyriakides, S. and De Martino, F. (eds.). 2004. *Middles in Latin Poetry*. Bari.

Kyriakou, P. 1997. 'All in the Family: Present and Past in Euripides' *Andromache*'. *Mnemosyne* 50: 7–26.

Lacan, J. 1977. *Ecrits. A Selection*, tr. A. Sheridan. New York.

Lada-Richards, I. 1997. 'Neoptolemus and the Bow'. *JHS* 117: 179-183.

Lada-Richards, I. 1999. *Initiating Dionysus: Ritual and Theatre in Aristophanes'* Frogs. Oxford.

Lada-Richards, I. 2002. 'The Subjectivity of Greek Performance'. In E. Hall and P. E. Easterling (eds.), *Greek and Roman Actors*. Cambridge, 395–418.

Laird, A. 2007. 'The *Ars Poetica*'. In S. J. Harrison (ed.), *The Cambridge Companion to Horace*. Cambridge. 132–143.

Lakoff, G. 2008. 'The Neural Theory of Metaphor'. In R. Gibbs (ed.), *The Cambridge Handbook of Metaphor and Thought*. Cambridge. 17–38.

Lakoff, G. 2016. 'Language and Emotion'. *Emotion Review* 8: 269–273.

Lakoff, G. and Johnson, M. 1999. *Philosophy in the Flesh. The Embodied Mind and Its Challenge to Western Thought*. New York.
Lamb, J. 2004. 'Modern Metamorphoses and Disgraceful Tales'. In B. Brown (ed.). 2004. 193–226.
Lami, A. (ed.) 1996. *Ippocrate. Testi di medicina greca*. Milan.
Lanata, G. 1967. *Medicina magica e religione popolare in Grecia fino all'età di Ippocrate*. Rome.
Lanata, G. 1968. 'Linguaggio scientifico e linguaggio poetico. Note al lessico del *De morbo sacro*'. *QUCC* 5: 22–36.
Landels, L. G. 2000. *Engineering in the Ancient World* (revised edn). Berkeley/Los Angeles.
Lang, F. G. 2004. 'Ebenmass im Ephesierbrief: Stichometrische Kompositionsanalyse'. *Novum Testamentum* 46: 143–163.
Lanier, J. 2010. *You Are Not a Gadget. A Manifesto*. New York.
Lapidge, M. 2010 [1989]. 'Lucan's Imagery of Cosmic Dissolution'. In C. Tesoriero, F. Muecke, T. Neal and S. M. Braund (eds.), *Lucan*. Oxford. 289–323.
Larivée, A. 2012. 'Eros Tyrannos: Alcibiades as the Model of the Tyrant in Book IX of the *Republic*'. *IJPlTr* 6: 1–26.
Lateiner, D. 1989. *The Historical Method of Herodotus*. Toronto.
Lateiner, D. and Spatharas D. (eds.). 2016. *The Ancient Emotion of Disgust*. Oxford.
Latimer, J. and Miele, M. 2013. 'Naturecultures: Science, Affect and the Non-human'. *Theory, Culture & Society* 30 (7/8), 5–31.
Latour, B. 1993. *We Have Never Been Modern*, trans. C. Porter. Cambridge, MA.
Latour, B. 2005. *Reassembling the Social. An Introduction to Actor-Network Theory*. Oxford.
Latour, B. 2009 [1999]. 'A Collective of Humans and Nonhumans. Following Daedalus's Labyrinth'. In D. M. Kaplan (ed.). 156–172.
Lattimore, R. 1965. *The* Odyssey *of Homer*. New York.
Lattimore, R. 2011 [1951]. *The* Iliad *of Homer*. Chicago.
Lawrence, S. 1978. 'The Dramatic Epistemology of Sophocles' *Trachiniae*'. *Phoenix* 43: 288–304.
Leach, E. W. 1974. 'Ekphrasis and the Theme of Artistic Failure in Ovid's *Metamorphoses*'. *Ramus* 3: 102–142.
Leary, T. J. 1996. *Martial Book XIV. The* Apophoreta. *Text with Introduction and Commentary*. London.
Leary, T. J. 2001. *Martial Book XIII. The* Xenia *with Introduction and Commentary*. London.
Lebeck, A. 1971. *The* Oresteia. *A Study in Language and Structure*. Washington.
Lebrère, M. 2015. 'L'artialisation des sons de la nature dans les sanctuaires à automates d'Alexandrie, du IIIe s. av. J.C. au Ier s. ap. J.C.'. *Pallas* 98: 31–53.
Lee, M. 2004. 'Evil Wealth of Raiment: Deadly Πέπλοι in Greek Tragedy'. *CJ* 99: 253–279.
Lee, M. 2015. *Body, Dress, and Identity in Ancient Greece*. Cambridge.
Lefebvre, L. 2017. *Le mythe Néron: la fabrique d'un monstre dans la littérature antique Ier–Ve s.* Villeneuve d'Ascq.
Leigh, M. 1997. *Lucan: Spectacle and Engagement*. Oxford.
Leigh, M. 2013. *From Polypragmon to Curiosus: Ancient Concepts of Curious and Meddlesome Behaviour*. Oxford.
Leonard, M. 2005. *Athens in Paris: Ancient Greece and the Political in Post-War French Thought*. Oxford.
Leonard, M. 2015. *Tragic Modernities*. Cambridge, MA.
Lesher, J. H., Nails, D. and Sheffield, F. (eds.). 2006. *Plato's* Symposium. *Issues in Interpretation and Reception*. Cambridge, MA.
Letoublon, F. 2010. 'Des traces sur la peau'. In P. Hameau, C. Abry and F. Letoublon (eds.), *Les rites de passage, 1909–2009*. Grenoble. 259–268.
Letoublon, F. 2016. 'Entre lions et loups. À propos des comparaisons homériques'. *Gaia* 19: 127–150.
Levaniouk, O. 2000. 'Aithôn, Aithon, and Odysseus'. *HSPh* 100: 25–51.
Levaniouk, O. 2011. *Eve of the Festival. Making Myth in* Odyssey *19*. Washington.
Leveringhaus, A. 2016. 'What's So Bad About Killer Robots?'. *Journal of Applied Philosophy* 2: 341–358. https://philpapers.org/rec/LEVWSB.
Levi-Strauss, C. 1963. 'Split Representation in the art of Asia and America'. In C. Levi–Strauss, *Structural Anthropology*, trans. C. Jacobson and B. Grundfest Schoepf. New York. 245–268.

Levinas, E. 1957. 'La philosophie et l'idée de l'infini'. *Revue de Métaphysique et de Morale* 62: 241–253.

Levinas, E. 1968. 'Humanisme et An-archie'. *Revue Internationale de Philosophie* 22: 323–337.

Levinas, E. 1974. *Autrement qu' être ou au-delà de l'essence*. Paris.

Levine, D. B. 2003. 'Sophocles' *Philoctetes* and *Odyssey* 9: Odysseus versus the Cave Man'. *Scholia* 12: 3–26.

Levine, D. B. 2015. 'Hephaestus' Winged Shoes and the Birth of Athena'. In A. Clark, E. Foster and J. P. Hallett (eds.), *Kinesis: Essays for Donald Lateiner on the Ancient Depiction of Gesture, Motion, and Emotion*. Michigan. 262–280.

Levy, D. 2007. *Love and Sex with Robots*. New York.

Levy, D. 2012. 'The Ethics of Robot Prostitutes'. In P. Lin, K. Abney and G. Bekey (eds.), *Robot Ethics*. Cambridge, MA. 223–232.

Levy, D. and Loebner, H. 2007. 'Robot Prostitutes as Alternatives to Human Sex Workers'. In IEEE International Conference on Robotics and Automation, Rome. http://www.roboethics.org/icra2007/contributions/LEVY%20Robot%20Prostitutes%20as%20Alternatives%20to%20Human%20Sex%20Workers.pdf

Lewis, D. 1973. 'Causation'. *Jph* 70: 556–567.

Lewis, S. 2017. 'A Lifetime Together? Temporal Perspectives on Animal–Human Interactions'. In T. Fögen and E. Thomas (eds.). 19–38.

Lewis, S. and Llewellyn-Jones, L. 2017. *The Culture of Animals in Antiquity: A Sourcebook with Commentaries*. Abingdon/New York.

Liapis, V. 2006. 'Intertextuality as Irony: Heracles in Epic and in Sophocles'. *G&R* 53: 48–51.

Liebeschuetz, W. 1965. 'Beast and Man in the Third Book of Virgil's *Georgics*'. *G&R* 12: 64–77.

Liessmann, K. P. 2002. *Günther Anders. Philosophieren im Zeitalter der technologischen Revolutionen*. Munich.

Lippit A. M. 2000. *Electric Animal: Toward a Rhetoric of Wildlife*. Minneapolis/London.

Lissarrague, F. 1990. *L' autre guerrier. Archers, peltastes, cavaliers dans l'imagerie attique*. Paris/Rome.

Liveley, G. 1999. 'Reading Resistance in Ovid's *Metamorphoses*'. In P. Hardie, A. Barchiesi and S. Hinds (eds.), *Ovidian Transformations*. Cambridge. 197–213.

Liveley, G. 2006. 'Science Fictions and Cyber Myths: Or, Do Cyborgs Dream of Dolly the Sheep?'. In V. Zajko and M. Leonard (eds.), *Laughing with Medusa. Classical Myth and Feminist Thought*. Oxford. 275–294.

Llewellyn-Jones, L. 2007. 'House and Veil in Ancient Greece'. *British School at Athens Studies* 15: 251–258.

Lloyd, G. 1984. *The Man of Reason: 'Male' and 'Female' in Western Philosophy*. Minneapolis.

Lloyd, G. E. R. 1996. *Aristotelian Explorations*. Cambridge.

Lloyd, M. 1994. *Euripides.* Andromache. Warminster.

Lloyd-Jones, H. 1990. *Pindar and the Afterlife*. In H. Lloyd-Jones, *Greek Epic, Lyric, and Tragedy. The Academic Papers of Sir H. Lloyd-Jones*. Oxford. 80–109.

Lloyd-Jones, H. 1996. *Sophocles. Fragments*. Ed. & trans. Cambridge, MA.

Lloyd-Jones, H., and Wilson, N. G. (eds.). 1990. *Sophoclis Fabulae*. Oxford.

Lohr, S. 2015. *Data-ism: The Revolution Transforming Decision Making, Consumer Behavior, and Almost Everything Else*. New York.

Lóio, A. M. 2014. 'Inheriting Speech. Talking Books Come to Flavian Rome'. In A. Augoustakis (ed.), *Flavian Poetry and Its Greek Past*. Leiden. 373–391.

Long, A. A. and Sedley, D. N. 1987. *The Hellenistic Philosophers*. Cambridge.

Longo, O. (ed.). 2007. *Sofocle.* Edipo Re. Venice.

Lonie, I. M. 1981. *The Hippocratic Treatises* 'On Generation', 'On the Nature of the Child', 'Diseases IV'. Berlin.

Lonsdale, S. 1979. 'Attitudes towards Animals in Ancient Greece'. *G&R* 26: 146–159.

Lonsdale, S. 1990. *Creatures of Speech: Lion, Herding, and Hunting Similes in the* Iliad. Stuttgart.

Loraux, N. 1978. 'Sur la race des femmes et quelques-unes de ses tribus'. *Arethusa* 11: 43–87.

Loraux, N. 1990. 'La métaphore sans métaphore. À propos de l'*Orestie*'. *Revue philosophique de la France et de l'Etranger* 180: 247–268.

Lovatt, H. 2013. *The Epic Gaze: Vision, Gender and Narrative in Ancient Epic*. Cambridge.
Lowe, D. 2010. 'Medusa, Antaeus, and Caesar Libycus'. In N. Hömke and C. Reitz (eds.). 119–134.
Lowe, D. 2015. *Monsters and Monstrosity in Augustan Poetry*. Ann Arbor.
Ludwig, P. 2002. *Eros and Polis. Desire and Community in Greek Political Theory*. Cambridge.
Lukács, G. 1971. *History and Class Consciousness*. London.
Lummerding, S. 2005. *Agency @? Cyber-Diskurse, Subjektkonstituierung und Handlungsfähigkeit im Feld des Politischen*. Vienna/Cologne.
Luppe, W. 2006. 'Sex mit einem Esel (P.Oxy. LXX 4762)'. *ZPE* 158: 93–94.
Luraghi, N. 2015. 'Anatomy of the Monster: The Discourse of Tyranny in Ancient Greece'. In H. Börm (ed.), *Antimonarchic Discourse in Antiquity*. Stuttgart. 67–84.
Lyne, R. O. A. M. 1983. 'Lavinia's Blush'. *G&R* 30: 55–64.
Lyne, R. O. A. M. 1989. *Words and the Poet. Characteristic Techniques of Style in Vergil's* Aeneid. Oxford.
Lyotard, J.-F. 1991. *The Inhuman*. Stanford.
Mac Góráin, F. 2013. 'Virgil's Bacchus and the Roman Republic'. In D. Nelis and J. A. Farrell (eds.), *Augustan Poetry and The Roman Republic*. Oxford. 124–145.
Mac Góráin, F. 2018. 'The Poetics of Vision in Virgil's *Aeneid*'. *HSCP* 109: 383–427.
MacCormack, P. 2012. 'Posthuman Teratology'. In A. S. Mittman and P. J. Dendle (eds.). *The Ashgate Research Companion to Monsters and the Monstrous*. Aldershot. 293–309.
MacCormack, P. 2012a. *Posthuman Ethics: Embodiment and Cultural Theory*. Farnham.
Macdonald, C. 2017. 'Take-away Art. Ekphrasis and Appropriation in Martial's *Apophoreta* 170–82'. *CA* 36: 288–316.
Mackay, A. T. (2019) *Animals and Animal-Human Dynamics in Valerius Flaccus'* Argonautica. PhD. Diss. University College London.
MacLeod, M. D. (trans.). 1967. *Lucian Soloecista. Lucius or The Ass. Amores. Halcyon. Demosthenes. Podagra. Ocypus. Cyniscus. Philopatris. Charidemus. Nero*. Cambridge, MA.
MacLeod, M. D. (ed.). 1974. *Luciani opera. Tomus II, libelli 26–43*. Oxford.
Macpherson, C. 1962. *The Political Theory of Possessive Individualism*. Oxford.
Madeleine, S. and Fleury, P. (eds.). 2017. *Autour des machines de Vitruve. L'ingénierie romaine*. Caen.
Mader, G. 2015. 'The Final Simile in the *Aeneid*: Mechanics of Warwfare and Textual Mechanisms'. *Mnemosyne* 68: 588–604.
Maehler, H. 1997. *Die Lieder des Bacchylides. Zweiter Teil: Die Dithyramben und Fragmente*. Leiden/Boston.
Maehler, H. 2006. 'Io auf der Bühne. Bemerkungen zum Aufführungsdatum des *Gefesselten Prometheus*'. In C. A. Láda and C. Römer (eds.), *Schrift, Text und Bild. Kleine Schriften von Hervig Maehler*. Munich/Leipzig. 43–52.
Mahon, P. 2017. *Posthumanism: A Guide for the Perplexed*. London.
Maines, R. 1999. *The Technology of the Orgasm: 'Hysteria', the Vibrator and Women's Sexual Satisfaction*. Baltimore.
Maiullari, F. 2001. *Sogno e omertà nell'* Edipo *Re: una tragedia per tutti e per nessuno*. Venice.
Makowski, J. 1996. 'Bisexual Orpheus: Pederasty and Parody in Ovid'. *CJ* 92: 25–38.
Malafouris, L. 2008. 'Is it "Me" or Is it "Mine"? The Mycenaean Sword as a Body-part'. In D. Boric and J. Robb (eds.), *Past Bodies. Body-Centered Research in Archaeology*. Oxford. 115–124.
Malamud, M. A. 2003. 'Pompey's Head and Cato's Snakes'. *CP* 98: 31–44.
Malamud, M. A. and McGuire, D. T. 1993. 'Flavian Variant: Myth, Valerius' *Argonautica*'. In Boyle (ed.). 192–217.
Männlein-Robert, I. 2014. 'Schmerz und Schrei: Sophokles' *Philoktet* als Grenzfall der Ästhetik in Antike und Moderne'. *A&A* 60: 90–112.
Manuwald, G. (ed.). 2015. *Valerius Flaccus:* Argonautica *Book III*. Cambridge.
Manuwald, G. and Voigt, A. (eds). 2013. *Flavian Epic Interactions*. Berlin.
Marchesini, R. 2017. *Over The Human. Post-Humanism and the Concept of Animal Epiphany*. Cham.
Marinis, A. 2008. *Mortals and the Divine. A Study in Religious Mentality and Epinician Poetics*. PhD. Diss. Cambridge.
Marinis, A. 2018. 'Pindar's Sixth *Paean*: Conceptualizing Religious Panhellenism'. In A. Kavoulaki (ed.), πλειών *Papers in Memory of Christiane Sourvinou-Inwood. Rethymnon*. Heraklion 145–177.

Marks, L. 2000. *The Skin of the Film: Intercultural Cinema, Embodiment, and the Senses*. Durham.
Mason, H. J. 1994. 'Greek and Latin Versions of the Ass-Story'. In *ANRW* II 34.2. Berlin/New York. 1665–1707.
Masson, J. M. and McCarthy, S. 1995. *When Elephants Weep: The Emotional Lives of Animals*. New York.
Massumi, B. 2002. *Parables for the Virtual: Movement, Affect, Sensation*. Durham.
Masters, J. 1992. *Poetry and Civil War in Lucan's* Bellum Civile. Cambridge.
Masterson, M. 2014. 'Studies of Ancient Masculinity'. In T. Hubbard (ed.), *A Companion to Greek and Roman Sexualities*. Malden. 17–30.
Mastronarde, J. 1988. *Euripides.* Phoenissae. Leipzig.
Mauss, M. 1950. *Essai sur le don*. Paris.
May, R. (ed. & trans.). 2013. *Apuleius:* Metamorphoses *or* The Golden Ass. *Book 1*. Oxford.
May, T. 2005. *Gilles Deleuze: An Introduction*. Cambridge.
Mayor, A. 2018. *Gods and Robots. Myths, Machines and Ancient Dreams of Technology.* Princeton.
Mayor, J. E. B. (ed.) 1888. *Thirteen Satires of Juvenal.* 2nd ed. London/New York.
McCall, M. 1972. 'The *Trachiniae:* Structure, Focus, and Heracles'. *AJP* 93: 142–163.
McCandrick, K. M. 2008. 'Sheep Senses, Social Cognition and Capacity for Consciousness'. In C. M. Dwyer (ed.), *The Welfare of Sheep*. New York. 135–157.
McClure, L. 1999. *Spoken Like a Woman: Speech and Gender in Athenian Drama*. Princeton.
McGlew, J. F. 1993. *Tyranny and Political Culture in Ancient Greece*. London/Ithaca.
McGurl, M. 2012. 'The Posthuman Comedy'. *Critical Inquiry* 38: 533–553.
McKirahan, R. 2012. 'Philolaus on Number'. *Proceedings of the Boston Area Colloquium in Ancient Philosophy* 27: 211–232.
McLuhan, M. 1962. *Gutenberg Galaxy*. Toronto.
McLuhan, M. 2001 [1964]. *Understanding Media. The Extensions of Man*. Oxon.
Meier, C. 1980. *Die Entstehung des Politischen bei den Griechen*. Frankfurt.
Meillassoux, Q. 2010. *After Finitude: An Essay on the Necessity of Contingency*. London.
Melegari, D. 2012. 'La politica nel regno illimitato del limite. Foucault e Laclau, tra ontologia del politico e problematizzazione del presente'. *Materiali foucaultiani* 1: 205–234.
Méridier, L. 1928. 'Euripide et l'Orphisme'. *BAssBudé* 18: 15–31.
Merleau-Ponty, M. 1964. *The Primacy of Perception*, trans. W. Cobb. Evanston.
Merleau-Ponty, M. 1968. *The Visible and the Invisible*, trans. A. Lingis. Evanston.
Merleau-Ponty, M. 2012 [1945]. *Phenomenology of Perception*, trans. D. A Landes. Abingdon.
Mertlitsch, K. 2016. *Sisters-Cyborgs-Drags. Das Denken in Begriffspersonen der Gender Studies*. Bielefeld.
Michelini, A. N. 1982. *Tradition and Dramatic Form in the* Persians *of Aeschylus*. Leiden.
Michelini, A. N. 1987. *Euripides and the Tragic Tradition*. Madison.
Midson, S. A. 2018. *Cyborg Theology. Humans, Technology and God*. London/New York.
Miles, G. B. 1975. '*Georgics* 3.209–94: Amor and Civilization'. *CSCA* 8: 177–197.
Miller, H. W. 1944. 'Medical Terminology in Tragedy'. *TAPA* 75: 156–167.
Mills, C. W. 1997. *The Racial Contract*. Ithaca.
Minh-ha, T. T. 1987. 'Difference. A Special Third World Women Issue'. *Feminist Review* 25: 5–22.
Mitchell-Boyask, R. 2007. 'The Athenian Asklepieion and the End of the *Philoctetes*'. *TAPA* 137: 85–114.
Mitchell-Boyask, R. 2012. 'Heroic Pharmacology: Sophocles and the Metaphors of Greek Medical Thought'. In K. Ormand (ed.), *The Blackwell Companion to Sophocles*. Chichester. 316–330.
Mitchell, W. 2003. *ME++: The Cyborg Self and the Networked City*. Cambridge, MA.
Moles, J. 2002. 'Herodotus and Athens'. In E. J. Bakker, I. J. F. de Jong and H. van Wees (eds.), *Brill's Companion to Herodotus*. Leiden. 33–52.
Mondi, R. 1986. 'Tradition and Innovation in the Hesiodic *Titanomachy*'. *TAPA* 116: 25–48.
Mondolfo, R. and Duncan, D. S. 1954. 'The Greek Attitude to Manual Labour'. *Past & Present* 6: 1–5.
Montaigne, M. de. 2003 [1580]. 'An Apology for Raymond Sebond'. In Chafer, C. (ed.), *The Complete Essays*. London.
Moore, J. W. (ed.) 2016. *Anthropocene or Capitalocene? Nature, History, and the Crisis of Capitalism*. New York.
Moraña, M. 2017. *El monstruo como máquina de guerra*. Madrid/Frankfurt.

More, M. 2013. 'The Philosophy of Transhuman'. In M. More and N. Vita-More (eds.), *The Transhumanist Reader*. Sussex. 3–17.

More, M. and Vita-More, N. (eds.). 2013. *The Transhumanist Reader*. Sussex.

Moreau, A. 1985. *Eschyle: la violence et le chaos*. Paris.

Moret, J.-M. 1990. ''Ἰὼ ἀποταυρουμένη'. *RA* 57: 3–26.

Moretti, G. 2010. '*Xenia* e *Apophoreta* di Marziale fra ekphrasis retorica e tradizione iconografica della "natura morta"'. In L. Belloni, A. Bonandini, G. Ieranò and G. Moretti (eds.), *Le immagini nel testo, il testo nelle immagini*. Trento. 327–372.

Morgan, K. 2000. *Myth and Philosophy from Pre-Socratics to Plato*. Cambridge.

Morrell, K. S. 1997. 'The Fabric of Persuasion: Clytaemnestra, Agamemnon, and the Sea of Garments'. *CJ* 92: 141–165.

Morris, S. 1992. *Daidalos and the Origins of Greek Art*. Princeton.

Morton, T. 2013. *Realist Magic: Objects, Ontology, Causality*. Ann Arbor.

Morton, T. 2017. *Humankind: Solidarity with Nonhuman People*. London & New York.

Most, G. 1983. 'Of Motifemes and Megatexts. Comment on Rubin/Sale and Segal'. *Arethusa* 16: 199–218.

Most, W. G. (ed. & trans.). 2006. *Hesiod. The Shield, Catalogue of Women, Other Fragments*. Cambridge, MA.

Motta, G. and Pizzigoni, A. 1998. *L'orologio di Vitruvio. Introduzione a uno studio della macchina di progetto*. Milan.

Moulton, C. 1977. *Similes in the Homeric Poems*. Göttingen.

Mousley, A. 2007. *Re-Humanising Shakespeare: Literary Humanism, Wisdom and Modernity*. Edinburgh.

Mozley, J. H. 1934. *Valerius Flaccus:* Argonautica. Cambridge, MA.

Muecke, F. 1982. 'A Portrait of the Artist as a Young Woman'. *CQ* 32: 41–55.

Mueller, M. 2009 [1984]. *The* Iliad. London.

Mueller, M. 2016. *Objects as Actors: Props and the Poetics of Performance in Greek Tragedy*. Chicago.

Mueller, M. 2016a. 'Recognition and the Forgotten Senses in the *Odyssey*'. *Helios* 43: 1–20.

Mühll, P. von der, ed. 1993 [1946]. *Homeri Odyssea*. Stuttgart.

Müller, S. 2004. 'Untätig in der Mitte?: die Rolle des Senats in der Fabel von "Magen und den Gliedern" (Liv. 2,31,7–32,12)'. *Gymnasium* 111: 449–475.

Müller, V. C. 2016. 'Autonomous Killer Robots Are Probably Good News'. In E. Di Nucci and F. Santonio de Sio (eds.), *Drones and Responsibility: Legal, Philosophical and Socio-Technical Perspectives on the Use of Remotely Controlled Weapons*. Aldershot. 67–81.

Mumford, L. 1967. *Technics and Human Development. Vol. 1: The Myth of the Machine*. London/New York.

Mumford, L. 1970. *The Pentagon of Power*. New York.

Munson, R. 2001. *Telling Wonders: Ethnographic and Political Discourse in the Work of Herodotus*. Ann Arbor.

Muraro, M. 2006. *L'ordine simbolico della madre*. Rome.

Murgatroyd, P. 2009. *A Commentary on Book 4 of Valerius Flaccus'* Argonautica. Leiden.

Murnaghan, S. 1987. *Disguise and Recognition in the* Odyssey. Princeton.

Murray, A. T. (rev. W. F. Wyatt). 1999. *Homer:* Iliad. *Books 13–24*. Cambridge, MA.

Murray, M. 2011. 'The Underdog in History: Serfdom, Slavery and Species in the Creation and Development of Capitalism'. In N. Taylor and T. Signal (eds.), *Theorizing Animals: Re-thinking Humanimal Relations*. Leiden. 85–106.

Musti, D. 2000. 'L'automatismo in Omero. Note sulla decorazione dello scudo di Achille'. In O. Reverdin (ed.), *Homère chez Calvin. Figures de l'hellénime à Genève. Mélanges Olivier Reverdin*. Geneve. 401–409.

Musurillo, H. 1961. 'Fortune's Wheel: The Symbolism of Sophocles' *Women of Trachis*'. *TAPA* 92: 372–383.

Mutschler, F.-H. 2015. '*De vita beata*'. In A. Heil and G. Damschen (eds.), *Brill's Companion to Seneca, Philosopher and Dramatist*. Leiden. 141–146.

Mynors, R. A. 1990. *Virgil.* Georgics. Oxford.

Nagy, G. 1990. *Pindar's Homer. The Lyric Possession of an Epic Past*. Baltimore.

Nagy, G. 1999 [1979]. *The Best of the Achaeans. Concepts of the Hero in Archaic Greek Poetry*. Baltimore.
Naiden, F. S. 2015. 'The Sword Did It: A Greek Explanation for Suicide'. *CQ* 65: 85–95.
Nancy, J. L. 2000. *Being Singular Plural*, trans. R. Richardson and A. O'Byrne. Stanford.
Nappa, C. 2005. *Reading after Actium: Vergil's* Georgics, *Octavian, and Rome*. Ann Arbor.
Nayar, P. K. 2014. *Posthumanism*. Cambridge/Malden.
Nelis, D. 2001. *Vergil's* Aeneid *and the* Argonautica *of Apollonius Rhodius*. Leeds.
Nestle, V. W. 1927. 'Die Fabel des Menenius Agrippa'. *Klio* 21: 350–360.
Newell, W. R. 2013. *Tyranny. A New Interpretation*. Cambridge.
Newell, W. R. 2016. *Tyrants. A History of Power, Injustice, and Terror*. Cambridge.
Newiger, H.-J. 1957. *Metapher und Allegorie: Studien zu Aristophanes*. Munich.
Newmyer, S. T. 2006. *Animals, Rights and Reason in Plutarch and Modern Ethics*. New York.
Newmyer, S. T. 2017. *The Animal and the Human in Ancient and Modern Thought*. New York/London.
Neyrat, F. 2015. *Homo Labyrinthus. Humanisme, Antihumanisme, Posthumanisme*. Paris.
Neyrat, F. 2017a. 'Transhumans, Posthumans, Androids, and Cyborgs'. *Palais* 25: 124–31.
Neyrat, F. 2017b. 'Escaping Humanism'. *Stream* 4: 60–64.
Ngai, S. 2005. *Ugly Feelings*. Cambridge, MA.
Nicolay, E. 2001. 'Homère et l'âme des bêtes'. In F. Niewöhner and J.-L. Seban (eds.), *Die Seele der Tiere*. Wiesbaden. 51–58.
Nilsson, M. P. 1935. 'Early Orphism and Kindred Religious Movements'. *Harvard Theological Review* 28: 181–230.
Noë, A. (2004). *Action in Perception*. Cambridge, MA.
Noel, A. S. 2013. 'Le vêtement-piège et les Atrides: metamorphosis d'un object protéen'. In S. Milenezi and B. Le Guen (eds.), *L'appareil scénique dans les spectacles de l'antiquité*. Saint-Denis. 161–182.
Nooter, S. 2012. *When Heroes Sing. Sophocles and the Shifting Soundscape of Tragedy*. Cambridge.
Nooter, S. 2017. *The Mortal Voice in the Tragedies of Aeschylus*. Cambridge.
North, H. 1994. 'Opening Socrates. The Eikon of Alcibiades'. *ICS* 19: 89–98.
Nousek, D. L. 2008. 'Turning Points in Roman History: The Case of Caesar's Elephant Denarius'. *Phoenix* 62: 290–307.
Nussbaum, M. 1999. 'Foreword'. In M. Schofield, *The Stoic Idea of the City*. Chicago. xi–xvi.
Nussbaum, M. 2001. *The Fragility of Goodness. Luck and Ethics in Greek Tragedy and Philosophy*. Cambridge.
Nussbaum, M. 2002. 'Eros and Ethical Norms: Philosophers Respond to a Cultural Dilemma'. In M. Nussbaum and J. Sihvola (eds.), *The Sleep of Reason*. Chicago/London. 55–94.
Nussbaum, M. 2009. 'Stoic Laughter: A Reading of Seneca's *Apocolocyntosis*'. In S. Bartsch and D. Wray (eds.), *Seneca and the Self*. Cambridge. 84–105.
Nuzzo, L. 2018. *Il mostro di Foucault. Limite, legge, eccedenza*. Milan.
Oakley, S. P. 2018. 'The Expansive Scale of the Roman Antiquities'. In R. Hunter and C. C. De Jonge (eds.), *Dionysius of Halicarnassus and Augustan Rome*. Cambridge. 127–160.
O'Brien, J. V. 1993. *The Transformation of Hera. A Study of Ritual, Hero and the Goddess in the* Iliad. Lanham.
O'Connell, M. 2018. *To Be a Machine: Adventures Among Cyborgs, Utopians, Hackers, and the Futurists Solving the Modest Problem of Death*. London.
O'Connor, J. F. 1974. *Disease Imagery in Aischylos and Sophocles*. Columbus.
O'Donnell, E. L. and Talbot-Jones, J. 2018. 'Creating Legal Rights for Rivers: Lessons from Australia, New Zealand, and India'. *Ecology and Society* 23. https://doi.org/10.5751/Es-09854-230107
O'Hara, J. J. 1994. 'They Might Be Giants: Inconsistency and Indeterminacy in Vergil's War in Italy'. *Colby Quarterly* 30: 206–266.
O'Sullivan, P. 2003. 'Victory Statue, Victory Song: Pindar's Agonistic Poetics and its Legacy'. In D. Phillips and D. Pritchard (eds.), *Sport and Festival in the Ancient Greek World*. Swansea. 75–100.
O'Sullivan, P. 2005. 'Pindar and the Statues of Rhodes'. *CQ* 55: 96–104.
OED. 2019. https://en.oxforddictionaries.com/definition/sheep
Ogden, D. 2013. *Drakōn. Dragon Myth and Serpent Cult in the Greek and Roman Worlds*. Oxford.
Ogilvie, R. M. 1965. *A Commentary on Livy: Books 1–5*. Oxford.

Oleson, J. P. (ed.). 2008. *The Oxford Handbook of Engineering and Technology in the Classical World.* Oxford.
Oliensis, E. 1998. *Horace and the Rhetoric of Authority.* Cambridge.
Olivieri, A. (ed.). 1897. *Pseudo-Eratosthenis Catasterismi (= Mythography Graeci, 3.1).* Leipzig.
Olsen, B. 2010. *In Defense of Things. Archaeology and the Ontology of Objects.* Lanham.
Opelt, I. 1965. 'Esel'. *Reallexikon für Antike und Christentum* 6: 564–595.
Ormand, K. 1993. 'More Wedding Imagery: *Trachiniae* 1053ff'. *Mnemosyne* 46: 224–227.
Osborne, C. 2007. *Dumb Beasts and Dead Philosophers.* Oxford.
Otis, B. 1964. *Virgil: A Study in Civilized Poetry.* Oxford.
Owsianik, J. 2017. 'State of Sex Robots: These are the Companies Developing Robotic Lovers'. https://futureofsex.net/robots/state-sex-robots-companies-developing-robotic-lovers/
Oyama, S. 2000. *Evolution's Eye: A Systems View of the Biology–Culture Divide.* Durham.
Padel, R. 1992. *In and Out of the Mind. Greek Images of the Tragic Self.* Princeton.
Padel, R. 1995. *Whom Gods Destroy.* Princeton.
Pagán Cánovas, C. 2011. 'The Genesis of the Arrows of Love: Diachronic Conceptual Integration in Greek Mythology'. *AJP* 132: 553–579.
Pagden, A. 1983. *The Fall of Natural Man: the American Indian and the Origins of Comparative Anthropology.* Cambridge.
Palmisciano, R. 2009. 'Il primato della poesia sulle altre arti nello scudo di Achille'. *AION* 31: 47–64.
Park, A. 2013. 'Truth and Genre in Pindar'. *CQ* 63: 17–36.
Parker, H. N. 2003. 'The Myth of the Heterosexual. Anthropology and Sexuality for Classicists'. *Arethusa* 34: 313–362.
Parker, R. 1996. *Athenian Religion. A History.* Oxford.
Parry, A. 1963. 'The Two Voices of Virgil's *Aeneid*'. *Arion* 2: 66–80.
Parry, R. D. 2007. 'The Unhappy Tyrant and the Craft of Inner Rule'. In G. R. F Ferrari (ed.), *The Cambridge Companion to Plato's* Republic. Cambridge. 386–414.
Paschalis, M. 1997. *Virgil's* Aeneid*: Semantic Relations and Proper Names.* Oxford.
Pattoni, M. P. 1987. *L'autenticità del* Prometeo Incatenato *di Eschilo.* Pisa.
Pavese, C. 2009 [1949]. *This Business of Living: Diaries 1935–1950.* London and New York.
Pavlou, M. 2008. 'Metapoetics, Poetic Tradition, and Praise in Pindar *Olympian* 9'. *Mnemosyne* 61: 533–567.
Pavlou, M. 2010. 'Pindar *Nemean* 5: Real and Poetic Statues'. *Phoenix* 64: 1–17.
Payne, M. 2010. *The Animal Part. Human and Other Animals in the Poetic Imaginaton.* Chicago.
Payne, M. 2016. 'Teknomajikality and the Humanimal in Aristophanes' *Wasps*'. In P. Walsh (ed.), *Brill's Companion to the Reception of Aristophanes.* Leiden. 129–147.
Pearl, J. 2000. *Causality.* Cambridge.
Pearson, K. A. 1991. *Germinal Life. The Difference and Repetition of Deleuze.* New York.
Peers, G. 2012. 'Object Relations. Theorizing the Late Antique Viewer'. In S. F. Johnson (ed.), *The Oxford Handbook of Late Antiquity.* Oxford. 970–987.
Peers, G. 2013. 'Byzantine Things in the World'. In G. Peers (ed.), *Byzantine Things in the World.* New Haven. 41–84.
Peil, D. 1985. *Der Streit der Glieder mit dem Magen: Studien zur Überlieferungs – und Deutungsgeschichte der Fabel des Menenius Agrippa von der Antike bis ins 20.* Jahrhundert. Frankfurt.
Pelling, C. 2002. 'Speech and Action: Herodotus' Debate on Constitutions'. *PCPS* 48: 123–158.
Pelling, C. 2006. 'Speech and Narrative'. In J. Marincola and C. Dewald (eds.), *The Cambridge Companion to Herodotus.* Cambridge. 103–121.
Pelling, C. 2016. 'Preparing for Posterity: Dionysius and Polybius'. In A. Lianeri (ed.), *Knowing Future Time In and Through Greek Historiography.* Berlin/Boston. 155–173.
Peradotto, J. 1990. *Man in the Middle Voice.* Princeton.
Peris, M. 1982. 'Greek Elements in the Vijaya Legend'. *JRASSLB* 26: 43–66.
Perkell, C. 1978. 'A Reading of Vergil's Fourth *Georgic*'. *Phoenix* 32: 211–221.
Perry, B. E. (ed.) 1952. *Aesopica. A Series of Texts Relating to Aesop or Ascribed to Him. Vol. 1: Greek and Latin Texts.* Urbana.

Perry, B. E. (ed.) (ed. & trans.). 1965. *Babrius and Phaedrus. Fables*. Cambridge, MA.
Petegorsky, D. 1982. *Context and Evocation. Studies in Early Greek and Sanskrit Poetry*. PhD Diss. Berkeley.
Peterson, C. 2018. *Monkey Trouble. The Scandal of Posthumanism*. New York.
Petropoulos, J. C. B. 2011. *Kleos in a Minor Key. The Homeric Education of a Little Prince*. Washington.
Peuker, B. 2010. 'Akteur-Netzwerk-Theorie (ANT)'. In C. Stegbauer and R. Häußling (eds.), *Handbuch Netzwerkforschung*. Wiesbaden. 325–335.
Philipp, H. 1968. *Tektonon Daidala. Der bildende Künstler und sein Werk im vorplatonischem Schriftum*. Berlin.
Phillips, C. 2007. *Seneca. Selected Philosophical Letters*. Cambridge.
Plotnik, J. M. and de Waal, F. B. M. 2014. 'Asian Elephants (Elephas Maximus) Reassure Others in Distress'. *PeerJ* 2: e278. https://doi.org/10.7717/peerj.278.
Plumwood, V. 1995. 'Human Vulnerability and the Experience of Being Prey'. *Quadrant* 29: 29–34.
Pollard, J. 1977. *Birds in Greek Life and Myth*. London.
Pollitt, J. J. 1995. 'The Canon of Polykleitos and other Canons'. In W. Moon (ed.), *Polykleitos, the Doryphoros, and Tradition*. Madison. 19–24.
Pöschl, V. 1962. *The Art of Vergil: Image and Symbol in the* Aeneid, trans. G. Selingson. Ann Arbor.
Pötscher, W. 1987. *Hera. Eine Strukturanalyse im Vergleich mit Athena*. Darmstadt.
Potter, P. (ed.) 1995. *Hippocrates. Vol. 8: Places in Man*. Cambridge, MA.
Power, T. 2011. 'Cyberchorus: Pindar's Κηληδόνες and the Aura of the Artificial'. In L. Athanassaki and E. Bowie (eds.), *Archaic and Classical Choral Song*. Berlin. 67–113.
Pozzi, D. C. 1986. 'The Pastoral Ideal in the *Birds* of Aristophanes'. *CJ* 81: 119–129.
Pozzi, D. C. 1994. 'Deianira's Robe: Diction in Sophocles' *Trachiniae*'. *Mnemosyne* 47: 577–585.
Pratt, L. 1993. *Lying and Poetry from Homer to Pindar*. Ann Arbor.
Preciado, P. B. 2008. 'Pharmaco-Pornographic Politics: Towards a New Gender Ecology'. *Parallax* 14: 105–117.
Precope, J. 1954. *Medicine, Magic and Mythology*. London.
Prince, G. 1990. 'On Narratology (Past, Present, Future)'. *French Literature Series* 17: 1–14.
Pritchard, J. S. 1969. *Ancient Near Eastern Texts Relating to the Old Testament*, 3rd edn, Princeton.
Pucci, P. 1986. 'Les figures de la Mètis dans l'*Odyssee*'. *Mètis* 1: 7–28.
Purves, A. 2010. *Space and Time in Ancient Greek Narrative*. Cambridge.
Purves, A. 2014. 'Thick Description. From Auerbach to the Boar's Lair (*Od.* 19.388–475)'. In M. Skempis and I. Ziogas (eds.), *Geography, Topography, Landscape. Configurations of Space in Greek and Roman Epic*. Berlin. 37–61.
Purves, A. 2015. 'Ajax and Other Objects: Homer's Vibrant Materialism'. *Ramus* 44: 75–94.
Purves, A. (ed.). 2018. *Touch and the Ancient Senses*. New York.
Putnam, M. C. J. 1965. *The Poetry of the* Aeneid. Cambridge, MA.
Putnam, M. C. J. 1979. *Virgil's Poem of the Earth: Studies in the* Georgics. Princeton.
Putnam, M. C. J. 2001. 'The Ambiguity of Art in Virgil's *Aeneid*'. *PAPS* 145: 162–183.
Putnam, M. C. J. 2011. *The Humanness of Heroes. Studies in the Conclusion of Virgil's* Aeneid. Amsterdam.
Quessada, D. 2013. *L'inséparé. Essai sur un monde sans autre*. Paris.
Quint, D. 1993. *Epic and Empire. Politics and Generic Form from Virgil to Milton*. Princeton.
Rabelais, F. 1996 [1532]. *Pantagruel*. Paris.
Rabinow, P. (ed.). 1984. *The Foucault Reader*. New York.
Race, W. H. 1997a/b. *Pindar. Olympian Odes, Pythian Odes/Pindar: Nemean Odes, Isthmian Odes, Fragments*. Cambridge, MA.
Ready, J. L. 2011. *Character, Narrator, and Simile in the* Iliad. Cambridge.
Reale, G. 1999. *Corpo, anima e salute. Il concetto di uomo da Omero a Platone*. Milan.
Reay, B. 2003. 'Some Addressees of Virgil's *Georgics* and their Audience'. *Vergilius* 49: 17–41.
Reckford, K. 1974. 'Phaedra and Pasiphae: The Pull Backward'. *TAPA* 104: 307–328.
Reckwitz, A. 2010. *Das hybride Subjekt. Eine Theorie der Subjektkulturen von der bürgerlichen Moderne zur Postmoderne*. Weilerswist-Metternich.
Redfield, J. M. 1994 [1975]. *Nature and Culture in the* Iliad: *The Tragedy of Hector*. Chicago.

Reed, J. D. 2007. *Virgil's Gaze: Nation and Poetry in the* Aeneid. Princeton/Oxford.
Regier, W. G. 2005. *Book of the Sphinx*. Stroud.
Rehm, R. 2006. 'Sophocles on Fire - To Pyr in Philoctetes'. In I. J. F. de Jong and A. Rijksbaron (eds.), *Sophocles and the Greek Language*. Leiden. 95-107.
Reitz-Joosse, B. 2016. 'The City and the Text in Vitruvius's *de Architectura*'. *Arethusa* 49: 183–197.
Reitzammer, L. 2016. *The Athenian Adonia in Context. The Adonis Festival as Cultural Practice*. Madison.
Renehan, R. 1981. 'The Greek Anthropocentric View of Man'. *HSPh* 85: 239–259.
Renger, A. B. 2013. *Oedipus and the Sphinx: The Threshold Myth from Sophocles through Freud to Cocteau*. Chicago.
Renger, C. 1985. *Aeneas und Turnus. Analyse einer Feindschaft*. Frankfurt/Bern.
Revel, J. 1996. *Foucault, le parole e i poteri. Dalla trasgressione letteraria alla resistenza politica*. Rome.
Revel, J. 2003. *Michel Foucault. Un'ontologia dell'attualità*. Soveria Mannelli.
Revel, J. 2008. 'Identità, natura, vita: tre decostruzioni biopolitiche.' In M. Galzigna (ed.), *Foucault*. Milan. 134–149.
Rice, E. 1983. *The Grand Procession of Ptolemy Philadelphus*. Oxford.
Richardson, K. 2015. *An Anthropology of Robots and AI: Annihilation Anxiety and Machines*. London.
Richardson, L. 1992. *A New Topographical Dictionary of Ancient Rome*. Baltimore.
Riedweg, C. 2011. 'Initiation – Death – Underworld. Narrative and Ritual in the Gold Leaves'. In R. G. Edmonds III (ed.), *The 'Orphic' Gold Tablets and Greek Religion*. Cambridge. 219–256.
Rimell, V. 2008. *Martial's Rome. Empire and the Ideology of Epigram*. Cambridge.
Rimell, V. 2015. *The Closure of Space in Roman Poetics*. Cambridge.
Ringer, M. (1998). *Electra and the Empty Urn. Metatheater and Role Playing in Sophocles*. Chapel Hill.
Robert, I. 1890. *Der Pasiphae-Sarkophag*. Halle.
Roberts, D. H. 1988. 'Sophoclean Endings: Another Story'. *Arethusa* 21: 177–196.
Roden, D. 2015. *Posthuman Life. Philosophy at the Edge of the Human*. London.
Rodríguez Adrados, F. 2003. *History of the Graeco-Latin Fable. Vol. 3: Inventory and Documentation of the Graeco-Latin Fable*. Leiden.
Roessel, D. 1989. 'The Stag on Circe's Island. An Exegesis of a Homeric Digression'. *TAPA* 119: 31–36.
Rogers, B. M. and B. E. Stevens (eds.). 2015. *Classical Traditions in Science Fiction*. Oxford.
Rohman, C. 2009. *Stalking the Subject: Modernism and the Animal*. New York.
Rose, N. 2007. *The Politics of Life Itself. Biomedicine, Power, and Subjectivity in the Twenty-First Century*. Princeton.
Rosella-Schluderer, L. 2018. 'Imitating the Cosmos: The Role of Microcosm–Macrocosm Relationships in the Hippocratic Treatise on *Regimen*'. *CQ* 68: 31–52.
Roselli, D. K. 2013. 'The Work of Tragic Productions: Towards a New History of Drama as Labour Culture'. *Ramus* 42: 104–121.
Roselli, D. K. 2014. 'Social Class'. In M. Revermann (ed.), *The Cambridge Companion to Greek Comedy*. Cambridge. 241–258.
Rosenberger, V. 1998. *Gezähmte Götter. Das Prodigienwesen der römischen Republik*. Stuttgart.
Rosenbloom, D. 2006. *Aeschylus.* Persians. London.
Rosenmeyer, P. 2018. *The Language of Ruins*. Oxford.
Rossi, A. 2004. *Contexts of War. Manipulation of Genre in Virgilian Battle Narrative*. Ann Arbor.
Rossini, M. 2017. 'Bodies'. In B. Clarke and M. Rossini (eds.). 153-169.
Rostovtzeff, M. I. 1941. *The Social & Economic History of the Hellenistic World*. Oxford.
Roth, P. 1969. *Portnoy's Complaint*. New York.
Rothwell, K. S., Jr. 2006. *Nature, Culture, and the Origins of Greek Comedy. A Study of Animal Choruses*. Cambridge.
Royakkers, L. and van Est, R. 2015. 'A Literature Review on New Robotics: Automation from Love to War'. *International Journal of Social Robotics* 7: 549–570.
Rubin, N. F. and Sale, W. M. 1983. 'Meleager and Odysseus. A Structural and Cultural Study of the Greek Hunting-Maturation Myth'. *Arethusa* 16: 137–171.
Ruck, C. A. 1968. 'Marginalia Pindarica'. *Hermes* 96: 129–142.

Ruffell, I. 2001.'The World Turned Upside Down: Utopia and Utopianism in the Fragments of Old Comedy'. In D. Harvey and J. Wilkins (eds.), *The Rivals of Aristophanes*. London. 473–506.

Rühl, M. 2006.'*Saturnalicio lusit et ipse luto*. Martial und die Kunst in den *Apophoreta*'. *RhM* 149: 287–309.

Rumpel, J. 1961 [1883]. *Lexicon Pindaricum*. Hildesheim.

Russo, J. 1993.'*Odyssey* 19, 440–443, the Boar in the Bush. Formulaic Repetition and Narrative Innovation'. In R. Pretagostini (ed.), *Tradizione e innovazione nelle cultura greca da Omero all'età ellenistica*. Rome. 51–59.

Russo, J., Fernandez-Galliano, M. and Heubeck, A. 1992. *A Commentary on Homer's* Odyssey. *Vol. 3: Books XVII–XXIV*. Oxford.

Rusten, J. S. 2013.'The Mirror of Aristophanes: The Winged Ethnographers of *Birds* (1470–93, 1553–64, 1694–1705)'. In E. Bakola, L. Prauscello and M. Telò (eds.), *Greek Comedy and the Discourse of Genres*. Oxford. 298–318.

Rutherford, I. 2001. *Pindar's* Paeans. Oxford.

Rutherford, I. 2009.'Hesiod and the Literary Traditions of the Near East'. In F. Montanari, A. Rengakos and C. Tsagalis (eds.), *Brill's Companion to Hesiod*. Leiden. 9–35.

Rutherford, R. B. 1992. *Homer.* Odyssey. *Books XIX and XX*. Cambridge.

Rutherford, R. B. 1995. *The Art of Plato. Ten Essays in Platonic Interpretation*. London.

Saïd, S. 1977.'Les Combats de Zeus et le problème des interpolations dans la *Théogonie* d'Hésiode'. *REG* 90: 183–210.

Salemme, C. 2005. *Marziale e la poesia delle cose*. Naples.

Salviat F. 2007a.'La pensée de Pindare et la 2e *Olympique*. Première partie: Victoire, mort et visions d'au-delà'. *Journal des savants* 1: 3–85.

Salviat, F. 2007b.'Deuxième partie: Dieu cosmique, harmonie, sagesse'. *Journal des savants* 2: 173–259.

Sanders, E., Thumiger, C., Carey, C. and Lowe, N. (eds.), *Eros in Ancient Greece*. Oxford.

Santamaría Álvarez, M.A. 2008.'Píndaro y el orfismo'. In A. Bernabé and F. Casadesús (eds.), *Orfeo y la tradición órfica: un reencuentro*. Madrid. 1161–1184.

Sautel, J. 2016. *Denys d'Halicarnasse*. Paris.

Savino, E. 1991. *Sofocle.* Aiace, Elettra, Trachinie, Filottete. Milan.

Šćepanović, S. 2016.'Wisdom and Human Temporality in Pindar's Victory Odes'. *A&A* 62: 18–37.

Schapp, W. 2012 [1953]. *In Geschichten verstrickt. Zum Sein von Mensch und Ding*. Frankfurt.

Scheid, J. and Svenbro, J. 2014. *La tortue et la lyre: dans l'atelier du mythe antique*. Paris.

Schein, S. L. 1970.'Odysseus and Polyphemus in the *Odyssey*'. *GRBS* 11: 73–83.

Schenk, P. 1984. *Die Gestalt des Turnus in Vergils* Aeneis. Königstein.

Schenk, P. 1991.'Cyzicus, Perses und das Eingreifen der Götter'. In: Korn and Tscheidel (eds.). 139–153.

Schiefsky M. J. 2007.'Art and Nature in Ancient Mechanics'. In B. Bensaude-Vincent and W. Newman (eds.), *The Artificial and the Natural: An Evolving Polarity*. Cambridge. 67–108.

Schlesier, R. 2002.'Der Fuss des Dionysos: zu PMG 871'. In H. F. I. Horstmanshoff, H. W. Singer, F. T. von Straten and J. H. M. Strubbe (eds.), *Kykeon. Studies in Honour of H. S. Versnel*. Leiden/Boston. 161–191.

Schmitt, R. 1967. *Dichtung und Dichtersprache in indogermanischer Zeit*. Wiesbaden.

Schmitz, S. and Degele, N. 2010.'Embodying – ein dynamischer Ansatz für Körper und Geschlecht in Bewegung'. In N. Degele, S. Schmitz, M. Mangelsdorf and E. Gramespacher (eds.), *Gendered Bodies in Motion*. Opladen/ Farmington Hill. 13–38.

Schnapp-Gourbeillon, A. 1981. *Lions, héros, masques. Les représentations de l'animal chez Homère*. Paris.

Schneider, H. 2007.'Technology'. In W. Scheidel, I. Morris and R. Saller (eds.), *The Cambridge Economic History of the Greco-Roman World*. Cambridge. 144–172.

Schofield, M. 1997.'Ἀρχή'. *Hyperboreus* 3: 218–36.

Schofield, M. 2012.'Pythagoreanism: Emerging from the Presocratic Fog'. In C. Steel (ed.), *Aristotle's* Metaphysics *Alpha*. Oxford. 141–160.

Schomberg, A. 2008.'Ancient Water Technology: Between Hellenistic Innovation and Arabic Tradition'. *Syria* 85: 119–128.

Schor, N. 1989. 'This Essentialism Which Is Not One. Coming to Grips with Irigaray'. *Differences* 1: 38–58.

Schork, R. J. 1986. 'The Final Simile in the *Aeneid*: Roman and Rutulian Ramparts'. *AJP* 107: 260–70.

Schrijvers, P. H. 1998. 'Le regard sur l'invisible'. In P. J. Schrijvers, *Lucrèce et les sciences de la vie*. Leiden. 183–213.

Schultze, C. 1986. 'Dionysius of Halicarnassus and His Audience'. In I. S. Moxon, J. D. Smart and A. J. Woodman (eds.), *Past Perspectives. Studies in Greek and Roman Historical Writing. Papers Presented at a Conference in Leeds, 6–8 April 1983*. Cambridge. 121–141.

Smart and A. J. Woodman (eds.) 2007. 'Dionysius of Halicarnassus: Clothing Cincinnatus'. In J. Marincola (ed.), *Blackwell Companion to Greek and Roman Historiography*. Oxford. 404–410.

Schumacher, J. 1940. *Antike Medizin, Vol. 1: Die Naturphilosophische Grundlagen der Medizin in der griechischen Antike*. Berlin.

Schwindt, J. P. 2014. 'Ordo and Insanity. On the Pathogenesis of Horace's *Ars Poetica*'. *MD* 72: 55–70.

Schwinge, E-R. 2014. 'Aristophanes' *Thesmophoriazusen* – eine Homage an Euripides'. *WJA* 38: 65–100.

Scodel, R. 1994. 'Odysseus and the Stag'. *CQ* 44: 530–534.

Scoon, R. 1922. 'Philolaus' Fragment 6 Diels'. *CP* 17: 353–356.

Scranton, R. 2015. *Learning to Die in the Anthropocene. Reflections on the End of a Civilization*. San Francisco.

Scullard, H. H. 1974. *The Elephant in the Greek and Roman World*. London.

Scully, S. 2003. 'Reading the Shield of Achilles: Terror, Anger, Delight'. *HSPh* 101: 29–47.

Seaford, R. 1984. *Euripides:* Cyclops. *With Introduction and Commentary*. Oxford.

Seaford, R. 1994. *Reciprocity and Ritual. Homer and Tragedy in the Developing City-State*. Cambridge, MA.

Sedgwick, E. K. 2003. *Touching Feeling. Affect, Pedagogy, Performativity*. Durham.

Sedley, D. 1995. 'The Dramatis Personae of Plato's *Phaedo*'. In T. J. Smiley (ed.), *Philosophical Dialogues: Plato, Hume, Wittgenstein*. Oxford. 3–26.

Sedly, D. 2004. *The Midwife of Platonism. Text and Subtext in Plato's* Theaetetus. Oxford.

Seely, S. 2012. 'How Do You Dress a Body Without Organs? Affective Fashion and Nonhuman Becoming'. *Women's Studies Quarterly* 41, FASHION: 247–265.

Seewald, M. 2008. *Studien zum 9. Buch von Lucans* Bellum Civile: *Mit einem Kommentar zu den Versen 1–733*. Berlin.

Segal, C. 1977. 'Sophocles' *Trachiniae*: Myth, Poetry and Heroic Values'. *YCS* 25: 99–158.

Segal, C. 1986. *Interpreting Greek Tragedy, Myth, Poetry, Text*. New York.

Segal, C. 1995. *Sophocles' Tragic World. Divinity, Nature, Society*. Cambridge, MA.

Severyns, A. 1946. 'Simples remarques sur les comparaisons homériques'. *BCH* 70: 540–547.

Shackleton Bailey, D. R. 1977. *Cicero: Epistulae ad familiares*. Cambridge/New York.

Shackleton Bailey, D. R. (ed.). 1993. *Martial:* Epigrams, *Vol. 3. Books 11–14*. Cambridge.

Shanahan, M. 2015. *The Technological Singularity*. Cambridge, MA.

Sharpe, A. N. 2010. *Foucault's Monsters and the Challenge of Law*. London.

Sharrock, A. R. 1991a. 'Womanufacture'. *JRS* 81: 36–49.

Sharrock, A. R. 1991b. 'Reviewing Pygmalion. The Love of Creation'. *Ramus* 20: 169–182.

Shaviro, S. 2014. *The Universe of Things. On Speculative Realism*. Minneapolis.

Sheffield, F. 2006. *Plato's* Symposium. *The Ethics of Desire*. Oxford.

Shelton, J.-A. 1999. 'Elephants, Pompey, and the Reports of Popular Displeasure in 55 BC'. In S. N. Byrne and E. P. Cueva (eds.), *'Veritatis amicitiaeque causa': Essays in Honor of Anna Lydia Motto and John R. Clark*. Wauconda. 231–271.

Shelton, J.-A. 2004. 'Dancing and Dying: The Display of Elephants in the Ancient Roman Arena'. In R. B. Egan and M. A. Joyal (eds.), *'Daimonopylai': Essays in Classics and the Classical Tradition Presented to Edmund G. Berry*. Winnipeg. 363–382.

Sider, D. 1978. 'Stagecraft in the *Oresteia*'. *AJP* 99: 12–27.

Silk, M. S. 2003. 'Metaphor and Metonymy: Aristotle, Jakobson, Ricoeur, and Others'. In G. R. Boys-Stones (ed.), *Metaphor, Allegory, and the Classical Tradition: Ancient Thought and Modern Revisions*. Oxford. 115–148.

Simon, E. 1985. 'Zeus und Io auf einer Kalpis des Eucharidesmalers'. *A&A* 100: 265–280.

Simondon, G. 2004. *Deux leçons sur l'animal et l'homme*. Paris.
Simondon, G. 2012. *Du mode d'existence des objets techniques*. Paris.
Simondon, G. 2013. *Sur la Technique*. Paris.
Sinclair, R. K. 1988. *Democracy and Participation in Athens*. Cambridge.
Singer P. 1975. *Animal Liberation: A New Ethics for our Treatment of Animals*. New York.
Sklenář, R. 2003. *The Taste for Nothingness: A Study of Virtus and Related Themes in Lucan's* Bellum Civile. Ann Arbor.
Slater, W. J. 1969. *Lexicon to Pindar*. Berlin.
Slings, S. R. 2003. *Plato.* Respublica. Oxford.
Small, S. G. 1959. 'The Arms of Turnus: *Aeneid* 7.783–892'. *TAPA* 92: 243–52.
Smith, R. 2007. 'Pindar's Poetry, Patrons, and Festivals from Archaic Greece to the Roman Empire'. In S. Hornblower and C. Morgan (eds.), *Pindar, Athletes, and the Early Greek Statue Habit*. Oxford. 83–139.
Smith, S. D. 2014. *Man and Animal in Severan Rome: The Literary Imagination of Claudius Aelianus*. Cambridge.
Smyth, W. R. 2002 [1920]. *Greek Grammar*. Cambridge, MA.
Snell, B. 1975 [1953]. *The Discovery of the Mind*, trans. T. Rosenmeyer. Oxford.
Sobchack, V. 1992. *The Address of the Eye. A Phenomenology of Film Experience*. Princeton.
Solmsen, F.1957. 'The Vital Heat, the Inborn Pneuma and the Aether'. *JHS* 77: 119–23.
Sommerstein, A. H.1989. *Aeschylus.* Eumenides. Cambridge.
Sontag, S. 1978. *Illness as Metaphor*. New York.
Sontag, S. 1989. *AIDS and Its Metaphors*. Toronto.
Sorabji, R. 1993. *Animal Minds and Human Morals*. Ithaca.
Sörbom, G. 1966. *Mimesis and Art. Studies in the Origin and Early Development of an Aesthetic Vocabulary*. Stockholm.
Spaltenstein, F. 2004. *Commentaire des* Argonautica *de Valérius Flaccus* (books 3, 4 and 5). Brussels.
Sparrow, R. 2015. 'Robots in Aged Care: A Dystopian Future?' *AI and Society* 31: 1–10.
Spielvogel, J. 2001. *Wirtschaft und Geld bei Aristophanes*. Frankfurt.
Spivey, N. 1995. 'Bionic Statues'. In A. Powell (ed.), *The Greek World*. London. 442–461.
Spurr, M. S. 2008, 'Agriculture and the *Georgics*'. In K. Volk (ed.), *Vergil's* Georgics. Oxford/New York. 14–42.
Squire, M. 2015. 'Corpus imperii: Verbal and Visual Figurations of the Roman "Body Politic"'. *Word & Image* 31: 305–330.
Stafford, E. 2012. *Herakles*. Abingdon.
Stafford, E. 2013. 'From the Gymnasium to the Wedding. Eros in Athenian Art and Cult'. In E. Sanders, C. Thumiger, C. Carey and N. Lowe (eds.), *Eros in Ancient Greece*. Oxford. 175–208.
Stahl, H.-P. 2016. *Poetry Underpinning Power. Vergil's* Aeneid*: The Epic for Emperor Augustus. A Recovery Study*. Swansea.
Stähli, A. 2014. 'Sprechende Gegenstände'. In: R. Bielfeldt (ed.). 2014a. 113–141.
Stanford, W. B. 1939. *Ambiguity in Greek Literature*. Oxford.
Stanford, W. B. 1996. *Homer:* Odyssey *XIII–XXIV. Edited with an Introduction and Commentary*. London.
Stavrinou, A. S. 2016. 'Hermione's Spartan Costume: The Tragic Skeue in Euripides's *Andromache*'. *ICS* 41: 1–20.
Steeves, H. P. (ed.). 1999. *Animal Others: On Ethics, Ontology, and Animal Life*. Albany.
Stehle E. 2002. 'The Body and Its Representations in Aristophanes' *Thesmophoriazousai*: Where Does the Costume End?' *AJP* 123: 369–406.
Steiner, D. 1996. 'For Love of a Statue. A Reading of Plato's *Symposium* 215a–b'. *Ramus* 25: 89–111.
Steiner, D. 2001. *Images in Mind. Statues in Archaic and Classical Greek Literature and Thought*. Princeton.
Steiner, D. 2007. 'Feathers Flying: Avian Poetics in Hesiod, Pindar and Callimachus'. *AJP* 128: 177–208.
Stern, J. (ed.). 1902. *Palaephatus.* Peri Apiston. Leipzig.
Stern, S. 2012. *Calendars in Antiquity*. Oxford.

Stevens, B. 2006. 'Aeolism: Latin as a Dialect of Greek'. *CJ* 102: 115–144.
Stewart, D. J. 1967. 'The Poet as Bird in Aristophanes and Horace'. *CJ* 62: 357–361.
Stewart, P. 2007. 'Gell's Idols and Roman Cult'. In R. Osborne and J. Tanner (eds.), *Art's Agency and Art History*. Malden. 158–178.
Stieber, M. C. (2011). *Euripides and the Language of Craft*. Leiden/Boston.
Stiegler, B. 1998. *Technics and Time. Vol. 1: The Fault of Epimetheus*. Stanford.
Stiegler, B. 2011. *Ce qui fait que la vie vaut le peine d'être vécue. De la Pharmacologie*. Paris.
Stiegler, B. 2012. 'Die Aufklärung in the Age of Philosophical Engineering'. *Computational Culture* 2. http://computationalculture.net/die-aufklarung-in-the-age-of-philosophical-engineering/
Stiegler, B. 2016. *Dans la disruption*. Paris.
Stiegler, B. and Sauvêtre, P. 2007. 'Entretien avec Bernard Stiegler'. *Tracés-Revue de sciences humaines* 13: 249–276.
Stinton, T. C. 1990. 'Heracles' Homecoming and Related Topics: The Second Stasimon of Sophocles' *Trachiniae*'. In T. C. Stinton, *Collected Papers on Greek Tragedy*. Oxford. 426–429.
Stoddard, K. 2004. *The Narrative Voice in the Theogony of Hesiod*. Leiden.
Stohn, G. 1993. 'Zur Agathonszene in den *Thesmophoriazusen* des Aristophanes'. *Hermes* 121: 196–205.
Stone, M. 2011. 'Law, Ethics and Levinas's concept of Anarchy'. *Australian Feminist Law Journal* 35: 89–105.
Stover, T. 2012. *Epic & Empire in Vespasianic Rome. A New Reading of Valerius Flaccus'* Argonautica. Oxford.
Strasburger, H. 1955. 'Herodot und das perikleische Athen'. *Historia* 4: 1–25.
Strathern, M. 1988. *The Gender of the Gift: Problems with Women and Problems*. Berkeley.
Strauss, B. 2004. *The Battle of Salamis*. New York.
Strauss Clay, J. 1983. *The Wrath of Athena. Gods and Men in the* Odyssey. Princeton.
Strauss Clay, J. 1993. 'The Generation of Monsters'. *CP* 88:105–116.
Strauss Clay, J. 2003. *Hesiod's Cosmos*. Cambridge.
Striker, G. 1983. 'The role of *oikeiosis* in Stoic ethics'. *Oxford Studies in Ancient Philosophy* 1: 145–167.
Stroup, S. C. 2006. 'Invaluable Collections. The Illusion of Poetic Presence in Martial's *Xenia* and *Apophoreta*'. In R. R. Nauta, H.-J. Van Dam and J. Smolenaars (eds.), *Flavian Poetry*. Leiden. 299–313.
Sullins, J. P. 2012. 'Robots, Love, and Sex: The Ethics of Building a Love Machine'. *IEEE Transactions on Affective Computing* 3: 298–409.
Swift, L. A. 2009. 'Sexual and Familial Distortion in Euripides' *Phoenissae*'. *TAPA* 139: 53–87.
Sykes, N. 2014. *Beastly Questions. Animal Answers to Archaeological Issues*. London.
Szasz, T. S.1970. *The Manufacture of Madness*. New York.
Tabacco, R. 1985. *Il tiranno nelle declamazioni di scuola in lingua latina*. Turin.
Tanner, R. G. 1982. 'The Case for Neo-Stoicism Today'. *Prudentia* 14: 39–51.
Taplin, O. 1977. *The Stagecraft of Aeschylus: The Dramatic Use of Exits and Entrances in Greek Tragedy*. Oxford.
Tarnopolsky, C. H. 2010. *Prudes, Perverts, and Tyrants. Plato's* Gorgias *and the Politics of Shame*. Princeton.
Tarrant, R. 2012. *Virgil.* Aeneid *Book XII*. Cambridge.
Taylor, L. A. 1968. 'Republican and Augustan Writers Enrolled in the Equestrian Centuries'. *TAPA* 99: 469–486.
Telò, M. and Mueller, M. (eds.). 2018. *The Materialities of Greek Tragedy. Objects and Affect in Aeschylus, Sophocles, and Euripides*. London.
Terada, R. 2001. *Feeling in Theory*. Cambridge, MA.
Thibodeau, P. 2011. *Playing the Farmer: Representations of Rural Life in Vergil's* Georgics. Berkeley.
Thomas, R. 2007. 'Fame, Memorial, and Choral Poetry: The Origins of Epinikian Poetry'. In S. Hornblower and C. Morgan (eds.), *Pindar, Athletes, and the Early Greek Statue Habit*. Oxford. 141–166.
Thomas, R. F. 1982. *Lands and Peoples in Roman Poetry*. Cambridge.
Thomas, R. F. 1988a. 'Tree Violation and Ambivalence in Virgil'. *TAPA* 118: 261–273.
Thomas, R. F. 1988b. *Virgil:* Georgics III–IV. Cambridge.

Thomas, R. F. 1998. 'The Isolation of Turnus; *Aeneid* Book 12'. In H. P. Stahl (ed.), *Vergil's* Aeneid: *Augustan Epic and Political Context*. London. 271–302.

Thompson, D. W. 1895. *A Glossary of Greek Birds*. Oxford.

Thomson, G. S. 1955. 'The Shepherd-Ruler Concept in the Old Testament and its Application in the New Testament'. *SJT* 8: 406–418.

Thumiger, C. 2008. 'anagkês zeugmat' empeptôkamen: Greek Tragedy Between Human and Animal'. *Leeds International Classics Seminar* 7: 1–21.

Thumiger, C. 2013. 'Mad Eros and Eroticized Madness in Tragedy'. In E. Sanders, C. Thumiger et al. (eds.). 27–40.

Thumiger, C. 2014. 'Animals in Tragedy'. In G. Campbell (ed.), *Oxford Handbook of Animals*. Oxford. 84-98.

Tiffany, D. 2004. 'Lyric Substance. On Riddles, Materialism, and Poetic Obscurity'. In B. Brown (ed.). 72–98.

Tilg, S. 2014. *Apuleius'* Metamorphoses. *A Study in Roman Fiction*. Oxford.

Tilliette, X. 1992. *Schelling: une philosophie en devenir. Vol. I: Le système vivant*. Paris.

Timofeeva, O. 2018. *The History of Animals: A Philosophy*. London.

Torrance, I. 2005. 'Andromache Aichmalotos: Concubine or Wife?' *Hermathena* 179: 39–66.

Torrance, I. 2013. *Metapoetry in Euripides*. Oxford.

Toynbee, J. M. C. 1973. *Animals in Roman Life and Art*. London.

Trabattoni, F. 2012. 'Myth and Truth in Plato's *Phaedrus*'. In C. Collobert, P. Destrée and F. J. Gonzalez (eds.), *Plato and Myth. Studies on the Use and Status of Platonic Myths*. Leiden. 305–322.

Tralau, J. 2016. 'The Justice of the Chimaira. Goat, Snake, Lion, and Almost the Entire *Oresteia* in a Little Monstrous Image'. *Arion* 24: 41–67.

Tralau, J. 2017. 'Cannibalism, Vegetarianism and the Community of Sacrifice. Rediscovering Euripides' Cretans and the Beginnings of Political Philosophy'. *CP* 112: 1–21.

Tralau, J. 2018a. 'Deg, smet, kakor, slaktoffer och politikens grundvalar hos Aischylos och Euripides'. *Aiolos* 59–60: 117–128.

Tralau, J. 2018b. *Havets väldiga ryggar. Offret och de flytande bildernas gåta*. Lund.

Tueller, M. 2008. *Look Who's Talking. Innovations in Voice and Identity in Hellenistic Epigram*. Leuven.

Turcan, R. 1986. 'Bacchoi ou bacchants? De la dissidence des vivants à la ségrégation des morts'. In O. de Cazanove (ed.), *L'association dionysiaque dans les sociétés anciennes*. Rome. 227–246.

Turing, A. M. 1950. 'Computing Machinery and Intelligence'. *Mind* 49: 433–460.

Turkle, S. 2011. *Alone Together: Why We Expect More From Technology and Less From Each Other*. New York.

Turpin, W. 1998. 'The Epicurean Parasite. Horace, *Satires* 1.1–3'. *Ramus* 27: 127–140.

Ulf, C. 1990. *Die homerische Gesellschaft. Materialien zur analytischen Beschreibung und historischen Lokalisierung*. Munich.

Unterthurner, G. 2012. 'Abnormality and Monstrosity in Foucault'. In G. Unterthurner and E. M. Vogt (eds.), *Monstrosity in Literature, Psychoanalysis and Philosophy*. Vienna/Berlin. 199–218.

Usher, S. 1982. 'The Style of Dionysius of Halicarnassus in the *Antiquitates Romanae*', *ANRW* 2: 817–838.

Utzinger, C. 2003. *Periphrades Aner*. Göttingen.

Van den Eersten, A. 2015. 'To Yoke a Bridge: Poetical Implications of The Subjugation of Nature in Herodotus' *Histories*'. *Proceedings of Anchoring Innovation In Antiquity*, 17–20 December 2015, https://www.Ru.Nl/Oikos/Anchoring-Innovation/Anchoring-Scholarship/Anchoring-Antiquity-International-Conference/

Van Gennep, A. 1909. *Les rites de passage*. Paris.

Van Nortwick, T. 1980. 'Aeneas, Turnus, and Achilles'. *TAPA* 110: 303–314.

Van Nortwick, T. 1992. *Somewhere I Have Never Travelled. The Second Self and the Hero's Journey in Ancient Epic*. New York/Oxford.

Varela, F. J., Thompson, E. and Rosh, E. 1991. *The Embodied Mind. Cognitive Science and Human Experience*. Cambridge, MA.

Vasunia, P. 2001. *The Gift of the Nile: Hellenizing Egypt from Aeschylus to Alexander*. Berkeley.
Verdenius, W. J. 1976. 'Pindar's Seventh Olympian Ode: Supplementary Comments'. *Mnemosyne* 29: 243–253.
Verdenius, W. J. 1987. *Commentaries on Pindar. Vol. 1: Olympian Odes 3, 7, 12, 14*. Leiden.
Verity, A. 2007. *Pindar. The Complete Odes*. Oxford.
Vermeule, E. 1979. *Aspects of Death in Early Greek Art and Poetry*. Berkeley/Los Angeles.
Vernant, J.-P. 1974. 'Le mythe Prométhéen chez Hésiode'. In J.-P. Vernant, *Mythe et société en Grèce ancienne*. Paris. 178–194.
Vernant, J.-P. 1979. 'A la table des hommes'. In M. Detienne and J.-P. Vernant (eds.), *La cuisine du sacrifice en pays grec*. Paris. 37–132.
Vernant, J.-P. 1990. 'The Lame Tyrant: From Oedipus to Periander'. In J.-P. Vernant and P. Vidal-Naquet (eds.), *Myth and Tragedy in Ancient Greece*, trans. J. Lloyd. New York. 207–326.
Vernant, J.-P. 1996. 'Les semblances de Pandora'. In F. Blaise, P. Judet de la Combe and P. Rousseau (eds.). *Le métier du mythe: Lectures d'Hesiode*. Lille. 381–392.
Vernant, J.-P. 1999. *L'Univers, les dieux, les hommes. Récits grecs des origines*. Paris.
Vernant, J.-P. 2001. 'Pandora'. In J-C. Schmitt (ed.), *Eve et Pandora. La création de la femme*. Paris. 29–37.
Vernant, J.-P. 2006a. 'The Figuration of the Invisible and the Psychological Category of the Double: The Kolossos'. In J.-P. Vernant, *Myth and Thought Among the Greeks*. J. Lloyd and J. Fort, trans. New York. 321–332.
Vernant, J.-P. 2006b. 'From the "Presentification" of the Invisible to the Imitation of Appearance'. In J.-P. Vernant, J. Lloyd and J. Fort, trans. *Myth and Thought Among the Greeks*. New York. 333–352.
Vernant, J.-P. and Vidal-Naquet, P. 1972. *Mythe et tragédie en Grèce ancienne*. Paris.
Vernant, J.-P. and Vidal-Naquet. 1986. *Mythe et tragédie deux*. Paris.
Vernant, J.-P. and Zeitlin. F. I. 1991. *Mortals and Immortals. Collected Essays*. Princeton.
Vernant, J.-P, Lloyd, J. and Fort, J. 2006 (trans.). *Myth and Thought Among the Greeks*. New York.
Veyne, P. 1988. *Did the Greeks Believe in Their Myths?* Trans. P. Wissig. Chicago.
Viveiros de Castro, E. 2014. *Cannibal Metaphysics*, trans. E. P. Skafish. Minneapolis.
Viveiros de Castro, E. 2015. 'The Relative Native'. In E. Viveiros de Castro, *The Relative Native*. Chicago. 333–349.
Voelke, P. 2001. *Un théâtre de la marge. Aspects figuratifs et configurationnels du drame satyrique dans l'Athènes classique*. Bari.
Volk, K. 2002. *The Poetics of Latin Didactic: Lucretius, Vergil, Ovid, Manilius*. Oxford/New York.
Von Arnim, H. 1903–5. *Stoicorum Veterum Fragmenta*. 3 vols. Leipzig.
Von Uexküll, J. 2010. *A Foray into the World of Animals and Humans*. Minneapolis.
Vorberg, G. 1932. *Glossarium Eroticum*. Stuttgart.
Wachter, R. 2010. 'The Origin of Epigrams on "Speaking Objects"'. In M. Baumbach, A. Petrovic and I. Petrovic (eds.), *Archaic and Classical Greek Epigram*. Cambridge. 250–260.
Waits, T. et al. 1993. *The Black Rider*. New York.
Waldau, P. and Patton, K. (eds.). 2006. *A Communion of Subjects: Animals in Religion, Science and Ethics*. New York.
Waters, K. H. 1971. *Herodotos on Tyrants and Despots: A Study in Objectivity*. Wiesbaden.
Watkins, C. 1995. *How to Kill a Dragon. Aspects of Indo-European Poetics*. Oxford.
Watson, L. 2003. *A Commentary on Horace's* Epodes. Oxford/New York.
Webster, T. B. 1967. *The Tragedies of Euripides*. London.
Wecowski, M. (1996). 'Ironie et histoire. Le discours de Soclès (Hérodote V 92)'. *AncSoc* 27: 205–258.
Weil, K. 2012. *Thinking Animals: Why Animal Studies Now?* New York.
Weiler, I. 2002. 'Inverted kalokagathia'. *Slavery & Abolition* 23: 9–28.
Weiss, N. 2016. 'The Choral Architecture of Pindar's Eighth *Paean*'. *TAPA* 146: 237–255.
Wellbery, D. E. 1996. *The Specular Moment. Goethe's Early Lyric and the Beginnings of Romanticism*. Stanford.
Wennerscheid, S. 2018. 'Posthuman Desire in Robotics and Science Fiction'. In D. Levy (ed.), *Love and Sex with Robots*. London. 37–50.
Werner, D. S. 2012. *Myth and Philosophy in Plato's* Phaedrus. Cambridge.

West, D. 1974. 'The Deaths of Hector and Turnus'. *G&R* 21: 21–31.

West, D. 1979, 'Two Plagues: Virgil, *Georgics* 3.478–566 and Lucretius 6.1090–1286'. In D. West and T. Woodman (eds.), *Creative Imitation and Latin Literature*. Cambridge. 71–88.

West, M. L. (ed. & comm.). 1966. *Hesiod.* Theogony. Oxford.

West, M. L. (ed. & comm.). 1978. *Hesiod.* Works and Days. Oxford.

West, M. L. (ed.). 1990. *Aeschyli Tragodiae cum incerti poetae Promethio*. Stuttgart.

West, M. L. 1997. *The East Face of Helicon. West Asiatic Elements in Greek Poetry and Myth*. Oxford.

West, M. L. (ed.). 1998. *Homeri* Ilias. *Volumen Prius Rhapsodias I–XII Continens*. Stuttgart.

West, M. L. (ed.). 2000. *Homeri* Ilias. *Volumen Alterium Rhapsodias XIII–XXIV et Indicem Nominum Continens*. Munich.

Whitaker, R. 2010. *Anatomy of an Epidemic: Magic Bullets, Psychiatric Drugs, and the Astonishing Rise of Mental Illness in America*. Broadway.

Whitby, B. 2012. 'Do You Want a Robot Lover? The Ethics of Caring Technologies'. In P. Lin, K. Abney and G. Bekey (eds.), *Robot Ethics: the Ethical and Social Implications of Robotics*. Cambridge, MA. 233–248.

White, D. 1993. *Rhetoric and Reality in Plato's* Phaedrus. Albany.

Whitley, J. 2017. 'The Material Entanglements of Writing Things Down'. In L. C. Nevett (ed.), *Theoretical Approaches to the Archaeology of Ancient Greece*. Ann Arbor. 71–103.

Whitmarsh, T. 2018. 'Sappho and Cyborg Helen'. In F. Budelmann and T. Phillips (eds.), *Textual Events*. Oxford. 135–149.

Whittaker, G. R. (ed.). 1988. *Pastoralism Economies in Classical Antiquity*. Cambridge.

Wiater, N. 2011. *The Ideology of Classicism: Language, History, and Identity in Dionysius of Halicarnassus*. Berlin.

Wickkiser, B. 2010. 'Hesiod and the Fabricated Woman: Poetry and Visual Art in the *Theogony*'. *Mnemosyne* 63: 557–576.

Wieser, M. 2012. *Das Netzwerk von Bruno Latour, Die Akteur-Netzwerk-Theorie zwischen Science & Technology Studies und poststrukturalistischer Soziologie*. Bielefeld.

Wilamowitz, U. v. 1907. *Berliner Klassikertexte, vol. V*. Berlin.

Wilamowitz, U. v. 1932. *Der Glaube der Hellenen, vol. II*. Berlin.

Wildberger, J. 2006. *Seneca und die Stoa. Der Platz des Menschen in der Welt*. Berlin.

Wildberger, J. 2008. 'Beast or God? – The Intermediate Status of Humans and the Physical Basis of the Stoic scala naturae'. In A. Alexandridis, M. Wild, and L. Winkler-Horaček (eds.). Wiesbaden. 47–70.

Wildberger, J. 2010. 'Praebebam enim me facilem opinionibus magnorum uirorum: Platonic Readings in Seneca, Ep. 102'. In V. Harte, M. M. McCabe, R. Sharples and A. Sheppard (eds.), *Aristotle and the Stoics Reading Plato*. London. 205–32.

Wilkes, J. J. 1996. 'The Danubian and Balkan Provinces'. In A. K. Bowman, E. Champlin and A. Lintott (eds.). *The Cambridge Ancient History X: The Augustan Empire 43 B.C.–A.D. 69*. Cambridge. 545–585.

Wilkinson, L. P. 1969. *The* Georgics *of Virgil: A Critical Survey*. Cambridge.

Willcock, M. M. 1995. *Pindar. Victory Odes:* Olympians *2, 7 and 11;* Nemean *4;* Isthmians *3, 4 and 7*. Cambridge.

Willekes, C. 2016. *The Horse in the Ancient World. From Bucephalus to the Hippodrome*. London.

Willi, A. 2010. 'Hera, Eros, Juno Sororia'. *IF* 115: 234–267.

Williams, C. 2010. *Roman Homosexuality*, 2nd ed. Oxford.

Williams, R. 1977. *Marxism and Literature*. Oxford.

Wills, D. 2016. *Inanimation: Theories of Inorganic Life*. Minneapolis/London.

Winfield, A. 2012. *Robotics. A Very Short Introduction*. Oxford.

Winkler, J. J. 1991. 'The Constraints of Eros'. In C. A. Faraone and D. Obbink (eds.). New York/Oxford. 214–243.

Winograd, T. 1991. 'Thinking Machines: Can There Be? Are We?' In J. J. Sheehan and M. Sosna (eds.), *The Boundaries of Humanity. Humans, Animals, Machines*. Berkeley. 119–223.

Wittels, F. 1924. *Sigmund Freud: His Personality, His Teaching, and His School*, trans. E. and C. Paul. New York.

Wittgenstein, L. 1995 [1953]. *Philosophische Untersuchungen*. Wekausgabe Bd. I. Frankfurt.
Wohl, V. 1998. *Intimate Commerce: Exchange, Gender, and Subjectivity in Greek Tragedy*. Austin.
Wohl, V. 2005. 'Beyond Sexual Difference: Becoming-Woman in Euripides' *Bacchae*'. In V. Pedrick and S. M. Oberhelman (eds.), *The Soul of Tragedy: Essays on Athenian Drama*. Chicago. 137–154.
Wohl, V. 2010. 'A Tragic Case of Poisoning: Intention Between Tragedy and the Law'. *TAPA* 140: 33–70.
Wohl, V. 2012. 'The Politics of Enmity in Euripides' *Orestes*'. In D. Rosenbloom and J. Davidson (eds), *Greek Drama IV: Texts, Contexts, Performance*. Oxford. 244–269.
Wohl, V. 2015. *Euripides and the Politics of Form*. Princeton.
Wohl, V. 2018. 'Stone Into Smoke: Metaphor And Materiality In Euripides' *Troades*'. In M. Telò and M. Mueller (eds.). 17–34.
Wolfe, C. (ed.). 2003. *Zoontologies: The Question of the Animal*. Minneapolis.
Wolfe, C. 2009. *What is Posthumanism?* Minneapolis.
Wolfe, C. 2009a. 'Human, All Too Human: "Animal Studies" and the Humanities'. *PMLA* 124: 564–575.
Wolfe, C. 2012. *Before the Law: Humans and Other Animals in a Biopolitical Frame*. Chicago.
Worman, N. 2000. 'Infection in the Sentence: The Discourse of Disease in Sophocles' *Philoctetes*'. *Arethusa* 33: 1–36.
Worman, N. 2002. *The Cast of Character. Style in Greek Literature*. Austin.
Worman, N. 2012. 'Cutting to the Bone: Recalcitrant Bodies in Sophocles'. In K. Ormand (ed.), *The Blackwell Companion to Sophocles*. Oxford. 351–366.
Worman, N. 2018. 'Touching, Proximity, and the Aesthetics of Pain in Sophocles'. In Purves (ed.). 34–49.
Worman, N. 2020. *Embodiment and the Edges of the Human in Greek Tragedy*. London.
Woytek, B. 2003. *Arma et nummi: Forschungen zur römischen Finanzgeschichte und Münzprägung der Jahre 49 bis 42 v. Chr.* Vienna.
Wrenhaven, K. 2012. *Reconstructing the Slave: The Image of the Slave in Ancient Greece*. London.
Wynter, S. 2003. 'Unsettling the Coloniality of Being/Power/Truth/ Freedom: Towards the Human, After Man, Its Overrepresentation – An Argument'. *The New Centennial Review* 3: 257–337.
Yalouris, N. 1986. 'Le mythe d'Io: les transformations d'Io dans l'iconographie et la littérature grecques'. In L. Kahil, Ch. Augé and P. Linant de Bellefonds (eds.), *Iconographie classique et identités régionales*. Paris. 3–23.
Yalouris, N. 1990. 'Io'. *LIMC* 5: 661–676.
Yates, F. 1964. *Giordano Bruno and the Hermetic Tradition*. Chicago.
Yeoman, I. and Mars, M. 2012. 'Robots, Men and Sex Tourism'. *Futures* 44: 365–371.
Young, D. C. 1968. *Three Odes of Pindar. A Literary Study of* Pythian *11,* Pythian *3, and* Olympian *7*. Leiden.
Young, D. C. 1987. 'Pindar and Horace against the Telchines (*Ol.* 7.53 & *Carm.* 4.4.33)'. *AJP* 108: 152–171.
Young, I. M. 1980. 'Throwing Like a Girl: A Phenomenology of Female Body Comportment Motility and Spatiality'. *Human Studies* 3: 137–156.
Yudkowsky, E. 2008. 'Artificial Intelligence as a Positive and Negative Factor in Global Risk'. In N. Bostrom and M. M. Ćirković (eds.), *Global Catastrophic Risks*. Oxford. 308–345.
Yudkowsky, E. 2011. 'Complex Value Systems in Friendly AI'. In J. Schmidhuber, K. R. Thórisson and M. Looks (eds.), *Artificial General Intelligence: 4th International Conference, AGI 2011*. Heidelberg. 388–393.
Zafiropoulos, C. A. 2009. 'What Did Elephants Fear in Antiquity?' *Les Études Classiques* 77: 241–266.
Zatta, C. 2017. *Interconnectedness. The Living World of the Early Greek Philosophers*. Sankt Augustin.
Zeitlin, F. I. 1965. 'The Motif of Corrupted Sacrifice in Aeschylus' *Oresteia*'. *TAPA* 93: 463–508.
Zeitlin, F. I. 1996. *Playing the Other: Essays on Gender and Society in Classical Greek Literature*. Chicago.
Zhmud, L. 1998. 'Some Notes on Philolaus and the Pythagoreans'. *Hyperboreus* 4: 243–70.
Zhmud, L. 2012. *Pythagoras and the Early Pythagoreans*, trans. K. Windle and R. Ireland, Oxford.
Zissos, A. (2004). 'Terminal Middle: The *Argonautica* of Valerius Flaccus'. In S. Kyriakides and F. De Martino (eds.). 311–344.

INDEX

Note: Locators for notes are given in the format 343 n.5.

www.ingramcontent.com/pod-product-compliance
Lightning Source LLC
Chambersburg PA
CBHW081354090726
47908CB00011B/2669

9781350231542